KU-282-287

THE GREAT WAR

VOLUME 3

Frontispiece. Vol. III. "THE GREAT WAR".

From the Painting by C. M. Sheldon.

The Capture of the German Trenches at Neuve Chapelle.

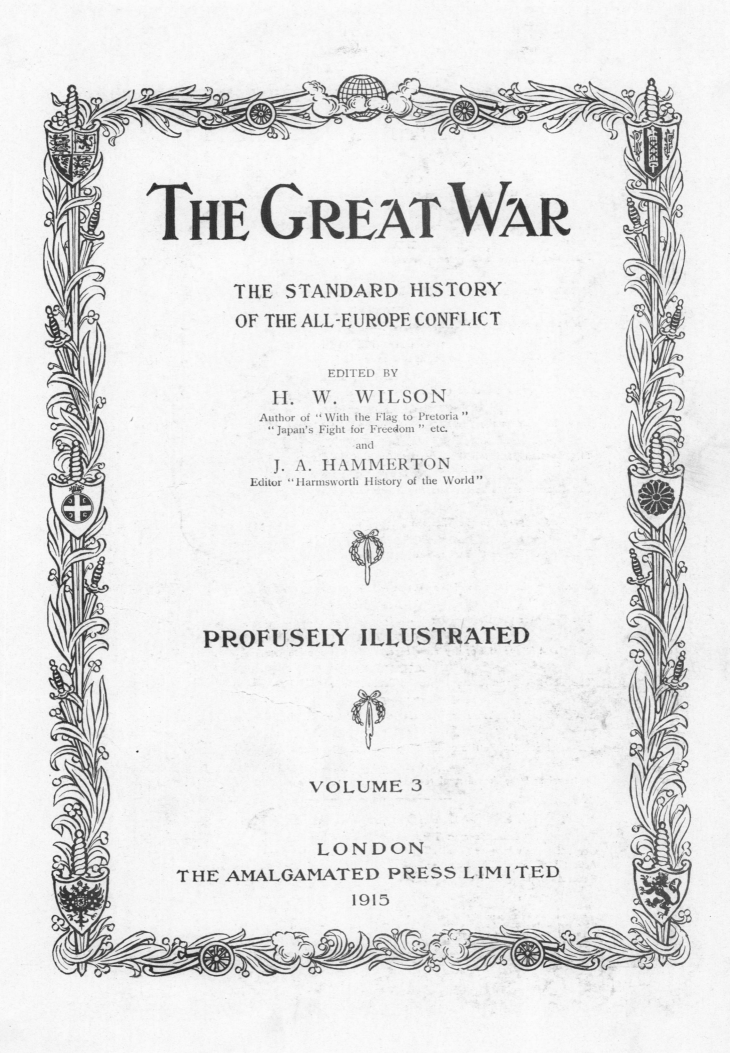

THE GREAT WAR

THE STANDARD HISTORY
OF THE ALL-EUROPE CONFLICT

EDITED BY

H. W. WILSON

Author of "With the Flag to Pretoria"
"Japan's Fight for Freedom" etc.

and

J. A. HAMMERTON

Editor "Harmsworth History of the World"

PROFUSELY ILLUSTRATED

VOLUME 3

LONDON
THE AMALGAMATED PRESS LIMITED
1915

CONTENTS OF VOLUME 3

SPECIAL PHOTOGRAVURE PLATES

ERRATA.—*Page 149.—Nine lines from foot, the sentence should read : " But both General Hertzog and Mr. Steyn," etc. We deeply regret the unhappy slip, although the error is obvious, the whole chapter paying tribute to the splendid loyalty of General Botha.*
Page 166.—Photograph showing arrival of troopship in home waters should be entitled: " The coming of the Australians. Arrival of Australian Reservists at Plymouth."

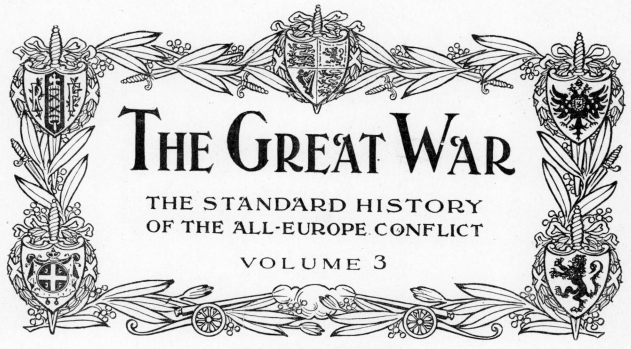

THE GREAT WAR

THE STANDARD HISTORY OF THE ALL-EUROPE CONFLICT

VOLUME 3

CHAPTER XLVII.

EAST COAST RAIDS AND THE DOGGER BANK BATTLE.

First Vain Attempt on Yarmouth—German Armoured Cruiser Sunk by German Mines—Fog Saves the Raiders from Our Fleet—Scarborough and Whitby Massacres—Attack on the Hartlepools—The Third Raid upon the British Coast—Sir David Beatty Catches the Hostile Squadron—Derfflinger Set on Fire and Battered—German Admiral's Flagship Half-Sinking—The Terrible End of the Blücher—The Lion Damaged at Bows—Action Broken Off as Enemy Ships are Nearly Sunk.

I T was on Monday, November 2nd, 1914, that the German Admiralty received news of the victory of their China Squadron over the Good Hope and Monmouth in the action off Coronel. It was then decided to launch the battle-cruiser squadron at once across the North Sea, and to bombard the East Coast of England, with a view to increasing the panic among the civil population of our country. The Staff of the German Admiralty took it for granted that the loss of the chief ships in Admiral Cradock's squadron would produce a panic, and it was hoped that the bombardment of Yarmouth and Lowestoft would increase violently the perturbation of the British people.

It was also expected that our battle-cruiser squadron, under Sir David Beatty, would try to engage the raiding warships under Rear-Admiral Funke. So a new mine-field was laid between Heligoland and Jahde Bay, where Wilhelms-haven is situated. The idea was to draw the counter-attacking British ships into the minefield, where a large flotilla of German submarines was also acting. For nine years this plan of provoking a naval engagement with the fast wing of the British Navy had been elaborated. Each German vessel designed for the operation had been provided with an unusual number of stern guns of large calibre. The Blücher, vainly planned in 1906 to counter

ADMIRAL FRIEDRICH VON INGENOHL.
Former Commander of the German High Seas Fleet, superseded for lack of dash and initiative.

our first battle-cruisers, was able to bring six large guns to bear astern. Then the first true German battle-cruiser, the Von der Tann, also had a stern fire of six large guns. The Moltke and Goeben were still more heavily gunned for a retreating fight, for they had each eight 11 in. guns astern, and only six ahead. The heavy armament of the Seydlitz was arranged in the same manner.

All these ships, in short, were built to run away, and yet fight terrifically while they were running, and lure the British squadron into a minefield.

Being well aware of the cool and even fighting temper of the ordinary British admiral, the Germans looked about for some means of working our seamen up to a heat of blind passion, in which such a thing as a minefield at the end of a long fighting chase might be overlooked.

The bombardment of some of our coast towns was selected as the best means to this end. It would rouse our sailors to anger, as well as create a feeling of widespread uncertainty and apprehension in our civil population.

So, as evening fell on Monday, November 2nd, a German squadron of three armoured cruisers and three battle-cruisers came out of Wilhelmshaven, and threaded the minefield around Jahde Bay, and then tore at high speed due west for the East Anglian coast. There they arrived at dawn on Tuesday morning, November 3rd. One of

THE " SMOKE BLANKET " WHICH SAVED THE HALCYON.
When, about seven o'clock on the morning of November 3rd, 1914, a German squadron appeared off the Yarmouth coast, the only British warship on view was the old gunboat Halcyon. The great German ships rained shells on the little vessel, but she was only hit eight times ; and a British destroyer arriving on the scene, sent up a screen of thick smoke, behind which the battered but uncrippled Halcyon got safely away.

our steam-trawling fleets, fishing about eight miles off Lowestoft, saw the warships steam by just at dawn, all lights out and no ensigns flying. A skipper of a steam-drifter was so sure that they were British boats that he waved his teapot at them as a morning greeting. He got in reply a line of shaking fists and angry faces on the deck of the nearest enemy ship.

About seven o'clock the bombardment began. The only British warship in view of the Germans was the old gunboat the Halcyon, lying ten miles off the English coast on fishing patrol duties. The great German ships rained shells upon the gunboat, which had only two 4·7 in. and four 6-pounder guns. She could scarcely do eighteen knots, being more than twenty years old ; but her captain, running her on a zigzag course, only had his boat hit eight times. Then a British destroyer arrived, and sent up a screen of thick smoke, behind which the battered but uncrippled little Halcyon got safely away.

Meanwhile, the bombardment of Yarmouth proceeded with much noise and fury, but with no damage. For the Admiralty had thoughtfully anticipated German tactics by providing the raiders with a minefield at the end of their outward journey. Nearly all the German shells fell with a mighty splash into the sea some two miles from the famous Yarmouth beach, where holiday-makers used to resort, as it was dangerous for the attackers to come much closer. For nearly an hour flashes of flame were visible along the seaward horizon, and the murderous missiles sent up towering cascades as they approached the shore. Nearer and nearer sounded the firing, and it was gravely feared that the town at last would suffer. But a little before eight o'clock, after a hundred shots had been uselessly fired, the hostile squadron disappeared into the haze.

Their destroyers, scattered northward and southward, had got into touch with the outer guard of our advancing battle-cruiser squadron. A wireless message came to the German admiral, and learning that a far superior force was closing down upon him, he turned for home at top speed, and escaped having to fight by getting into a thick mist. Some of his ships also started dropping mines as soon as they left Yarmouth Roads. As the result of this mine-dropping there was a chapter of accidents to some British vessels. About ten o'clock in the morning a steam-drifter, the Fraternal, was blown up eight miles off the coast, midway between Lowestoft and Yarmouth. She sank slowly, and her crew were rescued by other steam-drifters. Then the Copious, arriving from the herring-grounds, was struck, and sank quickly with the loss of most of her men. A few minutes afterwards two British submarines, moving in pursuit of the Germans, came in sight. One of them was submarine D5, a boat of 630 tons, built in 1910. She was travelling on the surface, with Lieut.-Commander Godfrey Herbert in charge, and the skipper of a Yarmouth trawler spoke him, and told him of the danger of mines. But as D5 shot over to the other **Loss of** submarine to carry the warning to her, **Submarine D5** she herself struck one of the mines. Her bow went up in the air, and she sank immediately, nearly all her crew of twenty men being lost.

But what we lost on this occasion by German mines was little in comparison with what the raiders themselves lost. For the thick fog that saved the hostile squadron from the attack of our battle-cruisers was a death-trap to the modern armoured cruiser the Yorck. Built just before the Scharnhorst and Gneisenau, she was sister-ship to the Roon, having an armament of four 8·2 in. guns and ten 6 in. guns, with a 4 in. armoured belt and 6 in. turrets

Hornsey Smith

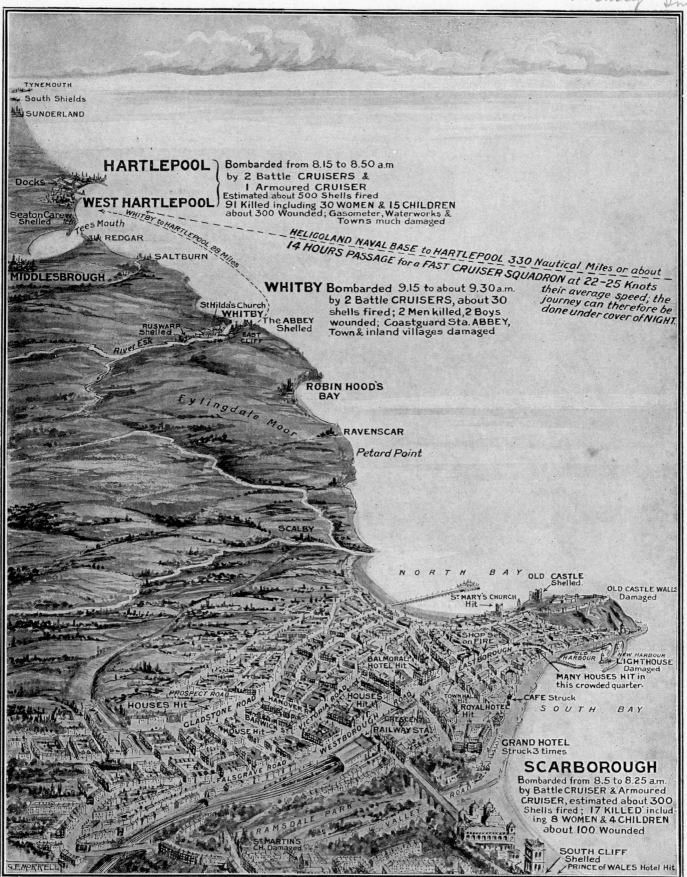

TYNEMOUTH
South Shields
SUNDERLAND

HARTLEPOOL } Bombarded from 8.15 to 8.50 a.m
by 2 Battle CRUISERS &
WEST HARTLEPOOL } I Armoured CRUISER
Estimated about 500 Shells fired
91 Killed including 30 WOMEN & 15 CHILDREN
about 300 Wounded; Gasometer, Waterworks &
Towns much damaged

Docks

Seaton Carew
Shelled
Tees Mouth
REDGAR

WHITBY to HARTLEPOOL 28 Miles

HELIGOLAND NAVAL BASE to HARTLEPOOL 330 Nautical Miles or about
14 HOURS PASSAGE for a FAST CRUISER SQUADRON at 22-25 Knots
their average speed; the journey can therefore be done under cover of NIGHT.

SALTBURN

MIDDLESBROUGH

St Hilda's Church
WHITBY
RUSWARP
Shelled
River Esk
EAST CLIFF

WHITBY Bombarded 9.15 to about 9.30 a.m.
by 2 Battle CRUISERS, about 30
shells fired; 2 Men killed, 2 Boys
wounded; Coastguard Sta. ABBEY,
Town & inland villages damaged

The ABBEY
Shelled

ROBIN HOOD'S BAY

Eylingdale Moor

RAVENSCAR

Petard Point

SCALBY

N O R T H   B A Y

OLD CASTLE
Shelled.
OLD CASTLE WALLS
Damaged

St MARY'S CHURCH
Hit

SHOP Set
on FIRE
EASTBOROUGH

NEW HARBOUR
OLD HARBOUR
LIGHTHOUSE
Damaged

BALMORAL
HOTEL Hit

HOUSES
Hit

MANY HOUSES HIT in
this crowded quarter.

PROSPECT ROAD
HANOVER ROAD
VICTORIA ROAD
ROAD
CAFE Struck

HOUSES Hit
GLADSTONE ROAD
BARWICK St
HOUSE Hit
CRESCENT
RAILWAY STA.
TOWN HALL
Hit
ROYAL HOTEL
Hit

S O U T H   B A Y

WESTBOROUGH

FALSGRAVE ROAD

GRAND HOTEL
Struck 3 times

RAMSDALE PARK

St MARTIN'S
CH. Damaged

VALLEY

ROAD

SCARBOROUGH
Bombarded from 8.5 to 8.25 a.m.
by Battle CRUISER & Armoured
CRUISER, estimated about 300
Shells fired; 17 KILLED including 8 WOMEN & 4 CHILDREN
about 100 Wounded

SOUTH CLIFF
Shelled
PRINCE of WALES Hotel Hit

G.F. MORRELL

[Drawn by G. F. Morrell.

BARBARIC KULTUR: GERMAN NAVY'S BOMBARDMENT OF OUR EAST COAST HOLIDAY RESORTS.

The bombardment by German warships of Scarborough, Whitby, and the Hartlepools, on the morning of December 16th, 1914, was described by a German paper as affording " further proof of the gallantry of the German Navy." The exploit, so graphically recalled to us in the above pictorial plan of the bombarded coast-line, supplied, rather, evidence that the German people had forgotten the lesson of their own Thirty Years' War, that the conventions of civilised warfare are based not merely on humane sentiment, but on sound general common-sense. In the three towns named above German shells killed, altogether, seventy-eight women and children, and wounded two hundred and twenty-eight.

ON THE LOOK-OUT FROM A SPLINTER-PROOF TRENCH ON THE EAST COAST.

occasion they prepared to risk the whole fighting power of their Fleet. For they brought out their latest, swiftest, and most powerful battle-cruiser, the Derfflinger, and used with her the Seydlitz, the Moltke, the Von der Tann, the Blücher, and two of their small remaining stock of fast lighter cruisers. The chief of these ships formed the battle-cruiser wing of the German Fleet, and on them would fall in a general fleet action the task of preventing the envelopment of the slower and more unwieldy battleships by our swift battle-cruisers.

It will thus be seen that the German Admiralty was taking a tremendous risk merely for the sake of killing and wounding a few hundred children, women, and

Losing her way in the mist while returning to Wilhelmshaven, she took the wrong path through the minefield, exploded a mine, and sank just in the entrance to Jahde Bay, thereby blocking it. Owing to the fog, the rescue of her crew was impeded, and only one hundred and seventy-seven men out of a complement of six hundred **Yorck blown up** and twenty-nine were saved. She was a **by mines** more modern ship than the Good Hope, with a more powerful armament, and in regard merely to ship power, her destruction did much to restore the balance we had temporarily lost three days before in the action off Coronel.

And as their victory at Coronel had provoked the German Admiralty to make their first vain raid on our East Coast towns, so their crushing defeat in the Battle off the Falkland Islands aroused them to make a more desperate attempt to carry out the scheme for which their battle-cruiser wing had been designed. On this second

EXTERIOR VIEW OF THE ABOVE SPLINTER-PROOF.

GUARDING THE CABLE STATION AT CUNARD BAY, ISLE OF WIGHT.

Admiral Jellicoe, in reply to certain alarmists, stated that the Isle of Wight was "the safest place in the world." Certainly, when this statement was published, in March, 1915, the island had so far escaped injury. The other photographs on this page illustrate the work of men of our new armies in trench-digging at home, either for practice or in view of the possible if not probable German invasion of these islands.

non-combatant men in certain towns on our East Coast. In actual matter of fact, the rôles of Germans and Britons in the proposed stern-chase action across the North Sea had been already reversed from the original intention of the German Staff. The leaders of the British Navy were just as cool and as scientific in both their strategical dispositions and their manner of handling their ships in action as they had been at the outbreak of the war. It was the German admirals who had been worked up into such a passion of rage, and subjected to such political and social pressure, that they had ceased to calculate forces or to try to organise a victory. Not only were the fighting seamen of Germany losing their spirit, but the long inaction of the High Seas Fleet was one of the

A NOVEL SIGHT ON THE CLIFFS OF OLD ENGLAND.

ANOTHER VIEW OF A SPLINTER PROOF ON THE EAST COAST.

factors of depression upon the minds of the overtasked German soldiers. Something striking had to be done to revive the courage of every German.

Therefore, about five o'clock in the evening of Tuesday, December 15th, the great German battle-cruiser fleet steamed out of Wilhelmshaven, and for fourteen hours made at a speed of twenty-five knots for part of the Durham and Yorkshire coast which was known to be unprotected by a minefield.

Of course, it seemed very negligent of our Admiralty not to have mined the approaches to the busy commercial port of the Hartlepools. But our entire coast could not be defended by mines without hampering our Navy and crippling our commerce. Certain risks had to be taken, but we were prepared to strike, if our risks tempted the Germans to cross the sea. It was all planned by the subtlest and most brilliant mind in our Navy—by the man who had won his position as Commander

The sea-raiders' second venture

BRITISH CAVALRY PATROL ON THE SANDS AT SCARBOROUGH AFTER THE RAID.

The murders at Scarborough began a little after eight o'clock in the morning. The Moltke, with her 11 in. shells, and an armoured cruiser firing 6 in. shells, came up in the mist, and opened fire at close range, the smaller vessel steaming up to within a quarter of a mile of the beach. The bombardment lasted about twenty minutes. Four children, eight women, and five men were killed, and some hundred were wounded.

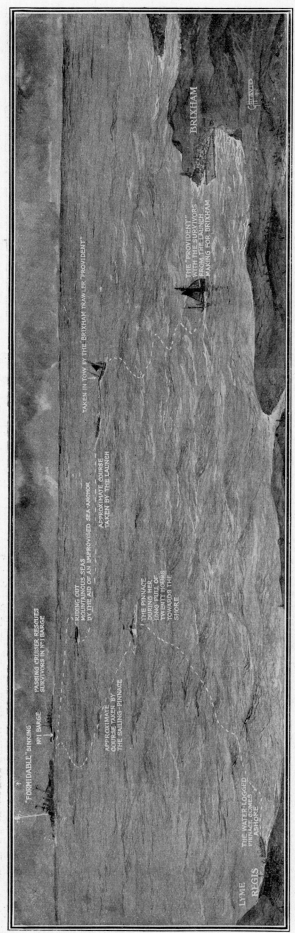

LYME REGIS

BRIXHAM

THE WATER-LOGGED PINNACE COMES ASHORE

APPROXIMATE COURSE TAKEN BY THE SAILING-PINNACE

THE PINNACE DURING HER LONG PULL OF TWENTY HOURS TOWARDS THE SHORE

APPROXIMATE COURSE TAKEN BY THE LAUNCH

RIDING OUT MOUNTAINOUS SEAS BY THE AID OF AN IMPROVISED SEA-ANCHOR

TAKEN IN TOW BY THE BRIXHAM TRAWLER "PROVIDENT"

THE "PROVIDENT" WITH THE SURVIVORS FROM THE LAUNCH MAKING FOR BRIXHAM

"FORMIDABLE" SINKING

PASSING CRUISER RESCUES SURVIVORS IN No.1 BARGE

No.1 BARGE

LOSS OF H.M.S. FORMIDABLE OFF TORBAY: FATE OF THE BOATS WHICH GOT AWAY FROM THE SINKING BATTLESHIP.

The Formidable was torpedoed off Torbay on New Year's Day, 1915. Five hundred of her men were sleeping in their bunks at the time. Nearly six hundred lives were lost. Of the four boats launched, one capsized. The second, also a barge, got away with about seventy men, who were picked up by a light cruiser. The third, a pinnace, with some sixty men, got ashore at Lyme Regis. The fourth, a launch, with some seventy men, was rescued by the Brixham trawler Providence. Many of the men died from exposure. Only one hundred and fifty lived to tell the tale.

of our Grand Fleet through never having been beaten in any battle manœuvres in which he took a leading part. Sir John Rushworth Jellicoe divined generally what the German Admiralty intended to do. He divined exactly how far the scope of the German Intelligence Department would reach. In fact, he may have allowed it to reach as far as the knowledge that there was no minefield protecting the Hartlepools. But by a curious coincidence, as soon as the German battle-cruiser squadron left Wilhelmshaven on its night voyage to the Durham coast, there was a stir of activity throughout our Grand Fleet. Not only did our First and Second Battle-Cruiser Squadrons put out to sea, but, on a remote point of the northern British coast, eight of our fastest super-Dreadnought battleships got up steam and turned southward.

It was all done in absolute silence. No easily decoded wireless messages could be picked up by spies in Norway, or by adventurous German boats scouting round Scotland. The British counter-stroke was arranged with so absolute a mastery that it is the greatest **The British counter-stroke** stroke of pure ill-luck in the history of naval strategy it did not come off. It reminds one of Huxley's satirical definition of a tragedy according to Herbert Spencer—a beautiful theory, killed by a wicked fact. It was a beautiful battle-plan, prepared with subtle genius and arranged with admirable skill. A tremendous array of forces was exquisitely adjusted for the rapid and complete annihilation of the raiding warships, but at the critical moment a heavy fog blanketed the scene of action, and allowed the enemy to escape.

Meanwhile, the surprised and stricken townspeople of Scarborough, Whitby, and the Hartlepools had to bear the brunt of the raiders' murderous attack. Of the three towns, only the Hartlepools—East and West, lying in a crescent on the Durham coast, with their tidal basins, docks, and shipbuilding yards—were legally liable to bombardment, for they were defended by forts. The case was entirely different in regard to Whitby and Scarborough. In Whitby was merely a coastguard look-out, with a signalling apparatus. At Scarborough was preserved as a curiosity a Russian 64-pounder captured in one of the old wars, and as useful against modern warships as a bow and arrow. The old garrison batteries had been dismantled when Lord Haldane provided the Volunteer Artillery with field-guns.

Moreover, in both the ancient fishing town and the picturesque watering-place, the enemy ships were able to approach quite close to the shore. Thus there was no minefield putting them technically among fortified places. The bombardment of them, and the killing and wounding of babes, children, women, and civilian men, was not an act of war. It was piracy.

The murders began at Scarborough a little after eight o'clock in the morning. The Moltke, with her 11 in. shells, and an armoured cruiser firing 6 in. shells, came up in the morning mist, and opened fire at close range, the smaller vessel steaming up to within a quarter of a mile of the beach. The first shell tore up the promenade and foreshore. Then the Grand Hotel and other prominent buildings were struck. The walls of the ancient castle, ten feet thick, were shattered in places, and the **Scarborough under fire** keep was also damaged. Happily, the old barracks on Castle Hill, at which the Germans continually aimed, were unoccupied. Naturally some of the churches were shelled, for no German gunner could see a Christian temple without wanting to destroy it in the interests of Deutsche Kultur.

It was a dark morning, and most people were either just getting up or breakfasting by gaslight. Women, barefooted, with wraps thrown over their nightdresses, ran into the streets, carrying their frightened children in their arms, with the only thought of getting out of the firing zone. A servant-girl was killed while cleaning a doorstep, a postman, who was about to deliver a letter at the same house being also blown to bits. Children with their mothers were killed with terrible suddenness in their wrecked homes, while fancying that the noise of the firing was only a thunderstorm. The bombardment lasted for about twenty minutes, and at times ten shells fell every minute. In all, four children, eight women, and five men were killed outright, and over a hundred were wounded. It was rather a small result for the expense of ammunition and the risk to the German battle-cruiser and her consort, for sufficient shells were used to have sunk a British battleship if they had all got well home. Far from terror-ising the Yorkshire people by this act of piracy, the Germans only increased the population of the beau-tiful shattered water-ing-place, producing a special bombardment season in the dullest part of the winter, when thousands of

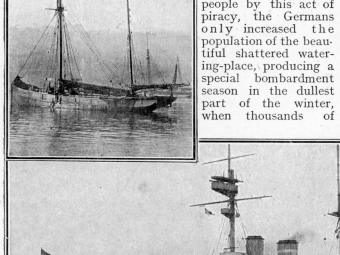

THRILLING EPISODE OF HEROISM AT SEA.

Heroism characteristic of the finest traditions of the sea marked the conduct of Captain Loxley and the crew of the Formidable after she had been torpedoed; and the same remark applies to the captain and crew of the trawler Providence, which was instrumental in saving some seventy lives. Above is a photograph of the lost battleship. Inset: (1) The trawler; and (2) the crew of the little craft—left to right, back row: W. Carter, Captain W. Pillar, J. Clark; front row: Dan Taylor, L. Pillar.

visitors came to see with their own eyes what the baby-killers had done.

It was the same at Whitby, where a coastguard and a vanman were killed and two boys wounded by two battle-cruisers firing 11 in. shells. They opened fire a little after nine o'clock, half a mile south of the Whitby Bell Buoy, and nearly opposite the point **The baby-killers at** on the reef where the hospital-ship **Whitby** Rohilla had struck in the previous October. The old Abbey of St. Hilda and the parish church were injured, and some women and children were wounded. At Whitby the fire was directed chiefly upon the signal station; but the general intention of the baby-killers was to slay as many non-combatants as possible, and to do the utmost damage to private property. This is quite clear from the number of rounds they fired, and from the manner in which they swept Scarborough, especially in the most crowded parts of the town.

At the Hartlepools the bombardment began at the same time as at Scarborough. The weather was very hazy, and the three enemy ships are said to have come in under the British flag, and to have fired first out to sea and signalled that a German squadron was approaching. This was a trick of war which, owing to the sea mist, apparently deceived the forts until the ships opened fire. The three battle-cruisers got within a range of about four thousand yards. But except for one shot that destroyed the gas-holders, little military damage was done. The coast batteries, though dominated by the heavier naval guns, maintained an artillery duel all the time, and inflicted some loss on the enemy. The shipbuilding yards were   **Homes shattered** not hit, and three small British vessels   **at Hartlepool** that engaged the enemy were not sunk. They were the light cruiser Patrol, with nine 4 in. guns, and two destroyers, the Doon and the Hardy, with a few guns of a similar calibre. The destroyers made a gallant and desperate attempt to get near enough to the great hostile battle-cruisers to torpedo them, but were, naturally, unsuccessful. Only on a dark night and by a surprise attack can frail destroyers sufficiently elude observation to bring their torpedo-tubes into play. But only seven sailors were killed and about two dozen seriously wounded. In the land batteries, where Colonel Robson performed prodigies of bravery and skill against the overpowering, longer-ranged ordnance of the enemy, six men of the Durham Light Infantry were killed, and seventeen of the Durhams, the Yorkshire Regiment, and the Royal Engineers were wounded.

The slaughter of non-combatants in this seaport, however, was serious. A hundred children, women, and men were killed, while nearly four hundred and fifty were wounded. Altogether, in the three towns, the men, women and children killed or wounded numbered six hundred and seventy-one. One dauntless little innocent mite set out for school, careless of the rain of shells, saying, "I must get that medal, mother." It was the medal for regular attendance she desired to win, but she was blown to pieces in Crimdon Street. Babies of six and fourteen months perished in agony. Three frightened children, running out into the street, were killed by a single shell, and kindly working women, trying to carry their neighbours' children to a place of safety, were slain with their frail, living burdens during the bombardment which a Berlin newspaper proclaimed to be " a further proof of the gallantry of the German Navy."

Scores of homes in the old town of Hartlepool were blown into fragments. Roofs were lifted off, the walls thrown down, and all that remained of them was, here and there, a heap of broken bricks and plaster, from which protruded portions of bedsteads and other pieces of domestic furniture. The German gunners were well informed as to the lie of the town. After trying to blow down the dock-basin gates they swept the sea front, and then shelled the gasworks, the railway-stations, the electricity works, the waterworks, and the shipbuilding yards. But only the gasworks and Messrs. Furness, Withy & Co.'s works

SURVIVORS OF THE FORMIDABLE BEING TAKEN ON
BOARD THE PROVIDENCE.

After being in their open cutter for nearly twelve hours, two officers and
some seventy men of the torpedoed battleship Formidable were rescued by
the Brixham trawler Providence. Inset: Sectional view of the side of the
Formidable, showing the point probably struck by torpedoes.

The principal conventions of
civilised warfare are not based
on simple, humane feeling.
They are based on the common
interests of the combatants.
The Germans first learned this
in their terrible Thirty Years'
War, when the armies starved
through the ill-treatment of
non-combatants, resulting in
the country through which the
soldiers moved becoming an
uncultivated and foodless
waste. It was for the soldiers'
sake that non-combatants were
afterwards spared in ordinary
civilised land warfare. In the
same way the British and
French, in the old days,
worked out in long practice
the humane conventions of
naval warfare. At first the
fleets raided each other's coast
towns. Then gradually they
saw that this was folly. The
fleet that wasted costly ammunition, carried abroad with
much trouble, on damaging
property and slaying non-
combatants, left itself so much
the weaker when it faced the
rival fleet on the seas. Therefore the contending admirals
learned to keep strictly to
business, and to save their
powder and shot for naval
action.

But the Ger-
mans, being with-
out experience in
the exercise of sea-
power, went back
at once to the
foolish barbarism
of the ancient days.
The Goeben and
Breslau began it in
the Mediterranean,
by wasting their
ammunition in
bombarding Alge-
rian coast towns
soon after the out-
break of hostilities,
when there were
powerful French
and British squad-
rons seeking an
action with them.
The same ships
adopted a like
policy afterwards
in the Black Sea. If the Germans had any clear idea of obtaining any definite military advantage by the wanton massacre of civilians, it could only have been that at which the
Assyrians used to aim when they impaled prisoners outside
a besieged town in order to frighten the garrison.

We have learned at first-hand in this war something
that Danes and Frenchmen knew a full generation ago.
There has been revealed to us all the parvenu quality of
German civilisation—all that was concealed in those
pedantic efforts at culture which are traceable even in
Goethe's career. For a hundred and fifty years the Germans,
imitated, painstakingly imitated, the veritable leaders of

appear to have suffered severely, and in addition Messrs.
Richardson, Westgarth & Co.'s engineering works were
somewhat damaged. In all, about five hundred houses
in the Hartlepools were hit, in a bombardment at close
range lasting some forty minutes.

It was not good gunnery. Taking into consideration
the number of shells fired by the three hostile warships,
the loss of life was much less than might have been expected,
and the damage to the seaport was not as great as it might
have been. Seeing that one of the vessels
attacking Hartlepool with 12 in. shells
was the latest German battle-cruiser, the
Derfflinger, which, at the range she fired,
should have been able to sink a ship of her own weight,
size, and armament in a quarter of an hour or less, the
Germans must have fired wildly. Either the men were
thoroughly ashamed of the work which they were doing,
or they were disturbed by the risks they ran.

In regard to the bombardment of Whitby and Hartlepool,
it was something worse than a crime—it was a blunder.

**Wild German
gunnery**

European life. But they did not grasp the vital wisdom in the old, rich traditions they so earnestly at times endeavoured to vainly absorb. They were learned barbarians. The wars for territory between their petty dynasties, which followed on the religious movement of the Reformation, left them stripped of culture while Western Europe was building up modern civilisation. Their efforts to acquire by study what they lacked in experience made them only uninspired pedants. When they were thrown back on their own stock of ideas and feelings, in the sudden stress of a supreme national struggle for dominion, they at once let go all that was to them mere convention. They then displayed that cruel stupidity, still innate in their minds, which had hitherto been masked by their docile and snobbish imitativeness.

Thereupon it remained for their opponents to teach them anew the forgotten lessons of their Thirty Years' War. They had to be shown that the conventions of civilised warfare were based, not merely on humane sentiment, which a conqueror might on occasion afford to disregard, but on sound, general common-sense. For if our modern civilisation, the best on the whole yet seen in the world, were merely founded on good feeling, its progress would not be sure. Happily, it is built on reason and experience. Therefore it can resist even the terrible organised attack of all the resurgent forces of ancient savagery, directed by a feudal militarism, clad in the armour - plate of industries.

In the present case the badly-needed lesson was prepared by Sir John Jellicoe. For when the last vessels of the German cruiser squadron steamed away from Whitby, about 9.30 o'clock on Thursday morning, December 17th,

Accidents to the raiders

a considerable part of the Grand Fleet was waiting for all the raiders. There was some brilliant manœuvring by certain British admirals, and then the desired positions were obtained, amid the uncertainty of the drifting fog-banks. On one side of the German squadron was Sir David Beatty with our First Battle Cruiser wing. On the other side of him was our Second Battle Squadron wing, with eight of our super-Dreadnought battleships, all ready for instant attack. It was as complete a trap as our fighting seamen of any period have ever got an enemy into. Our Second Battle Squadron suddenly saw the Germans about eight miles away, coming out of a fog-bank. Our fire-control officers marked the ranges, and the loaded guns were laid on the mark. Then just when our ships were about to open fire, the fog came down again heavily and entirely hid the enemy. Apparently the Germans saw the British ships, and altered course as they sped away through the fog. For nothing more could be seen of them. But they did not escape quite without hurt. For as the battle-cruiser the Von der Tann was fleeing fast in the thick fog she rammed the light cruiser the Frauenlob,

SCENE OUTSIDE THE WRECKED BAPTIST CHAPEL AT WEST HARTLEPOOL DURING THE SECOND BOMBARDMENT OF OUR EAST COAST.

A German shell, after going clean through the chapel, rebounded from the roadway into the first-floor bed-room of the house seen on the right. One woman was struck down. A Territorial, rushing to her assistance, had his rifle blown out of his hand. The scene outside the chapel was piteous in the extreme. People came rushing from the adjacent houses, through a haze of dust, and all the windows in the vicinity were shattered.

damaging herself badly in the bows, as well as half sinking the lighter vessel.

The Von der Tann was a newish ship, completed in 1909, with a displacement of 21,000 tons and an armament of eight 11 in. guns and 7 in. armour amidships. Her injuries were to prove a serious factor in the naval engagement in the North Sea, which the Germans were provoking and yet eluding. The Frauenlob, a light cruiser, built in 1902, with ten 4·1 in. guns, and a crew of 264, was most seriously damaged, increasing the weakness of the German Navy at its weakest point. All this, however, was no compensation for the befogging of our Grand Fleet at the critical moment off our East Coast. But for the extraordinary stroke of ill-luck in regard to weather conditions, the Grand Fleet would have sunk every German ship that had taken part in the raid. So terrific were the odds that Sir John Jellicoe had brought against the enemy that there would not have been a battle but a rapid and overwhelming annihilation. However, this was not to be.

Vengeance delayed by fog

> "The best-laid schemes o' mice and men
> Gang aft agley."

And with all his skill in battle manœuvres, Sir John Jellicoe was unable to control the winter fogs of the North Sea. It was reported that all the officers of the German raiding squadron and a number of the men were given the Iron Cross on returning to Wilhelmshaven. In a way the baby-killers deserved the cheapened decoration which had

B

THE GERMAN BOMBARDMENT OF HARTLEPOOL.
Shells falling on the battery at the end of the pier.

THE PIER AND LIGHTHOUSE, HARTLEPOOL.

VIEW OF HARTLEPOOL DOCKS.

been distributed wholesale among the land forces of Germany. For they certainly had had a narrower escape from total destruction than had most German soldiers.

But their luck was apparently unfailing. For when they were next sent forth to cross the North Sea, only one of their armoured cruisers met the full fate again prepared by the British admiral for the entire squadron. For the third time, on Saturday afternoon, January 23rd, 1915, the remaining battle-cruisers of the High Seas Fleet of the German Empire put out to sea. First the destroyer flotilla steamed out in fan formation beyond the minefields in the Bight of Heligoland. Then, as twilight was falling, a line of long, narrow shapes—six light cruisers—threaded their way between the mines to support the destroyers, While the last glimmer of daylight lasted the destroyers

and light-cruisers continued their work of months by hunting about for some sign of a British submarine. But none was visible. So as the early winter night drew on, the defences of Wilhelmshaven opened, and four vast grey fighting ships, with the sharp bows of ocean racers, came out at full speed, under the guard of the wide-flung destroyers.

The Von der Tann, the flagship of Rear-Admiral Funke—a curious name in the circumstances—had, as we have seen, been temporarily put out of action during her flight from our Second Battle-Cruiser Squadron. On the third raid Rear-Admiral Hipper, the senior officer in the German cruiser squadrons, with his flag in the Seydlitz, led the line, consisting of his flagship the Derfflinger, the Moltke, and **The enemy's third** the Blücher. Owing to the incom- **attempt** pletion of the new battle-cruiser the Lützow, the loss to the German Navy of the sistership of the Moltke, the Goeben, and the injury to the Von der Tann, the four ships which Admiral Hipper led on this raid represented all that Germany could bring out to face our battle-cruisers.

For even her latest battleships were too slow for anything like a running fight, and their armament was so inferior in range that our swifter ships would have them at our mercy. We had available seven battle-cruisers of the Dreadnought and super-Dreadnought type, with speeds varying between twenty-eight and thirty knots.

Germany, in her supreme effort at a fast running action, could only bring up three battle-cruisers, with smaller guns than ours, together with one misbegotten, would-be battle-cruiser of the Dreadnought type—the Blücher. In the year 1906, when Lord Fisher was working out his plan for a fleet of all-big-gun capital ships, the German Admiralty heard a rumour of the creation of a British ship of the new type—the battle-cruiser. With much trouble and expense the Intelligence Department of the German Admiralty obtained a forecast of the plan of our Invincible. On this plan the design of the Blücher was carefully modelled with the same draught of about 15,500 tons as the British ship would possess. She was armed with what was thought to be an overpowering armament for a cruiser—twelve

THE QUEEN OF NORTHERN WATERING-PLACES—TWO VIEWS OF SCARBOROUGH—YORKSHIRE'S FASHIONABLE SPA.

Valentine.

8·2 in. guns—and engines were made to give her a speed of a little over twenty-six knots. But all the information obtained at considerable cost by German spies was false. The Blücher was laid down in October, 1906, and was not completed until September, 1909. In the meantime our first three battleships of the Invincible class were completed in 1908. They were not cruisers in the old sense of the word, but racing battleships, with two and a-half knots more speed than the Blücher, a tonnage of 17,250 tons, and—the grand surprise—eight 12 in. guns apiece. The best existing German battleship at the time had only 11 in. guns. Our battle-cruisers, with superior speed and longer range, could outfight any of them. Such is the story of the ill-fated Blücher that now steamed out on her last voyage.

SCARBOROUGH CASTLE RUINS.

Photochrom.

Admiral Hipper made full preparations for a running fight. He laid a new minefield north of Heligoland, and arranged for the Zeppelins on that island to come out and drop bombs, with the assistance of a squadron of seaplanes, laden with smaller shells. He also concentrated a large flotilla of submarines between the minefield and the Dogger Bank, with a view to torpedoing his possible pursuers, while his own ships were threading the mine area. All this, however, was only a precautionary measure, like the entrenchments along the Aisne heights which General von Kluck made in his rear when he advanced to attack the French in the valley of the Marne. Admiral Hipper seems to have hoped to have been able to start a different operation at some distance from the northern

SHELLS FROM GERMAN WARSHIPS BURSTING OVER SCARBOROUGH SEA-FRONT.

According to the Berlin "Lokalanzeiger," defenceless, pleasure-loving Scarborough is "the most important harbour on the East Coast of England between the Humber and the Thames." The "Berliner Tageblatt" also described Scarborough as being an important port!

British coast, during which one or more of his fastest battle-cruisers would be able to slip out on to the trade routes, while the British squadron was being hammered in an unexpected way. The minefield, submarines, Zeppelins and flying machines were arranged to protect the weakened but successful squadron as it turned homeward after the accomplishment of the first part of the design.

But by the same curious coincidence as marked the second German sea-raid, as Admiral Hipper left Wilhelmshaven in the Seydlitz, Sir David Beatty left a certain port in Scotland in his flagship the Lion. He took with him the

A fateful Sunday morning Tiger, commanded by Captain Henry B. Pelly; the Princess Royal, under Captain Osmond de Beauvoir Brock; the New Zealand, flying the flag of Rear-Admiral Sir Archibald Moore, and commanded by Captain Lionel Halsey; and the Indomitable, under Captain Francis W. Kennedy. This magnificent battle-cruiser squadron was accompanied by four light cruisers of the town class—the Southampton, the Nottingham, the Birmingham, and the Lowestoft. They steamed on the port beam of the big ships, on the left-hand side looking forward from the flagship. Then, far ahead of the squadron, were our destroyers with their mother ships of the fleetest and

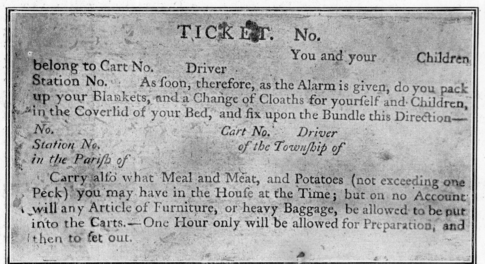

AN INTERESTING SOUVENIR OF THE NAPOLEONIC SCARE.
Facsimile of a ticket issued to the inhabitants of North Shields in the days of Napoleon.

newest cruiser class—the Arethusa, the Aurora, and the Undaunted.

The Aurora, under Captain Wilmot Nicholson, led, and about seven o'clock on Sunday morning, January 24th, her look-out sighted the leading German light cruisers near the Dogger Bank. At twenty minutes past seven the Aurora opened fire with her two 6 in. guns, and wirelessed her flagship that she was engaging the enemy. Sir David Beatty at once altered course towards the direction of the gun flashes, which were south-south-east, ordered all his battleships to increase speed, and commanded the light cruisers and destroyers to get in touch with the enemy.

But there was no need for this last command. For as soon as the Germans had been seen, all our scouting force had flung forward on to the enemy. Admiral Hipper had been steering north-west. Without waiting to see clearly what he had to meet, he at once turned his ships about, and went full speed on a south-east course. Meanwhile the British light cruisers kept closely in touch with the hostile ships and wirelessed all their movements to Sir David Beatty. Our battle-cruiser squadron was working up to full speed, and was steering south-eastward to close with the enemy. The weather this time was extremely favourable from the British point of view. A north-east

wind swept sea and sky clear of mist, and allowed a long vision over the grey-foam-flecked waste of waters. At half-past seven the German squadron was sighted from our flagship. It was seen leftward, on the port bow, about fourteen miles away, steaming fast, and steering towards the south-east.

The tail-end ships of the enemy's line were preparing to drop contact mines in their wake, on the chance of blowing up some of the pursuing British vessels. But this simple trick was easily countered, for the first thing Sir David Beatty did, on receiving the report of the enemy's position, was to steer his ships outside the enemy's track, getting on their quarter. In other words, he so altered his course as to pursue them on a line parallel to theirs, instead of following directly behind the hostile squadron. Thus the course of the fugitives and the line of the pursuers formed two parallel lines at least six or seven miles distant from each other. No mines dropped by the enemy could drift anywhere near the attacking squadron. All this, of course, was merely the usual battle tactics of every British squadron. Nevertheless, the hopeful Germans seemed to have brought quite a heavy cargo of floating mines. If they could not damage our fighting ships, there was at least a chance of sinking some neutral merchant-ship or fishing-smack, and generally increasing the perils of commerce in the North Sea.

The British squadron settled down to a long, stern chase, all the battle-cruisers working up their speed until they reached a pace of thirty-two ordinary miles an hour. This was an easy speed for the new ships, the Lion, Tiger, and Princess Royal. They were, indeed, able to add another couple of miles an hour to it. But for the Indomitable, a battle-cruiser of the oldest type, it was a great excess over her normal rate of movement. She would have tailed away out of the line, but for the tremendous exertions of her black squad. Her engineers and stokers sent her along in a way that excited the admiration of the entire squadron, and Sir David Beatty expressed the general feeling when he signalled : " Well done, Indomitable stokers !" Even the New Zealand, completed in 1912, four years after the Indomitable, had some difficulty in keeping up with the three leading ships. For while the Tiger could do over thirty knots, the Princess Royal thirty knots, and the Lion nearly thirty knots, the older New Zealand could only do a fraction over twenty-nine knots at her best. But her black squad also drove her along at a pace that kept her fairly in line.

It was a battle between British engineers and stokers and German engineers and stokers in the first place. The Germans had fourteen miles start, which our engine-room men had to wipe out long before the danger spot was reached. The speed **Our " black squad's " grand work** of the newly completed Derfflinger was not known, but it was certainly less than that of our latest battle-cruisers. The speed of the Seydlitz, a 1913 ship, was about equal to that of our Princess Royal, a 1912 ship. The Moltke, completed in 1911, was just a little faster than the New Zealand, completed a few months later. And the Blücher, with an actual sea speed of about twenty-five knots, was quite out of the running. It was a blunder to have brought her out on a fast-raiding action. For the speed of a squadron that holds together is naturally that of its slowest ship.

It only took our sailors eighty-two minutes to close

Damage wrought by a German shell to the rear of a house in Hunter Street.

At the gasworks shells penetrated two gasometers, and the engine-house was hit. The escaping gas caught fire, and eight workmen were injured.

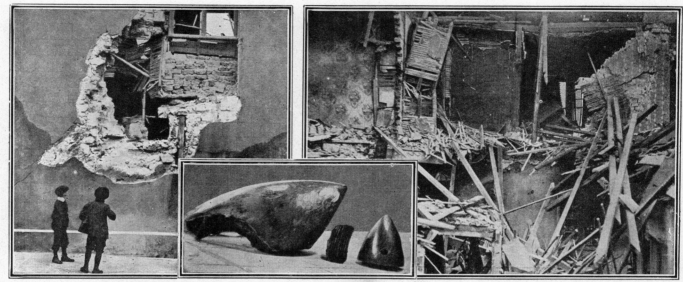

The first of these photographs gives another view of the Baptist chapel shown on page 9. In the house in William Street (on the right) four children were killed and two injured. The third photograph is of fragments of shell fired from the German warships.

Two houses in Cleveland Road which were completely demolished. The bombardment of the Hartlepools levied a total of nearly a hundred lives.

Private dwelling-houses, the upper parts of which were shattered by German shells.

CAMERA RECORDS OF THE SEA HUNS' VISIT TO THE HARTLEPOOLS.

Interior of All Saints' Church, Scarborough, showing the wreckage which was caused by a shell that came through the roof.

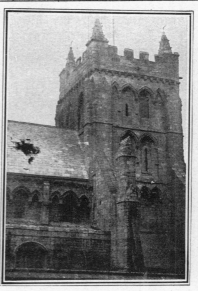

The historic Church of St. Hilda, showing damage to the roof.

What a boarding-house on St. Nicholas companion cruiser

Gap in the wall of the Town Hall, made by a shell which passed through the Council Chamber.

A corner of the Royal Hotel, showing damage caused by a German shell during the bombardment.

Scarborough's "fortifications." Gaps in the walls of the ancient castle caused by the German shell fire. Dating from the reign of King Stephen, the castle was dismantled by Cromwell.

The Harbour Lighthouse at Scarborough the German gunners availed th

TS WERE FIRED UPON THIS DEFENCELESS TOWN.

iff looked like after the Moltke and her
d steamed away.

A house in Commercial Street which
was wrecked by a German shell.

The walls of the ancient castle, ten feet thick, were shattered in places, and the
keep was also damaged by the bombardment.

Where a family perished. House in Wykeham Street, where
Mrs. Barnett and two children were killed.

Photograph showing the work of the Sea Huns on a house
in Lonsdale Road.

rovided a conspicuous mark, of which
mselves with the effect shown.

The Grand Hotel, one of the most prominent buildings from the sea, was struck by three shells. Our photograph
shows the destruction caused in the restaurant and buffet.

15

The ancient ruins of St. Hilda's Abbey, standing near the cliff's edge, afforded congenial "sport" for the German gunners.

The damage caused by German shell-fire to these two houses suggests that the cellars were not invariably the safest of hiding-places.

The ancient Abbey of St. Hilda, the torn shell of which is famous wherever the English language is known, stands on the site once occupied by the monastery of Streonshalh. This, according to Bede, was established in 657, when Hilda became abbess, building her abbey on ground granted by King Oswy. It was during the reign of Hilda that Whitby became the cradle of English poetry. Of the two smaller views inset, the upper one shows the damage done to the old abbey, and the lower one the wreckage of Whitby coastguard station,

DEVASTATION WROUGHT IN ANCIENT WHITBY, THE CRADLE OF ENGLISH POETRY.

within twenty thousand yards of the rear German ship. At this distance the Lion fired a single ranging shot, but it fell short. The enemy at this time were steaming in single line ahead, with their six light cruisers tearing away in front of them, and a large number of their destroyers on their starboard beam—that is, on the right-hand side.

First shell on doomed Blucher At nine minutes past nine, when the ships were about ten miles apart, the Lion got her first shell home on the Blücher. A terrific mass of high explosive and hardened steel, weighing more than half a ton, screamed through the air at a speed of more than a mile in two seconds, and crashed on the armour of the doomed Blücher. A blue light showed where steel struck on steel, and then came the smoky explosion of the lyddite tearing open the six-inch thickness of Krupp armour-plate. Eleven minutes afterwards shells from the Tiger also began to fall on the Blücher. Seeing this, the chief gunnery lieutenant of the Lion took another target, and, with the help of his fire-control officers, dropped the shells from his four bow guns on to the third ship in the German line, the Derfflinger, and struck her with salvo after salvo, from a distance of eighteen thousand yards.

The British gunnery was of unparalleled excellence. Much credit was, of course, due to the designer of our superb 13·5 in. naval gun, and to the directors of the ordnance factories who constructed it in its exquisite trueness and incomparable strength. But, after all, the best weapon of war can be impaired or enhanced by the men who handle it in the battle. And the way our men fought their guns was a revelation in warlike efficiency. Everybody worked with high and yet cool energy, many of them thinking at times of the massacred women and children of Scarborough. To Gunnery-Lieutenant-Commander Gerald F. Longhurst, of the Lion, Gunnery-Lieutenant-Commander Evan Bruce-Gardyne, of the Tiger, and to Gunnery-Commander Roland C. S. Hunt, of the Princess Royal, fell the most important work of the action; for their twelve forward guns mainly decided the action.

The position at thirty-five minutes past nine was that the Blücher had dropped astern, and had come within the range of the four forward 12 in. guns of the New Zealand, where Lieutenant-Commander Cecil B. Prickett was gunnery officer. The unfortunate Blücher had been terribly bombarded in turn by the Princess Royal the Tiger and the Lion. They had crippled her, set her on fire, and even knocked one of her gun turrets out of its holdings, and hurled it with its guns and its crew into the sea.

Now the three leading British battle-cruisers passed over the doomed rear ship of the enemy's line, and steaming ahead on their parallel course, attacked the more powerful and swifter German vessels. Our flagship had gained so much on the enemy that she could now straddle the

German flagship, the Seydlitz, leading the enemy's line. To straddle an enemy vessel means to pitch a number of shells at her simultaneously, some of them perhaps falling short or going over, but some of them hitting. She is not straddled unless the middle shells, at least, get home on her armour, turrets, funnels, and conning-tower or fighting top. The Tiger also massed her guns on the Seydlitz, while the Princess Royal continued to batter the Derfflinger, the third ship in the German line.

Only the second German ship, the Moltke, escaped much damage. The reason for this was that she was, during the earlier part of the fight, hidden in smoke. Smoke was the great trouble that our gunners had to contend against. When the action opened, our flotilla cruisers, the Arethusa, Aurora, and Undaunted, with their destroyers, were steaming ahead of our line. They

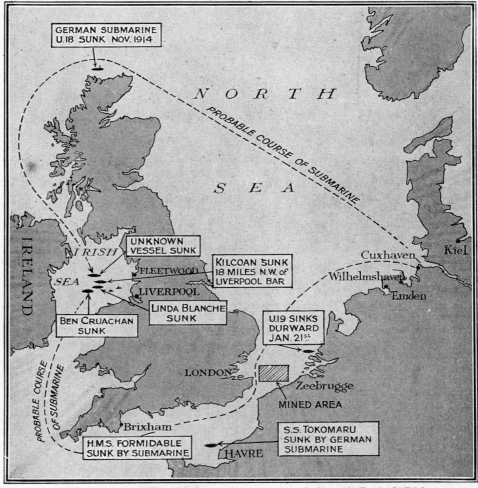

PROBABLE ROUTES TAKEN BY GERMAN SUBMARINE RAIDERS.
This sketch indicates the probable course of German submarines in their attacks on British vessels in the opening weeks of 1915.

immediately dropped back so as not to foul our range with their smoke. At a distance of about ten miles, when the Lion first got home on the Blücher, the target was extremely small. The principal German ships were from six hundred to six hundred and fifty feet long, and about ninety-five feet wide **Perpetually changing** amidships. On the skyline they make a **targets** mark that could be covered by a large pin's point. Hold a lead pencil by the point, one and a half feet from the eye, and the small black centre of it will more than cover the target presented by the whole German battle-cruiser squadron. Naturally, therefore, any drift of smoke between this remote target and the fire-control stations on our leading battle-cruisers seriously interfered with the aim of our gunnery officers.

They were moving at something over thirty miles an hour, and the enemy's ships were driving along at nearly that pace. Thus the calculations for throwing a shell at a pin's-point target ten to eight miles away were continually changing. The battle was really fought by mathematicians, armed with various kinds of range-timing and range-finding instruments. In most cases the man who actually aimed and fired the great guns never saw the guns he fired or the mark at which he aimed. Other men supplied him with visual information, and all he had to do was to make his rapid calculations, then give his guns the right elevation and traverse, and fire them by an electrical signal when his chronometer marked the fraction of a second to which he had calculated.

Getting a gun on the mark is now a fairly easy matter with modern telescopic sights and range-finders. The trouble is to calculate the elevation at which the shot

length, it is extremely difficult to hit. The explanation lies in the old problem of raising the gun to its right elevation. When a fleeing ship is fighting bows-on or stern-on the entire length of its deck comes under fire. A shell pitched at its bow, but falling short, will strike amidships or aft. In the same way, a shell pitched at its stern, and falling over the mark, will strike amidships or forward. In short, when a ship fights broadside-on, there is only the narrow breadth of her deck as a **The odds against Hipper** target. When she fights a running action, showing her bow or stern, the entire length of her deck forms a receptacle for the enemy's shells.

For this reason a fighting admiral will not usually run away when he meets the foe, but will turn and engage in a sound, regular broadside action. In so doing he exposes his ships less to the enemy's fire than if he ran away. He puts spirit and courage into his men, and if he wins the victory it is an absolutely decisive one. To steam away, trying to escape at full speed, and expose the entire length of the ships' decks to the salvos of a confident enemy, exhilarated by the feeling of mastery, is to ride for a fall.

shall be pitched into the air, so that, at the end of its curve, it shall plump down right on the mark. A gun may be truly brought into line with the target, but if the elevation is not correct the shell will pitch harmlessly into the sea, either in front or behind the enemy's ship. At a distance of ten miles, a 13·5 in. shell would be about twenty seconds making its aerial voyage. During this time, a twenty-nine or thirty knot target would have shifted an appreciable distance. So the shell has to be pitched at the spot a vessel will reach in about a third of a minute. To make quite sure of hitting it, all the attacking guns are fired at once by the chief officer of the fire-control, with the result that if his calculations are correct he straddles his target, and gets at least one terrible wrecking shell full on the mark.

Both the British and the German squadron began the action under the best conditions for good gunnery effects, for each of the principal opposing ships presented only her bow or stern at the target as a mark. This **Conditions for good gunnery** meant that each ship could be more easily hit by the opposing guns than if it had shown one of its long sides to the enemy. This is a curious paradox, well known to all fighting seamen, but scarcely understood by the general public. When a ship shows only its bow or stern, leaving merely the beam of ninety to ninety-five feet clear on the skyline, it is easy to shell it. If a ship fights broadside-on, showing its long grey side, six hundred to six hundred and fifty feet in

THE WAR AT SEA THROUGH GERMAN EYES.

The upper picture is an essay in imagination on the part of Professor Paul Teschinsky, of Hamburg, and purports to represent German torpedo-boats attacking British coast defence ships. The other picture is from a painting by Professor W. Malchin, and was painted to show the German people how their " gallant " Navy bombarded Scarborough.

Rear-Admiral Hipper had four ships against five, and thirty-six big guns against forty. His guns were all of smaller calibre than the British. The odds in gun-power were, we may admit, fully two to one against him. But this is only a paper calculation. It was up to him, by skilful manœuvring, to get certain massed fire effects, which would give him the advantage. Nelson was always ready to fight against heavy odds, and yet, by his genius in handling his ships, to bring superior forces to bear on the enemy at the critical point. Only a few weeks before, Admiral Cradock, with only two large old guns, had gallantly faced an enemy with eight times his gun-power. He attempted the impossible, perhaps, but Admiral Hipper was offered a fighting chance that any British squadron would have gladly taken. His precipitate flight looked like being both a bad move from the German

The German Press, the German people, and the German Navy appear to have been immensely satisfied with their wild work on our East Coast. This illustration is taken from a picture based by Professor F. Lindner on a sketch by a German naval officer who took part in the bombardment of Scarborough. British feeling was faithfully expressed by Mr. Winston Churchill, who wrote: " Whatever feats of arms the German Navy may hereafter perform, the stigma of the baby-killers of Scarborough will brand its officers and men while sailors sail the seas."

The above picture, by Professor Höger, of " The Panic at Scarborough," was painted to commemorate the bombardment of our East Coast towns. The deaths numbered over one hundred, and over five hundred were wounded, many severely. A large number of the victims were women and children, and all but a few dozen were unarmed civilians. The effect of this example of German " frightfulness " was to give a remarkable impetus to recruiting in London and many other parts of the country, and this impetus would have been more marked had the time not been so near Christmas. Lord Kitchener expressed his pleasure at the calmness and absence of panic among troops and civilians.

GERMAN ARTISTS' VIEWS OF THE EFFECTS OF " FRIGHTFULNESS " AT SCARBOROUGH

THE LION LEADS THE LINE: SIR DAVID BEATTY'S BOLD AND DARING PLAN OF ACTION.

When on January 24th, 1915, the German raiding squadron under Admiral Hipper was caught unawares and turned in frantic haste for home, Sir David Beatty took a bold and daring line of action. Leaving the New Zealand and the Indomitable to get along and support him as fast as they could, he put the Lion along at her top speed, and, followed by the Tiger and the Princess Royal, faced all the guns the Germans could bring to bear upon him. The Lion got her first shell home on the Blücher when the ships were about ten miles apart. Our picture is from a drawing by Charles Dixon, R.I.

point of view and an additional dishonour to the squadron of baby-killers. It seemed to mark more clearly than anything which had occurred on land or sea up to that time how low the fighting spirit of Prussia had declined since the days of Frederick the Great. But, as we shall afterwards see, there is just a possible explanation of his apparent want of fighting energy. He may have been trying to lure Sir David Beatty into a trap.

The only other manœuvre of importance that Admiral Hipper attempted was to sacrifice his destroyers in the hope of saving his battle-cruisers. This movement began at a quarter to ten, when our two leading ships were pounding the flaming Seydlitz, while the Princess Royal was hammering the flaming Derfflinger, and the New Zealand was crippling the Blücher. Our flotilla cruisers and destroyers had previously withdrawn from the front to the left of our line, to prevent their smoke from obscuring the chief targets, and the enemy's destroyer flotillas now swept away from their battle-cruisers and charged across at our leading ships. In answer to this movement the lieutenant-commander in charge of the destroyer Meteor, steamed out to meet the enemy's mosquito attack, backed by the M Division of our destroyers, handled with splendid ability by Captain the Hon. H. Meade.

All through the critical period of the remaining part of the action the position of the little Meteor was terrifying. She was clean in the line of fire, shells whistling over and all around her, with now and again an enemy's broadside aimed directly at her. Try to imagine a frail little vessel, steaming thirty-five knots, with four battle-cruisers on either side belching forth flame and smoke continually, and the screech of the projectiles flying overhead seeming to tear the air into ribbons. Twelve and 11 in. shells, dropping perilously near, sent columns of water a hundred feet above the sea, just a few yards away from her deck, and the descending spray drenched every man. All around was the awful crashing noise of the great guns, the yellow explosions, the blue flashes, as the shells struck the armour-plate, with massive tongues of fire shooting up, and dense clouds of black or yellow smoke, which obliterated the whole ship from view when the shells burst upon her.

The terrible grandeur of the scene made the men on the destroyer forget their personal danger. For sublimely spectacular interest, their position was worth the peril they ran. They were hit twice without suffering any material damage, though most of the crew continually missed death by inches. It seemed as though they possessed a charmed life, until they tried to torpedo the Blücher. She had at last fallen out of the line, a raging furnace amidships, helpless, and the German admiral left her to her fate. She had been battered by the 13·5 in. guns of our three leading ships. Then the New Zealand turned her 12 in. guns upon her; and lastly the heroic stokers of the Indomitable brought up their vessel in time to do the final killing.

This was about noon. To hasten the job, the little Meteor circled round the doomed ship that was settling down, though still on an even keel. But **The Blucher's last shot** even then she was not dead. For, firing her last round, she sent an 8·2 in. shell into the Meteor, which killed four men and wounded another. What next happened is not clear. On the one hand the Meteor, two minutes after the shell struck her, discharged her torpedo. On the other hand, the Arethusa had also approached the stricken enemy ship, with the same idea of finishing her off, and of releasing the Indomitable for more important work. The Arethusa likewise discharged a torpedo. As at this time

the poor old Blücher was almost stationary, it is possible that both torpedoes got home, for the crew of the Arethusa admit that the doomed ship had a terrible list before they fired their first torpedo. The Arethusa used her second torpedo quite close, steaming up within two hundred yards of her prey before she delivered her blow.

The German crew was game to the last. They lined up to the taffrail, standing rigidly to attention, and in this attitude they would have met their death if a British sailor had not warned them. But one of the officers of the Arethusa took up **Airmen bomb** a megaphone and shouted to them to **drowning seamen** jump if they wanted to save their lives. They understood him, and after gallantly waving their caps and cheering as their ship went down, they all took headers into the water.

In the meantime the last torpedo got home. The explosion was appalling, and the Blücher slowly turned over on her port side, showing her starboard side. Then for some minutes she floated bottom upwards, and at

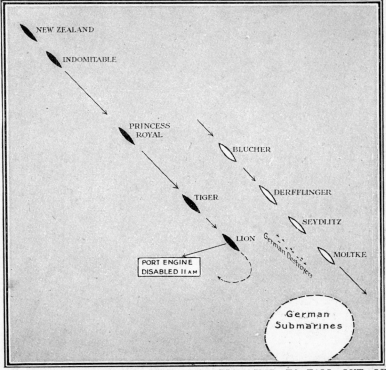

SKETCH PLAN SHOWING WHEN THE LION HAD TO FALL OUT OF LINE.

In the above plan are indicated the approximate positions of the British and German battleships in the Dogger Bank Battle, when one of the enemy vessels got a shot in on her bow, which damaged the feed tank, stopped the port engine, and made it necessary for her to turn.

last sank slowly, leaving the survivors of her crew struggling in the water. Most of the Germans wore india-rubber airbags, fitting in front of their chests, and these floats kept over a hundred and twenty-five of them up in time to be rescued. More would have been saved; but while our boats were picking up the survivors, a Zeppelin airship and a German seaplane soared above the scene of rescue and began dropping bombs upon the men who were being given their lives. One bomb fell among the drowning men, and blew four of them to pieces as they were clinging to one of the hundreds of planks which the British sailors had thrown overboard to help them till the boats came along. It is unlikely that even German airmen would deliberately kill their own defeated men as they were struggling in the water. In the distance they must have mistaken the Blücher, which had been battered out of all recognition, for a sinking British ship, thus giving rise to the extraordinary report

Courtesy of "The Daily Mail."

THE BURNING BLÜCHER, ABANDONED TO HER FATE, SANK LIKE A TIN CAN FILLED WITH WATER.

The above unique photograph, taken from a British cruiser, shows the Blücher at the moment when the great ship was about to take the final plunge. The bow of the leviathan is on the right of the picture. A remnant of the ill-fated crew clustered astern, and many slid down the ship's side in the hope of being picked up from the sea. The shattered tripod mast is observable on the right. Four 8·2 in. and two 6 in. guns are to be seen pointing passively skywards. The fore-shortened mainmast appears abaft two of the 8·2 in. guns, but both funnels had disappeared under the deadly British fire.

Reproduced by permission of " The Illustrated London News."

THE CRIPPLED BLÜCHER, A RAGING FURNACE AMIDSHIPS, WAS GAME TO THE LAST.

Fought to a standstill as the Blücher was, her crew were game to the last. They lined up at attention, and in this attitude would have met their death, had not an officer of the Arethusa shouted to them to jump to save their lives. Over one hundred and twenty-five of them were rescued.

afterwards made by the German Admiralty, that a British battle-cruiser had been seen to sink. In any case it was not chivalrous of the German airmen to bombard drowning seamen, and the fact that these seamen were their own countrymen, with whose rescue they interfered, was in a way a providential punishment for their national manner of warfare. The conduct of the Zeppelin, in regard to warlike operations, was visible. For when two shots had been fired at her, she made off with frantic haste, amidst the derisive cheers of our fighting seamen.

Screen of enemy destroyers While the affair of the Blücher was proceeding, the enemy's destroyer flotillas got between the opposing battle-cruiser lines, and emitted vast columns of smoke to screen their beaten and flying remaining big ships. Then, under cover of the thick drifting curtain of smoke, the three German battle-cruisers turned northward in order to increase their distance from our Lion and Tiger. But the manœuvre was at once discerned by Sir David Beatty, and he ordered his squadron also to alter course, form a line bearing north-north-west, and drive on at utmost speed.

Thereupon the commander of the German destroyer flotillas attempted a very brave but impossible thing. He sent his frail small boats full steam ahead at the two leading British battle-cruisers, with the intention of closing for a torpedo attack. On a dark cloudy night with a little mist, these mosquito tactics might produce an important result. It was for such work in the darkness that destroyers were partly designed. But to attempt it on a clear bright winter morning, in an air of extreme visibility, was not gallantry, but utter desperation. For the battle-cruisers had each a broadside of eight 4 in. guns, directed by a special subsidiary system of fire-control, for beating off destroyers. The small guns on the German destroyers were useless, and for **A brave but desperate effort** two reasons. In the first place they had to be laid in the old-fashioned way simply by a gunlayer, as there is no room on a destroyer for a proper system of fire-control. In the second place, the destroyer guns could not send a shell of sufficient size and penetrative power to get through the armour-plate of our new big ships. So when the Lion and the Tiger both opened fire on the enemy's mosquito craft, the effect was so over-whelming that all the German destroyers withdrew from the tempest they had drawn down upon themselves, and resumed their original course alongside their own battle-cruiser line.

Reproduced by permission of " The Illustrated London News."

THE BLÜCHER GOES TO HER DOOM: ANOTHER VIEW OF THE SINKING LEVIATHAN.

At the moment when the above striking photograph was taken the fore-turret of the great German cruiser had gone by the board, the funnels had been battered out of place, and the hull was holed from stem to stern. On the left of the photograph a British torpedo-boat destroyer is seen waiting to pick up survivors. In firing her last round the Blücher sent an 8 2 in. shell into the Meteor, killing four men and wounding another.

BOATS FROM THE ARETHUSA RESCUING MEN FROM THE SINKING BLÜCHER.

Most of the German sailors wore india-rubber airbags, fitting in front of their chests, and these kept up over one hundred and twenty-five of them from drowning before help arrived. More would have been saved, but while our boats were picking up the survivors a Zeppelin airship and a German seaplane soared above the scene of rescue and began dropping bombs among the men who were struggling in the water, one bomb blowing four of them to pieces. The airmen apparently were under the impression that the battered and now unrecognisable Blücher was a sinking British vessel.

Reproduced by permission of " The Illustrated London News."

H.M.S. LION, VICE-ADMIRAL BEATTY'S FLAGSHIP, GOING INTO ACTION.

But soon after they withdrew, about six minutes to eleven, when the Blücher was a fiery, shapeless wreck, a new source of danger to our squadron was observed. Enemy submarines were reported to be steering under water towards our cruisers from the starboard bow—that is, coming forward on the right of our line. Sir David Beatty personally observed the wash of a periscope two points on the starboard bow of his flagship. He immediately had his ship swerved round to the other side to escape the invisible torpedo. The peril of this underwater attack, however, was not great in the circumstances. For our leading ships were then being driven along at a pace of thirty-two miles an hour. No sub-

Peril of under-water attack

marine was quick enough in action to get a torpedo on a target going at this speed. Sir David had already met and evaded a hostile torpedo attack in misty weather in the Bight of Heligoland. In the present Battle of the Dogger Bank the air was clear and the water calm enough for even the wash of hostile periscopes to be discerned.

Everything was going excellently from the British point of view. From 9.20 o'clock to 11 o'clock the Lion had been hurling her terrible shells at the three German battle-cruisers From 9.45 o'clock the Tiger and the Princess Royal had also been hammering the Seydlitz, Moltke, and Derfflinger; and the New Zealand had also brought her 12 in. guns to bear on the rear enemy ships. For the last seventy-five minutes the Seydlitz and the

Derfflinger had been continually on fire, and the Moltke, which had first been obscured by the drifting smoke of her flagship, had also become a clear target. There were more than a thousand men dead and wounded in the three ships, and some of their guns were out of action. An hour more and the three of them would have been at the bottom of the sea.

But the luck which had enabled the raiders to escape from Sir John Jellicoe in person again favoured them, but not to the same extent.

The enemy's concentrated fire was especially directed upon our flagship, which therefore suffered the most in Sir David Beatty's squadron. Owing, however, to her armour and to the great range at which she fought, the Lion suffered no material damage, though a

Action suddenly broken off

few of her men were wounded. One of the crew afterwards remarked that the noise of the falling German shells was like the rattle of peas on a corrugated-iron roof. The distance was too great for the German gun fire to take effect.

But at three minutes past eleven, as the Lion was going at her topmost speed, firing as she went, her bow lifted high out of the water as it tore through the seas, one of the enemy's ships, by a stroke of luck, got a shot in on her bow, which damaged the feed tank, and thus stopped the port engine.

Materially it was only a slight injury that could soon be repaired in a shipbuilding yard. But the immediate

AFTER THE BATTLE: THE INDOMITABLE TOWING THE LION BACK TO PORT.

By permission of "The Illustrated London News."

THE DOGGER BANK BATTLE: SIR DAVID BEATTY ON THE BRIDGE OF THE TORPEDO-BOAT DESTROYER ATTACK.

During the Dogger Bank Battle on January 24th, 1915, it was reported to Admiral Sir David Beatty at 11.3 a.m. that the injury to his flagship the Lion was incapable of immediate repair. He then directed the Lion to shape course N.W. At 11.20 he called the destroyer Attack alongside, shifting his flag to her at about 11.35 a.m. He then proceeded at utmost speed to rejoin the battle-cruiser squadron, and met them at noon retiring N.N.W. He then boarded and hoisted his flag in the Princess Royal at about 12.20 p.m., amidst the enthusiastic cheering of the crew. Admiral Beatty paid a notable tribute to the good seamanship of Lieut.-Commander Cyril Callaghan, of the Attack. The above remarkable photograph shows the gallant admiral on the bridge of the Attack approaching the battle-cruiser Princess Royal.

effect was that it reduced the speed of the flagship and compelled her to fall out of the line under a guard of destroyers. Though Sir David Beatty at once transferred his flag to one of these fast little boats, the Attack, it was some time before he could rejoin and lead his squadron. In fact, he did not shift his flag to the Princess Royal until about twenty minutes past twelve. Meanwhile, the other British cruisers pursued their flaming foes for some minutes as they fled eastward.

Then the action was suddenly broken off and the British squadron withdrew under the orders of Rear-Admiral Sir Archibald Moore. Of the three enemy battle-cruisers, one was seriously damaged, and the other two, according to German reports, were able to make good their injuries. Some damage was also done to the German destroyers, and one of their light cruisers of the town class,

the Kolberg, was engaged by our light cruiser the Aurora, and much battered. It was at first thought that she had been sunk, but the Berlin authorities denied this. Our loss in lives was very slight. Six men were severely wounded in the Lion, but none killed. In the Tiger, Engineer-Captain Taylor and nine men were killed, and four men lost their lives on the destroyer Meteor.

At two o'clock in the afternoon the Germans had one slight final chance of partly redressing the balance against them. For the starboard engine of the Lion then began to give trouble. Owing to priming, it gradually stopped, and at thirty-eight minutes past three the Indomitable was ordered to take the Lion in tow. Under difficult circumstances this task was accomplished in a seamanlike manner, and the former flagship was brought safely to port.

This description of the semi-decisive battle-cruiser action in the North Sea, which partly crippled **Rival accounts of** the fast wing of the German High Seas **the battle** Fleet, is necessarily incomplete, for no official information has been published concerning the reason why Sir Archibald Moore, in the temporary absence of Sir David Beatty, broke off the action while we still had the odds in ships and guns on our side.

The unofficial report, issued by the Press Bureau soon after the battle, stated that the action had been broken off because of the vicinity of German submarines and minefields. On the other hand, the later British official despatches did not give this explanation, and the German

naval authorities asserted that the fight ended some seventy miles from their minefields and Heligoland. The German Admiralty, however, went on to allege that the action was broken off because the British squadron had lost a battle-cruiser and two destroyers.

Entirely false was the enemy's statement that we lost any ships. But it is impossible to deny that when Sir David Beatty, owing to the injury to his flagship, had to leave, at the critical **Admiral Moore and** moment, the handling of the squadron **the critics** to Sir Archibald Moore, the battle ended a few minutes afterwards, though the Germans were badly beaten and in dire distress many miles from their minefields. No clear explanation has yet appeared of the reason why the battered enemy ships were allowed to escape from our still much superior force.

Nelson used to say that if he had sunk ten ships and allowed the eleventh to escape, he should not think he had done well. If this remark is in any way applicable to the leadership of our First Battle Cruiser Squadron at the critical moment, Sir David Beatty at least cannot come under any censure. For while he was in the destroyer the Attack, the handling of the squadron had to be left to Sir Archibald Moore in the New Zealand.

There was, however, a rumour that the battle-cruiser action off

GERMAN SUBMARINES IN DOCK AT WILHELMSHAVEN.
The submarines seen in the above photograph are of the 1910-12 class, and we get a clear view of the position of the twin torpedo-tubes at the stern. In the earlier types the torpedoes were discharged only from tubes in the bow. Inset: The British submarine D5, sunk by a mine laid by one of the German cruisers returning after the raid on Yarmouth.

the Dogger Bank was only part of a possible larger operation, in which Admiral von Ingenohl with his battleships intended to engage. It was reported that the German main fleet came out eastward, and tried to close round our First Battle Cruiser Squadron, while Admiral Hipper was luring our ships towards Heligoland.

This movement by Ingenohl, it was said, was countered by the unexpected appearance of the advance guard of destroyers of our Battle Fleet, whereupon Ingenohl turned at full speed for his base. It was then alleged that in the brief interval between the promise and non-fulfilment of the hope of a general fleet action, our First Battle Cruiser Squadron, under the temporary command of Sir Archibald Moore, hesitated just for ten minutes between the larger and smaller force of enemy ships, and thus allowed the

DIAGRAM ILLUSTRATING THE WORK OF OUR 12 IN. GUNS AT FIFTEEN MILES RANGE.
Owing to the distance at which the battle-cruisers fought on January 24th, 1915, the shells from the British 12 in. guns had to take a curved path, reaching a very high point before beginning to fall towards their objectives. Admiral Sir Percy Scott has estimated that in firing at a range of fifteen miles the shot would attain an altitude of 22,500 feet, or some 6,000 feet over the summit of Mont Blanc.

Seydlitz, Moltke, and Derfflinger to escape. All this, however, was mere rumour, and a long time may pass before the full facts are made public.

It is worthy of note, however, that soon after the action Admiral von Ingenohl was superseded from the command of the German High Seas Fleet. This looked as though Rear-Admiral Hipper had played well the part assigned to him, but had failed to receive proper support from his chief. Somewhere about the same time Sir John Rushworth Jellicoe was promoted. These two changes of command and rank in regard to the contending leaders of the opposing fleets were fairly indicative of the results of the British and German naval operations at the end of the first six months of the war. The German commander had failed ; the British commander had succeeded. So extreme then

REAR-ADMIRAL HIPPER.
Commanding German battle cruiser squadron.

REAR-ADMIRAL FUNKE.
Second in command to Rear-Admiral Hipper.

was the desperation of the German Admiralty that it designed the extraordinary plan of trying to torpedo, in submarine attack, all the neutral ships trading to our shores. The barbaric, lawless, murderous nature of this last piratical venture of the enemy was a fair measure of the results of the Dogger Bank action. The battle had definitely established our superiority in gunnery, and for this reason it was decisive.

"This combat between the finest ships of both navies," said Mr. Winston Churchill on February 15, "is of immense significance and value, in the light it throws upon rival systems of design and armament. Although the German shell is a most formidable instrument of destruction, the bursting, smashing power of the heavier British projectile is decidedly greater, and—this is the great thing—our shooting is *at least* as good as theirs!"

OFFICERS OF H.M.S. LION. VICE-ADMIRAL SIR DAVID BEATTY (MARKED WITH AN x) IN CENTRE OF THE GROUP.

CHAPTER XLVIII.

THE FIRST PHASE OF TURKEY'S SHARE IN THE WAR.

By A. H. Trapmann, Special War Correspondent in the Balkan Wars.

The Too Gentle Treatment of the Sublime Porte—Mission of the Goeben and Breslau—Festive Reception of German Sailors in Turkish Waters—Dilemma of the Young Turks—Germany's " Happy Expedient "—Goeben's Commander Threatens to Bombard Constantinople—Enver Pasha and his Co-Plotters—The Balkan Wars and Turkish Intrigues with Bulgaria—British Naval Missions in Greece and Turkey—Enver Engineers the Proclamation of a Jehad—Loyalty of Indian and Egyptian Mohammedans to the British Raj—Faulty Turkish Mobilisation—German's Short-Sighted Policy and Turkish Armaments—The Modernised Turkish Army—The Ottoman Fleet—Isolation of the Turkish Empire—Armenian and Arabian Factors—The Egyptian Campaign—Turkish Disaster in the Caucasus—Invasion of Persia—The Allies Knocking at the Gates of the Dardanelles.

O N November 5th, 1914, Great Britain declared war upon Turkey, and thus Asia Minor and North-East Africa became potential areas for the waging of the Great War, which hitherto had been confined to Europe and the immediate vicinity of German colonies. The declaration of war came as a surprise to no one ; indeed, the only surprise was that the Porte had been allowed to defy for so long the first international principles of neutrality. The patience displayed by the Entente Powers under the most exasperating circumstances did more credit to their desire for peace than to their knowledge of the workings of the Oriental mind. Incident after incident of an unfriendly, and even of a directly hostile nature, was allowed to pass with little more than a gentle diplomatic protest. Such action was construed by the Sublime Porte as an admission of weakness.

The incidents referred to were of a sufficiently unusual nature to occasion as much surprise as annoyance. The declaration of war between the Entente and Germanic Powers found two German warships in the Mediterranean—the Goeben and the Breslau.

The Goeben was one of the latest Dreadnought cruisers. Completed in October, 1912, she had a displacement of 23,000 tons and a main armament of ten 11 in. guns. On her steam trials she attained a speed of 27 knots per hour, but she had

MEHMED V., SULTAN OF TURKEY.
Born on November 3rd, 1844, he was proclaimed Sultan on April 27th, 1909, after the deposition of his brother Abdul Hamid II.

since attained a speed of 28·4 knots on several occasions. The Breslau was a light cruiser completed in April, 1912, with a displacement of 4,550 tons, carrying twelve 4·1 in. guns, and was capable of steaming 27·5 knots.

These two swift cruisers had been allotted the task of cruising the Indian Ocean and holding up the British main steam routes to the East beyond the Suez Canal in the event of Britain joining the Entente Powers in the war. Owing to the miscalculation of German statesmanship these vessels were still in the Western Mediterranean on their way to the Suez Canal when Britain declared war on Germany.

In the Straits of Messina they were nearly run to earth in August by a British squadron commanded by Admiral Sir A. Berkeley Milne and Rear-Admiral Troubridge. The Goeben and Breslau, thanks to their superior speed, managed to effect their escape after making a somewhat dramatic exit from the straits, which they left with decks cleared for action, crews piped to stations, and the ships' bands playing " Die Wacht am Rhein " and " Deutschland über Alles."

It was common knowledge that the Goeben, at least, was manned entirely by a crew of skilled ratings and petty-officers. Her stokehold was worked exclusively by chief stokers, and her boats' crews consisted entirely of petty-officers. It had been the intention of the Goeben to put the majority of her crew ashore at Smyrna and there pick

THE BRITISH CRUISER GLOUCESTER IN ACTION.

Photograph of the second-class protected cruiser Gloucester firing a broadside while going at full speed. The gun crew is almost obscured by the spouts of water from a burst hose-pipe. Hose-pipes were laid along the decks, keeping them constantly wet, as a safeguard against fire. The Gloucester was in pursuit of the Goeben when that vessel sought safety in the Dardanelles.

up a substitute crew of less skilled German sailors who had been sent out in two merchant vessels beforehand for the purpose. The skilled ratings were then to have proceeded to the Golden Horn and staffed the whole Turkish Fleet.

The German battle-cruiser, however, was obliged to alter her programme. Chased by the British fleet she raced at her highest steaming power for the Dardanelles, and, with her little consort, gained the protection of the Turkish forts just in time to give her wash to the British pursuing squadron on August 10th. In exchanging shots with H.M.S. Gloucester the Goeben had been seriously damaged, and had sustained several casualties.

The Turkish military authorities stage-managed a most cordial reception for the two fugitive war vessels. The captain of the Goeben was received in special audience by the Sultan, and the crews were fêted (by order) by the whole population, military and civil, of the Turkish capital.

For three days the German crews gave themselves up to the delights of Oriental festivity, while the Ambassadors of the various Powers to the Sublime Porte wrangled over the point of international law raised by the vessels' stay in Turkish

THE TURKISH CRUISER HAMIDIEH.
The Hamidieh bombarded Novorossisk, in the Black Sea, on October 28th, 1914. Inset. Captain Rauoff.

waters. As usual the Porte was prolific with excuses and procrastinations. After the exchange of many terminological inexactitudes, Turkey eventually announced to a disbelieving world that she had arranged to purchase the two vessels and to intern their crews. It was soon apparent that this announcement was nothing but a mere subterfuge, for the vessels still continued to be manned by German officers and men wearing Turkish uniforms and flying the Turkish flag. In order still further to complicate the situation, the Goeben held up various British, French, and Italian vessels in a most arbitrary manner. Note after Note was exchanged between Britain and the Porte, but with no tangible effect. Finally, on October 28th, 1914, the Goeben, Breslau, and Hamidieh bombarded the Russian coast at Theodosia and Odessa, causing inconsiderable damage it is true, but placing the remedy of the situation beyond the reach of diplomacy. The Entente Powers delivered an ultimatum simultaneously, the terms of which were not complied with, and Britain, Russia, and France declared war upon the Sublime Porte, the Ambassadors having already left Constantinople on November 2nd.

Mobilisation scene near Constantinople. Once the finest of fighting men, the Turks fared badly in the Balkan War. Under German officers they rallied again in October, 1914, against the cause of civilisation in Europe.

Recruits from Anatolia leaving a steamer at Constantinople. Formerly only the Moslem Turk was liable for military service, but the Young Turks instituted a law making every Turkish subject liable to be called up.

Turkish Lancers leaving the Ottoman capital on their way to the front. Our photograph is eloquent of the change in uniform and equipment brought about by the German military mission. But the change did not extend very far. When Turkey threw in her lot with the cause of Kaiser Wilhelm, the arrangements for providing the troops with clothing broke down entirely, and one result was that the men had to undertake a winter campaign in cotton summer garments, and suffered terribly, especially in the Caucasus. Inset: Turkish infantry on the march.

THE "SICK MAN OF EUROPE" RALLIES AT THE KAISER'S CALL.

Germany, Turkey hoped no doubt to be able to threaten Greece with war unless Greece abandoned the lost Ægean Islands, while at the same time the astute Turk hoped to sail a middle course between the two groups of belligerent Powers—borrowing money from Germany, while putting off the Entente Powers with endless prevarications and subterfuges.

When the German officers, who doubtless had very definite instructions from Berlin, found that the Turk was disinclined to make common cause with the Germanic Alliance, they hit on the happy expedient of compromising him by bombarding the Crimean coast with the vessels which they themselves commanded, flying the Crescent from the masthead. The Entente Powers demanded an ample apology, and terms which included the interning of the Goeben and Breslau as well as the dismissal of all German officers from the Turkish Navy.

Persian leader in Constantinople announcing the Sultan's proclamation of a "Holy War." Inset: Prayer meeting, led by the Sultan (on left), and attended by German and Turkish officers, for the success of the Turkish arms.

It is now known that the Turkish executive during this period was upon the horns of a dilemma. With that love of intrigue which is the backbone of Oriental diplomacy, the Young Turk Party had flirted and coquetted with Imperial Germany to such an extent that at the crucial moment it was unable to extricate itself from the Kaiser's clutches. By allowing thousands of German officers, soldiers, and sailors to take up duties in the Ottoman Army and Fleet, and by purchasing vast supplies of war material from

Mass meeting in the Turkish capital after the announcement that Turkey had taken the side of Germany in the Great War. The flag bearing the device of a lion and a drawn sword is Persian.

SULTAN MEHMED'S PROCLAMATION OF A "HOLY WAR."

Even in the Turkish Cabinet this ultimatum gave rise to two distinctly opposite views, and the fate of Turkey hung in the balance until the commander of the Goeben intimated to the Turkish Cabinet that unless they rejected the ultimatum he would at once proceed to bombard Constantinople itself, commencing with the Sultan's palace. The situation was too strong for the Turkish Cabinet. The waverers followed the line of least resistance, and preferred to offend their quondam friends beyond the gate rather than their newfound ally-enemy who had so firmly established himself in the very citadel of the Empire.

The history of the world has few more tragic moments to offer to the consideration of posterity than those dramatic hours when those who had banished Sultan Abdul Hamid, and usurped the reins of power under the thin disguise of setting up a constitutional government, eventually found themselves outwitted and helpless, obliged to do the bidding of a German naval officer.

To this end Enver Pasha, the arch-schemer, had undoubtedly plotted, so that the situation came as no surprise to him nor to the narrow circle of astute but unscrupulous men who for close upon a decade had controlled the suicidal foreign policy of the Ottoman Empire, but to all those who did not enjoy Enver's confidence—and at least half the members of the Cabinet must be included in this category—the blow was an exceedingly bitter one, shattering all their day-dreams of a revivified Turkey and replacing them with the worst fears of a black

Arrival of H.H. Prince Hussein Kamel Pasha in Cairo on the occasion of his proclamation as Sultan of Egypt on December 18th, 1914. His Highness was described as the eldest living prince of the family of Mehemet Ali.

nightmare. Ever since the so-called Party of Union and Progress (the " Young Turk " Party, as it was familiarly known) came into power, and by a military coup de main deposed Sultan Abdul Hamid, the Ottoman Empire had commenced to travel downhill at a greater rate than had ever been attained hitherto. Abdul Hamid, with all his wicked ways, his callous massacres of Armenians and oppression of Macedonians, his outrageous dishonesty and admitted shiftiness, was at least a ruler who had known how to keep the Ottoman Empire intact, and by skilfully playing upon the jealousies of the Great Powers had managed to misgovern his disjointed Empire without undue interference from the outside world.

When he wanted money, which was a chronic obsession, he found little difficulty in obtaining it

Hoisting the flag of the new Sultan of Egypt at the Abdin Palace, Cairo. Inset: The new Sultan, accompanied by his Prime Minister, H.E. Sir Hussein Ruchdi Pasha, on their way to the Abdin Palace.
PROCLAMATION OF PRINCE HUSSEIN KAMEL PASHA. THE NEW SULTAN, AT THE ABDIN PALACE, CAIRO.

in Paris or London by hypothecating revenues and granting monopolies. When he got into trouble with either of the groups of Great Powers, he invariably played his cards in such a manner that the other group came to his rescue. So that while Europe wrangled and Christian Ottomans suffered,

Diplomacy of the Sublime Porte

Abdul Hamid continued duly to mis-govern the land. While he amassed personal wealth, it must be admitted that by his brilliant diplomacy he in-variably managed to maintain the prestige and integrity of the Ottoman Empire.

The Young Turk Party came into power, like most oppositions, with fine-sounding promises of reform. They would, so they declared, make Turkey into a modern European State, with all the advantages of Western civilisation grafted upon an inexhaustible Oriental imagina-tion. Whether at first the Young Turks were sincere in their protestations it is difficult to say, but the fact remains that the moment they had usurped the power they fell into the same faults which have ever characterised Oriental government. It is possible to change rulers frequently, but to change the character of a nation is a process that requires centuries.

The new men at the helm committed all the old, flagrant errors of their predecessors, besides inventing a completely new set of their own. The diplomacy of the Sublime Porte was framed not by one master diplomat, as hitherto, but by a caucus of infinitely less astute men, each of whom was jealous of his neighbour, and desired more his own personal advancement than that of the Ottoman Empire. In quick succession followed the war against Italy, when Turkey lost Tripoli and Cyrenaica as the result of a year of war; and before peace had been declared with Italy, the Balkan League —Bulgaria, Serbia, Greece,

THE EX-KHEDIVE ABBAS HILMI.
Who threw in his lot with Germany.

SIR FRANCIS WINGATE.

and Montenegro—had de-clared war on Turkey on Octo-ber 13th, 1912. In that cam-paign the Porte lost nearly the whole of her European provinces, including Crete, and only retained the narrow strip of territory in advance of the Chataldja lines, sufficient to safeguard Constantinople itself from a surprise attack.

The outbreak of war be-tween the Balkan Allies on July 2nd, 1913, when Bul-garia treacherously attacked her former allies, was a heaven-sent opportunity to the Young Turk to re-estab-lish his vanishing prestige. To do him credit he made the most of it. Hastily gathering together an army of 150,000 picked troops, Enver Pasha marched on Adrianople and, scarcely firing a shot, retook that most important city and fortress. The armistice, which began on July 31st, ended in the signing of the Treaty of Bucharest, which gave Eastern Thrace back to Turkey. It is now known that during the early summer of 1913 Turkey was intriguing with Bulgaria to enter into a war against Greece and Serbia. Turkey demanded as her share of a possibly successful campaign the restitution of Adrianople and of Albania. Bulgaria was only willing to agree to Turkey retaking Albania if the European Powers would allow it, wherefore Turkey broke off these somewhat delicate negotiations and made war on Bulgaria. It is characteristic of Ottoman policy, however, that before entering upon this campaign entirely on her own account, she offered an alliance to Greece, which

Greco-Turkish "incidents"

M. Venizelos, the Greek Premier, refused on the ground that it would be unseemly to unite with so recent an enemy to make war upon a former ally—a sentiment which perhaps was more honourable than profitable, as the sequel tended to prove; for hardly had the Treaty of Bucharest been signed than Turkey began to make trouble with Greece. The islands of Chios and Mitylene were two of the stumbling-blocks. "Incidents" were frequent. The Porte applied

GENERAL LIMAN VON SANDERS.
The German Commander-in-Chief of the Turkish Army. The portrait of Sir Francis Reginald Wingate, in supreme command of the Egyptian Army, is given in the centre of this page.

the screw of massacre and oppression upon the Greek inhabitants of Thrace and Asia Minor, and daily relations became more and more strained. The two countries vied in their endeavours to outbid each other for the purchase of two Dreadnought battleships from South American republics at fancy prices, until it was obvious to all intelligent spectators that the danger of war was very imminent.

An interesting feature of the Greco-Turkish situation was that the navies of both countries were being trained by British naval missions. Early in 1914 the Turkish Government signed a contract with a combination of British armament firms to build and maintain a dock and arsenal at Constantinople capable of dealing with the largest types of battleships afloat, while two British admirals, assisted by a well-chosen staff of naval officers, were devoting all their energies to reorganising the Turkish Fleet and dockyards. At the same time, another large British naval mission, consisting of no fewer than nineteen officers under Rear-Admiral Mark Kerr, C.B., had for several months taken in hand the reorganisation of the Greek Navy.

Into this eddy of Balkan politics fell the bombshell of the Great European War. The greater issue drowned all minor strife, but the population and bureaucracy of the Ottoman Empire were incensed against the British Government because on the outbreak of hostilities the British, according to their declared rights, commandeered all war craft building in British dockyards for

foreign Governments. Now among these were two Dreadnought battleships building for Turkey, the first instalments on the price of which had been paid by Turkey out of "voluntary" contributions subscribed by private individual citizens of the Ottoman Empire. As a matter of fact, the vast majority of the sum thus "voluntarily" collected consisted of six months' pay stopped from the salaries and wages of all Turkish Government employees, both military and civil; and these shorn lambs knew only too well that, although Great Britain would refund the money to Turkey, the Turkish Government would never reimburse the subscribers.

Enver gambling for high stakes

Once the Entente Powers had declared war upon Turkey the die for her was cast. None knew better than Enver Pasha the vital issues at stake. Success might bring a recrudescence of Turkish power, and a rehabilitation of her sovereignty over the Balkans and Northern Africa; while defeat would mean the dissolution of the Ottoman Empire into its component parts of Greek, Armenian, Circassian, Syrian, and Arab. Enver was gambling for the highest possible stakes, but so far as he himself was concerned it was a gamble well worth the risk. In the blackest days of the Balkan Wars he had rallied all the polyglot fragments of the patchwork Empire around the Crescent by an appeal to Ottoman patriotism. He invited Syrian, Jew, and Christian alike to forget their diverse creeds and to concentrate their whole energies on winning back from Bulgaria the fair

TURKEY'S EVIL GENIUS.
Enver Pasha, the leader of the Young Turks. He threw himself heart and soul into the quarrel which was forced upon Turkey by her German masters, and it was he who induced the Sultan to proclaim a Jehad, or "Holy War," against the British Empire.

DEFEATED IN THE CAUCASUS.
Shukri Pasha, commander of the Turkish troops in the Caucasus, a badly-defeated general. Inset (left): The eldest son of the Sultan of Turkey and (right) Colonel Halil Bey, commander of the Constantinople garrison.

PERSIA

Desert

Seaman signalling enemy's position

Merchant ship at anchor

BRITISH SLOOP Port Battery in action

Enemy's Bullets striking the water

RIVER SHATT-AL-ARAB

Fire from Turkish snipers

Line of trenches from which enemy was firing

Mud forts partially destroyed down our fire

Reeds

TURKEY

Thick Palm wood.

OPENING STAGES OF THE WAR WITH TURKEY—BRITISH RAID AT THE MOUTH OF THE SHAT-EL-ARAB, PERSIAN GULF.

On November 8th, 1914, the British Admiralty announced a successful operation against Fao, at the mouth of the Shat-el-Arab, a waterway which, formed by the junction of the Euphrates and the Tigris, falls into the Persian Gulf about sixty miles below Basra. The operation was conducted by a military force from India, covered by H.M.S. Odin (Commander Cathcart R. Wason), the armed launch Sirdar, a force of Marines with a Maxim-gun party, and a boat from the Ocean. The enemy's guns were silenced after an hour's resistance, and the town was occupied by the troops and the naval brigade.

lands of the Maritza valley. In part the appeal succeeded, and when the recapture of Adrianople came to flatter this first effort, Enver found his personal prestige— which had been sadly in need of a stimulant—go soaring once more into the zenith. Prestige, however, of this kind is only fed on victory. To maintain his political ascendancy in Constantinople it was necessary for Enver to be able to boast of some new conquest biennially. He was plotting a victorious war against Greece when the German intrigues suddenly pitched him into the seething cauldron of the Great European War. He was far too astute a man to miss his opportunity. War of some kind, against somebody—it mattered not whom—was essential to him personally; he threw himself heart and soul into the quarrel which Turkey had had forced upon her.

In view of the fact that Enver completed his military studies in Germany, it is probable that there was a good deal of reality in the warmth with which he espoused the cause of the new Triple Alliance. **Proclamation of a "Holy War"** On the other hand, clever man as he was, he readily realised that the adversary from whom Turkey had most to fear, or most to gain in the event of final victory, was Britain. It was against Britain, therefore, that expediency and strategy combined to suggest that he should make his greatest effort. It may be imagined how cordially such a strategic doctrine was welcomed by his German ally. Since at first he was powerless to strike at Great Britain effectively either by land or by sea, he determined to strike at her morally. In a moment of exuberant optimism he induced the Sultan to proclaim a Jehad, or Holy War, against the British Empire.

Whether Enver was hypnotised by the political miscalculations of Germany (who throughout the war proved herself as impotent in diplomacy and appreciation of national character as she showed herself capable in military organisation), or whether he was merely risking a false lead in the hope that it would draw a trump, it is impossible to conjecture, but there can be no doubt that in fomenting a holy war Enver placed the seal of finality upon the crumbling destinies of the Ottoman Empire. Religious fanaticism is not a force which can be lightly invoked; when once aroused it is calculated to carry all before it, overstepping, as it does, all considerations of nationality, race, and language. So long as the Sultan of Turkey did not mix politics with his religion he remained the head of the Moslem world; and no matter what might befall the Ottoman Empire the Sultan would have always retained a great power in the world as head and leader of the Mohammedan faith, just as the Vatican still has a large voice in the council of nations despite the fact that the Empire of Rome has long since crumbled into the dust.

Had the Sultan, when proclaiming a Jehad, been able to rally the faithful to his standard by calling a war on Christianity, the move might have proved a feature of great strength, but all that he could do was to proclaim that as the ally of two Christian Empires he proposed to make war upon a group of Christian States, one of which— Britain—ruled over a vast Mohammedan Empire in India, and had nursed ten million Moslems in Egypt into a state **Moslem loyalty to the British Raj** of prosperity and religious freedom which they had never enjoyed under Turkish rule. Not unnaturally the Jehad was a fiasco. The Moslems of India and Egypt saw through the shallow device and refused to be entrapped into a pseudo-religious fanaticism against their benefactors. All the great Moslem institutions and societies throughout Egypt and the British Empire hastened to assure the British Government of their unswerving loyalty to the Raj, and openly deplored the fact that the Sultan, the chief of the Moslem faith, should have dragged their sacred religion into so sordid a political intrigue.

Thereafter, it was clear that by his folly in proclaiming a Jehad, the Sultan had lost the confidence of his co-religionists throughout the world, and that in future Mohammedans would look elsewhere for their spiritual guidance. The Sultan had let his mantle of sanctity fall away from him. It will fall upon the shoulders of a prince or rajah subject to the British throne.

In the bad old days of Abdul Hamid only the Moslem Turk was liable for military service, but the Young Turk Party altered the conscription laws, making every Turkish subject liable to be called up, irrespective of creed or race. The war against the Balkan League showed the utter futility of this new régime, for it was found that only a small percentage of the Armenian and other Christian races answered the mobilisation summons, while the vast majority of these who actually joined the colours seized the first possible opportunity to desert or to go over to the enemy. Again, another cause which contributed even more potentially to the collapse of the Turkish armies was their faulty mobilisation scheme. In order the better to make clear the vital importance to a nation of having a carefully thought out scheme of organisation, it may be as well to describe roughly the process of mobilisation. In peace time it is the object of the army organiser to maintain the largest number possible of skeleton formations, which in war time can be clothed with reservists, and thus made into a complete fighting machine; but these skeleton formations must be able to train men in peace time as well as providing a nucleus in war time. For instance, if it is desired to have a battalion of 1,200 bayonets in time of war, a conscript country need only maintain some three hundred of the men in peace time. When mobilisation takes place these three hundred are medically examined, and those who are unfit, under age, or insufficiently trained are left behind at the depot, while the battalion is brought up to war strength by calling up the various classes of reservists. Any surplus that is still left over remains at the depot and is drafted out to replace the casualties. Now, in all European countries since the Franco-Prussian War, this process of mobilisation is completed before any attempt is made to send the unit on service. A unit does not leave its mobilisation centre until it is complete to the last detail in men, arms, equipment, stores, ammunition, and transport. This, however, was not the case with the Turkish Army in the autumn of 1912. Units were sent direct from their peace stations to the firing-line, their reservists and stores being sent out to join them at the front.

To give an example. The 23rd Independent Division, stationed at Janina, in Albania, had a war strength of some 15,000 men. In peace time it actually numbered about 6,000 all told, one-third of whom had less than one year's service. The reservists, stores, and equipment for this division were supposed to come from Smyrna, in Asia Minor, and as a matter of fact never reached their destination—which is hardly surprising.

Ever since January, 1913, the Turks under German guidance had been making desperate efforts to put their house in order, to remodel and equip their Army, to replenish their military stores, and to recast their entire mobilisation scheme. Each of the Active (Nizam) Divisions was allotted a mobilisation centre. At these centres the

Remodelling the Turkish Army

Nizam units were brought up to war strength and fully equipped, and to each Nizam Division a Redif (or Reserve) Division was affiliated. It was part of Germany's commercial policy to discourage the Turks from creating a large arsenal capable of constructing guns or ammunition on a big scale, since the firm of Krupp wished to sell such warlike stores to Turkey. But the Germans had reason to regret their short-sighted policy, for as soon as war broke out it became impossible to ship further ordnance stores from Essen to Constantinople; there was a great shortage of guns and artillery material in the new Turkish Army. The arrangements for providing the troops with clothing broke down entirely, with the result that the men had to undertake a winter campaign in cotton summer garments. This was their foretaste of the joys of German organisation.

Short-sighted German policy

The modernised Turkish Army of 1914 was organised as follows:

The Army on a peace footing was to consist of twenty-five Nizam (or Regular) Divisions each, consisting of thirteen battalions of infantry, twenty-four guns, one squadron of cavalry, and various details. In all about 15,500 men.

VISIT OF THE SULTAN'S HEIR TO POTSDAM.
An interesting record of the Turco-German entente. The fourth figure in the group is Youssouf Izzedin, heir-apparent to the Turkish throne. Mustapha Pasha is the bearded man in the dark overcoat.

Five of these divisions (i.e., two at Adrianople, one at Constantinople, one in Turkish Caucasia, and one in Arabia) were to be maintained at full strength. The remaining twenty divisions, however, while kept nominally at about half strength were, for one reason or another, allowed to fall to anywhere from one-third to one-quarter of the established strength. On mobilisation all these divisions were to be brought up to full strength by drafts of reservists who had recently left the colours, or by men supposed to be serving, but who were actually on permanent leave; and, moreover, the strength of each battalion was to be augmented from a nominal 1,000 to an actual 1,250. Thus it was contemplated that the twenty-five Nizam Divisions of about 19,000 men each would muster 475,000 men. It was, moreover, schemed to add one Redif (Reserve) Division to each Nizam formation, each pair making an army corps; the men of the Redif formations being either middle-aged reservists who had finished their service or younger men who, by hook or by crook, had escaped the net of conscription. The army corps were to be grouped into five armies, each consisting

GERMANY'S TURKISH ALLIES IN TRAINING FOR THE FIELD.

Our first photograph shows a number of Turkish soldiers engaged in fixing wire entanglements. They are wearing their new military head-dress, half fez and half helmet. In the lower picture we see some of the Sultan's troops digging trenches. It was reported at the time that the men went about their work under German supervision with a marked lack of enthusiasm.

of five Nizam Divisions, five Redif Divisions, a mixed Cavalry Division composed of regulars, reservists, and irregulars, and two regiments (forty guns) of artillery, both light and heavy. This organisation was calculated to bring the effective field armies up to about 1,150,000, the remaining 50,000 men being accounted for in garrison artillery and gendarmerie.

There is reason to believe, however, that the utmost Turkey could hope actually to arm and muster during the present war would be the following:

It must be borne in mind and emphasised that the Redif organisations were of little military value, and their numbers were in many cases fictitious.

The troops of the Nizam and those of the five Redif Divisions raised in Anatolia were fine fighting material if any time and money had ever been spent on their training; but the days were now past when sheer courage alone sufficed to make a good soldier. Some ninety-five per cent. of the Turkish rank and file were illiterate and of low intelligence; their musketry was inferior, and their knowledge of entrenching most elementary. The vast majority of the officers had very little education, either military or otherwise. There were, however, some 1,500 officers in the Turkish Army who had either studied abroad or completed their military education under German instructors. These officers for the most part were very intelligent and eminently capable. Before the war had progressed far the old régime of incompetent pashas had been done away with, and bright westernised young officers of the new school held those superior commands which the Germans had not reserved for themselves.

The chief characteristic of the Turk as a fighting man is his wonderful doggedness in defence, even when vastly

ESTIMATED TOTAL STRENGTH OF THE TURKISH ARMIES.			
			MEN.
The Army of Europe (Adrianople)	5 Nizam Divisions, 2 Redif Divisions, and 3,000 Cavalry		say 140,000
The Reserve Army (Constantinople)	5 Nizam Divisions (under strength) .. .. say	70,000	
	3 Redif Divisions (under strength) .. .. ,,	35,000	
	Irregular Cavalry	2,000	
			say 110,000
The Caucasian Army (with part of Smyrna Army)	8 Nizam Divisions (under strength)	120,000	
	8 Redif Divisions (under strength)	80,000	
	Mixed Cavalry	5,000	
			say 210,000
Arabian Garrison	2 Nizam Divisions (1 under strength)	30,000	
	2 Redif Divisions (probably unarmed, and very doubtful if they would mobilise at all .. .. say	10,000	
			40,000
Smyrna Garrison	1 Nizam Division (under strength and badly armed).. .. .. ,,	12,000	
	3 or, perhaps, 4 Redif Divisions (under strength and badly armed ,,	40,000	
	Cavalry and Details .. .. ,,	8,000	
			60,000
Available against Egypt	4 Nizam Divisions (under strength) .. .. ,,	60,000	
	1 strong Redif Division (for lines of communication) .. .. ,,	20,000	
			80,000
	TOTAL AVAILABLE		640,000

outnumbered. His tactics are clumsy and devoid of originality, and he is terribly slow in seizing an opportunity.

Taught by the bitter experience of the Balkan League War, Turkey had at last realised the value of sea-power, and had determined to create a fleet which would at least secure her own home waters, and keep open the fairway through the Ægean Sea. During the campaign of 1912-13, the Greek Fleet had kept the Turkish Navy mewed up in the Sea of Marmora, an **Turkey's bid for sea-power** impotent onlooker, while Greek shipping furrowed the narrow seas and Greek warships effectively blockaded the Turkish coasts. Turkey had suffered bitterly by reason of her inability to dispute the mastery of her own home waters, and she had determined not to be caught napping again. Under the guidance of the British naval mission at Constantinople, she had bought or laid down two Dreadnoughts, and these were being completed by the Armstrong and Vickers yards when war broke out between Great Britain and Germany, and the British authorities promptly took over the two battleships. These were :

The Sultan Mehmet Rechad V. (now H.M.S. Erin), 23,000 tons, ten 13·5 in. and sixteen 6 in. guns, designed for a speed of twenty-one knots ; and the Sultan Osman (ex-Rio de Janeiro, and now H.M.S. Agincourt), 27,500 tons, fourteen 12 in. and twenty 6 in. guns, designed for a speed of twenty-two knots.

Thus the two principal units that Turkey had counted upon were not available ; but by way of consolation the German vessels Goeben and Breslau (previously described in detail) were henceforth to form part of the Turkish Fleet, which consisted of the following obsolete units :

The battleships Barberossa and Torgud Reis, built in 1891 for the German Navy, and sold by Germany under the Naval Law to Turkey in 1910, of 10,000 tons, with six 11 in., and eight 4·1 in. guns each, and probably capable of steaming seventeen knots on occasion.

The Messudiyeh, built in 1874, and reconstructed in Genoa in 1903, was of 9,250 tons displacement, could steam sixteen knots, and carried two 9·4 in guns as her main armament, and twelve 6 in. guns in her secondary battery. The Messudiyeh was sunk by a British submarine which, passing under five minefields in the Dardanelles, torpedoed the ship while riding at anchor, and in imagined security. This was one of the most daring and unique naval enterprises of the war, and was performed by Lieutenant Holbrook in the B11.

The Muin-i-Zaffir, built in 1869 and refitted in 1907, was really little better than a gunboat. Of 2,400 tons displacement, she could only steam twelve knots, and was armed with four 6 in. guns.

The light cruisers Hamidieh and Medjidieh, of 3,500 tons, could only steam twenty-two knots, and carried each two 6 in., and eight 4·7 in. guns. Fifteen obsolescent gunboats, four modern destroyers and older ones, together with fifteen torpedo-boats, completed the Turkish Navy.

As a fighting force it was entirely a negligible quantity, since had it been possible to coax it into a fight in the open, one British cruiser of the armoured class would have sufficed to sink the **A weird collection of scrap-iron** whole weird collection of scrap-iron in a very short space of time.

Nothing could have been less sound than was the Turkish strategical situation. On all sides Turkey was isolated and surrounded by superior hostile elements. In the Black Sea she was face to face with a Russian squadron which made up in efficiency for what it lacked in paper strength. Outside the Dardanelles was concentrated a vastly superior Franco-British naval force. In European Turkey the Balkan situation was so unstable that Turkey had of necessity to keep a large army ready in order to cope with any recrudescence of a Balkan coalition. The Balkan States fully realised that should the Germanic Alliance come victorious out of the war, Turkey would be paid for her

THE ARABIAN FACTOR IN THE GREAT WORLD WAR.

For centuries the Arab has suffered under Turkish domination, and for generations he has striven by local rebellions to discard the yoke. When Turkey formally yielded to Teutonic pressure, she called upon her Arabian troops to mobilise. Our illustration shows a party of these soldiers of the desert, distinguished still by their traditional head-dress, but wearing European uniforms, and carrying German-made bugles and drums.

aid at the expense of the other Balkan Powers. So long as the Allies of the Entente continued to hold their own, so long would Rumania and Greece remain neutral, but a successful Austrian invasion of Serbia would automatically bring Greece, Rumania, and perhaps Bulgaria into the field to drive the Austrians out of Balkania

Although Turkey had to keep at least 300,000 men under arms in the vicinity of Constantinople, in order to deal
Turkey's hopeless isolation
with the Balkan political situation and to safeguard the capital against a sea-borne expeditionary force, this army could not hope in any way to co-operate with those of Turkey's allies in Europe. Turkey was left entirely to work out her own salvation, or to march in lonely solitude to her doom.

In the Caucasian area she was called upon to put into the field an army capable not only of holding back any Russian invading force, but also of maintaining Turkish suzerainty over the Armenian Christian population, long since seething with revolt. In this one theatre of war alone Turkey had more than enough to occupy all her remaining resources, for Russia could put in the field the whole of her Caucasian army of three-quarters of a million of men, troops

of a new Arabian Empire, with Arabic as its official language, Mohammedanism as its official religion, and King George as its official protector, would be welcomed throughout the length and breadth of that vast tract known to geographers as Arabia; and since every Arab is a born irregular soldier, Turkey would have found her south-eastern provinces over-run by an Arab army which would have needed at least a quarter of a million men to oppose it.

We have thus seen that the strategical situation of the Ottoman Empire was hopelessly unsound. An Empire with an extensive seaboard, she had no fleet capable of opposing serious naval operations, while all her greatest cities were on the coast. In the Black Sea she was faced by a very powerful Russian fleet, and in the Mediterranean by a still more powerful Franco-British fleet, while in the Red Sea, the Indian Ocean, and the Persian Gulf she was at the mercy of the British or Japanese navies.

All her land frontiers were also menaced, with the possible exception of the Persian frontier. Inspired by her German advisers, Turkey determined to forestall her troubles, and, applying the axiom that a vigorous offensive is the best defence, she prepared two armies of invasion. The one, based on Erzerum, was to cross the Caucasus and invade Russian territory; the other, based on Damascus, was to cross the Sinai Desert and invade Egypt. Both of these ambitious expeditions were fore-doomed to failure, but the fact that they should ever have been undertaken at all is strong testimony of the wonderful driving power of the German officers attached to the Ottoman Army.

WHERE EUROPE AND ASIA ALMOST MEET.
Sketch map indicating the relationship of the Dardanelles to the Sea of Marmora and the Bosphorus, and the route by which it was hoped ships trading between Russia and her Allies in the Great War would be able to pass to and from the Black Sea.

The Egyptian campaign had these ostensible reasons:

1. A vigorous offensive by land was necessary to counter-balance the Allies' predominance of sea-power in Near Eastern waters.

2. To strike at the very spring of British trade, wealth, and power—the Suez Canal.

3. By extending the authority of the Turkish Raj over a Moslem Egypt, the holy war might be partially justified in practice.

that otherwise would not have been drawn into the maelstrom of Armageddon.

Again, in the Arabian theatre of hostilities was a huge sub-continent, all the important cities of which were at the mercy of a sea-borne army or of a naval power; and here again, as in Armenia, there was a local population only too anxious to throw off the hated yoke of the Turkish tax-collector. The Arab had little in common with the Turk, under whose domination he has suffered for many centuries all the hardships of misgovernment and over-taxation. The one sentiment Turk and Arab shared in common was the religion of Mohammed, but the fact should not be lost sight of that Mohammed himself was an Arab, and it was the Arabs who built up the great Empire of which Constantinople was the centre.

For many generations local rebellions had strived, and sometimes succeeded, in shaking off the Turkish yoke both in Africa, Asia Minor, and Arabia. Had Disraeli been alive in October, 1914, we can imagine him humbly petitioning King George to proclaim himself Emperor of the Arabs, much as he persuaded Queen Victoria to assume the Imperial crown of India. Those who know the Arab well, who know his language and his aspirations, who are aware of the immense prestige enjoyed by Britishers amongst Arab populations, will agree that the proclamation

The real reasons of the ambitious invasion were dictated, not by a council of war, but by a council of political schemers in Constantinople who had become the tools of the Kaiser. The true reasons for the invasion of Egypt may be summarised as follows:

1. Every British soldier retained to garrison Egypt would mean one man less on the Allies' line in Belgium and France, and therefore would set free a Prussian soldier to march on Warsaw and to liberate Eastern Prussia from the heel of the invading Russian host.

2. The war was already sufficiently unpopular in Turkey, and if a revolution were to be avoided, then an early success for Turkish arms was essential. Although the prospects of success in Egypt were extremely meagre,
Decision to invade Egypt
there was at least a faint possibility of achieving some military feat of arms; while in the only other area of war available to Turkish armies—the Caucasus—there was no possibility of success whatever, owing to the rigours of the climate in winter and the known superiority of the Russian armies both in organisation and numbers.

Having once decided upon the invasion of Egypt, it must be admitted the Turco-German Staff set about their task in a most businesslike manner. All Turkish officers suspected of political intrigue against the Young Turk

SINKING OF THE TURKISH BATTLESHIP MESSUDIYEH BY SUBMARINE B11.

On December 13th, 1914, the British submarine B11 (Lieutenant-Commander Norman D. Holbrook, R.N.) entered the Dardanelles, and, in spite of the current, dived under five rows of mines and torpedoed the Turkish battleship Messudiyeh, which was guarding the minefield. Although pursued by gun fire and torpedo-boats, B11 returned safely, after being submerged on one occasion for nine hours. Lieutenant-Commander Holbrook was awarded the V.C. on December 21st, just a year after he had been appointed to the command of the B11 at Malta.

Inspired by her German advisers, Turkey determined to forestall her troubles; and, applying the axiom that a vigorous offensive is the best defence, she prepared two armies of invasion. The one. based on Erzerum, was to cross the Caucasus and invade Russia; the other. based on Damascus, was to cross the Sinai Desert and invade Egypt. Both of these ambitious expeditions were foredoomed to failure. For the Caucasian venture three armies were formed, each of about 55,000 men. The campaign was planned to allow two columns to advance, while a third was kept two days' march in the rear to act as a

general reserve. Snow was already thick on the uplands when a start was made, and owing to faulty staff work and the appalling climatic conditions, one of the columns outdistanced the other. In turn both were driven back in hopeless disorder, pursued by the victorious Russians, who struggled waist-deep through the mountain snowdrifts. The arrival of the Turkish reserves synchronised with a terrific snowstorm ; and during this the remnants of the Turkish army of invasion, reduced to about one-quarter of its original effectives, managed to find their way back to their base at Erzerum.

Lieutenant-Commander Norman D. Holbrook being invested by a brother officer with an " Iron Cross " on board H.M.S. Indefatigable. It will be noticed, on comparing the bottom photograph with the small one, that the gallant commander of B11 had grown a beard during his daring exploit in the Dardanelles.

After the ceremony on board the Indefatigable. Lieutenant-Commander Holbrook displaying his " Iron Cross." A few days after the humorous interlude above depicted, the King was pleased to signalise Lieutenant- Commander Holbrook's conspicuous act of heroism by bestowing upon him the V.C.—the first award of this coveted distinction to a naval officer during the Great War.

"IRON CROSS" FOR THE COMMANDER OF B11: HUMOROUS INTERLUDE AT SEA.

Party were drafted to the army of Syria, while those who were known to have Anglophile tendencies were drafted to the army of the Caucasus. It is impossible to obtain definitely detailed information regarding the troops told off to form the army of Egypt, but the following estimate is approximately correct :

ADVANCE GUARD.—A Redif Division from Arabia, consisting chiefly of Arab Bedouins, who had no

Bedlam of nomad irregulars

military training whatever, and no organisation save on paper —about eight to ten thousand. This bedlam of nomad irregulars was concentrated between Jerusalem and Akabah, and it is estimated that at least fifty per cent. of them deserted before the advance even began.

MAIN BODY.—Four Nizam Divisions, drawn from Asia Minor, consisting of the best fighting material in the Turkish Army, but considerably under strength. These Divisions were numerically strengthened but morally weakened by attaching to each certain Redif formations, raised in Syria and Palestine. This combined force, amounting to about 60,000 Nizam (regulars) and 10,000 Redifs, were concentrated at Smyrna and Damascus, and were moved forward, when completed, by successive half-divisions along the Hedjaz railway, through Jerusalem, and thence by steady marching toward the Sinai Peninsula, where, on the confines of the desert wastes, an immense camp was formed during the middle of December, 1914.

From then onwards the Turkish army came under the almost daily supervision of the British reconnoitring aircraft. The movements of the Bedouin camelry and horsemen were watched also by patrols of the Egyptian and Bikanir Camel Corps. During December and January two very minor skirmishes took place between the opposing desert riders, the advantage in each case being ludicrously to the advantage of the British.

The Turco-German army commenced a general forward movement from its rest camp at the end of December, striking out into the wilderness on the march that Moses had taken forty years to accomplish, but which, with modern organisation, was completed in as many days.

ANGLO-RUSSIAN COMMUNICATIONS.
Map showing the three routes between Russia and Great Britain, with distances in miles between Petrograd and London.

Some features of the German arrangements are worthy of being placed on record. The guns and limbers of the artillery were equipped with cast-iron wheels, some six inches wide on the tread, in order to distribute the weight of the guns on the sand of the desert. Some two thousand draught animals, other than the six thousand baggage-camels employed in carrying food and ammunition, were utilised in dragging sand-sledges. A Turkish bridging train of thirty-six galvanised-iron pontoons, German Army pattern, was intended for bridging the Suez Canal. These pontoons, somewhat resembling an iron punt, pointed at one end, were nineteen feet by four-feet-six, and could be used either as boats or as floating piers for the construction of a bridge, or bridges, wherewith to span the Suez Canal. Each pontoon was furnished with wide rollers to act as wheels on uneven ground ; but where the surface of the sand was smooth, the rollers were unshipped, and the pontoon with its iron bottom slid like a sledge across the desert behind its team of draught animals. The pontoons were also used for the transport of stores, and thus served the double purpose of cart and boat — a thoughtful economy of matériel.

Fortune at first appeared to favour the Turkish venture. During the months of November, December, and January there had been plentiful rains—in fact, the best rainfall that had occurred for seven years—and the water-holes (or wells) of the desert were unusually well sup-plied with precious liquid,

Season of plentiful rains

vegetable in taste, grit-ting to the teeth, café au lait in colour, which people in this part of the world call water.

A well in the desert is very different from what we are accustomed to call a well in Western Europe. The desert " well " may belong to either one of two varieties. The visible well, or waterhole, is reminiscent of an English horse-pond, and is the result of innumerable generations of industrious digging on the part of desert wayfarers and of long-forgotten convict gangs in the days of the Pharaohs. Usually with a steep bank at one end and steps reaching down to the waterside, the water level may be six to sixteen feet below the level of the bank. At the other end, however, a shelving ramp runs down to the water, so as to enable

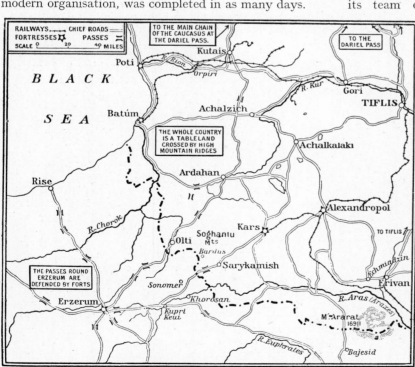

THE TURKISH INVASION OF THE CAUCASUS.
Key map of the passes by which the Turkish forces invaded Russian territory. They suffered utter rout at Sarykamysch (or Sarykamish), and at Ardahan.

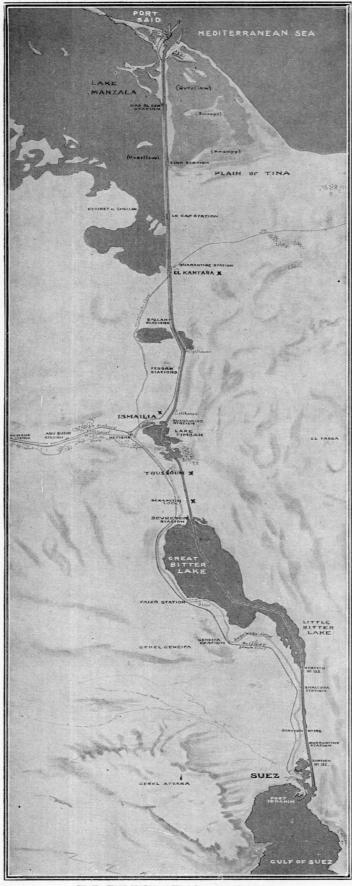

THE TURKISH ATTACK ON EGYPT.
In the above diagrammatic plan are clearly seen the points against which
Djemal Pasha directed his attack—El Kantara, Ismailia, Toussoum,
and Serapeum.

beasts of burden to drink. A large well will be sometimes as big as a tennis-lawn, with four or five feet
of water in it after heavy rains ; but in summer time this
same well will be reduced to the size of a dining-room table,
in which eight to ten inches of water does its best to boil
under the scorching rays of the sun. The other, the
invisible variety of " well," is nothing more nor less than
the damp surface of an underground streamlet. In order
to obtain water, it is necessary to dig down anywhere
between two and twelve feet, when the supply will be fairly
constant but very small in quantity. A trench six feet
in length by three feet broad, for instance, will not yield
water, as a rule, at a greater rate than about a half a pint
a minute. In the rainy season, however, these hidden
streams will often run above ground for
twenty-four hours or so after a down-   **Night attack in a**
pour. The comparatively copious   **sandstorm**
rainfalls at the end of 1914 and in
January, 1915, greatly facilitated the invidious task of
the invading army, and solved their principal administrative
problem—transport.

During the early spring there is a desert wind that blows
at times for a period of two or three days at a stretch. It
comes charged with all the intolerable heat and minute
sand particles of the surrounding desert, and is called the
khamsin (fifty), because from its first to its last visit
is supposed to be a compass of fifty days. When this
hell-breath blows the atmosphere is superheated and is
surcharged with sand. Even though there is no cloud in
the sky, it is impossible even to guess the direction of the
brilliant Egyptian sun, so thick is the sand fog. To face
the gale, which often reaches a velocity of fifty miles an
hour, is an impossibility, unless eyes and mouth be firmly
closed.

On February 2nd, 1915, the first khamsin of the New
Year blew in from the east by south, and that night the
Turkish forces coming from the north-east determined to test
the defences of the Suez Canal, trusting, no doubt, to the
darkness and noise of the sandstorm to hide their approach,
and to the biting sand particles to serve as their allies.

The British force in Egypt, under General Maxwell, at
this time consisted of a strong force of Indian troops,
with a fine Lancashire Territorial division. The latter
were somewhat weedy and only partially trained when
they first arrived in early September, but had grown into as
fine a body of well-disciplined, lusty manhood as might be
wished.

There was also a very strong contingent from the
Antipodes, splendid specimens of manhood from Australia
and New Zealand. Splendid though these men were in
physique, they had not, however, at this time been
sufficiently trained to that iron discipline which is essential
in modern warfare to serve in garrison on the canal. They
were held in reserve in the garrisons of Cairo, Alexandria,
Mansourah, Tanta, and Zagazig.

To complete the truly Imperial nature of this composite
force, the native Egyptian Army also furnished a not
inconsiderable quota of its effectives to
the force either holding the canal or   **Foredoomed to**
immediately in reserve. Thus, along   **failure**
the western bank of the canal, in
trenches which had been carefully prepared and
strengthened for months previously, was a British force
of about 50,000 men, with another 40,000 men behind
it as a reserve.

It was against this highly-trained army, perfectly
equipped in every detail, completely entrenched and
serenely confident, that Djemal Pasha, the Turkish commander, launched his attack at dawn on February 3rd,
1915, under cover of a khamsin sandstorm. The issue
was never in doubt for a moment, for even had the Turkish
general obeyed the first rules of tactics and strategy instead
of setting them at defiance, he could have hardly hoped
to have overcome the obstacle of the Suez Canal and take

THE FORT OF SEDDEL BAHR, AT THE MOUTH OF THE DARDANELLES.

ONE OF THE HILL FORTS GUARDING THE ENTRANCE TO THE DARDANELLES.

CONSTANTINOPLE, WITH THE FAMOUS MOSQUE OF SULEIMAN SHOWING AGAINST THE SKY.

Rarely within living memory has the narrow channel separating Europe from Asia, known to us as the Dardanelles and to the ancients as the Hellespont, ceased to occupy the world's attention. Both sides were strongly fortified, and the safety of the Ottoman capital depended on the power of the Turks to defend the forty-mile strait. Xerxes and Alexander crossed the Dardanelles in 480 and 334 B.C., the first named to enter Europe, and the last named to enter Asia. Tradition has it that Leander, to visit Hero, nightly swam across, and Byron actually performed the feat.

PICTURESQUE SCENES ALONG THE SHORES OF THE STORIED HELLESPONT.

THE OPERATIONS IN EGYPT: OUR INDIAN TROOPS REPELLING A NIGHT ATTACK BY THE TURKS ON TOUSSOUM. The main effort of the enemy was directed against the entrenched force of Punjabis. The main effort of the enemy was directed against the Turkish force, advancing from the direction of Bir Murra, attempted unsuccessfully to launch boats across the canal under cover of their artillery fire. On the Egyptian side of the canal defences between Toussoum and Serapeum, where it culminated in a disastrous retreat.

the British trenches with the ill-clad, march-weary army at his disposal. As it was, however, he neglected two fundamental principles, either because he underrated his adversary, or else, as is far more probable, because there were dissensions between the Turkish and German officers. When on February 1st he arrived within striking distance of the Suez Canal, the obvious thing for him to have done would have been to push forward reconnoitring columns to ascertain the strength of the British positions. He could hardly hope to take these by surprise, since British aeroplanes had dogged his footsteps across the desert. If, on the other hand, rejecting this obvious precaution, he was determined to attack at all costs, he should have struck with all his available force. He did neither. He blundered up against the British defences with his advance division, a second division being some three miles in rear as a support, and the rest of his army might just as well have never left Syria for all the assistance they afforded.

Aeroplanes over the desert

It seems extremely probable that the German Staff officers, for reasons which will be easily appreciated in Berlin, urged Djemal to attack at once in the sandstorm without making a preliminary reconnaissance, but trusting rather to their luck, and hoping for a laxity in British vigilance. It may well be that Djemal was over-persuaded to fall in with these views, but, not wishing to risk his whole army in such a hazardous adventure, he decided to compromise and attack with a part of his strength only. Like most military compromises the effort was fore-doomed to failure. The battle itself, if battle it can be called, offers very few points of interest. The British force allowed the enemy to come on well within close range before they opened fire upon them with murderous precision. At one point, indeed, the Turks were actually allowed to bring two of their pontoons up to the canal bank and to launch them on the water before the defenders started to massacre them. The Turks fought pluckily, as is their wont, but they had no chance from the very first.

At Serapeum, where the main Turkish attack culminated in a disastrous retreat, a Turkish 6 in. gun opened a fairly effective fire upon the British position and some of the war vessels lying in Lake Timsah, off Ismailia. The Indian Marine Service vessel Hardinge was struck twice by shells; a gallant old pilot of the Canal Company, Captain Carew, was stand-ing on the bridge piloting the ship when a great 6 in. shell burst on the bridge, tearing off his leg and wounding him in no less than nineteen places. With that heroic devotion to duty and sublime fortitude that has always characterised the sailors of Britain, he called down to those who were still alive amongst the débris: " Bring me a chair, and I'll take her into port ! " The spirit was willing, but, alas ! the flesh was weak, and he was carried below in a fainting condition. It is pleasing

Heroism of Captain Carew

Line of entrenchments along the Egyptian side of the Suez Canal. These trenches were prepared and carefully strengthened months before Djemal Pasha, under Teuton tutelage, launched his ill-starred attack on the night of February 2nd, 1915.

British battleship in the Suez Canal, with decks cleared for action and sand-bag barricades fixed up to defend the crew from stray shots. The Indian Marine Service vessel Hardinge was hit twice by shells, and Captain Carew was severely wounded.

A British encampment. There was a British force estimated at about 50,000 along the western bank of the Suez Canal, while some 40,000 were held in reserve. The native Egyptian Army contributed a not inconsiderable quota to the defensive forces under General Maxwell.

THE DEFENCE OF EGYPT AGAINST THE TEUTONISED TURKS.

A FORCE OF GURKHAS—THE HIGHLANDERS OF INDIA—TAKING PART IN EGYPT'S DEFENCE.
A camera impression of our warlike Gurkhas resting, but on the alert and eager to try conclusions with "the unspeakable Turk."

to reflect that this grand specimen of Britain's mercantile marine recovered from his terrible injuries.

A short while afterwards, however, one of the warships on Lake Timsah took an ample revenge on the Turkish gun, killing the crew and silencing the gun with a well-aimed salvo from its 12-pounder guns, while the old French battleship Requin shelled the enemy's positions with 10·8 in. guns.

By six o'clock, as night was falling, the enemy's reserves were also in full retreat, but it was not considered advisable to follow them up into the desert. However, after nightfall, sniping broke out from the eastern bank of the canal, and two companies were sent across the canal next morning to round up the snipers. These were met by a quite unexpected fire from a deep trench which had been well screened from view. The two companies sat tight and fought well until further reinforcements were

PLAN OF THE TURKISH ATTACK ON EGYPT.
Specially drawn to show the direction in which the attempts were made to test the defences of the Suez Canal.

brought up, when the trench was cleared with the bayonet. All who remained of the original occupants were captured, some two hundred and fifty prisoners, all of whom were picked men. It will never be known what losses the Turks actually incurred in the battle of the canal, for many hundreds of fugitive soldiers must have been lost in the subsequent retreat; but, in any case, their losses were not less than four thousand officers and men in killed, wounded, and prisoners, while the British casualties barely totalled threescore.

It is interesting to note that four Turks actually succeeded in swimming across the canal, and were discovered the following day hiding miserably in the vicinity of El Ferdan. Perhaps the most bitter blow of all to the Turks was the loss of practically the whole of their bridging train, which was partly destroyed and partly captured, for they did not make any attempt to save it. The

WITH OUR INDIAN TROOPS BEHIND SAND-BUILT BARRICADES IN THE EGYPTIAN DESERT.
Sikhs holding an entrenched outpost commanding one of the desert roads to the Suez Canal.

INDIAN TROOPS MARCHING ACROSS THE DESERT NEAR SUEZ.
In their first encounter with the Turks near Suez our gallant Indian troops scored a notable success. Advance parties of Indians and Turkish soldiers came into touch in the desert, and the result was entirely to the advantage of the Indians.

EGYPTIAN CAMEL CORPS GALLOPING ACROSS THE DESERT.
This splendid force formed a part of the native Egyptian Army which fought side by side with their British and Indian fellow-subjects in defending their country against the German-Turkish raiders from across the Sinai Peninsula. Long journeys across the vast Eastern sand wastes would be impossible but for the services of " the ship of the desert."

CAVALRY AND INFANTRY OF OUR EGYPTIAN ARMY ON PARADE.
Lord Kitchener's work in Egypt and the Soudan has borne wonderful fruit in the loyalty and fitness of one of the most efficient native forces in the world. Horse and foot, the Egyptian Army affords remarkable evidence of the British genius for turning coloured races into first-rate soldiers.

A UNIQUE REVIEW NEAR THE PYRAMIDS.
Sir George Reid, High Commissioner for Australia, reviewing the Australian troops as they marched past the motor-car in which he is seen acknowledging the salute.

THE RALLY FROM NEW ZEALAND.
With their Australian comrades the New Zealand contingent were halted at Egypt on their journey to Europe, to complete their training and, if necessary, to take part in the fighting against the Turks.

loss of these pontoons precluded the possibility of any further Turkish attack upon the canal for many a long week, even if the Turks had stomach for more fighting.

In the same bright, optimistic way that characterised the Egyptian Expedition, the

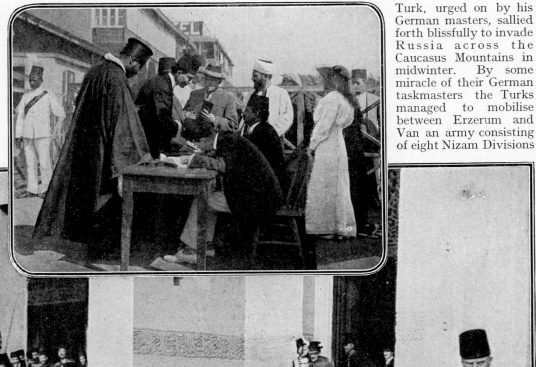

Turk, urged on by his German masters, sallied forth blissfully to invade Russia across the Caucasus Mountains in midwinter. By some miracle of their German taskmasters the Turks managed to mobilise between Erzerum and Van an army consisting of eight Nizam Divisions

ARRIVAL OF THE BRITISH HIGH COMMISSIONER AT CAIRO.
Sir Henry McMahon, the new High Commissioner for Egypt, arriving at Cairo on January 9th, 1915, with General Sir John Maxwell. They are seen leaving the railway-station by the Royal entrance, followed by Sir Milne Cheetham, Governor of Alexandria. In the foreground is Lewa Herbert Pasha, the commander of the Egyptian garrison in Cairo. Inset : Examination of passports at Port Said.

AUSTRALIANS IN CAMP IN THE LAND OF THE PHARAOHS.

The contingents from Australia and New Zealand were splendid specimens of manhood. They were held in reserve in the garrisons of Cairo, Alexandria, Munsourah, Tanta, and Zagazig.

A GLIMPSE OF THE ARID WASTES OF THE SINAI DESERT.

Our photograph affords a graphic impression of the plain of El Tih, near Tor. This was the scene of one of the early skirmishes between British scouting parties and advanced troops of the enemy.

FORT OF ABOUKIR, NEAR ALEXANDRIA, NOW A BRITISH NAVAL BASE IN THE MEDITERRANEAN.

TURKISH ARTILLERYMEN.
They are seen wearing their new campaign uniform.

TURKISH GUN IN ACTION.
The Turkish field artillery are armed with 7·5 cm. Krupp guns.

and eight Redif Divisions. The mobilisation was hopelessly incomplete owing to the difficulties of transport and communication and to the disinclination of fifty per cent. of the men to answer the summons. The exact numbers mustered are not known, nor are they ever likely to be, but eventually three armies were formed, each consisting of two Nizam

Turkish debacle in Caucasia

Divisions and one composite Redif Division, and numbering about 55,000 men each. The remainder of this group of Divisions, mustering about 15,000 of the Nizam and 25,000 of the Redif, were retained at Erzerum and used on the lines of communication. The plan of the campaign, if such it may be termed, was to advance simultaneously upon the Russian frontier in two columns, a third column being retained two days' march in rear to act as a general reserve.

The Russians, out of an available Caucasian army of three-quarters of a million men,

contented themselves with pushing up 200,000 men towards the passes and awaiting the results of the Turkish offensive. The two Turkish columns had been timed to advance simultaneously over an exceedingly difficult country where already, in November, the snow lay thick on the uplands. Owing to faulty staff work and the appalling climatic conditions one of the Turkish columns outdistanced the other.

Waist-deep in snowdrifts

The Russian advance guard drew back, luring the enemy onwards, which is a time-worn trick of Russian strategy. The Turks fell into the trap, and having for two days announced a wondrous victory in optimistic telegrams to Europe, they struck, on the third day, the real Russian main body. A disastrous action followed; over 20,000 Turks were slain on the battlefield or were lost in the subsequent rout, and the remainder fell back in hopeless disorder. The second Turkish column met with no better success

CHEWING THE CUD OF BITTER REFLECTION: TURKISH PRISONERS IN EGYPT.
On another page is given a tabular statement of the units of the Sultan's Army. From this it appears that the total force available numbered 640,000 men. The above photograph is a souvenir of the disastrous attempt of Djemal Pasha to invade Egypt, and shows Turkish prisoners in the hands of the British. Inset: Prisoners being assisted by native railway guards to board the hospital train on their way to Cairo.

and an almost exactly similar fate. Both columns fell back in hopeless disorder, hotly pursued by the victorious Russians, who struggled waist-deep through the mountain snowdrifts. At the critical moment the Turkish reserves came up. Their junction with the fugitive columns synchronised with a snowstorm of unusual violence, during which the remnants of the Turkish army of invasion, reduced to about one-quarter of its original effectives, managed to effect their escape to Erzerum, while the Russians contented themselves by consolidating their positions and going into winter quarters.

In the meanwhile a subsidiary Turkish column had, with Teutonic disregard of international rights, invaded North-Western Persia and entered Tabriz. When the general Turkish retreat set in, a Russian cavalry force marched on Tabriz and, with very little difficulty, drove the Turkish invaders before them, being assisted thereto by the Persian mountain robbers of the vicinity, who joined in right merrily in the pillage of the convoys and transports which the Turks were obliged to abandon in their retreat. At the end of February the allied fleets were heard knocking at the door of the Dardanelles.

TURKISH INVASION OF NORTH-WESTERN PERSIA.

While the Germanised Turkish forces were making their way across the Sinai Peninsula and into the heights of the Caucasus, a subsidiary column, with utter disregard of international rights, entered Tabriz, the capital of the Persian province of Azerbijan. But with very little difficulty a Russian cavalry force drove out the invaders, being assisted in this enterprise by the native mountaineers, who were rewarded by the pillage of the convoys and transports which the Turks were obliged to abandon in their retreat. Inset. A Bedouin on his steed.

NIGHT OF A GERMAN DEFEAT: INVADERS OF POLAND MARCHING INTO CAPTIVITY.

A column of German infantry taken prisoners by the Cossacks after a Russian advance into Poland. A vigorous and impressive picture of the appalling devastation of war under modern conditions. The picture from which our illustration was taken is the work of M. André Devambez, and its exhibit in the French capital attracted crowds of spectators.

CHAPTER XLIX.

FIRST GREAT CLASH OF SLAV AND PRUSSIAN.

How France Helped Russia—Russians only Faced by Inferior German Troops—Russia Half Crippled by Lack of Guns, Rifles, and Munitions—Closing of Dardanelles Cuts Off her War Supplies—Hindenburg's Rise to Power—The Kaiser Comes to Graievo to Watch Triumph of his Siege Guns—Hindenburg's Essay in Grand Strategy—Tries to Conquer Main Russian Armies by Cutting their Railway Line—General Situation of the Two Teutonic Empires—Russian Recoil from the Niemen Front—Battle of the Augustovo Forest—How the Cossacks Ringed and Routed their Enemies—Victory at Raczka—Siege of Osoviec—Russian Cavalry's Magnificent Charge against Siege Guns—Hindenburg Alters his Plan and Attacks Warsaw and Ivangorod—How the German Spies Helped the Russians—The Battle of Warsaw—Retreat of Northern German Army—The Battle of Kozienice—The Defence of Ivangorod—How the Austrians were Outplayed—General Defeat of the Entire Austro-German Armies.

AFTER the first-line armies of Austria-Hungary had been thrown back confused and dispirited from Poland the position of Germany became insecure. She had about twenty-two army corps round her eastern frontier, but the number of these troops was more remarkable than their quality. All the first-line soldiers of Germany were retained before the French, British, and Belgian lines, and there they remained for many months. The early rumours of the movement of large bodies of the best German troops from France to Prussia or Poland were afterwards proved to be misleading. These rumours were put about by German agents with the intention of deceiving the French Military Staff as to the strength with which the Allies in France were still opposed. It was not until the early spring of 1915 that the presence of a single first-line German army corps was clearly traced by the Russians amid the hosts facing them.

In the original design of a defensive league between Russia and France, it was supposed by both parties that the mighty forces of the Tsar would protect the French nation from their aggressive and traditional enemy. But as things worked out, it was the smaller but more progressive and inventive Republic of Western Europe which protected the vast Russian Empire. The Russians never felt the full weight of the German military machine. For the French

fought with such amazing vigour and unrelenting tenacity that the German Great Staff was never able to swing its best armies into the eastern theatre of war. Germany at no time had more than her left hand free to deal with Russia. She had engineered the war directly against Russia, with a view to extending the Teutonic Empire to Constantinople, and from thence to the undeveloped wheat-lands of Mesopotamia. France was not directly threatened. The struggle was the final clash of Slav and Teuton in regard to Constantinople, the prospect of which had disturbed Europe for two hundred years.

In former days the strife and intrigue over the heritage of the declining Ottoman Turks had been chiefly confined to Austrians and Russians, with Napoleon I. and Napoleon III. intervening, and Great Britain keeping a watchful eye upon the situation. In the opening years of the twentieth century Austria still remained nominally Russia's competitor for the succession to Constantinople. But everybody except the Austrians themselves was well aware that the House of Hohenzollern had become the principal opponent of the claims of the House of Romanoff. The strong, upstart, enterprising Prussian Emperor was merely using the Hapsburgs as a battering-ram, with a view to absorbing both the conquering Austrian and the conquered Turk in a mighty Teutonic Empire, stretching from the North Sea to the Persian Gulf. It was because the Russians were resolved to perish rather than permit

KAISER WILHELM'S MISPLACED CONFIDENCE.
Just as the German Emperor visited the outskirts of Nancy fully confident that he would be able to witness the fall of that place, so he went east to see the fall of Osoviec—again to be bitterly disappointed. He is the figure on the left of the above photograph, the officer in the centre facing the camera being General von Mackensen. The Emperor's motor-car stands in readiness on the left.

PREPARING FOR THE WINTER CAMPAIGN.
Scene outside a store in East Prussia. Germans fitting themselves with waterproofs and oilskins.

Germany to take, through Austria, the first important step to dominate Constantinople by the possession of the Serbian river valley running towards Salonica, that the Great War broke out.

France was dragged into it as a matter of honour, through a treaty at first intended merely for her protection. But the aid which she gave to her mighty ally was of incomparable value. Germany went into the long-deferred struggle for Empire between Slav and Teuton with her right arm rendered absolutely useless. Six weeks after the war broke out the ally on whom she had strongly relied for help was shrilly clamouring for assistance. For the main Austro-Hungarian armies had been shattered, and were being shepherded into the river marshes of the San and the

Vistula by the victorious Russians. At that time Germany herself was in considerable difficulty. For all her first-line armies in France had been repulsed, and were retreating before the French and British troops. Had Russia been as strong as she seemed, the war might then have come to an end quickly. Germany was in such a position that she could not do more for Austria than she had arranged to do. Her twenty-two army corps of troops of only second and third quality, concentrated round her eastern frontier, were alone available. **German aid for beaten Austria** They covered the retreat of the Austrians and Hungarians, provided officers who reorganised the beaten armies of the House of Hapsburg, and took over the entire control of these re-formed troops and of the new formations. Otherwise not a man or a gun could be spared from the western theatre of the war.

In spite of this fortunate condition of affairs, the Russian Commander-in-Chief could not press home the advantage he had won. For months afterwards the most he could do was to hold his own. He had trained men in overwhelming numbers and an abundance of food for them. But, in the circumstances, millions of these men were practically

RETREAT OF THE KAISER'S TROOPS IN EAST PRUSSIA.
German troops resting, during their retreat, in a town that had suffered severely from Russian bombardment. Inset: German supply column passing through a deserted town in East Prussia.

useless at the critical time. The war-machine of Russia was too small to absorb them. There were no rifles for them, no cartridges. Vast parks of field-guns and immense stores of shell and shrapnel were needed to form the absolutely vital artillery power of the great unemployed new Russian armies. So long as the ports of Archangel and Vladivostok remained free from ice and the Dardanelles was open to our cargo steamers, it was possible for Great

Russia's lack of war stores

Britain to set some of her factories working for her ally. To some extent, also, military stores could be obtained from the armament and ammunition firms of the United States and from Japan. But our country had also to assist France in the production of munitions of war, and to build up likewise a great machine for our army of two millions or more. As a matter of fact, our newly-raised troops went for some time without actual musketry training, because we were so busy supplying the fully-trained and ready troops of France and Russia that our own raw levies had to wait for their arms.

Slowly but carefully the Russians began to extend their

COMMANDEERING BREAD FOR THE KAISER'S TROOPS.
Detachment of the German commissariat corps making a bread levy from a bakery in East Prussia.

military machine; but before they could bring the whole weight of their men to bear upon the Teutons and Magyars there was a complete interruption in the armament supplies by a telling stroke of policy that greatly prolonged the war. The Germans succeeded in dragging the Turks into their camp, and thus closing the Dardanelles all through the winter. Soon afterwards the northern Russian port of Archangel, with very feeble railway communication, was closed by ice.

Russia—being mainly an Empire of agriculturists, lacking the great, costly, and slowly built-up plant needed in making guns and rifles rapidly in large quantities—was half crippled by the closing of the Dardanelles. Her existing

EAST PRUSSIAN CONVENT AS A SUPPLY STORE.
Convoy of supplies arriving at German headquarters and being stored in a convent. Inset: German field kitchens that, with other impedimenta, fell into the hands of the Russians during the German retreat from Warsaw.

GERMAN TRENCH ON THE ANGERAP RIVER, IN EAST PRUSSIA.
Camera record of the operations near Darkehmen, East Prussia. The
Prussians were armed with mitrailleuses.

hundreds of German generals included in
" Wer Ist's "—the German " Who's Who."
He was one of the laughing-stocks of the
modern fashionable soldiers who took part
in the Kaiser manœuvres. All he was
known for was his curious hobby for
keeping the wild Masurian Lakes region
in East Prussia in its original state of un-
cultivation. The only thing that moved
him to leave his Hanoverian café and go
to Berlin, in the days
before the war, was a   **Problem of the**
politician's proposal   **Masurian Lakes**
for the drainage and
cultivation of the Masurian Lakes. He
called on deputies, he called on party
leaders, he pleaded before committees;
and when all these efforts of his proved
vain he went to the Emperor and begged
that the scheme for reclaiming the lakes
should be abandoned.

The ruling German military school
regarded the old man as a nuisance and
a fool, and as somewhat of a coward. They
agreed with the administrators who
wanted to drain the lakes, and thus to
open up to cultivation and to inhabi-
tation an immense region which had been
unproductive from the primeval age of
the world. Over the drained and populated ancient waste of marsh and water
the German Staff intended to march their
armies across the Niemen River and cut
the railway communication between

factories were barely sufficient to keep her field armies
supplied with raw material, and to continue the construction
and munitioning of her new fleet. The result was that the
Grand Duke Nicholas had to continue to fight the Teutons
with the odds still heavy against him.

All through the first seven or eight months of the war the
Russian field armies were inferior in numbers and artillery
power to the hosts opposed to them. Germany was able
to give a million rifles to the new Austrian levies and to help
to fit them out with field-guns. She had collected enormous
stores of armament in preparation for the great struggle.
As Russia, like France and Britain, had kept her military
stores at the ordinary low level, she also was taken at a
general disadvantage. Like her western allies, she had to
fight for time, and to look forward to
Where the Prussians a defensive action throughout the
were stronger winter. Only in the spring of 1915, when
she would at last be well supplied with
rifles and guns and ammunition, could she seriously undertake a grand offensive movement. Meanwhile, the Russian
steam-roller could not get up full steam.

All this, of course, was well known to the German Great
Staff. They were weakest at the point at which the
Russians were strongest, and strongest at the point at
which the Russians were weakest. All their infantry
in the eastern field of battle was of inferior quality, but
they had more ammunition and more weapons, and what
was of still more importance, they had a commander with
a genuine talent for war. More by luck than by skill
in selection, the circle of courtiers and intriguers gathered
about the Emperor Wilhelm and constituting the directing
minds of his Great Staff hit on a good man for the
command of their eastern armies. This man was
General von Hindenburg. His name is not given among

DEVASTATING EFFECT OF A GERMAN BOMB ON A RUSSIAN
RAILWAY TRACK.
Prussian airmen successfully dropped a bomb which shattered the rails
and burrowed deeply into the permanent way.

Warsaw and St. Petersburg. But, moved by the entreaties
of the old warrior, Kaiser Wilhelm stopped the scheme for
draining the lakes, and in the ancient watery wilderness
Hindenburg continued to spend his holidays every year.

Nobody in authority remembered him, even when the
Emperor and his Staff were thrown into deep perturbation
by General Rennenkampf's sudden raid into East Prussia.
The command of the new army of defence would have
been entrusted to another untried courtier-general who
had succeeded in pleasing the Emperor but for the
patriotism of General von Ludendorff, a fairly able man of
the younger generation connected with the Great Staff.
He is said to have urged the claim of his old master in
military studies, with the result that Hindenburg was
given all the forces he required for his long-thought-out
operations in the Masurian Lakes. There, towards the

end of August, as already related, the old general trapped the Russian army under General Samsonoff and captured one corps with a large number of guns.

The grizzled, bull-necked old fighting man at once became the darling of all the Teutonic peoples. The popularity of the Kaiser, the Crown Prince, Kluck, Moltke, and Heeringen paled before that of the saviour of Prussia. Meanwhile, Rennenkampf with his cavalry forces, outstretched between Königsberg and Kovno, continued a stubborn rearguard action all through the month of

OBSERVATION WORK IN A RUSSIAN TRENCH IN EAST PRUSSIA.
While his comrades kept a sharp look-out, the soldier with the notebook entered the results of his observations for the use of the Staff.

September, with Hindenburg vainly trying to force the main Russian army of invasion into the lakes and marshes. Rennenkampf was greatly outnumbered in both men and guns, for his opponent had nearly half a million troops, with their artillery corps increased by guns worked by part of the garrison forces of Thorn and Graudenz.

So sure was the German commander of victory that the Kaiser Wilhelm left the western theatre of war, where he had been sadly disappointed, and came in his special train to Lyck, amid the Masurian Lakes, to watch the great triumph over the Russians. From Lyck the Emperor advanced to Graievo, over the Russian frontier, immediately behind his only successful army. Just **The Kaiser at** fourteen miles south- **Graievo** east of Graievo was the Russian river fortress of Osoviec, guarding the high, dry road across the marshlands of the Bobr River. This was the critical point in all the dispositions of Russian troops made by the General Commander-in-Chief, the Grand Duke Nicholas, and by his Chief of Staff, General Sukhomlinoff.

Something like two million Russian troops, operating far away on the southern reaches of the Vistula against the main eastern forces of Germany and Austria, depended for food and ammunition chiefly on their railway-head at Warsaw. Warsaw in turn depended on its railway communication with Petrograd, and as the line to Petrograd ran close to Osoviec, and actually touched the River Bobr a few

miles northward at the town of Grodno, where the Bobr flows into the Niemen, there was good reason for the interest which the Kaiser took in the attack upon Osoviec.

Hindenburg was no mean strategist. Early in life he had seen that the Masurian Lakes system, which extends far into Russia to the banks of the Niemen and Bobr, was the key to Russian Poland. By cutting the Russian railway at Osoviec or Grodno he could win Warsaw, and throw the main Russian armies back from Silesia and Posen without a battle. For if the railways were cut, starvation and lack of ammunition would force all the Russian troops in the bend **Von Hindenburg's** of the Vistula to retire towards the new **railway strategy** railway-heads of Siedlce and Brest Litovsk. And even before they could withdraw, the Siedlce line, close to the Warsaw line, could also be cut. Without a general battle the main Russian forces could be thrown back on Brest Litovsk, nearly two hundred and forty miles from the German frontier.

It will thus be seen that, in his fierce and ceaseless attacks upon Rennenkampf's Cossacks, maintained all through the month of September in the swamps and woods and waters of the Masurian Lakes system, Hindenburg aimed at more than freeing East Prussia from the invader. It was no wonder that the Kaiser melted in pride and gratitude for the one man among his millions of men who appeared to possess a gift for grand strategy. It seemed as though

"MUSIC HATH CHARMS"—BUT NOT TO SOOTHE THE PRUSSIAN BREAST.
German troops in a trench on the Angerap, singing national songs during a lull in the fighting.

MEMEL TILSIT
WIRBALLEN
BAKLARZEYO
SUWALKI
GUMBINNEN
INSTERBURG
GOLDAP
KONIGSBERG
LYCK
SPIRDING
LAKE
JOHANNESBURG
BALTIC SEA
LAKE MAUER
DANZIG
RASTENBURG
OSTERODE

SCENE OF THE GREAT STRUGGLE BETWEEN SLAV AND TEUTON IN THE WILD MASURIAN LAKES REGION.—THE LAND OF THE DISMAL SWAMP.
A proposal for draining this watery wilderness was vetoed by the Kaiser at the earnest request of General von Hindenburg, who had long ago studied its defensive possibilities. The whole of this region is dotted with lakes, and the roads between them are comparatively few and unreliable. This immense tract of country has been unproductive since the primeval age of the world.

the road to Petrograd, along which the Kaiser had never hoped to travel, would be more easy of access than the road to Paris. If General Joffre would only have allowed it, the original German war plan, drawn up by the elder Moltke, might have been reversed. The French, British, and Belgian forces would merely have been held by an immense line of entrenchments, while the chief immediate effort of conquest would have been directed by Hindenburg against the Russians.

As we have seen, General Joffre would not allow this to be done, but continued to make rapid outflanking attacks on all the first-line German armies, till the opposing **Allies in close co-operation** fronts stretched to the North Sea, and half a million new German formations had to be railed westward to keep Sir John French from breaking through between Ypres and Lille. As a matter of fact, neither General Joffre nor the Grand Duke Nicholas was fighting for his own hand by the third week in September. Both the allied Commanders-in-Chief then began to act in closer co-operation, and many an important stroke of war in France or Belgium was aimed directly at Hindenburg. In the same way many a stroke of war by the Russians, though apparently directed at Hindenburg, was aimed at Falkenhayn and struck him in Flanders. This close and intimate co-operation was born of the loyalty, the comradeship, and the superb skill in strategy which marked the operations of the Allies.

There were no separate fields of struggle in Europe. One immense connected battle raged in and around the lands of the Teutonic Empires. The allied front stretched from Holland to Courland and the marshes of Eastern Prussia. **Situation of the Teutonic Empires** In the middle it was broken by the neutral territories of Switzerland and Italy; but to the west of Italy the Serbian advance formed another part of the besiegers' front, with a lessening gap between it and the Russian columns which had invaded the Hungarian plain. Then from the Carpathian heights the main Russian armies stretched through Galicia and Poland to the Niemen River. At sea the British fleet under Sir John Jellicoe cut Germany off from the food-producing countries of America, while Admiral de Lapeyrère, operating in the Adriatic with a Franco-British fleet, cut off Austria and Hungary

REFRESHMENT BY THE WAY.
Prussian cavalry patrol about to sample some refreshment at a stall in a Polish village.

RUSSIAN RED CROSS TRAIN IN POLAND.
Soldiers of the Tsar, wounded in the fighting against the Prussians, returning by train to a base hospital.

from the Suez and Mediterranean supply routes. The naval power of the Allies was also exerted in an increasing stringency of examination into the destination of cargoes in neutral vessels. By this means the points of contact which the besieged Empire had with the neutral territories of Scandinavian, Dutch, Swiss, Italian, and Rumanian Powers were lessened in importance.

No attempt was made to counter Hindenburg's attack on the Warsaw-Petrograd railway line and recover the ground lost in Prussia. Instead, the Russian Chief of Staff sent up another army to hold the line of the Niemen and Bobr Rivers, and there retain Hindenburg as long as he cared to continue attempting vainly to break through. Russia, in short, began that process of stonewalling every German and Austro-German attack, which marked her strategy all through the winter and into the spring.

Russian feint and counter-stroke Remarkable as was the talent for war of Hindenburg, he was powerless to make any progress against the new scheme of operations which the Russian Chief of Staff rapidly organised on the Niemen and Bobr river-fronts. General Rennenkampf extricated his troops at Stallupöhnen by the end of September, and withdrew towards Kovno. But this withdrawal was only a feint. The Russian commander only moved two miles from the German frontier in order to get into touch with a large reinforcement awaiting him. Then he swung back with a force as heavy and unexpected as that with which Hindenburg had originally swung forward. The German tried to hold the Russians in the north and to counter at three distant points farther south. He sent one strong army through the Forest of Augustovo, a second still stronger force

against Osoviec, and a third unusually large force was concentrated at Mlava, to the north of Warsaw.

The new battle began about the end of September on a front of about two hundred miles. It extended from the point at which the Niemen enters Prussia to the point at which the Ukra River, a tributary of the Narew, flows out of the district of Plock. All along this line of attack the Warsaw-Petrograd railway line continued to occupy the mind of Hindenburg. In the northern section, amid the woods and swamps of the Suwalki Government, Rennenkampf turned on his pursuer, with a terrible surprise for him. His Cossack forces had been sadly wanting in artillery power, but they were now provided, not only with an abundance of ordinary field artillery, but with heavy siege-guns from Kovno.

The German Landwehr and Landsturm troops were lured, in close formation, to attack the entrenched Cossacks

A HUMBLE SERVITOR OF THE ALLIES.
The donkey seen in the above photograph, in charge of a Russian infantryman, is helping to convey supplies to an outpost patrol.

close to the concealed positions of the new guns. At the same time Russian aviators, working with their gunners, reconnoitred for advancing columns of German supports behind the attacking line. Then the unexpected bombardment began. The Germans broke and fled, with shrapnel bursting over them for eight miles of their flight. The light German field artillery which Hindenburg used in this section of the lake country was completely overmastered by the heavy Russian guns, which had taken a week or more to haul into position in the arranged ambush.

As the guns cleared their path, the Cossacks, heading their reinforcements, drove again towards the hostile frontier. The hottest fighting took place on September 30th and October 1st at Mariampol and Kalvaria. Here the Germans were driven back two days' march nearer their own country than they had been at the beginning of the week. Their retreat was conducted in a heavy and continual rainstorm, which, in the swamp country, made the worst possible conditions for fighting against men so practised in guerilla methods of warfare as the Cossacks. In spite, however, of the adverse conditions,

Hindenburg held on desperately to the important town of Suwalki by reason of its railway connections north and south with the Warsaw line. But dearly did he pay for his inability to admit the complete defeat of his plans.

South of Suwalki was the great dense Forest of Augustovo, a primeval waste of lakelets and morasses. There were no roads, but only a few narrow winding passages, running between water and bog, with all the approaches screened by the autumnal foliage of brushwood and trees. Only a few hundred Russian woodsmen knew all the safe ways through this prehistoric wilderness, where herds of aurochs, the cattle of the stone ages, used to roam down to modern times.

The Battle of Augustovo

Led by the woodsmen, the Cossacks and their artillerymen with light guns threaded the unmapped wilderness where the Germans had entrenched on the principal paths. This was the sort of fighting the Cossack liked. By woodcraft and scouting tactics he quietly discovered the enemy's positions. The Russian guns were hauled up and trained on the forest defences, while companies of Cossacks worked round by unknown ways and got on the flank and rear of the enemy. They were Don Cossacks, the fighters in the Augustovo Forest, men who reckoned themselves the flower of the Russian forces. They were opposed by four to five times the number of Germans; but these were mostly Landwehr and Landsturm men, the latter being often either seventeen to eighteen years old or over forty. Many of them were armed with rifles dating back to 1880 or to 1899, and they had only had a few weeks' musketry practice before they were entrained for the defence of East Prussia.

There is no need to describe what happened, for only the slaughter of the new formations at Ypres can compare

SIDELIGHTS ON THE MUSCOVITE POSTAL SERVICE.
Sleigh heavily laden with postal packages for the Russian troops in the field. Probably never before have the postal services of great armies attained such huge proportions as in the British, French, Russian, and German commands during the Great War; and the transport difficulties that had to be surmounted by the Russian officials in Poland were even greater than those confronting the others.
Inset: A soldier of the Tsar posting a letter home.

GIVING THE POPULATION OF EAST PRUSSIA A TASTE OF BELGIUM'S SUFFERINGS.

In East Prussia alone, during the first six months of the war, was Germany made to feel the terror of invasion. Our picture is of a street in an East Prussian town which was wrecked by Russian guns. But the damage done was in the main confined to buildings, and even here restraint was exercised, the Tsar's artillerymen making a point of sparing the churches. And non-combatants were treated with a consideration never shown to their victims by the German invaders of Belgium and Northern France.

with it. Mile by mile the Cossacks worked through the forests, avoiding the easy known paths in their advance, and ambushing rearguard after rearguard, bivouac after bivouac. It was hard, slow work, scouting for the enemy and encircling him, but the actual fighting was a fairly safe and easy job. By the end of the first week in October the Don Cossacks had reached the village of Raczka, close to the German border. The river separated them from the forest where a brigade of German troops had retired, with two batteries of guns and eight armoured motor-cars.

Cossacks over the German border

In the night the Cossacks swam the river on horseback, and made a turning movement against the hostile brigade, and then at daybreak they charged into their lines at the rear. They took three thousand prisoners, together with the batteries and all the armoured cars. This left a breach in the defences of the German frontier, and the Cossacks, sweeping over the border, seized the German town of Biala on October 7th. Three days afterwards, the more important town of Lyck was captured by General Rennenkampf, by an outflanking movement on both sides of a German force to the north, which had held too long on to Suwalki.

Meanwhile, the principal German attack, conducted against the fortress of Osoviec under the eyes of the Kaiser, had not prospered. The Germans advanced by a single narrow road running alongside the railway line, with marshes on either hand. They posted their heavy artillery about five miles from the chain of forts, and their infantry entrenched some three miles closer to the threatened fortress. For four days the forts were bombarded night and day by 11 in. and 12 in. howitzers. But nothing happened. Russian fortress engineers had had a little experience at Port Arthur, and they had not designed Osoviec in the manner of Liège, Namur, and Maubeuge. The fortress was scarcely injured by the thousands of great shells hurled at it, and the Russian commander patiently waited until all the German forces available for the operation were concentrated against him, and comfortably entrenched and sited.

He knew exactly what was happening. For a Russian artillery officer, Colonel Martinoff, was hidden with a telephone near the German lines, watching all their movements, and directing the artillery fire of the fortress. When everything was ripe for the Russian counter-move, the colonel, who had not slept for eighty hours, telephoned his final observations. In the darkness of night, in a violent downpour of rain, two strong columns of Russian infantry advanced into the swamp on either side of the road held by the Germans. Guided by shepherds, who used the dry parts of the morasses as pastures, the soldiers picked their way over the winding track of firm land. When daylight came they were well on the flank of the enemy, but still hidden from observation. As they moved out to attack, a superb force of Russian cavalry crossed the bridge over the Bobr River at Osoviec, and gathering

The defence of Osoviec

RUSSIAN CAVALRY IN ACTION: BRILLIANT CHARGE BY THE FINEST HORSE-SOLDIERS IN THE WORLD.

A German artist's impression of an engagement between a body of Russian cavalry, some of the gallant men who crossed the Carpathians from Galicia, and a force of Germany's Austrian allies. In the early days of November, 1914, to the east of Neidenburg, near the station of Muschaken, about two miles from the East Prussian frontier, the Tsar's redoubtable horsemen routed a German detachment which was guarding the railway, captured their transport, and blew up some bridges. In the same month a German cavalry division, supported by rifles, was driven back towards Kalisz.

RUSSIA'S OLDEST VOLUNTEER.
Ivan Trufanoff, aged sixty-two, a Cossack, who has taken part with distinction in three wars.

INTERESTED SOLICITUDE FOR THE PRISONER.
A Siberian prisoner in the hands of Germans, who, after supplying him with food, are anxiously putting questions, the answers to which they hope to turn to their advantage.

PRAYING FOR RUSSIA'S SUCCESS.
A Jew, of Bukovina, inspired by new hope for his race, praying for a Russian victory.

by the flanking infantry attack the Russian horsemen got halfway to the guns before the German foot soldiers were ready to oppose them. Meanwhile, the alarmed gunners tried to shatter the charging squadrons. But a siege-gun is not a rifle. It takes some time to alter its range. The first salvo of shells flew over the Cossacks. The second salvo was aimed too hurriedly and fell short. By this time the Cossacks were fully halfway to the batteries. The hostile artillerymen did not try a third salvo, but bent all their energies to getting their guns safely away by motor traction. Their infantry moved forward to hold off the cavalry. But it was too late. For the two flanking Russian infantry movements culminated at this minute as the Russian cavalry reached the foremost guns. Three pieces of ordnance were captured, and the force sent to defend the guns was killed or taken. Then, breaking through this rearguard, the Cossacks swept for ten miles along the road, overtaking the motor-vehicles with the guns and limbers.

A wonderful cavalry charge

The extraordinary success of this wonderful cavalry charge against siege artillery is indicated by the fact that not one horseman was killed. There were only sixteen casualties, and most of the wounds were slight. The two flanking infantry attacks across the swamps completely shattered the nerve of the Germans. Their gunners, with a five-mile field of fire to work over, could not place one shell or case-shot amid the advancing squadrons. In all some forty heavy guns, and a far larger number of

speed as they went through the town, swept between their own forts and charged the German siege-guns.

In the confusion caused

RUSSIA'S YOUNGEST VOLUNTEER.
Constantin Malafeef, aged fifteen, promoted sergeant on the field, and for his bravery made a knight of the military order of St. George.

IN THE HANDS OF THE ENEMY.
Prisoners hailing from remote districts of Siberia captured in the early days of the fighting round the beleaguered fortress of Przemysl.

light quick-firers and machine-guns, were taken on the East Prussian front between October 1st and October 7th. The Battle of Augustovo began on September 25th and ended on October 4th. The siege of Osoviec began on September 26th and ended on October 1st. An attempt to pierce the Niemen defences at Drusskeniki, eastward of the town of Suwalki, was made on September 26th, but it failed, too. In less than a week the victorious Russian forces were again operating in East Prussia.

Thus, in spite of the preliminary success of Hindenburg at Tannenberg against the wing of the Russian invading force, the acclaimed saviour of Prussia had not been able to save his country from invasion. He had come up against Rennenkampf with numbers, railways, and artillery in his favour. But far from trapping the main Russian army of invasion, he had been completely defeated himself, and had had to give ground in his own country before the new victorious advance of his opponents.

Hindenburg has to give ground

Hindenburg, however, was not personally responsible for the series of German defeats around the Niemen River, for he had left all these operations to a subordinate general soon after the affair with Samsonoff. Hindenburg was an able man. It is not saying too much to credit him with the strength and force of character of Blücher and the skill in strategy of Gneisenau, but in the Grand Duke Nicholas he met a man superior to himself in ability and in the efficient force which he wielded.

Hindenburg did not have things all his own way as Moltke did. He had better communications, superior artillery, and larger numbers

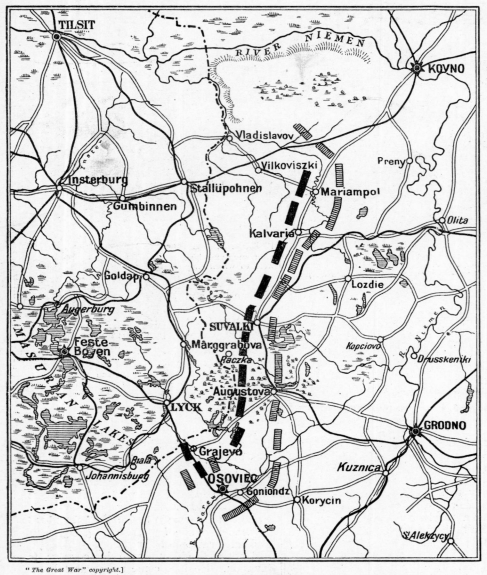

" *The Great War* " copyright.]

MAP OF THE TERRITORY BETWEEN THE NIEMEN AND THE MASURIAN LAKES.
Showing the area of the fighting which ended in the Russian victories at Augustovo and Osoviec,
the relative positions of the opposing armies being represented by solid black lines for Germans
and shaded lines for Russians.

the Grand Duke Nicholas, Ivanoff, and Russky. The important consequence was that all the chief moves of Hindenburg were continually anticipated by the Russian Staff, and that preparations were made against them. Early in October it was known to the Russians that the attack on their Niemen defences was partly a distraction intended to have the effect of inducing them to make a very great concentration of troops to protect their railway line of communication between Warsaw and Petrograd. Hindenburg was ready to push home his offensive in this region so long as it promised success. But when he found, in the first week in October, that his men were very firmly held, he adopted another plan of attack.

Leaving in the Masurian Lakes district what seemed to be a sufficient force of troops to continue a swaying battle with the Russians, he drew off about half his forces and railed them down to Thorn. Some weeks before this he had been strengthening his main force on the Warta River in Russian Poland. There he had brought up new formations from Central Germany, and reorganised the Austro-Hungarian armies at Cracow and the Galician heights. Only General Dankl was allowed to retain a veritable power of high command over part of the beaten armies of the Southern Empire. There was a wholesale dismissal or reduction in rank of officers, and in many cases the subjects of the Emperor Francis Joseph were displaced by men who owed allegiance to the Emperor William. Only the Hungarian officers escaped from this Prussianisation of the war-machine of the Hapsburg house.

The Northern Teutons treated the Hungarians as comrades, but dealt with the Austrians as with serfs. But it must be admitted that this sudden, rigorous, and **Reorganisation of Austrian forces** thorough absorption and reorganisation of the Austrian forces by the German Great Staff was an effective and businesslike measure. It put a new power both of attack and resistance into the battered and broken armies of Austria-Hungary, and it is an achievement on which the Germans can justly pride themselves. It was mainly the enormous store of war material which the German Great Staff had prepared, when it decided on an aggressive attempt to dominate Europe, that enabled this achievement in reorganisation to be carried out on the spur of the moment.

By the first week in October Germany had a million and a quarter of her own men on the Polish front, with a quarter of a million Austrian troops immediately joining with them in front of Cracow. Fully another million of Austrian and Hungarian effectives were working against the Russian lines on the Galician battle-front, concentrating towards the upper course of the Vistula and the San Rivers. There were also a million troops of the third line collecting in the Hungarian plain for action against the Russian raiders

of troops than had the Russian commander. But, on the other hand, the Russians possessed more experience of war under modern conditions, troops of a finer quality, and somebody with a very high genius for strategy —probably the Chief of Staff, General Sukhomlinoff.

In addition, the chief Russian armies were commanded by men like Russky, Dimitrieff, Brussiloff, and Ivanoff, all of proved strength of character and genius of mind. Then the Grand Duke Nicholas had shown himself as remarkable an exception to the rule regarding the warlike ability of princely leaders as the young Austrian Archduke Charles did in 1796, when he beat both Jourdain and Moreau in the Wars of the Revolution. It will be seen that we have to go **Emergence of an Imperial captain** back fairly far into history to find some parallel to the emergence of an Imperial captain of the stamp of the Grand Duke Nicholas. Having threshed the weak elements of command out of her armies during the Manchurian campaign, Russia was immeasurably stronger than Germany and Austria in regard to leadership.

Hindenburg was a very good man faced by still better men. In the main area of the struggle there were always at least four prime minds against his—those of Sukhomlinoff,

OPENING OF THE WINTER CAMPAIGN IN RUSSIAN POLAND.
Russian soldiers at work breaking ice on a Polish river.

THE GERMAN ADVANCE ON THE CAPITAL OF RUSSIAN POLAND.
Troops of the Kaiser, confident of victory, advancing over the East Prussian border to be broken against the Russian defences west of Warsaw.

German transport column in a Polish quagmire and attacked by Siberian horsemen. In his desperate effort to get his army back to his own frontier, the German commander buried many guns, and quantities of stores. But he found the Siberians more deadly in attack than in defence. The retreating Teutons threw out strong rearguards, but one half of the German northern army had to be sacrificed to save the other half in the harassed retreat from Warsaw

During General von Hindenburg's attack on Warsaw a force of German cavalry was sighted by a Cossack patrol. To avoid a fight at close quarters, the Teutons dismounted and opened fire with their carbines. On came the Cossacks, and as they got nearer, one after the other, adopting their favourite manœuvre, dropped beneath the girths of their steeds. Thinking they had killed their adversaries, the Germans mounted, with a view to capturing

o the Warta.   The pursuit was planned so that each Russian attack was made by fresh bodies of troops, and by the end of October, 1914, mounted Cossacks were threatening the frontier of German Poland at Kolo.   Hindenburg's retreat was very like that of Napoleon from Moscow in 1812, and their tactics in 1914 demonstrated that the Tsar's soldiers retained many of the characteristics of their forefathers a hundred odd years ago.

at they supposed to be riderless horses. As they approached the latter, wever, the Cossacks suddenly reappeared, and attacking the Germans with eat fury, cut them to pieces.   The Cossacks, like the Arabs, are superb horsemen, and their horses are as highly trained as the riders themselves.   The Cossack lives for battle, and to him is due the Russian conquest of the whole of Northern Asia.

WATCHING THE FLAMES RISE FROM A BURNING VILLAGE IN NORTHERN POLAND.

The Russian general seen in the above photograph is watching a necessary, but to him regrettable, of the Tsar in their struggle with General von Hindenburg's forces in Northern Poland and East work of destruction. Only where it was imperative were villages committed to the flames by the soldiers Prussia, though the Germans proved as lustful of destruction in Russian territory as in Belgium.

who had crossed the Carpathians and had occupied Munkacs, Ungar, and other Hungarian towns. In both Hungary and Eastern Prussia the Russians were pressing against the flanks of the two Teutonic Empires. The obvious answer to these side pressures was a strong thrust against the Russian centre in Poland.

Against this centre the Germans had, in fact, concentrated at the opening of the war. They had crossed the border and had captured Czestochowa and Kalisz, and entrenched along the Warta River. Their position formed a long flat curve in Russian territory menacing Warsaw and Ivangorod. The Russian commander had scarcely 50,000 bayonets and 10,000 sabres operating in the rolling Polish plain—an immense region dappled and belted with forests, scantily provided with good roads, and served only by few railways. The Russian horsemen, with their infantry and light artillery supports, were little more than a reconnoitring and patrolling force, in just sufficient strength to discover any serious forward movement by the enemy. The Russian General Staff, indeed, deliberately left its line weak and yielding immediately in front of the main German armies. And the pressure that the Russians exerted on both their enemy's wings was also designed to induce the Germans to take the line of least resistance, and to attack from their centre in Poland.

So when Hindenburg advanced in the required direction he was only obeying his masters in strategy—the Russian Staff. The fact was, the Russians could not afford to attack the Germans on the Warta entrenchments. The Russian railway lines from Warsaw and Ivangorod were

MAP OF THE COUNTRY EAST OF THE WARTA.
"The Great War" copyright.
Illustrating the relative positions of Warsaw, Ivangorod, and Cracow. The black lines show the approximate positions of the German forces, and the shaded lines the Russian, when Hindenburg's army made its futile effort to reach the Polish capital.

Moltke's battle-railway tracks not sufficiently developed to supply a Russian army operating near the German frontier. In particular, there was no cross-country railway running parallel with the frontier by which the Russians could shift their troops swiftly and thus concentrate them for a series of feints and frontal attacks. The Germans, on the other hand, had two parallel railway systems running close to the Russian frontier. These railways were designed by the elder Moltke for the purpose of a border campaign with Russia. As a consequence the Grand Duke Nicholas refused to fight near the German frontier railways. He kept his main armies nearly a hundred and forty miles east of Moltke's battle-railway tracks. He left all Poland up to Warsaw and Ivangorod open to the enemy, merely occupying the country with reconnoitring forces based on the two Polish railway systems in the bend of the Vistula.

All this was known to Hindenburg. The manner in which he dealt with the situation is a fair measure of his powers. He made a remarkably swift attack, and so provided against possible defeat that when he was defeated he got away without losing any notable number of guns.

His first campaign on the Vistula was a tiger's leap, and though the tiger struck against a stone wall, he at least escaped from the pit dug for his doom. For Russia, six weeks after mobilisation, could not put into the field sufficient armed men to win the full advantage of her superior strategical position. She had millions of fairly well-trained troops waiting for rifles, artillery, and munitions. The Siberian railway formed the line of communication with ordnance works and ammunition factories in Japan and the United States. But it was choked with troops and Russian stores, and before American material reached it this material had to cross the American continent and the Pacific Ocean.

Russia, therefore, lacked the strength to hit back hard, even when she was apparently in a position to do so. Her Commander-in-Chief **Russian front of** and Chief of Staff were occupied all the **1,100 miles** autumn and winter in solving the difficult problem of using three million fine troops to counter a series of attacks by four million soldiers of inferior quality. Considerable genius was required to divine where the two enemies would concentrate their forces, so as to be able to meet them without delay before they could break through the comparatively weak line of the Russian defences.

THE "LAVA": A UNIQUE AND FAVOURITE METHOD OF ATTACK USED BY THE COSSACK CAVALRY.
Of all the distinctively racial methods of warfare the Cossack "lava" remains unique, and it was used with terrible effect against the Teutonic cavalry. The Cossacks allow the enemy to make the first move. Then they advance, three squadrons ahead extended in line, and two squadrons massed in close formation in the rear. This advance is made at a pace which renders any necessary turning movement to be carried out with ease and celerity. When some two hundred yards from the enemy, the pace is quickened to a gallop, and the front line divides into two sections, each of which swings outwards and spreads rapidly in file to attack the flanks of the foe. Coincidently the rear squadrons, now in the centre, engage the enemy in front.

From Memel on the Baltic to Czernovitz near the Rumanian border the Russians had to hold a front of about eleven hundred miles against the two Teutonic Empires. At any point along this immense line there was the constant danger of an unexpected concentration in overwhelming force by the enemy. The wonder is not that the Russians did not advance, but that they were able to hold on to their recovered province of Galicia, and to compel Hindenburg to attack them at the time and the place that they selected. In his first Vistula campaign Hindenburg divided his forces into four groups. The first army, formed of men drawn from East Prussia, worked up from Thorn, by the left bank of the Vistula. The second came from Kalisz and moved eastward through Lodz. These two armies concentrated against Warsaw. The third army, starting from Breslau, passed through Czestochowa, and following the southern bank of the Pilica River, turned towards the Ivangorod region. The fourth army, consisting of Austrians and Germans based on Cracow, moved up towards Kielce and Radom, and advanced north-eastward by the left bank of the Vistula.

Hindenburg's four invading armies

Up till October 3rd the movement was a strategic deployment rather than an offensive attack. At this date the main Teutonic forces occupied a line running through Kutno, Lodz, Petrokoff, and Kielce. This was rather more than half-way between the German frontier and the Russian positions on the Vistula. At this time the German offensive movement against the right Russian flank on the Niemen was being defeated. But, as the Russian commander knew, his victory on his right wing denoted a withdrawal of the enemy's force for a stupendous attack against his centre. There then arose a ticklish problem for the Russian Staff. They had to foresee the point at which Hindenburg would hurl his main force. Would he try to cross the Vistula by the bridge at Warsaw or by the bridge at Ivangorod? At one place there would be a strong demonstration; at the other a long and desperate battle, where Hindenburg in person would launch some three-quarters of a million men on a wide front, strongly supported by artillery.

A victory at Ivangorod would be the more decisive; it would give a larger range for future operations against the Russian forces, and allow a turning movement against Warsaw, and another against the Russian position southward in Galicia. For this and other reasons the Russian Staff decided rightly that Ivangorod would be the critical point in their line of defence. But the trouble was that the troops which they were withdrawing from the Niemen front, in answer to the similar withdrawal of Hindenburg from this part of the battle-field, were collecting at Warsaw. This was their nearest point of concentration, and as the light railway between Warsaw and Ivangorod was heavily loaded with war traffic, the new re-inforcement would have to march for a week to get into action at the decisive spot.

It was a situation of extreme difficulty; but the Grand Duke Nicholas coped with it by means of a very simple but yet effective trick. Nearly all the Jews in Russian Poland were eager for their country to be conquered by the Germans. In their view, there was more to be hoped for men of their creed from the Empire in which brilliant Jews like Ballin, Dernberg, Rathenaus, and hundreds of Jewish bankers and manufacturers had risen to eminence and power, than from the Russian rule that still prac-tically confined Jews in a pale, and prevented them from fully developing their gifts for finance and politics. The majority of the peasantry of true Polish race favoured the Russian cause, looking confidently to the re-establishment of the ancient kingdom of Poland under the suzerainty of the Tsar. The majority of the Jews, however, regarded this prospect with deep fear, and many of them became passionately willing to act as Secret Service agents of the invaders.

German-Jewish secret agents

This condition of things seemed to add to the difficulties of the Russian Commander-in-Chief. But, by a stroke of genius, he transformed the German-Jewish system of espionage into a splendid instrument of Russian strategy. Warsaw was prepared for evacuation. Many of the Government officials left the city, and the troops, thrown out in front to entrench and guard the bridge, looked like a forlorn hope. About October 17th German aeroplanes began to soar over Warsaw. At first they dropped pamphlets in Polish, telling the people that the armies of redemption were at hand, and that Poland would soon be recovered from Russian tyranny. The Germans did not go on to state that all Russian Poles would then be treated as kindly as were their countrymen in Prussian Poland. The Poles were left to draw this conclusion for themselves when the German airmen returned and began to throw bombs on the town. Women, children, and peaceful townsmen were killed, but no Russian soldier, for there were practically no Russian soldiers in Warsaw. The people, frightened by their defenceless condition, were swept by a terrible panic and poured out eastward to escape from the coming struggle. Nothing more hopeless than the appearance of Warsaw at this time was seen in any other field of the war. It was a combination of Paris, when the French Government was removing to Bordeaux, and Antwerp.

Civilian panic in Warsaw

Naturally, everything that went on at Warsaw was soon known to Hindenburg and his Headquarters Staff. It led them to change their plan of attack somewhat, and to weaken their main offensive against Ivangorod, by detaching the second column to co-operate with the first, in a veritable attempt to carry Warsaw by storm. Nearly a quarter of a million men were assigned to this purpose, and what had only been intended as a demonstration was transformed into a real attack.

With the idea of making the most by this change in his plan, Hindenburg launched his two armies swiftly on the capital of Russian Poland before he began to threaten Ivangorod. By this means he hoped to distract the Russian Commander-in-Chief, and to induce him to attempt at the last moment to reinforce Warsaw at the expense of Ivangorod. The Grand Duke Nicholas must have smiled when he learned this last essay in strategy on the part of the enemy. For, as we have seen, Hindenburg had done everything that the Russians had wanted him to do. His army of spies in and around Warsaw pursued their work and communicated with the Germans, under the fostering attention of the Russian secret police. Every facility but one was placed in their way. It was only when they left the city in an easterly direction, and tried to find if anything were behind the crowd of fugitives, that their careers were suddenly closed. The country north and east of the Bug River was an immense Bluebeard's chamber, from which spies were not allowed to return. For in this region and on the Petrograd railway running through it was the Siberian army, with Cossacks and infantry from the Niemen front and wild, warlike Moslem horsemen from the steppes.

"An immense Bluebeard's chamber"

Unaware of the immense ambush before them, the quarter of a million Germans opened the battle with a series of skirmishes on Sunday, October 11th. The weak Russian

BIRD'S-EYE VIEW OF THE OLD AND NEW CITIES OF WARSAW, LOOKING NORTH-WEST ACROSS THE VISTULA.

Something like a million Russian troops, operating far away on the southern reaches of the Vistula communication with Petrograd. German airmen dropped bombs over the city, the windows in which against the main eastern forces of Germany and Austria in October, 1914, depended for food and rattled for eight days with the concussion of artillery fire. By order of the Russian Generalissimo ammunition chiefly on their railway-head at Warsaw. Warsaw in turn depended on its railway Warsaw was prepared for evacuation. This was done to counteract the German spy-service.

WHERE HINDENBURG WAS CHECKED.
Portion of railway track marking the spot where General von Hindenburg was compelled to retreat.

advance guard fell back, continually fighting, between the Vistula and the northern bank of its tributary the Pilica. The Russian force was first composed of masses of cavalry, supported by infantry detachments; but at every stand they made the infantry and artillery power increased, especially on their northern wing.

The enemy, however, was always thrusting forward with remarkable impetuosity to find the weak section in the Russian line. This section they discovered far away from Warsaw, by the northern bank of the Pilica. Here they drove in till they passed the town of Varka, and reached the Vistula at the point where the Pilica flows into it. It was rainy weather; the roads were in a terrible state; the rivers were in flood and their valleys turned into morasses. It **The Battle of** was not a river but a great lake to **Warsaw** which the northern German army was allowed to penetrate with its southern wing. There it was permitted to rest, while the decision was being fought out round Warsaw—some days' march northward. There, backed by a converging system of railways and with the only bridge across the river in his hands, the Russian commander played with the enemy; for on his right was Novo Georgievsk, one of the strongest fortresses in Russia, worth an army for the support it gave to the right flank of the Russians.

The Russian advance guard continued to retire till its lines swung back a few miles from Warsaw. It entrenched at just sufficient distance from the city to prevent the large German field-guns from bombarding the Polish capital. The Russian artillery had already been sited in sufficient number and power to engage on at least equal terms the guns which the Germans were

GERMAN ENGINEERS INSPECTING A DAMAGED RAILWAY LINE ON THE ROAD TO WARSAW.
The single-track line shown in the above photograph is apparently that running between Warsaw and Kalisz, a branch of which runs into Lodz. It had been torn up by the Russians and was repaired by the Germans. Inset: Destruction on the main Russian Kalisz-Lodz-Warsaw line.

GERMANS IN WARSAW—BUT NOT AS THEY EXPECTED TO BE.
Marching German prisoners through the streets of the Polish capital.

hauling forward. As the Germans brought up their guns and their ten or eleven infantry divisions, there was a remarkable hardening of the Russian resistance. Every night large bodies of Russians crossed the Vistula bridge and took up their positions in the trenches. The Germans were never allowed to slacken in their attack. If they tried to do so, there followed a tremendous infantry charge against their positions, which compelled them to counter-attack with all available forces. For eight days the windows of Warsaw rattled with the concussion of artillery fire, and the thunder of the neighbouring batteries rolled over the picturesque, historic city.

The Germans fall back The Russians made their first attack in the middle of October. This brought the Germans out of their trenches in massed formation on Saturday and Sunday, October 17th and 18th. Swept by shrapnel, mowed down by rifle fire, and at last driven in by the bayonet of the Siberian troops, the Germans fell back. To strengthen their lines before Warsaw, their commander was obliged to call in part of the army corps resting on the Pilica and the Vistula. He did this on the night of Monday, October 19th. About the same time a very strong Russian column marched south along the right bank of the Vistula, while the Germans were marching north on the left bank. The Russian column reached Goura-Kalvaria, a little more than half-way between Warsaw and Pilica River. Bringing up guns to dominate the crossing of the broad, swirling waters of the Vistula, the troops made a pontoon bridge on Monday night, October 19th. On Tuesday morning men and guns crossed the river and attacked the weakened wing of the German northern army. At the same time another Russian column was sweeping northward round by Novo Georgievsk, and menacing the right wing of the Russian army.

A WAYSIDE LUNCH IN RUSSIAN POLAND.
Russian generals partaking of a frugal meal during the operations along the Vistula.

ON THE TRACK OF THE FLYING FOE.
Cossacks examining some empty barrels left in a Polish village by the retreating Germans.

77

RECONSTRUCTING A BROKEN RAILWAY BRIDGE IN POLAND.
German engineers reconstructing the railway bridge at Sieradz, east of Kalisz. The gap has been temporarily filled by pontoons.

The effect of these two movements was to bring the German attack upon Warsaw to an abrupt end; for on the night of October 20th the enemy began to evacuate his position on the Goura-Kalvaria front, and to prepare a general retirement. The elaborate scheme of fortifications, intended to hold the Russians across the Vistula during the winter campaign, was abandoned without a struggle. All that the German commander then hoped and worked for was to get his army back to his own frontier with little loss. He buried many guns and stores of shells as he withdrew. But he could not avoid terrible losses in men, for the Siberians were even more deadly in attack than they were in defence. Like most of the colonial troops of the white races, they were the picked spirits of their mother country, distinguished from the stay-at-home population by their initiative, enterprise, and venturesomeness. Born sharpshooters, and as fond of the bayonet as the French, they were irresistible in attack. And as the Russian artillery skilfully and thoroughly prepared the ground for them, they worked forward very quickly.

Fate of Northern German Army

Two German army corps—the 17th and 18th—tried to make a stand at the villages of Bloni and Pasechno, the first sixteen miles west of Warsaw and the second twelve miles south of it. There were 60,000 German bayonets holding the two villages, and fed and munitioned by the railway from Skernievice. But the Siberians got on their left flank, operating from the fortress of Novo Georgievsk. Then came the slaughter. There was only one way for the German commander to prevent his retreat from becoming a rout. He had to throw out continually strong rearguards to enable his heavy guns to be buried or got away before the Cossack horsemen got in front of the batteries. In fact, half the northern German army had to be sacrificed to save the other half and the guns. For the Russians were in such force, and were moving so quickly over the rolling prairies and forests, that a continual enveloping movement went on against each German rearguard.

Every village which the Germans tried to hold was shattered by the light field artillery of the pursuers. And while the shells were falling, the Russian impi—infantry in the centre and horse at the horns—advanced, and began to lock round the smaller hostile force. It was something more than a retreat and something less than a rout. It was a race for the German entrenchments on the Warta. Between this river and the Vistula there was only one river-line on which the Germans could have made a stand—the line of the Bzura River, running through Lodz. But the trouble was that Lodz was a rich, industrial town, financed by the Germans, and run by them and by their Jewish sympathisers. So Lodz and Lowicz had to be surrendered without a struggle for the sake of German commercial interests. Moreover, the Cossack cavalry still continued to ride down the Vistula on its flanking movement. There

Surrender of Lodz and Lowicz

GUARDING THE RUSSIAN FLAG.
Armed escort of the Tsar's soldiers bringing in colours to the Russian Headquarters.
Inset : Austrian prisoners in Galicia, on their way to a Moscow concentration camp.

were many places where German sappers prepared extremely elaborate positions along the ridges of the rolling country, with deep trenches, abatis of felled forest trees, and gun-sites with a clear sweep for fire as far as field artillery could carry. Yet the rearguard did not stay one day at many of these points. At the first

From Warsaw to the Warta threat of an outflanking movement they fled to save the guns.

The general method of the Russians in these rearguard actions could be studied at the pretty little Polish city of Skernievice. On a ridge six and a half miles from the town were the German fortified lines; they had been abandoned without a struggle. Half a day's march farther west was another ridge near a forest. A Russian infantry brigade crept forward under the cover of its guns, took the forest at the point of the bayonet, and then turned the German trenches. The victorious troops rested for a day on the field they had won, while another brigade took up the pursuit, with the Russian cavalry spread out before it. In this way each Russian attack was made by fresh bodies of soldiers always on the march. At the same time the more fatigued, victorious brigades and divisions also advanced after a brief rest, in case the enemy should attempt a general stand. But this the Germans did not do, and by the end of October the mounted Cossacks were threatening the frontier of German Poland.

While the northern German army was thus being defeated and pursued from Warsaw to the Warta, the main central German force attacked Ivangorod. The general situation was very interesting. Swift and overwhelming as had been the defeat of the German northern wing before Warsaw, this did not bring about the retirement of the whole German front. The stronger central army of invasion, massed against Ivangorod, still hoped to retrieve the situation by forcing the passage of the Vistula and wedging itself between the Russian lines.

In this part of the field the Russian troops were commanded by General Russky, the victor of Lemberg. His army held more than a hundred and fifty miles of the winding course of the Vistula, from the point where the Pilica falls into it to the point where the Kamienna flows into the great river near Jozefov. These geographical details are of vital importance, for the distance from Russky's left wing to the battlefield of Warsaw was equal to seven days' hard marching. That is to say, Hindenburg had a week's grace in his operations round Ivangorod, in which he could attempt to

Battle for the Central Vistula force the Vistula with no fear of any attack on his rear by part of the conquering Russian force from the Warsaw section. If Hindenburg won, the retreat of his northern wing would be an affair of no importance. He would still be master of the whole of Russian Poland, Warsaw being his to take when he liked to concentrate upon it, and the Russians of the southern reaches of the Vistula and the San Rivers would be at his mercy.

As a matter of fact, a strong Russian

NEWSPAPER CORRESPONDENTS' "WAR SPECIAL" IN THE EAST.
A number of war correspondents were allowed to follow the Russian armies in the field. Among those invited was Professor Pares, of Liverpool University.

A WELCOME GIFT FROM A FRIENDLY SLAV.
Russian soldier providing a German prisoner with "something to smoke," much to the interest of the onlookers. Inset: A bombarded town in Galicia, where the church was spared.

ENEMIES UNITE IN AIDING
THE WOUNDED.
Russian and Austrian Red Cross doctors
attending a wounded Austrian soldier.

column had set out from
Warsaw to reinforce General
Russky's army. Marching
through the rain and mud at
an amazing speed, it came up
at the critical point in the
central battle, and took the
enemy by surprise. An un-
paralleled vigour of movement
in bad weather over bad roads
enabled this column to beat
Hindenburg at his own game of
unexpectedly swift concentration. But whereas the Germans relied on the handling of
railways in these strategic
feats, the Russians trusted to their feet.
It was their physique that enabled them
to get the winning move.

Meanwhile the battle for the Central
Vistula was conditioned by the dense
forests in this region. There were only
three large open spaces of nearly level
country available for army operations with
a clear field for gun fire. The chief of
these open spaces was the plain of
Kozienice, running fourteen miles along
the Vistula, with a breadth of less than
six miles. It was about a day's march
from Ivangorod. Beyond it, in the
            direction of Warsaw,
German semicircle was the open space of
round Ivangorod Glovachev, with a clear
            battle-plain fifteen
miles long by ten miles broad. Then south
of Ivangorod was the open space of
Politchna. In all three heavy Russian
guns were placed on the opposite side
of the Vistula, while troops entrenched on
the plains to hold back the enemy. The
Germans moved forward under the cover
of the forests on the southern bank of
the Pilica. They occupied the town of
Glovachev and the larger town of Radom,

and deployed until their forces formed a
mighty semicircle round Ivangorod. Their
intention was to clear the plains of
Glovachev and Kozienice of Russian
troops, and then to force the passage of
the Vistula at these points and envelop
Ivangorod from the north, while making
also a frontal attack and a southern
enveloping movement from Radom. Here
the open space of Politchna by the Vistula
was the principal scene of struggle.

The battle opened with a series of small
successes for the Germans. Each of the
three open spaces was held by only small
bodies of Russian troops, the main defending armies being drawn up on the other
side of the great river. The idea was to
hold the open spaces as
bridge-heads, where the **Fierce fighting in**
principal Russian forces   **forest paths**
could cross by pontoons
when the army of invasion had been forced
to reveal its attacking dispositions and had
been shaken by bombardments from the
            numerous concealed Russian
            batteries firing over the river.
            But small though the Russian
            advanced bodies were, they did
            not act passively and simply wait
            to be attacked. In all the forest
            paths were fierce and desperate
            encounters with each thrusting
            wedge of Hindenburg's armies.
            With Maxim, rifle, and bayonet
            the Russians continually kept
            the enemy off, until the Ger-
            mans brought up their field-guns
            and shelled the Russians out of
            their positions.

Then at Kozienice the Russian
troops entrenched and the battle
was joined in a general fury.
The small line of advanced

A TOUCH OF NATURE IN LEMBERG.
When the Russians captured Lemberg they allowed their prisoners to be visited by their
friends. We are able to give above an interesting camera record of this act of kindliness
on the part of the victorious Muscovites. Inset: Homely interlude in a Russian trench;
cheery Slav soldiers preparing a meal.

troops became a bait to the mighty attacking force, and for nearly fourteen days it had to fight, like our 7th Division at Ypres, against a continual bombardment of shells, varied by infantry attacks in dense, deep lines. But about Thursday, October 22nd, reinforcements began to arrive from the opposite bank of the Vistula. The resisting Russian line lengthened out and thickened, and began to threaten a flank attack on the enemy. The Germans retired from the

The Battle of Kozienice open space into the forest, which was so dense with trees and underwood that a man could hardly see fifty feet around him. In this jungle the Germans had about forty-two guns to the mile, and every possible path was defended by rifle pits, with machine-guns and abatis defences. The Russian artillery was no longer able to support its infantry, as it was only wasting shell and shrapnel to try and search for the hostile positions. All that the Russian commander could do was to send his foot soldiers into the forest to poke the enemy out with the bayonet. Day after day brigade after brigade of Russians entered the tangle of trees and vanished from sight. Companies, regiments, battalions lost touch with each other, and in places brigade was cut off from brigade. Few Russian colonels there knew what was going on anywhere, except in the patch of ground on which their men were fighting. But every Russian knew that the only thing required of him was to push the enemy out. This he did yard by yard, and hour by hour, in one of the fiercest hand-to-hand struggles in his-

RUSSIAN CHARITY IN GALICIA. Russian priest, assisted by soldiers, distributing money to poor children in Galicia.

tory. It was a soldiers' battle, won by bullet and bayonet—mainly the bayonet.

The Germans left 16,000 of their dead in the woods and thickets of Kozienice when they broke and fled on Monday, October 26th. On this day the German retreat from Ivangorod was general. At Glovachev their Twentieth Army Corps and Reserve Corps of the Guards were defeated and driven along the southern bank of the Pilica. In the centre the Russians carried the forest villages at the bayonet point. At Politchna, on the left wing, the enemy's defences were stormed, thousands of prisoners were taken with many guns, and the invading army thrown back to Radom.

While this frontal attack by the Teutons upon the Ivangorod bend of the Vistula was being repulsed, still more interesting things were happening farther south up the river at Jozefov. Here the Austro-Hungarian army, under General Dankl, was opposed by part of the southern Russian army, under the Bulgarian General Dimitrieff. Farther away was General Brussiloff, holding Lemberg and the greater part of Galicia, with part of Hungary, against the attacks of the new militia forces of the Dual Monarchy. General **Austria's new formations broken** Brussiloff had especially to protect the railway line, running from Lemberg to Kieff, by which his troops were provisioned and munitioned. He was greatly outnumbered by the new Austrian and Hungarian levies operating in the extreme south. Yet he had to hold Lemberg and the railway line against them, and at the same time help to defeat General Dankl's

A MEAL A LA RUSSE IN THE OPEN. Russian soldiers snatch a hasty meal on the Galician plain while one of their number keeps a look-out. Inset: Russian officer making observations in Galicia.

BRIDGE DESTROYED BY THE GERMANS BEFORE LODZ.
The invading army under General von Hindenburg made strenuous but unsuccessful efforts to intercept the Russian railway communication at this point.

forces on the Vistula. He split his armies up. About half of the troops were left in Galicia under the personal direction of Brussiloff; the other half was sent up towards the Vistula, under the command of Dimitrieff. Brussiloff abandoned the siege of Przemysl, retired from Jaroslav, and, entrenching between these towns and Lemberg, he held out against all the assaults of the new armies of the southern Teutonic Empire. South of Przemysl, on October 27th, one of these new armies attempted a flank attack on the Russian line. The battle took place fifteen miles south of the town of Sambor, in a hollow plain amid the foot-hills. But the Russians also had newly-formed regiments, railed from Kieff, to counter the enemy's new formations. The Russian recruits shepherded their foes into the river valley and then rushed up the heights, from which they poured a terrible fire, until the Austro-Hungarian force was practically annihilated. Only a few hundreds escaped, in small squads, by the paths used by the mountain sheep. All their guns and convoys were captured. While breaking the enemy up in this manner in the valleys, General Brussiloff continued to send raiding brigades of Cossacks over **Cossacks over the Carpathians** the passes of the Eastern Carpathians to menace the Hungarian wheat-plains of the Danube, and to force the enemy to concentrate against him all along the mountains. His scheme of operations completely succeeded; for though the Russian raiders had at last to draw back to the mountain passes, they continued for months to detain large forces of the enemy in the ravines and high valleys. Meanwhile Lemberg was safely and firmly held until the siege of Przemysl could be renewed.

This magnificent and stubborn defence, conducted by the extreme southern wing of the Russian forces, allowed the neighbouring army, under the Bulgarian General Dimitrieff, to act more freely. Dimitrieff, who had led the Bulgarians in their victories against the Turks, and was acting as Bulgarian Minister in Petrograd on the outbreak of war, had accepted a Russian command, though he was promptly disgraced by the Bulgarian Government. His glorious achievements, performed for his brother Slavs, were one of the principal factors in swaying the minds of the Bulgarian democracy away from Austria towards Russia. Dimitrieff was engaged in the preliminary operations for the siege of Cracow until Hindenburg attempted to get the whole line of the Vistula as a base for a winter campaign. The Russians then had to retire, leaving the upper reaches of the Vistula in the hands of the enemy.

THE MOBILISATION IN SIBERIA: COSSACKS IN MODERN SERVICE UNIFORM.
Inspection of a squadron of Cossacks in a little Siberian town prior to their departure for the battle-front in Poland. Inset: A Russian battery working under the direction of an observation officer, who is locating the enemy's position from a field-ladder.

RUSSIAN ARTILLERY IN ACTION DURING THE PRUSSIAN
ATTACK ON WARSAW.

RUSSIAN RED CROSS WORKERS REMOVING WOUNDED
AUSTRIANS FROM A GALICIAN BATTLEFIELD.

Apparently the strength of the defending forces was over-taxed by the great numbers brought against them, for there was a gap of more than sixty miles along the Vistula and the San Rivers. All that Dimitrieff left was a thin cavalry screen to test the strength of the enemy's movement and watch the course of their advance. The Austro-German troops might have made things difficult for the Bulgarian general had they tried to curve round him from the north. But, as he had rightly divined, they used the gap, under the direction of Hindenburg, to strike at the more important objective of Ivangorod. They crossed the Vistula near Jozefov, the last point held by the Russians in strength. Meeting with no opposition, for the Russian cavalry retired as they advanced, the Austrians marched northward through the Lublin district, with the intention of taking the main Russian army gathered about Ivangorod suddenly in the rear.

The extraordinary success of their manœuvre must have been very exhilarating to them. Alone of all the invading armies they had crossed the Vistula, practically without a struggle, and there remained no obstacle between them and the Russian forces entrenched farther down the river, around whom they were curving. But the alluring gap through which they had first passed was only a mouse-trap on a large scale. At the southern end of the gap General Dimitrieff was in wireless communication with the Russian commander at Nova Alexandria, some fifteen miles south-west of Ivangorod. As the trapped Austrian army moved northward, Dimitrieff followed them and closed the gap ; and at the same time a strong Russian force moved south from Ivangorod.

The long-prepared surprise

The long-prepared surprise occurred with fine exactitude on the fatal Monday, October 26th, when Hindenburg's main army was being pushed back to Radom. The Austrians across the Vistula were marching hard to time with the already defeated movement by the German Commander-in-Chief. After a long stretch of level country with squashy, parish roads, varied by patches of marsh, the troops making the turning movement came, weary and yet unsuspecting, to the hilly country near Nova Alexandria. There they struck against a considerable force of Russians, who had done their marching the day before, and were well rested, well fed, and eager for the fight. The Russian guns were posted on the heights, with all the ranges nicely marked beforehand. Under the cover of a furious shrapnel fire the defending infantry attacked with the bayonet. So swift and fierce was the onset that the Austrians were killed before they could make up their minds to surrender. Every one of them fell, and their guns and train were taken.

As this action opened, Dimitrieff, farther up the river near Jozefov, crossed the Vistula and advanced along its tributary, the Kamienna, towards the Polish mountain range of Lysa Gora. This long line of heights extends in front of the city of Kielce, and Dimetrieff designed to forestall the main German army by occupying the heights and the rivers north and south of them—the Kamienna and the Nida. His extraordinary situation, some forty miles in the rear of the retreating main forces of Hindenburg, is evidence of the assured skill and reliant foresight with which the Russian operations were planned. By letting through the doomed Austrian force without a struggle, he co-operated in closing the trap on it, and at the same time, by sweeping across the Vistula in turn, he unexpectedly arrived behind the main army of invasion on its day of defeat.

So great was the menace of this move against his rear that Hindenburg had to withdraw from the line of the Vistula and huddle his troops westward along the southern bank of the Pilica. And there, amid the forests, they were harried by Russky's men. Some of the troops of the main Russian army got behind a wood in which one of Hindenburg's rearguards was entrenched with artillery, and fired it in four places while a strong wind was blowing. Few of that rearguard escaped from the most terrible of deaths. They died in thousands from suffocation or from fire.

It was in these circumstances that Hindenburg took a

step which is likely to sully his fame, and to prevent the Catholic Teutons and Magyars from ever forming again a warlike federation with the Protestants of Prussia. For in the terrible week of the first great retreat from Russian Poland the Prussian Commander-in-Chief deliberately sacrificed the Austrians and Hungarians in tens of thousands in order to give his own countrymen an opportunity of escaping. It is quite likely that Hindenburg found that the Austrians were already so much shaken by their early defeats that their fighting value was of

Rearguard action round Kielce small importance. But even so, it was hardly fair to weed them out of his army for continual rearguard actions, in which they scarcely won a day's respite for the fugitive forces of Germany.

The chief rearguard action of this sort took place round Kielce on the night of Monday, November 2nd. The Austrian army, under General Dankl, held a long line of heights, with woods screening them from artillery fire and streams moating their positions. But the Russians under General Dimitrieff did not trouble about clearing their path with shrapnel. They had been driving the enemy along for a week at the speed of fifteen or twenty miles a day. The hero of Kirk Kilisse was well acquainted with the feeling of demoralisation in the ranks of an opponent. When evening fell he sent his troops forward in open order with fixed bayonets. Under the deepening darkness they crept close to the enemy's lines, and groping for him in the night they stabbed their way through his trenches and broke his front. When dawn came, and General Dankl was able to gather clearly what had occurred, no orderly retreat was possible. His entire line had been crumpled up. It was a rout. The last troops of the enemy left the city of Kielce at ten o'clock the following morning. Before noon the Russian soldiers were marching into the square. For hours they swung through the streets in their dirty grey coats, stained with the mud of trench and battlefield. Then, as daylight began to fade, the rumble of artillery fire came from the south. Dimitrieff and his men were working southward amid the hills and woods of the Nida to the upper reaches of the Vistula by Cracow. They entrenched on a southern tributary of the great river which they were to make famous by their long swaying movement of attack and defence against the troops holding Cracow.

The tributary they held was the Dunajec, which runs by the city of Tarnow, to Neu Sandez, in the Eastern Carpathians. There the remnants of what was once one of the main Austrian armies was now reduced to three army corps. Strengthened by a German division, it formed the eastern garrison force of Cracow. Eight miles beyond it were two 16·5 in. siege-guns of Krupp manufacture, and

closer to the Russian trenches were some hundreds of 6 in., 8 in., and 12 in. howitzers. On some days a thousand shells were pitched into the Russian lines. But Dimitrieff did not lose many men. So well were the Russian shell-proof trenches constructed that it took on the average a hundred Austrian shells to kill one Russian soldier.

All through the winter and far into the spring the strange siege went on. It was difficult at times to discover whether Dimitrieff was besieging the Austrians in Cracow or whether the Austrians were besieging him on the Dunajec. General Dimitrieff, however, had no doubt in the matter. He professed himself ready to carry the Austrian trenches and to break open the gate into Silesia at the word of command from the Grand Duke Nicholas. But the Russian Commander-in-Chief preferred to keep the enemy attacking through the mud of the Polish plain and the marshland of the lake region round the Prussian frontier. Russia was not ready to strike her great blow until arms and ammunition for her new armies arrived in the late spring of 1915. Meanwhile, scope was allowed to Hindenburg to make another attempt on Warsaw, and to maintain an offensive movement in the long, terrible, wearing Russian winter weather, in which the forces of Nature operated on the side of the hardy, enduring, patient, armed peasantry of the great agricultural Empire. Being practically in a state of siege, with an almost complete deadlock in the western theatre of the war, Germany and her unfortunate ally could not allow the Russians also to hem them in. The pressure on them was so great that they had to attempt sorties on a tremendous scale. Thus, under favouring conditions for the Powers of the Triple Entente, the struggle went on through the winter, with Russian Poland, the Masurian Lakes, and the snow-covered passes of the Carpathians as the chief scenes of conflict.

In the western theatre of war the Allies had definitely won the initiative, and, while holding the enemy all the winter, the French and British armies were improving their artillery.

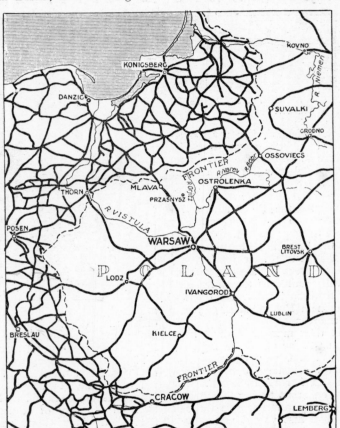

THE SECRET OF GERMANY'S MILITARY MOBILITY.
Even the best maps of the military areas do not show all the railways with which Germany, in pursuance of her long-established intention of making war, had covered her frontiers. This sketch map shows all the known strategic railways and branch lines on her eastern frontier, and it will be seen at a glance how terribly handicapped the Russians were in concentrating against the German forces, whereas Germany could swing her armies about from any part of the frontier.

In the eastern theatre of war the Russians could not reduce the fortress of Przemysl, which was relieved by the Austrian forces during Hindenburg's first vain advance against Warsaw and Ivangorod. But when Dimitrieff swung down again towards Cracow, Brussiloff also closed once more round **The siege of Przemysl** Przemysl, and entrusted the task of reducing the fortress to one of his best subordinate officers, General Selivanoff, a veteran of the Turco-Russian War. Early in November General Selivanoff entrenched his troops on a thirty-mile circle round Przemysl, out of range of the fortress, and waited. He had a more terrible weapon than a gun—famine. It was slow but deadly sure.

JAPANESE ARTILLERY | CHAPTER L. | AT SHANTUNG.

JAPAN'S INTERVENTION IN THE GREAT WAR: THE STORY OF TSINGTAU.

By F. A. McKenzie, Author of "From Tokyo to Tiflis," "The Unveiled East," etc.

Facts Behind the Ultimatum to Germany—How the Japanese People Nursed their Wrongs and Prepared for Reprisals—Rise of the City of Tsingtau, "The Brighton of the Far East"—Terms of the Ultimatum—The Imperial Rescript—Japanese Moderation—Strength and Weakness of the Japanese Army—The Kaiser's Message: "Defend to the Last Man"—Chinese Coolies Pressed into German Service—Combined Naval and Military Operations—Perils of Mine-Sweeping—Position of China—Landing of the British Force under General Barnardiston—A British Officer's Impressions of Trench Work—The Bombardment—Experiences of Civilians—The Fall of Tsingtau—Rejoicings in Japan—Congratulatory Messages—Germany's Threat of Vengeance—General Kamio's Appointment—The British General in Tokyo—Work of the Japanese Navy.

EARLY in August, 1914, before the actual outbreak of war, the Japanese Government announced that it was prepared to do its part to aid Great Britain, as laid down in the Anglo-Japanese Alliance. The Japanese Army and Navy made ready, and on August 15th an ultimatum was presented to Germany requiring her withdrawal from the Far East. No reply being received, war was declared, and a Japanese expedition set out to capture the German protectorate of Kiao-chau, in China.

In the days to come, when the world has reshaped itself under its new conditions, historians may well regard this Japanese intervention as one of the vital points in the struggle of the nations. Its results will be as far-reaching in Asia as will be the overthrow of German militarism in Europe. To understand its real meaning and purpose it is necessary to go back for a few years in the history of the Far East.

Less than half a century ago Japan was a mediæval land. For hundreds of years her people had shut themselves altogether apart from foreigners. When at last Commodore Perry, the American naval officer, broke down the barriers of exclusion, Europeans were still regarded with suspicion and distrust. Had anyone foretold in 1871,

when Germany concluded her triumphant peace with France, that in the years to come Japan would humiliate and defeat the forces of Germany, it would have seemed as fantastic as if anyone to-day were to say that fifty years hence the South Sea Islanders would be in a position to attack and defeat Great Britain.

Once the Japanese people came in contact with the West they were clever enough to realise that their civilisation could not stand before ours, any more than men with arrows and spears can fight Maxim guns. They set themselves to learn from Europe and America. At first the West refused to take them seriously. When Gilbert wished to pick a land of absurdity and fantasy, he selected Japan, and his generation laughed with him at the drolleries of "The Mikado." Europe heard of Japan modernising her Army, buying a Navy, and hiring distinguished men to teach her people the arts of peace and war. But it was not until 1894-5 that the world began to realise what all this meant. In 1894 Japan declared war upon China. Men expected the Mikado and his people to be swallowed up like a mouthful by the fierce and hungry Chinese giant. In place of that, the Japanese Navy wiped out the Chinese Fleet, and the Japanese armies defeated the great Chinese hosts with a celerity and a

THE EMPEROR OF JAPAN.
Yoshihito, born August 31st, 1879; succeeded his father Mutsuhito, July 30th, 1912.

precision which few European troops could have equalled and none surpassed. China was glad to make peace on terms dictated by Japan herself, paying an indemnity of two hundred million taels (thirty-three millions sterling) and handing over large sections of territory to Japan, including the south of Manchuria, Port Arthur, and the great island of Formosa.

In the very hour of Japan's triumph, Russia, France, and Germany intervened and robbed her of the fruits of victory. They sent their warships to the Yellow Sea, cleared them for action, and advised her "in the interests of peace" to restore the territory she had taken on the Chinese mainland. They refused to allow her to retain the great fortress of Port Arthur, which she had captured

GENERAL NATHANIEL W. BARNARDISTON, M.V.O.
The commander of the British Expeditionary Force at Tsingtau with two officers of his Staff.

after a brilliant siege. The people of Japan were furious, but the Japanese Government recognised that to risk a war with Russia, Germany, and France would be to invite its own destruction. It gave way, but it gave way reluctantly, bitterly, and resolute on revenge.

Great Britain had refused to join the three Powers in coercing Japan, although they did their utmost to persuade her. Germany and her partners defended their action on the plea that they were guarding the integrity of China. They were soon to prove the insincerity of their claim. Two years afterwards the Germans found an excuse in the murder of some German missionaries in Shantung to demand territory for themselves. A German force

The "mailed fist" in Shantung

was landed in China, and Prince Henry of Prussia was sent to the Far East with a fleet. Germany put forward a series of demands, of which the chief was the occupation of Kiao-chau and the recognition of Shantung as a German sphere of influence. Everyone, even in Germany itself, recognised that the plea of inflicting punishment for the murder of the missionaries was merely an excuse to obtain a foothold in China. The German Press frankly declared that it was necessary for the German Fleet to secure a Chinese Gibraltar and for

German commerce to have a Chinese Hamburg. The town, harbour, and district of Kiao-chau were formally transferred to Germany on a ninety-nine years' lease in March, 1898, and were made a German protectorate. Shortly afterwards Russia took possession of the very fortress of Port Arthur from which she and her allies had ousted Japan.

The Japanese people nursed their wrongs. They increased their fighting forces and entered into a formal alliance with Great Britain, the Power which had **Japan's first act of revenge**
refused to join the others in despoiling them. In 1904-5 they took their revenge against Russia, defeated her armies, sank her fleet, and wrested Port Arthur from her. They still had a score to pay off against Germany. Their statesmen believed that the real hand in the operations against them after the Chinese War was the Kaiser himself. Little was said. A new policy of friendship was adopted towards Russia, and Japan conserved her resources and made ready for the next struggle.

Germans regarded the seizure of Kiao-chau by their Government with great satisfaction. The spot was carefully chosen. There was a good harbour, with an entrance about two miles wide, which could be well defended from the high hills around. The whole protectorate had an area of about two hundred miles. It was a natural outlet for the trade of Shantung, one of the richest provinces in China. The seizure of Kiao-chau was among the first moves in the new policy of Imperial world-expansion adopted by the German Government. Men who had dreamed of a great German Empire, rivalling in extent the British Empire, now came to the fore. The occupation

LADY BARNARDISTON IN TOKYO.
The wife of the British General, accompanied by the wives of two officers of his Staff, who took part in the attack on Tsingtau, and a Japanese lady.

of this Chinese port was made an excuse for building a larger navy. The benefits that would be reaped from it were the subject of thousands of articles and speeches throughout Germany. In other words, when Germany seized Kiao-chau she set out on the road that led her finally to war with Great Britain.

Everything was done to make Kiao-chau an example of what Germany could accomplish in Imperial colonisation. It was placed under the command of the German Navy and vast sums were spent on it each year. It became the headquarters of an important group of Chinese railways and the centre for spreading German ideas, German authority, and German products throughout the Far East. The little old town of Kiao-chau itself, on the inside of the bay, was made secondary to Tsingtau, a modern city which the Germans erected at the harbour

LIEUTENANT-GENERAL KAMIO, THE "GENERAL FRENCH" OF JAPAN, AND GENERAL BARNARDISTON.
General Kamio was in command of the Japanese Expeditionary Force at Tsingtau, of which place he was afterwards appointed Governor-General.

mouth. Tsingtau became one of the show places of China. It was a delightful holiday resort, with fine bathing sands, and was known as the "Brighton of the Far East." It was kept distinctively European. Poorer class Chinese were not allowed to stay in it at nights, but had to go beyond the city limits. The houses were in European style. All the luxuries of civilisation abounded, from the best hotel in Asia to model schools. The place was in excellent sanitary condition, a great gain in Asia; it had electric light and pure water; there were—as in every white settlement in the Far East—good **"The Brighton of** clubs. The trade of Tsingtau grew by **the Far East"** leaps and bounds. Factories and works began to arise. The harbour was improved, with breakwaters and dry docks, repairing yards, floating docks, and as good a mechanical equipment for the loading and unloading of ships as could be found east of Suez. The bare hills around the city were planted with trees, and nursery establishments flourished, sending trees and bushes by the thousand throughout China.

In the early summer of 1914 the Germans were very proud of what they had done at Tsingtau. Here was a model city, with wide streets, fine public buildings, abundant gardens, and comfortable houses. Tsingtau had been built on a system. It was as orderly, as exact as

mechanically perfect as any new town in Germany itself. Above all the place was a fortress. It was under the command of a naval governor, Captain Meyer-Waldeck, and the chance visitor was almost overwhelmed by the numbers of officers everywhere. Every second man one met in certain circles had his rank—kommandant or hauptmann, intendant or oberleutenant, or the like. There were two strong forts, called after the Kaiser and Bismarck, on the hills overlooking and commanding the city. Bomb-proof batteries and concealed entrenchments abounded, making the place a fortified zone. The Germans claimed afterwards **Fortifications of** —apparently correctly—that apart from **Tsingtau** the two main forts, many of the gun positions held only weapons of an older type. In addition to the land fortifications, there were naval works, and there were almost always several warships in the harbour.

When Great Britain declared war against Germany, Japan realised that her hour for vengeance had come. The Japanese ultimatum was presented to Germany on August 15th, demanding the immediate withdrawal of German warships from Chinese waters, and the handing over to Japan of the complete territory of Kiao-chau for eventual restoration to China. The Japanese, as though to remind Germany that they had not forgotten past wrongs, drew

up their note in exactly the same style and with the same phraseology as the note delivered to Japan by the three Powers in 1895.

The text of the ultimatum was as follows:

We consider it highly important and necessary in the present situation to take measures to remove the causes of all disturbance of peace in the Far East, and to safeguard general interests as contemplated in the agreement of alliance between Japan and Great Britain.

In order to secure

problems for Great Britain. For some years the commercial and political policy of Japan has been a source of uneasiness to the British community in China, and to the people of Australia, New Zealand, and Western Canada. A strong anti-Japanese sentiment has developed in recent years in Western America. It was feared that the entry of Japan into the fighting ranks might be used to alienate American sympathy from the Allies, and to kill the ardour of the Canadian and Australasian peoples for the war. It was recognised that German propagandists might use it to inflame **Formal statement by** fears of Japan forcing herself to a place **Great Britain** where she could despoil China and dictate the future of the Far East. To lessen such alarms the British Government made a formal statement, soon after the ultimatum was issued, that Great Britain and Japan had been in communication with each other, and were of opinion that it was necessary for each to take action to protect the general interests in the Far East contemplated by the Anglo-Japanese Alliance, keeping specially in view the independence and

MAJOR-GENERAL YAMADA, AT THE ENTRANCE TO HIS "DEN" IN THE JAPANESE LINES. ABOVE: VICE-ADMIRAL YASHIRO, JAPANESE NAVAL MINISTER.

firm and enduring peace in Eastern Asia, the establishment of which is the aim of the agreement, the Japanese Government sincerely believes it to be its duty to give advice to the German Government to carry out the following two propositions:

1. To withdraw immediately from Japanese and Chinese waters the German warships and armed vessels of all kinds, and to disarm at once those which cannot be withdrawn.

2. To deliver on a date not later than September 15th to the Japanese authorities, without condition or compensation, the entire leased territory of Kiao-chau, with **Japan's ultimatum** a view to the eventual restoration of the same **to Germany** to China.

The Japanese Government announces at the same time that in the event of its not receiving by noon on August 23rd an answer from the German Government signifying unconditional acceptance of the above advice offered by the Japanese Government, Japan will be compelled to take such action as it may deem necessary to meet the situation.

The intervention of Japan in the war created special

integrity of China. "It is understood," the official communication continued, "that the action of Japan will not extend to the Pacific Ocean beyond the China Seas, except in so far as it may be necessary to protect Japanese shipping lines in the Pacific, nor beyond Asiatic waters westward of the China Seas, nor to any foreign

LIEUTENANT-GENERAL OKA, JAPANESE MINISTER OF WAR.

ONE OF THE JAPANESE SIEGE-GUNS THAT HELPED TO BRING ABOUT THE FALL OF TSINGTAU.
The men of the artillery detachment are receiving orders by telephone from Headquarters, preparatory to opening the bombardment.

JAPANESE SIEGE-GUN IN ACTION AGAINST THE GERMANS.
The dense, black smoke rising in the background is from one of the oil-tanks set on fire in the bombardment of Tsingtau.

THE JAPANESE IN TSINAN-FU.
Japanese advance guard arriving on trolley and trailer at the West Station, Tsinan-fu, on the Shantung Railway.

BRINGING UP SHELLS FOR THE JAPANESE GUNS.
Japanese artillerymen hauling shells for the siege-guns by means of a light railway, specially laid down for the purpose.

territory except territory in German occupation on the continent of Eastern Asia." This British declaration did much to allay uneasiness, particularly in the United States. Washington had confidence in the word of Great Britain.

At the expiration of the time given in the ultimatum, no reply having been received, war was declared. The Imperial Rescript declaring war was an interesting document. It has been summarised already (see Vol. II., p. 72), but may be given here *in extenso* :

"We, by the Grace of Heaven, Emperor of Japan, on the throne occupied by the same Dynasty from time immemorial, do hereby make the following proclamation to all Our loyal and brave subjects.

"We hereby declare war against Germany and We command Our Army and Navy to carry on hostilities against that Empire with all their strength, and We also command all Our competent authorities to make every effort in pursuance of their respective duties to attain the national aim within the limit of the law of nations.

"Since the outbreak of the present war in Europe, the calamitous effect of which We view with grave concern, We, on our part, have entertained hopes of preserving the peace of the Far East by the maintenance of strict neutrality, but the action of Germany has at length compelled Great Britain, Our Ally, to open hostilities against that country, and Germany is at Kiao-chau, its leased territory in China, busy with warlike preparations, while her armed vessels, cruising the seas of Eastern Asia, are threatening Our commerce and that of Our Ally. The peace of the Far East is thus in jeopardy.

"Accordingly, Our Government, and that of His Britannic Majesty, after a full and frank communication with each other, agreed to take such measures as may be necessary for the protection of the general interests contemplated in the Agree-

ment of Alliance, and We on Our part, being desirous to attain that object by peaceful means, commanded Our Government to offer, with sincerity, an advice to the Imperial German Government. By the last day appointed for the purpose, however, Our Government failed to receive an answer accepting their advice.

"It is with profound regret that We, in spite of Our ardent devotion to the cause of peace, are thus compelled to declare war, especially at this early period of Our reign and while we are still in mourning for Our lamented Mother.

"It is Our earnest wish that, by the loyalty and valour of Our faithful subjects, peace may soon be restored and the glory of the Empire be enhanced."

The Japanese people behaved at the opening of the war with the greatest correctness and moderation. There were few displays of noisy patriotism. Germans living in Japan were left unmolested. Immediately the ultimatum was issued, every Japanese subject in Germany itself was arrested and kept in prison, the German Government explaining that this was done for their protection. The Japanese Government money deposited in the Deutsche Bank in Berlin was seized. The Japanese attempted no reprisals. German money was untouched and German subjects walked freely about Japan. The German Ambassador in Tokyo evidently expected **Treatment of Germans** that his Embassy might be attacked by a **in Japan** mob, as the British Embassy in Berlin was attacked by Germans. His fears only made him seem somewhat ridiculous. Instructions were issued that German subjects in Japan were not to be injured in any way so long as they conducted themselves properly. The people of Tokyo were informed by the chief of police that although the two Governments had entered into hostilities for good reasons, the people individually were not to cultivate animosity, but were to treat the Germans who chose to continue among them with kindness. The German Ambassador remained in Tokyo until August 30th, when he sailed away with his staff and other officials. A number of Germans had left Japan previously to join the defenders at Tsingtau. A certain number of others elected to live on in Japan itself, and were allowed to continue their work there. "Of twenty-four German teachers in Government employ," says one writer, "only three left to join the colours at Tsingtau. Over fifty German teachers remained in private employ, and no students or classes showed disrespect or turbulence. No German property was injured, no German molested. No one's

German governess, valet, or employee of any kind was interfered with or imprisoned. Germans naïvely wrote their names in the lists for tennis tournaments, unconscious of the fact that not a British woman or child would tread the same court with them."

The Japanese plan of campaign was twofold—to drive the German warships from Eastern waters and to capture Tsingtau. The latter would give the Army once more an opportunity to prove its mettle.

The Japanese Army had showed its right, in the operations during the Boxer trouble in 1900 and in the war against Russia in 1904–5, to rank among the great armies of the world. The bravoes and fighting men who rallied around the clan chiefs in the middle of the nineteenth century, the heroes with their two-handed swords, the men in armour, the picturesque Oriental warriors with **Strength of the** bows and arrows, disappeared long ago as **Japanese Army** completely as though they had never existed. But the spirit of supreme courage, of personal discipline, of self-sacrifice, and of unquestioning obedience to superiors, the loyalty of the clansmen for their chiefs, the splendid simplicity of the life of the Samurai— all these factors have gone to the making and the strengthening of Japan's modern Army. Strong in numbers, up to date in equipment, keen in professional zeal, the Japanese Army reveals in marked fashion both the strength and the weakness of the nation. Its routine side, its armament, transport, uniforms, medical service, are models of their kind. Every military movement is carried out with the mechanical precision of a perfect machine. The individual soldier has the ideal spirit for a fighting man. He is full of initiative and exceedingly brave. The retention of the old clan spirit maintains a friendly rivalry between different regiments, which often leads the men to accomplish the apparently impossible. The whole Army is fired with an intense, burning patriotism. The weak points of the Army are twofold. The first is the lack of good cavalry, a lack due mainly to Japan being a rice-growing country and consequently unsuitable for much hard riding. The second and more serious drawback of the Japanese Army is a certain lack of boldness in the higher generalship. The Japanese soldier individually is willing to take any risks; the Japanese general plans above all things to ensure the safety of his operations.

WIRE ENTANGLEMENTS IN FRONT OF THE FIRST LINE OF THE GERMAN DEFENCE.
At a quite early stage of the bombardment of Tsingtau the barbed-wire entanglements in front of the first line of the German defence were scattered into fragments by the Japanese shells. Inset. A quaint Japanese sentry-box at Tsingtau.

At the first sign of war orders were issued for all German reservists in the Far East to report themselves at Tsingtau. Not all of them obeyed. Many women and children left, and before the final bombardment the remainder were sent out of the place, and very few civilians remained. The garrison numbered between 5,000 and 6,000 men, all told, including the new arrivals and the crews of some gunboats and destroyers in the harbour. The posi-

The Kaiser's message to Tsingtau tion had been planned more for defence against sea attack than against land attack, and the German authorities afterwards admitted that they had not anticipated hostile Japanese action. The Kaiser sent messages bidding the place defend itself to the last. "God be with you," was his last message. "I shall bear you in remembrance in the imminent hard struggle. Defend to the last man."

The garrison prepared to obey orders. Partial reports received in Europe immediately after the surrender caused some doubts to be cast at first on the stubbornness of the defence. Europe understood the place to be much stronger than it actually was, and was surprised at the briefness of its resistance. But, as the facts became better known, it was seen that the Tsingtau garrison defenders were not lacking in courage. They were overwhelmed by superior force, superior numbers, and superior artillery. That, however, is anticipating.

The entire waters for a

SPADE-WORK IN THE FAR EAST.
Japanese soldiers actively engaged digging trenches.

radius of eight miles around the place were thoroughly mined. All tall structures in the protectorate which might afford assistance to an attacking fleet by giving them sighting-points were dynamited. The railway bridge at the boundary of the German territory was blown up, and all houses or woods offering shelter to an enemy approaching from the land side were razed to the ground. Feverish work was begun on three lines of defence works. Thousands of Chinese coolies were pressed into service and set to work digging fresh emplacements and strengthening old ones. The countryside was mined. Barbed-wire entanglements were erected at many spots and were attached to the local electric works, so that they could be charged with fatal current whenever necessary. The ladies turned the houses into hospitals and made ready to nurse the wounded. When the Japanese called for the surrender of the place the Governor, Captain Meyer-Waldeck, replied: "Never shall we surrender the smallest bit of ground over which the German flag is flying. From this place we shall not retreat. If the enemy wants Tsingtau he must come and fetch it."

The Governor's "No Surrender"

The Japanese professed to look upon the order of the Kaiser to the garrison to defend itself to the last as inhuman, although doubtless they would have acted in the same way in similar circumstances. They let it be known at the start that they did not propose to make any spectacular assaults upon the town, such as those which caused such heavy losses at Port Arthur. The operations against Tsingtau were to be slow, gradual, cautious, and were to be carried out with a view of minimum loss to either side.

The Japanese were willing, and it is believed desired, to undertake the fighting against Tsingtau by themselves, but it was thought better that the operations should be carried out by a combined Japanese-British force. Two British vessels, the battleship Triumph and the destroyer Usk, shared in the sea fighting in co-operation with a number of Japanese ships. The Japanese expeditionary

JAPANESE BLUEJACKETS.

A CAPTURED GERMAN TRENCH.
One of the German trenches at Tsingtau, captured by the Japanese troops, who are seen occupying it. Centre: Japanese bluejackets lending a hand with the spade outside the besieged city.

force numbered 22,890 officers and men and 142 guns. It was under the command of Lieutenant-General Kamio, with Major-General Yamanashi as Chief of Staff. The force was mainly composed of the 18th Division, the 29th Brigade of Infantry, the Siege Artillery Corps, Marine Artillery, and a Flying Corps. The British force under Brigadier-General Nathaniel W. Barnardiston, M.V.O., commander of the British troops in North China, included 910 South Wales Borderers and 450 men of the 36th Sikhs.

The day that the ultimatum expired the Japanese were ready to advance upon Tsingtau. The blockading fleet took up position on August 25th, and a blockade of the coast was declared as from August 27th. It was hoped to bottle up the German fleet in the harbour, but some of the ships slipped out. Several vessels, however, were left behind, including five gunboats, a destroyer, and a minelayer. The Austrian light cruiser Kaiserin Elisabeth was ordered to join the force **Opening phases of** at Tsingtau, and succeeded **the attack** in doing so.

The first task of the attackers was to clear the seas of mines in order that the allied ships might approach. A number of Japanese women shell-divers from the province of Ise begged that they might be permitted to join in the work of mine-searching. These women, who are accustomed to stay for some minutes under water while searching for pearls, could undoubtedly have accomplished good work. But Japan is not the land of the New Woman, and the offer was emphatically and instantly rejected. The mine-clearing was done in much the same way as mine-clearing

around the British coast, the waters being swept by vessels moving in pairs some three hundred yards apart and pulling thick wire ropes stretched between them, wire ropes which sweep the waters and indicate, if they do not instantly explode, any mine on their path. Work like this is among the most dangerous known in modern war, and before Kiao-chau Bay, as around the North Sea, many a mine-sweeper paid the price of the search with his own life. The danger of the **Heroism of the** work made it the more attractive to **mine-sweepers** many Japanese, and the crew of one boat, when applying to be engaged, wrote the letter in their own blood, as a sign of their resolution.

The early operations of the fleet were greatly hampered by the minefields. The Japanese suffered some losses in attempting to get near the coast, and two torpedo-boats and one cruiser were unofficially reported as blown up or

A ROUGH-AND-READY MEAL AFTER THE TAKING OF GERMANY'S PROTECTORATE IN THE FAR EAST.
The hardy Japanese soldiers, who, like the allied troops in France and Flanders, had to undergo the rigours of flooded roads and rain-filled trenches, are seen in the above photograph regaling themselves with rice-balls. Above: A luncheon more at leisure.

L

JAPANESE RED CROSS
WORKERS.

sunk. When, however, the ships got within reasonable range they maintained a constant fire on the forts and on some outlying redoubts. People inside Tsingtau during the siege declared that most of the ships' fire was ineffective because the great distance —about nine miles— at which the ships mainly lay prevented good marksmanship. This criticism is not altogether borne out, however, by some of the known facts. The naval guns succeeded in destroying a 4 in. gun on the fortification at Mount Iltis, one of the most **Destructive work** important points, **of naval guns** and a lucky shot destroyed another gun, killing most of its crew. It was reported during the siege that the Triumph put the Bismarck fort out of the fight with seven well-directed shells.

The Japanese expeditionary force landed at Laichow Bay, to the north of the Shantung Peninsula, and advanced through Chinese territory on to Kiao-chau. Their progress was exceedingly difficult owing to phenomenal floods—heavier, it was said, than Shantung had known for sixty years. The floods hindered the landing of the heavy guns and supplies, and made it impossible to move them forward quickly. They were bad also for the Germans, for they filled their trenches, rendered many of their mines useless, and destroyed much of the results of their work of careful preparation.

Laichow is Chinese territory, and is therefore nominally neutral. The Japanese, however, knowing that China was in no position to resist, swept Chinese neutrality on one side. Their troops advanced to the town of Weihsien, and from there spread through a large part of the province, even taking possession of the town of Tsinan-fu. They seized the Shantung Railway, and dealt with a large part of the Chinese province as though it were conquered territory occupied and held by their troops. Yuan Shi-kai, the Chinese President, and his Cabinet were powerless to do anything else **Chinese protests** than protest. **disregarded** They consented to the Japanese control of the railway between Weihsien and Tsinan-fu, but declared themselves opposed to any occupation of Tsinan-fu Station itself. When Tsinan-fu was occupied, despite the objection, the Chinese Cabinet requested Japan to withdraw her troops. Japan took no notice. Chinese telegraph and post-offices were taken over; Chinese military establishments were used for Japanese soldiers; armed guards were placed at every railway-station. The German Government

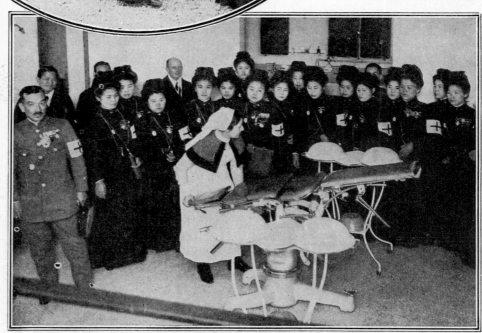

EXPLAINING THE MECHANISM OF THE OPERATING-TABLE.
Nurse of the 4th Divisional Hospital explaining to a group of Japanese nurses the working of the operating-table. Inset: Red Cross nurses departing for Tsingtau. The Japanese Red Cross Society, one of the most highly-organised institutions of its kind in the world, dates from 1877, and was originally called "The Society of Benevolence" (Hakuaisha).

BRITISH-INDIAN AMMUNITION TRAIN CROSSING A RIVER ON THE WAY TO THE FRONT.

WOUNDED JAPANESE SOLDIERS BEING TAKEN TO THE REAR ACROSS THE BESHA RIVER.

THE JAPANESE EXPEDITIONARY FORCE LANDING AT LAICHOW.

The first division of the Japanese force landed at Laichow Bay, to the north of the Shantung Peninsula, and advanced through Chinese territory on to Kiao-chau, taking possession of Weihsien and Tsinan-fu. The advance was rendered difficult by extraordinary floods—heavier, it was said, than Shantung had known for sixty years. This condition of affairs limited the rate of advance to eight miles a day.

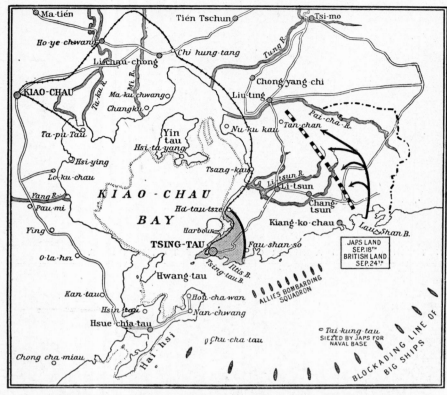

SKETCH-MAP OF THE ATTACK ON THE GERMAN STRONGHOLD.
The early operations of the fleet were greatly hampered by minefields. When, however, the ships got within reasonable range they maintained a constant and deadly fire on the forts and on some outlying redoubts.

now turned on the unhappy Chinese, and declared that since they had allowed their territory to be used against them, Germany would consider herself free to deal as she pleased with China at the end of the war.

The beginning of the end   The Germans threw out scouting parties at various points beyond Tsingtau in order to discover the Japanese approach. The Japanese advance guard at times scarce succeeded in marching eight miles a day. Streams were swollen to torrents impossible to cross; fields were turned into seas of mud; there was nothing to do but to wait for a few days. By September 13th, however, the Japanese scouts reached and attacked the railway-station of the little town of Kiao-chau itself, twenty-two miles from Tsingtau. Japanese aeroplanes began to soar over the German positions. Day after day they dropped bombs on the fortifications, the electric-light works, and the harbour.

A battle started on September 26th. Guns were hurried into position, and a very heavy bombardment opened on the German front. Three Japanese warships—the Suwo, Iwami, and Tango—assisted by the British battleship Triumph, bombarded Tsingtau from the sea, and then came an advance on land. The Japanese set themselves to clear the outer works of Tsingtau, and completely succeeded. Point after point was stormed. Two gunboats in the

harbour—the Jaguar and the Kaiserin Elisabeth—poured shell fire on the Japanese troops as they rushed forward. At one or two points the Japanese were caught by heavy machine-gun fire, and in one case, according to German accounts, a large body of them were swept down as they came unexpectedly under enfilading fire. The Germans estimated the Japanese loss that day at a thousand, an absurdly excessive estimate, as was proved by the total casualties later. By the morning of the 28th the Germans had been driven right into their inner fortified position in Tsingtau, behind the line of hill forts. Here it was that they were to make their real defence on a comparatively small peninsula, roughly triangular in shape, with the sea on one side, Kiao-chau Bay on the other, and the land on the third, their defences centring around the Moltke, Bismarck, and Iltis Hills.

On September 30th the Germans made a desperate attempt to drive the Japanese back, attacking from land, sea, and air. Their effort was altogether vain. Their troops were driven in, one of their destroyers was sunk, and it was clear that they were completely held. The Japanese were now content to wait for a few days while some of their heaviest siege-artillery was brought up into position. At the first approach of the Japanese the Germans opened a very heavy artillery fire which was maintained day after day. Occasionally a Japanese position was located by means of the German aeroplanes, and was promptly bombarded. But much of the gun fire was mere aimless shooting. Every independent observer agreed that the big-gun ammunition was thrown away in the most reckless and careless fashion. Thus in twenty-four   **German waste of ammunition**
hours alone, early in October, the forts on the three hills fired 2,015 shells, and correspondents with the Japanese force

WITH THE JAPANESE RED CROSS IN THE FIELD.
Bringing in the wounded. One section of the Japanese army paid a heavy price for the victory.

LANDING-PARTY OF JAPANESE BLUEJACKETS AT TSINGTAU.

In the long siege of Tsingtau, carried out deliberately in order that the loss of life might be reduced to the minimum, an important part was played by the Japanese Navy. Our photograph shows a number of sailors from the warship in the offing approaching the shore.

JAPANESE INFANTRY STORMING A HILL POSITION.

A vivid camera-picture of one of the charges that carried the German positions before Tsingtau. At dawn on November 7th, 1914, the Japanese made ready for a grand final assault, but before the whole line moved forward a white flag fluttered from the observatory. The Germans had surrendered.

Mine and hand-grenades captured from the Germans at Tsingtau. The first task of the attacking force was to clear the seas for the approach of the warships.

Japanese artillery landing for the bombardment of the German port. The heavy guns got to work on October 31st, 1914, the birthday of the Emperor of Japan. Our ally had one hundred and forty-two guns in position, guns of a calibre more than sufficient to deal with the heaviest pieces of ordnance

Japanese and British landing at Laoshan Bay. While the first Japanese landing took place at Laichow Bay, the second, with the British troops, disembarked on the south of the Shantung Peninsula. The British force included 910 South Wales Borderers and 450 men of the 36th Sikhs.

Tsingtau on fire. Almost every German posi stood, was knocked to bits by the bombardm The electric-light works were destroyed, and for

Of the four illustrations at the foot of the page, the first, taking the views from left to right, is of a heavy gun taken from the Germans at the foot of Moltke Hill. In the second a section of Japanese infantry is seen advancing across a river in the attack on Tsingtau. One man is carrying

in the German forts. They had every range, and they knew exactly where to hit. The bombardment opened at dawn, and one of the first shells set fire to enormous oil-tanks in the naval docks, sending up a pillar of smoke that spread like a pall over the city.

A corner of the shattered Bismarck fortress. This, with the fortified position at Iltis, fell into the hands of the Allies with the minimum of opposition.

the bomb-proof casements in which the guns bs from Japanese aeroplanes fell everywhere, days the people had nothing but candle light.

Shell-shattered oil-tanks at Tsingtau. The tanks of the Standard Oil Company and the Asiatic Petroleum Company caught fire. Most of their contents had been run off before the bombardment, but enough oil was left in them to add flame and smoke to the surrounding conflagration.

bicycle. Our third picture is of the formal entry of the victorious troops into the surrendered ity, the camera being exposed at a moment when Japanese infantry were marching past the Commander and his Staff. The last photograph displays a ruined cupola and dismounted gun.

WHERE THE "MAILED FIST" WAS BROKEN AND THE HUN HUMBLED IN THE DUST.

All that was left of one of the German fortresses at Tsingtau after the Japanese siege-guns had done their work. From the first hour the major operations began it became evident that the German resistance would be smashed by mere weight of metal. The Germans replied bravely but vainly, and when they had fired their last shot they destroyed their guns with explosives. Ammunition gave out before the food supply.

THE VICTORS INSPECTING ONE OF THE FALLEN GERMAN FORTS.

By September 13th, 1914, the Japanese were attacking the railway-station, twenty-two miles from Tsingtau. Then their aeroplanes began to soar over the German positions. Three Japanese warships and a British battleship took part in the bombardment. By the 28th the Germans had been driven right into their inner fortified position. Thence they maintained a heavy but largely futile artillery fire day after day.

declare that the entire firing during that twenty-four hours inflicted no damage on the Japanese whatever. This waste of ammunition is difficult to explain, and undoubtedly was a leading factor in the early surrender of the place, for before many days were over the shells for many of the guns ran short. The besiegers noticed in the second

week of October that artillery fire fell off in surprising fashion; some forts that had formerly been keeping up an almost incessant bombardment now allowed hours to go by without a single shot. One battery of guns in

GERMAN PRISONERS UNDER JAPANESE GUARD.
The top circular photograph is of Captain Meyer-Waldeck, the German Governor of Kiao-chau, which was a naval command; and the lower shows that officer on his arrival in Tokyo.

particular, that had specially annoyed the Japanese, did not fire a single shot for three days. The attackers not unnaturally imagined that this was some trick of war on the part of the Germans, calculated to trap them.

A story was told in China early in October that when the Japanese had fixed their siege-guns in position and were ready to begin the more serious operations, they first shelled the warships in the harbour, and put them out of action without touching a slate in the town. Then they gave twenty-four hours' notice for the real bombardment to begin and for non-combatants to clear out. When the notice expired they signalled: "Are you now quite ready, gentlemen?" "The reply," said one, "came in the shape of a whizzing bullet which took **Prinz Heinrich Hill** three hairs out of the signalman's **captured** moustache, leaving eight remaining."

The difficulty, however, in accepting this story, widely as it was circulated at the time, is that at the date the description was written the real bombardment of Tsingtau had not yet begun.

The Japanese captured with comparative ease a position, Prinz Heinrich Hill, from which they could mount their guns to bombard the forts. During the latter part of October the Japanese hold on the city steadily increased, and the artillery fire grew daily in intensity. The Japanese and British warships maintained a constant fusillade on the forts and on the infantry works near the sea. On the

30th the Japanese opened a heavy fire on a dismantled gunboat, the Tiger, which lay anchored outside. One shell took her funnel away, and the others fell all around her, inflicting serious loss.

When their heavy siege-guns were ready, the Japanese circulated a message to the defenders of Tsingtau. It was printed in German on handbills, and was dropped by the thousand from **Aeroplane protest** an aeroplane on to the forts in the **to the defenders** town. It read as follows:

"To the honoured officers and men in the fortress.

"It is against the will of God, as well as the principles of humanity, to destroy and render useless arms, ships of war, merchantmen, and other works and constructions, not in obedience to the necessity of war, but merely out of spite, lest they fall into the hands of the enemy.

"Trusting as we do that, as you hold dear the honour of civilisation, you will not be betrayed into such base conduct, we beg you, however, to announce to us your own view as mentioned above.—THE BESIEGING ARMY."

The British contingent under General Barnardiston left Tientsin on September 19th, and after calling at Wei-hai-wei for transport mules, landed in Shantung on the 21st. Our authorities were careful to select a point of landing in the German protectorate in order that no question of violating Chinese neutrality might arise. The weather was very trying, a strong

southerly gale blowing, heavy rain falling, and a very heavy sea running. It seemed, when the troops landed, as though earth and sea and sky had contrived to make their work as difficult as possible. They set out on a forty-mile march, and came up behind the Japanese as they were driving in the German advance positions. It was intended that they should participate in this attack, but the German resistance at this point was so slight that their help was not wanted. On October 30th the entire British force moved up to the front.

The British now occupied one part of the allied front, a front extending to about five miles, and there they took part with the Japanese troops in the work of digging an approach by sapping right up to the German redoubts. Night after night officers and men worked with feverish energy, digging their zigzag trenches in the direction of the enemy. It was exceedingly dangerous and trying work. The Germans constantly fired star shells, illuminating the entire position, and as they saw the allied soldiers at work, immediately opened fire on them with shells of every kind and with machine-guns. Day by day the Japanese and the British, notwithstanding all resistance, made their way like moles towards the doomed city.

In a letter to "The Times," a British officer in the expeditionary force gave a vivid description of his experiences in this work. "I left Headquarters and took over a double company," he wrote. "That night we were working in trenches along a river-bed at the bottom of the slope, where the others had been wounded, and *sans doute* most darnation close to the enemy. A beginning had been made on this trench the night before, so there was a little cover. The two redoubts were about eight hundred yards on our right and left respectively, the enemy's trenches about three hundred and fifty yards to our front. Well, for the first hour after getting down we were left severely alone. Then they started throwing star rockets and sort of Roman candle things which lit up the place like day, and at the same time they peppered us with Maxims, pom-poms, and rifle fire from all three places. We had some men hit farther back in the communication trench, but,   **British officer's** funnily enough, none in the forward line.   **experiences** The Borderers left early, and we were working by ourselves for about an hour. Then, in a lull, I withdrew to what was called the 'first position of attack,' a similar line of trenches about a thousand yards up the slope, where my double company was in position during the day. We were entertained to a certain amount of shell fire during the rest of the night. Next night we were due to leave for the forward trenches, at dusk, to carry on, having had our usual entertainment in the afternoon from the Germans, when suddenly they began throwing shrapnel at our trench. For about half an hour it was all over us, and I'm blest if I know why nobody was hit. It was the overhead cover, I fancy, that saved us this time. We came out like a lot of rabbits when it was over, and proceeded to get down below. The Japanese artillery was supporting us that night, as we were working on the enemy's side of the river, within two hundred yards

JAPANESE WARSHIPS WHICH TOOK PART IN OUSTING GERMANY FROM CHINA.
The above photograph was taken from a Japanese battleship. Among the vessels of our Far Eastern ally taking part in the operations off Tsingtau were the pre-Dreadnoughts Suwo (laid down in 1898), Iwami (1900), and Tango (1892). They were assisted by the British pre-Dreadnought battleship Triumph (upper photograph), which was acquired by purchase from Chili in 1903, and the destroyer Usk.

HYDROPLANE EMPLOYED IN SCOUTING AND RANGE-FINDING FOR THE JAPANESE-BRITISH FORCES.

of their advance trenches. Never have I felt a more comforting sensation than when watching those Japanese shells bursting just over our heads, a little in advance, the shrapnel from them going slap into the Germans every time. I must say it was a magnificent sight when the Japanese guns were going, the German rockets, etc., and their machine-guns and rifles joining in when they could get their heads up. One had to shout to make oneself heard, and those who saw it from the top of Heinrich Hill in rear said it was very fine."

The bombardment with the heavy siege-artillery opened on October 31st, the birthday of the Emperor of Japan. Everything had been arranged for the occasion. The Japanese had one hundred and forty-two guns in position, guns of a calibre more than adequate to deal with the heaviest guns on the Tsingtau forts.

The heavy guns open fire They had every range, and they knew exactly where they meant to hit. There was no wasteful firing here. From Prinz Heinrich Hill, where the staff of the Japanese and British expeditionary forces had betaken themselves, it was possible to see the operations like a great panorama spread out under one's feet. That morning Japanese and British cruisers lay out at sea, waiting for the signal to begin. The British and Japanese troops held their entrenched positions, and at every point concealed great guns were directed on to Tsingtau itself. The bombardment opened at dawn. One of the first shells set fire to enormous oil-tanks in the naval docks, sending up a pillar of smoke that spread like a pall over the city. Then shells burst over the forts, and under the almost ceaseless rain of heavy metal the gun emplacements seemed to melt and to crumble. The barbed-wire entanglements were scattered into fragments; the trenches were broken, filled in here, expanded there, and blurred elsewhere by the high-explosive shells constantly falling among them. Under the shelter of this fire the infantrymen

ANTI-AIRCRAFT GUN MOUNTED ON A BRITISH WARSHIP.

continued to push up their saps and trenches. While the artillery were at their deadly work from the shore, the naval guns of both the Allies were pouring their messengers of death on the town from the sea. It was evident from the first hour the major operations began that the German resistance would be smashed by the mere weight of metal.

The Germans replied bravely, but vainly. A Japanese observation balloon overhead signalled the positions and the result of the firing. The tanks of the Standard Oil Company and the Asiatic Petroleum Company caught fire. Most of their contents had been run off before, but enough was left to add to the blaze. "The noise of the whistling and exploding shells was tremendous," wrote one observer. "They covered the summits of the hills with dust and smoke."

The artillery fire was incessantly maintained for seven days, night and day. Non-combatants in the town herded themselves in cellars to escape the bursting explosives. The wounded were taken from their wards into the cellars and cared for there. The men in the German bomb-proof casements replied till all their shells had gone. Almost every German position, save the bomb-proof casements in which the guns stood, was knocked to bits. The ground was everywhere pitted and torn. The troops in the trenches between the forts were in many cases wiped out by the rain of bursting shrapnel and high explosives. Meanwhile the Japanese and British infantry had advanced by means of their trenches to

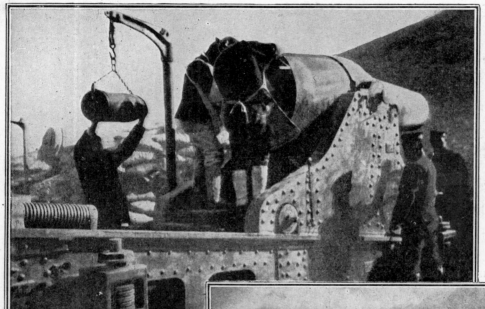

JAPANESE SIEGE-GUNS IN ACTION.

points right under the forts. Here they lay watching, and picking off any man who in the least exposed himself. To add to the horrors in the place, Japanese aeroplanes were constantly soaring overhead, dropping bombs on every possible position. The Japanese fire destroyed the electric light works, so that for the last few days the people had nothing but candle light. The wireless apparatus was rendered useless. Life in Tsingtau for those few days was a concentration of all possible horrors.

What were the experiences of the few civilians left in the place? Happily we are able to answer this question from the very vivid despatches of Mr. A. M. Brace, the staff correspondent of the Associated Press, who was the only foreign correspondent in Tsingtau itself. At first, he says, in spite of the fact that the city was almost empty, the **Civil life during the siege** life of those who remained was quite normal. There were enough shops open where purchases could be made. Cafés continued business, and tiffin and dinner were served without interruption at the German Club throughout the whole siege, although towards the end the number who came to the club dwindled to a few of the administrative officers and civilians. On the second day of the heavy

bombardment, at dinner-time, one shell struck in the street in front of the favourite café, the Kronprinz, two in the side street next to it, and two more a hundred yards from the club. "There was just a sign of uneasiness among a few at a table, but when the final crash came near by someone lifted his glass and started a scrap of a song, which was taken up around his table and had a decidedly heartening effect."

During the last days the streets were **Water scarce but** practically deserted. A few men hurried **beer plentiful** along on necessary errands. The people stopped the windows of the cellars in which they slept with bags of sand, or in some cases even with newspapers. While the supply of running water ceased in the middle of October, there was an abundant stock of beer which lasted amply until the very end. News from the outside world came through until November 5th, news that usually told of the ruin of England. "I remember one evening the roar of laughter that went up in the German Club when the news was read that England had asked Portugal for assistance. For two or three days it looked, according to the news, that the British Empire was going to pieces. We heard of revolutions in India, riots in Alexandria, mutiny and martial law in South Africa, and even disaffection in Sarawak and North Borneo."

It became clear to everyone inside that the end was drawing

very near. The warships in the harbour were blown up and sunk in order that they might not fall into Japanese hands. The big guns in the forts were fired many of them to the last shot, and then the gunners, acting under orders, destroyed them with explosives. There was no shortage of food, and when the city was captured provisions were found there sufficient to feed five thousand persons for three months. But provisions without ammunition were of no use.

Bismarck Fort, one of the most powerful of all, had been destroyed at the beginning of November, as was told

A NOVELTY IN MILITARY COSTUME.
British soldiers wearing "shorts"—and attracting thereby the noticeable interest of their Japanese allies.

earlier, by the British battleship Triumph. Other forts became more and more silent. On the night of November 6th some troops advanced to attack a redoubt, and entered it with comparatively little difficulty. Encouraged by this success, the Japanese Commander ordered a general advance. Japanese and British battalions crept up silently in the darkness to point after point. The two great mountain positions of Iltis and Bismarck fell into the hands of the Allies with a minimum of opposition. At one ridge they came on a small party of Germans in charge of a searchlight. They did not fire on them, for to do

BRITISH AND JAPANESE IN ARMS AGAINST THE COMMON ENEMY.
A British field kitchen at work not far from Tsingtau. The circular photograph was taken after the fall of the city, and shows a British and a Japanese officer on their way to Headquarters.

so would be to betray themselves, but they fell on them with spades and pickaxes and killed them. At other parts they took up positions covering the exits of the forts, so that should any Germans try to emerge they could shoot them down. How the Japanese were allowed to advance that night as they were across the elaborate land defences of the Germans, practically without resistance, remains to this day a mystery. They expected to have to make a grand assault and lose possibly thousands of men. They found, so to speak, the door left open for them to enter at their ease. Were the Germans stupefied and deadened by the continuous hail of shell fire? It was said at the

THE BATHING BEACH AT TSINGTAU.

time that Captain Meyer-Waldeck was wounded a few hours before the end. The feeble resistance before the Japanese final advance is inexplicable.

When dawn broke the Japanese found themselves in command of some of the forts dominating the city. Now was the moment for a grand final assault. They made ready, but before the whole line moved forward a white flag was seen fluttering from the observatory, followed by white flags raised at other points. The Germans were going to surrender. It may safely be said that no one was so much surprised at this inglorious final collapse as the Japanese themselves.

It was seven o'clock in the morning when the white flag was raised, and as the little Japanese soldiers saw it they set up a loud shout of "Banzai! Let great Japan live for ever!"—the national cry. As they looked around their ranks they saw that even though the capture of the city had been very much easier than they expected, yet some parts of the Army had paid a heavy price. Thus the company that attacked Redoubt 2 had been caught under the fire of machine-guns, and out of two hundred and fifty men only eighty-seven were left. This was the heaviest loss of any, the total Japanese casualties in the final assault being four hundred and fifty killed and wounded. The British casualties were slight.

Casualties in the final assault

Much regret was felt over one accident. The Governor had resolved to surrender the place at six in the morning, and sent Major von Kayser, his adjutant, to approach the Japanese and to negotiate terms. Major von Kayser, accompanied by a trumpeter and another officer, left the staff headquarters bearing a white flag. The white flag was not observed, and as they got into the region of fire the trumpeter was killed and the major's horse shot under

him. According to the letters of some of the officers sent home at the time the major himself was shot.

The formal surrender of the place was arranged. The Japanese immediately took possession, and on November 16th a ceremonial entry was arranged, when a memorial service was held for the dead. The Germans before surrender had done all they could to spoil supplies likely to be of use. The warships had been sunk and the great guns damaged or destroyed. The trophies of war that were taken included 2,500 rifles, 100 machine-guns, 30 field-guns, some ammunition, cash to the amount of £1,200, 15,000 tons of coal, 40 motor-cars, and a considerable quantity of provisions. The prisoners taken numbered 4,043, including the Governor, 201 German officers, and 3,841 non-commissioned officers and men. The Japanese casualties were 236 killed and 1,282 wounded. The British casualties were 2 officers wounded, 12 men killed, and 61 wounded. These figures were surprisingly small. The Germans estimated their losses during the siege at about 1,000 men.

Rival gains and losses

The fall of the city was naturally the occasion for great rejoicing throughout Japan. The capital was decked out with flags, the Union Jack alongside of the Rising Sun. Lantern processions, a very picturesque Japanese form of rejoicing, were held in towns and villages and cities alike, where long lines of men marched in their native dress through the streets of bamboo-sided houses, bearing paper lanterns and waving banners.

Numerous congratulatory messages were received. Lord Kitchener sent his felicitations to the Japanese Minister of War at Tokyo: "Please accept my warmest congratulations on the success of the operations against Tsingtau. Will you be so kind as to express my felicitations to the

GERMAN HOTEL AT TSINGTAU.

UP IN THE HILLS BEHIND GERMANY'S LOST COLONY.

Japanese forces engaged? The British Army is proud to have been associated with its gallant Japanese comrades in this enterprise." The Board of Admiralty also sent heartiest congratulations "on the prosperous and brilliant issue of the operations." The Emperor of Japan sent a message to the Japanese forces telling his appreciation of "the faithful discharge of their duties." He further sent a message to the British forces "deeply appreciating the brilliant deeds of the British Army and Navy which, co-operating with the Japanese, have fought for and bravely achieved one of the objects of the war."

The Germans tried to explain away their loss. Captain Meyer-Waldeck, interviewed when removed as a prisoner

THE PRUSSIAN PASSION FOR
MONUMENTS.
This is exemplified in the Imperial insignia
which was found cut in the rock on the
heights above Tsingtau.

of war to Japan, said that many
of the guns at Tsingtau were old,
and the Germans had not calculated on having to resist the
Japanese Army. Dr. Kaempf, the
President of the Reichstag, sent
a telegram to the German Emperor
condoling with him on the surrender, and expressing the hope
that the day might come when
German civilisation would re-
occupy its place in the Far East.
The Germans circulated an account
in their Chinese subsidised newspapers in which they stated that
the fortress of Tsingtau was not
stormed at all but capitulated
voluntarily, on receipt of orders
from the Kaiser, to obviate the
useless shedding of Japanese blood.
The account added that the
Kaiser intended, after peace had
been established, to extract an
enormous indemnity from Japan.
The Berlin "Lokalanzeiger"
threatened vengeance: "Never
shall we forget the bold deed of
violence of the yellow robbers or
of England that set them on to
do it. We know that we cannot
yet settle with Japan for years to
come. Perhaps she will rejoice
over her cowardly robbery. Here
our mills can grind but slowly.
Even if the years pass, however,
we shall certainly not often speak

of it, but as certainly always think of it. And if eventually
the time of reckoning arrives, then as unanimously as what
is now a cry of pain will a great shout of rejoicing ring
through Germany, 'Woe to Nippon.'"

General Kamio was appointed Governor-General of
Tsingtau. The Japanese started clearing the land and
sea of mines and preparing the city for fresh life under the
new administration. The prisoners were
moved to concentration camps in Japan.   **British General**
A new series of problems now arose,   **in Tokyo**
problems connected with the permanent
occupation of Tsingtau and the future relations between
Japan and China. These matters, however, hardly come
within the scope of this history.

General Barnardiston, the Commander of the British
Forces, visited Tokyo early in December, and his visit was
made the occasion of a great national demonstration.
When he reached the Japanese capital the station was
decorated and thousands of school children were waiting
to greet him. Dense crowds lined the entire roadway
to his hotel, and a week of entertainment was mapped out
for him in the lavish fashion which the Japanese understand
so well. He was received in audience by the Emperor,
dined by the municipality, and treated as Great Britain's
representative who had helped to seal closer the Anglo-

THROUGH GERMAN EYES: IMPRESSION OF THE FIGHTING AT TSINGTAU.
A striking picture by a German war artist representing the final phase of the fighting before the surrender
of Tsingtau. It will be noticed that the caps worn by the sailors on the right of the drawing bear the
name of the Austrian light cruiser Kaiserin Elisabeth.

FUNERAL OF THE CAPTAIN AND OFFICERS OF THE TORPEDOED JAPANESE CRUISER TAKACHIHO.

The Takachiho was one of the two oldest cruisers in the Japanese Navy. She was sunk off Tsingtau by a German torpedo. Her commander (Captain Ito) and seven other officers were accorded a naval funeral, which, as may be gathered from the remarkable photograph we are able to give of a part of the procession, was of a most solemn and impressive character.

Japanese Alliance. Military bands had not played in Tokyo since the death of the Dowager-Empress until he arrived, when "See the Conquering Hero Comes" was played for him.

The Japanese have helped the Allies in two other ways. It is well known that at the beginning of the war there was a considerable shortage of rifles and guns among the Allies, and sufficient weapons could not be manufactured in time to supply the suddenly raised armies. The Japanese arsenals aided the Allies, and tens of thousands

ONE OF THE BEAUTIFUL TRIUMPHAL CARS IN THE PROCESSION AT TOKYO.

of stacks of arms were manufactured and despatched to different countries. The Japanese Navy co-operated in the campaign against the German cruisers in the Pacific and in convoying the Australian contingent to Europe. Japanese warships took prominent and arduous part in sweeping the seas, and it was only by the accident of war that the Emden met the Australian cruiser Sydney in place of one of the Japanese warships.

"IO TRIUMPHE!" JAPAN'S ENTHUSIASTIC WELCOME HOME TO GENERAL KAMIO.

Perusal of the opening paragraphs of Mr. F. A. McKenzie's account of Japan's grievance against Germany will explain the joy which spread throughout Nippon on the receipt of the news of the surrender of Tsingtau. The return of General Kamio to Tokyo was made the occasion of a general holiday all over the Empire. With the Japanese Commander, General Barnardiston was received in special audience by the Emperor. The fervour of the popular reception of the victors is shown in the remarkable photographs given above of the processions through the streets of the capital.

ARTILLERY OF THE

CHAPTER LI

RUMANIAN ARMY.

GERMANY'S WORLD-WIDE CAMPAIGN OF INTRIGUE.

Influence of Italy and Rumania on the Conduct of the War—Bülow's Intrigues with the "Black" Families—Prussia as the Mainstay of the Anti-Democrat Movement throughout the World—The Pro-German Belgian Nuncio and Cardinal Mercier—Signor Giolitti's Startling Revelation of the Teutonic War Plot—Rivalry of Signor Salandra and Signor Giolitti—Bülow at Last Makes a Bid for Italian Friendship—Discovery of German Mischief-Makers in the Tripoli Risings—Italy at the Crisis of Her Destiny—Rumania Makes a Fighting Convention with Russia—Why the Rumanians Hesitated all the Winter—Conflict between Tsar and Premier of Bulgaria—Conflict between King and Premier of Greece—Disadvantage of Foreign Dynasties in the Balkan States—People Ready for Action, but Checked by their Rulers—Greece Loses her Great Chance—Bulgaria Becomes Half Inclined to Act against Turks—The General Position of Neutral Countries in Europe—United States Protests against Stopping and Searching of Ships—Convincing Answer by Sir Edward Grey—Mr. Bryan Rebukes American Partisans of Germany and Austria—Difficulties of President Wilson with the German-American League—Financial Alliance of the Powers of the Triple Entente.

THERE is often seen around a great whirl of the forces of the air a series of minor disturbances which gradually become involved in the central vortex. So it was in the Great War. Around the vast scene of actual conflict was a series of smaller disturbances, nearing the point at which thunder and lightning would appear while they now approached, and now receded from, the great centre of collision. All through the autumn and winter of 1914 and the opening months of 1915 the intricate and subtle play of the smaller outer forces of disturbance continued.

There was a gathering storm centre in Italy, and influenced by it was a movement for war in Rumania. Then, balancing Rumania to some extent, was a small reverse vortex in Bulgaria, which also had a strong effect upon the clashing currents of feeling in Greece. Across the Atlantic was another system of cyclone and anticyclone in the United States. All these outer movements of warlike currents exerted considerable pressure upon the course of the fighting on the battlefields. Indeed, some of the principal strategical moves of the rival commanders-in-chief were conceived with a view to swaying Italy and Rumania, Bulgaria and Greece. Field-Marshal von Hindenburg, especially, fought through the autumn, winter, and early spring

PRINCE VON BÜLOW.
Leaving the German Embassy in Rome.

with one eye on Italy and Rumania and another on Russia. The unexpected movement of his southern wing into Bukovina and to the Rumanian frontier was aimed as much at the hesitating Rumanians as at the alert and unperturbed Russians. In the same way, the second disastrous invasion of Serbia by the Austrians was intended to shake and demoralise the Greeks and reassure the Bulgarians, and force them into an alliance with the Turks, while putting the entire Serbian Army out of action. And the later Franco-British bombardment of the forts of the Dardanelles was a movement against the Teutonic party in Bulgaria, as well as a stroke against Turkey, and an attempt to force a warm-water passage for the munitioning of Russia.

Had the Powers of the Triple Entente desired in the late autumn of 1914 to obtain military help at any cost, they could undoubtedly have purchased it; for Italy and Rumania were eager to take the field against Austria-Hungary on certain large conditions. The recovery of their unredeemed territories in Austria and Hungary did not at the time seem to them to be sufficient compensation for the heavy sacrifices in men and treasure which they would be compelled to make. Rumania desired also some voice in shaping the future of Constantinople and the Dardanelles. Italy had magnificent ambitions in regard to her position as one of the chief Mediterranean Powers.

The Russian Commander-in-Chief could perhaps have induced the Rumanians to take the field by greatly strengthening his southern wing, and holding Bukovina strongly while pressing down upon the Hungarian plain.

Instead of doing so, he kept strictly to the purely military aspect of the conduct of the campaign, and manœuvred his troops as though Rumania and Italy were as steadfastly neutral in feeling as Denmark and Holland. The explanation was perhaps that Russia was so confident of her strength, and felt so capable of bearing the burden of a long war, that she would not relinquish in advance any of the fruits of victory for the sake of a quicker end to the struggle. Now that Turkey had entered the field against the Triple Entente, Russia had her eyes fixed upon Constantinople and the Dardanelles, and upon her future new and higher position as one of the great Sea Powers of the Mediterranean. At the cost of a longer war, and even of another million men, she was resolved to realise at last the plan of all her great Tsars, and to establish herself in the seat of Constantine and Justinian.

Russia and Constantinople

Italy was then left to come to a decision in her own interests without any pressure at all from Russia, Britain, and France. This was the opportunity for which Prince von Bülow had been waiting. Under the skilful direction of this brilliant ex-Chancellor of the German Empire, all the forces of reaction in Italy were organised in favour of the Teutonic cause. The first stroke that came from Italy against the Powers of the Triple Entente was in appearance a small and unimportant matter. Soon after the fall of Antwerp, the Papal Nuncio to Belgium gave a banquet to some of the generals and officers of the German armies in Belgium. When Cardinal Mercier of Malines was arrested on January 2nd, 1915, for writing his famous pastoral letter to his stricken and downtrodden people, the Papal Nuncio misrepresented this noble act in the confidential advice which he sent to the Vatican.

Then, when the Belgian Government brought about the dismissal of the Nuncio, and obtained the appointment of a more impartial representative of the Vatican, the chief organ of the Vatican itself, the "Osservatore Romano," republished, in a translation, a German newspaper article in which the new Nuncio was fiercely attacked because he was not a partisan of Protestant Germany. It will thus be seen that,

THE CONFLICT BETWEEN TSAR FERDINAND AND HIS PRIME MINISTER.

The top photograph is of Dr. V. Radoslavoff, the Bulgarian Premier; and immediately underneath is a photograph of Tsar Ferdinand. The large view is of Sofia, looking towards the Djumaia Pass (some forty-five miles away), from the front of the Parliament House, and showing the monument to Alexander II., at the foot of which on March 13th, 1915, Dr. Radoslavoff publicly laid a wreath in memory of "the Liberator's" death-day. The pro-German ruler of Bulgaria, like King Constantine of Greece, opposed the anti-Turkish policy of his Prime Minister.

temporarily at least, the Vatican became the active ally of the megalomaniac Protestant German Emperor, who, in some of his wilder speeches during the war, had claimed to be God's representative on earth. Pope Benedict himself tried to preserve a neutral attitude, but the Vatican as a whole was of Teutonic sympathies.

Allied with the ecclesiastical intriguers, against whom the British Cardinal Gasquet stubbornly, but apparently vainly, fought, were most of the descendants of the nobles that had wrecked Italy in the fifteenth and sixteenth centuries. These "black" families, as they are called, had for some centuries exercised the chief control over

LIEUT.-GENERAL CADORNA.
Chief of Staff of the Italian Army.
Inset: Baron Sonnino, Italian Foreign Minister.

THE WAR SPIRIT IN ITALY.
Scene in the Cathedral Square at Milan, where a demonstration in favour of Italian intervention in the war was held in check by Bersaglieri and Lancers.

standing with Prince von Bülow in regard to the temporal government of the world. They agreed to support the Germanic cause, and to assist by all means in their power the spread of the caste system of government for which Prussia stood. "You are aristocrats, and we are aristocrats," said Prince von Bülow in effect, "and we must work together to combat any democratic movement either in politics or in religion." As in Germany, so in Italy, some of the most powerful leaders in the fields of finance and industry were admitted into the camp of the new feudalists. And, what was more remarkable still, an apparently considerable body of Italian Socialists was induced to side, at least passively, with all the forces of reaction.

Having thus gathered, by his remarkable skill in intrigue, a great party round his Roman villa, Prince von Bülow tried to come to terms with those leaders of Italian political opinion who held the supreme power in the Government independently of both the ecclesiastical and Socialistic parties. He had to deal chiefly with both Signor Salandra and Signor Giolitti, the first the Prime Minister, and the second the leader of the largest party in the Chamber of Deputies. On November 6th Signor Salandra's position was strengthened by the appointment of Baron Sonnino, a Liberal aristocrat, to the position of Foreign Minister. Salandra and Giolitti were rivals for the control of the destinies of their country. Salandra was in office, and possessed, therefore, some means of controlling the General Election in the way usual in Italy. When menaced by an adverse vote from Giolitti's majority, he was able to reply by the threat of dissolution. In this manner he retained his position and power, and showed an impregnable front against the intrigues of Prince von Bülow.

BARON SONNINO.

Bülow openly made approaches to Giolitti. But the result was such a fierce movement of warlike patriotism in the general body of the Italian people that Giolitti himself drew back from anything that looked like an understanding with the German intriguer. The upshot was that Bülow found he could make no impression upon the ruling parties in the Government of Italy. He had made large promises of helping Italy at the expense of Austria. But these promises had only evoked some very plain criticism from the statesmen of Italy. They reminded Bülow that in 1866 Bismarck's agent in Rome, Usedom, had officially declared that: "If Italy resists the pressure of France, I am authorised to assure her in a confidential and precise manner that my Government will support her claim to the Southern Tyrol." And they reminded him of the insulting answer Bismarck is said to have made when asked by Italy to fulfil his promise.

Von Bulow's intrigues in Italy

SIGNOR SALANDRA.
Italian Prime Minister.

SIGNOR GIOLITTI.
The Italian leader who revealed the war plot of 1913.

the affairs of the Roman Catholic Church, and in recent years they had quashed a movement for the development of representative government in the Church which originated among the Catholics in the United States. In the winter of 1914 they came to an under-

Wyndham.

FINANCE MINISTERS OF THE TRIPLE ENTENTE DISCUSS THE PROBLEM OF THE "SILVER BULLETS."

In February, 1915, at the French Ministry of Finance in Paris, the Finance Ministers of the Allies—M. Bark, M. Ribot, and Mr. Lloyd George (seen from left to right)—met in conference, when it was agreed that the Allies should unite their financial equally with their military resources in order to carry the war to a successful conclusion.

Long had the Italians waited for their revenge for this double act of treachery and insult. But Bülow paid to the full on January 6th, 1915, for the act of bad faith by Bismarck in 1866. Then Signor Giolitti himself—the more pro-German in appearance of the two political leaders of Italy—went out of his way to reveal to the world the fact that the Germans had plotted to make the Great War in 1913, but that the plot then temporarily failed owing to the refusal of Italy to co-operate in an aggressive action directed through Serbia at Russia. This revelation was intended to shock Bülow into sincerity. It had that effect. By this time Italy had a million first-line troops ready for war, and it was plainly hinted that she was only waiting for the snow to melt on the Alpine passes in order to recover by force the lands of her people still held by the last and worst of all the conquerors of her territory in the days of her weakness— Austria. Bülow then ceased to promise, and began to make definite offers of the

THE QUEEN OF HOLLAND IN AMSTERDAM.
Her Majesty's German consort (Prince Henry of Mecklenburg-Schwerin) is seen taking his seat on her left.

immediate cession of ancient Italian territory. He entered into negotiations with Count Tisza, the Hungarian who was almost in the position of dictator in Austria-Hungary. He arranged with the count that Italy should receive the Trentino, in the Southern Tyrol, together with an increase of frontier towards the great seaport of Trieste. The Italians insisted on Trieste itself being included. "Impossible!" Bülow at first replied. "Trieste does not belong to Austria now. It is a vital outlet for Germany."

Signor Salandra said nothing, but accelerated his military preparations, and in some of his speeches to his own people he continued to say nothing, but to hint a great deal. Meanwhile the clever but baffled German intriguer pretended that the Emperor Francis Joseph would not hear even of the cession of the Trentino, but that Germany was still trying to induce her ally to arrive at a fair compromise with Italy. Then came the thunderclap of the Queen Elizabeth's guns at the gate of the Dardanelles. This was the

CONSTANTINE I.
King of the Hellenes.

kind of action which Italian statesmen could well appreciate after months of grappling with the phantasmal promises of Teutonic friendship. By the middle of March, 1915, both Germany and Austria-Hungary were eager to come to terms with Italy. They made the following offer: " I. The cession of the Trentino, and of all the frontier territory completing the basin of the Isonzo, including the new railway. 2. The concession to Trieste and the surrounding district of the modified form of self-government that existed at

these rebels would at last be conquered, weapons in hand, they sent them French rifles, with a view to involving France in difficulties with Italy The flagrant exposure of the plot in the critical days of the middle of March was as helpful to the Powers of the Triple Entente as a great victory in Bukovina would have been.

SIGNOR GIUSEPPE MOTTA.
President of the Swiss Confederation.

Fiume before this was withdrawn by the Hungarians. Fiume to have her rights restored. 3. Renunciation by Austria of all interference in the Italian control of Albania. 4. An agreement between Austria and Italy in regard to their respective influences in the Adriatic. A more effective co-operation of the two naval forces. A common opposition to any Serbian expansion on the Albanian coast.

M. VENIZELOS.
Greek Premier during the first phase of the Great War.

Italy thus arrived, after the war had gone on for seven and a half months, at the hour of crisis in her history which would determine all her future development. The Teutons had apparently made their final offer, and the snow was beginning to melt in the mountain passes of the Trentino. It was then that the Custom-house officers at Venice made a little discovery with some great political consequences. In some barrels about to be shipped through a German firm to the rebellious Arabs at Tripoli was found a large consignment of rifles of French manufacture. The Germans had aimed at bringing down two birds with one stone. They wished to increase Italy's Colonial troubles by arming the rebels; but seeing that

German Plot to delude Italy

The hesitating position of Rumania during the winter of 1914 was partly due to the immobility of Italy in that period. After the death of King Carol, on October 10th, 1914, the Rumanian people became eager to fight. But they wanted, if possible, to time their sweep into the Hungarian territory of Transylvania occupied by their race with the Italian advance into the Trentino and Trieste. By attacking the common foe together, during a renewal of the Serbian offensive movement, the

Apprehensions at Bucharest

Rumanians would have only a distracted foe to face, especially if the southern Russian army were attacking the Austrians and the Hungarians at the same time. When Italy held back, and the southern Russian army was forced away from Bukovina, exposing the Rumanian frontier to an Austro-German attack, the statesmen of Bucharest became apprehensive; for it was then well known that Rumania had entered into a fighting treaty with Russia. The negotiations had taken place towards the end of October, 1914, and had ended in a convention signed towards the close of the following month. One of the clauses of this conven-

CARDINAL GASQUET.
An opponent of German ecclesiastical intrigue.

tion was to the effect that: " In return for the neutrality of Rumania, Russia consents to her annexing, by occupying them, the territories of Austria-Hungary peopled in larger part by Rumanian populations." The terms are somewhat curious, but the real significance of this clause is not obscure.

The last military preparations of Rumania were completed. Her Army had not fought since its glorious campaign of 1877-78 against the Turks of Osman Pasha, but it had continually developed in strength. With

MR. WILLIAM JENNINGS BRYAN.
Secretary of State, U.S.A.

SENATOR GENERAL HORACE PORTER.
Formerly United States Ambassador to France.

BARON STEPHAN DE BURIAN.
Austro-Hungarian Foreign Minister.

A BIVOUAC IN THE BRUSHWOOD: FRENCH ADVANCE GUARD ENJOYING A TEMPORARY REST AT THE FRONT.

FRENCH ARTILLERY IN A WOOD.
The guns are cleverly hidden, the chimneys shown serving the double purpose of disguise and exit for the gases after firing.

INSPECTING A NEW TRENCH.
French officer making a final tour of inspection of a newly-constructed trench at an advanced point in the firing-line.

MAKING THE BEST—AND THE MOST—OF IT: A MEAL IN THE OPEN AIR.
When the above photograph was taken the weather was the reverse of congenial; but with characteristically French regard for the *convenances* of the table, this little detachment of soldiers had their refreshments in as much style as the means at their disposal would permit.

CLEANING UP: FRENCH SOLDIERS FIND A CONVENIENT SPOT FOR A LITTLE LAUNDRY WORK AFTER A HARD SPELL OF MARCHING AND FIGHTING.

feverish activity it had prepared for the great war of liberation. In number and in machinery Rumania had created the most notable military organisation of Europe, after those of the Great Powers. There was a first-line Rumanian Army of 400,000 men, well-organised and well-led, and to these, at the end of two or three months, another quarter of a million soldiers would

Rumania's great military strength be added. Both the Austrians and the Germans were well aware of Rumania's remarkable strength. For this reason they refrained from any act of hostility when they reached the frontier in their first successful advance through Bukovina. In the meantime the Rumanians went on increasing their stores of ammunition with the help of Italian armament firms.

The fact was that the Rumanians wanted to see the Russian troops firmly established on their frontier before they moved. Their great fear was that if they swept into Hungary while the Russian southern army was still being pressed back the Tsar of Bulgaria would attack them from the south. In 1913, 300,000 Rumanian troops had crossed the Danube, and by invading Bulgaria had brought the second Balkan War to a close quickly. Rumania had then taken an important tract of Bulgarian territory, to cover her expenses of mobilisation and military action. So it was only to be expected that the Bulgarians might now strike back if an opportunity offered.

The position of Bulgaria during the winter of 1914 and the spring of 1915 was extremely delicate. The people were angry with the Serbians and the Greeks for having deprived them of the rich province of Macedonia, where the finest kinds of Turkish tobaccos are grown. This region, with its port of Kavalla, was peopled by Bulgarians, who were being, it was said in Sofia, oppressed by their new Christian masters. If Serbia and Greece could have

been induced to give up their share of Macedonia, there would have been a solidarity of interests among the Balkan States. But apparently the representatives of the Powers of the Triple Entente could not bring about this arrangement. In the meantime the domestic politics of Bulgaria were as complex and troubled as those of Greece. In both kingdoms the King and the Court party favoured the cause of the Teutons, while the people were ready to fight on the side of Russia, Britain, and France. The Premier of Bulgaria, M. Radoslavoff, co-operated with the Premier of Greece, M. Venizelos, in preparing to act against the Turkish Army in Europe, and to thus win a place of power in the council chamber of the Allies when the partition of the Ottoman Empire was being decided.

But Tsar Ferdinand and King Constantine did not agree with the views of their respective Premiers. The German Tsar of Bulgaria, having lost Constantinople in the first Balkan War through listening to the treacherous voice of Austria, was still apparently more inclined to side with his betrayers than with the natural allies of his people. It was Austria and Germany who had induced him in 1913 to shatter his Army against the forces of Greece and Serbia. And now the inveterate intriguer of the House of Coburg **The German Tsar** still placed his hopes upon the eventual **of Bulgaria** success of the Teutons. He had been promised a share of Serbian territory—a share of the body of the small heroic nation which had fought faithfully with him against the Turks, until he had tried to destroy it at the bidding of Austria. His great general, Radko Dimitrieff, was winning new victories for Russia against the men who had deceived, betrayed, and broken his own country. Yet Tsar Ferdinand continued to oppose the wishes of his people and of their constitutional representatives.

WITH THE GERMAN ARMY IN POLAND.
General von Gropp, with his Chief of Staff. In the trench is a mitrailleuse which had been abandoned by the Russians.

AN ENEMY PATROL IN THE FLOODED AREA OF THE YSER.
German Lancer scout, armed with lance, sword, and rifle, looking over the waste of waters in a corner of Flanders. The circular view is of Prussian Hussars using the backs of their horses from which to survey the position of the foe.

FRENCH "75" WITH SHELTER FOR THE GUNNERS IN A WOOD IN THE ARGONNE.

FRENCH ARTILLERYMAN BRINGING UP A SHELL FOR A HIDDEN "75."
The smaller photograph is entitled by our French photographer "The Passing of Winter," a title suggesting not only the life beyond the grave and the approach of spring, but the advent of eventual victory.

It was in this critical period of their history that many of the Balkan States recognised the disadvantage of their foreign dynasties, all more or less accessible to the subtle and pervasive influences of Berlin and Vienna. It was a notorious fact that the German Emperor regarded the German monarchs of Bulgaria and Rumania, and the German-Danish King of Greece, as energetic and friendly vassals. It was their duty, from the German point of view, to prepare the way for the extension of the Teutonic Empire to Constantinople and the Persian Gulf. King Carol of Rumania had been bound to the Hohenzollerns; only his death liberated his people from the alternative of a revolution or a national decline. Greece and Bulgaria remained till the spring of 1915 in the sphere of Germanic influence.

The position of things was extremely unfortunate for the Greeks. For they had in M. Venizelos the greatest national leader since Pericles. This Cretan shepherd and guerilla soldier had fought his way to high command in his native island, and then had sailed to Athens and become the main force in the Balkan League, which would have turned the Turk out of Europe in 1913 if the Germans, Austrians, and Italians had not interfered. After breaking with his too-ambitious ally, the Tsar of Bulgaria, Venizelos had turned to the Germanic marionettes in his own national court, and, in spite of the efforts of King Constantine, the King's four sons, and his Prussian wife, sister to Kaiser Wilhelm II., had practically banished them. Unhappily, M. Venizelos allowed them to return when the Great War broke out, in the hope of arriving at a complete national unity. But by intriguing with some of the chiefs of the Army the Prussian Court party brought about the overthrow of the great Cretan patriot, at the very moment when he was about to take measures to build his country up into one of the great Mediterranean Powers.

A great Cretan patriot

All through the winter Greece had been watching Bulgaria in the interests of Serbia. Had Tsar Ferdinand attempted to attack the Serbians when they were hard pressed by the Austrians, Greece would have come to the rescue of her ally. In the spring a new arrangement of the Balkan problem was worked out by Russia and Britain. While waiting to enter the Great War, Rumania took over the task of protecting the Serbians. This left Greece with her hands free. A representative of the British Government then consulted with M. Venizelos, and in February, 1915, it was arranged that when the Franco-British fleet had opened the gateway of the Dardanelles, and had wrecked some of the chief forts in the Narrows, Greece would provide part of the landing-force for operations against the Turkish troops holding the Gallipoli Peninsula.

There remained only the apparently formal act of getting the consent of King Constantine to the policy arranged by his constitutional Premier. Then it was that the Kaiser and his sister, with his nephews, were well repaid for all the trouble they had taken to win over the chiefs of the Greek Army. King Constantine refused to send a single soldier to co-operate with the allied fleet in forcing the passage of the Dardanelles. The principal generals of the Greek Army agreed with their foreign King. M. Venizelos —surprised, consternated, bewildered—resigned. One of the chiefs of the Epirote clans tried to assassinate the King. He failed. In the meantime France prepared a large Mohammedan force in her North African dominions to supply the place of the Greek

BELGIAN RECRUITS IN TRAINING IN THE ENVIRONS OF PARIS.

Army, and Great Britain also organised in Egypt an army of invasion for transport to the Dardanelles. At the same time Russia prepared to launch a very considerable force north of Constantinople. By the end of March the Powers of the Triple Entente were

All King Constantine effected

well able to do without help from either the Bulgarians or the Greeks in the operations against Turkey. All that King Constantine effected was to delay for two or three weeks the Franco-British fleet's attack upon the forts in the narrowest part of the Dardanelles.

The general position at the opening of the spring campaign around the great central battlefield was that nearly three-quarters of a million of first-rate Rumanian soldiers were ready to invade Hungary. Italy had a full million troops of the first line seemingly waiting for the snows to melt in the Trentino in order to march into Austria. The old Austrian Emperor, who had once reigned over Lombardy, said that he would rather surrender the Duchy of Galicia to the Russians, and make a separate peace with the Triple Entente, than yield any more territory to the Italians. On the other hand, it was reported that the people of Austria-Hungary were anxious for the Italians to take the field, and thus quicken the ending of the war. They did not mind who won, so long as the terrible struggle was brought abruptly to a conclusion. It is thus that we see, more clearly in the field of diplomacy than in the field of battle, the progress made by the Allies after seven months of warfare.

To all appearance the opposing fronts were held as strongly as ever. But there was a large crack between the two Teutonic Empires. Germany was in such difficulties that she was eager to sell her fighting ally Austria

KING ALBERT'S NEW ARMY AT DRILL IN THE VICINITY OF THE FRENCH CAPITAL.
While Lord Kitchener's new army was getting into form in various parts of the United Kingdom, and new classes of the French Army were preparing for active service, Belgian recruits were in training in France. Our smaller view shows a section of them being reviewed by M. Carton de Wiart.

to Austria's deadliest enemy—Italy. To counter this move, Austria was almost ready to come to a separate arrangement with Germany's deadliest enemy—Russia. The war had been started directly with a view to enlarging Austria's power in the Adriatic Sea. But Germany had now given up all idea of a Byzantine-Ottoman extension of her Empire. She was ready to tear up another scrap of paper—her treaty with Austria—in the hope of being able to save herself at the expense of her partner in international crime.

This act of German faithlessness was worth more than a smashing victory to the Powers of the Triple Entente, for it was something that would tell on the future relations between the Northern and Southern Teutons for several generations. It would be very long before an Austrian would again trust the word of a Prussian.

There was also a wide division between the people of Vienna and the people of Budapest. The resignation of the Austrian Foreign Minister, Count Berchtold, on January 14th, 1915, was followed by the appointment of a Hungarian magnate, Baron Burian. It was well known that Burian was only an automaton controlled by his masterful fellow-countryman Count Tisza. The count

directed all the affairs of Austria-Hungary, and the Kaiser dealt with him in every important matter, instead of arranging things with the Emperor Francis Joseph. It was really Hungary that was trying to sell Austria to Italy.

The Hungarians were dominated by fear of the Rumanians. As masters of the Southern Teutonic Empire, they first insisted upon Germany sending soldiers to help in the defence of their country against the Russians. When this was done, they proposed to stave off the Italian attack at the expense of Austrian territory, in order that Rumania should not have any co-operating force if she persisted in attempting an invasion. The result of all these involved intrigues upon the deserted and betrayed Austrian populace was that many of them became ready to make peace with Russia, and even looked forward to the success of the **Austrians ready** Rumanians with a malicious joy. **to make peace** Mutinies became more frequent in the Austrian armies, and only the Hungarian forces continued to show any resolute courage. Even the Hungarians sometimes thought of breaking away from Germany and making a separate peace.

In fact, Count Tisza hinted this tendency of his countrymen to the Kaiser and his Staff in order to induce them to send special reinforcements into Hungary to throw the Russians back from the Carpathians. Tisza was a master in making menaces of this sort, and by means of them he kept the Germans faithful to the cause of Hungary during the winter and spring. As a matter of fact, his position in his own country was not secure. There was a very powerful movement for independence among the Hungarian magnates. The leaders of this movement proposed to make peace with Russia and to leave Austria to her doom.

It was this movement that told upon the Rumanians, for they knew that they would lose Transylvania if the Hungarians first concluded negotiations with Russia. This was why the Russian-Rumanian arrangement was signed early in the winter of 1914. Rumania was resolute

FRENCH SAPPERS ERECTING TEMPORARY TELEGRAPH WIRES IN THE NORTH OF FRANCE.
In the upper view are to be seen Belgian soldiers on guard by a famous old mill near Furnes.

EN ROUTE: STRIKING VIEW IN THE CHAMPAGNE COUNTRY.

THEIR LAST FIGHT: TRIBUTE OF RESPECT TO THE FALLEN FOE.

German dead in a field on the banks of the Oise. The young Frenchman, the only living being seen in the above pathetic camera-record of the wastage of war, is crossing the stricken field with bared head. The centre picture is of the new French cannon, a weapon with a calibre of a little over six inches. It is fitted with wheel-pads to facilitate transport over rough, roadless country.

PRESIDENT POINCARE, WITH SOME OFFICERS, AT
THE FRENCH HEADQUARTERS.

By the middle of March it looked as though the German loan would be spent in buying ammunition for use against Germany's latest ally. The Turk grew apprehensive of his northern neighbour, and began to concentrate troops around Adrianople. Altogether, the prospect, from the Teutonic point of view, was very gloomy in the field of diplomacy. On March 13th, the anniversary of the death of Alexander II. of Russia, the Tsar of the Liberation, the Bulgarian Premier publicly laid a wreath on the statue of the great Romanoff to whom Bulgaria owed her redemption from Turkish tyranny. It was a very significant act, especially on the part of the leader of the Government that had lately received a large sum of money from Germany.

In other countries of Europe there was little change of policy from the autumn of 1914 to the spring of 1915. What change occurred was not to the advantage of the spoilers of Belgium. Even the German-Swiss began to

to be first in the field on the side of the Triple Entente. Her claim to Transylvania was practically admitted by our Government on January 27th, 1915, when a British loan of £5,000,000 was made to her. Germany tried to counter this British move by making a similar loan to Bulgaria, for it was on Bulgaria that the Hungarians relied to prevent the Rumanian attack. The German loan was no doubt arranged by Count Tisza with this end in view.

Bulgaria temporises But by this time the Bulgarian Premier, M. Radoslavoff, was inclined to imitate the policy of Venizelos, of Greece. The reversion to Adrianople tempted him, as well as the tract of fertile land on the southern border of Bulgaria. When Greece drew back from the plan of co-operating in forcing the passage of the Dardanelles, M. Radoslavoff became still more tempted to let bygones be bygones in regard to Serbia, and to launch a Bulgarian army once more against the Turks.

FRENCH INFANTRY ON THE MARCH.

FRENCH RED CROSS WORKER RENDERING FIRST-AID TO A WOUNDED SOLDIER IN THE FIRING-LINE.

hesitate in their blind admiration for the men of their Prussianised race on the other side of the Rhine. There was an increasingly loud revolt of opinion against the Prussian methods of many of the officers of the Swiss Army, and the Swiss President, Herr Haffmann, of German stock, was replaced by a man of Italian stock, Signor Motta, from Southern Switzerland. The Swiss censorship, which at first had been grossly biased to the German cause, was also modified. By the spring Switzerland as a whole was inclined to look with more sympathy at Belgium, and to preserve a veritable neutral attitude.

The new Swiss President

In Sweden, the only other democratic country in Europe, which showed at first a strong sympathy with Germany, a similar revolution of feeling gradually took place in the winter months. While in Persia some of the Swedish gendarmerie were actively helping the Germans to arm certain of the tribes around the Persian Gulf to enable them to attack our friendly sheikhs there, and to raid our camp, the Swedes at home became less inclined to make trouble on the Russian frontier. There was a certain incident in November, 1914, which seemed to show that some Swedish sailors were ready to go further against us than even the Swedish gendarmerie were going in the Persian Gulf. But the nation generally became more averse from any understanding with Germany.

Naturally, this aversion was not diminished when Germany instituted her extraordinary submarine campaign against all neutral ships trading to ports in the United

NEW USE FOR LACE.

The guns in the above photograph were covered with lace curtains to hide them from aerial observation. Inset: British officers at the entrance to their bomb-proof shelter.

Kingdom. In fact, this murderous measure left Germany without a friend among the democracies of Europe. Only the monarchs of Bulgaria and Greece and the reactionary aristocratic and clerical parties of Italy and Spain continued to favour the Teutonic cause. The curious condition of things in Spain, where the King and Queen stood out for the Allies against their own Court, with only part of the Spanish democracy siding with them, attracted the notice of the Portuguese Republicans. It may have been with a view to reviving the old Republican movement in Spain that the Portuguese Parliament became eager to

"SHELLS, MORE SHELLS!" THE INSATIABLE APPETITE OF THE GUNS.

Unloading ammunition immediately behind the line of fire. As the spring of 1915 approached it became more and more evident that the progress of operations depended on an increased supply of ammunition for the guns. The official French review of the first six months of the war frankly stated that the consumption of projectiles was so enormous as to cause for a moment an ammunition crisis, but that this had been completely overcome. Anxiety in Great Britain on this score was accentuated by labour disputes attributed in part to German agency.

PHOTOGRAPHIC PROOF OF THE DETERIORATION OF GERMAN EXPLOSIVES.

Extreme interest attaches to these camera-records of German gunfire. They were sent to us by a French artillery officer. In the left-hand photograph, taken in January, 1915, a 15-cm. German explosive is seen bursting at a distance of two hundred metres in front of the battery. The haziness of the view is caused by the mass of débris hurled over the earthworks on the right. Great damage was done, and the good quality of the German ammunition is shown by the quantity of smoke. Contrast this with the effect to be seen in the second photograph, of a 15-cm. German shell exploding at only thirty metres' distance from the camera. This second photograph was taken some weeks later. Had our correspondent attempted to take his first photograph at thirty metres, we should not have been able to place these interesting records before our readers.

send its Army into the battlefield of France. On November 24th the Portuguese deputies authorised their Government to support Great Britain in accordance with the old alliance between the two nations. It was a gallant gesture on the part of the Portuguese, but for reasons which are still obscure it did not result in any active measures of a warlike kind. Probably the continual disturbances which had followed the revolution had left Portugal with so empty an exchequer that she could not, even to put to shame the reactionary Spanish parties, raise the money to equip an army for the field. Still the will to fight in the great struggle for the principle of freedom was there, though the means may for the time have been lacking.

The greatest of all democracies in the world—the United States of America—continued to be divided in its sympathies. The native-born American, who owed his national independence largely to France and the greater part of his culture to the islands whose language he inherited, had to walk warily. His chief representative, President Woodrow Wilson, son of a Scots Presbyterian minister, seemed inclined to bear openly against the contraband policy of the Allies. With that peculiar conscientiousness of the Anglo-Celtic temperament, he was more troubled about the mote in Britain's eye than about the beam in the Teutonic vision. So, at least, it appeared on December 30th, 1914, when the American Note to Great Britain in regard to neutral shipping was presented in London. The Note contended that American ships, and neutral vessels carrying American cargoes, should not be taken into British ports and detained there for the purpose of search, unless our warships had, before they stopped each vessel, sufficient evidence to justify belief that contraband goods were being carried. The American Note also protested against the seizure of contraband articles consigned to neutral countries,

America's Note to Great Britain

even in cases where it was fairly patent that the neutral importers would forward the goods to Germany or Austria.

The manner in which the Note was first published, in a short, sharp résumé printed in American newspapers before the complete document was seen by Sir Edward Grey, helped to increase the bad impression made in our country. The tragic year of 1914 closed in gloom. For it looked as though President Wilson had adopted the method of President Cleveland in the former dispute about Venezuela, and was about to put us in the difficult position of resigning our proper rights or drifting into war with the United States.

The doctrine of continuous voyage

What especially saddened British feeling was the fact that we were conducting our search for contraband in accordance with the principles established by the United States. Abraham Lincoln and his advisers, in their blockade of the Southern States, gave a remarkable extension to the doctrine of continuous voyage, which had first been heard of in the French revolutionary war. Under this doctrine goods which were shipped to a neutral port, but which were intended ultimately to reach the enemy, were to be regarded as if on one continuous voyage to the enemy's ports or frontiers, and were therefore liable to seizure in neutral ships. Thus the American courts ruled that goods shipped to the Mexican port of Matamoras were liable to seizure, if those goods were intended for the Southern States, and they admitted suspicion as sufficient evidence of such a destination. There can be no doubt that the doctrine of continuous voyage was established justly, and it seemed extremely unfair that President Wilson should seek to hinder our Navy from adopting the instrument that Abraham Lincoln had once used rightly against our own shipping. For a few days there was a tendency in

IN THE ALLIES' TRENCHES BEFORE YPRES.

"THE PATHS OF GLORY LEAD BUT TO THE GRAVE."

That "there is no moderation in arms" is a thought as old as Seneca. But the above camera-picture of a handful of Frenchmen compelled to take their part in repulsing the enemy over graves and by the side of a shattered mortuary is calculated to send an icy chill to the hearts of the least impressionable of those who look at the conflict from afar. In one case the Germans actually dug deep trenches among graves.

MEN OF DESTINY: THE TWO LEADERS OF THE ALLIES IN THE WEST.

An artist's impression of a consultation between the French Generalissimo and the Commander-in-Chief of the British Forces in France. President Poincaré, in presenting General Joffre with the Military Medal, referred in glowing words to his " force of soul that nothing disturbed," and his " serenity, the salutary e of which spread confidence and hope everywhere." The confidence of his c men in Sir John French is only equalled by that of the French people in Genera

THE BRITISH UNDER FIRE—AND ALMOST UNDER WATER.

During the incessant rain in Flanders the lot of our men in the trenches was such that they had to be relieved as quickly as possible. Rubber boots and leggings were but slight palliatives, and coke braziers, while they cast a ruddy glow around, gave comparatively little warmth. Where this could be done, corruga structures were used for protection, and the ground was covered with br and straw. Sometimes it was possible to pump out the water.

SCENE AT A BLUE CROSS RECEIVING DEPOT IN NORTHERN FRANCE.

ry doctors attached to the Blue Cross service receiving a wounded war- Red Cross workers on behalf of the men. First-aid having been rendered, the
r treatment. In dealing with casualties among our four-footed friends, wounded animals were drafted to depots for surgical and medical attention. Later
Cross organisation developed on lines identical with those adopted by the the horses were placed in meadows, to complete their recovery there.

IN THE THICK OF A BITTER CONTEST IN THE ARGONNE.

contested hand-to-hand fighting went on in the forest region of the Argonne by yet more desperate encounters with the determined foe. The situation was one
ut the winter. The trench shown in the above drawing was fought for of prolonged strain, through which, however, the survivors emerged with smiling
d again. Brilliant work on the part of our brave ally had to be followed faces if tired frames. The struggle in the vicinity of Verdun was most exacting.

BIG GUNS USED BY THE BRITISH IN THE YSER DISTRICT—CAREFULLY SCREENED FROM BOMB-DROPPING
ENEMY AIRCRAFT.

ANOTHER EXAMPLE OF THE METHOD ADOPTED BY BRITISH GUNNERS TO CONCEAL THEIR PIECES FROM
HOSTILE OBSERVATION.

Britain to regard the modern American nation, as represented by the activities of its responsible Government, as a purely commercial community, eager to overthrow its own contribution to international law as soon as this law was found to interfere with its pursuit of wealth at any cost. But, as we shall see in the course of this chapter, this view of American policy did not cover all the facts of the case.

Meanwhile, Sir Edward Grey prepared to reply to the American Note. His preliminary answer was sent to the American Ambassador in London on January 7th, 1915.

He began by pointing out that the figures in regard to American trade, which he had seen, did not show that commerce with neutral countries had been affected by our process of searching ships. In November, 1913, the exports from New York to Denmark were worth 558,000 dollars.

In November, 1914, Denmark was taking over 7,100,000 dollars' worth of goods. In the same way, Sweden increased her New York imports from 377,000 dollars to 2,858,000 dollars; Norway from 477,000 dollars to 2,318,000 dollars; Italy from 2,971,000 dollars to 4,781,000 dollars. The increase of American copper exports to the neutral countries of Europe was very striking. Italy received more than double the amount she had done in 1913; and, with the exception of Holland and Italy, the other European states received in 1914 *nearly five times the amount of American copper* which they had taken in 1913. Sir Edward Grey pointed out that there was a very strong presumption that the bulk of American copper consigned to Norway, Sweden, Denmark, and Switzerland was intended for use in Germany and Austria. Our Government had, in fact, at the time of writing, positive evidence that four copper and aluminium consignments, then on **Copper to Germany** the way from the United States to **via Sweden** Sweden, were definitely destined for Germany. This American copper, it must be remembered, was being employed by the Germans and Austrians to make shells for the slaughter of Belgians, Serbians, Frenchmen, Russians, and British troops. In conclusion Sir Edward Grey stated:

"We are confronted with the growing danger that neutral countries contiguous to the enemy will become, on a scale hitherto unprecedented, a base of supplies for the armed forces of our enemies and for materials for manufacturing armament. The trade figures of imports show how strong this tendency is, but we have no complaint to make of the attitude of the Governments of those countries, which, so far as we are aware, have not departed from proper rules of neutrality. We endeavour, in the interest of our own national safety, to prevent this danger by intercepting goods really destined for the enemy, without interfering with those which are bona fide neutral.

"Since the outbreak of the war the Government of the United States have **America's** changed their previous practice, and have **shipping policy** prohibited the publication of manifests till thirty days after the departure of vessels from the United States ports. We had no locus standi for complaining of this change, and did not complain. But the effect of it must be to increase the difficulty of ascertaining the presence of contraband, and to render necessary, in the interest of our national safety, the examination and detention of more ships than would have been the case if the former practice had continued.

"Pending a more detailed reply, I would conclude by saying that his Majesty's Government do not desire to contest the general principles of international law on which they understand the Note of the United States to be based, and desire to restrict their action solely to interference with contraband destined for the enemy."

The reply of Sir Edward Grey was friendly in tone, but masterly in argument. It swayed the minds of a large number of American people who were not anxious to fight on the side of Germany against Britain, France, Russia, and Japan. Soon after it was received in America, President Wilson and his Secretary for Foreign Affairs consulted together in regard to the charges made by German-Americans about their shipping policy. A letter of inquiry had been received from Senator Stone, who had a large German

AS THE SOLDIER SEES THE BATTLEFIELD.
These photographs, sent to the Editor by soldiers in the front trenches, are most interesting. They are snapshots taken through the loopholes of the trenches. In the first a battle is raging. Note the distant smoke, while the dim figures in the foreground are dead Germans who fell in attacking the trench days before. The second shows a row of houses held by Germans, towards which the French engineers had stealthily sapped and mined; and in the third we have the same scene after the mine was fired—the whole of the houses destroyed and the German position made untenable

electorate in St. Louis, the chief city of his State. He was chairman of the Committee on Foreign Relations, and he stated in his letter of inquiry that many of his electorate sympathised with Germany and Austria, and believed

THE PRICE OF THE TRENCH: CHARGE OF TURCOS OVER FIRE-SWEPT OPEN COUNTRY.

In Champagne the French offensive was taken part in by Zouaves, Colonial infantry, Algerian sharpshooters, and Turcos. Our artist depicts a charge by the last-named. The Moroccans have taken one trench, and, leaving their dead and wounded with dead and dying Germans, are advancing under shell and shrapnel fire across the coverless country, to be engulfed again in another trench melée farther on. In addition to the awful price in flesh and blood paid for a slight advance, the ground between the trenches was ploughed and scarred by the tempest of fire and flame, which had also levelled any trees that formerly stood between the opposing armies. One observer tells us that in the intervals of artillery firing "larks could be heard singing continuously in joyous chorus."

PAY DAY ON THE BATTLEFIELD.
German infantry being paid in notes. In the circular photograph we see a French soldier assisting an unhappy German who was found practically naked in a captured trench.

that the United States Government was showing partiality to Britain, France, and Russia.

The letter from Senator Stone brought to a head the German-American agitation against the munitioning of the Allies by American armament firms. It was a notorious fact, for example, that the Bethlehem Steel Works were making 16 in. guns for Britain, and a considerable amount of the shells used against the German front in the western theatre of the war came from America. Something like twenty million men, women, and children of Teutonic stock, settled in the United States, looked at this position of affairs with much anger and

Mr. Bryan's reply to agitators bitterness. But in the letter in reply, drawn up by the President and the Foreign Secretary, and signed by the latter, it was pointed out that the situation was simply the inevitable sequel to the British control of the sea.

"If," said Mr. Bryan, "any American citizens who are partisans of Germany and Austria-Hungary feel that this Administration is acting in a way injurious to the cause of those countries, this feeling results from the fact that on the high seas German and Austro-Hungarian naval power is thus far inferior to the British. It is the business of a belligerent operating on the high seas, not the duty of a neutral, to prevent contraband from reaching the enemy.

"Those in this country who sympathise with Germany and Austria-Hungary appear to assume that some obligation rests upon this

WINTER FASHIONS IN THE KAISER'S ARMY.
German soldier of the Landsturm wearing a fur coat with a Medici collar.

Government in the performance of its neutral duty to prevent all trade in contraband, and thus to equalise the difference due to the relative naval strength of the belligerents. No such obligation exists. It would be an unneutral act—an act of partiality on the part of this Government —to adopt such a policy, if the Executive had the power to do so."

Mr. Roosevelt also intervened in the discussion with considerable effect. He remarked that any restriction of the export of armaments and ammunition would weaken his country. The Government factories were inadequate to supply American needs in case of war, and it was only by allowing American business men to develop their plant for supplying any foreign nation able to maintain a sea-borne traffic that the United States

INDIAN TROOPS IN ACTION—CAUTIOUS ADVANCE OF A MAXIM-GUN DETACHMENT.

could grow in warlike strength with no increase of taxation for military purposes.

But some German-Americans were still eager to work mischief between America and the Powers of the Triple Entente and Japan. Chief among them was Mr. Edward Breitung, a German-American trust magnate of Michigan. He purchased the steamship Dacia, of the Hamburg-Amerika Line, and prepared to send her out under the American flag with a cargo of cotton to Germany or Holland. It was expected that a British warship would seize the vessel, and that in due course she would be sold as a prize. Then Breitung, and the men working with him, hoped to work the American people into a state of indignation over the insult to the flag. If, on the other hand, our Government were so daunted by the threat of trouble with America as to let the Dacia pass, it was intended to transfer all German merchant ships sheltering in American ports to German-American capitalists. When, however, the Dacia at last appeared near the English Channel, she was captured by a French warship and taken to Brest. By this very simple method our Government avoided all complications with the American people, and prevented the pro-German intriguers

The case of the Dacia

INDIAN INFANTRY ON THEIR WAY TO THE FIGHTING-LINE IN NORTHERN FRANCE.
The smaller photograph is of members of the Sirhind Brigade of the British Indian troops in France. These sturdy fighting men were specially mentioned in Sir John French's despatches.

from arousing the ancient jealousy of the great Trans-Atlantic Republic in regard to our mercantile marine.

By this time the leaders of the Teutonic agitation in the United States began to attract seriously the attention of the loyal American people. At a conference held in Washington by fifty-eight representative German-Americans under the leadership of Richard Bartholdt, of Missouri, a nation-wide organisation was created on January 30th, 1915, to act in a partisan way in American politics. Chief among the leaders of the new party were five congressmen, Bartholdt, Vollmer, Barthfeld, Lobeck, and Porter. In addition were Dr. C. J. Hexamer, president of the German-American National Alliance of Phila-

The Teuton menace in America

delphia, claiming a membership of two millions; Professor W. R. Shepherd, of Columbia; Professor Von Mach, of Harvard; Professor Faust, of Cornell; Mr. John Devoy, editor of the New York "Gaelic-American"; and many editors of German-American papers connected with German-American societies. The organisation claimed to represent some twenty million German-Americans, with certain Irish-American sympathisers.

Their main published programme was: "1. We demand a free and open sea for the commerce of the United States, and unrestricted traffic in non-contraband goods, as defined by international law; 2. We favour, as a strictly American policy, the immediate enactment of legislation prohibiting the export of arms and munitions of war; 3. We pledge ourselves, individually and collectively, to support only such candidates for public office, irrespective of party, who will place American" (*sic*) "interests above those of any other country, and who will aid in eliminating all undue foreign influences from American life."

The immediate object of the organisation was to bring about an alliance between the German-American and German-Irish voters, and to defeat the native Americans in the approaching Presidential primaries and the 1916 campaign. It was intended to overthrow President Wilson and any other Democratic, Republican, or Progressive leader who refused to place

"HINDRANCES TO PROGRESS."
A field of stakes in front of a German position, designed to impale cavalry in case of a charge.

A DEVICE OF GERMAN MANUFACTURE.
Hundreds of these horrible implements were found on a road along which it was expected British cavalry would have to pass.

the insane German-American desire to provoke a war with Britain above the true interests of the peaceful, friendly majority of voters in the United States. The plan of action had been foretold by military writers in Germany, and it was notorious that the ex-German Minister, Dr. Dernburg, was the master-hand working in the background and weaving the plot. At times even the threat of another Civil War was uttered by some of the German-American hot-heads.

It was this movement that partly accounted for the Notes sent to our Government by President Wilson with regard to American shipping. The President inclined to state the American case over-strongly, in order to show that he was fighting with all his power for the true interests of all neutral nations. It did not matter much to him if, in his eagerness to champion the rights of neutrals, he laid himself open to an overpowering reply from Sir Edward Grey.

What he wanted chiefly to do **President Wilson's** was to show his countrymen **attitude** that he had gone as far as man could rightly go in trying to abate the rigour of search exercised by the British and French Navies. In short, he was preparing his case against the German-American organisation. If there were to be a fight at the next election, he intended to come into it with scrupulously clean hands, and, if necessary, to call for the co-operation of all loyal Americans to defeat the machinations of the German intriguers against their peace.

In spite of the great show of numbers of the Pro-Prussian League, it was doubtful if it could become a main force in American politics. Most of the

IN SEARCH OF A SPY.
An incident in Poland. A German officer and some of his men are searching a farmhouse in which they were led to believe a Russian spy had taken refuge.

older German emigrants to the United States had left their Fatherland in search of liberty after the overthrow of the German Liberal movement and the establishment of a policy of military aggression by Bismarck. For the last thirteen years the Kaiser had made great efforts to win over these fugitives from his scientific system of reactionary government. But only the latest multitude of German emigrants

The Kaiser and the fugitives

to America, who had mainly been attracted by the wealth rather than the freedom of the great Republic of the West, were inclined to listen to Prince Henry of Prussia and the other Ambassadors of Teutonic militarism who visited the States to inspire and organise the great intrigue.

Certain plutocrats of German and German-Jewish origin may have been won over, together with some of the younger generation of German-Americans, dazzled by the personality of the Kaiser, and swayed by the prestige of German achievements in technical industries and university education. Many of the older men of German stock, however, remembered very clearly the reason why they had left their country, and had no desire whatever to help towards the world-wide triumph of the principles of the Junker class, against which they had fought vainly in their unhappy Fatherland. For these and other reasons it was with a considerable amount of confidence in the ultimate issue that the true Americans faced the menace of the so-called German-American Neutrality League. It was generally reckoned that the result of the elections would be to bring odium and confusion upon the chief intriguers and upon all who stood with them. Indeed, it was the common belief that any show of hostility by the German-American organisation against a candidate would be sufficient to enable that candidate to win. For though the American people kept very quiet about the matter, their quietness was only that calm that sometimes goes before a storm. In the meantime the United States continued to protest about our interference with their shipping, and to supply the Powers of the Triple Entente with an enormous amount of war material.

The German intriguers then tried to make mischief in another direction. In January, 1915, Japan began to press China somewhat vigorously to make various large and profitable concessions. The United States was then urged by the German party to take warlike steps for the conservation of Chinese integrity, and challenged Great Britain in regard to the scope of the British-Japanese treaty. It was hoped either to make trouble with Britain's ally, or to detach the two island Powers of Europe and Asia from further co-operation. President Wilson, however, continued to negotiate calmly regarding all the difficulties exaggerated by the German-American Neutrality League.

In the domestic affairs of the British Empire during the autumn and winter campaign there was little of importance directly bearing

upon the course and duration of the war, with the exception of the financial position of our country. The State still continued to play the part of the rich uncle. There had been guarantees to the railways, the banks, and the Stock Exchange, and on November 3rd, 1914, it was announced that help would be given to traders with foreign debts which they could not collect. Solvent traders, with moneys due from foreigners, were enabled to realise immediately fifty per cent. of the amounts owing to them. Like the other measures of financial support undertaken by the British Government, this scheme helped to prevent the widespread bankruptcy of industrial firms and the closing of factories.

On January 19th, 1915, further measures for the organisation and conservation of our financial resources were put into force. No company thenceforward was allowed to obtain fresh capital, and no new companies were permitted to obtain public subscriptions, unless in each case our Government approved the intended use of the capital. Furthermore, no capital was allowed to go abroad for the financing of foreign concerns.

Early in February Mr. Lloyd George **Financial conference** and the Governor of the Bank of England   **in Paris** went to Paris to hold a conference with M. Ribot and M. Bark, the Finance Ministers of France and Russia. The outcome of this conference was one of extraordinary importance and originality. The three Powers of the Triple Entente resolved to unite their financial resources equally with their military resources for the purpose of carrying the war to a successful conclusion. With this aim in view, they decided to take over in equal shares all present and future advances to friendly countries which were then fighting with them or intending soon to do so. Financial measures were adopted for facilitating Russian exports, and for establishing, so far as possible, the par of exchange between Russia and her Allies.

It was expected that by December 31st, 1915, the combined expenses of the Allies would be about two thousand million pounds. The greatest expenditure would fall upon the British Empire, which had to maintain a huge Navy, and to create and maintain a new army of three million or more troops. Happily, as Mr. Lloyd George pointed out, Britain and France were the great bankers of the world. Merely out of the proceeds of our investments abroad we could pay for our huge war expenditure for five years, while allowing a substantial sum for depreciation. France could carry on the war for three years at least out of the proceeds of her foreign investments; and both countries would still have something to spare to advance to their Allies. At the time when the financial alliance between Britain, France, and Russia was made, the Allies were fighting the whole mobilised strength of Germany with less than one-third of their own strength. Hence the importance of the new agreement.

BAFFLING THE ENEMY SNIPERS.
The invention of the trench periscope, one of the innovations brought about by the war, made outlook work a matter of comparative safety except from shell fire.

CHAPTER LII.

THE BACK-VELDT REVOLT IN SOUTH AFRICA.

South Africa and the German Ambitions—How General Botha Worked for a Permanent Settlement—German South-West Africa the Centre of Intrigue—General Beyers at Berlin—Arrangements Made for Prussianisation of South Africa—General Hertzog Breaks with General Botha—Racial Ascendancy *versus* Union of Boer and Briton—Interventionists and Neutralists—Prophecies of Van Rensburg—Botha and Smuts Stand for Swift and Active Measures—Triumph of Loyalists in Union Parliament—Beyers Plots an Outbreak of Rebellion—Puts Maritz in Command on German Frontier—Death of Delarey Stops First Revolt at Potschefstroom—General Botha's Great Speech—Maritz Betrays Loyal Forces and Opens the Rebellion—Defeat of Maritz—De Wet and Beyers Revolt—Botha Takes the Field and Breaks Up Beyers's Forces—Pursuit and Capture of De Wet—Death of Beyers.

EVER since Bismarck remarked that South Africa would be the grave of Britain's greatness, the fourth-rate Machiavellis of the German Foreign Office had regarded the Cape as the clay foot of the Colossus of the British Empire. It was at this point that they began the process of undermining our Imperial power, which they afterwards vainly continued in India and in Egypt. It was mainly their machinations that brought about the South African War. Their secret service men were behind the Afrikander Bund, and President Kruger was encouraged to resort to the arbitrament of arms, in the quarrel over the rights of the Uitlanders, by receiving promises of help from the agents of the German Emperor. How sadly President Kruger was deceived, when he went in person to Germany to plead with the Kaiser to help him, is a matter of history. The President of the Transvaal was then merely a broken tool of German intrigue. There had never been any intention of helping his country, save in so far as damage could be done thereby to the British Empire, with no risk to the position of Germany.

After the generous and magnificent settlement of South African problems made by Sir Henry Campbell-Bannerman and his Cabinet in 1906, there seemed little room for any further German intrigue of a serious and widespread kind. The pacific settlement of the racial difficulties of the two white peoples was still further established by the result of the Union elections. These gave the Dutch party a working majority, with a Boer as Prime Minister. There was a considerable outcry from South Africans of British stock over the power that had been entrusted to the men with whom they had been fighting barely eight years before. But, happily, the unparalleled policy of magnanimity prevailed, and the Dutch and British parties were left to work together, without interference from Britain, and to grow by use and kindly intercourse into a combined nationality such as French and British Canadians had developed after a century of conflict

Had the Union of South Africa been as secluded from hostile outside intrigue as was the Dominion of Canada, all might have gone well. The solvent of free government and the recurring need for co-operative efforts in solving all kinds of social and industrial difficulties would gradually have grouped the nations together by classes, interests, and principles, cutting across the racial distinctions. For by the bounty of Providence the chief power had fallen into the hands of a man of noble character and enlightened mind—General Louis Botha. Eight years before he had been one of the ablest of Britain's enemies, and by his skill in war and the strength of his personality he had become the commander-in-chief of the

GENERAL LOUIS BOTHA AND HIS SONS.
The Premier of South Africa, with Captain Louis Botha, John Botha (who joined the Cape Town Highlanders), and Philip Botha, the General's youngest son.

Boers. But after the settlement, and his rise to the Premiership, he took a wide and long view of the destinies of his country, and worked with the single purpose of reconciling both races in a harmonious union. Born in Natal in 1863, he knew the Briton as well as the Boer. He had a generosity of soul and a largeness of mind similar to that of the Liberal British statesman who had suddenly transformed South Africa into the greatest of all experiments in democratic government. General Botha resolved that the experiment should not fail, while he controlled affairs, for want of fairness, goodwill, and foresight.

Naturally, this did not suit the views of the Governor of German South-West **German strategical** Africa. His colony had **railways** been provided with strategical railways for the invasion of Cape Colony. The railways ran from the ports of Swakopmund and Lüderitzbucht and connected with a central track that ended near the Orange River. The nearest line in the South African Union was over three hundred and fifty miles away, while the intervening country was thinly populated and poorly provided with roads. Their railways of invasion gave the Germans a somewhat similar advantage over the South Africans to that which they possessed, on the eastern frontier of their Fatherland, over the Russians. Of course, the expensive railway system of German South-West Africa, which did not pay for itself in a commercial way, was not planned merely to waste money. But the money would certainly have been wasted if the Dutch and British stocks in South Africa had been allowed to settle down in peaceful co-operation for the development of their country.

A war with Boer and Briton combined, with the British Navy in practical control of the seas, would result in overwhelming disaster for the Germans. They

GENERAL HERTZOG.

GENERAL CHRISTIAN DE WET. (In circle: GENERAL BEYERS.)

GENERAL SMUTS.

...

GENERAL MARITZ.

each other for German ends.

The Germans definitely began to prepare their colony north of the Orange River as a base of operations against British South Africa in 1908. The Germans had then been occupied for five years in a war with the natives of German South-West Africa, among whom the nomad cattle-breeders, the Hereros, were eminent. A very capable force of Boer auxiliaries had been employed in the native war. Some of them were men still unpropitiated by the grant of self-government to the Transvaal and Orange River Colony. The discontent of the irreconcilables of the back veldt was remarked by the German Governor of South-West Africa. He had formerly been German Consul-General at Cape Town, directing there the web of intrigue by which the agents of the Kaiser tried to keep the Boers ready for revolt at the word of command from Berlin.

When the Herero war drew to an end, many of the 19,000 German troops were retained as farmers. Most of their guns were kept, with huge stores of ammunition and food, and in 1913 the preparations were fairly complete. The Germans scarcely troubled to conceal the fact that they intended to combine the South African Union with German South-West Africa into a vassal colony under the control of the Prussian bureaucracy. It was not made clear what advantage the **General Beyers and** Boers would derive from ex- **the Kaiser** changing their status as a self-governing Dominion in a loose federation of progressive and liberal powers for the rule of the Hohenzollerns. But certain Boers were shown that they would profit by the success of the Prussians.

In the autumn of 1913 General Beyers, the Commandant-General of the Union Defence Force, went with his wife to Switzerland to study the manœuvres of the Swiss militia army. Kaiser Wilhelm II. also attended these manœuvres. Naturally, the two men met. Beyers had married a German lady remarkable for the intensity of her patriotism, and, like many of the women of her country, she was more embittered by the outcome of the South African War than were the Boers themselves. Beyers was a tall, manly, handsome man, with a strong, magnetic personality. The Kaiser was delighted with him, and some time after the Swiss manœuvres he was invited to Berlin, and there feasted

would lose their only dependency in Africa suited to colonisation by the white races, with its rich grass-lands in the north, its recently discovered diamond-fields by the shore, and its unexplored mineral resources. The Germans, therefore, resumed their old schemes of intrigue. Their intention was to set Boer and Briton again to fight

and flattered by the Court, until by some means he was won over.

Mere bribery was not likely to have undermined the honesty of character of this quiet, dignified man, for he was already rich ; but he was vain, and it was upon his vanity that the Kaiser and his ministers played. He was apparently offered the position of President of the Great South African Republic which was to be established under German " protection." He returned to Cape Town with his heavy black moustache turned up in the Kaiser style and the ideas of the Kaiser running in his head.

At that time the Germans intended to provoke the Great War immediately. As Signor Giolitti revealed in a speech which he made at the beginning of 1915, the attack on Serbia was first timed to take place in 1913. It was only because Italy refused at the last moment to join in the aggressive act of conflagration that Great Britain escaped being drawn into the war about the time when General Beyers first began to plot with the Germans. Meanwhile the policy of General Botha's party became troubled by the revival of a renewed movement for racial ascendancy.

The movement originated among some of the leaders of the Dutch people of the Orange River **General Hertzog's** Colony. Chief among them was General **new party** Hertzog, who had to leave the Cabinet, owing partly to a difference of opinion with General Botha concerning the Imperial responsibilities of South Africa. As a matter of fact, General Hertzog was moved largely by personal animosity to his more powerful colleague. But on breaking from him he gave his animosity a political colouring, and started a new Dutch party which aimed at racial ascendancy ending in absolute independence. General Hertzog was not prepared

to declare war against the rest of the British Empire. He thought that South Africa might remain nominally part of the Empire, until the time came for her to lapse, without any show of violence, from the British Crown. This would occur, in his view, whenever the interests of South Africa were likely to be sacrificed to the common cause of the Empire, as in the case of a war with Germany.

General Botha, on the other hand, took a high and honourable view of the obligations of his people. He intended to hold by the spirit **The ruling mind in** as well as by the letter of the grant of **the Union** free government. Quite likely the result of the treacherous intrigues of the Germans in the days of President Kruger weighed in the decision to which the South African Prime Minister came in 1913. Besides being the ruling mind in the Union, he was also the old commander-in-chief of the Boers. He had the patience and the tenacity of the race that produced Tromp, De Ruyter, and William of Orange. He knew well what were the intentions of Germany in regard to South Africa, and his efforts to reconcile Boer and Briton in the new Commonwealth were animated with a military purpose as well as with a generosity of view. As a Boer he had an account to settle with the Kaiser, who refused to see President Kruger in Berlin in the autumn of 1900. With fine Dutch patience, he did not go out of his way to seek a quarrel. But, as was seen in his break with Hertzog and De Wet, when he saw that the quarrel would be forced upon him, he began to prepare in 1913 to meet it with all the stubborn valour of his race.

He foresaw everything except the downright treachery of Beyers. There was an extremely difficult task before him and before his capable colleague, General Smuts, but

REPRESENTATIVE GROUP OF LOYAL BOERS WHO RESPONDED TO THE PATRIOTIC APPEAL OF GENERAL BOTHA AND RALLIED TO THE FLAG OF THE EMPIRE.

their courage only rose with their difficulties. The pro-
rogation of Parliament on July 7th, 1914, was a stroke of
good luck. For when war broke out the next month, the
Government was able to arrange its plan of action in
silence. The position in some of the country districts
was disturbing. For in those places the agents of Germany
had long been spreading the idea that when the time came
for the downfall of the British Empire by German hands,
a larger South African Republic would be created with
the help of the Teutons. In the Western Transvaal some
of the back-veldt Boers were ready to rise, and the rumour
ran that the Germans had invaded the Union, and that
the burghers were being called out on commando to act
with them.

At one place in the Western Transvaal a mass of armed
Boers collected for action. But General Delarey hastened
to the spot and spoke sternly to his countrymen, and
induced them to go back home. Only in the large towns
was there an instant and passionate demonstration of
loyalty to the Empire. In districts where settlers of
Dutch stock prevailed, the general attitude of the people
was that of bewildered expectancy. They were waiting

request that the famous old guerilla leader is said to have
made is that, before he was punished for his treason, he
might have a quarter of an hour and a rifle alone with
Hertzog.

While the party politics of the Dutchmen of South
Africa were in this confused condition, the Imperial
Government was troubled about German
South-West Africa. It was absolutely   **Peril to British**
necessary to attack this enemy colony.   **shipping**
Its mighty wireless station at Windhoek,
and its port of Swakopmund, made it a great danger to our
shipping. It was known that a system for coaling German
commerce raiders had been arranged at Cape Town, where
German agents had a carrier-pigeon scheme of communication with German South-West Africa. The large
number of soldiers retained in German territory, many
of them having settled down as soldier-farmers in the old
Roman manner, was fair proof of German intentions.
The German plan was to keep their colony safe from
attack, while using it as the organising centre for the
intrigues of rebellion in South Africa.

Much as the Imperial Government would have liked to
allow German South-West Africa
to remain undisturbed till its fate
was decided on the battlefields of
Europe, this could not be done.
For though the Empire might
thereby have been enabled to
content awhile the honestly-
mistaken section of Afrikanders,
the premature explosion of the
combined forces of intrigue and invasion might have been disastrous.
The proximity of a large German
military force was having a de-
moralising effect upon the border
folk of the Union. An attack
had to be made upon this force.

TRANSVAAL SCOTTISH PREPARING FOR THE ROLL-CALL AT THE
WANDERERS' CLUB.

to see what action their Government would take. Meanwhile a fierce and decisive struggle was going on between
General Botha and General Smuts on the one side, and
General Hertzog and ex-President Steyn on the other
side. Between them was General Delarey, with
Christian de Wet and Beyers trying to win Delarey
over to active rebellion. The situation was much complicated by personal feelings of disappointed ambition on
the part of General Hertzog and De Wet. Hertzog was
working to establish a Hertzog Cabinet, and his chief end
was to overthrow Botha rather than to
Complications and   provoke armed rebellion. But if he did
a mystery   not actively incite traitors like Beyers and
fools like De Wet, he was not displeased
to watch them proceed to shed the blood of British settlers.
The greater the trouble gathering round the Botha Cabinet,
the greater was the chance of General Hertzog getting
all the power of government into his hands. What
Hertzog intended to do, when he was controller of the
destinies of South Africa with the German nominee Beyers
as the nominal head of his party, is a mystery. We shall
perhaps know more about this when Christian de Wet
speaks. At the time of writing the only important

It was only a question whether
the operations should be conducted
by the Imperial Government with
British, Australian, New Zealand,
and Indian troops, or whether
the South African Government
would undertake the conquest of
the neighbouring hostile territory.
There was an Indian army corps
almost ready to sail, and composed
largely of hardy men, accustomed
to the kind of desert warfare that
would be waged in German South-
West Africa. And if the Indians had afterwards been
encouraged to settle on the land they had won, the neutralists
of the Union would have had no ground of complaint in the
matter. This was the critical position, as General Botha
afterwards pointed out to a great gathering of his constituents in the Transvaal. If the Boer was not willing
to co-operate with the Briton in striking against the
intriguer who intended to ruin their Commonwealth,
there were other fighting races in the British Empire who
would rejoice at the opportunity of conquering the finest
of all German colonies.

General Botha did not hesitate. Some Boers afterwards
said that he should have first of all asked permission of
the people of South Africa; but, as he replied scornfully,
what was the good of a Government which was not prepared to accept responsibility? He rejoiced in the power
constitutionally put into his hands, and brought to the
task of a fine statesman the swift decision and instant
action of a military genius. To him it had suddenly been
given to shape the destiny of a United South Africa.
German ambition and German intrigue, he saw, could be
transformed into a consolidating influence on the Union,
producing in the course of months a veritable sentiment

"FIRST-LINE TRANSPORT" OF THE RAND RIFLES: SLEIGHING OVER THE SAND IN SOUTH-WEST AFRICA.

GETTING A "LONG TOM" INTO POSITION: UNION ARTILLERY ON SERVICE IN SOUTH-WEST AFRICA.

WITH THE SOUTH AFRICAN UNION FORCES AT SWAKOPMUND: IN THE TRENCHES FACING THE GERMAN POSITION.

of common nationality not to be developed in peace time for several generations. The hammer directed at South Africa should be turned into an anvil, on which a greater South Africa could be swiftly fashioned—a South Africa including the German colony, and perhaps Rhodesia and part of German East Africa. From Table Bay to the source of the Nile, Briton and Boer could extend their sway, with an Imperial railway linking the Empire's ports on the Mediterranean with Egypt, the Soudan, Uganda, the Zanzibar hinterland, Rhodesia, and the Union of South Africa.

Botha had to deal with the most difficult people on earth—the last of the stern, passionately narrow, and fiercely ignorant race of Calvinists. They were men of the type of the old Scottish Covenanters, and

Van Rensburg's prophecies

even superior in the vigour of their fighting fanaticism to the Cameronians. They came from the two principal persecuted stocks of the European wars of religion—the Calvinists of the Netherlands and the Huguenots of France. Two hundred and fifty years of toleration and enlightenment in Europe had not affected them. Left to themselves they would have burnt a Darwinian with more readiness than Calvin burned Servetus. The back-veldt Boers especially were quite unchanged in mind and character from their ancestors. Except a man spoke to them in the terms of their own creed, they recognised no human authority. And the trouble was that they had a famous prophet, Van Rensburg, who lived at Lichtenburg, near General Delarey. He had won renown towards the end of the South African War by inducing Delarey to attack Lord Methuen, with the result that the Boers gained a remarkable victory. It was by a prediction, in which he actually named the day on which the movement should be conducted, that Van Rensburg brought about the capture of Lord Methuen. After this he made other prophecies, some of which did not fall out as he foretold, but his one great success made him a power among the back-veldt Boers.

As soon as war broke out Van Rensburg began again to see visions and to make prophecies. In one vision there was an ocean, and across the ocean five great bulls were fighting, and a blue bull gored a great hole in a red bull. The red bull was Britain, while the blue bull was Germany. In another vision some commandos of burghers were trekking across the Orange River into the desert northward. There they met the German troops, and talked with them, and came back home without firing a shot. This, being interpreted, meant that the soldiers of the Kaiser intended not only to restore the old Republic, but to add Natal and the Cape to it.

It was on Delarey that the prophet of Lichtenburg chiefly worked, and when the famous general came down to attend a special war session of Parliament, his friends found him in a state of mind bordering on religious mania. Delarey was a well-balanced, enlightened man of strong personality; and seeing what an effect the prophet of Lichtenburg produced on him, it is easy to calculate how profound and disturbing was the influence the preacher of rebellion exercised upon the narrow, ignorant country Boers. If the policy of neutrality had been maintained for some months, men like Van Rensburg and active intriguers like Beyers might have

completely undermined the settlement between Boer and Briton and created a terrible struggle, with German troops and Imperial forces intervening.

In these circumstances of extreme perplexity and danger General Botha, with the help of General Smuts, started a policy of extraordinary audacity. Nearly all their fellow-countrymen were inclined to draw together in a common aversion to any expedition against German South-West Africa. The majority of Botha's own followers were disinclined to take up arms against the Teutons. Even the Boers who were not willing to co-operate with the Germans in attacking British settlers were averse from letting any Boer blood be shed in the interests of the British Empire. Had General Botha been content to be merely the index to Boer sentiment, he would have tried to keep South Africa out of the war, and to prevent both loyalists and traitors from involving the Union in a conflict. But, as we have seen, Botha was not a follower of public opinion, but a director of the popular mind. When he saw that a majority of his countrymen were tending in the wrong direction, he rallied them by a magnificent stand for the honour, the true interests, and the right development of South Africa. On his own responsibility he entered into an agreement with the Imperial Government for the withdrawal of the Imperial troops, and undertook that the South Africans would out of their own resources launch an expedition into German territory.

General Botha was well aware of the intrigues going on about him. He did not suspect that the Commandant-General of the Union was a complete traitor, but he knew that he and various other men of position were hesitating over the course which they should adopt. So he gave a clear, bold, resolute lead, calculated to bring the domestic situation at once to a crisis that could immediately be dealt with. He revealed his plan on the opening of Parliament on September 9th, 1914. He moved a resolution to convey an address to King George, assuring him of the loyal support of the Union, and of the determination of the

Botha's bold and resolute lead

South Africans to co-operate in maintaining the security and integrity of the Empire. His speech, already touched upon in Chapter XXXVI., was something more than a challenge : it was a declaration of war against the pro-German party.

It must be remembered that he was speaking to men of a race of born fighters, whose minds were still deeply coloured by the tragic events of a long and terrible campaign, in which they had been overpowered by the superior numbers and superior organisation of their traditional opponents. As an example of the literature of power, his words are of high historic interest. After relating the agreement made with the Imperial Government for the invasion of German South-West Africa, General Botha said :

" To forget their loyalty to the Empire in this hour of trial would be scandalous and shameful, and would blacken South Africa in the eyes of the whole world. Of this South Africans were incapable. They had endured some of the greatest sacrifices that could be demanded of a people, but they had always kept before them ideals, founded on Christianity, and never in their darkest days had they sought to gain their ends by treasonable means. The path of treason was an unknown path to Dutch and English alike.

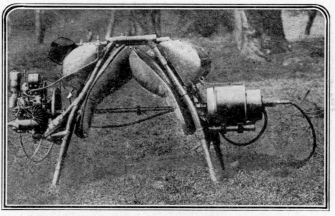

A MARCONI OUTFIT FOR MOUNTED CONVEYANCE.
Two of these sets of wireless for mounted conveyance, with equipment and operators, were offered by the Marconi Company to General Botha to present to the force under Brigadier-General Duncan Mackenzie. They were accepted, and proved of great value.

SOUTH AFRICA'S PATRIOTIC PREMIER TAKES THE FIELD.

One of the brightest features of the war in Africa was the splendid stand of General Botha against German aggression and Back-Veldt disaffection. He told his countrymen that to forget their loyalty to the Empire would blacken South Africa in the eyes of the whole world, and declared that the path of treason was an unknown path to Dutch and English alike. He then took the field in person.

"Their duty and their conscience alike bade them be faithful and true to the Imperial Government in all respects in this hour of darkness and trouble. That was the attitude of the Union Government; that was the attitude of the people of South Africa. The Government had cabled to the Imperial Government at the outbreak of war, offering to undertake the defence of South Africa, thereby releasing the Imperial troops for service elsewhere. This was accepted, and the Union Defence Force was mobilised."

In answer to this speech, General Hertzog moved an amendment to the effect that any act that would lead to an attack on German territory in South Africa would conflict with the interests of the Union and the Empire. In the speeches moved by members of the Hertzog party in support of this amendment doubts were cast on the justice of the British cause, bitter personal attacks were made on General Botha, and memories of the South African War were revived with a view to provoking racial hatred.

General Botha's Government, however, won a decisive victory by a majority of ninety-two votes against twelve votes. Of the seventeen members from the Free State, which was the Hertzog stronghold, only nine, including General Hertzog himself, voted for the amendment, and one of the nine afterwards recanted publicly.

Beyers' letter of resignation

So deep and widespread was the effect of the speeches of Generals Botha and Smuts that the leaders of the revolt became desperate. General Beyers, having more courage than General Hertzog, immediately took action. Parliament rose on Monday, September 14th, and on the following day Beyers wrote a letter of resignation of his position of Commandant-General of the Defence Force. The letter was written the day before it was dated, and a copy was given for immediate publication, so that it would be read by the people before the original letter reached General Botha and General Smuts in Cape Town. But by means of the Press censorship the Government prevented the publication of the letter until September 21st, when it was published together with the reply of General Smuts as Minister of Defence.

The letter of Beyers was not a mere resignation of his office and rank, but a practical declaration of war against the British Empire. It ran as follows:

Pretoria, September 15th.

Honourable Sir,—You are aware that during the month of August last I told you and General Botha by word of mouth that I disapproved of the sending of commandos to German South-West Africa for the purpose of conquering that territory. I was on the point then of resigning, but, hearing that Parliament would be called together, I decided to wait, hoping that a way out of the difficulty would be found. To my utmost surprise, however, Parliament confirmed the resolution adopted by the Government, namely, to conquer German South-West Africa without any provocation towards the Union from the Germans. The Government must be aware that by far the great majority of the Dutch-speaking people of the Union decidedly disapproved of our crossing the frontier, and that two conferences of commandants recently held at Pretoria bore eloquent testimony to this. I challenge the Government by an appeal to the people, without making use of compulsion, to obtain another result.

A challenge to the Government

It is said that Great Britain has taken part in the war for the sake of right and justice in order to protect the independence of smaller nations, and to comply with treaties. But the fact that three Ministers of the British Cabinet have resigned shows that even in England there is a strong minority who cannot be convinced of the righteousness of a war with Germany. History teaches us, after all, that whenever it suits her interests Great Britain is always ready to protect smaller nations; but, unhappily, history also relates instances in which the sacred rights of independence of smaller nations have been violated and treaties disregarded by that same Empire.

In proof of this I have only to indicate how the independence of the South African Republic and Orange Free State was violated, and of what weight the Sand River Convention was. It is said that war is being waged against the barbarity of the Germans. I have forgiven, but not forgotten, all the barbarities perpetrated in this our own country during the South African War. With very few exceptions all farms—not to mention many towns—were so many Louvains, of which we now hear so much. At this critical moment it is made known in Parliament that our Government was granted a loan of £7,000,000 by the British Government. This is very significant. Anyone can have his own thoughts about this. In the absence of legitimate grounds for the annexation

R   141

policy of the Government, you endeavour to intimidate the public by declaring that Government possesses information showing that Germany has decided, should opportunity arise, to annex South Africa.

My humble opinion is that this will be hastened if from our side we invade German territory without having been provoked thereto by the Germans. And as to the alleged German annexation scheme,

The alleged German scheme

this is nothing more than the result of the usual national suspicion attending such matters. The allegations made in Parliament —namely, that the Germans have already violated our frontier—are ungrounded. See the official report of the Information Bureau, corroborated by Lieutenant-Colonel Maritz and his officers, who are on and near the frontier.

Apparently Government longed for some transgression by the Germans of German South-West Africa, but have been disappointed in this, for so far not a single German soldier has crossed our frontier. As you know very well, the report is perfectly correct regarding an involuntary transgression of the frontier some time ago and the tendering of an apology for so doing. Whatever may happen in South Africa, the war will be decided in Europe in any case; so if Germany triumphs and should decide to attack us, then, even if Great Britain should be unable to help us, we shall at least have a sacred and clean cause in defending our country to the utmost, provided we stay inside our borders meanwhile. In case we are attacked our people will arise as one man in defence of its rights.

Besides, I am convinced that a commando of about 8,000 Germans, as at present stationed in German territory, will not be so foolish as to attempt an attack on our country. I have always said, and repeated at Booysens recently, that if the Union is attacked, Boer

A BIVOUAC IN THE ARID SOUTH-WEST AFRICAN SAND WASTES.
In their advance in German South-West Africa the Union forces had to cross country described as a heart-numbing ocean of soft white sand billows, rising in places to a height of one thousand feet or more. Our photograph shows troops in bivouac after a period of weary "sand-jamming" over this dry and dusty country.

and Briton will defend this country side by side, and in such case I will deem it a great honour and privilege to take up my place at the head of our forces in defence of my Fatherland. I accepted the post of Commandant-General under our Defence Act, the first section of which provides that our forces can only be employed in defence of the Union. My humble opinion is that this section cannot thus be changed by informal resolution in Parliament, such being contrary to Parliamentary procedure. So the Defence Act does not allow us to go and fetch the enemy over the frontier and to light the fire in this way, but should the enemy penetrate into our country it will be our duty to drive him back and pursue him in his own territory.

In his speech General Botha speaks about the help we had from the Belgians and French after the South African War. That assistance is still appreciated by us and by all our people, but we must not forget that the Germans also were not behindhand and have always been well disposed towards us. So why should we deliberately make enemies of them ? As circumstances are, I see no way of taking the offensive, and as I sincerely love my country and people, I must strongly protest against the sending of the Union Citizen Forces over the frontier. Who can foretell when the fire the Government has decided to light shall end ? For the reasons enumerated above I feel constrained to resign my post as Commandant-General, as also my commissioned rank. For me this is the only way of faith, duty, and honour towards our people,

of which mention was made by General Botha, I have always tried to do my duty according to my best convictions, and it sorely grieves me that it must end in this way.—I have, etc.,
(Signed)   C. G. L. BEYERS.

To this treacherous letter, with its calculated appeal to racial animosity, General Smuts made a telling, historic reply :

Pretoria, September 19th.

Sir,—It was with regret that I received your letter of the 15th inst., tendering your resignation as the Commandant-General, Union Defence Forces, and as an officer of the Union. The circumstances under which that resignation took place and the terms in which you endeavour to justify your action tend to leave a very painful impression.

It is true that it was known to me that you entertained objections against the war operations in German South-West Africa, but I never received the impression that you would resign. On the contrary, all the information in possession of the Government was communicated to you, all plans were discussed with you, and your advice was followed to a large extent. The principal officers were appointed on your recommendation and with your concurrence, and the plan of operations which is now being followed is largely the one recommended by yourself at a conference of officers.

My last instructions to you before I left for Cape Town to attend the special session of Parliament were that in my absence you should visit certain regiments on the German border, and it was well understood between us that immediately the war operations were somewhat further advanced and co-operation among the various divisions would be practicable, you should yourself undertake the chief command in German South-West Africa.

The attitude of the Government after this remained unchanged, and was approved by Parliament after full discussion. One would have expected that that approval would make the matter easier for you, but now I find that you anticipated that Parliament would disapprove of the policy of the Government, and that your disappointment in this became the reason for your unexpected action. In order to make your motives clearer, the reasons for your resignation were explained in a long political argument, which was immediately communicated to the Press and came into the hands of the Government long after publication.

I need not tell you that all these circumstances in connection with your resignation have made a most unpleasant impression on my colleagues and myself. But this unpleasant impression has even been aggravated by the allegations contained in your letter. Your bitter attack on Great Britain is not only entirely baseless, but is the more unjustifiable coming as it does in the midst of a great war from the Commandant-General of one of the British Dominions. Your reference to barbarous acts during the South African War cannot justify the criminal devastation of Belgium, and can only be calculated to sow hatred and division among the people of South Africa.

You forgot to mention that since the South African War the British people gave South Africa her entire freedom under a Constitution which makes it possible for us to realise our national ideals along our own lines, and which, for instance, allows you to write with impunity a letter for which you would without doubt be liable in the German Empire to the extreme penalty.

As regards your other statements, they have been answered and disposed of in Parliament. From these discussions it will be apparent that neither the British Empire nor South Africa was the aggressor in this struggle. War was in the first instance declared by Austria-Hungary, and thereafter by Germany, under circumstances in which the

General Smuts' historic reply

British Government employed its utmost powers to maintain the peace of Europe and to safeguard the neutrality of Belgium.

So far as we ourselves are concerned, our coast is threatened, our mail boats are arrested, and our borders are invaded by the enemy. This latter does not occur, as you say, in an involuntary manner and with an apology, which latter, at any rate, was never tendered to the Government.

Under these circumstances it is absurd to speak about aggressive action on the part of the Union, seeing that, together with the British Empire, we have been drawn against our wish and will and entirely in self-defence into this war. As regards your insinuation concerning the loan of £7,000,000 which the British Government

SOUTH AFRICAN TROOPERS ATTEND A CHURCH SERVICE BEFORE JOINING IN THE PURSUIT OF THE REBELS.
An animated scene outside the Dutch Reformed Church at Pretoria where a special service was held prior to the departure of the troops in pursuit of Beyers and De Wet. One of the officers is accompanied by a lady, evidently a privileged relative anxious to be by his side as long as possible.

BRITISH FORCE ENTERING GERMAN SOUTH-WEST AFRICA AT A POINT NEAR RAMAN'S DRIFT.
Shortly after the above photograph was taken there was a skirmish, as the result of which the enemy were driven from their positions. The nature of the ground and the conditions of the atmosphere are indicated by the rising dust, though the pace at which the troops were moving was a slow one.

THE MOTOR CHASE OF CHRISTIAN DE WET.
Special motor-car squadron of the Union forces passing through Vryburg. They played a most active part in the pursuit of Christian de Wet, and were especially praised by General Smuts.

CAPTURED AT LAST.
General de Wet knocking the ashes from his pipe on the mudguard of the motor-car in which he was conveyed part of the way to Johannesburg.

was kind enough to grant us, and for which the public of the Union, as evidenced recently in Parliament, are most grateful, it is of such a despicable nature that there is no necessity to make any comment thereon. It only shows to what extent your mind has been obscured by political bias.

You speak about duty and honour. My conviction is that the people of South Africa will in these dark days, when the Government as well as the people of South Africa are put to the supreme test, have a clearer conception of duty and honour than is to be deduced from your letter and action. For the Dutch-speaking section in particular I cannot conceive anything more fatal and humiliating than a policy of lip loyalty in fair weather and of a policy of neutrality and pro-German sentiment in days of storm and stress.

It may be that our peculiar internal circumstances and our backward condition after the Great War will place a limit on what we can do, but nevertheless I am convinced that the people will support the Government in carrying out the mandate of Parliament, and in this manner, which is the only legitimate one, fulfil their

duty to South Africa and to the Empire, and maintain their dearly-won honour unblemished for the future.

Your resignation is hereby accepted.

(Signed)   J. C. SMUTS.

But before this correspondence was published General Beyers made his first open stroke against the Government and failed. He had been actively engaged in organising rebellion weeks before he resigned his command. In the plan of operations which he drew up for the Government, and through the officers he appointed to carry out these pretended plans, he was treacherously arranging a large concerted scheme of operations in which the German force was to take part. His chief difficulty was to win over General Delarey, the leader of the Boers of the Western Transvaal. About a thousand armed Boers of Delarey's district were encamped at Potchefstroom, and as General Delarey returned from Cape Town on September 15th, **How Delarey was** he met General Beyers and **shot** arranged to motor with him that night and visit the camp of the Boers of the Western Transvaal.

The two generals left Pretoria by motor-car about seven o'clock in the evening, and took the road that led them through the mining city of Johannesburg. It happened that a gang of bandits, known as the Jackson gang, had been terrorising for several days the Witwatersrand Reef committing burglaries, and shooting at sight any one who interfered with them. On the afternoon of September 15th they had been traced to a house in the suburbs by some detectives; but on an attempt being made to arrest them, they shot dead one of the detectives and escaped in a motor-car. The armed police patrols were then ordered out on all the highways leading to Johannesburg, and instructed to stop and examine all motor-cars, and fire at once if their challenge were ignored. After nightfall a motor-car resembling that of the Jackson gang was

REBELS ON THEIR WAY TO PRISON.
Men of General de Wet's rebel commando being escorted
through Vryburg by mounted loyalists, on their way to captivity.

PIET DE WET GIVING INFORMATION.
Christian de Wet's loyalist brother Piet, telling Colonel Brits how his brother looted his
horses. The loyalists wore white armlets.

challenged at the east end of the city, as it went
along at high speed with a powerful headlight.
Again it was challenged twice as it flashed
through the western end of the town. For a
fourth time it was challenged by the western
boundary. One of the policemen then fired at
the wheel of the car in order to disable it, but
the bullet ricochetted and struck General Delarey,
killing him instantly. Almost at the same time
a well-known doctor on the East Rand, Dr. Grace,
was shot dead by the eastern boundary by the
police while travelling in another car resembling
that of the Jackson gang.

Probably the reason why General Beyers did
not answer the challenges of the armed patrol was
that he thought his plot had been discovered, and
that he was to be arrested for treason. As a
matter of fact, both Generals Botha and Smuts
were unsuspicious of his immediate purpose.

The plot at Potchefstroom Beyers had intended to start
the rebellion with the thousand
men in Potchefstroom Camp,
who had just come in from their
three weeks' training. Colonel Kemp had won
over their officers, and these had harangued the
troops that morning on parade, and had urged
them to refuse to volunteer for German South-West Africa.
All loyalists who objected were jeered at, and Kemp
collected what ammunition he could lay hands upon,
storing it in his tent. In the afternoon the loyalists
sent a warning message to General Smuts by a native runner,
while the conspirators gathered in a house in Berg Street and
sat there all night waiting for the sound of Beyers's car.
Beyers's plan was to confront General Delarey with the
accomplished fact of the opening of the rebellion in the
Western Transvaal, and by shock tactics to win him over
to the rebels.

But the death of Delarey completely unnerved and
cowed the arch-traitor. No doubt he wondered if the shot
had been meant for him, and if he would be arrested and
put on his trial. All night he waited in extreme anxiety,

doubtful whether to hush everything up, or to go to Potchefstroom and fight to the death. At three o'clock in the
morning he telephoned to his fellow-conspirators, reporting
the accident to Delarey, and explaining that he could not
come. There was something like a panic amid the plotters,
and dawn broke without the Vierkleur, the old Transvaal
flag, floating over Potchefstroom.

Colonel Kemp, who had sent in his resignation at the
same time as General Beyers, was so frightened that he
withdrew his resignation. Over the grave of Delarey,
and in the presence of General Botha, Beyers, lying to save
himself, proclaimed that he had no intention of causing or
advising rebellion. Yet the next day the forsworn traitor,
acting with General de Wet and other conspirators, held a
meeting at Lichtenburg, where Delarey had lived and

had exercised wide authority, and tried to win over the country people—the country Boers who had come to the funeral of their dead leader. Beyers and De Wet began by condemning in violent language the policy of General Botha. Then they went on to create a sort of mutiny by passive resistance; for they advocated that all their fellow-countrymen serving in the Defence Force should refuse to go on active service if the commandos were called out in accordance with the Defence Act.

Botha's call for volunteers

At this time none of the loyal Dutchmen would admit that Beyers and De Wet were engaged in any intrigue against the Union. At most it was thought that they were striving with General Hertzog to overthrow the Botha Cabinet, by making the utmost difficulties over the intended campaign against German South-West Africa. Had the Prime Minister let things drift, the conspirators would soon have organised a strong party on their new policy of passive resistance, and would then have suddenly swept most of their supporters into a plan of open rebellion by means of some dangerous incident. But General Botha was well

THE LEADER OF THE REVOLT IN THE ORANGE RIVER COLONY.
General Christian de Wet (in centre) ; a photograph taken just after his capture. He headed the rebellion in the Orange River Colony on October 21st, 1914, and surrendered at Waterburg on December 1st.

aware of the perils of the situation. The old generalissimo of the Boer forces kept to his plan of audacious and quick action, with a view to forcing a solution of the issue and compelling the conspirators to cease conspiring or take the field.

On the day when Beyers and De Wet began to preach their subtle scheme of passive resistance, General Botha called for volunteers, and announced that he would lead the South Africans against the Germans in person. By this brilliant masterstroke he rallied the whole British population and a large majority of the Dutch to the support of the Government. By his gift for grasping difficult situations and doing the thing that carried people with him, he turned the position of his opponents. To the men who had been his commandants in the former war his return to the battlefield was a flaming challenge, and stilled all doubts. The vehement activity of their old leader was a heartening influence, compared with which the underground intrigues of the hesitating rebel leaders were of no avail.

His speech on this occasion was a finer effort of persuasion and direction than his Cape Town declaration. He spoke at Bank to five thousand of his own people, among whom was a strong commando of burghers. The Prime Minister

asked his constituents to speak out freely and straight-forwardly. He wanted to know once and for all what was the good of talking as some people did and trying to create hostility against Great Britain. That could only provoke ill-feeling between Briton and Boer. Neutrality for South Africa was an utter impossibility. If a German warship came to Durban and imposed a levy of five millions on them, it would help them very little to say they were neutral. Would it be noble or honest to act as some people suggested that South Africa should act after the undertakings they had given in the past ? What would hostility to Great Britain mean to South Africa ? Ruin !

He was animated by a true and sincere love of his people, and yielded to no man in his patriotism to South Africa, and he wished them to understand clearly that there were only two courses open—the one that of loyalty and help, and the other that of disloyalty and treason. There was no middle course, and whoever said there was was trying to mislead them. Now, which course did they intend taking ? They must give him a straightforward answer. (Loud cries : " We want the loyal course. You have done the right thing.")

General Botha said he had information regarding German ambitions concerning South Africa which would make their hair stand on end. The fact of the matter was, General Botha declared, amid tremendous cheers, that the Kaiser wanted to go down to posterity as a second Napoleon. Incidentally he wanted a place to which to send Germany's surplus population, and South Africa appealed to him as a suitable place. German agents with their seditious talk were already doing a great deal of harm in South Africa. Surely the Government was there not to shirk responsibility, but to take responsibility, and to give the people a lead. People who shirked were people of no significance. The stain of treason had never touched South Africans, and would not now. To-day South Africa must prove to the British Empire, which was watching them, that they were worthy, and still more worthy, of trust. By doing so they would create for themselves a greater future than would ever otherwise be possible.

General Botha emphasised the importance of the gathering. He wanted them to speak with no uncertain voice. Their decision would have great influence throughout South Africa, and would go forth to the whole Empire. (Cries of " We support you.") Though the Dutch South African could not be expected to be so enthusiastic as the British South African, still he was loyal, and they did not want lip loyalists or fair-weather patriots. The people they wanted must be true patriots, men willing to do something and to make sacrifices. " The British Government must be able to look straight into our eyes and see what is in our minds." (Great cheering lasting several minutes.)

Lip loyalists not wanted

General Botha then referred directly to General Beyers. He said he was grieved that his old comrade, with whom he had gone through the South African war, should have taken up such an attitude. He had shaken the discipline of the Defence Force. He had issued a letter which was simply a political manifesto, evil in its effect, and by his conduct had greatly hurt him.

TEAM OF FORTY OXEN DRAWING A BRITISH GUN IN GERMAN SOUTH-WEST AFRICA.

General Botha continued : " But in all these difficulties I realise that God rules and will inspire the people to do what is right. Knowing and believing this, I said I shall assume responsibility and take command—(prolonged cheers)—and I ask you to strengthen my hands so that justice may be supreme." (Renewed cheers.)

After paying a moving tribute to General Delarey, General Botha said in conclusion that he wanted to serve his people. His time here might not be long, his hair was growing grey, and his health was not good, but he would continue to the end to do what he thought was in the true interest of the nation. In the past they had a clean and noble history ; let them continue so ; let there be no treason ; let them stand by the Government.

For some weeks the conspirators made no outward sign of their intention to take the field against General Botha and General Smuts. But Beyers, at least, was secretly acting in a vigorous manner against the constitutional Government of the Union. On September 26th a small force of South African Rifles, with a section of the Transvaal Horse Artillery, under Colonel Grant, was operating at Sandfontein by the German border. They had marched to a water-hole, through a narrow defile, into a valley surrounded by kopjes. Here both rifles and artillery were trapped by a couple of German battalions, who placed their guns on the ring of heights dominating the saucerlike basin in which the water-hole lay. The South African gunners fought till every man of both gun crews was either killed or wounded, and their ammunition had run out. Then, when the guns were put out of action by our men to render them useless to the enemy, the gallant little body of Britons and Boers surrendered.

Trapped by the Germans

The high-explosive shells from ten German guns on the surrounding kopjes wrought most of the slaughter. General Lukin, who had vainly tried to relieve the little trapped force, remarked at the time that no blame attached to Colonel Grant, who had fallen wounded into the hands of the enemy. It was afterwards discovered that the disaster had been brought about by the treachery of a Boer leader, who had been placed by General Beyers in command of the Union forces in the north-west territory. The traitor was Lieutenant-Colonel S. G. Maritz. He had distinguished himself in the South African War, and had then served under the Germans in the Herero campaign, but he came back in the guise of a loyalist, professing a detestation of his Teutonic neighbours. There was no doubt that he had been won over by a large sum of money, and the suspicion of him was so common that had it not been for the influence Beyers exerted on his behalf, he would never have been appointed to an important command on the German frontier. It was he who arranged that Colonel Grant's force should be trapped and slaughtered at Sandfontein, and as soon as this was suspected General Smuts ordered the traitor to give up his command and to report himself to headquarters. Maritz thereupon issued an impudent ultimatum, dated October 8th, in which he demanded to meet General Hertzog, General de Wet, General Beyers, Kemp, and Müller. He stated that if he were not allowed to receive instructions from these men he would attack Colonel Brits's force and invade the Union. He added that, in addition to his own troops, he had German guns and German soldiers, and that he had signed an agreement with the Governor of German South-West Africa, ceding Walfish Bay and other portions of the Union territory in return for a guarantee of the independence of the South African Republic.

Maritz won over by money

General Botha's reply was a proclamation of martial law throughout the Union. Maritz had arrested all his officers and men who were unwilling to join the Germans, and had sent them as prisoners into German territory. Colonel Brits, with the Imperial Light Horse, at once flung himself on the traitor, and the civil war opened on October 15th with an engagement at Ratedraai, ten miles

SOUTH AFRICAN TROOPS MOVING OFF IN THE ARDUOUS PURSUIT OF CHRISTIAN DE WET.

THE LAST CROSSING: TRAGIC END OF THE REBEL BEYERS WHILE TRYING TO CROSS THE VAAL RIVER.

General Beyers, who led the revolt in the Western Transvaal, met with a terrible end. Having divided his party into two groups, he fled with one of these in the direction of the Vaal. At daybreak on December 9th, 1914, they were trapped in the angle between the Zandspruit and the Vaal, and after a sharp fight Beyers, who was wounded, tried to swim his horse across the river. He and his companions were fired on, and it was seen that Beyers fell from his horse, but managed to grasp another animal by the tail. He was heard to cry for help, but was drowned before anybody was able to rescue him. In the above drawing he is seen in the water, with a guide who was shot. Near the river bank the remnant of Beyers' followers are holding up their hands in token of surrender.

SOLDIERS OF BRITISH
BORNEO IN KHAKI UNIFORM.

wounded, and fled into
German territory. Two
days afterwards some of the
rebels with German gunners
were again defeated at
Kakamas. Maritz fell into
disgrace with his German
masters, who began to suspect he was ready to reverse
the rôle he had played at
Sandfontein, and lead German troops into a trap in
the hope of being able in
this manner to make peace
with the South African
Government.

A TYPICAL FIJIAN IN
NATIVE DRESS.

The way in which Maritz's operations were defeated was
extremely significant. Colonel Van de Venter, with one
Staff officer, went to the town of Calvinia, in Northern Cape
Colony. He called for loyalists to come out on commando
for the sake of the honour and good name of the Dutch.
In a few days there were two thousand men ready to take
the field. Many of them were fathers and brothers of the
rebels. Under Colonel Van de Venter they co-operated
with the Imperial Light Horse and the
Transvaal Horse, under Colonel Brits,
and beat Maritz over the German
frontier.

A sinister silence

Meanwhile a friend of General Botha and General Hertzog
tried to get the two leaders to co-operate to end the revolt
of Maritz. There can be little doubt that if General
Hertzog had at once publicly repudiated the action of the
traitor, the disruptive warlike movement among the
Dutch would have been checked. But General Hertzog
and Mr. Steyn, the former President of the Orange Free
State, after closely consulting together, refused to denounce
the rebellion. General Smuts even allowed Beyers afterwards to pass through the lines of the Government forces,
and spend a night at Mr. Steyn's house outside Bloem-
fontein, with a view to giving the ex-President an opportunity of bringing the arch-traitor to his senses. But
both General Botha and Mr. Steyn continued to maintain

south of Upington, in
which seventy rebels
were taken prisoners.
On October 22nd Maritz
attacked the post of
Keimos, between Kaka-
mas and Upington.
There were only 150
loyalists at Keimos, and
Maritz had 1,000 rebels
and 70 German gunners.
He advanced at dawn,
but the small garrison
held out till reinforce-
ments arrived, and then
the rebels were so
severely handled that
Maritz offered to surren-
der if a free pardon were
granted. He was

a sinister silence at a time when a few strong words from them
would have prevented Dutchmen from shedding Dutch blood.

General Smuts, in a speech at Johannesburg, made a
direction allusion to the overtures which went on for a
fortnight after Maritz's ultimatum. " The rebels had their
own leaders, leaders to whom the people looked, and the
Government were anxious to give these leaders every chance
to show their patriotism and their powers of leadership
in this great crisis. Efforts were being
made, very serious efforts, by very important gentlemen to see whether it was
not possible to bring the rebellion to
a close without bloodshed." This was a plain reference to
General Hertzog and Mr. Steyn, and the refusal of these two
men to do what they could to prevent the rebellion from
spreading entailed on them a passive responsibility for
subsequent events.

Hertzog and Steyn

It was General Hertzog who, for two years, had set
Beyers and De Wet in jealous opposition to General Botha
and General Smuts. It was General Hertzog who had created
the intense personal malevolence with which De Wet
regarded his former companions-in-arms. De Wet
had never reconciled himself to the advantages
which Botha and Smuts had won over him.
Starting, like himself, as simple farmers, they had
become the leaders of a great nation, while he,
after an unsuccessful term of office as Minister of
Agriculture, had retired into the obscurity of the
back veldt. Thus there was a deep feeling of bitterness in his mind, upon which General Hertzog
was able to act, when trying to organise a party
strong enough to overturn the Botha Cabinet.
Then Beyers came along, with a plan for open
warlike action that caught the fancy of De Wet.
The famous old guerilla captain seems to have fancied

MEN OF THE FIJIAN CONTINGENT ON PARADE.

SOME OF THE MAORIS WHO VOLUNTEERED FOR SERVICE IN EGYPT.

that General Hertzog was behind the movement of rebellion, and being already himself compromised by Maritz's reference to him, he gathered a commando, and broke out in revolt on October 21st, 1914. He invaded Vrede, a town in the Northern Free State, and there he issued an amazing manifesto, in which he said :

" I signed the Vereeniging Treaty, and swore to be faithful to the British flag, but we have been so downtrodden by the miserable and pestilential English that we can endure it no longer. His Majesty King Edward VII. promised to protect us, but he has failed to do so, and has allowed a magistrate to be placed over us (he is one of the miserable and pestilential English) who is an absolute tyrant, and has made it impossible for us to tolerate it longer. I was charged before him with beating a native boy. I only did it with a small shepherd's whip, and for that I was fined five shillings."

This wildly ridiculous statement of the grounds of rebellion was a fair measure of De Wet's capacity for politics. The Vrede magistrate, " the absolute tyrant," who fined De Wet the sum of five shillings for an assault to which he had pleaded guilty, was a brother-in-law of Mr. Steyn, the former President of the Orange Free State. He had been appointed to his position at Vrede by General Hertzog, largely through the influence of Mr. Steyn. His act in fining De Wet a small sum for ill-treating a native boy **De Wet's motive for rebellion** was something less than justice—it was rather a favour to the fierce old Boer general. To start a great rebellion on such a ground was farcical. But, at the same time, De Wet, though ridiculous, was at least honest. For instead of trying to trump up a high-sounding case against the Union Government and the Imperial authorities, he frankly stated that his only cause of discontent was the slight measure of protection given by a magistrate to a black boy. His manifesto greatly helped to save the Union. It was believed at the time that two-thirds of the population in the Free State were either lukewarm or ready to rebel. In the Transvaal one-third of the population, drawn mainly from the Western Transvaal, were in a similar condition of ferment. But few of

GENERAL GODLEY ADDRESSING THE MAORIS UNDER HIS COMMAND. INSET: CAPT. PITT, A MAORI OFFICER.

them were willing to rise in arms because De Wet had been fined five shillings for beating a black boy, and though Beyers at once acted with De Wet, and tried to remedy matters by a more high-flown proclamation, the movement did not increase in a formidable way.

Three members of the Union Parliament came out in arms, and a member of the Defence Council, Mr. Wessel-Wessels, went over to the rebels, together with several ministers belonging to the seceders from the Dutch Reformed Church. The rebel leaders had about 10,000 men in detached groups in the Western Transvaal and the Northern Free State. In their original plan, Beyers, De Wet, and Kemp were to converge with

MAORI CHIEFS. TOP PHOTOGRAPH: MEN OF THE SAME VIRILE RACE TAKING PART IN A WAR-DANCE AT AUCKLAND BEFORE THEIR DEPARTURE FOR EGYPT.

their commandos, effect a junction, and then march westward and join with a force under Maritz from German South-West Africa. The Germans arranged to bring the artillery and ammunition, in which the rebels were deficient. After being properly munitioned, organised, and reinforced by some thousands of German troops, the rebel army was to march on Pretoria.

From a military point of view the situation was a serious one. Politically, however, the position of the rebels was very weak. For the traitors had completed failed to make the right sort of appeal to the fanatical section of their countrymen. Had it not been for the remarkable influence exercised by the prophecies of Van Rensburg over the back-veldt Boers, Beyers and De Wet would have made a feebler show of force than they did.

All the genius in statesmanship and the power of passionate appeal resided in the Government party. The extraordinary personal influence

TYPES OF MAORI WARRIORS IN BRITISH UNIFORMS.

of Botha and the energy and resource of Smuts enabled them to command the situation. In a few weeks they had 40,000 men in the field. Of these a few thousand were part of the little army sent to occupy the coast towns of German South-West Africa, and recalled when the rebellion broke out. But by far the larger number were commandos of burghers, who came forth to fight their own kith and kin for the sake of an Empire against which they had been fighting only twelve years previously side by side with the same kith and kin.

The strain on the loyal Boers was appalling. In the course of the campaign complaints were made here and there by South Africans of British stock that they were bidden to hold their fire—while the rebels were shooting them down—to the last moment. There is no doubt that the Dutch generals and commandants were anxious to spare the lives of their own kinsmen. The loyal Boers themselves often remained for a long time under fire without shooting in reply, in the hope that the rebels would be surrounded and forced to surrender. The loyalists of both races at times suffered heavy casualties, owing to the forbearing way in which they conducted their operations. But the blood that the Boer and Briton shed side by side in the common cause of honour was worth shedding. Their comrades, who often fell while holding back their fire, were something higher even than heroes in a righteous fight. They were martyrs for the Union. They died so that the two white races of South Africa should grow into one nation, united by a common tradition of self-sacrifice and of forbearance in the hour of victory.

The rebels were never able to link up their forces. General Botha proved that he still retained the qualities by which he had won the chief command in the old days. He never gave the traitors a moment's rest. General Beyers with his commando was acting round Rustenburg on Tuesday, October 27th. General Botha in person came up in the morning and drove the rebels in headlong rout the whole day.

By October 29th Beyers was a fugitive, and some of his scattered commandos were defeated southward at Lichtenburg by Colonel Alberts. There was another action at Zuitpansdrift on November 5th, in which the rebels were again scattered. By this time the rebellion in the Western Transvaal was practically crushed. Kemp, who had been

NEW ZEALANDERS IN EGYPT. WASHING-UP AFTER DINNER.

acting with Beyers, now separated, and moved with the larger force westward towards German South-West Africa, pursued by Colonel Alberts. Beyers, with a commando, tried to get into touch with De Wet, and leaving the Transvaal at Bloemhof, he crossed the Vaal River and entered the Orange Free State. He was pursued by a strong loyalist force under Colonel Lemmer. Colonel Lemmer attacked Beyers's commando near the Vet River on November 7th. The engagement occurred south-east of the Bloemhof diamond diggings, and though Beyers in person led the rebels, he was heavily defeated, three hundred and sixty-four of his men being captured, and some twenty killed and wounded. Most of the fugitives went on to Hoopstad, from which town Beyers tried to join De Wet.

By this time the poorly-organised forces that De Wet had collected in the northern districts of the Orange Free State were the only source of anxiety to the South African Government. But every centre of **Rebels in the Orange Free State** revolt had been masked by strong Union forces, concentrated with remarkable speed and secrecy by General Botha. For some days negotiations went on between De Wet and other Free State leaders, while the Government refrained from action in the hope of avoiding more bloodshed. De Wet, however, was too much inflated with pride in his own talent for war to lay down his

arms. The world-wide fame which he had won in the old days as a guerilla captain inclined him to overestimate his ability, and to underestimate that of General Botha. If his rival had been commander-in-chief of the forces of the Transvaal in the old days, he, De Wet, had been commander-in-chief of the forces of the Orange Free State. And he still thought himself the more skilful fighter. Nothing but the stern ordeal of battle could bring him to his senses. **The battle at Marquard**

He opened his campaign on November 7th by an action at Winburg, in which by superior numbers he managed to defeat a small loyalist commando under Cronje. One of his sons was killed in the fight. Then came the main battle between General Botha and General de Wet in person. It took place on November 12th at Marquard, about twenty-four miles east of Winburg. General Botha had arrived at Winburg the day before with his Transvaal commando, and by a splendid forced night march he came up with the forces of the rebel leader, and surrounded them in a north-eastern and easterly direction. At the same time Colonel Brandt, with another commando, also marched from Winburg towards Hoenderkop, where the men under De Wet were hemmed in. Then General Lukin and Colonel Brits moved from the west in order to complete the envelopment of the enemy.

If the operations had been carried out on the time-table drawn up by General Botha, the entire forces of De Wet would have been captured. But General Lukin and Colonel Brits were not able to take up their position at the appointed time. Meanwhile General Botha's commando attacked the rebels and defeated them with great loss, while Colonel Brandt also closed in on them. It was a smashing victory. The entire laager of De Wet was captured, with its stores of food and munitions, and a hundred carts, waggons, and motorcars. In addition, two hundred and fifty prisoners were taken.

De Wet fled up the Vet River, with a strong Boer commando pursuing him. Then he turned south, where the pursuit was continued by another loyal commando. The

NEWS FROM HOME.
A New Zealand trooper gets news from his far-away home. The charger by his side seems equally interested.

rebel leader at Boshof divided his diminishing force into two divisions. With one of these he doubled back north, and reached the Vaal River with only twenty-five men out of the two thousand he had commanded at the Battle of Marquard. He was beaten back by a loyal outpost, but on November 21st he got across the Vaal,

SIR GEORGE REID, HIGH COMMISSIONER FOR AUSTRALIA, INSPECTING A CONTINGENT FROM THE GREAT ISLAND CONTINENT.

AUSTRALIAN LIGHT HORSE RETURNING TO CAMP AFTER BREAKING IN REMOUNTS FOR ACTIVE SERVICE.

INSPECTION OF CANADA'S FIRST CONTINGENT PRIOR TO EMBARKATION.
The Duke of Connaught is passing down the lines.   Top centre : His Royal Highness leaving the parade ground after
the inspection.

THE AUSTRALIAN CONTINGENT ON THE SOIL OF THE MOTHERLAND.
Stalwart sons of Australia marching past the saluting point during an inspection at Romsey, Hampshire, by Sir
George Reid, the High Commissioner, before leaving for active service.

MAJOR-GENERAL SAM HUGHES ADDRESS
A scene at Toronto, the "City of Homes," as
assembly was composed of m

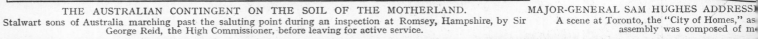

AUSTRALIAN INFANTRY RETURN FROM A SKIRMISH BY THE SUEZ CANAL.
The men are crossing the Nile Bridge, on their return to camp after a brush with the Turkish raiders along the eastern bank of the Suez Canal.

EMPIRE RALLY FROM OVERSEAS.

GRAND MARCH-PAST OF CANADIAN TROOPS JUST BEFORE THEIR DEPARTURE FROM HOME.
When the photograph was taken the Duke of Connaught was taking the salute as these stalwart sons of Empire passed before him.

RECRUITS OF THE TORONTO DIVISION.
second great city is familiarly known.   The
Second Canadian Contingent.

THE KING'S UNCLE TAKES THE ROYAL SALUTE.
The Duke of Connaught is seen taking up his position at the saluting base as the Royal Standard was being unfurled.
As Governor-General and Commander-in-Chief, he took the liveliest interest in the Dominion rally.

LADS OF THE RED ROSE AND SONS OF THE WATTLE.
A company of sturdy " Lancashire lads " marching past a guard composed of Australian troops at a spot in the vicinity of the Egyptian capital.

CITIZEN SOLDIERS OF AUSTRALIA'S SMALLEST STATE—VICTORIA—ON A ROUTE MARCH.

A CONTRAST IN IMPERIAL UNITY—ARABS UNLOADING SACKS OF CRUSHED BARLEY ON THE OUTSKIRTS OF THE NEW ZEALANDERS' CAMP IN THE EGYPTIAN DESERT.

NEW ZEALAND TROOPS ON FATIGUE DUTY.

followed by Commandant Dutoit with a special motor-car contingent from Witwatersrand.

So severe was the motor-car chase that De Wet's following was soon reduced to four men. But he managed to join another small commando of rebels, consisting mainly of fugitives from the Western Free State, who had gathered at Schweizer Reneke. With this force De Wet started westward, intending to follow Kemp and to join with Maritz in German South-West Africa. Fortune at first favoured him. For a series of heavy rainstorms reduced the roads to so bad a condition that the pursuing motor-cars could not keep up with him. On November 25th he crossed into Bechuanaland, over the railway line by Devondale. Here, however, another fresh loyalist force, under Commandant Brits, took up the pursuit. At the end of two days' chase about half of the fugitive force was captured. Then, on December 1st, Commandant Brits surrounded De Wet and the rest of the small commando at a farm at Waterburg, between the Molopo River and the Morokweni Reserve, about a

The capture of De Wet

hundred miles west of Mafeking. The rebel party, numbering fifty-two men, surrendered without firing a shot, and the former commander-in-chief of the Orange Free State forces was confined in prison pending his trial for high treason.

General Beyers came to a more terrible end. He remained in the northern districts of the Orange Free State with about seventy men, while loyal commandos harried him from every side and tried to force on an action, from which he continually escaped by scattering his force. At last, after an engagement near Bothaville on December 7th, he split his party into two small groups. With one of these he fled towards the Vaal River along the tributary stream of the Zandspruit.

He was pursued by Captain Uys and Field-Cornet Deneker, with a small loyalist force. At daybreak on December 9th the rebels were trapped in the angle between the Zandspruit and the Vaal, and after a

ARABS CLIPPING HORSES IN THE NEW ZEALAND CAMP IN EGYPT.

sharp fight of fifteen minutes Beyers with some of his men tried to swim their horses across the Vaal to the Transvaal. They were fired on, and it was seen that Beyers fell from his horse, but managed to grasp another animal by the tail. This horse was swimming back to the Free State side. Beyers began to cry for help; but fighting was still going on between the loyalists and some of the rebels, and the arch-traitor was drowned before anybody was able to rescue him.

His death, following on the capture of De Wet and the flight of Maritz and Kemp, practically brought the rebellion to a close. During the first week in December General Botha continued to conduct operations in the northern district of the Orange Free State, where fogs and heavy rains veiled the movements of the last main forces of the revolt. But in a few days the rebels were hemmed in on all sides, five hundred and fifty being captured, and two hundred surrendering to a single loyalist, Commandant Kloppers, who had been previously taken prisoner and released.

One of the chief reasons for the extraordinary speed with which a rebellion of ten thousand armed men, under famous and experienced leaders, was broken up was the amnesty offered to all rebels who surrendered voluntarily by November 21st. This merciful measure, in combination with the swift and wide-driving operations of General Botha, completely undermined the apparently formidable forces of Beyers and De Wet.

By Christmas the warrior Prime Minister of South Africa was able to enjoy a week's holiday at his farm, in preparation for the arduous and difficult campaign in German South-West Africa. From a military point of view the delay caused by the rebellion was fortunate. As originally planned, the expedition was dangerously **The Burgher Forces** inadequate in numbers; many of the men **trained afresh** were imperfectly trained; they had not sufficient artillery, and were entirely without aircraft. All these defects, partly due, perhaps, to the treachery of General Beyers as Commandant-General of the Union Forces, were made good by General Botha and General Smuts. The members of the first expedition consisted almost exclusively of South Africans of British extraction.

But on January 5th, 1915, the burgher forces reassembled, and thousands of Boers, trained afresh for war by their recent operations against their misguided fellow-countrymen, began to encamp on Green Point Common, on the way to German South-West Africa. All that German gold, German intrigue, and German lies had accomplished was to consolidate the Union of South Africa and raise a strong Boer army, under the greatest of Boer generals, for the invasion of the only German colony suitable for white settlers. The ultimate result of a generation of German intriguers in South Africa is one of the grand ironies of history. The Germans dug their own graves as a colonising race. They thought the feet of the British Colossus were made of clay. But the Imperial Government did not build on clay; it built on the honour, the conscience, and the virile integrity of the embattled farmers of the veldt.

And one of these farmers proved to be a statesman of supreme genius as well as a warrior of the finest Dutch type. Noble were the words he uttered at Pretoria when he went back to his farm: "For loyalist Boers in these later days it has been a tragic ordeal to hunt down and fire upon men—some of them their relatives, and many of them their friends—who were once their comrades-in-arms. The Dutch loyalists have discharged a painful duty out of a stern sense of honour, and they regard the whole rebellion as a lamentable business upon which the curtain should be rung down with as little declamation, as little controversy, as little recrimination as possible. For myself, personally, the last three months have provided the most sad experiences of all my life. I can say the same for General Smuts, and indeed for every member of the Government. The war—our South African War—is but a thing of yesterday. You will understand my feelings, and the feelings of loyal commandos, when, among rebel dead and wounded, we found from time to time men who had fought in our ranks during the dark days of that campaign. The loyal commandos have had a hard task to perform. They have performed **General Botha's** it. The cause of law and order has **noble speech** been, and is being, vindicated. Let that be enough. This is no time for exultation or for recrimination. Let us spare one another's feelings. Remember, we have to live together in this land long after the war is ended."

Thus spoke General Botha, the man who saved South Africa for both Boer and Briton. Let his words close the strangest, the most tragic, and yet the most glorious chapter in the history of the mighty Commonwealth that had suddenly been welded into a true nation, ripe for a great and happy destiny.

VISITING DAY IN THE CAMP OF THE VICTORIAN CONTINGENT JUST BEFORE EMBARKATION.

MARCH-PAST OF NEW ZEALANDERS AT A REVIEW NEAR CAIRO. AT THE SALUTING-BASE (LEFT TO RIGHT):
GENERAL GODLEY, SIR THOMAS MACKENZIE, AND GENERAL SIR JOHN MAXWELL.

NEW ZEALAND TROOPS PASSING SHEPHEARD'S HOTEL, THE FAMOUS FASHIONABLE RENDEZVOUS IN CAIRO.
INSET: NEW ZEALANDERS ARRIVING AT CHELSEA BARRACKS.

CHAPTER LIII.

HOW THE EMPIRE RALLIED TO THE FLAG.

Dissensions in the British Empire Calculated Upon by Germany—What the Potsdam Plotters Failed to See—The Question of the Empire as a Whole—Canada's Magnificent Rally to the Call—Her Splendid Contributions of Men and Material—Arrival of the First Canadian Contingent in England—In Training on Salisbury Plain—The "Patricia's" in Flanders—General Alderson's Message to the Dominion Troops at the Front—Praise from Sir John French—Second Contingent at Shorncliffe—The Australian Commonwealth's Fine Response—The First Contingent from "Down Under"—An Exciting Voyage—New Zealand's Noble Part—A Maori Incident—The Australasians Win Golden Opinions in Egypt.

ERMAN statesmen, in estimating their chances in a war against Britain, placed much weight on the advantages that would come to them from expected dissensions within the British Empire.

As soon as Britain was engaged in a life-and-death struggle her subject races would, these critics believed, throw off their yoke. There would be risings in Calcutta and Bombay; while from Nairobi to Singapore, and from Khartoum to Port Elizabeth, nations would seize the chance of slaying their British administrators and returning to their old, primitive freedom. Uganda and Ceylon, Basutoland and the Straits Settlements, the solemn marches under the shadow of the Himalayas, and the fever-haunted jungles of Central Africa were alike to witness the quick, savage revolt of their people against the British oppressors.

Nor was this all. Canada would refuse to bear the burden of a war of whose origin she knew nothing, and cared less; Australia would quietly "cut the painter," and secure at a stroke her independence, and her freedom from war's burdens; while in South Africa the Boers would raise the standard of rebellion again and sweep every Briton into the sea.

This was the dream of Germany. It seemed impossible to her precise and philosophic Empire-builders that an Empire that has grown like ours, without plan or premeditation, should stand a great strain. Even those Germans who knew something of Greater Britain and of our dependencies failed to comprehend the real strength of our position. They were ever dwelling on our disputes and differences. These, they declared, were bound to split the Empire.

They knew all about the line of cleavage between French Canadians and British Canadians; they were well informed of the differences in opinion between various political parties in the Dominions and at home on the question of naval defence; they had precisely recorded all the minor squabbles that must arise where independent and free peoples are working out their destiny.

What the German observers did not understand was that the differences were on the surface, and that underneath them lay a great fundamental unity. They did not realise that the French Canadians in Quebec, the British settlers in British Columbia, the Dutchmen in Cape Town, and even descendants of Germans in South Australia were one in their love of the freedom of British institutions.

Behind them stood men of a hundred nations, with skins of every hue, bound to the British rule, not by compulsion, but by their experience of generations of honest, capable, sincere, and disinterested administration.

Early in August, 1914, crowds gathered at every city in the Empire, day by day, waiting for news. Every phase was then followed with strained attention—the declaration of war upon Russia by Germany on August 1st, the invasion of French territory by German troops on August 2nd, and the mobilisation of the British Fleet on August 3rd.

When, on the evening of August 4th, war was declared between Great Britain and Germany the response was immediate. From end to end of the Empire controversies were forgotten, differences passed out of sight, and men united in one plea—"What can we do in this, our war?" This response has been the subject of incidental reference in Chapters Twenty-five, Thirty, Thirty-three, and

AT THE CANADIAN REMOUNT DEPOT.
Canadian Rough-rider showing his horsemanship.

FAREWELL MARCH OF CANADA'S SECOND CONTINGENT THROUGH THE STREETS OF MONTREAL.

WINNIPEG RIFLES CROSSING A PONTOON BRIDGE OVER THE JACQUES CARTIER RIVER.
Note how the lumber has been held up by the bridge, testing the work of the Canadian Engineering Corps.

161

GROUP AT THE DIVISIONAL HEADQUARTERS,
FIRST CANADIAN CONTINGENT.
Lieut.-General E. A. H. Alderson, C.B., in centre.

OFFICERS OF THE DIVISIONAL HEAD-
QUARTERS STAFF, FIRST CANADIAN
CONTINGENT.

Thirty-six, but demands more extended and particular treatment. Canada and Australia and New Zealand began to raise their armies to send to Europe; South Africa rallied her sons for fighting nearer to hand; the Indian princes mobilised their forces and offered their armed men, with themselves and their fortunes, to their King. Basuto and Zulu, Kanaka and Maori, Negro and Cingalese, clamoured to serve. Men in the heart of Africa, and in tiny Pacific Islands whose names were scarcely known to a handful of people in Britain, men who had never in their lives seen Great Britain or met more than a score or two of Britons, were found preparing themselves to fight for the Flag and Empire they had learnt to love. "Why should I, the King's servant, stand idle when the King is fighting his enemies?" asked one Basuto chief. And that was the question of the Empire as a whole.

In the dark days of early August, when Great Britain suddenly found herself confronted with her armed and well-prepared antagonist, the silver lining to the black clouds that hung over us was the splendid consistency of the people of the Empire. Everyone in Great Britain who knew anything of Greater Britain knew that the Dominions would be loyal and true. But even those who knew Greater Britain best could hardly have believed that

BRIGADIER-GENERAL LAWRENCE.
Appointed to assist General Alderson in the command of the Canadian Contingent.

at the first cry of danger to the Motherland old foes would sink ancient controversies, old antagonists would clasp hands, and men from East and West would flock to the Flag as Britain's sons did. The world had seen nothing like it before.

Even the seers who had visions, and the dreamers of dreams, had failed to imagine anything so great as what actually took place. From August 4th it was no longer a case of the people of Greater Britain helping Great Britain in her war. It was the people of Greater Britain taking their share in their own war, making common purpose and finding common strength in their unity.

Canada's great lead

The people in the Dominion of Canada regard theirs as the premier Dominion of the Empire, and they were resolved now to lead the way in Imperial zeal. The Government did not wait until war was declared. As soon as it became evident that Great Britain was likely to be dragged into the struggle, the Duke of Connaught, the popular and able Governor-General, then touring the west, started for Ottawa, and the Dominion Cabinet met to take action.

German cruisers were traversing the seas, and it was thought possible that some of these might attempt attacks on certain vulnerable Canadian points. There were large German colonies in the United States, and smaller ones in Canada itself. Would some of these Germans seek to open guerilla war on Canada, or try, by destroying bridges, blowing up cities, or damaging ships, to injure the Empire? All these things had to be guarded against. Canada had not given much time or care to military defence in the past. There was, it is true, a Department of Militia responsible for military matters, and at its head was a very active officer, Colonel (afterwards Major-General) Sam Hughes. But Colonel Hughes's power was limited until the approach of war by the apathy of the people. There were numerous militia regiments, and a small regular force, but the average young man had not thought it worth while to trouble to do militia training. The militia were little more than skeleton corps. But they were found, at the moment of emergency, to supply an invaluable groundwork on which a military organisation could be built up quickly.

As it became clear that war must come, steady processions of men poured from every point to the different militia headquarters offering their services. Farmers drove in twenty and thirty miles or more, cowboys left their prairies, city men, clerks and bank cashiers, owners of prosperous businesses and mechanics—young men, middle-aged, and old—moved by one common purpose, offered themselves. The militia officers found themselves suddenly overwhelmed. There were so many recruits that they could barely record their names. Soldiering, yesterday the amusement of a few, became to-day the settled work of the nation as a whole.

A truce to party strife

Party politics usually burn with a fierce heat in Canada, and the line of cleavage between Government and Opposition, both in the Dominion and the provinces, has always been clearly marked. Now, however, divisions were obliterated. Sir Wilfrid Laurier, the venerable ex-Premier and Leader of the Opposition, called his chief adherents together, and after consulting them, publicly announced that the Liberal Party would lend its support without reserve to all measures deemed necessary by the Government. "There should be a truce to party strife," said he, and he saw that the truce was declared. The statesmen of the different provinces echoed the same sentiment. The Duke of Connaught, who was to prove himself now, more than ever, a fitting leader for the Canadian people, summarised the national position— " Canada stands united from the Pacific to the Atlantic in her determination to uphold the honour and traditions of the Empire."

Parliament was assembled, and it unanimously resolved to raise an expeditionary force of 22,000 men, fully equipped, for despatch to Europe. The Dominion Government had already placed the two Canadian cruisers, the Niobe and the Rainbow, at the services of the Admiralty. The Government paid the cost of a hospital for the French wounded in Paris, and when news came from England that there was likely to be distress among the poor in the Motherland, it sent over a gift of a million bags of flour of ninety-eight pounds each to the people of the United Kingdom.

A great outburst of public and private generosity was witnessed. Provinces, cities, banks, business organisations, and individuals vied with each other in the extent of their gifts for the Empire. Less than eight weeks after war was declared a list was drawn up of what had been offered and given. Among the provinces, Alberta gave half a million bushels of oats to England, and her civil servants set apart five per cent. of their salaries up to £300

Canada's gifts in kind

a year, and ten per cent. beyond that, for the Patriotic Fund. British Columbia gave 25,000 cases of tinned salmon, Manitoba 50,000 bags of flour, New Brunswick 100,000 bushels of potatoes, Nova Scotia offered 100,000 tons of coal (afterwards changed to £20,000 in cash), Ontario 250,000 bags of flour, Prince Edward Island 100,000 bushels of oats, also cheese and hay, Quebec 4,000,000 pounds of

SUPPORT FROM BRITAIN'S OLDEST COLONY; SECOND CONTINGENT OF NEWFOUNDLAND VOLUNTEERS AND RESERVISTS PARADING IN GOVERNMENT HOUSE GROUNDS, ST. JOHN'S.

The Colony of Newfoundland, as was specially noted in the King's message to his Overseas Dominions, doubled the numbers of its branch of the Royal Naval Reserve, and in addition contributed a force of two hundred and fifty men to take part in the operations at the front.

cheese, and Saskatchewan 1,500 horses. Then the cities made their presents : Montreal, £30,000 to the Patriotic Fund and a battery of quick-firing guns ; Ottawa, £10,000 to the Patriotic Fund, and £60,000 for a machine-gun section ; Toronto, £10,000, and other gifts. Calgary sent 1,000 men for the Legion of Frontiersmen. These were typical. The women of Canada were building, equipping, and maintaining a Canadian women's hospital of a hundred beds to supplement the British naval hospital at Haslar, near Portsmouth. They had raised altogether within between two and three weeks close on £60,000, partly as presents to the War Office for hospital purposes,

were as keen as those of British descent. Americans living in Canada clamoured to serve. Towns mainly inhabited by German emigrants led the way in loyalty. The white men were not alone. American Indians brought their gifts, of money and in kind, and offered themselves as scouts, boatmen, and woodmen.

Canada was undoubtedly handicapped at the beginning of the war by her absence of naval and military preparations. The Canadian people had for some time recognised that it was their duty to take part in the defence of the seas, but they had been unable to agree on

The Canadian Navy

their naval policy. The Government of Sir Wilfrid Laurier proposed to build a Canadian Navy, as Australia was building an Australian Navy. Preliminaries were being actively discussed when the Liberals were defeated, and the Conservatives, under Sir Robert Borden, returned to power. Sir Robert Borden and his Ministry, acting under the advice and with the support of the British Admiralty, proposed not to build, for the time, a separate Dominion Navy, but to provide a certain number of ships to form part of the regular British Navy. An ambitious

A GIFT TO THE FIRST NEW-
FOUNDLAND REGIMENT.
Mr. R. G. Reid, of the Reid-Newfoundland
Co., with one of the two guns presented
to the First Newfoundland Regiment by
Mr. W. D. Reid.

and partly for their own hospital. The Canadian Red Cross raised vast sums. The banks gave donations to the Patriotic Fund, from £2,000 from the Montreal City and Districts Savings Bank to £20,000 from the Bank of Montreal.

The public teachers of Winnipeg sent £6,000. The individual gifts of many rich Canadians were on a princely scale. Thus, Mr. J. K. L. Ross, of Montreal, presented £100,000 to the Patriotic Fund, paid the cost of taking the 5th Royal Highlanders to England, and gave a steam-yacht. Mr. Hamilton Gault,

NEWFOUNDLANDERS LEAVING ST. JOHN'S.
The s.s. Stephano, with two hundred and fifty men of the First Newfoundland Regiment and nearly
one hundred for the Navy, leaving their island home for Europe.

another millionaire, raised and equipped at his own cost a regiment—Princess Patricia's Light Infantry—soon to win wide fame. Crowds of rich men came together and raised many hundreds of thousands of dollars to purchase machine-guns and armoured motor-cars for the troops. The Canadian Pacific Railway gave £20,000, and the men on the line gave another £20,000, in addition to promising one day's pay monthly during the war.

Princess Patricia's Regiment

It was not alone the rich who gave. Canada was at this time passing through a trying period of industrial depression. Many of her business men were having a desperate fight, and at the time that the war broke out the streets of many cities were full of unemployed. Yet the poorest managed to find something for King and Empire. French Canadians

programme was drawn up, but the Government was unable to carry it through the Senate. There was an exceedingly bitter and sustained controversy, and in the end a deadlock ensued.

Hence at the outbreak of the war the Royal Canadian Navy consisted of two training ships—the Niobe and the Rainbow. The work of raising the first contingent, and of completing its equipment, was made much harder by the smallness of the Dominion military establishment, useful as that small establishment was. Despite this, the speed with which the contingent was equipped surprised the world. Canada determined to make up for lost time, and set itself with its whole heart to become a nation in arms.

It was soon found that the first contingent could not be kept within the 22,000 originally intended In a few weeks

NEW ZEALAND GUN TEAM: INSPECTION DAY IN THE CAMP NEAR CAIRO.
Men, horses, and guns were found to be in the very pink of condition.

SUPPLY WAGGON OF THE NEW ZEALAND ARMY SERVICE CORPS IN EGYPT.
Even in the photograph one can see how well the horses were selected and cared for.

A CHURCH SERVICE IN THE LAND OF THE PHARAOHS.
A remarkable camera picture of one of the many striking contrasts brought about in Egypt by the Great War.

an army of 33,000 men was raised. The different regiments of militia immediately placed their services at the disposal of the Government. The wave of passionate loyalty that swept over the country gathered strength day by day. The determination of the people showed itself, not so much in great meetings and in public demonstrations, but in strenuous preparations and willing self-sacrifice. Two quotations from Canadian newspapers, written before war was actually declared, will testify the feeling of the nation. The first is from the Toronto "Globe," a leading Opposition journal:

THE COMING OF THE CANADIANS.
Landing of the First Canadian Contingent at Plymouth.

If Canada is called upon to speak in the midst of the wild war babel, let her voice be strong, responsible, and authoritative —the voice of the whole Parliament of Canada. Of one thing let there be no cavil or question; if it means war for Great Britain, it means war also for Canada. If it means war for Canada, it means also the union of Canadians for the defence of Canada, for the maintenance of the Empire's integrity, and for the preservation in the world of Great Britain's ideals of democratic government and life. When that issue is raised all differences of party and race merge into one positive and unwavering unity. Before the world Canadians are not divided. With Great Britain and all the British dominions we stand, whatever needs to be done. Sir Robert Borden may be confident that the Canadian people are not only loyal to their obligations, but soberly and resolutely ready to do their solemn duty as citizens and as a nation.

The next is from "Canada," a French Liberal newspaper published in Quebec:

Country before parties

When the country is in danger the time for political quarrels, for the conflict of interests or classes is past, and everyone must rally around the one who holds the national Flag. In England the country comes before parties, and we approve with all our hearts. We are certain it will be the same in Canada, and if the occasion presents itself the Liberal party will second all measures which patriotism can dictate to Sir Robert Borden. When the country is in danger political arguments must cease, and if now the danger is come Canada will be found united in this sentiment.

A message from the King, explaining how Great Britain had been forced into war, brought forward fresh demonstrations of loyalty.

The various regiments raised throughout the Dominion were assembled at a newly-created camp, Valcartier, outside Quebec. Valcartier was a marvel of its kind, a camp built up from nothing in a very few weeks, with permanent buildings, shower-baths, electric light, a good water supply throughout the lines, and conveniences lacking in many camps that have been established for years. The army that arrived here had features of its own.

The camp at Valcartier

There were regiments of regulars, cavalry like the Royal Strathcona Horse and the Royal Dragoons, largely composed of veterans from the South African War. There were Highland regiments drawn from cities like Toronto, Montreal, and Vancouver, regiments affiliated with famous Highland corps in the United Kingdom—Seaforths, Gordons, and Camerons—full of the pride of tradition and race. There were scouts from the west; plainsmen trained to pioneer work in the desolate lands of the north, cowboys accustomed to life in the saddle, trappers and hunters, and farmers. There were many townsmen, but the Canadian townsman, as a rule, sees much more of the open air than the townsman in Europe, and possesses much more initiative. A very large proportion of the men were British born, young fellows who had gone out to Canada, lived there for some years, and had, at the first call of duty, volunteered to return and fight for the land of their birth.

The Dominion Government resolved that the first contingent was to be completely equipped in a way surpassed by no other army in the world. No money was to be spared. Accordingly, the personal equipment of the men was brought to a point of excellence that excited general admiration on their arrival in Europe. They were amply provided with machine-guns, their artillery was abundant in quantity and of the best. They had a splendid park of motor-transports, and the mechanical equipment was as good as could be.

The hospitals of Canada had been searched to select a strong corps of trained nurses to accompany the army. There was a complete medical department, chaplains were given military rank, and—at that time an unusual feature—secretaries to the Y.M.C.A. were given rank as officers and attached to the regular forces.

By the end of September the expeditionary force was complete, from a very carefully chosen Intelligence

WITH THE FORCES IN AUSTRALIA.
Guarding a river bridge in New South Wales.

BRITISH BULLDOGS IN EGYPT.
Corporal and private of the Australian Contingent in Egypt with their bulldog pets, in which the natives displayed a sympathetic interest.

Department to the hospital orderlies. Then one day the men heard the bugle calling them to attention. They set out as though on a route march, but this time their steps were directed towards the St. Lawrence, and they did not look back.

A fleet of great ships had been assembled there, the expeditionary force marched aboard, its guns and supplies were slung into place, and it sailed for Europe.

The voyage of the contingent across the Atlantic was watched with anxiety by the people on both sides of the ocean. Would the raiding German cruisers succeed in attacking them en route? A complete veil had been drawn over the movements of the troops. For some weeks no Canadian newspapers were allowed to be circulated abroad.

How the Canadians came to England No word was breathed of where, or how, or when the Canadians had started.

Early in October a report was circulated in England that the contingent had landed at Southampton. People rushed down to give them a great greeting. The report turned out to be false. Then, on October 14th, the people of Plymouth were surprised in the early morning to see transport after transport arrive in the Sound, and drop anchor there. The people, looking across the waters, could hear singing and shouting and cheering from the boats, and could see thousands of khaki-clad men on the ships' sides looking towards the shore. The word went round the town that the men on the crowded decks were

Canadians, and Plymouth and Devonport thereupon set out to give the unexpected new comrades a right royal reception. The Canadians had thought they would have a cordial greeting when they reached England, but as they one and all admitted afterwards, they had never dreamed of such a demonstration as awaited them.

The coming of the Canadians was felt throughout Britain to be something more than the mere addition of some tens of thousands to our armies, important as that was. It was the visible evidence that in her great world-struggle Britain did not stand alone. Her sons had rallied to her **An enthusiastic reception** side. "We know that they indeed come of the right breed," said "The Times," voicing the national sentiment, as it welcomed them. "If they did not, they would not have flocked of their own free will to the Flag, as they have done, and as they are still doing with unabated ardour. We remember their work and the work of their brothers from Australia and from New Zealand in South Africa. There, for the first time, the troops of the daughter nations proved their valour and their skill in a common Imperial enterprise. Now they are about to prove their soldiership for the first time in a great European war. We welcome their assistance with gratitude and with pride. We welcome it for the addition which it brings to our numbers in the field, and for the exceptionally fine quality of the troops which it gives us. We are deeply sensible of its high military worth. But we welcome it far more for the incalculable moral support which it lends us in this great struggle. Our enemies thought that a war would divide us. They have been foolish enough to utter their thoughts, and even to base their calculations upon these vain imaginings. All of us, whether at home or beyond the seas, knew that nothing could do so much as war to reveal

A CANADIAN GUN FOR THE FRONT.
Field-piece being hoisted on board a transport at Montreal.

our real unity and to foster it. We have been right, as we were sure we should be right. The coming of the Colonial troops is the proof that the peoples of this Empire understand each other better than all the spies and investigators whom Germany has sent out to study them."

A group of camps had been arranged for the contingent on Salisbury Plain, and the men were immediately moved there. The young recruits hoped to proceed to the front within a week or two. The British military authorities

SAND ARTISTS IN THE DESERT.
Queenslanders inscribe the arms of their State in the sands of Egypt.

had other ideas for them, and gave them an exceedingly hard course of training, which, starting in October, continued well on into February. It had been intended to transfer the troops before the winter weather came on from their tents to huts, but the shortage of labour in England and other causes prevented the completion of the huts, and most of the troops were still under canvas when the New Year opened. The life of the Canadian troops during those weeks on Salisbury Plain was, it must be admitted, wearisome and trying. The camps were one great sea of mud. It was an unusually wet winter. The roads had not been made to stand the strain of the heavy military traffic that fell on them, and in places they became **Wearisome and trying work** almost impassable. The camps were miles away from any villages, and fourteen miles from a town, in the loneliest, most exposed, and dullest part of England. The soldiers had nothing to do during the long winter nights but crouch in the semi-darkness in their tents, listening to the unceasing rain outside, unless they were able to get into the Y.M.C.A. marquee, which would not hold them all. They had plenty of money, the private soldier receiving

about five shillings a day, including allowances, but there were few or no rational ways of spending it.

The young recruits found it hard to understand military discipline. The result was that in a short time the Canadian Contingent was the object of some criticism. Those who knew the Canadians well knew that the faults, such as they were, were all on the surface. In the hasty enlistment of so many men a **The King and the** small proportion of unsuitable recruits, **Canadians** not more than five per cent. of the whole, had been accepted. Some of these were not physically fit, others had not the moral stamina. The weeks of waiting and of preparation on Salisbury Plain enabled the authorities to weed these out, and relentlessly weeded out they were.

Lieut.-General E. A. H. Alderson was given command of the contingent shortly after its arrival. The King visited the camp on November 4th, accompanied by the Queen, Lord Kitchener, and Lord Roberts, and was greeted with immense enthusiasm. Lord Roberts, as Colonel-in-Chief of the Colonial Forces, paid a special visit by himself to the Canadians, and made a speech, which was long remembered. "We have arrived at the most critical moment of our history, and you have generously come to help us in our hour of need," he told the assembled soldiers. "I need not urge you to do your best, for I know you will, for you will be fighting in the greatest of all causes—the cause of right, of justice, and of liberty."

By early in February the time of preparation in England was finished. Those who saw the troops on their arrival at Plymouth, and who saw them shortly before their departure for France, could

AUSTRALIAN FIELD ENGINEERS AT WORK.
Laying a field telegraph.

not fail to be struck by the difference. They had now experienced four months of the most rigorous military life and discipline. They had lived under surroundings of the greatest hardships, exposed to the worst weather possible, with few comforts and few conveniences, in their isolated camp on Salisbury Plain. They had been tried, hardened, and strengthened. No man of military knowledge who walked through the Canadian camps at the beginning of February could doubt but that here were men who, given opportunity, would bring glory to the Dominion and victory to the British arms.

SMART WORK OF THE NEW ZEALANDERS IN EGYPT: BRIDGE-BUILDING NEAR THE NILE.

The contingent had been accompanied on the journey to Europe by a special regiment, Princess Patricia's Light Infantry, largely composed of veteran British soldiers. Four hundred and fifty men in the ranks had the right to wear war medals. Its commander was Colonel Farquhar, D.S.O., who went to Canada as Military Secretary to the Duke of Connaught in 1913, and Mr. Gault who, as has been already stated, paid the cost of raising and equipping the regiment, served as an officer under Colonel Farquhar. The Patricias were named after the Duke of Connaught's daughter, and they were quickly nicknamed "Princess Pat's." They remained a short time with the first contingent, and then in November were transferred to Winchester, and from there were sent in December to Northern France. They were at once moved up to the fighting zone, and were first given a spell of very heavy work, digging one of the rear line of trenches. Then they set out for the fighting front.

Princess Patricia's Regiment

The arrival of the Patricias in Flanders was watched with keen interest in all parts of the Empire, for they were the first troops from the Dominions to take part in Continental fighting. At first nothing was heard of them, and then rumour after rumour spread through England and America of their fate. Mysterious stories arose, no one knew how, of how they had been wiped out in the fighting, of how they set out in charges in hundreds and returned in tens. One newspaper published a story of how, at the first opportunity, their slouch-hatted ranks had charged the German trenches with a shout "For God and Canada!" and had captured large sections of the German lines.

What actually happened to them was this. After finishing their work at trench-digging, they had two days of heavy marching of sixteen miles each day over broken, muddy roads. Then, at half-past ten one night, they were led quietly into the front line of trenches, relieving French troops there. The following description, written at the time in the "Toronto Star" by Mr. F. A. McKenzie, who saw something of their life, tells their experience:

It was pitch dark, with heavy rain. The darkness was frequently illuminated by German star shells, which fell along the front, making the position as light as daytime. Some soldiers could not immediately realise the absolute necessity of dead silence while advancing, and the noise of their movements brought a heavy, but futile, German bombardment on the lines. The first and second companies occupied the front trenches, the third and fourth companies supporting in secondary lines. The trenches were mud-holes holding from fifteen inches to three feet of water, and at some points deep, concealed cavities, into which the men plunged up to their chests in water. The Canadians took up their positions without lights, commands being whispered along the line. Some men occupied observation points ahead, crouching in the mud, searching through the darkness for any signs of a German advance. Others crouched behind parapets ready for instant action.

Face to face with the foe

Amid pauses in the almost incessant din of artillery fire they could hear Germans conversing and baling water out of their trenches scarcely a stone's throw away. The artillery on both sides kept on during the night. There was an occasional ping of a single rifle shot, which told of the activity of snipers.

Star shells fell frequently. Several times the men, believing the Germans were approaching, opened a rapid rifle fire into the darkness. Here and there along the trenches were rough tops of tarpaulins or tarred paper, beneath which some stood to escape the rain. Others were busy baling water from the trenches. It was a night none there will ever forget. The next morning gave the Canadians a fuller view of their position. They were occupying long, hidden lines in a sea of mud. The German lines, scarcely visible, were from fifty to one hundred and fifty yards away. Between both fronts were wire entanglements. The soldiers had hoped when approaching the trenches that they would have an

A GLIMPSE OF THE NEW ZEALANDERS' STIRRING CAMP NEAR CAIRO.

opportunity of charging the enemy's position and driving them back. One glance showed that an advance either by the Germans or ourselves was at this point practically impossible. The contested space between the lines was a morass of mud, into which any man attempting to cross would instantly sink.

Scouts and sharpshooters on either side instantly fired upon any indication of human life. It was impossible for a man to raise his head above the trenches without a quick bullet coming. The Germans evidently knew the position of every British dug-out. They had rifles so fixed as to cover them exactly, enabling the trigger to be pulled without taking time to aim.

A fatal deed of heroism — Two of the most popular officers in the regiment—Captain Newton and Captain Fitzgerald—were killed in the early fighting. Captain Newton, like Colonel Farquhar, had been formerly attached to the Duke of Connaught's staff. Soon after the Patricias arrived at the front he was moving around the trenches at night time, inspecting the lines. It was pitch dark, and a heavy storm made it scarce possible to observe anything around. Newton lost his way in the darkness in going from one trench to another, and stumbled to a place in front of our own lines. A sentry challenged him, and receiving no reply, shot him. The officer was brought in, and died some hours afterwards. Captain Fitzgerald, a former officer in the regular British Army, had won early the goodwill of all by his cheerfulness, his daring, and the careful way he looked after the men under him. One soldier had been shot by a German sniper, and his dead body lay in the trenches outside. Fitzgerald declared that he was not going to see one of his comrades lying there. He made a dash to pick up the body, but before he could grasp hold of it, a German bullet got him, and killed him. "He was a hero, and he died a hero's death," said the soldiers, as they told afterwards of how he had fallen.

Life in the trenches in these early days in January was trying and arduous. It was the custom then to keep the troops for forty-eight hours in the front line, then forty-eight hours in the reserve lines, and afterwards to send them back for a rest. The trenches were horrible. The air was charged with the sickly odour of bodies of men who had fallen weeks before, lying in spots where it was impossible to get to them. There was mud everywhere, mud sometimes up to a man's knees, sometimes up to his waist. Here and there was a deep mud-hole, caused by the explosion of a "Jack

Johnson." A man who fell into it could not release himself, but had to be dragged out, his comrades standing at the side, and putting their rifles so that he could clutch hold and be pulled up. The drinking water was brackish, making some of the men ill with stomach troubles. Frost-bite, the terrible frost-bite of the trenches, took its toll of the Canadians. It was found, however, that they stood the exposure better than most troops, and the proportion of sick among them was below the average. The first period in the trenches was not spectacular. It was a time of waiting and endurance.

The Patricias did not appreciate the work of the German snipers, and they quickly formed their own corps of snipers, who, creeping around, repaid the Germans with interest. Then came duels between the individual snipers on either side. In February, when again in the trenches, the Patricias found an opportunity to make a gallant dash and to capture a German trench. A storming party, consisting of the corps of snipers and thirteen picked men, started out at midnight to explore the German position. They crept up until they were within twenty yards of the enemy's trench, fixing their bayonets as they approached. Then, as the order was given to charge, they leaped right into the German trenches, bayoneting the men still left there. There was fierce fighting with picks and shovels, and whatever came first to hand. Hand bombs were thrown on either side. The Germans counter-attacked with a fresh force, but the Patricias held their own, losing, however, a number of men, Major Hamilton Gault himself being one of the wounded. A few days after this, in further fighting, Colonel Farquhar was killed. The Patricias had by this time won their reputation with the British Army. They had been widely chaffed at first because of their name and because of the Canadian tendency to magnify their doings. The British soldiers found, however, that they were of the right stamp, hard-bitten fighting men.

Colonel Farquhar killed

To return to the first contingent. Early in February the word was passed that the time of departure was approaching. The King paid another visit to Salisbury Plain, this time a visit of farewell. Nothing was said in the Press about the coming departure of the troops, and even the King's visit

THE FLEETING SOLACE OF A HASTY GAME DURING AN INTERVAL IN CAMP.

was not allowed to be mentioned for some weeks afterwards. The Canadians themselves understood that they were going to Rouen, where they were, they thought, to spend some weeks before proceeding to the front. Their expectation was, however, disappointed.

German submarines were very active in the Channel at this time, and it was well known that the Germans particularly aimed at destroying some of the Canadians on their way across. They entertained a particular hatred for them, for they had disappointed German hopes by taking part in the war. The British Admiralty took ample precautions to guard the sea-way. The Canadians embarked at Avonmouth and set out—not as they had expected for a trip of a few hours across the narrow waters, but towards the Atlantic Ocean. A few ships, carrying some part of the heavy military train, dodged the waiting submarines and reached Havre. Most of the vessels never tried for Havre, but made for St. Nazaire, hundreds of miles away, on

AN ARAB BOY ENJOYS THE LIGHTER SIDE OF EUROPEAN CAMP LIFE.

NEW ZEALANDERS IN EGYPT AT SIGNALLING WORK ON THE ROOF OF THEIR "DINING-HALL."

the west coast of France. There was to be no more waiting now. As the troops stepped ashore they found officials in attendance, with great stacks of fur coats, mountains of big gloves, and other equipment for the front. The men were fitted with their new garments on the spot, and at once started off for a railway journey from the extreme west to the far north-east of France. Three days later they stepped out of their trucks at their destination, somewhere in the neighbourhood of Ypres. They were where they had long wanted to be—at the actual front.

Here they settled down to the everyday work of war, taking their turn in the trenches, after first going through a preliminary course with older troops. The Canadians soon won a character for themselves with the British Army, and a character wholly good. Their one difficulty at first was a certain recklessness. The boys off duty would start and keep on with a football match, for example, under heavy German artillery fire. While they were in the trenches

it was hard for them to realise the necessity of keeping under cover. The Germans, with their amazing intelligence service, learned this characteristic of the Canadians, and on the first night they were in the trenches they tried by taunts and cries to draw them out to their death. "Come out, you Canadians! Come out and fight!" they called.

But the Canadians soon learned to abide by war conditions. The Dominion soldiers were filled with admiration for the British Tommies, whose trenches they shared. Letter after letter sent back to Canada was charged with praise of the British. "These English regulars are just fine," wrote one young Canadian, in a typical letter. "They're full of notions, they have all sorts of devices; they joke over the hardest luck; they never grumble. I tell you, when I thought of how I had grumbled over the mud of Salisbury Plain, and when I saw what they had gone through without a kick, I just felt ashamed of myself." The British were as emphatic in their praise of the Canadians. **General Alderson's message**

General Alderson, who commanded the Canadian Division at the front, as he had done at Salisbury Plain, circulated a soldierlike message to the troops before they first occupied their own line of trenches :

ALL RANKS OF THE CANADIAN DIVISION.—We are about to occupy and maintain a line of trenches. I have some things to say to you at this moment, which it is well that you should consider. You are taking over good, and, on the whole, dry trenches. I have visited some myself. They are intact, and the parapets are good. Let me warn you first that we have already had several casualties while you have been attached to other divisions. Some of those casualties were unavoidable, and that is war. But I suspect that some—at least a few—could have been avoided. I have heard of cases in which men have exposed themselves with no military object, and perhaps only to gratify curiosity. We cannot lose good men like this. We shall want them all if we advance, and we shall want them all if the Germans advance.

Do not expose your heads, and do not look round corners, unless for a purpose which is necessary at the moment you do it. It will not often be necessary. You are provided with means of observing the enemy without exposing your heads. To lose your life without military necessity is to deprive the State of good soldiers. Young and brave men enjoy taking risks. But a soldier who takes unnecessary risks through levity is not playing the game, and the man who does so is stupid, for whatever be the average practice of the German Army, the individual shots whom they employ as snipers shoot straight, and screened from observation behind the lines, they are always watching. If you put your head over the parapet without orders, they will hit that head. There is another thing. Troops new to the trenches always shoot at nothing the first night. You will not do it. It wastes ammunition, and it hurts no one. And the enemy says, " These are new and nervous troops." No German is going to say that of the Canadian troops.

" The Canadians never budge " You will be shelled in the trenches. When you are shelled, sit low and sit tight. This is easy advice, for there is nothing else to do. If you get out you will only get it worse. And if you go out the Germans will go in. And if the Germans go in, we shall counter-attack and put them out, and that will cost us hundreds of men instead of the few whom shells may injure. The Germans do not like the bayonet, nor do they support bayonet attacks. If they get up to you, or if you get up to them, go right in with the bayonet. You have the physique to drive it home. That you will do it, I am sure, and I do not envy the Germans if you get among them with the bayonet.

There is one thing more. My old regiment, the Royal West Kent, has been here since the beginning of the war, and it has never lost a trench. The Army says : " The West Kents never budge." I am proud of the great record of my old regiment. And I think it is a good omen. I now belong to you and you belong to me ; and before long the Army will say : " The Canadians never budge." Lads, it can be left there, and there I leave it. The Germans will never turn you out.

Sir John French, in an emphatic message to the Duke of Connaught, praised the Canadians :

The Canadian troops having arrived at the front, I am anxious to tell your Royal Highness that they have made the highest impression on us all. I made a careful inspection the week after they came to the country, and was very much struck by the excellent physique which was apparent throughout the ranks. The soldierly bearing and steadiness with which the men stop in the ranks on a bleak, cold, and snowy day are most remarkable. After two or three weeks' preliminary education in the trenches, they have now taken over their own line, and I have the utmost confidence in their capability to do valuable and efficient service.

The Princess Patricias arrived a month earlier, and since then have performed splendid service in the trenches. When I inspected them also, in pouring rain, it seemed to me that I had never seen a more magnificent-looking battalion, Guards or otherwise. Two or three days ago they captured a German trench with great dash and energy. I am **Sir John French's tribute** writing these few lines because I know how deeply indebted we all are to the untiring and devoted efforts your Royal Highness has personally made to ensure the despatch in the most efficient condition of this valuable contingent.

From now on, the work of the Canadian Contingent proceeded with that of the regular forces, the troops being first attached for training for a few days to brigades in the 3rd Corps' trenches. The Canadian artillery took part in the fighting around Neuve Chapelle, and the infantry were in the trenches. Although they did not share in the main attack, they rendered valuable help by keeping the enemy engaged in front of their trenches. The Princess Patricias shared in the battle around St. Eloi. Everywhere the Canadians won high praise for their physique, and their splendid soldiery. " If we're good enough to fight by the side of the British soldiers at the front, we're proud," said they.

Sir John French, in his despatch of April 5th, 1915, describing the Battle of Neuve Chapelle, told how he inspected the Canadian Division a few days after it arrived at the front. " They presented a splendid and most soldierlike appearance on parade. The men were of good physique, hard and fit. I judged by what I saw that they were able to take their places in the line of battle. Since then the division has justified the good opinion

SIDELIGHTS ON THE CAMP LIFE IN EGYPT OF OUR KINSMEN FROM OVERSEAS.

PONTOON-BUILDING UNDER THE SHADOW OF THE PYRAMIDS.

REMOVING WOUNDED FROM THE SUEZ CANAL FRONT TO THE HOSPITAL TRAIN.

I formed of it. All the soldiers of Canada serving in the army under my command have so far splendidly upheld the traditions of the Empire, and will, I feel sure, prove to be a great source of additional strength to the forces of this country."

While the first contingent was completing its training, a second and a third contingent were formed. The second contingent arrived in England in March, and was given headquarters at Shorncliffe. A distinguished Canadian officer, General Sam Steele, who took a prominent part in the Boer War, was chosen to command it. It was easily observable that the authorities had learned much from their first experience. Shorncliffe was a much better site for the troops than Salisbury Plain, and there was no whisper of disorder from the start with the second contingent. By the middle of April Sir Robert Borden was able to say that Canada had 101,000 men under arms. Her people were standing, to their last shot and their last dollar, if need be, behind the Motherland.

At the beginning of the war the Commonwealth of Australia had one great advantage over Canada. The people of each of the great sister nations were equally loyal, equally eager to help, equally determined to sacrifice all they had, if necessary, for victory. But Canada started her real preparations for war when war began, while Australia had been preparing for close on ten years.

Australia's advantage over Canada

A generation ago Australia was the least military of nations. Her people, placed by their geographical position out of the current of European controversies, had felt no necessity for arming themselves. Then the developments of the world, the rising of the new Asia, and the partitioning of the Pacific, made every thoughtful citizen from Cape York to Greenbushes realise that Australia must be ready to defend herself. The flood of emigration from China, from India, and from Japan set in southwards, and Australia built barriers against it. The Japanese Fleet sailed into Sydney Harbour, and held manœuvres around the northern coasts of Western Australia. Men were quick to realise that Australia had no defences of her own against Japan. As a result Australia started to build a navy, and to establish universal military training for her young men. At the outbreak of the war the Royal Australian Navy consisted of one battle-cruiser, five light cruisers, two gunboats, six destroyers. and two submarines. In November the Minister for Defence was able to declare that Australia had a total of 164,631 men under arms.

There was no question of what Australia should do. "Our duty is quite clear," said the Federal Premier. On the Monday preceding the declaration of war the Governor-General of Australia sent on behalf of the Commonwealth Government the following offer to Great Britain. "In the event of war the Commonwealth of Australia is prepared to place the vessels of the Australian Navy under the control of the British Admiralty, if desired. It is further prepared to despatch an expeditionary force of twenty thousand men of any suggested composition to any destination desired by the Home Government, the force to be at the complete disposal of the Home Government. The cost of the despatch **The Commonwealth's** and maintenance would be borne by this **generous offer** Government. The Australian Press has been notified accordingly." Mr. Harcourt, the British Secretary for the Colonies, replied: "His Majesty's Government greatly appreciate the prompt readiness of your Government to place their naval forces at the disposal of the Admiralty and their generous offer to equip and maintain an expeditionary force. I will telegraph further on the latter point."

Shortly after the outbreak of war there was a general election in Australia, the Cook Ministry was overthrown and a Labour Government, under Mr. Andrew Fisher, succeeded it. Apprehension was entertained in some quarters in Australia lest the Labour Government should be less keen on giving assistance in the war than its predecessor. This fear was wholly groundless. The Labour leaders during the election pledged themselves in the most complete fashion. Mr. Andrew Fisher declared at the beginning of the war that Australia should support Great Britain with her last man and her last shilling. When he became Prime Minister he acted on the declaration. Senator Pearce, who had done very much to create and to mould the new defence movement in Australia, was made Minister of Defence in the Labour Cabinet, and showed himself the right man for the place.

There was absolutely no division of opinion in the country. Even the descendants of German settlers met to declare their unswerving loyalty and affection to the King and their determination to sacrifice, if necessary, their property and lives for the welfare of the British Empire. Private and public philanthropy were active.

Australia's active philanthrophy Hundreds of thousands of pounds were raised for war funds, and enormous sums were given for medical and charitable purposes. Thus the Commonwealth Government gave £100,000 to the Belgian Relief Fund, and various State Governments contributed. Gifts of food were sent to England, scores of thousands of carcases of mutton, great quantities of port wine, butter, bacon, cheese, condensed milk, and the like. One newspaper sent three shiploads of foodstuffs. Sydney raised £20,000 for the Belgian Relief Fund; £50,000 was raised in a comparatively short time for the British Red Cross. These are typical cases.

The first Australian contingent consisted of 20,338 men, trained in equal proportions according to population, from the different cities of the Commonwealth. Arrangements were made to send regular monthly reinforcements of between 2,000 and 3,000 each to make up for casualties and wastage, and no sooner was the first con-

transports was kept as secret as possible. But it was impossible to suppress the overwhelming enthusiasm of the people in Melbourne and elsewhere as the boys marched down to the front. When Brigadier-General Bridges, who was responsible for the expeditionary force until it was later on taken over by General Birdwood, left Melbourne with his Staff on Trafalgar Day, he was given a reception that kings might have envied. Senator Pearce, the Minister for Defence, sent a formal message to the troops: "Upon the force devolves the honour and responsibility of representing Australia, and of performing Australia's share in the great Imperial effort in the interests of justice, honour, and international integrity. The ultimate issue of that undertaking can never be in doubt, but its attainment demands steadfast display of the British qualities of resolution and courage, which are yours by right of heredity. The people of Australia look to you to prove in battle that you are capable of upholding the traditions of the British arms. I have no fear that you will worthily represent the Commonwealth's military forces. Your presence among the Imperial forces has, however, a wide significance, as representing the solidarity of the Empire and the Imperial spirit of loyalty to the King."

Brigadier-General Bridges sent a message to the people of Australia: "I hope to report that the conduct of the Australian troops, both in camp and on the field, is worthy of the trust imposed upon them by the people of the Commonwealth. The men are a fine lot, soldierly and patriotic. I am grateful to the soldiers and citizens for the help they have given me in organising and preparing the force now about to do its part for the good of the Empire. I venture to express the hope that, no matter how great the demands on their patience, the Australian people will see to it that there is no diminution of their determination to face their responsibility. This spirit cannot fail then to pervade the troops."

A PEEP BEHIND THE SCENES: AUSTRALIAN FIELD KITCHEN IN EGYPT.

tingent ready than a second contingent of over 10,000 was prepared. Then in October the Commonwealth Government offered another brigade of light horse with brigade train and field ambulance, and the offer was gratefully accepted by the Army Council.

The work of preparing the first contingent proceeded automatically. Every man was a volunteer, for soldiers of the citizens' army cannot be called upon to serve outside the Commonwealth unless they wish. The soldiers were paid what would seem to the British "Tommy" on a princely scale, starting with 6s. a day and 1s. allowance. General Birdwood, a well-known British officer who had served with Kitchener in India, was given charge of the contingent. The first force, when it left Australia, was made up as follows. There was a light horse brigade, consisting of three regiments of cavalry, a field artillery battery, and an ammunition column, signal troop, and train and field ambulance. There was a division composed of three infantry brigades, two light horse squadrons, headquarters divisional artillery, three field artillery brigades, engineers and the accompanying train of ammunition column, signal company, field ambulance, etc. There were 9,000 horses and seventy guns.

The embarkation of the division began on October 17th and lasted five days. Nothing was allowed to be published outside Australia concerning it, and the departure of the

Much uneasiness had been caused by the presence of the Emden and other German cruisers in the Pacific Ocean, and it was believed, not without reason, that they intended to attempt a raid upon the expeditionary force on its way to Europe. The Royal Australian Navy at the outset of the war had been handed over by the Commonwealth Government to work in co-operation with the British Navy under the Admiralty, and it was already operating in the Pacific. British ships, Japanese ships, and Australian ships manœuvred to convoy and protect the vessels bearing the troops. The voyage was not to pass, however, without some excitement.

The rendezvous of the transports was Albany, Western Australia. Here not only the Australians, but also the New Zealanders arrived. "It is the most wonderful sight an Australian ever saw," said one who witnessed it. The long line **Memorable scene at Albany** of transports set out, a great string of ships, each keeping its distance behind the other, a couple of cables' lengths away, moving on, a steady, unceasing procession, the pace of all being fixed at the pace of the slowest. Around were the guardian warships. Mr. A. B. Paterson, the well-known Australian writer, described the scene: "Away ahead of the whole fleet, just in sight on the edge of the horizon, is a pillar of smoke—a cruiser is clearing the way for us, setting the pace, giving the direction, and keeping a watchful eye out for enemies. Far away to

VOLUNTEERS OF THE GREAT COMMONWEALTH IN TRAINING FOR THE FRONT.

their silent way scarce out of hearing of the gunshots in her final battle.

The Australian contingent believed that it was going to Europe. Great was the surprise, when the ships arrived at the Suez Canal, to find that orders had come for them to disembark there, to complete their training in Egypt, and to help to guard that country from the coming attack by the Turkish army that even then was crossing the desert.

New Zealand, like Australia, was in the fortunate position of being ready by land and by sea for war. There had been for some time before the outbreak of war compulsory military training for all male citizens between the ages of twelve and twenty-five, and there was a fine defence force thoroughly trained, armed, and organised, with ample guns, transports, and scientific corps.

Australia had elected to keep her Navy under her own control in times of peace, New Zealand had chosen to pool her resources with those of the Mother Country. **New Zealand's defence force** Many people in the Dominion would gladly have seen their battle-cruiser New Zealand around their own waters; but it was with the British Fleet, helping to guard other seas at the outset of the war.

Some days before war was declared, the Prime Minister of New Zealand, Mr. Massey, declared that the Government intended, if necessary, to offer an expeditionary force to the Imperial Government, and an understanding already had been arrived at concerning the number and constitution of that force. The announcement was made the occasion for a remarkable display of enthusiasm. For

starboard, just visible on the skyline, is another pillar of smoke and a dimly-seen, low-lying vessel on the horizon to port shows where a cruiser is day and night keeping her watch over our movements. So we move across the ocean like a large regatta of great steamships, always the same order being inflexibly kept. It is sometimes hard to believe that a hundred and twenty miles have been covered since one saw them last—they seem to be so exactly in the same place."

As the contingent was passing the Keeling Cocos Islands word went round that an attack was imminent, and the troops were to be prepared. The men were paraded on deck, bare to the waist, with trousers rolled up to the knees and lifebelts donned.

Meanwhile, the Australian battle-cruiser Sydney was that very day seeking out the Emden not a hundred miles away. Had there been a little less care, a little less precaution, the Emden might have cut into the convoy and possibly sunk several of the ships. As it was, the Emden herself went to her doom, while the transports passed on

AWAITING THE ORDER TO ADVANCE AGAINST THE TURKISH RAIDERS: STRIKING CAMERA PICTURE OF THE
AUSTRALIAN CAMP NEAR THE THREATENED BANK OF THE SUEZ CANAL.

once Parliamentary etiquette was forgotten, and everyone in the House of Representatives, whether member, visitor, or official, cheered to the echo. The leader of the Opposition, Sir Joseph Ward, declared, as soon as silence was secured, that the entire Opposition would co-operate with the Government in the defence of the Empire. The news of the declaration of war was made in dramatic fashion. The Governor appeared on the steps of Parliament House on the great afternoon and read a cablegram from the King thanking the Dominions for their loyal messages. Then he proceeded, almost as though by an afterthought: "I have yet another message—England and Germany are now at war."

The usual features familiar in other parts of the Empire followed. Men everywhere volunteered for service. The well-to-do gave their gifts of money and supplies. One of the most notable of national gifts was £20,000 divided between the National Relief Fund and the Belgian Relief Fund. In April, 1915, the Postmaster-General was able to announce that the total contribution to the Belgian Fund was £133,000 in cash, and goods and produce worth £65,000. The cash and produce sent for the poor of Great Britain and Ireland amounted to £138,000. The Maori people demanded that they should be allowed to share with the white races in the defence of the Flag. They offered to raise some thousands of men, and when news came that the British Government had decided to employ Indian soldiers in the war, it was impossible to refuse the Maoris the opportunity of doing their share.

In a very short time an expeditionary army of 8,000 was ready, and on September 24th the troops went on shipboard for Europe. "Time was, not very long ago," said Lord Liverpool, the Governor, "when the sight of a troopship in the New Zealand harbour denoted the arrival of troops from the Old Country. To-day the position is reversed. England has need of all her sons to-day, and the young Dominion is sending home to the Motherland of her best."

Lord Liverpool did not exaggerate. The young men who had volunteered for service in Europe were the very pick of the manhood of the Dominion. One found in the ranks university graduates, a large proportion of public schoolboys, the sons of statesmen and responsible business men. New Zealand, like the other parts of the Empire, gave her best.

New Zealand's splendid tribute

The expedition was timed to sail on September 25th, but probably on account of the activity of the German cruisers in the Pacific, the sailing was postponed at the last moment. The troops and horses were landed, and waited another twenty days. Then they got away.

The New Zealand Government made ample arrangements to keep the first contingent up to full strength. Shortly afterwards a further body of troops left for the front, and in February a third party sailed. The third party was notable on account of a corps of five hundred Maoris in its ranks—magnificent and eager fighting men. The Maori mothers and sisters, who came down to see them off, sent them to the front with every sign of cheerful courage. "Be brave. Do your duty. Kaiora" (farewell), one Maori mother telegraphed to her son. "No tangi"

PRINCESS PATRICIA'S CANADIAN LIGHT INFANTRY IN CAMP ON SALISBURY PLAIN.
Distribution of cigarettes to the men. In circle: Captain H. C. Buller, of the Rifle Brigade, who was appointed Lieutenant-Colonel in command, in succession to Colonel Farquhar, killed in action at Neuve Chapelle.

NOT THEIR OWN ROLLING PRAIRIE.
Canadian troops engaged in field operations on the Wiltshire uplands.

A HALT BY THE WAY.
Men of the First Canadian Contingent : A photograph taken during a halt on the way to the railway-station shortly after their disembarkation in England.

(no lamentation), said another mother. "Only too glad that my sons are serving the King."

One little incident may serve to show that this spirit was not confined to the people of the greater isles. Niue (Savage Island) is one of the Cook group, annexed to New Zealand in 1901. It has a population of about 4,000, nearly all natives. These could talk no English, and had seen very few Europeans. But when the news of war came they collected £164, and counted their young men. Two hundred of their picked youths were ready to go. So they sent the gift of money to Wellington, and the offer of their two hundred sons in a letter signed by twelve chiefs. Here is a translation of their message :

"To King George V., all those in authority, and the brave men who fight.

"I am the small island of Niue, a small child that stands up to help the King to stand fast.

"There are two portions we offer—(1) Money, (2) Men."

The Australians and New Zealanders landed along the Suez Canal and camped, many of them right at the foot of the Pyramids. He would have been dull, indeed, whose spirit was not stirred, and whose emotions were not aroused by the sight of these men, strong sons of the newest of white nations, coming their many thousands of miles to stand between the oldest of nations, Egypt, and its ancient Turkish oppressor.

The Colonial troops in Cairo   The Australasians won golden opinions during their stay on account of their giant stature, their fine equipment, and their orderliness. General Sir John Maxwell, the commander of the troops in Egypt, said after he inspected them that it would be impossible to find better material than this. "The Colonial troops are, as a whole, a really fine body of men," wrote one who saw them in Cairo. "Broad of shoulder, deep in the chest, and sun-burnt to a rich dark brown, they are the picture of rude health, and chock-full of animal spirits, which even the climate of Egypt cannot eliminate."

When Abbas Hilmi Pasha was deposed from the Khedivate of Egypt, and Prince Hussein appointed Sultan of Egypt, under the protectorate of the British, the presence of the Australasians helped to force the friends of Abbas to silence. On the day of the accession of the new Sultan a large number of the Australians and New Zealanders formed part of the forces for the military review. The Australian and New Zealand Light Horse, the New Zealand artillery, and the infantry made a deep impression by their splendid bearing on Europeans and natives alike.

The tale of how the Australasians, their work in Egypt done and well done, left for England, will belong to a latter part of this history.

The people of New Zealand witnessed with the greatest interest the departure of a small force, working in co-operation with the Australian Navy, for the capture of German islands in the Southern Pacific. New Zealanders had long regretted that Germany was ever allowed to acquire a foothold in Samoa. Now New Zealand troops quietly occupied Samoa, destroyed German wireless stations, and raised the British flag. The Australian Navy, having co-operated with New Zealand **Fine work in the Southern Pacific** in this removal of an unwanted neighbour, went on to island after island under German rule, raising the British flag everywhere. How they succeeded, the record of the useful work of the Australian Fleet, and its moral for the Empire at large belong to the naval sections of this book.

Australia and New Zealand felt, as they witnessed the triumphs of their ships and the advance of their armies, that they had stepped at last into full nationhood. They had reason for their pride and exultation. The community of sentiment in the Overseas Dominions was emphasised by the congratulatory message received from General Botha by the new Australian Premier, who in turn congratulated the General on taking the field against "the common enemy."

Elliott & Fry.

COMMANDER CHARLES RUMNEY SAMSON, D.S.O., R.N.

Commanding the Aeroplane and Armoured Motor Support, Royal Naval Air Service of the British Expeditionary Force.

178

HOW THE WAR IN THE AIR DEVELOPED.

How Kluck's Swerve from Paris was Observed—France Brings Her Brave Civilian Pilots to the Front—German Supremacy in Aerial Fire-Control Tactics—How Our Private Aeroplane Makers Saved the Situation—Defects of Our Royal Aircraft Factory—The Small, Swift Machine of British Aerial Victories—French Invent the Terrible Air-Arrow—Losing a German Army Corps in the Woods—German Airmen Search for British Reinforcements—Sudden Improvement in German Airmanship —Due to Use of Newly-Built Machines—Our Hard and Long Struggle to Recover Aerial Supremacy—Insufficient Number of British Airmen at the Front—How Our Men were Overworked—Adventures with " Archibald " and " Cuthbert "—" Mother " and the British Aviator—Part Played by the Wind—Duels in the Air—German Airmen Commanded to Avoid Fights— Achievements of the Crack French Airmen—The Significance and Aims of the Air Raiders—Superiority of the Aerial Observation Officers—Airmanship at Neuve Chapelle—The Vital Work of the Naval Air Patrol—Air Raids on Zeppelin Sheds, Aircraft, Factories, and Submarine Bases—The Combined Operations off Cuxhaven.

I N the first month of the war the military use of aircraft was in an experimental stage. The Germans had the advantage in material, numbers, and organisation. Their airmen co-operated with their field batteries in a practised manner during the retreat of the allied troops from the Sambre to the Marne. It was largely owing to the great number of German aerial observers that the heavy German field artillery dominated many of the early battlefields.

At the opening of the campaign the military aviation system of France was sadly defective. It was not until the dashing and superbly-trained civilian air pilots of France came to the front that the German airmen were held in check by our Allies. Then General Hirschauer, a strong and businesslike reformer, was given control over the aviation system, and he soon raised the general standard of French military airmanship by a wholesale dismissal of men who had joined the flying branch of the French Army for other reasons than a liking and talent for flying.

In our own Royal Flying Corps there were happily no defects of personnel to be remedied. Our men were magnificent. It was they who discovered on September 4th that the main columns of General von Kluck's army had swerved from Paris, and had moved in a south-easterly direction towards the Marne River in an attempt to turn or break the Fifth French Army. And it was this achievement that elicited General Joffre's message of high praise for the work done by our pilots and observers. In the subsequent German retreat to the Aisne our airmen reconnoitred the movements of the enemy, and by the mastery obtained over their flying foes they managed to prevent the hostile aerial scouts from discovering the movements of our troops. During this happy turn in the fortunes of the Franco-British army, the crack French civilian aviators were allowed to go to the front and supplement the efforts of the somewhat small number of efficient French military pilots. When the heroes of French aviation got to work on either side of our small but deadly Flying Corps, the German airmen lost the command of the sky all along the western front of the war.

The results of this aerial supremacy of the Allies were not at first apparent, for the military airman only does his best work when he is harnessed to a battery of powerful pieces of ordnance. At least, such was the condition of affairs when the lengthy campaign of trench warfare opened on the Aisne. So long as the British and French armies had only their ordinary artillery corps firing against the great siege train which the Germans brought from Maubeuge to reinforce their magnificent field-guns and howitzers, the allied airmen worked at a disadvantage; for often when they discovered the enemy's chief gun positions,

WARDERS OF THE SEAS.
Navy men keeping a bright look-out for enemy aircraft.

179

OUTWITTING THE ENEMY: THRILLING INCIDENT OF THE AIR RAID ON CUXHAVEN.
One of our seaplanes coming down short of its rendezvous, a British submarine shipped the pilot, destroyed the damaged machine, and dived, its captain gaining time by waving his hat to the crew of the Schütte-Lanz airship hovering aloft, and so making them think he was a German capturing a British airman. Immediately the submarine was submerged those on board felt the shock of bombs dropped by the disappointed enemy. Our picture is from a sketch made by an officer who took part in the action.

as little successful in aeronautics as in dye-making. But several private manufacturers in our country struggled on under severe discouragement from our official organisation. Prevented for a time from assisting our Army, they yet impressed, by the uncommon merits of their machines, some enlightened men in our Admiralty. A little Admiralty work enabled them to carry on, and continue their progress in construction, with the result that they produced at last the finest flying machines in existence.

One of the most important instruments of British aerial supremacy was the small, high-speed scouting aeroplane manufactured by the Sopwith and Bristol companies. Then there was the pretty, fast Manchester-built aeroplane, the Avro, with various other swift makes by other private British firms, such as the Short, Wight, and Martinsyde. In addition, the Vickers and Sopwith companies constructed splendid gun-carrying biplanes. These machines beat the Germans in speed, which was what our French comrades were at first generally unable to do, owing to the slowness of their "'buses." The French aviators were very plucky, and, as was well known before the war, they were incomparably skilful. But for some time their machines were not fast enough to enable them to fight air duels with as much success as our men. Happily, the new Voisin biplane and the Caudron machine lifted the French aviator, in regard to material, on a level with his foemen, and at the beginning of October the new French types of aircraft seemed to be superior to anything possessed by the Germans. Their production was a striking instance of the manner in which the French mind, when encompassed with dangers, can improvise a brilliant achievement, eclipsing all that the plodding, patient, organising talent of the Teuton has accomplished after years of preparation.

As the Allies improved both the material and the organisation of their aircraft, the increasing power of their artillery enabled their airmen to show to more advantage. The work of the aerial scouts went on incessantly. They preceded both armies in the long race to the sea which began west of the Aisne in the third week in September and ended on the Yser in the second week in October. **Aerial observers behind each front**

For a hundred miles or more behind each front the aerial observers of the opposite camp watched the movement of columns of troops and trains, the collection of rolling-stock, and the crawling lines of motor-vehicles.

They studied the size and situation of the enemy's bivouacs, parks, supply depots, and other facts giving a clue to the intentions of the hostile commanders. All this was aerial strategical reconnaissance, by far the most important part of the airmen's work. Then they had to make tactical observations. These were confined to a

their own gunners lacked the weapons to smash the enemy. Meanwhile, our artillery and that of our Allies had a hard fight against the German airmen. In all cases the guns of the Allies had to be hidden from aerial observation with extreme ingenuity and care. When a hostile air-scout appeared above our lines it was usually dangerous for our gunners to try to bring it down with shrapnel. For, thereby, they only revealed their emplacement, and the German flier signalled this to one of his distant batteries of great howitzers, which at once began to shell our guns. The situation was mainly saved by the fighting of our flying men, and by the excellent qualities of some of their machines. Indirectly, it was the inventiveness and the tenacity of character of a score or two of men connected with several private British firms manufacturing flying machines that defeated the great organised effort made by the Germans to obtain the control of the air.

Our official centre of aeronautic research and construction—the Royal Aircraft Factory—was in many ways behind the German aircraft organisation. Some of the machines it first produced seemed to show that the direction of scientific industries by our Government was

THE PICTURESQUE EFFECT OF SHELLING AN AERIAL MARAUDER.

Almost as remarkable as the triumph of the aeroplane has been the ingenuity in devising anti-aircraft weapons. In the above, sketched at the front by Mr. Seppings-Wright, the well-known war artist, a German "Taube" is speeding away from the too close attention of an anti-aircraft gun, which fires shells so rapidly that they burst in a long stream, and are effective at a height of between four and six thousand feet.

The great things anticipated of German Zeppelin airships when they would first come into touch with British warships failed entirely to materialise on Christmas Day, 1914, when seven British naval seaplanes, escorted by a light cruiser and destroyer force, together with submarines, made their famous attack on the German warships lying in Schillig Roads, off Cuxhaven. To quote the official despatch relating to that episode : " As soon as the ships were seen by the Germans

om Heligoland, two Zeppelins, three or four hostile seaplanes, and several hostile bmarines attacked them. It was necessary for the British ships to remain in e neighbourhood in order to pick up the returning airmen, and a novel combat ensued between the most modern cruisers on the one hand and the enemy's aircraft and submarines on the other. By swift manœuvring the enemy's submarines were avoided, and the two Zeppelins were easily put to flight."

NECESSITY TO SHELTER FROM AERIAL ATTACK IS THE MOTHER OF INVENTION.

In this photograph from the front, what looks at first glance a harmless haystack, with a ladder laid against it, contains a door beneath the ladder, and this door leads into a fair-sized farmhouse, the whole of which has been ingeniously covered by British soldiers with hay to disguise it from enemy aircraft. The farmhouse within was made to serve as an important intelligence post, with telephone connections.

A BRITISH GUN IN ACTION IN THE NORTH OF FRANCE.

The above particularly clear and very interesting photograph shows on the right a British gun in firing position, while to the left is its caisson, from which one of the gunners is withdrawing shells, while the sergeant stands by calmly giving orders. There is no evidence of warlike excitement; yet the photograph was taken while the gun was in action at a severely contested portion of the British front.

BRITISH AEROPLANE FLYING OVER A VILLAGE
IN NORTHERN FRANCE.

small area, which perhaps was about to be
assailed, or from which an attack was expected.
The flying observers had to locate the enemy's
trenches, gun emplacements, reserves, headquarters,
supply parks, and railheads. In some cases they
took photographs of the hostile positions. Then
there was the unceasing work of directing the
fire of our artillery. Now and then, when occasion
offered, the airmen came out in large machines,
carrying a store of bombs, with which they tried
to injure the railway communications of the foe.
They also worried any mass of hostile troops, the
French airmen having small boxes of steel arrows
for dropping on the enemy.

This new aerial weapon, introduced by the French
in October, was a terrible thing. It was a piece
of steel rod a third of an inch in diameter, and
about seven inches long. One end was pointed
like a pencil for an inch or so, while the other end
was machined out for five inches like the feathers of an
arrow. They were packed in boxes of fifty, and released
by the aviator opening the bottom of the box with a string.

The terrible aerial arrow Then the speed at which the aeroplane
was travelling distributed the arrows
thoroughly, while the force of gravity
endued the missiles, as they fell from
a great height, with horrible power. The effect on infantry, when in close formation or when lying behind low
trenches, was far more deadly than the same weight of
bombs.

By lying flat on the ground a fighting man could escape
the effect of a bomb unless it made a direct hit, which was
extremely unlikely. But men lying flat, or even crouching,
beneath a shower of aerial arrows, only exposed more
surface to the missiles. The effect on cavalry was worse
than on infantry, for there was a larger surface to hit.
Altogether, it was a horrible weapon. But it was not more
horrible than long-range gun fire, against which infantry
was quite as defenceless, and its wounds were no worse
than those made by shell splinters. Some of our officers
of the Royal Flying Corps, however, objected to the employment of these air arrows, as they thought the use of
them was unsportsmanlike. As the French airmen were
not fighting for sport, but to free their country from
a decivilised, inhuman race of invaders, notorious for the
murder of thousands of non-combatants, they proceeded
to develop the use of their new weapon.

Meanwhile, the allied aerial scouts continued their work
of reconnaissance around the advancing armies. They

IN READINESS FOR ENEMY AIRCRAFT.
British anti-aircraft guns on a motor-lorry cunningly concealed by the side of a
haystack.

were not always successful. An extraordinary case of an
entire German army corps being lost by our airmen took
place in the movement towards Arras. Two hostile army
corps were seen marching through the forest at Vermand.
A sharp look-out was kept on their movements. One
corps was traced as it went to reinforce the German troops
at St. Quentin. The other, however, vanished in a
mysterious manner. A similar disappearance of a German
army corps under the eyes of aeroplane scouts occurred
some time before at Compiègne. In both cases it is supposed that the large mass of men, 40,000 to 50,000, concealed themselves in the forest, where their movements
could not be observed by the aerial scouts. Then they left
the woods in small numbers at different times, and collected
at a prearranged rendezvous. But the fact that the
Germans had to undertake this lengthy
and difficult operation of marching an **Telling example of
aerial efficiency**
army corps to a forest and scattering it,
and then arranging for it to join together
again by a time-table, after a long night march, is a telling
example of the way in which the aerial reconnaissance of
the Allies increased the difficulties of the enemy.

Towards the middle of October there was a series of
German aeroplane raids on St. Omer, Dunkirk, Calais, and
Boulogne. But though the popular mind was struck by
the murderous bomb-dropping exploits of the enemy fliers,
this was only an amusement of the barbarians. Their real
business was the reconnaissance of the approaching movements of British troops. It is clear that the German
General Staff expected the landing of a stronger British

reinforcement than the 7th Division and the 3rd Cavalry Division under Sir Henry Rawlinson. It was feared that a considerable number of our Territorials would at once be transported and help in strengthening the seaward front. Hence the far-ranging activities of the German airmen, who also went bomb-dropping to Paris while reconnoitring for General Joffre's reserve forces.

Improvement in German aircraft It was about this time that a German cavalry division was defeated by a few airmen, as has already been related. The large force of horsemen were pursued and harassed from the sky during the whole of October 15th, and as evening drew on a well-aimed bomb completed their discomfiture. The allied airmen, however, did not have another amazing success of this sort. For on the same day a chase occurred at St. Omer, in which three of our aeroplanes tried to hunt down one German machine. It was expected that the enemy would be overtaken and put out of action. But two of our machines proved to be slower than the Germans', and the other one met with an accident and had to give up the chase.

This was the first significant sign of a general improvement in German aeroplanes, that caused the allied commanders a considerable amount of trouble in the early part of the winter. Several things seemed to show that the superiority in the air, won by us at the beginning of the war, was partly due to the fact that our opponents, drawn from the frontier air-stations, were at first using machines they had kept there for six, twelve, or eighteen months. They had mainly old-type T a u b e monoplanes, Aviatik biplanes, early-type Albatross, L.V.G. biplanes, and Jeannin monoplanes. These machines were heavy and slow, and many of them had only four-cylinder engines of 70 h.-p., instead of the 100-h.-p. six-cylinder engines of the new type.

But in the middle of October a large supply of superior machines arrived in the western German lines. Some of them had been building before the war, others had been completed after the great struggle opened. The effect of this sudden and important improvement in the most useful kind of the enemy's aircraft was soon remarked. Our pilots were surprised to discover that many of the German airmen began to climb better and fly more quickly than they used to. We had, in fact, only a few machines that could keep up with them. Our main problem in aerial warfare then rested with our manufacturers. Fortunately we had various new makes of aeroplanes capable of overtaking the best of the newest German types. The Germans had largely recovered their lost ground by modelling their new machines on ours. Their latest type of tractor biplanes were almost indistinguishable from ours by an untrained observer. The Ago tractor resembled our Sopwiths or Avros, the new Aviatik, Albatross, and L.V.G. looked like our B.E.'s. The popular chart, contrasting the silhouettes of German and British machines, and issued with the authority of our Government, was therefore misleading in regard to modern types. The old-fashioned Taube especially, so continually mentioned in our newspapers, was rarely employed by the enemy. The new Aviatik seems to have been the common German machine.

But while the Germans were imitating our inventive manufacturers, progress in construction had continued in our country. We had the Sopwith Scout, the Bristol Scout, the remarkable Avros, so light and yet so strong, and the new Martinsyde Scout, possessing some fine qualities. Then the Royal Aircraft Factory had developed out of the Sopwith and Bristol Scouts a small machine with the enormous speed of one hundred and fifty miles an hour. It was indeed so fast that it was hard to find pilots for it. One expert reckoned that there were only two men in the world who could m a n a g e it safely.

Thus, in combination with French makers, our aeroplane manufacturers were able to maintain a superiority against the better-organised efforts of the German aviation authorities. It was the old contest between the loose, free-branching activities of our muddling and yet finely-gifted race and the careful, comprehensive, and efficient system of Government control on which the Germans have relied for the last hundred years. We continued to retain the defects of our virtues. For no attempt was made to transform the Royal Aircraft **The better-organising Teuton** Factory into a general centre of aircraft research and construction, in which all the brilliant minds in our enterprising private firms could co-operate. Though Sir John French pointedly asked for greater efforts in providing our growing armies with an overwhelming superiority in the machinery of the new arm, there was no complete and really efficient organisation of the splendid resources we possessed. We still went

Flight-Commander F. E. T. Hewlett.

Flight-Commander D. A. Oliver.

Flight-Lieut. A. J. Miley.

Flight-Commander C. F. Kilner.

Flight-Sub.-Lieut. V. G. Blackburn.

Flight-Commander R. P. Ross.

Flight-Lieut. C. H. K. Edmonds.

A GROUP OF INTREPID BRITISH AIRMEN.

WONDERFUL CAMERA RECORD OF A FRENCH AEROPLANE PURSUING A GERMAN AIRSHIP.

This unique view was developed from a " snapshot " taken from a second aeroplane, and the incident thus recorded took place after one of the German airship raids on Paris. The aeroplane shown, in which two men can be discerned quite plainly, was in reality a considerable distance from its quarry. The distance can be gauged by the relative sizes of the two rivals for the dominion of the air. The airship is ascending and turning away from the camera, hence the foreshortening of the rear part of the immense craft, which here seems smaller than it is in reality.

along in the old free-and-easy way, managing on the whole to keep about level with the less inventive but better-organising Teuton.

The work of our Army pilots and observers was less spectacular than the raiding expeditions of our naval airmen ; but the work which our soldier fliers did was more laborious and more important. The number of pilots we had was really very small, but they made up in skill, courage, and endurance for their scanty numbers. It was reckoned that in the first month of the war their air mileage amounted to 87,000 miles—an average of 2,000 miles a day. Had we possessed a hundred pilots, the official figures given would have meant that each of them had only been in the air about half an hour a day. But, as a matter of fact, our men were overworked. So it is easy to see that they numbered much less than a hundred pilots.

Contrasts in aerial fire-control

The result was that we had not at first sufficient airmen with our Expeditionary Force to establish a general system of aerial fire-control for the batteries of our two army corps. The Germans, on the other hand, were excellently equipped on the Aisne, and the subsequent trench warfare, for the aerial control of their guns. They had a sausage-shaped balloon, known as the Parseval-Siegfeld, which was ridiculous in appearance, but admirable for observation purposes. The Germans protected their balloons from any aeroplane attack by posting a battery of anti-aircraft guns near them, often with airmen defenders. The anti-aircraft guns, however, were not very effectual against our dashing and adventurous flying men, who nicknamed them " Archibald " and " Cuthbert." Some of " Cuthbert's " shells burst at the tremendous height of 22,000 feet. It was impossible to execute reconnaissance work and escape from their range.

But our men were not daunted by " Archibald " and " Cuthbert." The German gunmaker had been very ingenious. Both the gun and the shrapnel shells which it fired were masterpieces of Teutonic science. The gun was semi-automatic ; it let off one shell, in which was a sort of parachute. When the shell burst, this parachute floated out in the air, making a conspicuous mark by which the gunner could correct his range and the timing of his fuse. Then, with startling rapidity, six more shells followed. Often the Germans arranged their aircraft guns in a triangular formation. When one of our machines appeared above their line, a gunner at the nearest point of the triangle fired a shell, making a burst of red smoke. From this red smoke, and from the flying machine, the second gunner got a more exact range, and tried a shell giving out a black smoke. If this missed, the third gunner had three marks from which to calculate his aim, so he tried a third test shot, and then the triangle of guns shot up their stream of shells by their semi-automatic device.

The trouble was that the German gunners were not sportsmen. They acted like amateur game-shots, who shoot at a bird, instead of aiming at the position the bird will occupy when the shot arrives. After a good deal of practice, the Teutons did get to understand what a game-shot was. Instead of firing at our machine, they fired at the place the machine would occupy if it continued flying in the same direction at the same height. But, naturally, our airmen were somewhat more intelligent than a pheasant.

Work of the German gunners

heavy pieces of ordnance, enabled our force to cope with the siege-artillery brought against our lines from Antwerp. At the same time an increase in the number of our aviators at the front enabled General Henderson to detach single machines for duty with artillery. We, in fact, then began to progress to that desirable stage of development in the use of aircraft when each artillery brigade would have its own aviators permanently attached to it. The pilots would be artillery officers in flying machines, and not merely Royal Flying Corps officers who happened to know something about guns.

A splendid beginning was made by attaching an aeroplane observer to our remarkable 9·2 in. howitzer, which our soldiers affectionately called their "Mother." It was their protection against the heavy siege-artillery of the enemy, from which they had suffered since the German stand above the Aisne. One aviator working with this great piece was at last able to direct it on a train moving behind the German lines eight miles away. The artillerymen simply loaded and fired according to wireless instructions, and got a direct hit on a moving mark far beyond their field of vision. Before the increasing use of wireless communication between the flying officer and the hidden guns which he controlled, the work of observing targets was signalled by means of smoke bombs, coloured lights with rocket tails, and other visible devices.

The artillerymen had to have an observation officer near their emplacement, watching their aeroplane observer with special instruments; for it was mainly from the study of the position of the aeroplane giving the visible signal that the situation of the hostile target could be calculated. But early in November the winter fog began

IN THE FORWARD "GONDOLA" OF A ZEPPELIN AIRSHIP.
The pilot and his assistants were accommodated in the forward end of the front "gondola," being in telephonic communication with the captain in the centre cabin. The windows were made of some flexible, transparent substance, such as mica, which was strong, thin, and light.

As soon as "Archibald" spoke, they dived, soared, or swerved, and even altered their speed. All our machines were hit by shrapnel bullets or rifle fire, but it was very seldom that either "Archibald" or "Cuthbert" brought them down. Our men relied mainly upon the high speed of their machines. The slowest of our "'buses" went at a mile a minute; the quickest of our "scouts" did well-nigh three miles a minute. The pilot and observer usually sat on a shield of bullet-proof steel, and though many holes were made in the planes of their machines they were rarely compelled to descend within the enemy's lines. Even when their petrol tank or some more vital part was injured, when they were making attacks or reconnaissances, they usually managed to volplane down to their own lines.

By the beginning of November, when we were at last holding the Germans firmly from Ypres to La Bassée, the co-operation between our airmen and artillery was perfected. The arrival of "Mother," our new great howitzer, and other

to veil the Flemish plain. The dense, grey clouds sagged lower and lower, so that the machines on both sides had to dive close to the ground for the purpose of a reconnaissance. "Archibald" became very busy, and it was assisted by rifle and machine-gun fire from the German trenches. Our darting, swerving, dancing aeroplanes were often screened by mist or cloud from the eyes of our artillerymen. Visible signalling became very chancy, with the happy result that the more scientific and exact method of wireless communication was developed.

Wireless communication developed

The military aerial work performed by our Army in the winter of 1914–15 was of supreme importance. The sodden, boggy condition of the ground between the two opposing fronts was a boon to the Allies. For in conjunction with their increasing power in artillery aircraft, it enabled them to beat back with little loss any further offensive movement by the enemy. Thus the great deadlock in the western theatre of war came about. The Germans had been so severely handled in all their vain attempts to break through that they resigned themselves to a defensive position. The Allies, on the other hand, were not yet strong enough to resume in turn their attacking movement. They needed some months' time to train their new army, to improve still further their artillery, and to increase their munitions of war. If the ground had been firm, the Germans could have worried them continually, and have compelled them at least to make frequent costly counter-attacks. But owing to the state of the soil there were few movements of importance on either side till the porous, chalky ground of Champagne began to recover from the winter rain.

The winter campaign was extremely arduous, both for the men in the air and for those in the pits and trenches.

The cold at high altitudes The cold at high altitudes was occasionally intense, fifty degrees of frost being marked in some early morning flights. At times the pilot and observer had to be lifted from their seats when they came down. They were quite numbed by the cold, in spite of the fact that they were very warmly clad. But it was not so much the cold as the high wind that troubled our airmen. On one occasion a pilot was going at full speed in a fast machine when he found himself returning to his own lines at the pace of ten miles an hour. He had flown into a tempest which was so overpowering that it annulled the power of his engine and blew him back. It was this reduction of speed by adverse winds that made aerial reconnaissance dangerous. At times our speediest scouts could only crawl along against a gale like lumbering, old-fashioned " 'buses," and they then became an easy target for their dear old friend " Archibald."

On the whole, however, the wind was more favourable to the Allies than to the Germans. The prevailing wind was westerly, so it usually increased the speed of our machines on their outward journey. The German pilots, on the other hand, often had the wind against them when they came over our lines, and the slackening of their speed enabled them to be brought down in greater numbers than were our own men. In addition to this, our remarkably swift scouting machines enabled many of our men to maintain a rapid flight even against a fairly strong head wind.

The direction of the wind was often one of the decisive factors in the aerial duels that took place. The Germans usually waited until a strong wind was blowing from their lines to ours. This gave them a very rapid flight over the area of danger. Our attacking pilot then had to rise, at a disadvantage, with the enemy above him and firing at him. There was a thrilling duel of this kind about a week or so before Christmas. A fast German biplane of a new type flashed in a northerly wind above our lines. One of our pilots rose to meet him on an Avro. The German used rifle and revolver without effect, for the British airman

got on the same level as his foeman. The German then tried to make for home. But the gale, which at first befriended him, now brought about his downfall. He could not make any headway against it, while the Avro machine steadily gained upon him, the British pilot shooting as he came on. The German dodged from side to side, planed down and swerved, reminding one of the twisting trail of a beaten fox. Our man countered every move. He was like a hawk circling round a crow. At last the German gave in, and. descending into our lines, was taken prisoner. He was not wounded, but utterly beaten in spirit. As our airmen put it in their expressive slang : " He came down through cold feet." There. were many other duels in the air, in which the enemy was either shot or brought down by damage to his machine. But this fight was especially remarkable in that it was the nerve of the German pilot that gave way.

As a matter of fact, the German airmen appeared to have received a general order to avoid fights in the air. In the circumstances this was simply a businesslike precaution on the part of the commander of the hostile air corps. His trained men were more useful to him in scouting and in gunfire-control than in direct operations against our airmen. We had proved ourselves the better aerial fighters early in the war. It may have been due to our qualities as a nation of islanders, with fine seamanship traditions and an instinct for dangerous sports. The air was only another sort of sea, and though the Germans began with thirteen hundred aeroplanes against a hundred machines capable of service in our country, while the French had only a few hundred really effective aeroplanes,

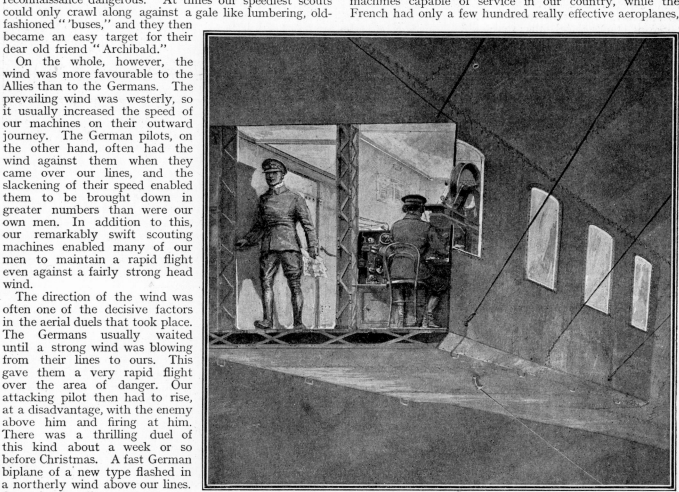

HOW THE RAIDING ZEPPELIN KEPT IN TOUCH WITH BERLIN.
View of the silence room in the centre cabin of a Zeppelin. The aerial telegraph line consists of 750 feet of phosphor-bronze wire which, when not in use, is wound round the wheel seen in the picture. At night, when the wireless waves have their fullest efficiency, a Zeppelin over England would be well in touch with the wireless stations in Germany.

the result was similar to that of the great Armada against the small ships of Sir Francis Drake. Our men had more zest for chancy, daring fighting than the cautious, calculating Teuton. He excelled in long, patient preparatory work, being bred up in blind reliance on his all-pervading State organisation. Naturally, some sense of sportsmanship marked the Germans who took to flying before the war; and the splendid records they made in the length of their flights and the altitudes they attained proved that they had an uncommon ability in the handling of their machines. But fighting in the skies from aeroplanes did not stir their sense of adventure. At least it ceased to do so when they met the still more daring Briton and found themselves outclassed.

The French aviators had the same zest for aerial warfare as our men, and on their improved machines they harried the enemy almost continuously at times. For instance, on September 18th, 20th, 21st, and 22nd they chased the German pilots on their front and compelled them to land. M. Pegoud, the famous inventor of the "looping the loop" operation, was one of the lords of the air. He took to night flying over the German lines, doing terrible damage in the darkness, and using a petrol flash on returning to land behind his own trenches. Sergeant Louis Noel, the well-known Hendon flier, also became remarkable for his nocturnal flights. The whole of his squadron followed his example in habitually flying at night, much to the

the next day they destroyed Fort Carnot. The forts were being used as magazines by the enemy and were important as points of support in the enemy's line of entrenchments. Their sudden destruction by aerial bombardment was an affair of some significance. Marksmanship in bomb-dropping was one of the peculiarities of the allied aviators. It was born of the same qualities as made them the victors in most of the aerial duels. They had more imperturbable daring than their opponents; they swooped lower to get well on their target; in short, they risked their lives more frequently, and at the same time they lessened the risk by the brilliance with which they handled their machines.

MILITARY AIRMEN OVER THE CLOUDS.
The remarkable photographs on this page, taken from an aeroplane over the clouds, help us to realise the difficulties of the airmen, whose observation while at a great altitude was limited to the brief glimpses they could get between the cloud-drifts of the enemy's positions on the ground below.

The air raids of the flying men of the French and British armies were seldom so spectacular in interest as the expeditions of some of our Naval Air Service aviators. They worked for the most part against the railway communications of the enemy, dropped bombs upon the motor transport columns of the German army, or attacked the German headquarters—striking at the brains of the enemy's forces. At the beginning of the war little or nothing was done by the Allies in these directions. What machines they had were urgently needed for other purposes, and the small experimental bombs first employed did not do enough damage. But when the battle of the trenches reduced modern warfare to strange new conditions, the quick-minded French had a machine ready for air raids on the enemy's communications. It was a large metal-built biplane, with a motor of 200 h.-p. It carried only a couple of very heavy bombs, charged with a new secret explosive. In the first experiment one of them made a hole in the ground ten yards wide and five feet deep. They were used for breaking down railway bridges and attacking trains. They were also employed in breaking up the permanent way in such a manner as to delay for days the supply of food and ammunition to the German front.

These great bombs weighed about one hundred and thirty pounds. A smaller bomb of twenty pounds weight could

New secret explosive

annoyance of the Germans, who would not imitate him. Noel, in the winter of 1914, was working on the Rheims section, where he achieved a great success. For it was by his efforts that the German fortress of heavy guns west of the cathedral city was put out of action.

Some weeks before this a combined squadron of British and French airmen made an attack upon the old forts of Lille. On November 4th they blew up Fort Englos;

THE WAR ZONE AS SEEN BY THE AIRMAN.

Two wonderful photographs indicating in each case how great an exercise of judgment is called for on the part of the airman, whether his mission be bomb-dropping, reconnoitring, or range-indicating. In the upper view, taken somewhere in France, a squadron of cavalry is seen passing. The lower photograph, taken from an aeroplane somewhere in Flanders, shows the flat nature of the country, every object being clearly detailed.

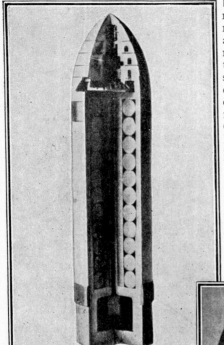

SECTION OF GERMAN SHRAPNEL SHELL FOR AERIAL USE.

be carried in larger numbers — in fact, most of the light and very swift machines could only take a few of the small missiles. The damage they did could quickly be repaired by the German engineers. But when a squadron of these light bomb-throwers attacked a certain important point, in a circular movement to and from their base of supplies and their point of attack, the continual aerial bombardment be-

came an important affair. When the Germans got their new machines, about the middle of October, 1914, they adopted the same tactics. In the middle of November especially they devoted much attention to our Army Service Corps, killing some of our men and transport horses. It seemed as though we had then lost for awhile our supremacy of the air through not having enough fast and powerful aeroplanes to attack all the German pilots who approached our lines. In the first week of December the German airmen were again very active. They attacked the town of Hazebrouck, hoping to destroy one of our headquarters, but only killed three children and three adult civilians. More effectual was their bombardment on December 7th of the junction of the Armentières-Dunkirk and Ypres-Calais railway line. Their bombs were small, and the damage they did was slight, but the operation was well planned. It showed, at least, that the Germans grasped the lesson **Narrow escape of** of the Allies' repeated attacks upon their **the Kaiser** communications. We had previously attacked the German headquarters at Thielt on November 1st, when it was reported that the Kaiser narrowly escaped death from the thirty-two bombs thrown on the building in which he met his generals.

All the military air raids on either side, however, did no more than annoy and worry the respective enemy. Owing, perhaps, to the lack of machines and pilots, no men could be spared from reconnaissances and artillery direction duties in order to make a grand air attack on some point of importance. As cavalry reconnaissance was prevented on both sides by the barrier of the trenches, only the spy and the airman could obtain any information as to the

movements of the enemy. The airman, therefore, became exceedingly valuable. It is not too much to say that he dominated the battlefield. In fact, he gave modern trench warfare its extraordinary character. It was to escape his observation that the life of the artillerymen became a laborious round of digging holes and hiding from sight. The entrenched infantry had continually to burrow deeper, and to conceal their burrows by all manner of devices in order to **Aerial control of** escape the notice of the airman. His **howitzer fire** bombs and air arrows were of small importance. What made him so terrible was the fact that he was the eye of distant batteries of hidden howitzers.

Without aerial fire-control, the indirect fire of the howitzer would not have been the main influence upon the later western battlefields. The trench protected the soldier fairly well from the direct fire of ordinary guns. If he could have also avoided the almost vertical bombardment of high-explosive howitzer shells, the character of the fighting would have been changed. In particular, the French would probably have won the first turning movement they made under General Castelnau towards the end of September. It was the heavy German guns and howitzers, directed by aerial observers, which saved the enemy's main line of railway communications at St. Quentin and east of Cambrai. And then, when the trenches along the Aisne were prolonged to Arras, Lille, and Nieuport, the long-range howitzer and its flying controller, with his range-finding instruments and camera, still remained the master-spirit of the campaign.

BOMBS DROPPED FROM A ZEPPELIN ON ENGLISH SOIL.

His vision reached a hundred miles or more over the opposing front. The war became to him an intellectual pursuit of absorbing interest. If he had a genius for his work, he could read the mind of a hostile commander from the size and position of the bivouacs and the direction of the long string of motor-vehicles.

No reconnoitring cavalry or scouts on motor-cycles could have accomplished what he accomplished. Beneath his eagle eye the fog of war was dissipated. The old grand, decisive element in strategy—the use of new large forces in unexpected times or places —became impracticable. The Germans effected one overwhelming thing of this sort at the opening of the war in the west by their vast, swift concentration of armies from the Sambre and

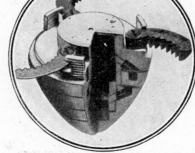

SECTION OF THE NOSE (FUSE) OF AERIAL SHRAPNEL SHELL.

Meuse. And the British army afterwards took General von Kluck by surprise by hiding in the forest near Paris, and chasing away his aeroplane scouts. But with these two exceptions, and the evasion of certain German army corps from aerial reconnaissance by scattering in thick woods, the mystery of war no longer obtained in the western field of struggle.

General Joffre knew what General Falkenhayn was doing in a large way, and also what he intended to do in the immediate future. General Falkenhayn was in a similarly enlightened position in regard to his opponent. From the point of view of strategy, each commander knew what cards his opponent had in his hand. It was only by small tactical manœuvrings of troops, conducted under cover of night, that the surprise attacks could be made. These had only a local importance, and by openly bringing up reinforcements the opposing commander always stopped the forward movement of the enemy.

This remarkable simplification of the art of war was the supreme achievement of the military airmen during the first nine months of the campaign. Next to it was the increased importance of long-range howitzer fire, and the general improvement in the destructive power of artillery due to fire direction from aeroplanes. In the third place came the long-range power over the enemy lines of communication, derived from the bomb-dropping art of the airmen. This line of development in the use of the new arm was not, however, followed up, for reasons already given. The best example of it was seen in the part played by our Royal Flying Corps during the attack on Neuve Chapelle in March, 1915.

This was, in plan at least, the first classic airmen's battle. But for an accident it might have resulted in the breaking of the German front and the recapture of Lille. Much time was spent in preparation. The enemy's trenches were minutely studied and photographed from the air.

ZEPPELIN HOLDING UP A MERCHANT VESSEL IN THE NORTH SEA.
Several Zeppelins took part in the German " blockade " of the British coasts ; and some of them came to grief, two (the L3 and L4) being wrecked in a storm off Denmark. Near the Haaks Lighthouse a Zeppelin came close to a Dutch steamer, the Helena, but on seeing the Dutch flag, reascended.

The artillerymen had simply to calculate the elevation of their howitzers, so as to drop an enormous number of high-explosive shells into the German line. While the guns and munitions were being secretly accumulated, the outpost duties of our airmen became very rigorous, for, naturally, no German aerial scouts could be permitted to make a reconnaissance. Each hostile flying man had to be met as soon as he appeared, and prevented from crossing our line, or brought down if he did so.

Then, when the terrific bombardment opened, and our infantry advanced, our Royal Flying Corps was used, probably for the first time in the history of warfare, in a masterly manner. They flew behind the enemy's lines and bombarded the railway station at Don and the railway bridge at Menin, by which reinforcements could have been sent to the breaking-point of the German front. The idea was superb, and marked a new and highly-important advance in general strategy. Our airmen got behind the fighting German force and attempted to isolate it from the rest of the German army. They were not in sufficient number to control all the roads, but they seriously interfered with the working of any railway transport of fresh guns or munitions. When a grand

An advance in strategy

army counts its airmen in tens of thousands instead of in scores, this aerial bombardment of the enemy's rear, in co-operation with an artillery and infantry attack on his front, will be widely employed. The engagement at Neuve Chapelle thus marked a new era in modern warfare. In it was developed the design of interrupting the enemy's communications, in the heat of an action, which our Allies had been employing a few weeks before in their attack upon the enemy's lines at Perthes, in Champagne. By this time both General Henderson and General Hirschauer had fully worked out the tactics of the new arm. It was only their lack of thousands of airmen and of thousands of machines which prevented them from dealing the enemy a series of terrific blows from the air.

Happily, the Germans were in no better condition than the Allies in regard to the number of men and machines on the front. The continual air raids which the Germans made upon Dunkirk in January, 1915, were only a sign of the growing weakness of German airmen. About this time they were concentrating the greater part of their aerial force in Champagne and Lorraine, being apprehensive that General Joffre would make his grand offensive movement in the spring from one of the sides of Verdun. Then, to mask this withdrawal of pilots and machines from the westernmost sectors of their lines, the Germans began to make furious raids upon our provisioning base at Dunkirk.

But none of these raids was successful. On January 22nd, for instance, a squadron of twelve German aeroplanes attacked Dunkirk, and only Captain F. V. Holt, of the Oxford and Bucks Light Infantry, was on patrol duty.

Air duel at Dunkirk But, on his little Martinsyde Scout, Captain Holt chased and fired at the two leading German machines and drove them off. By the time the other ten German aeroplanes came up, two more officers of our Royal Flying Corps, Captain Mills and Lieutenant Morgan, had ascended to a height of 6,000 feet, at which the action was taking place. Our three airmen then attacked the German machines, each of which had two men aboard. One enemy aeroplane was brought down by a bullet through one of its cylinders, and the pilot and observer were captured, with eight unexploded bombs, the observer being armed with a double-barrelled pistol for firing chain-shot. Having regard to the heavy odds against them, the achievement of Captain Holt and his two assistants was a remarkable example of the personal ascendency established by our

AIR - SCOUTING OVER THE DARDANELLES.
British seaplane, after a flight, about to be taken in tow by a ship's cutter.

SEAPLANE BEING HOISTED ON BOARD A CRUISER.
The machine had been on a flight over the Turkish positions in the Dardanelles. The pilot (seen standing) was French and the observer British.

by a fortunate chance their efforts were, to some extent, helped by the enlightened policy of our Admiralty.

As an organiser in war, Mr. Winston Churchill was not without defects, but he certainly had some inspiriting qualities of dash and originality. Early in the campaign, under his direction, the Royal Naval Air Service proved to be as efficient as the other branches of our naval force. This may partly have been due to the fact that the Admiralty relied less upon the Royal Aircraft Factory than our War Office did, and kept our enterprising private aeroplane makers going by Admiralty orders. Many of the best machines of the Sopwith Company and the Avro Company were taken up by the Naval Air Service and put to excellent use. The Admiralty also had, though it did not advertise the fact, a superb fleet of air destroyers, manned by men who were very anxious to try conclusions with the craft of Count Zeppelin. Our air destroyers were, indeed, the finest in the world.

But it is not yet possible to discuss the part which they played in the Great War. This is one of the things of which full details will only appear when the great struggle is over. Our naval aircraft patrolled the east coast of the North Sea and the Strait of Dover by daylight. The airships often kept aloft twelve hours, and, with the assistance of seaplanes working from a carrier steamer, the naval airmen kept continually under observation all the waters off the enemy's western coasts.

This laborious, unending, unspectacular reconnaissance work, carried out, as the war proceeded, in bitter, dangerous weather, constituted the most important achievement of the men of our Naval Air Service. Public attention was naturally fixed upon a few happy naval officers engaged in air raids. But these men were only able to be spared for picturesque and exciting work through the steady, silent, unnoted, but more important labours of their comrades.

men. Captain Holt was appointed a Companion of the Distinguished Service Order, in recognition of his gallantry and skill.

It was reckoned that from November, 1914, to February, 1915, our Army airmen flew altogether a hundred thousand miles. They always attacked any enemy craft which they sighted, except on the occasions when they were on some special duty from which they could not turn aside just for a sporting fight. Had we but possessed more machines and men, the ascendancy over the enemy would have been far more completely maintained. As it was, our overworked men did the best they could to interrupt continually the reconnaissance work of the enemy, and

On both sides the airship became, in regard to North Sea operations, a great auxiliary of the fleets. The Zeppelin and other large airships were soon found to be ineffectual in land warfare. The French brought the first Zeppelin down in a wood near Epinal on August 20th, 1914. No special anti-aircraft gun was necessary. The rigidly-built composite balloon was wrecked by a 3 in. shrapnel shell from one of the light French field-guns. Several of the rigid and semi-rigid German airships were destroyed by French and Russian soldiers, while our army never caught a glimpse of a Zeppelin or Parseval.

WRECKED IN A SNOWSTORM.
The German Airship L3, which came to grief in a snowstorm on the Danish island of Fanoe. Its size may be judged by that of the two men seen standing on the left of the wreck.

The airships were at last withdrawn into their sheds, and the German land forces worked almost entirely with the speedier and handier flying machines. A night raid on a French coast town, a voyage to Paris, and a little bomb-dropping at Antwerp and round the eastern French frontier constituted the sum of activities of the Zeppelins in regard to land warfare in the western theatre of battle. The huge dirigible balloons were but huge failures. Their construction was an extremely laborious task, and also highly expensive having regard to the results obtained. Large aeroplanes, carrying each a couple of heavy bombs, were much speedier, much safer in all weathers, and much less costly in life, labour, and treasure. A single pilot, combining great daring and great skill and **Failure of the Zeppelins** using a scouting machine travelling at a hundred and fifty miles an hour, was likely to be able to wreck a Zeppelin. So the Zeppelins, Parsevals, and other German airships retired from the battle-front.

Some of them were preserved as bogies, intended to frighten nervous people in London. One or two of them seem to have at last reached our country on January 19th,

1915, in a nocturnal voyage to Yarmouth and certain Norfolk villages. They dropped bombs in water-butts and other places. A shoemaker and an aged woman were killed at Yarmouth; a lad of fourteen and a soldier's widow were murdered at King's Lynn; and one soldier at Yarmouth, belonging to the Essex Regiment, was wounded, being the first military victim of hostile aircraft in the British Isles. The affair **Night flight over** was of no importance whatever. It took **Norfolk villages** place on a rainy, foggy, night, when our naval air patrol was impeded by the weather from observing the advance of enemy aircraft. But the fog that prevented the Germans from being seen also hindered their operations. The few deaths and injuries of innocent non-combatants in East Anglia were a loss that might have occurred in an everyday street accident.

Apparently the intention of the Zeppelin commander was to recover the prestige lost by the German airships in the North Sea on Christmas Day, when they failed against our combined air and sea raid off Cuxhaven. The proper course for the Germans would have been to make a similar attack on our great shipyards or war manufacturing centres. The latest Zeppelins were

INGLORIOUS END OF ANOTHER "AERIAL DREADNOUGHT."
The framework of this aerial monster, which met with disaster on French soil, was cut up by French soldiers. Pieces of the aluminium frame were on sale in Paris as souvenirs of the German raids.

capable of a flight of thirty hours at their full speed of fifty miles an hour. Their range of action, in favourable weather, was therefore about twelve hundred miles, allowing for loss of power against wind on part of the journey. There was no part of the British Isles they could not have reached, partly by daylight travel; and even between evening and dawn they could have flown at full speed from Heligoland or the German coast sheds, bombarded some of our larger towns, and returned through the veil of darkness.

But they made no attack on any important centre of warlike activity, such as our Naval Air Service had continually selected in Germany. They dared not, in their first raids at least, take the risk of facing the various means of defence and offensive-defence concentrated at British places of national importance. All they attempted was an easy reconnaissance in force over an unprotected area of no military importance, where they could cheaply re-establish their prestige in their own country by a little bomb-dropping on England, with little danger to themselves.

The Zeppelins seem to have left their base about 11.30 a.m. on Tuesday, January 19th, 1915, and arrived over the East Anglian coast about 8.30 p.m. They used only half their power, for fear of encountering later either adverse air conditions or our naval airmen. As a matter of fact, they had a favouring wind on their return, and went back faster than they came. The airships appear to have travelled together towards Mundesley, and then separated, one going to Yarmouth and another to Cromer. At 8.30 p.m. Cromer was missed, but Beeston was bombarded without result, and another bomb was dropped at Sheringham, but it did not explode. The same airship seems to have travelled on past Hunstanton at 10.30 o'clock, and whirred over

BRITISH SEAPLANE IN FLIGHT DURING THE RAID ON CUXHAVEN.

Airship attack on Yarmouth

Heacham, where a water-butt received a shell, and on to Snettisham, where the village church was missed by sixty yards by a bomb. Then about 11 o'clock at night King's Lynn received a series of bombs, a soldier's widow was killed and a lad of fourteen was slain in his bed, his father and mother and their baby child being injured.

Yarmouth was attacked from another direction about 8.30 p.m. The airship passed rapidly over the town from south to north, the crew throwing bombs for ten minutes at points all in a line about a hundred yards from each other. The streets were full of people, taking the air in the winter evening, but only three persons were struck. Two bombs thrown by St. Peter's Church killed an old lady who was fetching her supper, and a middle-aged shoemaker, while a soldier was injured. The townspeople, far from being panic-stricken, were inclined to remain in the streets, looking at the first Zeppelin bombardment of Britain ; but the borough engineer cut off the lighting, as a measure of precaution against the return of the raider. This was well done, for about midnight the whir of an airship was again heard from the sky, but the hostile craft turned out to sea without attempting more slaughter or damage.

It is doubtful if the reported presence of King George and Queen Mary at Sandringham led to the second airship raiding southward from Hunstanton. The bomb may have been dropped at Snettisham in mistake for Sandringham. But, as a matter of fact, their Majesties had left Sandringham, without public

notice, so there was no danger to them—though the foe may have intended to follow the tactics of the Zeppelin raid on Antwerp, when the Royal palace was attacked, in the hope of killing King Albert and Queen Elisabeth of Belgium.

To achieve the insignificant results of the Norfolk aerial raid, the German airships, in their journeys over the waters, had to run grave risks. What these risks were was more clearly seen in the third week of February, when a Zeppelin and a Schütte-Lanz were wrecked by a storm in the North Sea. One came down, on February 17th, 1915, on Fanoe Island, and was there burned, the officers and men being arrested and interned by the Danish authorities. On the same day another German naval airship was wrecked off the west coast of Jutland, four of the crew being saved and eleven drowned.

This double disaster was a matter of supreme significance to the people of the British Isles. The two airships seemed to have been overtaken by a snowstorm. The snow that fell on their coverings, amounting perhaps to a ton in weight, pressed them down, and led to the wrecking of them. The direct cause of the disaster was a lack of knowledge of the probable weather conditions on February 17th. Our meteorological authorities controlled the situation.

From our weather stations on the edge of the Atlantic it is possible to foretell fairly the conditions of the air in the North Sea and the Channel. Thus our naval airships were able to operate with comparative safety. But as soon as the war broke out our Meteorological Department kept its main weather information a secret, and in particular ceased to transmit to the Continent the facts gathered in our observing stations in Ireland and elsewhere. The result was that our country, through its happy position on the edge of the storm-brewing Atlantic Ocean, was as supreme over Germany in regard to aerial operations as in regard to naval operations. And this was the chief reason why no squadron of Zeppelins attempted all the autumn, winter, and spring of 1914-15 to bombard London.

Our supremacy in weather-lore

Not only had they to face our air destroyers, flying machines, and anti-aircraft corps, but they had to take the immense risk of meeting adverse weather conditions. The extraordinary advantage enjoyed by our country in regard to weather-lore was providential. Nearly all anti-cyclones, representing mainly stable weather conditions, spread from the European continent to our islands. Nearly all cyclones, representing weather disturbances, sweep across the Atlantic and affect our country a day before they spread to the Continent. Thus it looks as though Britannia need not fear the coming era of aerial warfare.

TROOPERS ENDEAVOURING TO FOLLOW A DUEL IN THE AIR BETWEEN A BRITISH AEROPLANE AND A GERMAN AVIATIK.

ARMED BRITISH BIPLANE STARTING FROM HEADQUARTERS NEAR HOLLEBEKE.

The Union Jacks on the under side of each of the upper planes were for the guidance of the gunners in the allied lines. The gun in front of the observer was a Colt automatic. The bombs, suspended independently at the side of the car, were released by pulling a cord and thus withdrawing a pin in the neck of each missile. Our illustration was made from photographic material received from a British officer.

The British supremacy in weather lore was the main factor in the success of our Naval Air Service. The German airships were superior to ours in range of action. When the weather seemed to be quite settled they could venture far out into the North Sea, and there, at a height beyond the reach of our destroyers' guns, they could watch the movements of our ships and telegraph their observations by wireless to the German naval base.

German airship superiority Our smaller patrolling craft, with a less range of flight, could not operate from our coast and keep all the waters between Denmark and Holland under constant observation. We had to use steamers fitted up as aircraft carriers in order to approach the German naval bases and to watch what went on round there. It was really our knowledge of coming weather conditions that enabled us to cope with the better-equipped German naval reconnaissance officers.

Count Zeppelin had served his country well. Though his dirigible balloons were ineffectual in land warfare, they were superb instruments of reconnaissance in naval operations. In fair weather they were able to watch over five hundred or more miles of sea. Floating at a high altitude above the Dogger Bank, they could prevent any daylight surprise by our battle squadrons. If we had also possessed a large fleet of Zeppelins, employed in accordance with our knowledge of weather conditions, the task of our naval patrol would have been greatly facilitated. Yet in spite of their inferior material our men also kept good watch and ward. The result was that the preliminary movements of both fleets usually took place at night. Our raid into the Bight of Heligoland and the German raids on our East Coast were both conducted in darkness. Such was the effect of the new aerial arm upon naval manœuvres.

Our Admiralty recognised the sterling worth of the Zeppelin by directing Wing-Commander Samson to bombard some of the airship sheds along the Rhine. We have already related the first attack on the airsheds at Düsseldorf and Cologne. This was only in the nature of a preliminary reconnaissance, and a more effectual operation was conducted from Antwerp on October 8th. Squadron-Commander Grey and Lieutenant Marix, on Sopwith Scouts, and Lieutenant Sippe went to Antwerp when the siege began. When they started on the raid Lieutenant Sippe's engine gave trouble, being an example of Royal Aircraft Factory adaptation. He was unable to complete the journey, while the two other men on their fast, private-built machines reached their mark.

It was not an easy expedition, as the country was veiled by thick weather. When Lieutenant Marix came down to discover where he was, he found himself only a hundred feet above some tree-tops. On reaching the Rhine Lieutenant Marix dived five hundred feet at the airshed, and released his bombs amid the heavy fire of high-angle guns and rifles. He set the shed alight and destroyed the Zeppelin inside it. Meanwhile, Squadron-Commander Grey whirred higher up the Rhine to Cologne. But all over this city the mist was so thick that the aviator could not find the position of the airship shed. So after circling above the city, much to the amusement of the townspeople, who did not imagine he was an enemy, he launched his bombs on the central railway-station, and considerably damaged this main centre of the German line of communications.

Squadron-Commander Grey got back safely to Antwerp, but Lieutenant Marix had to alight in Belgium, through his supply of petrol running out. A Ghent newspaper at the time reported that the Belgian patrol saw a machine alight and hurried to the spot. There they found a young man, who thought he had fallen into the hands of the German soldiers and was coolly waiting for death. He was taken in an armed motor-car to Antwerp by the admiring Belgians, just in time to escape with the Belgian Army and the British Naval Division. **Marix's exciting adventure**

The next base of our raiders of the Royal Naval Air Service was Belfort. There, on November 21st, Squadron-

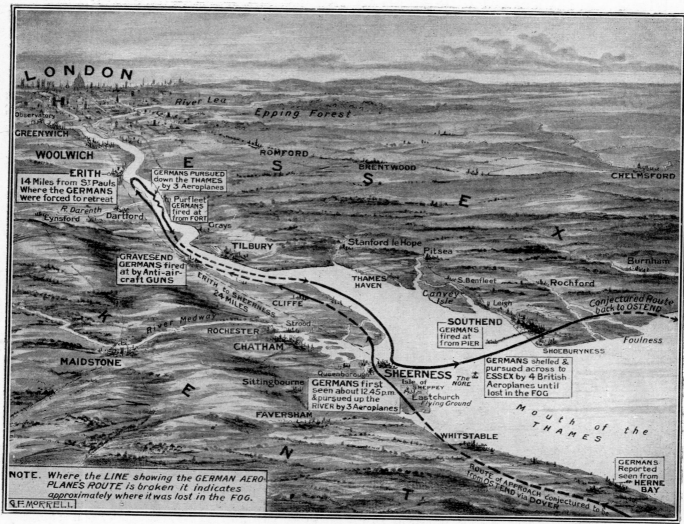

GERMANY'S CHRISTMAS DAY AIR RAID ON LONDON.
Owing to fog, the German aeroplane which flew over the Thames to within fourteen miles of St. Paul's Cathedral, on December 25th, 1914, escaped from its British pursuers. The flight, with Woolwich perhaps as its objective, caused some excitement, but no damage was done.

Commander E. F. Briggs, with Flight-Commander Babington and Lieutenant Sippe, set out on Avro machines on a round voyage of two hundred and fifty miles towards the centre of the Zeppelin industry. The three airmen had to cross the mountainous tract of the Black Forest in thick weather, and to fly over the misty waters of Lake Constance to the lakeside town of Friedrichshafen. At Schaffhausen Commander Briggs lost sight of his companions in the fog.

He was the first to arrive at the Zeppelin factory, where he dived through the fire of the machine-guns and quick-firers and dropped his bombs. Commander Babington and Lieutenant Sippe came out of the mist, and also attacked through a heavy fire. Most of the bombs were skilfully aimed at the Zeppelin works, but one or two dropped on the airshed and damaged the latest Zeppelin. The gasworks were exploded, sending up gigantic flames into the sky, and for an area of seven hundred square yards in and around the Zeppelin works considerable damage was done. The machine of Squadron-Commander Briggs was badly injured by the enemy's fire, forcing the naval aviator, who was wounded, to alight. An attempt seems to have been made to lynch him when he landed, and a German soldier attacked him; but he was rescued by an officer and taken to the hospital, some of his foes being full of admiration for the daring courage which he had displayed. Commander Babington and Lieutenant Sippe had each a dozen holes in their machines, but the fuselage and important fittings were untouched, and both officers got back safely to their starting-point.

The next air raid was conducted by French aviators. They also selected one of the principal aircraft construction

Briggs' daring courage

works in Germany. The best German aeroplane was the Aviatik, which had been manufactured at Mulhouse at the beginning of the war. But when the French Army entered Alsace, and threatened to capture Mulhouse, the aeroplane works were removed across the Rhine to Freiburg in the Black Forest. Here they were repeatedly bombarded by French aviators, the first raid taking place in the first week in December. Considerable damage was done, and the German Government had the impudence to protest that, as Freiburg was an open town, the aerial bombardment was contrary to international law. This protest was made after German airmen had for months been busy killing civilians, mainly women and children, with the sole object of creating a panic among the French people. Important centres of military activities like Freiburg or Friedrichshafen were regarded by the Germans as sacrosanct, while quiet villages in Norfolk and unfortified historic towns in France were treated as the proper objects of German bomb-throwers. The way in which the new barbarians combined a screaming foolishness in regard to attacks on their own country and a cold-blooded lust for murder of Belgian, British, and French children and women can be explained.

The explanation was obtained from Düsseldorf. There the German civil population was terrified by the success of our naval airmen. Many well-to-do families left their homes after the destruction of the Zeppelin shed and Zeppelin and settled in Central Germany. The General in command, Baron von Bissing, issued a long proclamation, in which he stated that the British raid " produced in certain circles of the population a feeling not in accordance

Repeated raids on Freiburg

THE ANTI-AIRCRAFT CORPS IN ACTION: "WINGING" A GERMAN TAUBE NEAR YPRES.

Ten Anti-Aircraft men were out scouting near Ypres with an anti-aircraft gun mounted on a motor-chassis. Immediately the Taube appeared they opened fire, with the result that the machine, spouting flame and smoke, zigzagged to earth about a mile away, where it was captured.

BIRD'S-EYE VIEW OF CUXHAVEN HARBOUR, AT THE MOUTH OF THE RIVER ELBE.

Scene of the daring exploit by seven British naval airmen, assisted by H.M.S. Arethusa and Undaunted and submarines, on December 25th, 1914, when many enemy warships were attacked.

with the active and vigorous character of the German people." He went on to say that "the German people has been partly spoiled by the successes of the German armies, so that many of them suffer nerve shock when the enemy obtains some slight success anywhere in Germany." He concluded by praising the strictly censored newspapers for not showing "the same excitement and nervousness as the **Civilian terror in** great part of the **Düsseldorf** people of Düsseldorf."

Thus it looked as though we were fighting an empire of cowards, dragooned into a warlike attitude by an aristocracy of bullies.

What especially made the German people nervous was the fact that they were able to see with their own eyes the destruction of the most acclaimed and cherished part of their great war-machine—the Zeppelins. They had been told that London would be completely paralysed by a terrific aerial bombardment by a mighty fleet of Zeppelins. Children of well-to-do German families had been provided with a toy London, which they were able to destroy, with the slaughter of millions of lives, by means of a fleet of toy Zeppelins. Merely a slight attack upon certain military points of importance at Düsseldorf, Cologne, Friedrichshafen, and Freiburg made the great, brave German people feel that two could play at the aerial war-game; and those two, it seemed to them, were Britain and France. No wonder then that Baron von Bissing had to issue a stern proclamation, even at a time when no German civilian had been killed by accident in our first raids.

By way of heartening their people the Germans sent one or two airmen on aeroplanes to attack Dover, and if possible to reach London. The most important attempt of this kind was baffled by an air patrol at Dunkirk; and none of the large squadron of German flying men even managed to cross the Channel.

At Christmas a single **Christmas raider** raider came up the **up the Thames** Thames as far as Erith, but was chased away by our naval airmen.

On the same day our Admiralty gave the Germans a lesson in the proper handling of a small naval air force engaged in reconnaissance work. Our Navy was anxious to know what the Germans were doing in the Schillig Roads, off Cuxhaven, and as our submarine scouts could not obtain full information, our naval patrol took the matter in hand. Seven seaplanes, piloted by Flight-Commanders Oliver, Hewlett, Ross, Kilner, Miley, and Flight-Lieutenants Edmonds and Gaskell Blackburn, sailed with their machines to a spot near Heligoland.

WANTON DESTRUCTION TO MAKE A GERMAN HOLIDAY: EFFECT OF BOMB-DROPPING IN A STREET IN KING'S LYNN, NORFOLK, ON JANUARY 19TH, 1915.

The carrier steamers were convoyed by a light cruiser and destroyer force, with submarines in attendance. The attack was delivered in daylight, and as soon as our ships were seen by the look-out on Heligoland Island, two Zeppelins and three or four German seaplanes, with several hostile submarines, were ordered to counter-attack.

Reconnaissance off Cuxhaven Our seaplanes were slung outboard and lowered with their pilots and observers at daybreak. With a rush the planes were off, and quickly climbed to a height of over 2,000 feet. As they approached the shore the land batteries and warships opened fire. But our men sailed on through the low-hung clouds, and then dived to extraordinarily low positions. This made it easier for them to strike their targets, and it did not really increase their danger, for their high-speed machines were as hard to hit when low as when high up. Our airmen made a valuable reconnaissance and bombarded the German fleet. But one flier, having used his last bomb on a big battleship, met another when he was quite out of ammunition. Throttling his engine, he dived straight to the ship's deck as if to ram it, and just before he used his control and soared upward he hurled at the enemy ship the only throwable thing within reach—a large woolly golliwog which he had carried as a mascot.

After studying the condition of things in Heligoland and Cuxhaven, and doing considerable damage in a round flight of three hours, our men returned to their

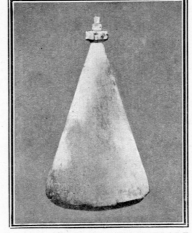

A BOMB THAT DID NOT EXPLODE.
Found at Yarmouth in January, 1915.

carrier steamers. Three of the seven airmen got back to their machines. Three others, returning later, had their machines sunk, and were picked up by our submarines. Commander Hewlett was rescued by a Dutch trawler. after losing his way in a fog and floating about the sea for six hours, when his motor went wrong.

While the airmen were enjoying **Commander Hewlett's** themselves at the first historic bom- **rescue** bardment of battleships by seaplanes, their protectors — the British light cruisers and the flotillas of destroyers and submarines—had an interesting time with the enemy aircraft. The two vast, silvery Zeppelins came floating over the British vessels, appearing in and out of the clouds. But there was no fight in the airship crews. Our cruisers opened on them with common shell from their 6 in. guns. One of our seaplanes also interrupted its special work in order to have an interview with a Zeppelin. But, as the pilot remarked, "Zeppy almost sat on her tail with fright when she was attacked." That is to say, the immense airship put up her nose, and began to climb for dear life. The seaplane, being unable to spare the time for a long manœuvring fight, whirred away towards Cuxhaven. Our ships then had to face their aerial enemies with no help from our Naval Wing. Some of the seaplane-carriers had a difficult time of it. They were attacked by aircraft and submarines. But they dodged the bombs by skilful seamanship, and our destroyers helped to keep off the German underwater craft

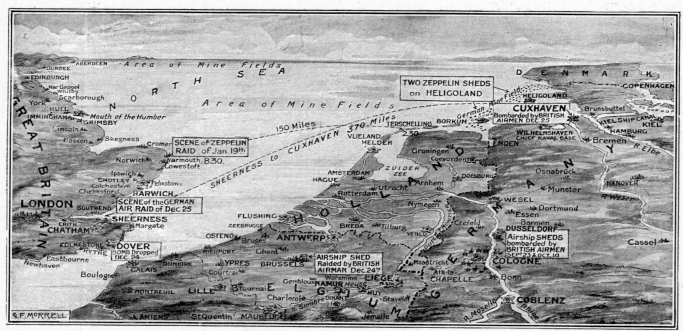

DIAGRAMMATIC MAP OF THE AREAS CHOSEN RESPECTIVELY FOR THE BRITISH AND GERMAN AIRCRAFT
RAIDS IN SEPTEMBER—DECEMBER, 1914, AND JANUARY, 1915.

The hottest work was done by Lieut.-Commander Nasmyth, commanding submarine E11. He was watching inshore, to assist any seaplane which might get into difficulties. Towards him descended the airmen Oliver, Miley, and Blackburn, who had run short of petrol. The submarine officer rose and went to their help, but one of the Zeppelin look-outs saw him and the three floating aviators, and the great airship shot overhead and began dropping bombs. But by his coolness and resource Lieut.-Commander Nasmyth rescued the three pilots, and all our ships and men got safely back to the East Coast after one of the greatest adventures of the war.

The reconnaissance work accomplished was of high military value. Then, in addition to the damage done, the experience gained in the novel combined operation by light cruisers, destroyers, seaplane-carriers, and submarines was of importance. Commodore Reginald Tyrwhitt, well known for his work in the Battle of the Bight, was in command of the ships, and Commodore Roger Keyes directed the submarines. Lieut. Erskine Childers, of the Naval Volunteer Reserve, acted as one of the aerial reconnaissance officers, a position which this author had earned by his close study of the German coast in times of peace. Flight-Commander Kilner and Flight-Lieut. Edmonds, with Chief Petty-Officers Bell and Budds, especially distinguished themselves. The two officers were made companions of the Distinguished Service Order, while the two chief petty-officers received the Distinguished Service Medal.

The last work of importance by the Royal Naval Air Service, undertaken during the period covered by this chapter, was directed against the increasing activities of enemy submarines. On January 22nd, 1915, in answer to a German air raid on Dunkirk, Squadron-Commander Davies and Flight-Lieut. Peirse flew to Zeebrugge, the seaport of Bruges, which the Germans were using as a submarine base. They found two submarines in harbour, one of which they destroyed by bombs. They also dropped bombs on the heavy batteries on Zeebrugge Mole, and killed or wounded many of the guns' crews. Squadron-Commander Davies was wounded in the thigh on his flight towards Zeebrugge, but proceeded to his objective, carried out his work, and returned without further injury.

On February 12th a larger aerial operation was conducted against Zeebrugge and other hostile positions on the Belgian coast. Thirty-four naval aeroplanes and seaplanes set out under the command of Wing-Commander Samson. Another submarine was damaged at Zeebrugge, and several batteries near the fort were put out of action. Railway communications along the coast were temporarily deranged by the destruction of the track in places, and the bombardment of the railway-stations at Ostend and Blankenberghe. A Zeppelin shed with its contents was reported to have been completely destroyed, and the electricity works at Zeebrugge had to be repaired before any more electricity could be produced.

On February 16th another strong air raid was conducted by forty aeroplanes and seaplanes. The German batteries along the Belgian coast were again bombarded; the Mole at Zeebrugge, already breached by our airmen, was further damaged; the locks of the sea canal between Bruges and the sea were partly blown up; and German mine-sweeping trawlers in the harbour were attacked. During this coast raid the German aeroplane centre at Ghistelles was bombarded by French airmen, who thus prevented the German aircraft from attempting to cut off our machines. We lost no men in these operations, though two of our airmen got out to sea, where they were picked up.

On March 7th another air attack was made on Ostend, where the German submarine repair base was bombarded. On April 1st the townspeople of Antwerp were gladdened by a break in the monotony of their lives as temporary subjects of the Kaiser. An outburst of gun fire in the morning brought them to their windows. Flight-Sub-Lieut. Frank Andreae was attacking the German submarine factory at Hoboken, near Antwerp, while the German anti-aircraft guns vainly tried to frighten him away or bring him down. According to a delighted eye-witness, the aviator dived within fifty yards of the shipyard, and dropped three or four bombs on two completed submarines and on two others in a half-constructed state. Not only were they all destroyed, but a fire broke out in the shipbuilding works, and there were numerous dead or wounded men among the band of expert German mechanics engaged in submarine construction. The people of Antwerp cheered the aviator, especially when they saw him make his daring low dive to launch his bombs. On the same day Flight-Lieut. Wilson, reconnoitring over Zeebrugge, observed two submarines lying alongside the Mole. He dropped two bombs on each of them with happy results. But the vital achievements in airmanship were performed by the anonymous officers and men directing the fire of the artillery, scouting over the enemy's territory, and patrolling our coast, the Channel, and the North Sea.

The attack on Hoboken

British bombs on Zeebrugge

THE BRITISH NAVAL AIR RAID ON THE GREAT GERMAN PORT OF CUXHAVEN.
An impression of the scene as it might have been witnessed from the foredeck of H.M.S. Undaunted when its guns and those of H.M.S. Arethusa (seen in centre of picture) drove the German aircraft back to Heligoland.

START OF THE FIRST OF THE BRITISH AIR RAIDS ON THE ZEEBRUGGE-OSTEND COASTLINE.
Squadron of naval aero-planes and seaplanes crossing the sea for the first great air raid in history, under the direction of Commander Samson, on February 12th, 1915. The object of the Admiralty was the preventing of the establishment of submarine bases at Zeebrugge and vicinity.

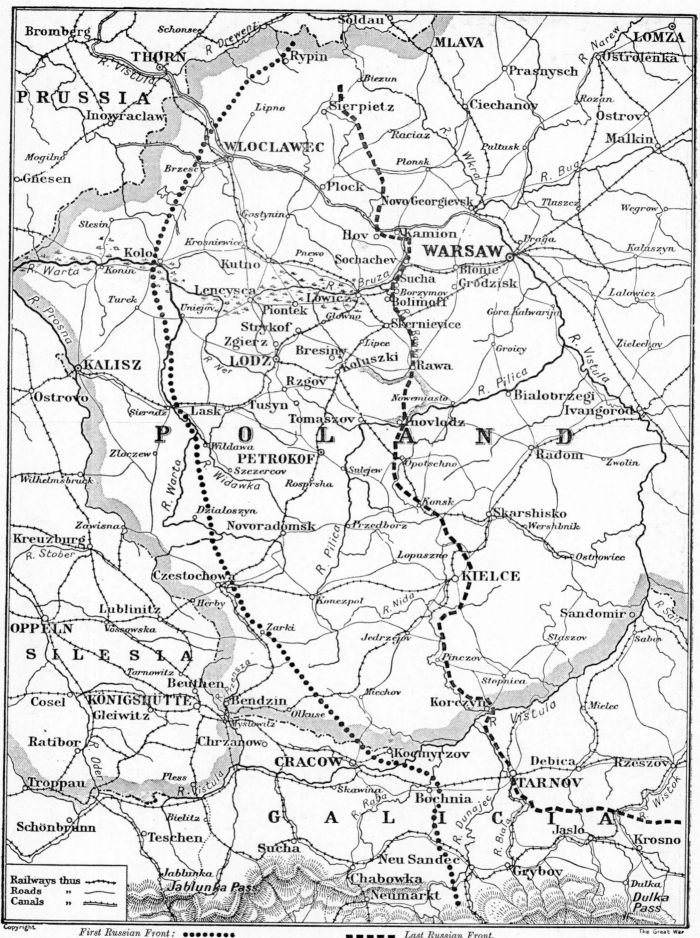

Copyright

First Russian Front: ••••••••   ▬ ▬ ▬ ▬ ▬ *Last Russian Front.*

The Great War

MAP OF MAIN EASTERN THEATRE OF WAR IN NOVEMBER AND DECEMBER, 1914.

Showing the position of Russian armies after their pursuit of first invading force, and their later position on the river system of defences after Hindenburg's second lunge at Warsaw.

CHAPTER LV.

THE RUSSIAN STAND ON THE FIVE RIVERS AND THE BATTLE OF THE CARPATHIANS.

Russian Advance to the Gate of Silesia—Germany in Danger of being Half Crippled—Russky and Ivanoff Try to Force a Decisive Conflict before Cracow—How Hindenburg Evaded the Conflict and Forced Ivanoff to Retreat—Germans Make a Sudden and Powerful Lunge at Warsaw—Heroic Stand by Russians Round the Marshes of the Bzura—Terrible Struggle for the Causeway of Piontek—Germans Break Through and Half Envelop the Central Russian Army—Russky's Struggle for Life—Abrupt Transformation of the Field of Battle—Victorious German Force Cut Off and Encircled—Failure of General Rennenkampf to Carry Out His Orders—General von Mackensen again Breaks the Russian Line and Releases His Trapped Troops—General Russky Withdraws from Lodz—General Ivanoff Retires from Cracow—All the Russian Armies Entrench Behind a Formidable System of River Defences—Ghastly Scenes of Slaughter on the Bzura and Rawka Rivers—Würtemberg Brigade Forces a Passage only to be Annihilated—Magnificent Fighting Qualities of the Siberian Riflemen—Battles of Bolimoff and Inovlodz—Austrians Broken and Captured on the Nida—General Dimitrieff's Decisive Victory on the Dunajec—Russians on Dukla Pass Threatening to Invade Hungary—Opening of the Battle of the Carpathians—Hindenburg's Attempt to Avoid the Mountain Conflict.

 Y the middle of November, 1914, the German offensive had exhausted much of its strength. The retreat of the Teutonic armies of invasion in Poland and the repulse of the Prussian Guard in Belgium were full of menace for Germany and Austria-Hungary. Had the Teutonic and Hungarian peoples then had any means of knowing the situation and controlling it, they might have asked for terms of peace. Of the two allies in the terrible war of aggression, Germany had suffered the less, owing to her incomparable war-machine and her superb body of one hundred and twenty thousand well-trained and masterful non-commissioned officers. The war-machine of Austria-Hungary had been shaken, and nearly all the first-line armies and a part of the second-line forces had been disintegrated. The casualties of the Dual Alliance amounted to at least two million men. The loss had fallen most heavily on the first-line armies.

Germany's best troops were indeed almost as shattered as those of Austria. But the German war-machine still worked as well as ever, and the Ersatz and Landwehr soldiers were drafted into the framework of the fighting armies and turned, by working with the remaining veteran troops, into good first-line material. Into the German war-machine the new levies of Austria-Hungary were also poured, and reorganised there into what afterwards proved to be an admirable fighting force. Yet all this was but a glittering stucco façade masking the ruin of the striking power of two mighty empires. The Teutons were no longer living upon the income of their vital energies, upon the annual increase of their population, upon the savings and profit of their labours. They had already spent much of the capital of their vital energies. Germany, it was reckoned by an impartial American observer, had crippled her national life for generations to come.

To sue for peace, however, was to overthrow the power of the aristocracies in Germany, Austria, and Hungary. It was well known what terms the Allies would demand, and peace on those terms would have resulted in the overthrow of the governing classes in the Teutonic and Hungarian countries. Their rule had only been suffered, during the growing influence of democratic forces in neighbouring nations, because the majority of people in the two empires were gratified by the supposedly invincible military power they derived from their modern feudalistic form of policy. The acceptance of peace with defeat would have been an act of suicide by the governing parties.

Being made of mortal clay, with all their human frailties increased by the irresponsible exercise of power, the leaders of Germany and Austria-Hungary resolved to sacrifice their peoples in the hope of saving their class and dynastic interests. An attempt was made to detach France from the Triple Entente. The French nation was offered part of Alsace, and, if necessary, part of Belgium, in return for its recognition of the German annexation of Flanders and Liège.

GENERAL RADKO DIMITRIEFF.

But, as the French themselves remarked at the time, the Germans, having no sense of honour themselves, thought that other peoples were in the same condition.

Then an attempt was made to convince the Russian Court that the Germanic principle of aristocratic and Imperial government was the only safeguard for Russia against the spread of democratic ideas of a revolutionary sort. But as the Russians were beginning

A Holy War of liberation

to see at last that their empire was an experiment in communism, with the communes organised for defence under a hereditary dictator or imperator, the Tsar was not moved by the Kaiser's sudden renewal of interest in his domestic politics. It is said that the Tsar sent the German proposal, without a word of explanation, to the Grand Duke Nicholas. The Grand Duke returned it with the remark that all his troops would mutiny and turn into armed revolutionaries if an easy peace were made with the foes against whom they were waging a Holy War of liberation.

As a matter of fact, the Tsar himself was most resolute to fight to a finish, and thus settle all the outstanding difficulties in Russian foreign affairs. For the possession of Constantinople, in particular, the Tsar and his

November, 1914, the Russians were sweeping towards the German frontier at Rypin, between Thorn and Graudenz, in the north, and in the south they were close against Cracow. The Austro-Hungarian army had ventured too far in its movement on the San River, supporting Hindenburg's movement against Warsaw and Ivangorod. By the capture of Sandomir the Russians had cut off part of the Austrian forces, and then in a swift northward advance they had driven a wedge into the Teuton-Magyar army round Cracow.

The position was then a paradoxical one. Austria had lost most of Galicia, and Hungary was in danger

A GERMAN SLEIGH AMBULANCE.
Horse-drawn sleigh used by Germans on the Russian frontier in taking wounded to hospital in the winter of 1914-15.

of invasion. Yet Austria and Hungary were comparatively strong. Their immediate situation was merely uncomfortable. Germany had lost only a few miles of territory in East Prussia, and she still possessed a large, rich, and important part of Russian soil, most strongly held by entrenched lines along the Warta River. Yet it was Germany who was in immediate and dire peril.

From the beginning the position of the German Empire had been remarkably curious. It resembled a great, powerful creature of a mythical kind, which could survive repeated stabs through the heart, but would die if its skin were pricked in a certain place. Let

RUSSIAN INFANTRY ADVANCING THROUGH THE SNOW BEFORE CRACOW.
This striking photograph demonstrates the perilous nature of such an advance. The men made startlingly prominent targets for the enemy's fire, their figures standing out like silhouettes on the surface of the snow.

peasants were ready to fight, if need be, for a lifetime. Its possession would crown the long, painful, wonderful efforts made by the Russian village communities, under the leadership of men of the House of Rurik, for a thousand years. Throughout this period Constantinople had been their Holy City. Thirty years of war would not be too high a price to pay for it. Yet Germany and Austria were intriguing for a patched-up peace, when it was becoming clear that they could not resist longer than two years at the most.

So the war went on. By the end of the first week in

us put it that Germany had two lungs from which her supply of oxygen was derived. One of these lungs was the western frontier land of Westphalia, and

Germany's two vital points

particularly the Black Country stretching from Düsseldorf to Dortmund, with the iron mines of Lorraine. The other lung was the eastern frontier land of the Black Country of Silesia, that extended into Russian territory above Cracow. No advance to Berlin was necessary to overthrow the Germans. The occupation of Silesia would half cripple them, and, if followed by the occupation of Westphalia,

AN INCIDENT IN THE CARPATHIANS: VIENNA-BOUND TRAIN HELD UP BY COSSACKS.

it would probably reduce them to helplessness. They would lack the means for carrying on the war. It was for this reason that the Russian Commander-in-Chief threw only a couple of army corps towards Posen, on the road to Berlin, in the second week of November, while he massed his two chief armies against Silesia.

It was expected that a tremendous battle for Silesia would take place along the frontier rivers, the Warta and Przemsza. Such appears to have been the belief of General Russky and General Ivanoff, commanding the central Russian armies. But General von Hindenburg showed an undoubted talent in the manner in which he countered the impending Russian offensive movement.

Hindenburg's advantages

He had the fatigued, disappointed, and somewhat mangled army of invasion which had retreated towards the Warta River. He had also the large new formations, which had been training since the outbreak of hostilities, less the multitude of recruits slaughtered at Ypres and elsewhere before they had been made into good soldiers. He had also large bodies of fresh Hungarian and Austrian Territorials, fired with high courage by the imminence of invasion.

His forces considerably outnumbered those at the disposal of Generals Russky and Ivanoff. What was still more important, he possessed, close to the rear of his lines, the finest system of strategical railways in the world. It was with these railways that he fought. At the beginning of the second week in November large bodies of men were withdrawn from the German lines, and reinforced by fresh troops. They were formed into some seven army corps, under the command of General von Mackensen, and were railed up towards Thorn. It was arranged for further army corps to follow them as soon as possible, bringing up Mackensen's strength to nearly three-quarters of a million men. Hindenburg's plan was a simple one. Instead of fighting a defensive battle for Silesia in front of Cracow, he swiftly recovered the offensive by lunging out again at Warsaw. In withdrawing from his first movement of invasion he had thoroughly destroyed the few railway lines running across

the territory which the Russians reoccupied. This had been done with a view to the execution of the plan which Hindenburg was now carrying out.

He had placed the victorious Russians in considerable difficulty. For their supplies they had to rely entirely upon strings of country carts, crawling over bad, swampy tracks. All movements of troops had to be carried out by marching through Polish mud. Hindenburg could move his armies by railways, which bent in a semicircle round the advancing Russians like a gigantic net. At need, the Russian soldiers could march thirty miles a day, but the German soldiers could move two hundred miles a day by train, and come absolutely fresh into the fight.

The power of manœuvring, therefore, rested entirely with the Germans, and everything favoured their strategy. The fighting-line extended from the north of Tilsit to the south of Czernovitz. With all its curves and irregularities it was about a thousand miles long. It was impossible for either side to entrench its troops on this tremendous front. Neither Teuton nor Slav had then sufficient men to garrison trenches of such a length. So in the eastern theatre of war the battles of manœuvres in the open field went on. On each side there were gaps between the main concentrations of forces, and in these gaps the reconnoitring mounted troops were continually skirmishing against each other. The Russians, of course, expected a grand counterstroke from the enemy, but they **Odds against the Russians** could not concentrate in advance for it, because they did not know at what point Hindenburg would launch his railway-speeded attack. All they could do was to try to force on the great decisive battle at the place where their own troops were most numerous. And this, as we have seen, they did by driving in upon Cracow. But it was at a spot nearly two hundred miles north of Cracow that Hindenburg again took the field.

Mackensen's army swung forward from Thorn and Kalisz. It had a scissorlike action. One blade worked along the Vistula and the other along the Warta River. Some part of the advanced guards of Russians was caught between the blades of the scissors and destroyed. From November 11th to November 13th the Germans won a series of successes at Wloclat, Wloclawec, and Kutno. It was at the last-named town that the main battle was fought. Two Russian army corps were faced by seven German army corps. The odds against the Russians in both men and guns were terrible. But they could not retreat. The entire strategy of all the allied commanders, and of the Grand Duke Nicholas in particular, was opposed to anything like a retreat under such conditions. The outnumbered and almost enveloped Russians had to stand their ground till they were completely destroyed as a fighting corps.

The action took place on the Bzura River, between the towns of Lowicz and Lencysca. From Lowicz to Lencysca, a distance of thirty-five miles, there **Battle of the marsh** stretched a great river marsh, which con-**at Kutno** tinued for nearly another twenty miles beyond Lencysca. There were only two causeways over this marsh, one being at Piontek, nearly midway between Lencysca and Lowicz. The small Russian army lined out along the marsh in front of the causeways, and just behind the town of Kutno. They had to hold the causeways until General Russky, with the main Russian forces, could come to their assistance. This was the only way in which the Russians could fight the German railway system of manœuvring. They lacked the mechanical means of transport necessary for the constant countering of Hindenburg's terrific rushes. In France, Joffre could work his railways as quickly as—and sometimes more quickly than —Falkenhayn.

Each German rush there was stopped before it went more than a few miles. But, in Russian Poland, Russian flesh and blood had to recover the advantages won by German trains and railway tracks. The Germans had always the advantage of surprise, and to win time Russian commanders had often to lose a great number of men.

So it was in the battle of the marsh at Kutno. The Germans won an easy victory in front of the town, and the Russian troops retired behind the long river marsh midway between Thorn and Warsaw. Their way of fighting was peculiar, and it overthrew the German plan. According to German ideas conscript troops had to be handled very carefully.

It was disastrous, on the German theory, to try to make them fight for long against superior numbers and superior artillery. So Napoleon's method of sacrificing a tenth or more of an army in order to hold an enemy was impossible under modern conditions. But it was just this impossibility, which the Russians on the Bzura, like the British at Ypres, turned into an accomplished fact.

The Russian troops fought magnificently. In the end they held up the Germans until first General Russky, then the commander of the Warsaw reinforcements, and lastly General Rennenkampf brought their armies, by forced marches over the muddy plain, to their help. The struggle in the marsh went on for a week. The stretch of bog, with its islands of dry land, extended for nearly sixty miles, and formed a better defence than a river—for you cannot bridge a bog with pontoons. The guns could only advance behind the infantry, over the

narrow causeways, where the Russians were able to concentrate against them, while carrying on a series of semi-disconnected fights on all the patches of firm ground.

In these circumstances, the Russian Commander-in-Chief used the most extraordinary tactics. He did not reinforce his small, battered advance army, desperately struggling to hold the marsh. But as Russky's troops marched up from the south, and new formations poured eastward from Warsaw, he drew them up in a line stretching from Sochachev, on the Bzura, through Lowicz, and then along the railway to Zgierz, and other smaller towns west and south-west of Lodz. Through lack of time to connect the converging Russian armies, a gap was left behind the Russian troops fighting in the marshes. After tremendous efforts and terrible sacrifices of life, General von Mackensen succeeded in capturing the Piontek causeway on November 19th. Thereupon the Germans poured in a broad avalanche through the gap They took the roads to Strykof, Bresiny, and Koluszki. This last small town was right behind the Russian front at Lodz, and close to it was the main railway junction, where three Russian-Polish railways connected. It seemed as though the Germans were winning the grandest victory in the war. Round Lodz they were outflanking the principal Russian army under General Russky, who had been suddenly stricken with illness. South of Lowicz and Skernievice they were turning the northern Russian armies. At the same time another main German force had advanced from Kalisz, and was engaged in turning General Russky's southern flank at Lask. The situation was extremely critical. It was almost as critical as the position in France after the Battles of Charleroi and Mons. Never was Hindenburg so near to a grand Napoleonic success. But dangerous as was the position of General Russky, he kept his head. He threw his reserves northward from Petrokof to Tusyn. There they stopped the main German movement of envelopment, and forced the enemy to

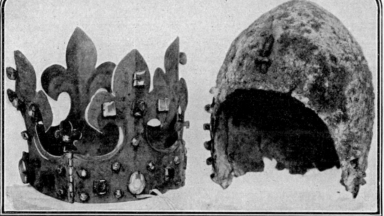

RELICS OF A GLORIOUS PAST.
The ancient crown of the Polish kings, and the iron helmet in which it was found under an old oak-tree in a Polish village about four years ago. The crown, which is in four parts and adorned with sixty-five precious stones, is preserved at Cracow.

stand on the defensive. At the same time Russky's active troops at Lask fell upon the second German army and flung the hostile columns back in disorder. Then came the mighty counterstroke, engineered by the Grand Duke Nicholas in person. He ordered General Rennenkampf to march with all haste to the decisive scene of conflict, and wheeled the army defending Warsaw from Lowicz and Skernievice south-westward. The army used Lowicz as a pivot, and swung over the hills of Central Poland for twenty-five miles till it reoccupied **Russky's advance** Strykof and Bresiny. While this move-**from Lodz** ment was going on, General Russky advanced westward from Lodz, and inflicted terrible losses on Hindenburg's central army, and forced it to withdraw back towards the Warta and entrench.

By November 23rd the situation in the eastern theatre of war had undergone a most remarkable change. The two German army corps which had forced the passage of the marshes, and almost enveloped General Russky's force, had their lines of communication cut. They were being bottled up in the region of Bresiny, some miles *behind* the Russian front. The Russians had opened and let the attackers through, and then had joined together again,

Russell & Sons.

Lieut.=General W. P. Pulteney, K.C.B., D.S.O., Commanding Third Army Corps.

Austrian General Steger Steiner and Staff watching operations in Galicia.

Russian Infantrymen entrenched on outskirts of wood in Galicia.

Twenty=eight ton Austrian siege=howitzer which fires a thousand=pound projectile.

Where Austrian trenches faced Russian across a morass in East Galicia.

Stubborn fighting on the heights carried by the Russians south of Dukla in the Carpathians.

snapping off a mass of Germans as large as the British Expeditionary Force at Mons.

The trap was as complete as a thing of man's shaping could be. But for some reason which is not yet clearly known, General Rennenkampf did not carry out his part of the operation. He delayed to march his men to the scene of action at the time when General von Mackensen was speeding up reinforcements to rescue his entrapped army corps. General Rennenkampf had been always unfortunate in his operations, though the Russian Chief of Staff had given him some of the most brilliant of Russian troops and had designed his course of action with the greatest care. Rennenkampf was one of the German barons in the Russian Empire who fought well against the Japanese, but seemed incapable of winning in any circumstances against men of his own original stock. Twice in East Prussia the Russian offensive movement had failed in a most curious manner. The troops under Rennenkampf's immediate command had been extricated with some difficulty from Hindenburg's and Eichhorn's attacks, but the Russian generals acting with Rennenkampf had on each occasion been strangely trapped in the Masurian Lakes. Now, at the Battle of Strykof, Rennenkampf himself failed to co-operate with the Russian generals in inflicting a tremendous defeat upon the Germans.

Owing to the slowness with which Rennenkampf moved, the action failed, and he was relieved of his command. From November 23rd to November 26th General von Mackensen's main army hammered fiercely and continually at the Russian line between Lowicz and Strykof. The desperate German attacks went on night and day, and as Rennenkampf's army did not arrive in time to reinforce the Russians, the final closing-up of the ring around the trapped German army corps was prevented. Mackensen succeeded in reopening the gap, and flinging in two more corps, which rescued the entrapped columns. The Germans got out, but in doing so they had to force a passage under cross-fire from the Russian machine-guns and rifles, and retreat through an area almost enclosed by Russian troops. Many of the German battalions lost three-fourths of their men; and the remnant of the columns, when they at last reached their own lines, were completely demoralised as a fighting force. They were withdrawn from the front of the battle, to be filled up with new drafts and reorganised.

Costly German retreat After Sedan military experts concluded that a large force entirely enveloped by an enemy would do wrong to surrender. It was calculated that if courageously led and strongly handled it could cut its way out with a loss of two-thirds of its number. This is what the Germans did, and their additional losses, bringing up their casualties to two hundred and ten bayonets out of two hundred and eighty in a company, seem to have been due to their early casualties at Piontek. It will be remembered that the Second Austrian Army under General Auffenberg was surrounded by Russky and Ivanoff between the Vistula and Bug Rivers towards the middle of September, 1914. But it also cut its way out through the marshes of the San, with a similar loss of about two-thirds of its effectives.

Altogether, the extraordinary Battle of Strykof was a grave disaster to Hindenburg's main army. The German commander had to ask for more reinforcements, and another six army corps, with five more divisions of cavalry, were thrown into the German lines. It was this arrival in mass, which began on November 25th, that enabled Mackensen to rescue the remnant of his attacking columns at Strykof, and to **The Battle of** continue to beat against the Russian **Strykof** front on the Bzura and Lodz line. Farther south, at Czestochowa, the Russian front continued between the Warta and Pilica, and from hence on towards Cracow and Tarnov and the Carpathian Mountains. Then far away in the north it ran from the Vistula, some forty or fifty miles in front of Warsaw, and skirted the German frontier of East Prussia at Mlava, and continued through the Masurian Lakes region to the Baltic coast.

By reason of his railway system Hindenburg could make surprise concentrations against any point or points in this far-stretched line. That he intended at any cost to obtain a decision was perfectly apparent; for some part of his new reinforcements had been obtained from the western theatre of war. The German lines in Belgium and France had at last been weakened in order to obtain a decisive result in Russia. There had been rumours of this transfer throughout the war, and Rennenkampf's first campaign in East Prussia had been reported to have caused the Kaiser to alter his plan of campaign. But this was a false statement put about by the German General Staff in order to delude the French Commander-in-Chief. Joffre, as we know, was not deluded; but about the middle of December, 1914, he received information from the Russian Staff that the Germans contemplated weakening the forces on his front, and he was also warned that the Russians had found on the field of battle the bodies of men in first-line German units which had apparently formed part of army corps on the Franco-Belgian front. The result was that in mid-December General Joffre published an order indicating his intention of opening a general offensive. This order he cleverly permitted to fall into the enemy's hand. Its effect was remarkable. It stopped the transfer of troops from west to east and held the first-line German armies on the western front.

Hindenburg could not fairly complain of any insufficiency in his forces in the circumstances. He had considerably more men than the Grand Duke Nicholas, and he had his railway system, designed by the elder Moltke for the struggle that was now taking place. But his only strength was his strength of character; he had no constructive imagination, no interplay of intuition and intellect. His one method of attack was a bull-like rush from some point on his railway system.

The fighting that followed the German defeat at Strykof was wild, confused, and disorderly. Hindenburg seemed

BEHIND A PRUSSIAN BARRICADE.
The Germans in Poland constructed barricades of wood. In the above photograph the German officer is seen about to look through his field-glasses over the barricade for signs of the Russian troops.

GERMAN TRANSPORT ON PACK-HORSES CROSSING THE SNOW-COVERED PLAINS OF POLAND.
Thousands of horses were employed in this arduous service in the winter of 1914-15 with the result that there was a marked disappearance of German cavalry from Western Poland. Our picture was drawn by Mr. Charles W. Simpson, R.I., from the description supplied by an eye-witness.

to have had no method indicating a co-ordinated plan. He simply lunged in a most desperate way at points wide apart on the Russian line. One day he would thrust in on the Bzura ; the next he would lunge out at Prasnysch, a village to the north of Warsaw ; and then, hundreds of miles away, he would try to break the Russian front at Czestochowa, or Petrokof. The Russian Staff went so far as to remark, in its communiqués, on the disconnected nature of Hindenburg's attacks. He was throwing his men away in tens of thousands with no clear aim in view.

It seems as if the iron nerves of the old German drunkard were giving out under the strain of repeated failure. It was, indeed, his Chief of Staff, Ludendorff, who supplied him with the brains for the Russian-Polish campaign. And Mac-

Mackensen as Kaiser's favourite kensen, the leader of the Ninth Army, fighting on the Bzura, became the Emperor's favourite, owing to the unexpected and brilliant way in which he rescued his trapped army corps from Russky's net. But no unexpected and brilliant stroke of strategy could avail Mackensen in the position in which he was. Along the Bzura, and in front of Lodz, the situation was similar to that in the western theatre of war.

The two great armies were now entrenched against each other, on a flat, marshy, muddy country, with their batteries behind them, directed by aeroplanes and observation balloons. The Russians had no occasion to move ; they were defending Warsaw and their lines of communication, and being mostly peasants accustomed to hard winter work, directed by officers with abundant experience of trench warfare in Manchuria, they were, on the whole, more comfortable than any of their Allies. It was for the Germans, if they wished to capture Warsaw,

to advance, and come under the tempest of shrapnel shell and bullets from the Russian line.

Mackensen made continually a series of infantry charges across the muddy No Man's Land between the trenches. In some places the Germans got within two hundred paces of the Russian lines, and hauled their guns within eight hundred yards of the opposing trenches. Their pluck and their determination were magnificent, but, unfortunately for them, the armed peasantry of Russia rose to a height of heroism that even the German in the supreme moment of his valour could not equal. Each attempt at a German advance along the front between Lowicz and Lodz was checked at once by a counter-charge of an incomparable kind.

The state of mind of the fighting peasantry of Russia was abnormal and unique. Nearly all of them were very sincere Christians, with an uncommon humility of soul. They had little or **Russia's fighting** nothing of the aggressive spirit of the **peasantry** ordinary fanatic warrior—of the Arab fighting under the Sword of God, or of the English Brownist fighting under Cromwell. There was nothing about them of the feudal Crusader, though, like him, they were fighting for their Holy City—Constantinople. These strange peasants, with their kindly communal ways, were a most peculiar mixture of a Christian martyr and a common-sense infantryman. They wanted to die in their grand Holy War, but they did not want to perish before they brought down one or two enemies. Under shell fire they were wonderfully patient, praying most of the time. They did not often joke about " Jack Johnsons " and " saucepans," as the British and French soldiers did, though the Germans brought 11 in. howitzers against the Russian positions on the Bzura. They were very serious and very prayerful, and they did not budge. When the order came to rise and charge, they went forth rather to seek death than to win a victory; but, as they used their rifles with great skill at the same time, they usually accomplished the task set them.

Only at Lask, in the first week of December, did they give ground. Here they were suddenly assaulted by dense columns of Germans secretly concentrated by Hindenburg's Staff. The Russians held out till the afternoon, but were at last forced to retire towards Lodz. But, in the meantime, the Russian Staff had prepared an unusual kind of counter-attack. As night fell, a squadron of armoured motor-cars with machine-guns and quick-firers rushed southward and penetrated the enemy's new line. From their modern war chariots the Russians poured a hail of shrapnel shell and bullets into the German troops and scattered them in all directions. Then the Russian infantry arrived and reoccupied the position.

Within gunshot of Cracow

At the beginning of December, however, the chief Russian armies were still in an awkward position. General Ivanoff won an important victory on the Upper Vistula, which brought him within gunshot of Cracow. With one more great blow he could have opened the gate to Silesia, and compelled Hindenburg's main armies to withdraw and defend their own country. The Russian Commander-in-Chief was therefore inclined to continue the pressure against Cracow, feeding and supplying Ivanoff's troops from Ivangorod. But the tremendously increased pressure of the German forces on the Bzura endangered the Russian scheme. The immediate risk to Warsaw was nothing. Warsaw could be held firmly just a few miles in front of the city, as had been done in October. It was Ivanoff's army which was in peril. If Russky's men had to give ground suddenly — as was quite a likely thing — the Germans would be able to get between Russky and Ivanoff and cut Ivanoff's communications. For this reason Russky, in the first week of December, suddenly surrendered Lodz to the enemy without a fight, and withdrew by a night march to a fresh position nearer Warsaw. This was only a veritable strategical retreat. It was carried out in co-operation with General Ivanoff's right flank, before the grand German attack was made. Huge new German forces had been felt on the Bzura, indicating at last clearly what Hindenburg's plan was. He was attacking Russky with the intention of smashing

The surrender of Lodz

AT GRIPS WITH DEATH ON THE BZURA: GHASTLY WORK WITH THE BAYONET.
During the German attacks on Warsaw the bayonet fighting was of the most desperate character. Many of the combatants were found locked together in pairs, the one transfixed by the weapon of his opponent. The above picture was drawn by Mr. Charles W. Simpson, R.I., from details given by an eye-witness.

HISTORIC CRACOW: BIRD'S-EYE VIEW OF THE ANCIENT CAPITAL OF THE POLES SHOWING THE DIRECTION OF THE RUSSIAN ADVANCE ON THE CITY.

Ivanoff. The feeble resistance offered to Ivanoff around Cracow was intended to lull him into security until he could be attacked unexpectedly on the right flank, or even taken in reverse.

What made all this manœuvring on a vast scale very difficult was the state of the ground. Though muddy on the surface, it was frozen hard at a depth of a foot. The troops on either side could only make kneeling trenches on the battlefield. It was thus inadvisable to leave a well-prepared and deeply dug position—and, after surrendering Lodz, the Russians were inclined to stand firm. By December 8th their situation seemed to have improved, so Hindenburg struck out in a fresh direction, and swung two army corps from East Prussia against the railway line connecting Warsaw with Petrograd. This was a further menace to the main line of communications of the Russian army. But when the German force reached Prasnysch it was so fiercely attacked that it was forced to entrench, and then its trenches were stormed, and it was thrown back over the Prussian frontier at Soldau.

German attack near Lowicz

All this, however, was only a diversion. It masked the further reinforcement of Mackensen's army on the Bzura-Lodz front; and at the beginning of the second week in December the Germans made a terrific attempt to break through the Russian lines near Lowicz. On some days there were seven attacks in twenty-four hours, delivered by columns in solid formation, advancing at point-blank range of the Russian position. The terrible onsets continued, day and night, for more than a week, and on December 17th Berlin and Vienna were beflagged, and German school children had a holiday. It was announced that, after a most desperate battle, the Russians were everywhere retreating and being vigorously pursued.

A few days afterwards, however, the German General Staff, which had sent the news of the great victory, rebuked the German and Austrian public for rejoicing before the battle was won. All that had really happened was that the Grand Duke Nicholas had begun to rearrange the Russian lines on a purely defensive system. The threat to General Ivanoff's line of communication had become more apparent. For more than a week an army of peasants, directed by Russian engineers, had been digging into the frozen ground beneath the Polish mud. The new lines ran from the Bzura along its tributary the Rawka. Thence they continued over some hills to the Pilica River, and from the Pilica they extended to the Nida stream, and then across the Vistula to the Dunajec.

Rearrangement of Russian lines

AUSTRIA'S COMMANDER-IN-CHIEF.
General Conrad von Hoetzendorf in the field, in conversation with a German officer.

material at many of the points where they attacked, and the men fell in such large numbers that the army doctors and nurses could not tend the wounded. At the fording places on the Polish river front the streams were often dammed by the dead bodies of the invaders. The ghastly horrors and searing miseries of Hindenburg's troops in the winter of 1914 were unparalleled in modern history. To the Kaiser the second Russian campaign must have been almost as terrible as Napoleon's retreat from Moscow.

But the Germans could not retreat. They had to fight on until they were exhausted. For the confessed failure of a retreat would at once have brought Rumania and Italy into the field. The extreme desperation of the efforts made by the German commanders to obtain a decision was indicated by the appearance of the Divisions of Death. The best German regiments were picked out and brigaded into forlorn hopes, every man in them knowing that he was practically doomed. And they died heroically, but in vain. Our officers and men at Ypres had remarked upon the extraordinary access of courage in their attackers. **The " Divisions of** They ceased to fight with the prudence **Death "** and individual skill that usually distinguish the civilised man. Instead, they came on in lines in a dervish-like charge, trying to choke our rifles and guns in a blind, gregarious, maddened rush. It was a sort of disciplined mob-valour, in which the real spirit of modern Germany, created by the all-absorbing machinery of State organisation, was fully displayed. Most of the regular troops, carefully trained to individual effort by manœuvres in which a battalion was taught to go on fighting when all its officers were out of action, had been shattered. The principal fighting forces of Germany now consisted of troops of the second and third line, who were moved by the instinct to collective action which had been fostered by their semi-socialistic system of government.

This way of fighting had been a special Russian characteristic. The armed moujik, with his traditions of village communism, had always fought at his best when he felt his neighbour close to him. He was not so formidable when fighting in widely-extended formation as when packed behind a trench two to a yard, or when closing for a desperate charge. He still used the bayonet more frequently than did the

Most of the Russian armies were thus moated as well as entrenched against the invaders. It was no wonder that the German Staff discounted the victories it had announced when the strength of the Russian position was seen. By giving up the attack on Cracow and withdrawing towards Ivangorod, General Ivanoff linked up at last strongly with Russky's troops on his right and Radko Dmitrieff's men on his left. Hindenburg had lost his chance. The Russians were now even more strongly entrenched than their Allies in the western theatre of war.

Their vast river system of defences, stretching from Ilov on the Lower Vistula to Tarnov in Galicia, was the most formidable series of military works ever constructed in the heat of action. It was to cost the Germans and Austrians half a million men merely to discover that the Russian lines were impregnable.

All the principal disadvantages now lay with the Germans. They were farther away from their railway-heads and struggling in a land of mud and rain. When they attacked they had to entrench feverishly before the Russian positions, and while they were digging at the hard ground the Russian guns slaughtered them. In addition to their slow and laborious cartage of food and munitions, they needed bridging

AUSTRIAN AMMUNITION SLEIGH.
The whiz of a bullet had come so near the shaggy-haired pony just before the photograph was taken that the animal was quivering with fear. The sleigh was taking ammunition to the Austrian trenches.

COSSACKS IN ACTION TAKING COVER BEHIND THE BODIES OF THEIR HORSES.
Cossacks train their horses to lend all possible aid in warfare and to remain motionless under gun fire.

Sochachev, where they defended the high-road and railway to Warsaw.

Before them was the stream of the Bzura, one hundred and fifty feet wide, running between clay banks thirty feet high, with wooded shores. On the night of December 22nd the Germans simultaneously attacked at six points along the river, and at five places their columns, wading through the fords or crossing by pontoons, were destroyed, with the loss of thousands of men. But at Sochachev a brigade of Würtembergers, brought from the Yser in Flanders, got across the river, and drove the two new Russian regiments back along the Warsaw road. The little Russian force divided; one regiment crept forward on the right, the other crept forward on the left. They were no longer soldiers; they were hunters. They caught the Würtembergers on both flanks and shot them down; those who were not shot or bayoneted were drowned in the river. Little more than five hundred of the Würtembergers remained alive when the Russian infantryman and the Russian gunner had done

British soldier, instead of relying upon the deadlier—if well-directed—stream of bullets from his magazine rifle.

But along the Bzura, where the Divisions of Death tried to break through all Christmas week, there was a new type of Russian—the Siberian. This splendid rifleman was, so to speak, the Canadian or Australian of the Russian Empire. He had the individuality and self-reliance of the adventurous colonial and backwoodsman. The ancient traditions of village communism had no hold upon him; he stood on his own feet and saw things with his own eyes, the practical result of which was that he was a magnificent rifleman. Associated with him were marksmen from the hunting region of Russia. At one spot on the Bzura there were two regiments of recruits from the sporting district of Pskoff. They had only just completed their training and came fresh into the battle near

Siberia's splendid riflemen

WITH THE AUTOMOBILE SECTION OF THE RUSSIAN ARMY.
A rest and a meal by the way in a pleasant corner of Poland before the winter set in. The smaller view shows graves of Russian soldiers of the Greek and Roman Catholic Churches and the different crosses afford interesting evidence of religious toleration on the part of our Slav Allies. The Greek symbol has three cross-pieces.

with them. Those who escaped with their lives only did so by becoming prisoners.

At the same time a tremendous conflict raged incessantly farther up the Bzura, at Bolimoff on the Rawka, and at Inovlodz on the Pilica, a few miles below Tomaszov. When the main effort failed on the Bzura, the struggle at Inovlodz became extremely violent. It can only be compared with the battle at Ypres at the close of October. The forces engaged were larger on both sides at Inovlodz than at Ypres, and the unmitigated fury of attack and counter-attack continued for a longer period, for each side threw in fresh troops as the men in the fighting-line became worn out. In this section of the battlefield the German attempts to obtain a decision went on fiercely to the end of December. Inovlodz

GERMAN SOLDIERS IN A SNOW-COVERED TRENCH IN POLAND.
The centre man was about to fire at the moment the photograph was taken.

was the connecting-point between the army of Russky and the army of Ivanoff. This was why the Germans assailed it with such terrible persistency, pouring out fresh troops for the attack from Kalisz. At the same time the main front of Ivanoff's force was also assailed, and he was forced to give ground at Kielce at the close of the month.

But there was no break in the Russian lines. On the contrary, the Grand Duke Nicholas recovered the power of offensive on the Bzura. Towards the end of December he had a large force on the German side of the river, and there can be little doubt that if he had so wished he could then have forced the Germans to retreat; for the enemy had lost from 150,000 to 200,000 men on the Bzura section alone. And the German troops there knew they were defeated, for they had **"Give us Warsaw!** received, direct from the Kaiser, the **Or take Berlin!"** order to take Warsaw by Christmas. It was nearly a week after Christmas; they could see with their own eyes the shattered condition of their ranks, and their feelings were well known to the Russians. In their last despairing attack they had screamed as they ran: "Give us Warsaw! Or take Berlin!" They wanted the war to end, and they did not much care how it ended.

Yet the Grand Duke Nicholas refrained from a grand counter-attack. He had got the Germans where he wanted

COSSACK OUTPOST IN ACTION IN THE SNOW-COVERED GALICIAN PLAINS.
In the small photograph we get another interesting glimpse of the way in which rifle ammunition was conveyed during the winter to the Russian trenches along the Galician battle-front.

them to remain for months—in the middle of Poland, far away from their railheads, with a difficult series of rivers to cross. He did not want as yet to get to Thorn, Posen, or Berlin; more particularly he did not want to force the main German army back again on its railways, while his own troops lengthened the distance between themselves and their railway-head at Warsaw. So he left the exhausted Germans in comparative peace, having immobilised them for the winter under very harsh, wearing conditions, mitigated only by the use the Germans were able to make of the Lower Vistula for river transport service.

Dankl's army driven back

It was at the Austrians that the Russian Commander-in-Chief struck. On December 28th General Dankl's army attempted to help the exhausted main German forces by crossing the Nida near its junction with the Upper Vistula above Tarnov. But at this point the Russians were suddenly reinforced by a number of very gallant troops, who swam the icy stream, caught the attacking army on the flank, and drove it back with heavy loss, ten thousand Austrians being captured. About this time, when Radko Dimitrieff was operating thus successfully round Tarnov, General Brussiloff resumed his aggressive movement in Galicia. His army was fed and munitioned from Kieff, and nearly all the railway system of Galicia was at his

still farther eastward, General Brussiloff's army held out against a large Austro-Hungarian force, under the command of an Arab general—Ben Ermolli.

Ben Ermolli's main offensive movement was directed in December towards the relief of Przemysl. He reached Grybov, Krosno, Sanok, and Lisko, his lines running through these towns, forming a wedge driven in between the army of Dimitrieff and that of Brussiloff. At the same time he assailed Dimitrieff furiously from the east along the line of the Dunajec and the Biala. But the hero of Bulgaria was more than a match for the Teutonised Arab. He broke him on the Dunajec in Christmas week in the most brilliant of the smaller actions in the eastern theatre of war. Nearly thirty thousand Austrian and Hungarian troops were taken prisoners, with many of their guns; and by the opening of the New Year the Russian armies in Galicia were ready for the aggressive action planned by the Grand Duke Nicholas and his Staff.

Cracow had become practically impregnable. The gate-

LAYING A NEW MOTOR-TRACK.
The motor-track illustrated was made over the mud by the automobile section of the Russian Army. The pine-logs forming the surface of the track were brought up in the special carts seen in the background.

RUSSIAN SEARCHLIGHT CAR UNDERGOING REPAIRS.
Specially-designed searchlight cars were employed in the Russian Army. The particular car shown in the above photograph was dismantled for temporary repairs to be made. Its complicated appearance suggests the great strain placed by active service upon the mechanicians responsible for its efficiency.

way to Silesia was closed. Thus Hindenburg had achieved one of his main objects. He had forced the central Russian armies back, and prevented Germany being half crippled by the loss of one of her two mining and industrial centres. It had cost him 600,000 men merely to produce a deadlock of trench warfare about midway in the vast bend of the Vistula. Terrible as was the price for a half success of this sort, it may have been worth it from the German point of view. For there can be little doubt that if General Ivanoff and General Russky had fought and won the battle for Silesia in November, 1914, on the field they selected in front of Cracow, their continued forward movement would have brought Italy and Rumania into the struggle. Austria and Hungary would have been assailed by overwhelming forces from three sides, and when Austria-Hungary fell, the overthrow of Germany would have been imminent.

Hindenburg had at least prevented all this, and though his grand counter-attack had failed to break the Russian lines, it had political consequences of high importance.

Hindenburg's grand counter-attack

One consequence was that the Russian Commander-in-Chief selected Hungary as the next object of attack. His new plan was to bring direct pressure to bear upon Vienna and Budapest, and force first the Hungarians and then the Austrians to sue for peace. If they did not accept the terms of the Triple Entente, the Russian action would have the effect

service for troop manœuvres and the distribution of supplies. He had only about a quarter of a million men, but their fighting value was enhanced by the service of railways, and General Brussiloff was able to detach a large force under General Selivanoff for the investment of Przemysl.

Przemysl, however, was of no immediate importance. It commanded the railway leading past Tarnov to Cracow, and if Radko Dimitrieff's army at Tarnov had been attacking Cracow the railway would have been badly needed. But General Ivanoff's army had been compelled to retire some fifty miles north of Cracow, so the smaller force under Radko Dimitrieff could not do anything against Cracow from the east. It withdrew from the upper course of the Dunajec River and entrenched along its more westerly tributary, the Biala. From the Biala the Russian line stretched to the Dukla Pass in the snow-covered Carpathian Mountains. All along the lower valleys of the Carpathians,

of moving Italy and Rumania to invade the territory of their traditional enemies.

In these circumstances opened the long, terrible, and extraordinary Battle of the Carpathians, which remained for many months the crisis of the Great War. The Russians began with numbers against them but with a favourable position. They advanced on the Dukla Pass on Christmas Day, when the Austrians were still reeling from the blows delivered against them on the Dunajec and the Nida. The Russians only reached the mouth of the pass, but this was sufficient for their immediate purpose. All the way from the Dukla valley westward they then had Ben Ermolli's troops at a disadvantage. The Austro-Hungarian Army had first driven over the mountains the Cossack raiders who had begun to ravage the Hungarian plain. Then the main force of the enemy had won most of the passes and debouched from the

AUSTRIAN PRISONERS AND THEIR RUSSIAN GUARDS FRATERNISING AT LEMBERG.

FRIENDLY WRESTLING MATCH BETWEEN RUSSIAN SOLDIERS AND AUSTRIAN PRISONERS OF WAR.

of Galician railways at his service. From his new depot towns of Tarnopol and Lemberg he had two trunk lines with a series of cross-country tracks, each leading to the principal valley passes. To him the task of suddenly collecting artillery munition for a surprise attack at any point was an easy affair. It could be carried out in a few hours. In the same way his troops could be manœuvred by train over long distances and come fresh into the fight, while the Austro-Hungarian columns were separated from each other by inaccessible mountains. They could not concentrate quickly or manœuvre. The attacking front could only be strengthened slowly by reinforcing it from the Hungarian plain.

Battle of the Carpathians

So long as General Brussiloff had fewer men than his opponent commanded he was loath to advance to the summits of the Carpathians. Had he done so he would have lost the advantage of his railway system, and been compelled to divide his troops into columns, wedged for the most part in the mountain valleys. His chief object in the first six weeks of the Battle of the Carpathians

valleys as far as the line on which the towns of Sanok and Lisko stood.

General Brussiloff withdrew his men without offering battle, and allowed Ben Ermolli to occupy the foothills. This occurred on December 21st, with the result that when General Brussiloff resumed the offensive at the end of the month the Austro-Hungarian troops were in great difficulties. For between them and their depots of supplies was the high barrier of the wintry Carpathians. All their food and munitions had to be conveyed from Hungary over the passes. When they lost the low, easy Dukla Pass on Christmas Day, the provisioning of the troops became a slow and arduous business. The Russians had, naturally, destroyed the mountain railways during their raid in the autumn, and in some places there were six feet of snow in the river gorges that cut through the mighty wall of rock.

General Brussiloff, on the other hand, had the well-articulated system

SOME OF THE TSAR'S MILLIONS ABOUT TO ENTRAIN FOR THE FRONT.

RUSSIAN GUNS AWAITING TRANSPORT TO THE FIRING-LINE.

The guns and their limbers were swathed in straw to hide them from the eyes of enemy aviators, and the snow helped to make the disguise more effective.

was to disturb the Hungarians with the threat of invasion, while continuing to fight mainly on the Galician slopes of the mountains, with his railways immediately behind him.

Here it was that the famous fortress of Przemysl (pronounced *Pshemissle*, "rz" standing for "sh") served the turn of the Russians. There were in it 130,000 Austrian, Hungarian, and German troops, under General von Kusmanek. They had more than 2,000 pieces of artillery, many of which could have been used in field warfare, and their stores of munitions were enormous. Thus the relief of Przemysl would have brought into the battlefield of Galicia a very powerful Teuton-Magyar force, which was being wasted in defending a single railway junction which had become of secondary importance. Being well acquainted with all these facts, General Brussiloff made no attack upon the fortressed garden city of the Carpathians. Under his orders General Selivanoff

Investment of Przemysl

entrenched the Russian troops on a circle of hills, beyond the range of the 12 in. howitzers of Przemysl. The Russian commander could have obtained in January, 1915, a siege train of heavy howitzers from Russia. But he did not want them. They were kept for use in Russia until the beginning of March. The army of investment relied entirely upon its ordinary

INHABITANTS OF A POLISH VILLAGE WATCHING THE BURSTING OF A GERMAN SHELL.

A Russian soldier is pointing to the spot where the shrapnel is bursting. Inset: An open-air granary by the side of a strategic railway. The bags contained flour destined to form rations for part of the Russian forces.

RUSSIAN GUNS IN ACTION NEAR WARSAW.
Some of the gunners are seen holding their hands over their ears to lessen the effect of the concussion.

field artillery which it directed, not at the forts of the fortress city, but at all the valley paths by which the garrison could attempt a sortie.

Famine was the weapon of reduction which the Russian commander employed. All his trenches and gun positions were solely designed to drive the garrison back to the city whenever they attempted to escape. Extraordinary as the statement may seem, General Brussiloff did not appear to want Przemysl to fall during the winter months. He had fixed its fall for the spring, and until then the Russian siege train could be used to strengthen Osoviec and other weak spots on the Polish front of the Russian armies.

When March came, the Russians were certain of receiving large and continual supplies of munitions and general war equipment. This would enable them to put another million or more men into the field, and also to prosecute their attack with more vigour. Then it would be possible to advance from the Galician railway system and engage in the decisive struggle on the summit of the Carpathians. But until the Russians were fully equal in number and war material to their enemies, it was necessary for them to keep the Austrians fighting on the Galician slopes. So Przemysl was held out as a lure to the Austro-Hungarian Army. All through the winter and into the spring the enemy had to assail the Russian lines, under increasing difficulties as to the transport of their supplies over the mountain

TRYING TO KEEP THEMSELVES WARM.
Russian soldiers clad in heavy coats with hoods over their heads and straw around the trenches to temper the bitter cold of the wind and snow.

passes. Every movement they made was easily countered by General Brussiloff and General Radko Dimitrieff. The Austrian Commander-in-Chief maintained communications with Przemysl by means of daily aeroplane flights, and usually arranged for the garrison to make a sortie whenever the relieving army swept down the mountain valleys in an attempt to pierce the Russian line. But though the Przemysl garrison lost forty thousand men in trying to break through the ring of General Selivanoff's hill trenches, not a battalion cut its way through.

Losses of the Przemysl garrison

The slaughter of the relieving forces was more dreadful and equally vain. Neither from the Cracow side, where General Dimitrieff barred the way, nor from the southward side, where General Brussiloff dammed every mountain valley, could the Austro-Hungarian armies break through to the relief of Przemysl.

WITH THE RUSSIAN RED CROSS SERVICE IN WINTER.
Like the Germans, the Russians utilised sleighs in Poland for the purpose of conveying wounded to the hospital bases.

By the end of January the situation of Austria-Hungary had become difficult. The troops of the Dual Monarchy were exhausted by the dreadful severity of winter mountain warfare. Their transport service over the heights was often disarranged by snowstorms, and the condition of many of the wounded was horrible in the wild, desperate scenes of struggle far removed from the Hungarian railway system. Seldom in the history of warfare has the advantage of position been used to better account than by General Brussiloff when he left the Austrians in possession of most of the passes of the Carpathians in order to check, endanger, and slacken their supplies of food and munitions. Whenever they weakened

Budapest talks to Berlin in attack he pushed his light artillery forward from the railway and bombarded the mouths of the mountain passes. This forced them to counter-attack to prevent the invasion of Hungary. Then, as winter softened into spring, the clamour for help from Przemysl increased, as the store of food there grew smaller and smaller. The Austrians, therefore, had to maintain a series of attacks over the mountain rampart, until the continual heavy attrition of their forces incapacitated them from any further attempt.

This condition of things was reached about the first week in February. As it approached there was much intercourse between the leading statesmen of Budapest and Berlin. Count Tisza had a long interview with the Kaiser Wilhelm, and the Kaiser Wilhelm travelled to Schönbrunn Castle to talk matters over with Kaiser Franz Josef. Count Tisza, the Hungarian Dictator, was the dominating figure in all the discussions. What he wanted was half a million first-rate German troops to continue the Battle of the Carpathians and defend the Hungarian plain, with its immense stretches of winter wheat, from invasion. His view was that if Germany would not or could not help in the protection of Hungary, after wasting the flower of Hungarian chivalry in the plains of Poland, then the Hungarians would be compelled to save the food resources of their country by making terms with Russia.

In regard to the Austrians, whose interests were also represented by Count Tisza, they were in a similar situation.

By making terms with Russia they would not only save their land from ravage, but they would escape loss of territory to Italy. In fact, as things stood, with Rumania ready to pounce upon Hungary, and Italy ready to pounce upon Austria, a separate peace with the Powers of the Triple Entente was the best expedient in the circumstances. Some hundreds of thousands of Austrians and Hungarians had fallen in defence of the Prussian territory of Silesia —a Prussian territory, by the way, which had been taken by force from an Austrian Empress by a Prussian King.

The Germans hesitated. In the first week of September they sent a few army corps to the Carpathian front, but some time passed before they despatched the great number of fresh troops needed to resist the increasing pressure of General Brussiloff's army. In the meantime Field-Marshal von Hindenburg, who naturally disliked having to meet the Russians at a disadvantage in the mountains, tried to force the issue, on ground of his own choosing, by a new plan of attack.

His scheme was simple and effective in principle. The lines of the main Russian armies ran in a large curve from Warsaw towards Czernovitz. The Russians attacked from the central parts of this curve. It was in the centre that they were strongest. At the ends of the curve, near Warsaw and near Czernovitz, were vital railway communications, where a blow against them would tell most heavily. In the struggle on the Bzura Hindenburg had tried to take Warsaw by **Attack on Prasnysch** a frontal attack. His new plan was to **and Stanislav** make a swerving movement against both ends of the Russian lines. The village of Prasnysch, north of Warsaw, and the railway junction of Stanislav, south-east of Lemberg, were the points he aimed at. He sent an army into East Prussia to advance in two columns past Prasnysch, force the passage of the Narew, cross the Bug River, and cut the trunk railway between Warsaw and Petrograd. About the same time he launched another army over the easternmost Carpathians into Bukovina, on the Rumanian frontier, to fight its way towards Stanislav. This new operation was conducted while the main battle in the Carpathians raged with increasing fury.

NOVEL FORM OF AMBULANCE USED BY THE RUSSIAN RED CROSS SERVICE.
Where sleighs were unprocurable the Russians removed their wounded by means of a kind of sledge made of some half-dozen ski-sticks lashed together, with layers of straw or twigs on top. These ski-sledges were drawn by stout leathern thongs fastened to the belts of the bearers.

CHAPTER LVI.

THE RESURGENCE OF SERBIA AND THE RESISTANCE OF RUSSIA.

How the Austrian Second Army of Invasion Failed—Siege Warfare Along the Frontier Heights—Serbian Artillery Munitions Give Out—Retreat to the Central Mountains—Serbians Half Demoralised for Lack of a Helping Hand—France to the Rescue—Arrival of Ammunition and More Guns—Austrian Commander Over-confident and Neglectful—Brilliant Strategy of General Putnik and His Staff—General Mishitch Attacks Unexpectedly with a Beaten Army—Austrian Centre Surprised and Routed—Serbs Envelop the Austrian Centre and Southern Wing—Panic Flight of 150,000 Invaders—Most of them Killed or Taken—Serbs Concentrate Against Northern Austrian Wing—The Battle of Belgrade—How the Hungarian Division was Captured—New Austro-Hungarian Army Collected—Russia Interferes and Attracts this New Hostile Force—Battles in Bukovina—How the Divisions of Death Went to Their Doom—Great German Army Sweeps from East Prussia—Magnificent Stand by Russian Twentieth Corps—The Encirclers Encircled at Prasnysch—Defeat of Hindenburg's Plan and Resumption of Carpathian Battle.

WHILE the great struggle was going on between Slav and Teuton in Poland and Galicia, the position of the Serbians became of great importance to the Russians. For it was largely owing to a magnificently successful diversion made by the little Serb nation in December, 1914, that the great Slav Empire was able to make headway against the furious, desperate efforts of Germany and Austria - Hungary. On the other hand, the Russians were also able to help the Serbs at the most critical moment in Serbian history, in spite of the fact that they were hundreds of miles away from Serbia. On no field of the conflict was the subtle and comprehensive system of co-operation among the Allies so clearly displayed as in the central Serbian mountains at midwinter in 1914.

The entry of Turkey into the war, in the first week of November, 1914, endangered the position which the Serbians had heroically maintained. Twice had the Austrians attempted to conquer them. The first invasion in August had ended in the terrible Austrian defeat on the Drina, which we have already fully described. The second invasion began on September 8th, when six Austrian army corps were held up in the mountains and marshes west of the Drina, and round the

mountain of Matchkokanen, a few miles south of the town of Krupanje. At a cost of over thirty thousand men the splendid fighting peasantry of Serbia repulsed the invaders on Matchkokanen, or Cat's Leg Mountain, which was lost and regained eight times before it was at last firmly held by the defending army. Grave as were the Serbian losses, they were less than those inflicted upon the Austrians, and the second invasion ended in the Austrians entrenching by the Drina and maintaining a system of trench warfare similar to that which the Germans had started on the Aisne heights. The Austrians had only two footholds on Serbian territory, while the left wing of the Serbian forces was operating in Bosnia, on a mountain range to the north of the fortress town of Sarajevo.

The series of heavy defeats which the small Serbian nation inflicted upon its mighty adversary, who had brought about the Great War by an attempt to rob Serbia of the advantages she won fairly in the Balkan struggle, were bitter blows to the pride of the Hungarian aristocracy and to all the Teutonic people of Austria. Nothing more clearly revealed to the world the military weakness of the large, uncemented mosaic of empire known as Austria-Hungary. The smashing victories won by Russia in Galicia and in the Lublin district could be explained on the ground of the

KING PETER OF SERBIA.
A portrait taken in January, 1915.

SERBIAN CONTINGENT CROSSING THE RIVER SAVE NEAR BELGRADE.

THE WATCH ON THE RIVER SAVE, ON SERBIA'S NORTHERN FRONTIER.

overwhelming numbers of the Russian armies. But in regard to the disasters in Serbia, nothing could be said to explain them away. *Res ipsa per se vociferat ;* the fact itself shouted its meaning. And the German openly despised his ally by reason thereof.

So when Turkey entered the war, and Hindenburg planned his great counter-offensive against Warsaw for the protection of Silesia, measures were taken with a view to wiping out the shame of Shabatz, and settling the entire problem of the Balkans. The intention was to launch an overwhelming force in a third invasion of Serbia and conquer all the country. Then, from the valley of the Morava, the railway to Salonica would be acquired, and, with a little pressure on Greece, the forces of Turkey would be able to unite with those of Austria-Hungary. Bulgaria would be won over completely, with the result that the Rumanians would also be terrorised into a benevolent neutrality.

Serbia was thus the key to all the problems of the Balkans, and the overthrow of its heroic little people would be a deadlier stroke for Russia than the occupation of Belgium was for France and Britain. So important, indeed, was the success of the third invasion that a large number of troops was detached for the operation, at a time when every Austrian and Hungarian soldier was needed against the Russian armies. General Potiorek, the Austro-Hungarian Commander, was

given 300,000 troops for action against the Serbians. Bosnia was almost stripped of its garrisons, an army corps was removed from the Italian frontier, and fresh drafts were sent to the troops on the Drina.

The condition of the fatigued and battered Serbian Army was such as to justify the wildest hopes of the enemy. The Serbs had been caught unprepared for war. They had barely enough rifles for their men in the fighting-line, and their reserves only came into action as the rifles of their dead and wounded comrades were available. The Serbian light field artillery was excellent in wearing quality and in handiness, but it was dominated by the heavy siege-guns of the Austrians brought up along the Drina.

Serbian Army's main trouble

The main trouble with the little Serbian Army was ammunition. In the last four years the Army had fought first against Turkey, then against Bulgaria, and twice against Austria-Hungary. It had not had time to recover from the Balkan wars before it was attacked by one of the great military empires of the world. Its small arsenal could not meet the strain, and during the trench warfare on the Drina, in September and October, 1914, the Serbian supply of ammunition completely ran out.

It was this fact that stimulated the twice-beaten Austro-Hungarians to make a supreme effort to conquer the Serbian Army, and crush the Serbian people by systematic

THE SPIRITED DEFENCE OF BELGRADE.
Serbian artillery about to fire on the attacking Austrians from an entrenched position on the outskirts of the Serbian capital.

AT WORK IN A SERBIAN FIELD HOSPITAL.

atrocities eclipsing all that the Germans had done in Belgium and Northern France. In vain did the British Government attempt to help their weakened and almost disarmed little ally, by inducing Greece to come to the help of Serbia. Sir Edward Grey offered the Greek Premier large territories in Asia Minor, including the coast from behind Chios to Rhodes, when the resettlement was made after the war. But the King of the Hellenes was too much afraid of what Turkey would do before it was dismembered, to dare to fight

Britain's offer to Greece for his old comrades-in-arms, the Serbs, and for a future Greek Empire in Asia Minor. The extraordinary generosity of the British proposal was indeed regarded generally as a sign of the extreme desperation of the Powers of the Triple Entente. It only lent deeper colour to the wild rumours concerning the effect that the entry of Turkey into the war was having upon the fortunes of the Allies.

All that France and Britain could do they did. Their own campaign in the western theatre of war was slackened, some time after the repulse of the Germans at Ypres, in order to save ammunition for the use of the Serbs. Large supplies of French material of war were shipped across the Mediterranean and sent up from the Balkan coast to Nish, arriving on the front in the first week of December. Meanwhile the Serbian Commander-in-Chief, General Putnik,

IN THE OPERATING-THEATRE OF THE AMERICAN RED CROSS HOSPITAL AT BELGRADE.

and his tattered and outworn army tasted to the full the bitterness of an approaching overwhelming national defeat. For six weeks the Serbs had been holding nearly all their frontier line, including the rich and fertile plain of Machva, between the Drina and the Save. With the coming of winter their trenches in the Machva plain became full of water, and their thin line, outstretched far beyond its strength, could not resist the pressure of the new forces brought against it.

General Putnik was compelled to order a retreat to the mountains, especially as there was no ammunition for the guns. The retreat was not carried out in good order. The Serbian infantryman was one of the finest in Europe ; but he had been put to an ordeal beyond his strength. Owing to the overwhelming power of the Austrian artillery and the incessant charges of the Austrian infantry in the last weeks of the trench warfare, the Serbian soldiers had had to fight day and night without sleeping For their reserves still lacked rifles, and the 300,000 Austrians attacked furiously all along the frontier from Orsova to Visegrad. The Serb could have died where he stood, but when he was ordered to rise and make a long march back to the mountains he completely lost heart.

His rearguards could not hold back the enemy. They swept over the frontier and converged upon the

DR. DONNELLY AND SIR THOMAS LIPTON AT A SERBIAN VILLAGE HOSPITAL.
Dr. Donnelly, a heroic American, died of typhus while trying to relieve the sick.

important town of Valievo, commanding the roads to Belgrade Obrenovac, and other strategical points.   By the capture of Valievo, on November 11th, the Austrian commander surmounted the first series of mountain barriers which formed the natural defences of Serbia, and planted the centre of his great army in the middle of the Serbian highlands.   At the same time he swung his right wing over the heights far to the south, where his mountain brigades outflanked the Serbian wing.   Ridge after ridge was lost by the Serbs, who grew more demoralised as the superior numbers and irresistible artillery power of the enemy pressed them back continually.

All along the line the Serbs gave way.   Their centre was thrown back on the Kolubara River on November 20th, and on November 28th the great part of the mountain defences, including the passes of the Suvobor heights, were stormed or turned by the invaders.   Belgrade, the capital of Serbia, had fallen, and the line of the Austrian advance stretched for seventy miles from the Danube towards Cacac, or Chachak, in the Western Morava valley.

On December 1st the weakening Serbian **The disaster of Suvobor** Army held only the rocky wedge between the Morava valleys.   In the middle of this wedge was the arsenal town of Kragujevatz, defended on the north-west by the Rudnik ridge, with peaks rising from 3,000 to 4,500 feet.   Some fifteen miles westward of the Rudnik ridge was another high and snow-buried tract of mountain, the Maljen ridge.   Then between the Rudnik and the Maljen extended the lower heights of Suvobor, over which ran the passes to Cacac and Kragujevatz.

The ground at Suvobor rose in fold after fold to a height of 2,000 feet.   It was the gateway into the central highlands of Serbia, and the First Serbian Army had surrendered it to the enemy almost without a blow and withdrawn to the lower slopes.   All the ridges of Maljen westward were also lost to the Serbs on November 25th, and the Fourth Army was retreating up the valley of the Western Morava.   Far to the south, along the railway leading to Salonica, by which the Serbians usually received their supplies, armed bands of Moslems and other insurgents broke their line of communication with the outer

world, preparatory to an advance by the Turks and Bulgarians against their helpless and stricken common foe of former days.

In these circumstances the Serbian peasant began, by a marvellous power of recoil, to recover his confidence. The weakness of the First Army had led to the grave disaster of Suvobor.   But the soldiers were only worn out by want of sleep and dismayed by lack of ammunition, after holding the marshlands of Machva against the heavy Austrian artillery.   During their retreat they had at least been able to sleep off their physical weariness ; for the Austrian advance over the mountains had been remarkably slow.   With this restoration to ordinary fitness, the astonishing character of the Serbian people in the hour of their apparent doom was fully displayed.

They were the least Slavlike of all the Slav races.   In their ancient descent into the Balkans they had absorbed a large number of Celts occupying the highlands.   The result was that they lost the stolidity that marks the Russian and Bulgarian, and acquired a natural light-heartedness and vivacity **Serbia's power** which made them the Irishmen of the **of recoil** Balkans.   They had also quite an Irish zest for fighting.   First of all the Christian people of the Balkans they had risen in open revolt against the Turks, in 1804, winning their independence after a terrible struggle that lasted thirteen years.   They gained their freedom with their own hands, and all that the great Powers of Christendom afterwards did for them was to rob them of territory to increase the dominions of the German Prince of Bulgaria, and to block their trade routes and fight them down with tariff walls.

Serbia had thus learnt, for a hundred and ten years, to rely only on her own strength of soul.   Her peasants had a well-founded contempt for the veneer of good manners of the great neighbouring Christian nations. When they had a bad king and a bad queen they killed them without formality, and found in the exiled survivor of their older dynasty, King Peter, the military leader they needed in their difficult situation.   In our country the rough-and-ready regicides of the Balkans were for

IF ENGLAND WERE INVADED—WHAT SHE MIGHT SUFFER AT THE HANDS OF THE HUN.
Serbia's sufferings are comparable to those of Belgium.   The soldiers of the Emperor Franz Josef rivalled the troops of the Prussian Kaiser in their ruthless brutality.   Save for the bodies of massacred civilians lying in the foreground, the above photograph might be of a peaceful English village.   Actually it is a camera-record of the trail of death left by the Austrians in their retreat from Belgrade.

WITH THE SERBIAN ARMY IN THE FIELD—AN INTERVAL OF NEEDED REST.

The soldier in the centre of the photograph is displaying a Hungarian flag, a trophy of a recent engagement in which it was captured from the 32nd Regiment. Seated on the ground are some soldiers of that regiment who had been taken prisoners by the Serbians. These men do not appear much concerned as to their fate

some years regarded as the scandal of the world. We could not appreciate the perils of Austrian domination from which the Serbs had temporarily escaped by a sudden stroke at their bad king. Russia was ready to advance the cause of the independent mountaineers when they had freed themselves from Austrian influence, but the Russians could not give the Serbians the aid they needed. It was the Republicans of France who helped most, and by financing Serbia and supplying her with first-rate artillery had done much to ensure her triumph over the Turks and the Bulgarians. The admirable light French guns greatly assisted in the first smashing defeat of the Austrians, and, until the fall of Belgrade, the capital of Serbia was defended by a few French heavy guns worked by French artillerymen. To France the Serbians looked for aid in the days of their extreme peril in November 1914, and by a masterly effort some new

How France saved Serbia

batteries and twenty thousand shells were transported from France to the Adriatic coast, and thence to the Serbian highlands in the last days of November. By this means France saved Serbia. For though the Serbian Army of 200,000 men was ravaged by typhus and other infectious diseases, and the few hospitals were so choked with wounded that injured soldiers went home with their wounds undressed to perish, or died in the streets, the fighting spirit of the heroic highlanders was not broken. The roads along which they fought and manœuvred were blocked by hundreds of thousands of fugitives, terrorised by the awful atrocities committed by the victorious armies of invasion. The winter weather in the mountains was very rigorous and severely tried the retreating Serbian troops, when their supply columns were put out of working order by the block of fugitives and by the sudden and unexpected movements of the defeated troops. But the Serb had a remarkable strength of physique

and a still more remarkable resilience of soul. When the rumour ran through the ranks that the guns had been supplied with French ammunition, the infantry took heart and resolved to die fighting. Old King Peter came into the foremost firing-line in front of the Suvobor ridge, in order, if need be, to fall in the foremost line of the defence. It was a fine, picturesque act on the part of the King, who knew his people well, and understood the effect his attitude would have upon them. He was the grandson of Black George, the Serb shepherd, who had freed his country in 1804. When King Peter in his old age showed himself ready to die in the front trenches, battling against the new oppressors of Serbia, his attitude fired his soldiers with a flame of heroism that nothing else could have kindled.

The leaders of the Serbian forces were men of tried genius, able to take full advantage of the great and unexpected resurgence of spirit among their troops. The Commander-in-Chief, General Putnik, was a great strategist of the Napoleonic school. With him worked Colonel

Two great Serbian leaders

Pavlovitch, the son of a farm labourer, who had won a series of scholarships, enabling him to study at Berlin, and master the art of war. He had directed the military operations in the struggle against Turkey and Bulgaria, and he was doing the same thing under his old chief, General Putnik, in the struggle against Austria-Hungary. He was now struck by the slowness with which the armies of the enemy were moving. They had lost a week since their capture of the ridges of Maljen and Suvobor.

Colonel Pavlovitch came to the conclusion that the Austro-Hungarian armies were in the same condition as the Serbian forces—starving by reason of the disorganisation of their transport columns, and half demoralised by lack of food, the rigour of the wintry weather in the mountains, and the general hardships of the campaign. This view was well founded. The Austrian Staff was incompetent, and yet exceedingly hopeful. It thought that, with the forcing of the Suvobor ridges, the resistance of the Serbians had been completely broken, and that it was only a matter of rounding up a shattered and demoralised mob of fugitives. News of the supposed complete Austrian victory had been sent to Vienna, and Kaiser Franz Josef, in honour of the grand event, had instituted a new military decoration, which was bestowed upon General Potiorek.

General Potiorek fully shared in the illusion of his Staff. Besides the 300,000 troops with which he was operating, there seem to have been another 150,000 men at his disposal, if necessary; for the complete conquest of Serbia was a matter of extreme urgency to Austria-Hungary, and both of her allies, Germany and Turkey, required her to carry it out at any sacrifice of life. The Russian armies, however, were then pressing strongly upon Cracow from the north and the east, and a large reinforcement was badly wanted to hold up the Russians on the Dunajec River and the Dukla Pass. In fact, the Russian Commander-in-Chief was exerting all the pressure he could, by means of the three armies of Generals Brussiloff, Dimitrieff, and Ivanoff, with a view to forcing the Hungarians to put more men in the field against him. All this was done in the hope of relieving the terrible pressure which was being brought to bear upon Serbia. And the plan succeeded. For, owing mainly to the grave weakness displayed by the Serbian troops, Potiorek dispensed with the use of his three additional army corps, which were railed at once against the menacing Russian front.

This left the Serbians with about three to one against them. But General Putnik was a superb master of the art of strategy. In retiring his troops, he had got into such a position that he was able to work on short interior lines, while the enemy had to make large and arduous movements in trying to envelop the Serbian position.

The Serbians held, with their Second and **Potiorek's text-book** Third Armies, the western slopes of the **plan** Rudnik Mountains. Then, more southward, the First Serbian Army was entrenched in front of its lost position below the Suvobor ridge. Still farther southward, the Fourth Serbian Army, thrown back from the chaos of mountains by the Bosnian frontier, defended the lower reaches of the Western Morava.

General Putnik had to decide where the hostile commander would place his strongest forces. This was a question depending on the character of General Potiorek, and as he was known to be an uninspired, unoriginal man, with a firm faith in the routine methods of the Moltke school of war, it was not difficult to foresee what he would do. As a matter of fact, he followed out the text-book plan customary in the situation in which he was placed. Having broken the Serbian resistance on his centre—the Suvobor ridge—

SERBIAN INFANTRY GOING INTO ACTION AT ROJAGNE, TAKING ADVANTAGE OF THE COVER OF TREES ON THE HILLSIDE.
The photograph was taken by a Serbian officer. The circular view shows a section of the Serbian trenches, whence heavy artillery bombarded the Austrian position.

AUSTRIAN OFFICERS AS PRISONERS IN BELGRADE.

AUSTRIAN PRISONERS AT A STATION IN GALICIA.

he held this ridge with only one army corps, and placed two army corps on each of his wings. His idea was to drive round in the greatest force by the north of the Rudnik ridge, and along the valley of the Western Morava, and thus envelop the Serbian forces on both sides, and achieve a new Sedan.

But while his troops were moving with great difficulty through the deep snow on the mountains in order to get into the dumb-bell formation, General Putnik struck. One of his most brilliant Staff officers—General Mishitch—took command of the First Serbian Army, displacing the general who had badly conducted the retreat from the river marshes. General Mishitch was a peasant's son, who had fought his way to the front rank and acted as lieutenant to General Putnik in the three great modern wars from which his country had emerged victorious. Like his fellow-worker on the staff, Colonel Pavlovitch, the peasant general was a brilliant thinker, who had directed other commanders without taking the field himself. It was now given to him to show that he could conduct a battle as brilliantly as he could arrange one. Acting with him was General Sturm, commanding the Third Army, entrenched on the slopes of the Rudnik range.

Mishitch's plan was quite simple. He intended a surprise attack against the single Austro-Hungarian army corps holding the Suvobor ridge. While he launched the First Army against it in front, Sturm would sweep down westward from the Rudniks with the Third Army, and take

General Mishitch in command

the enemy on the flank. Then, as this was being done, the two other Serbian armies would have to hold back the two very powerful wings of the invading force.

General Mishitch, with the First Army, had halted on the little mountain stream—the Dicina. He suddenly advanced in a general attack, on the morning of December 3rd, 1914, and completely surprised the Austrians. He caught them leisurely moving along the valley paths. Capturing the overlooking hills, the Serbs shot the hostile columns down, while the Austrians were still wondering where they should place their artillery. Naturally, the Serbs knew every fall and rise of the ground, for Mishitch himself had been born and bred by the Suvobor, and his gun sites, skilfully captured by sudden strokes, commanded

HAPPY THOUGH CAPTIVE—AUSTRIANS RESTING UNDER GUARD ON A SERBIAN FARM.
In the smaller photograph we have evidence that the Serbians put their Austrian prisoners to serviceable but legitimate employment.

the paths along which he was driving the enemy. So overwhelming was the unexpected recoil of the nation of highlanders, that Potiorek and his Staff thought all the Serbian armies had been massed for the attack on the Suvobor. The Austrian commander, therefore, attempted in the heat of the action to alter entirely his dispositions for battle. He ordered both his wings to send large reinforcements to his centre. But the movement of large bodies of troops through snowstorms in the mountain chaos of the Balkans, intersected only by a few rough roads, was not a quick or easy matter. The guns were also held up, with the supply waggons, and most of the Austro-Hungarian troops had nothing to eat for two days or more. And this at a time when the searching coldness of the high altitudes, in which they were operating in midwinter, hourly lowered their vitality.

The Serbian artillerymen were at the top of their form. As soon as their infantry had rushed a good gun position for them, they got their pieces up by severe and yet enjoyable labour, and then opened with shrapnel on the enemy, bunched up in the valley, and plainly outlined against the snow. All the targets were large and extraordinarily clear, and with their long experience of mountain warfare, the Serbian artillerymen, with guns firing twenty rounds a minute, wrought terrible havoc. It was the remarkable increase in the destructive power of the Serbian artillery which made the Austrian Staff conclude that all the forces of Serbia were concentrated in front of Suvobor.

At the end of ten hours of fierce, incessant conflict, the Austrian first line was thrown back with the loss of some of its mountain howitzers. The troops retired on the positions defended by their heavy siege-guns. But the Serbians, exhilarated by their preliminary success, wanted no sleep or food. Onward they swept in the darkness, gaining ground over which it would have been impossible for them to advance in daylight in the teeth of the long-range Austrian guns. After midnight they snatched a little sleep, and ate what food could be brought up; and long before the slow winter dawn broke they had hauled their light guns closer to the enemy. Then came the grand attack, carried out with an impetuosity and tenacious fighting power unparalleled even in Serbian history.

The leadership of the company officers was magnificent. After a short struggle the enemy's front was broken, and his well-entrenched positions were enfiladed and captured. Line after line of rising crests, each commanding the other, and all with a wide field of fire dominated the ground which the Serbians approached. Each assault up the slopes, against machine-guns, artillery, and rifle fire, was an arduous business, and if the snow on the ground had not been trampled into mud by the retreating invaders, the

GENERAL BULGAROFF.
Commander of heroic Twentieth Russian Army Corps.

GENERAL POTIOREK.
Commander of Austrian Armies in Serbia.

GENERAL VON BULOW.

GENERAL VON EICHHORN.
Commanded German Armies in East Prussia.

GENERAL STEPHANOVITCH.
Victorious Serbian General.

storming parties could have been marked down miles away. But the mountaineers went up in widely extended order, throwing up little mounds at the end of every rush. Then, as their guns in the rear beat down the fire from the heights, the troops closed to the final charge, and broke through on the rise.

The end came near Gorni Toplitza, where the road runs round a great height, overhanging the river valley. On the edge of the mountain the Austrians had a battery of field-guns in a plum orchard. In the road below was a string of ammunition waggons, from which the guns were served. The Serbian artillerymen hauled up their guns on the flank of this position and poured on it a devastating enfilading fire. The torrent of shrapnel shot down men and horses, and the high-explosive shells which followed wrecked the batteries, limbers, and ammunition carts. Some men tried to escape, throwing away their packs as they made for the shelter of a neighbouring ravine. But they were all caught before they reached it. The French guns used by the Serbians had a semi-automatic device for slaughtering men in thousands, or tens of thousands, by a progressive movement in a given direction.

After the slaughter at Gorni Toplitza the central Austrian army became a terrorised rabble. All that the troops thought of was to get beyond the range of the Serbian guns. They did not stay even to put their own abandoned artillery out of action. They left their machine-guns and their unexhausted stores of ammunition in the trenches, and the paths over which they ran were marked by the trail they left behind them. It was a litter of accoutrements of every kind. There was one very significant incident. A pursuing Serb battery could not get its guns up quickly enough to help the infantry against an Austrian rearguard. The artillery officer ordered his men to leave their guns and charge with the riflemen. In about half an hour they had captured the Austrian battery opposed to them, and, hauling the guns round, they poured upon the fugitives round after round of Austrian shells.

At Valievo there was at last a rally of the best regiments of the Fifteenth Army Corps, and the several brigades of the Sixteenth Corps brought up to reinforce it. There were Hungarian regiments also, sent hurriedly down from the neighbourhood of Belgrade to stop the rout. The Hungarians and Austrians entrenched along the main road from the Suvobor region, and got their guns into position. The Serbs could be seen slowly advancing against them along the road. But a considerable time passed before an attack was made. Then it was an overwhelming surprise. For the Serbs who could be seen along the road were only a reserve, waiting to pursue the

UNIQUE WAR-TIME PHOTOGRAPH OF PRINCE ALEXANDER OF SERBIA.

The above photograph was taken during the bombardment of Belgrade by the Austrians, and shows Prince Alexander near a waterfall close to the forts, watching the result of the Serbian shells on the Austrian position. The photograph affords a glimpse of the picturesque beauty of the scenery in the vicinity of Belgrade.

BRITISH HONOUR FOR SERBIA'S PRINCE REGENT.
At Nish on March 19th, 1915, the Order of the Bath was conferred on Prince Alexander of Serbia by General Sir Arthur Paget, in the name of King George. Our photograph shows a group of officers who were present at the investiture. Left to right: Anto Mitrovitch, Colonel Harrison (British Attaché), and Colonel Yivko Pavlovitch (Governor-General).

broken the centre of Potiorek's front, the Serbian commander gave his chief attention to capturing the Austrian southern wing, operating in the Western Morava valley.

Here the Fourth Serbian Army, usually known from its base town as the Ushitza Army, was striding across the river valley above Cacac. For some days the Serbians in this sector of the front could only hold their own by a great effort against superior forces brought against them.

But when General Mishitch stormed the Suvobor rid es, the Austrian southern wing, connected by wireless with its centre, knew that it was in peril. So it began to withdraw on December 5th, but as the commander of the Fourth Serbian Army was even better acquainted with the general situation, he did not allow the withdrawal to take place in an orderly manner. Waiting till nightfall, when he knew the roads would be choked with the enemy's heavy artillery, he delivered an attack at midnight. As dawn came the Austrians were in full retreat. They threw out rearguards in the river valley, but the highlanders knew the mountain tracks, and dropped down behind the entrenchments, making continual hauls of guns and prisoners.

On December 7th some of Mishitch's men captured the summit of Maljen. Then, linked with the advancing edge of the Fourth Army that was curling south around Ushitza, they achieved the enveloping operation which the Austrian commander had vainly hoped to accomplish. The three

enemy when he was broken. The main force had crept over the mountains; they attacked on the flank and threatened the rear, with the result that the battle did not take place. Only the rout was intensified.

When the First Serbian Army, under Mishitch, was winning one of the best-handled battles in the Great War, the Third Army, under Sturm, and the Second Army, under Stephanovitch, came down from the slopes of the Rudniks. Sturm's men worked through the turned flank of the central Austrian forces on December 5th, 1914, and then broke off a large part of the enemy's northern wing by a night attack in which thousands of prisoners were taken. At the same time Stephanovitch, with the Second Army, drove hard into the middle of the Austrian northern wing, and caught it as it was still extended in its vain circling movement round the Rudniks towards Kragujevac.

But though the powerful northern wing of the Austrian Army was severed from its centre, and thrown back violently, no overwhelming victory against it was achieved. This was all according to the plans of General Putnik. Being much outnumbered, he could not spare the forces necessary to rout the enemy's strong northern force. Having

A SERBIAN OUTPOST ON THE DANUBE.
The condition of the fatigued and battered Serbian Army was such as to justify the wildest hopes of the enemy. But the astonishing recuperative qualities of the people were fully displayed after the earlier stages of the Austrian attack, and all that Britain and France could do to help they did. General Putnik was a great strategist of the Napoleonic school.

PREPARING THE DEFENCES OF BELGRADE.
Serbian soldiers completing trenches and putting up wire entanglements around the forts of their threatened capital.

fugitive army corps, which had constituted the centre and southern wing of the invading force, were cut off from the northern wing and shepherded to destruction. There was little fighting. It was merely a race towards the Drina and Save Rivers, through the labyrinth of mountains in North-West Serbia. The Austrians kept to the valley roads, and the Serbians cut them off in thousands by using the straighter mountain paths. The fact that these paths were buried in snow did not

Through mountain labyrinths seriously trouble the mountaineers, who had pastured their sheep there since boyhood. They could work their way across them in the dark. By November 10th Sturm with the Third Army was nearing Obrenovac, on the Save, a few miles below Belgrade. Far in the west the Fourth Army and the First Army were collecting a miscellaneous mob of the various races peopling the Empire of Franz Josef— Austrians, Hungarians, Bosnians, Mohammedans, Serbians, Bohemians, Moravians, Slovenes, Rumanians, and Russians. The captives were all starving, and two Serbian soldiers were a strong enough force to guard a column of two thousand of them. For captivity was welcome—

IN THE TRENCHES NEAR THE RIVER DRINA.

it meant food and shelter. In between the convoys straggled men who had fallen out by the way, most of them footsore creatures, paddling along through the freezing slush till they reached some place where they could get food, or till they dropped dead by the roadside.

Meanwhile, eastward, General Potiorek was trying to retain Belgrade with his detached northern wing. Formed of the Eighth and a mixed Army Corps, this force

SERBIAN PEASANT WOMEN BY THE GRAVES OF THEIR DEAD.
The photograph is of an improvised Serbian cemetery, and the women are seen paying a tribute of homage and respect to the fallen brave.

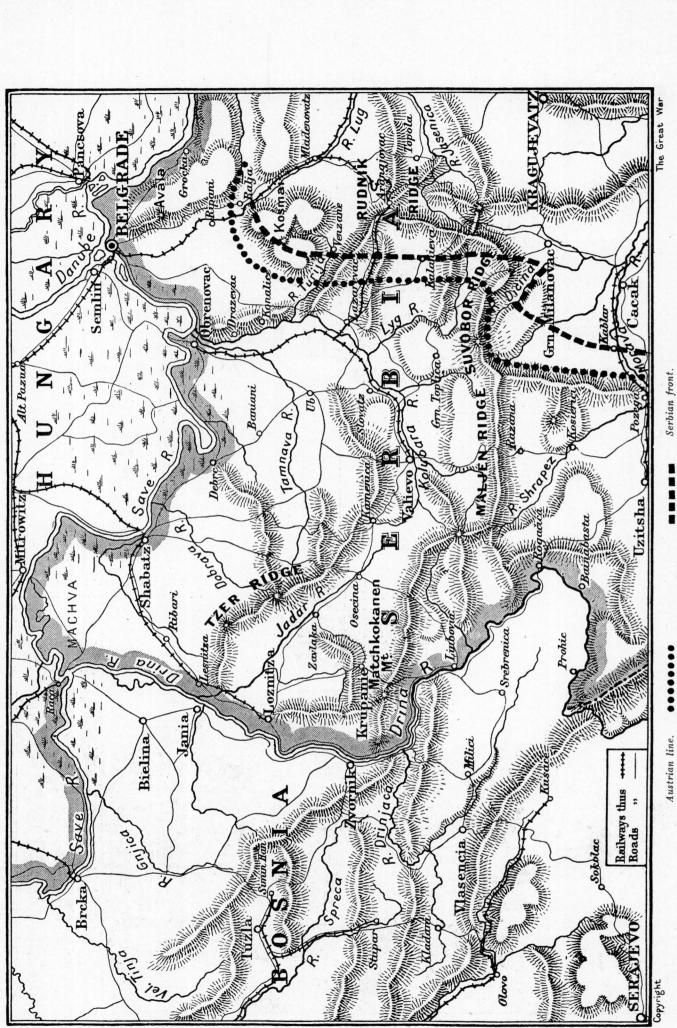

MAP OF THE THIRD AUSTRO-HUNGARIAN CAMPAIGN IN SERBIA.

Showing the position of the invading army and that of the Serbian troops just before the attack that broke the enemy's centre.

Austrian line. ●●●●●● Serbian front. ▬ ▬ ▬

Railways thus ┿┿┿
Roads   ,,   ────

The Great War

Copyright

Russian outpost going on duty carrying wood for fuel.

Russian officer testing the food at a travelling army kitchen.

Remarkable photograph of Austrian trenches near Jasionna, showing in lef

ground entrance to bomb=proof, and on the right communicating trenches.

Prussian Cavalry against Cossacks of the Don: Fierce encounter on the Dniester.

had checked the advance of the Second Serbian Army, under General Stephanovitch, and had pressed hard against the garrison of Belgrade. This garrison, on the fall of the Serbian capital, had retired to the mountain of Kosmai, north of the Rudnik range. Here it was attacked by part of the Austrian northern wing on December 7th, 8th, and 9th. On the last day, however, the complete

THE AGONY OF SERBIA.
Stricken soldier of the suffering little kingdom refused admission to hospital because it was already overcrowded with typhus patients.

overthrow of the main forces of the enemy enabled General Putnik to rearrange his forces. He moved part of his Third Army towards the Save, some twenty miles south of Belgrade. Another part he attached to his Second Army, and added his cavalry to it, and also the Belgrade garrison. This combined force was placed under the command of General Stephanovitch, famous for his victories in earlier campaigns.

By September 10th, when Stephanovitch assumed full command of the eastern operations, the Austrian forces had been bent back from the Rudnik ridge and the height of Kosmai. Their front stretched **Austrian invaders shattered.** from Grocka on the Danube to Konatice on the Kolubara River. Some fifteen miles behind them was the city of Belgrade, which they were endeavouring to retain for the honour and prestige of their empire. The failure of the movement of invasion was patent to the world. General Potiorek sorely needed the possession of Belgrade to palliate the overthrow of the third Austrian plan of conquest of Serbia.

General Putnik reckoned on this. The loss of Belgrade had become a gain to him. By means of his lost capital he was able, not merely to shatter the centre and southern wing of the invading armies, but also to make a new concentration of force against the powerful remnant of the enemy's strength. Right in the centre of the Austrian front was a hill through which ran the railway from Salonica to Vienna. General Stephanovitch brought his heavy guns up by this railway on the night of December 10th, and then at dawn he flung his troops forward, under the cover of his gun fire, and stormed the hill. At the same time his left wing advanced up the

Kolubara River towards its junction with the Save, some eight miles behind the Austrian front. The enemy had to draw back, for fear of being suddenly taken in the rear, and sent two monitors up the river to check the Serbian Cavalry Division, which was trying to work over the marshes and cut off the entire Austrian force.

But this movement of the Serbian left wing was only a feint. It was intended simply to make the Austrian line waver. While Potiorek was manœuvring his troops in answer to the feint, Stephanovitch made another frontal attack. Then for three days there was a most violent, swaying battle along the base of the little triangle of Serbian soil that ended in a point at Belgrade. The Austrians fought manfully, and, indeed, gave the Serbians one of the best fights in their long and warlike history. Instead of merely clinging to their hill entrenchments, they made fierce and tenacious attempts to break the Serbian front. But it was in one of these counter-attacks, near the central height where the railway entered a tunnel, that the resistance of the Austrians was broken. After the Serbian riflemen, with their machine-guns, had thrown back the enemy, the Serbian artillery caught the retiring troops.

This produced a panic in the dense retreating column, and the Serbian infantry left their trenches at a run, and formed into two streams, flowing on either side of the column of fugitives in the river valley. And as these streams ran uphill more quickly than the grey-blue flood moved, the Austrian rearguards, composed of heavy forces entrenched on strong positions, were turned. By December 14th the Serbians approached the line of

WAR-WORN, BUT BY NO MEANS BROKEN.
Mountain gun battery leaving Monastir for the front. The Serbian troops had been through two wars already, also a campaign against Albanian insurgents. But they responded cheerfully to the further call against the Austrian oppressor when it came to them.

hills forming the southern defence of Belgrade. Here General Potiorek had constructed a system of earthworks, consisting of deep trenches with shrapnel cover, and well-concealed gun positions, with numerous heavy howitzers and field-pieces. He intended to stand an indefinite siege on this fragment of Serbian territory, holding Belgrade as a bridge-head for another advance along the main Morava valley. In this way a rag of prestige would be saved from the debacle, enabling the campaign to be represented as a reconnaissance in force, similar to Hindenburg's first advance against Warsaw.

But his troops had received so terrible a punishment that they could not garrison the siege defences. The Serbians, steeled by victory after victory, and absolutely reckless of death as they drove in upon their capital, with their old King, the grandson of Black George, moving through their

THE FORTIFICATIONS OF BELGRADE.
The river in the foreground is the Danube, which forms a natural barrier between Hungary and Serbia.

1914—the pontoon bridge was destroyed by shell fire. A cloud of fog and rain veiled the scene, but the gunners knew the position of their mark, and, breaking down the bridge, they cut off the retreat of the remnant of the two Austrian army corps. The rearguard outside the city was destroyed, and then the Serbian cavalrymen, accompanied by King Peter, swept from the height of Torlak, and entered the streets of the capital, killed a detachment of Hungarians who would not surrender, and began to round up the prisoners to the number of ten thousand. As the street fighting between the cavalrymen and the Hungarians was going on, King Peter entered the cathedral of his capital to give thanks for the almost miraculous salvation of his small, heroic nation.

King Peter gives thanks

Of the army of 300,000 invaders who crossed the Drina and Save Rivers nearly half was put out of action. More than 41,500 prisoners were taken, together with 133 guns, 71 Maxims, 386 ammunition waggons, 3,350 transport waggons, and more than 3,250 horses and oxen. The

EFFECT OF SHELL FIRE ON A BRIDGE NEAR THE SERBIAN FRONTIER.

foremost ranks, charged up in the ring of hills. On the central height of Torlak, on the evening of December 14th, they shot and bayoneted two Austrian battalions. Then moving in the darkness they captured all the heights.

No Serbians slept that night. They dragged or man-handled their guns towards Belgrade, and placed them on heights commanding the pontoon bridges, by which the enemy were fleeing over the Save. At dawn, on the happiest day in Serbian history—December 15th,

ANOTHER VIEW OF THE DEFENCES OF BELGRADE.
General view showing the fortress of Belgrade and the Austrian position round Semlin.

TRAGEDY IN THE HOUR OF TRIUMPH.

A realistic photograph from the Serbian battlefield. Serbian gunners left dead at their posts while their comrades were pursuing the surprised and humiliated Austrians after the latter's brief occupation of Belgrade.

WHERE PRISONERS OF WAR ENJOYED COMPARATIVE LIBERTY.

Austrian prisoners purchasing cooking utensils at a popular store in Nish. They were allowed to enter the town to buy provisions and other necessaries.

AUSTRIAN PRISONERS ARRIVING AT NISH.
When Belgrade was bombarded the Serbians made Nish their temporary capital.

A MOVING STORY.
Wounded Austrian prisoner telling the story of the Battle of Mount Tyser to Serbian soldiers near Nish.

number of dead and wounded Austro-Hungarians left on the battlefields exceeded 60,000. These were only put out of action during the retreat and rout of the invading forces, when the enemy could not stay to bury his own dead and tend his wounded. His losses during the early part of the campaign were not known, but reports from Hungarian sources went to show that one-half at least of the entire fighting force had been destroyed, captured, or disabled.

In importance, the achievement of the Serbians ranks immediately after the Battle of the Marne and the Battle of Turobin, in which latter battle the first-line armies of Austria-Hungary were overthrown. For had Serbia fallen, the Teutonic Empires would have been **The Allies' debt** united with little delay to the Ottoman **to Serbia** Empire, with Bulgaria as their new ally, Greece reduced to vassalage, and Rumania and Italy definitely intimidated. Any operation to force the Dardanelles would then have become, not merely a hard task, but a practical impossibility, and the difficulties of the entire campaign of the Powers of the Triple Entente would have been greatly increased. The Dardanelles would have become an important submarine base for Germany and Austria, and the transport of troops and the movement of shipping along the Mediterranean and through the Suez Canal might have been very gravely impeded.

In any case the Balkans would have been dominated by the enemy, and transformed into a land bridge between Turkey and the Teutonic countries. But all this was prevented by the wonderful efforts of the small race of mountaineers, exhausted by three great wars, ravaged by deadly infectious diseases, and reduced to extreme poverty. A few thousand Britons recognised what they owed to Serbia, and came forward in the spring of 1915 with offers of money, clothing, medicine, and aid in doctoring and nursing. One London hospital, in particular, sent out a capable staff of surgeons and nurses. But up to the time of writing (May, 1915), the general British public, saved from

the horrors and miseries of invasion by a strong Fleet, had shown no practical appreciation of the achievement by which Serbia had shortened the war at an, as yet, untold sacrifice of the lives of her finest men, and of the health of half or more of her people.

The Austrians and Hungarians themselves were staggered by the extraordinary power of the Serbs. Their last disaster, indeed, left them half-stunned. Then a gust of desperate anger swept over them. Calling the Germans to their aid, they began to collect, in January, 1915, a new army of 400,000 troops of good quality—Bavarians, Hungarians, and German Austrians—who were ranged close to the Serbian frontier. **Austria's call for** It is, however, impossible to say whether **German aid** these preparations were seriously meant at the outset, and were subsequently overruled by Hindenburg, or whether the Prussian Commander-in-Chief completely controlled the situation from the beginning of the new movement, and used the new menace to Serbia as a feint. However this may be, the Russian commander of the south-west armies saw to it that the hard-pressed, over-

NOVEL SERBIAN GUN TEAM.
Oxen hauling a big gun along a rough cart-track across the fields.

BRINGING UP AMMUNITION BY HAND.
Owing to the difficult nature of the country, shells for the Serbian guns had frequently to be carried by hand. In circle: Serbian artillery entrained for the front.

THE TERRIBLE QUICK-FIRING GUNS WITH WHICH THE SERBS BROKE THE POWER OF THE INVADER.
These mobile field-pieces were made on the same principle as the famous French "75."

wrought, but victorious Serbians were given breathing space.

This was accomplished by bringing pressure to bear upon Hungary. On January 5th a Russian Division, equipped with mountain guns, came down from Galicia and captured Czernovitz, and began to work its way through Bukovina. By January 13th nearly the whole of Bukovina was in the hands of the Russians, and they were advancing by the Kirlibaba Pass over the Carpathian Mountains, which rise to a great height by the Rumanian frontier. Here the Russians attacked the last Austrian fortress guarding the path to Transylvania.

At the same time the main Russian armies in Galicia, under the command of General Brussiloff, **Russia's advance** a man of genius and courage, stormed **into Hungary** certain of the Carpathian passes, two hundred miles north-west of the Bukovina Pass. Brussiloff had to give up for the time his easy method of fighting with the Galician railway system immediately behind his line, and send several of his army corps over the snow-buried summits. In spite of the difficulties of their enterprise, they hurled back the great Austrian army, with its first reinforcement of three German army corps. The Dukla Pass and the Uzsok Pass were captured, and an advance was made into Hungary along the river valley leading to the town of Ungvar. In conjunction with the advance towards the Kirlibaba Pass, the Russian movement threatened to sweep over all the Hungarian plain to the east of Budapest. So no troops could be spared for another invasion of Serbia, and on January 23rd, 1915,

the new Austro-German army, gathered near the Danube, was sent up into the Carpathian Mountains.

Brussiloff then had all the work and excitement he wanted. Half his forces were entrenched around Przemysl, patiently waiting for it to fall by famine. This left him with about a quarter of a million men, and with them he had to meet and hold up the whole Austrian forces on the Carpathians, not less in number than his troops, reinforced by 400,000 fresh soldiers, many of them being first-rate German fighting men, with more tenacity of character than the light, gay, artistic Austrians. The Germans advanced towards the end of January on the Uszok and Beskiden Passes, and captured them. On this section of the front Brussiloff was compelled to fall back on the Galician slopes, where he could use **A month's fighting** his railways. He also withdrew from the **in Bukovina** Kirlibaba Pass the single division operating there. It slowly retired, fighting in the upland forest against two army corps which were trying to reach General Brussiloff's railway communications at Stanislav. The Russian Division had to fight for time, by ambushing the advance guards of Hungarian troops, and generally impeding the enemy's advance. This it did in a month's incessant fighting in the Bukovina, that only cost the Russians in dead, wounded, and prisoners 1,007 men.

Meanwhile, Hindenburg prepared in a very able manner for his more important attack on the Russian line of communication behind Warsaw. The Russians had four army corps, under General Baron von Sieviers, operating by the East Prussia frontier. It was Hindenburg's intention

OUTPOSTS ON A SNOW-COVERED SERBIAN HILLSIDE IN THE DEPTH OF WINTER.

AUSTRIAN PRISONERS OF WAR ENGAGED IN FARM WORK AT USKUB, IN SERBIA.

SOME OF THE MEN WHO DEFEATED THE AUSTRIANS: SERBIAN SHARPSHOOTERS IN ACTION.

to overwhelm this small army by a sudden superior concentration of force in the Masurian Lakes region. Then he designed to sweep across the Niemen and the Narew Rivers and cut the line of supplies for all the Russian troops in the bend of the Vistula. The German commander had first to make sure that no important part of the Warsaw army or of Russky's army was detached to reinforce the East Prussian front. The means by which he accomplished this end was dreadfully simple.

On January 31st, 1915, seven "Divisions of Death," composed of picked troops who did not expect to return from the attack, massed behind the troops holding the German line in front of Sochachev on the Bzura and Bolimoff on the Rawka. At the same time an unusual number of heavy and light batteries were concentrated on this section of the front,

Germany's explosive bullets and the Kaiser came to Hindenburg's headquarters at Kutno to watch the great offensive. The German ordnance authorities even went so far as to issue supplies of cartridges with explosive bullets to the 84,000 infantrymen designated to make the terrible demonstration. Then on the last day in January, after the Russian lines had been bombarded most heavily with high-explosive shells, many of them of 11 and 12 in. calibre, the attack was made.

Every German infantryman taking part in it went forth with high courage to die. He came on with his comrades in close formation and with strong supports, and bridged the Bzura in three or four places, and advanced on the eastern villages of Sucha, Borzimov, and Gumine, between Sochachev and Bolimoff. The Russians were forced back from the Bzura into the forest stretching to Warsaw. For a week the fight went on, with desperate tenacity and intensity. So long as the Divisions of Death retained their cohesion, they went forward, but at the edge of the forest the Russian guns caught them in dense masses, and broke them up. Then the Siberian riflemen swept down and recaptured their trenches, and by the middle of the week they won back the important position of Volya Shidlovska, near Gumine. Neither explosive bullets nor chlorine-gas bombs, both of which the Germans used freely, could stay the Russian counter-attack. At night the Russian searchlights revealed the last of the Divisions of Death marching to the support of their comrades ; but the columns were dispersed by field-guns and machine-guns, and by February 6th 45,000, out of the original 84,000 bayonets composing the seven divisions, were put out of action. Thereupon the most costly demonstration ever made in the history of war came to an end.

It may have been intended for more than a demonstration. But though it failed as an attack, it certainly succeeded in holding all the Russian armies before Warsaw, and thus facilitated Hindenburg's main plan. On the day it ended, the more important battle of East Prussia began. In three broad columns the great north-eastern German army, under General von Eichhorn and General von Bülow, advanced in the rear of Warsaw. The first column, containing an army corps of first-line troops railed from the French front, operated against Grodno. The second column advanced against the Russian fortress town of Osoviec and the important railway junction of Bielostok. The third column marched on Prasnysch, immediately north of Warsaw.

Russians held before Warsaw

At the beginning of the struggle the main battle raged round the forest town of Augustovo, and extended to the line of the Niemen. One Russian army corps was threat-

A TRAP FOR THE ENEMY: MOTOR-CYCLISTS IN AMBUSH AT A TURN OF THE ROAD.

MOTOR RECONNOITRING PARTY PASSING OVER ROUGH
GROUND.

·ened by an enveloping movement, and hurriedly retired
·on Kovno. It had formed the extreme right wing of the
Russian force, and its hasty retreat exposed the neighbouring Russian army corps at Augustovo to the fate from
which it had itself narrowly escaped. This was the Twentieth
Army Corps under General Bulgaroff.

The northern German column swerved southward and
half encircled Bulgaroff's men in the trackless wilderness
·of wood and water round Augustovo. Then, as the Russians
were fighting their way out, another German column
·crossed the frontier still more to the south, and engaged
them on the other side, completely cutting their line of
·communications. There were six German army corps
against the single Russian army corps. The Russians
were entirely encircled, and compelled to fight incessantly
·on four fronts. In an ordinary way they might have been
annihilated in twenty-four hours, but the ground favoured

**Six army corps
against one**

them. It was a wilderness of lakes,
swamps, and dense brushwood, above
which rose the gaunt boughs of the
great forest trees and the sombre ever-
·lasting foliage of the pines. In this spot a force of
·Cossacks had annihilated a large section of the former
German army of invasion in the autumn of 1914.

Bulgaroff still retained many of the Russian woodsmen
·of the district who·had guided the troops in the former
victory. This gave him a notable advantage in the use
·of the difficult and intricate system of paths across the
·swamp lands. Happily, there were no dominating heights
from which the enemy could bring to bear his overwhelm-
·ing number of field-guns. The Twentieth Army Corps
was clearly doomed, but this fact did not disturb the
Russian commander. To General Bulgaroff had fallen
the same task as that which the Russian commander of
the two army corps at Kutno had carried out in the same
·circumstances of peril. He had to put up so fierce,
stubborn, and long a resistance that when he fell the
victorious enemy would be checked by the arrival of
·stronger Russian forces. He had to fight for time, to
·enable the Russian Commander-in-Chief to alter his main
·dispositions, and bring up a great army to defend the
·Warsaw-Petrograd railway.

This Bulgaroff accomplished. As late as February
·24th battalions of the heroic Twentieth Corps were cutting their way through the German ring and rejoining the
·main Russian forces. Detachments continued to fight
their way out of the forest, after a struggle lasting three
·weeks. Most of the corps fought on until their ammunition

RUSSIAN MOTOR SCOUTS IN TOUCH WITH THE GERMAN
COLUMNS.

was exhausted, and then surrendered. The Germans
exaggerated this small success in a very extravagant way.
They claimed that they had overthrown and routed all
the four Russian army corps defending the East Prussian
front, and that they had rounded up the remnant in the
Forest of Augustovo. But, as a matter of fact, General
Bulgaroff, by his long and splendidly-
handled defence, had saved the situation. **The fall of**
By the time he was captured, the **Prasnysch**
Russian line along the Niemen and Narew
Rivers had been so greatly strengthened that Hindenburg's
last attempt to obtain a decision was verging upon disaster.

The disaster occurred at the village of Prasnysch. Here
the third force of invasion, operating in two streams from
Soldau and Willenberg, swept down towards Warsaw.
By Saturday, February 20th, a brigade of Russian troops
holding Prasnysch were partly forced back. The Germans
did not at first directly attack them, but swept in two strong
lines southward on either side of the village, in an encircling

RUSSIAN CAVALRY IN PURSUIT OF THE AUSTRIANS ACROSS THE SNOW-BOUND UZSOK PASS.

When Austria's invasion of Galicia was turned into a precipitate retreat back into Hungary, by way of the panic-stricken soldiers of the Dual Monarchy were followed by Cossack horsemen, who attacked them the Uzsok Pass, in the Eastern Beskid range of the Carpathians, in the bitter winter of 1914-15, in flank and rear, inflicting heavy losses and taking many prisoners.

movement. A third German force marched still more southward to capture a ridge on which part of the Russian brigade was retiring.

But though Prasnysch was about to fall, the men on the ridge, overlooking an endless waste of snow, held out with as desperate a valour as the heroes of the Twentieth Corps. One German column attacked them on the west, while another column tried to storm them from the east. Their food supplies began to run out, and the ammunition for their small number of field-guns got low. But from their dominating position they held out against terrible odds from February 20th to February 24th. It was on the last date that Prasnysch fell, with half the brigade involved in its fall. But the ridge was still defended by about a thousand Russians, with their dead and wounded lying near them, and all the slopes around strewn with the bodies of their enemies. For one day and one night more the band of heroes had to stand to their work. Just twenty miles away were the two Russian army corps that had escaped defeat, in spite of the resounding falsehoods of the German Staff. These two Russian corps were extended along the River Narew, where they were greatly reinforced by the new army brought up to defend the frontier rivers.

A thousand Russian heroes

Their general was using the remnant of the heroic brigade on the Prasnysch ridge to lure the enemy onward. When the village of Prasnysch fell, he crossed the Narew and advanced up the Orzec, and thence in a swift night march on Thursday, February 25th, he cut off the leading German army corps. The encirclers were encircled. The German commander tried to retrieve the position by swinging the whole of his force on the line of the Orzec. But the Russians were too strong for him. They captured half his first army corps and killed a great part of the other half. Then they turned upon the main German force, and fought it back from the Orzec River to the hills of Prasnysch, in an incessant battle of four days, and on March 1st their full victory was achieved.

Hindenburg had sacrificed in vain his seven Divisions of Death on the Bzura River. For the surprise he had thereby hoped to accomplish against the Warsaw line of communications had completely failed. His strongest column, with the first-line Twenty-first Army Corps from the French frontier, had forced the passage of the Niemen beyond Suwalki, but could do no more than make a bridge-head, from which it was unable to advance against the distant railways. The second column of invaders was entirely held up in front of the fortress of Osoviec, the garrison of which fought with magnificent skill as well as with superb courage.

Hindenburg's ineffective sacrifice

With the defeat of the Germans at Prasnysch, and their containment at Osoviec and the Niemen line, Hindenburg's first main attempt to create a diversion from the Battle of the Carpathians came to an end. Meanwhile, Przemysl was still holding out, and men were falling in hundreds of thousands on the high rampart of snow-covered rocks, defending the illimitable stretches of winter wheat in the Hungarian plain.

AUSTRIAN MACHINE-GUN IN ACTION IN THE SNOW.
The gun, which was of the Maxim type, was fitted with sleigh-runners so that it could be drawn along rapidly by hand.

PRUSSIAN "FRIGHTFULNESS" IN POLAND: HUNS WATCHING THE BURNING OF A VILLAGE THEY HAVE GIVEN OVER TO THE FLAMES.

It was announced in Petrograd in March, 1915, that the Germans had laid waste three-quarters of Russian Poland, ninety-five towns and large villages having been ruined, while 4,500 smaller villages were demolished, a thousand being burnt to ashes. The damage was estimated at over £100,000,000.

LONDON SCOTTISH BEHIND

CHAPTER LVII.

A SAND-BAG BARRICADE.

THE WINTER CAMPAIGN IN THE WESTERN TRENCHES.

The Bog Between the Trenches in France and Flanders—Winter Campaign Immobilised by State of Ground—How the Allied Armies Profited by the Standstill—France Acquires a Heavier Armament—Four Million French Troops under Arms, and another Half a Million Training—Reversion to Old-Fashioned Methods and Weapons of Warfare—The British Admiralty Provides the British Soldier with a " Mother "—Germany Tries to Shift her First-Line Armies from France to Russia—General Joffre's Subtle Counter-move—Gives Orders for a Grand Offensive Movement—How the Germans were Outmanœuvred and Held Up—Tne Strategy of the Allied Trench Attacks—The Battle of the Vosges—Reverse at Soissons—Action at Givenchy, and the Feat of Sergeant O'Leary—The Battle of Champagne—The Battle of Neuve Chapelle.

AFTER their heavy losses in the Battle of Ypres the Germans were obliged to stand on the defensive all through the winter. They were still more powerful in numbers and armament than the Allies. We had, for instance, only about 84,000 British bayonets in the field, just one more division than the little, reorganised Belgian Army mustered on our left flank. By the middle of November the French had to bring up round Ypres and Dixmude somewhat more men than we had put into the field, in order to save our line from being broken and enabling the enemy to capture Calais. Our Indian Army Corps, with 24,000 bayonets, lost ground around La Bassée, and had to be strengthened by our small body of overworked British troops. The position all along the western front at the end of the autumn campaign was still critical. Had the ground been firm and hard between the opposing lines and the air clear, the Germans might have been able to resume their offensive with some hope of success.

What chiefly checked them was the state of the soil between the hostile trenches and the pressure which the Russians were exerting against Silesia and Hungary. The ground in Flanders, after the soaking autumn rains and the mild, moist winter weather, was a bog. Any attack from either side ended in the storming party sinking up to its knees, hope-

lessly entrapped, and being shot down by its enemies. In conjunction with our French reinforcements, we tried to resume a vigorous offensive from Ypres about the middle of November, 1914, but the movement was checked by the Germans without much difficulty.

Sir John French, thereupon, resolved to remain upon the defensive until the spring winds dried the ground. He would not be even tempted into a counter-attack when he lost a trench or two south of Ypres. He made the enemy pay a severe price on every occasion for every few yards they slowly won, and drew back from Zandvoord, and even from Hill 60, and strengthened his lines and awaited more men, more guns, and more ammunition. This he had to do because the Germans were better prepared for trench warfare than were the Allies. The German Staff had been deeply struck by the lesson of Mukden, in the Manchurian campaign, and for years they had been arming their forces against such an occasion as now arose in the western field of war. They had an abundant supply of special weapons for trench fighting, most of which were a revival and improvement upon the instruments used in the old-fashioned war of earthworks in the days of Marlborough. They had numerous modern trench mortars for pitching huge bombs a few hundred yards into neighbouring hostile lines; they had peculiar steel catapults fulfilling the same purpose, and a vast

GENERAL GOURAUD.
The youngest General in the French Army. It was announced in May, 1915, that he had succeeded General d'Amade in command of the French forces in the Dardanelles in consequence of the last-named officer's illness.

store of hand-grenades, which were a deadlier form of the missiles used by our Grenadier Guards in the era before Napoleon.

The French Army was quite unprepared for this extraordinary reversion to the ancient way of war. Their generals had relied entirely upon the method of quick manœuvring in the open field, by means of which Napoleon had revolutionised the art of war and won rapid decisions, while his opponents were considering where they should entrench. Only Wellington, keeping to the old-fashioned system of long lines of earthworks at Torres Vedras, had been able to resist the new method of manœuvring used by Napoleon's brilliant marshals. Great modern French soldiers, such as General Foch, had studied the lesson of

OFFICERS AND MEN OF THE CAMERONIANS' 1st BATTALION IN WINTER ATTIRE BEHIND THEIR SNOW-COVERED DEFENCES.

Mukden from a point of view different from that of the Germans. Foch and his disciples had hoped to revive and extend the battle of open manœuvres, by rapidly handling hundreds of thousands of troops in railway trains. They kept their artillery as light and as mobile as possible, with a view to massing it with great rapidity. And though General Joffre just before the outbreak of war reluctantly came to the conclusion that France would have to spend some thirty million pounds on heavy, slow field artillery, hostilities suddenly opened before the French Chamber, as thrifty as the peasants it mainly represented, could be induced to vote the expense of the additional national armament.

General Foch justified all the ideas he had preached in regard to the extension of Napoleonic tactics. In spite of his fame as a professor of strategy he had only a small command in August, 1914, being the commander of a Lorraine army corps of some 40,000 men, operating round Nancy. First he had rescued from an overwhelming attack the broken French force trapped and routed by the Bavarians in the mountains. Then with his two divisions of infantry, including the famous Division of Iron, he had held the Grand Couronné de Nancy against the attack by the whole Bavarian army, directed in person by the Kaiser. Thereby he did more than any other one man to save France, and General Joffre rewarded him by giving him the command of the strongest French army, the new Ninth Army, holding the French centre in the Battle of the Marne. There General Foch again

General Foch's promotion

won an epoch-making victory. He alone of all the allied army commanders, from the Ourcq to Verdun, absolutely routed the Germans on his section of the front. He completely shattered the Prussian Guard Corps, and when he had finished with the Saxon army it was a disorganised rabble whose leading general was sent home in disgrace. Again at Rheims General Foch threw back the new main German army with which Field-Marshal von Heeringen tried to resume the offensive. Later the Battle of Flanders, from Nieuport to La Bassée, was won by the allied troops, acting under the general control of the brilliant Lorraine commander.

The Foch-French understanding

All through the autumn and winter of 1914 and the spring of 1915 General Foch was practically the high commander in Flanders, who co-ordinated the actions of the Belgians, British, and French forces from the North Sea to below Lille. Technically, of course, the famous French general was not the superior officer of the British Field-Marshal, commanding-in-chief our Expeditionary Force. But Sir John French and General Foch admired and understood each other, as did also General D'Urbal, directing the Belgian army corps. The troops of the three allied nations moved

PART OF A TRENCH OCCUPIED BY CAMERON HIGHLANDERS, THE SNOW REMINDING THEM OF A REAL OLD HIGHLAND WINTER.

as one machine of war along their front; they lent each other guns; they were even brigaded together at times, and always acted in complete and loyal harmony.

Until the Allies were as fully armed for trench warfare as was their common enemy, there was little movement of importance in the western theatre of war. The advantage at first rested with the Germans, who inflicted small but continual losses on the allied troops by means of short-range bomb-throwers and hand-grenades. Their sniping operations, performed by men with special rifles fitted with telescopic sights, were also a considerable annoyance. Some of our Indian troops retaliated by getting close to the German lines at night with the knife,

REMARKABLE CAMERA-PICTURE OF A BRITISH ENTRENCHED
POSITION AT THE FRONT.

LIVERPOOL SCOTTISH TERRITORIALS IN THE TRENCHES.

and doing some quick, silent slaughter. In a general way what little progress was made was affected by sapping. This was a complete return to the slow, old-fashioned method of warfare, such as is vividly described by Laurence Sterne in his scandalously amusing novel of the days of Queen Anne, "Tristram Shandy." All the strange terms of war used by Uncle Toby and Corporal Trim became full of meaning—ravelins, covered ways, approaches, saps, traverses, and the rest of the old glossary.

From the North Sea to Switzerland four million or more men were living like human moles. There were three to four thousand miles of excavated earthworks, curiously constructed to prevent more than a few yards of trench in any part being useful to an enemy who had captured it. The vast battlefield was a strange, empty desert. Not a living thing was visible on it. Even the heavy guns, far in the rear of the firing-line, were placed in large earthen cellars, from which only their muzzles protruded, and these were usually hidden by an artificial hedge or mass of brushwood. Most of the four million soldiers, when on duty in the trenches, rested and slept in subterranean caves. Their only glimpse of the battlefield was caught through the loophole in the parapet of the trench, from which they fired their rifles. As the intensity of sniping operations increased, even a peep through the rifle-hole became perilous in many places, and the ordinary work of observation was conducted usually by means of trench periscopes. The top mirror was often shattered, but it cost less than the human eye or the brain behind and far below it.

Four million human moles

The ingenious Germans sometimes employed gigantic telescopes in searching for targets and watching for signs of activity on the allied lines. One of these mighty instruments of astronomy was set up near Lille, with a sweeping vision over the British front near the Lys. It was also near this place that a battalion of French or British marksmen always came out at night, and swept with their fire a certain place behind the German firing

trench. Our heavy howitzers had smashed up the main communication trench of the Germans, compelling them to do the work of bringing up supplies and changing the trench garrison in the darkness. Now and then a volley from our lines would catch a large body of Germans as they were creeping at night out in the open.

Meanwhile the engineers from both sides drove tunnels through the enemy's front trenches, and then ran a side shaft under them and filled the shaft with dynamite. The result was an explosion, often followed by the capture of the wrecked trench. The enemy would then have to come out in the open, generally at night after a bombardment, and make a costly counter-attack. A subtler way was to mine one's own front trench, especially when it had been badly sited and was difficult to hold. The enemy was allowed to capture it and alter the parapets. A feint was made to attack him in his new position. Consequently, he packed more men into the ground he had proudly won, in preparation for the coming attempt to retake it by storm. Then there would be an explosion, and the allied troops would charge the moment after their engineer fired the mine. In the Argonne section especially a captured trench became regarded as a thing not worth having by either side. It was usually a mined trap.

Trenches as mined traps

BRITISH PIONEERS AT WORK WITH PICK AND SHOVEL "SOMEWHERE IN FRANCE."

The French were particularly good at this mole warfare. They drove their mining tunnels under many important points of support of the German lines at Vermelles, near Arras, at the Perthes furnaces in Champagne, and near the height of Eparges leading towards Metz. All this subterranean activity, however, had no large result. A few well-placed, large, high-explosive howitzer shells did as much damage in a minute as the sappers could do in a month.

Up to the middle of December, 1914, the two opposed and invisible armies practically marked time, doing what little work they safely could to keep each other occupied. All this was to the advantage of the Allies. It afforded them breathing space, during which they brought their heavy armament to an equality with that of the enemy, and then proceeded to surpass him in the general range and power of their howitzer fire. Our War Office was assisted by our Admiralty, from its stock of naval guns.

The arrival of "Mother"

Then came the arrival of that modern pet of the British soldier — his "Mother." This admirable heavy field-howitzer, with its calibre of 9·2 in., has already been described in connection with the wireless aeroplane service that found its target and directed its fire. Even heavier howitzers were brought up, christened by the soldiers "Grandmother."

The 9·2 had a range of more than eight miles; it was handier than the very heavy German howitzers, and much more formidable than their ordinary field-pieces. As a trench-breaker and an interrupter of hostile lines of communication, this gift of the British Navy to the British Army was a memorable thing. Like the naval 4·7 in. gun, used in a former war, it showed how the superb organisation of British sea-power could be made to tell quickly and directly in land warfare.

Small as our Army originally was, it had in artillery, at least, an important source of additional strength in our great naval arsenals. And Admiral Sir Percy Scott, renowned for his skill in mounting naval guns for action on land, was again at hand to help the British soldier in the day of difficulty.

The great French gunmakers were equally alert for the needs of the new situation. Since the Balkan War of 1912 they had proved to the world by the ordeal of battle that their guns were superior to those of Krupp. All the self-advertisement and intrigue of the German firm could not palliate the failure of their guns in the Turkish armies trained by German officers. The French **French gun-plant increased** gunmakers were able to increase their plant owing to the prestige they had won. The result was that, when the war opened, France possessed in the works of Creusot, Schneider, and other armament firms, a system of organised machinery for the production of ordnance which rivalled, if it did not eclipse, the German plant.

Each French battalion soon received an additional machine-gun, with an extra machine-gun party, and preparations were made to increase still further the war machinery of each battalion in this direction. At the same time large and increasing numbers of heavy howitzers were produced, with trained crews to work them, and railed to the front.

By the time the ground was dry enough for attack and counter-attack, General Joffre had two and a half million men at the front, another million and a half in the depots, and about half a million of new recruits training in camp. All the artillery corps had been strengthened by the addition of numerous long-range heavy cannon and heavy howitzers. The new pieces resembled the heavy artillery of the German Army, but the new French artillery was of a later and improved model, with special excellencies such as had distinguished the French 3 in. gun from its German imitation. The entire military forces of France had also been trained in new defensive tactics, without in any way diminishing their fine Gallic spirit of vehement attack.

All things considered, the comparative stagnation of the winter campaign in the western field of war was a boon to the Allies and a ban upon the Teutons. For it gravely diminished the fighting strength of Ger-

A boon to the Allies

many, by giving France and Britain time to build up a war-machine almost as formidable as the German organisation for battle. But as we have already seen in the study of the operations in Russia, the Great Staff of the Teutonic Empires made an attempt to profit by the bogged condition of the western front. They regarded the standstill as the temporary equivalent to a victory over the Franco-British-Belgian forces, and reverted the plan of the elder Moltke. It was their intention to garrison their trenches in France and Flanders with troops of inferior quality, and rail a large part of their first-line armies against Russia. By this means they hoped to win Warsaw, Ivangorod, and all the line of the Vistula by the spring of 1915. They thought that Galicia also might possibly be conquered by their first-line armies, whose power the Russians had never yet fully felt. Then in the spring they designed to entrench along the Niemen, Narew, and Vistula, and hold this front with troops of the second class, while they

swung back their first-line armies for operations on the wind-dried ground of Flanders and France.

Such was the situation on December 15th, 1914. But General Joffre was equal to it. As we have explained, he loudly proclaimed that France and Britain must, at all costs, advance to the help of Russia. In spite of the mud, mist, and snow of winter, a grand offensive movement had to be undertaken against the German lines. In certain places, a hundred thousand French soldiers were massed on a narrow section of the front, with a tremendous artillery power behind them, in order to cut a way through the German trenches at the cost of all their lives. The number of the British Expeditionary Force was doubled, and afterwards trebled for the great event. A general order was issued to the allied troops, and, by a sad accident, copies of it were found by the Germans on men taken prisoners in

Joffre's magnificent bluff

some of the preliminary attacks intended to feel the strength of their front. But the whole thing was a feint. General Joffre never meant to advance. All he wanted to do was to disconcert and alarm his opponent, General von Falkenhayn, by the threat of a grand offensive that might sweep the Germans out of Northern France and Belgium. The affair was a magnificent bluff. Its success was extraordinary.

By the winter of 1914 the Germans had formed sixty-nine army corps. Of these there were fifty-two army corps on the western front. So in the eastern field of battle Hindenburg had only seventeen German army corps, composed mainly of troops of the second and third line. After the wastage of the autumn campaign, these troops did not amount to half a million men. Naturally, Hindenburg wanted more, and especially more first-line

USED UP IN HEAVY MARCHING: DISCARDED RELICS OF MANY A WEARY MARCH.

troops. But little more than 180,000 first-line troops were removed from the Flemish and French front. Most of them were taken from the Yser line, where the inundations protected both sides from a sudden, serious attack. As the Germans did not know whether General Joffre was in earnest, and indeed thought he was so, they did not dare to weaken their forces in front of the French and British troops. Thus, without a battle, the French master of high strategy defeated the intentions of his enemy and imposed his will upon him.

It all sounds very simple when the main outlines of the great winter campaign are represented in this elementary fashion. But the execution of General Joffre's subtle and deceitful plan needed a master's hand to give it full effect.

took just to shake the German front. Sometimes the British troops sprang out of their trenches and waded through the mud and drove the Germans in at St. Eloi, a village between Ypres and Lille; or they made an assault against Neuve Chapelle, or a position near La Bassée. In almost every case they were unable to advance more than a few hundred yards. Often, indeed, they lost the short stretch of trench they captured, and had to draw back to their old position. For by weakening the German line in other places, and hurrying strong reinforcements up to the threatened point by railway train or motor-vehicles, the German commander was always able to stop the gap that had been made. But when he had thus made a concentration in the north, the Chasseurs Alpins, fighting on the heights and in the valleys of the Vosges far to the south, would mass and carry some small but important position in Alsace. Again the Germans had to rail up troops in order to outnumber and master the French attackers. By this time the Germans had strengthened both ends of their lines. So the next assault would be made somewhere near their centre—in the Aisne valley, in Champagne, or east of Verdun.

Testing the German reserves

And the trouble was that the German Staff knew exactly what General Joffre was doing. He was trying to find out

DEVELOPMENT OF THE ARMOURED TRAIN.
The armoured train, vastly improved since the South African War, was used largely by the rival forces on the Continent. Our centre photograph is of a British armoured train firing its big guns while running at a high speed. Top and bottom are shown respectively one of these Dreadnoughts on wheels passing through a wayside station, and two waggons of a French armoured car in action.

Mere talk and the issuing of orders were not sufficient to throw the German commander off his balance. He had to be made to feel the pressure of Franco-British forces, superior in number and armament to those of his command. The ostentatious collection of four million Frenchmen immediately at the front or in depots; busy movements and concentrations of trucks and engines at the manœuvring centres of the French railway system; the buying of large quantities of munitions from America, and their accumulation at places within quick reach of the firing-line—all these delusive devices were employed, with a pretty shrewd guess at their effect upon the Intelligence Department of the Great Staff of Germany.

Shaking the German front

Then began the more expensive pretence of searching for an opening for the grand attack. All the comparatively weak points in the German line from Ypres to Perthes, in Champagne, and from the hills round St. Mihiel, between Verdun and Toul, to the heights of the Vosges near Mulhouse, were continually tested and shaken. It is scarcely worth while relating in detail all the steps which General Joffre

if the Germans had an important reserve of troops, which they were using to stop the little gaps, or whether they had to weaken their line continually, in the sections that seemed safe, in order to strengthen their forces in the sections that were being attacked. Naturally, the Germans always tried to bring up reinforcements with such quickness as to suggest that they were working with a large reserve. But there is such a thing as intelligence men, working in or behind an enemy's lines, calculating the movements of his trains, the amount of supplies and ammunition he received, and deducing from this information the exact number of his troops. As the Germans were working in Belgian and French territory, all the precautions they took against espionage could not interfere with the working of certain channels of knowledge open to the commander of the

INDIAN TROOPS WITH TRANSPORT ON THEIR WAY TO AN ADVANCED POSITION IN FLANDERS.

LORD ROBERTS IN FRANCE, WHERE HE WENT TO GREET THE INDIAN TROOPS, OF WHICH HE WAS COLONEL-IN-CHIEF.

OUR GALLANT GURKHAS MARCHING THROUGH A TOWN ON THE CONTINENT.

GERMAN OFFICERS STUDY-
ING A WAR MAP.

allied armies. Moreover, General Joffre had a fine body of airmen, who kept watch upon the movements of trains and supply columns in the enemy's lines.

He knew exactly how the Germans stood, and the Germans knew that he knew; for he took occasion to prove to them the soundness of his knowledge. And this was the way he did it.

On December 18th our Indian Army Corps began the feint of a grand offensive movement by the Allies. Advancing from Givenchy, the Meerut Division swept upwards towards the out-lying German trenches round the rise of La Bassée.

TEUTON SNIPERS AT WORK IN A SHELL-WRECKED
BUILDING.

Then the Lahore Division went into action on the left. Their gallant leading brigades dashed through the deep slush into the German position, and captured it at the bayonet point.

Heroic Indians and Manchesters The men of the Meerut Division were at first equally successful on their side. But their advanced companies were soon thrown back by a heavy counter-attack by the enemy, and as they retreated at night to their own entrenchments the situation of the Lahore Division became desperate. It was not until morning broke on December 19th that the Lahore troops saw their danger. The German artillery at La Bassée put a shrapnel curtain behind them, and they were fixed in the captured trenches with their flank left in the air, owing to the retirement of the Meerut troops. They could be enfiladed on both flanks, and no reinforcements could reach them across the fire-swept zone in their rear. They could only hold on till nightfall and withdraw in the darkness.

Then the Germans counter-attacked in greater force with

the Prussian Guard and other reinforcements. They captured Givenchy on December 20th, and imperilled the entire British line. The 1st Manchesters by a splendid effort recaptured the village and the old trenches in the evening. But they, in turn, were cut off from all their supports by a curtain of shrapnel fire, falling everywhere, behind and around them, from the German guns. No troops could move out to them. Yet the Manchesters held out bravely, and at last fell back, after being continuously in action for twenty hours. Meanwhile, the British commander was hurrying up reinforcements, and the Indian Army Corps, with the support of the First Army Corps, recaptured the position. Nothing had been gained, apparently, but the effect **German concentration** was seen at once on the Belgian coast. **at La Bassee** The enormous concentration of German forces of the highest quality at La Bassée had exposed another part of the German lines to attack. It remained to be seen if the hostile commander could also reinforce his troops on the Yser as quickly as he had strengthened the garrison of the La Bassée trenches.

On December 22nd, 1914, the Allies only held a very narrow bridge-head at the Belgian town of Nieuport by the mouth of the Yser. In order to extend and strengthen this bridge-head, a fairly strong force of Zouaves and Turcos swept out and fought their way through the dunes by the sea, and captured the inland village of St. Georges. In about twenty-four hours the German commander made the answering move of collecting a similarly strong force, and launching it in violent counter-attacks against the new French trenches. But General Foch threw in more men from his reserves, and by December 30th the French troops had still further advanced to the flank of the main German position—the Grand Dune. Thereupon the Germans fell back and ceased to counter-attack, thus giving clear evidence of the general weakness of their line.

Then, on January 1st, 1915, the French Commander-

PRUSSIAN INFANTRY BEING INSPECTED BY AN OFFICER BEFORE RETURNING
TO THE TRENCHES.
They wore cotton trouser overalls and their rifles were bandaged to prevent the sights from being filled
with sand in the trenches.

LIEUT.-GENERAL EDWIN ALFRED HERVEY ALDERSON, C.B.
Commander of the Canadian Division of the British Expeditionary Force.

KING GEORGE AND KING ALBERT, ACCOMPANIED BY THE PRINCE OF WALES AND THEIR STAFFS, ON THEIR WAY TO THE BELGIAN LINES IN FLANDERS.

in-Chief ordered a movement of advance in Alsace at the extreme southern end of the German front. Here the Chauseurs Alpins, working through the snow, sleet, and frozen slopes of the Vosges Mountains, had a happy success. They placed most of their light guns in concealed positions on their front, so as to command the valley through which they were moving. On the lower ground they came out to attack, dragging a single battery with them. When the Germans, based on Mulhouse, counter-attacked with 6,000 men something like a French rout happened. The French fled, abandoning their guns, and the Germans, elated by their victory, swept down in full force to capture the battery. The result was that two thousand of the enemy were killed, two thousand surrendered, and most of the German guns were taken, the French losses amounting to scarcely more than two hundred men. It was one of the neatest little ambushes in the war. Having broken the defending hostile force, the French advanced in earnest, and captured the approaches to Mulhouse. This was the great sectional test action. For it took the German commander four days to collect a force capable of making a strong counter-attack.

Alpine soldiers' clever ambush

This long delay showed that he had no powerful reserves, but had to detach men by companies all along his line, some coming from such a distance from the scene of conflict that it took them four days to arrive at their new position. General von Falkenhayn, it was clear, had no large reserves or new formation on the western front. He was able to see that General Joffre was well acquainted with the fact, and was playing with him as a cat plays with a mouse.

It was then that Field-Marshal von Hindenburg was refused any more first-line troops. They were all needed badly in France and Flanders, and the Kaiser came to Laon, the headquarters of Field-Marshal von Heeringen, to hold a council of war. For the situation immediately in front of Laon, along the heights of the Aisne, was growing very serious. From the natural fortress, formed by the seamed and broken

plateau, most of the troops urgently needed north and south had been taken. The German commander relied upon his strong artillery power, sited on the most formidable line of heights in the western field of war, to beat back any attack. For both British and French troops had failed to carry the plateau in September, 1914, when they came to it, flushed with the victory from the Ourcq and the Marne. But in midwinter the new French army east of Soissons, which had replaced the British force when our men went to Ypres, had been supplied with the new armament of heavy howitzers, designed to keep down the fire of the German artillery. Along the whole of the front the enemy was losing the special advantage he had possessed in the matter of heavy ordnance.

French attack Soissons heights

For this reason the heights around Soissons had become more open to assault, and on January 8th, 1915, ten thousand French infantrymen crossed the Aisne by a series of pontoon bridges and attacked the hill, four hundred and thirty feet high, against which our Third Army Corps had failed the previous September. Since that date the Germans had strengthened their barbed-wire defences, and had extended their trenches. But the lines were now held so feebly that, after a terrific bombardment, the French carried the firing-line, the support-line, and the reserve-line at ten separate points, and then broke the counter-attack at the point of the bayonet. For forty-eight hours the struggle went on, the French General feeding, munitioning, and reinforcing his troops by a series of pontoons thrown over the Aisne.

On the night of January 9th two more strong German counter-attacks were repulsed, and then at dawn, after throwing the enemy back yet again, the French stormed two further lines of trenches, and captured also a copse on the plateau. A considerable body of Morocco troops, cut off two days before from the attacking French division, had managed to hide between the opposing armies. The new French advance released them, and it was their unexpected attack on the

KING GEORGE ON THE BATTLEFIELD.
During his six days' visit to the troops at the front in December, 1914, the King inspected almost every part of the British lines. He came across many mounds surmounted by wooden crosses, and in each case stopped to read the inscriptions.

enemy's flank that helped to decide the second battle. The next day was marked by an increasing violence in the German counter-attacks. General von Kluck, who was still commanding the remnant of what had once been the strongest of all German armies, was being reinforced. It appeared that a fresh army corps had been entrained to the western front to form the much-needed reserve. The Kaiser, who had a hand in the matter, sent it to reinforce Kluck's lines, and came to view the expected victory.

In the ordinary way the Kaiser would have had to suffer the disappointment which had become customary in these cases ; for French aviators had observed the movement of troops round Laon, and the French general commanding the Soissons army also brought up reinforcements. But on the night of January 11th the forces of nature worked against our gallant allies. A thaw set in, and the flood from the melting snow swelled the River Aisne into a fierce, broad torrent, and all the bridges except one at Venizel were swept away. Not only could the French commander send no reinforcements, but his troops fighting on the plateau, with the odds of more than four to one against them, were unable to retire.

Thaw causes a reverse

In the darkness they got some of their guns over the Venizel bridge, while the Germans were making their grand counter-attack under cover of a very violent fire from all their guns. Two pieces of artillery had to be rendered useless, and left in the hands of the enemy, but even when the French division sent most of its artillery back over the bridge, and could not hope for reinforcements, or even for a safe retreat, it fought on with heroic bravery for two days. On January 13th the French troops made a furious counter-attack against the hill, four hundred and thirty feet high, they had lost, and their comrades from Morocco advanced against the Hill of Crouy. In spite of the steepness of the slopes and the bogs of mud in the hollows, and the massed fire of the enemy's guns, the French captured a trench and a considerable number of prisoners. Then, having checked the enemy, they retired in good order on the night of January 13th, for the Germans had suffered so severely they were unable to press against them.

This affair was one of the most notorious in the history of the war. The German Staff proclaimed that they had won a great victory, which was compared with the Battle of Gravelotte. They claimed that they had killed five thousand French troops, had captured another five thousand two hundred men, with fourteen cannon. It followed that if they had killed five thousand Frenchmen they had wounded another fifteen to twenty thousand. So, all told, they had put out of action about thirty thousand French soldiers, in spite of the fact that there had only been a single wasted division of ten thousand men fighting against them ! In matter of fact, the French lost about half their small force and two pieces of their artillery, and they remained strong enough to counter-attack at the end of the battle, and install themselves in the curve of the Aisne, covering Soissons. They repulsed a counter-attack on St. Paul on January 14th, and in so far as the aim of General von Kluck was to cut the French force in two, or hem it in on the river, it did not succeed.

Extravagant German claims

For the Germans were still too weak to assume the initiative. By a violent effort they had massed forty thousand men near Soissons, and defeated the local attack of a single war-worn French division, cut off from its main army by a sudden flood, but after this small and loudly-advertised success they displayed no further activity on the Aisne. Even on the top of the plateau the French were

KING GEORGE PASSING DOWN THE BRITISH LINES AMIDST THE RESOUNDING CHEERS OF THE TROOPS.
This picture was drawn from a sketch and personal description by an eye-witness of the scene so graphically depicted. We are told that the cheers were not of the formal parade character but came from men "who could not await their strict turn to cheer." The King smiled back his acknowledgment to right and left as he passed along.

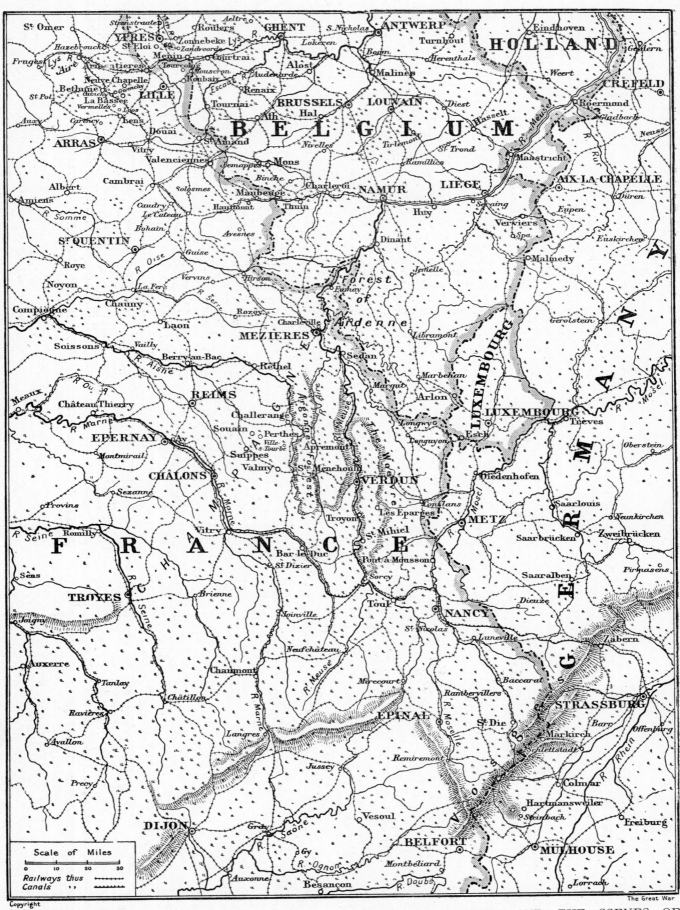

Copyright

The Great War

NORTH-EASTERN FRONTIERS OF FRANCE, SHOWING THE VOSGES AND THE SCENES OF
SOME OF THE FIERCEST FIGHTING IN THE WINTER CAMPAIGN.

German machine-gun section holding a barricade in Poland.

The thunder of the guns: French artillery in action.

German officers watching effect of incendiary shells on Rheims.

Field=Marshal Lord Kitchener arriving at a French railway=station.

The British War Minister with General Joffre and M. Millerand in France.

Armed canal boat on a once peaceful Flemish waterway.

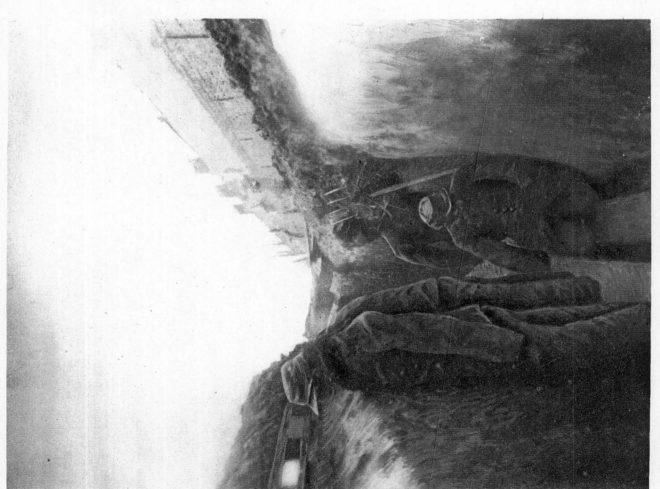

To deceive enemy airmen: Dummies in a French trench.

still entrenched at the sugar factory of Troyon, won by Sir Douglas Haig's men in September; and by the river, going towards Soissons, they held on to a bridge-head at Venizel and Missy, where Sir Horace Smith-Dorrien's troops had fought.

The manner in which the Germans exaggerated their success near Soissons was significant of a weakening of their spirit. In the earlier part of the campaign their official reports of the war had been as trustworthy as could be expected in the circumstances. But both sides had minimised defeats and done all they could to sustain the confidence of their public. After the strengthening of the allied line in France and Flanders towards the beginning of 1915 the French Staff became remarkably frank in regard to all old reverses as well as new sets-back, like that which occurred near Soissons, while the German Staff took to hiding all defeats and exaggerating in an extraordinary manner every small, temporary, local success. Berlin was beflagged in celebration of tremendous victories on the Russian front when no fighting had taken place, or when the supposedly victorious German army was being surrounded and set to struggle for very life.

And later, as the spring campaign opened **Capture of** in the western field of war, astonishing **Hartmannsweiler Hill** impudent claims were made in regard to the capture of important positions such as Hartmannsweiler Hill, in Alsace, from which the Germans had really been expelled. So insistent were the false claims made by the German Staff that the French Government had at last to allow an American war correspondent to visit the summit of Hartmannsweiler Hill in order to prove to neutral nations that it was held by French troops. The same condition of affairs obtained at the British position on Hill 60, near Ypres. With steady and unabashed mendacity the German Staff maintained that its soldiers held this hill, when, as a matter of fact, our men were entrenched upon the rise, and were slaughtering the Germans in thousands on the westward slopes and in the dip of land running towards Zandvoorde.

One cheering result of this war of words was that the French Staff drew up and published a statement of the military resources of both Germany and France at the end of January, 1915. Four million men were then known to be represented in German formations. At the outbreak of hostilities there had been nine millions of German men available for service, but of these half a million were needed for railways, administrative duties, and vital industries. Germany had lost on both fronts one million eight hundred thousand men in the first five months of the campaign, and out of these half a million had

"THERE HAVE BEEN ARTILLERY DUELS AT VARIOUS POINTS."

This sentence is repeated in nearly every official communiqué. Our photographs (from top to bottom) show respectively a French "75" sending its answer to a German challenge, one of Austria's heavy field-pieces at the moment of firing, and a Belgian gun in action. The incessant thunder of the guns led to innumerable cases of what is known as "shell shock."

AN ANGLO-GERMAN RIFLE CONTEST DURING A LULL IN THE BATTLE.

In the latter days of 1914 trench amenities became few and far between. Earlier in the campaign the contiguity of the trenches, some of which were no more than fifteen or twenty yards apart, lent itself to occasional rivalry of almost a friendly, or at least a sporting, character. The incident depicted above arose from the placing by a British soldier of an empty bottle on his trench edge as a challenge to the Teuton marksmen. When the Germans found no trap was intended they entered into the spirit of the thing, and provided marks for our men to fire at. On the occasion illustrated a German stepped boldly out of his trench, with an empty tin, upon which a bull's-eye had been roughly marked, and placing it on a branch in the snow, called upon the Britishers to fire at it.

been able to rejoin the Army after being cured. The definitive loss up to the middle of January was thus about one million three hundred thousand men, not counting the sick or the casualties in the last great battle in Poland. Therefore, Germany's available reserve in January amounted to three million two hundred thousand men. Many of them had been untrained in time of peace, and one quarter were regarded as inefficient by German military authorities, while eight hundred thousand of them were men of more than thirty-nine years of age. The French Staff concluded, somewhat optimistically, in their statement of the case, that the total available reserves of the German Empire were about two million men. These were just sufficient to fill the gaps on both fronts up to November, 1915. It was further estimated that Germany had in January, 1915, eight hundred thousand partly-trained men from this reserve available for a new offensive movement. If Germany could be induced to create new formations with these eight hundred thousand men, and launch them in a new attack to break the allied line instead of using them in an economical way to replace the wastage of two hundred and sixty thousand men a month which was being incurred on both fronts, then the end of the war would be brought nearer.

French estimate of German strength

Hence it became the aim of General Joffre to induce General von Falkenhayn to resume the offensive in France and Flanders. To this end he continued to exert an increasing pressure on the enemy's lines from the North Sea to the Swiss frontier. He threatened to break through in one of three places. Neuve Chapelle, near Lille, Perthes, near Rheims, and Eparges, between Metz and Verdun, formed the three points against which the Allies pressed. In between these foci of attack were several places of minor importance, from which railways and roads serving the German lines were imperilled. And far to the south the menace of a sweeping movement through Mulhouse to the Rhine was maintained for several months. Then there were many places of small importance in themselves, where a scarcely perceptible swaying movement went on all through the winter. The ferry town of Berry-au-Bac, on the Aisne, became world-famous through frequent mention in the official communiqués, and the Four de Paris, in the Argonne, acquired a similar renown. Tracy au Val, below the western slopes of the heights of the Aisne, and Cuinchy, near La Bassée, on the British section, were other little points of renown in the history of the interlocked wrestle between the first-line armies of France and Germany, with Belgium and Britain intervening.

Fresh German offensive

The first serious attempt by the Germans to renew their offensive was made on January 25th, 1915. Apparently the only reason it was made was that the birthday of the Kaiser was approaching, and the Duke of Würtemberg, on the Ypres front, and the Crown Prince of Bavaria, on the Lille front, wished to present their Emperor with a birthday gift of some valuable strategical positions. But the

GRAVES OF MEN OF THE 1st LOYAL NORTH LANCASHIRE REGIMENT: BRITISH PATROL HALT TO DO HONOUR TO THE DEPARTED BRAVE.

operation was not planned in a large way. The French troops holding the trenches near Zonnebeke, eastward of Ypres, were assailed at dawn by a German brigade, the leading companies of which advanced to the attack without any preliminary bombardment of the allied position. The French batteries opened fire when the Germans were hung up in the wire entanglements, and then formed a curtain of lead in front of the main force of attackers. The German reverse was as sudden as it was complete. None of the storming parties reached the French trenches. Three hundred German troops were killed round the wire entanglements, and many more were caught by the allied artillery as they retired at a break-neck run.

More serious was the attempt to penetrate through the allied line in front of Béthune, which town was a principal railway-head for the Allies' positions north
Strategic importance of the Lys River. Béthune was more
of Béthune important than Ypres ; for if it had been taken, the Germans would have been able to threaten the British communications with Boulogne and the French communications with Calais. Prince Rupert of Bavaria, therefore, thought that Béthune would be a handsome birthday present for his Emperor on January 27th. He began by attacking Neuve Chapelle at dawn on January 25th. This was only a feint to induce Sir John French to concentrate in the wrong direction. The grand attack was launched against the French and British trenches on the south of the canal from La Bassée to Aire. At the same time another fierce assault was made on the British position north of the canal at Givenchy.

The German guns round La Bassée massed their fire to clear a path for their infantry, but our artillery answered by shelling the enemy's gun positions ; and the artillery duel ended in our favour. At eight o'clock in the morning the German infantry attacks were made against Givenchy and Cuinchy, by the canal, and against the Béthune road, south of the canal. In both places the Germans succeeded in capturing some of the allied trenches. At Givenchy they swept over our firing-line and captured the village. But as they surged forward down the street our men met them with the bayonet, and in a desperate fight at close quarters, lasting for four hours, the enemy was driven back. Practically every German who penetrated our lines was killed or captured. But the Germans were remarkably resolute. After being bayoneted out of the village they made five attacks
on the north-east corner of our posi-   **Kaiser's ghastly**
tion, and the slaughter went on until   **birthday gift**
the enemy had had enough of it and withdrew. Our casualties in this part of the struggle were fairly light, while the losses of the enemy were heavy.

Meanwhile the German attack on the other side of the canal went on all day. As the Germans came along the main Béthune road they were caught by our machine-guns, till their bodies littered the ground over which they were advancing. But with fine determination the Bavarians held together, and took a part of our trenches in the brickfields near La Bassée. Then, at one o'clock in the afternoon, our troops made a counter-attack, with the help of a section of General Maud'huy's army, and

GRIM HARVEST OF A FRENCH "75"
These Germans were convoying the transport cart against which they are seen postured by the hand of Death when they were located by the gunners of a "75." A single, well-placed shell found them, and in an instant ended for ever their part in the war.

FRENCH SOLDIERS ABOUT TO SEND A BOMB HURTLING INTO
A GERMAN TRENCH THIRTY YARDS AWAY.

FIXING A BOMB AT THE END OF A MODERN CATAPULT.

BOMB-THROWING CATAPULT USED BY THE FRENCH.

ANCIENT ROMAN INVENTION ADAPTED FOR USE IN MODERN WAR.

Three of the photographs on this page illustrate how the catapult—an engine for hurling projectiles, first used as an implement of war by the ancient Romans—was adapted for use in the Great War. The bottom view is of British troops armed with rifle-grenades, the invention of Mr. Marten-Hale. Hand-grenades, first invented in the sixteenth century, were used with deadly effect by the Japanese at Port Arthur in 1904.

THE DESPERATE FIGHTING NORTH OF ARRAS: GERMAN ATTACK REPULSED.

Official French communiqués issued in February, 1915, reported continued fighting north and north- a number of violent counter-attacks such as that represented in the above spirited drawing.
west of Arras. On February 17th, north of Arras, our allies gained two lines of trenches and repulsed Numerous German officers were killed, while a mortar and several hundred bombs were captured. The
fighting was especially severe near the railway line at Blangy and Roclincourt.

BRITISH PRISONERS BEING MARCHED THROUGH DOBERITZ.
Döberitz, where one of the prisoners' camps was situated, is about twenty miles from Berlin.

drove the enemy back a considerable distance in furious hand-to-hand fighting. Our original trenches, however, were so strongly held by the Germans with machine-guns that our troops had to make a fresh line close behind the one they had lost. But the Germans paid dearly for one small and unimportant gain of ground they had achieved. It was reckoned that the total cost of the attempts made by the Duke of Würtemberg and the Crown Prince of Bavaria to win a birthday gift for their Emperor by January 27th represented the best part of the bayonets of a German army corps. The two points of attack, at Zonnebeke and Givenchy-Cuinchy, were twenty-eight miles distant from each other. There was no tactical

connection between the two advancing forces and no co-ordinated effort. The local defences of both Ypres and Bethune were so strong that an attacking force of some two hundred thousand men would have been necessary to defeat the armies of Sir Douglas Haig and Sir Horace Smith-Dorrien. The attacks were just wild, spasmodic, forlorn hopes, the result of which was that the Kaiser had the ghastly birthday present of 25,000 killed or badly-wounded soldiers.

And what little ground they won was soon lost. For on the night of January 27th our men made a nocturnal attack up the Bethune road and won back some of their trenches with little loss. This brought the Germans out

FRENCH AND BRITISH OFFICERS IN GERMAN HANDS.
The officer on the extreme left of the fore rank has been identified as Colonel W. E. Gordon, of the Gordon Highlanders.

NEUVE CHAPELLE IN RUINS.

on alone towards the second barricade, sixty yards behind the first, and captured it single-handed after killing three more German soldiers and taking two others prisoners. The remarkably small losses of our attacking party were due to the skill and audacity of the heroic Irish Guardsman. His feat was the most extraordinary individual affair conducted by any infantry-man in the British Expeditionary Force.

While our men were accomplishing this success at Cuinchy, the French were equally prospering on our right flank, south of the

again, south of the canal, on February 1st. Advancing also before dawn, they took one of our small trenches by the canal, but as soon as the sun rose and our airmen were able to direct our guns, the victors were shelled out of their position. Then our infantry swept out in strong force, and not only drove the Germans from the trench they had captured but seized one of the German posts upon the canal embankment. Our supports then came up, and, rushing through our firing-line, pushed on to the second German post, driving out the garrison at the point of the bayonet. From this position our men were able to take the enemy on the flank.

They fought their way along the German trench southward, throwing hand-grenades in it until they had dislodged the foe from a considerable length of his line, and captured two of his machine-guns. The hero of this dashing

Michael O'Leary's dashing exploit

and important little affair was Sergeant Michael O'Leary, of the Irish Guards. He was one of the leaders of the storming party who captured the German posts. Rushing ahead of his comrades, in the face of a sweeping rain of fire, he shot some of the Germans holding the first barricade and bayoneted the others. Then he went

ANOTHER VIEW OF THE HAVOC WROUGHT BY BRITISH GUNS AT NEUVE CHAPELLE.
Neuve Chapelle, the scene of the memorable British offensive movement in the second week of March, 1915, lies at the junction of the road from La Bassée to Estaires and the road leading via Croix Blanche and Fleurbaix to Armentières. It was strongly held by the Germans, and the British victory was prepared for by the massing of three hundred and fifty guns on a front of barely two thousand yards, the terrible effect of which is graphically shown in the above photographs.

Béthune road. Here the Germans made three attacks. The first two were beaten back by the French artillery, but in the third attack the enemy reached the trenches of our Allies. The French, however, had only been holding their fire, so as to give the Germans no means of escaping. They opened upon them at point-blank range, brought down all the front line, caught the supports as they rose, and then shrapnelled the last line of reserves. Only three Germans got back to their own trenches.

The reason for all this activity round La Bassée, at a time when the boggy ground was unfavourable to any

SHELL-SHATTERED BUILDINGS IN THE VILLAGE OF ST. ELOI.
St. Eloi is situated where two main roads meet—the road from Ypres to Armentières and that from Ypres to Warneton. The Germans occupied St. Eloi on March 14th, 1915, but the next morning the village and the whole of the trenches except one were recaptured by our troops.

HOW THE TABLES WERE TURNED ON THE GERMANS.
Above is another photograph showing the terrible effect of the massed British gun fire at Neuve Chapelle. The Germans, who prepared an overwhelming force of artillery before the war, and were the first to employ the concentrated action of heavy guns in field warfare, cried out bitterly when the tables were turned on them.

A SHATTERED GERMAN HOUSE-FORTRESS.
All that was left of a house outside Neuve Chapelle after the British victory. Many of these houses, in positions of vantage, were occupied by the enemy, who in some cases worked as many as half a dozen machine-guns from the doors and windows. These houses had to be taken one by one after desperate fighting at close quarters.

movement, was learned from the German prisoners. From our position on the canal we had brought to bear an enfilading fire on some of the German trenches. Our machine-gun officers could not see what damage they were doing, but according to the prisoners the German losses had been so grievous that it seemed worth while to risk the lives of thousands of men to capture Cuinchy. Our artillery, sited near this position, was also doing terrible damage. In two days, said one of the prisoners, his company lost thirty men from our shell fire. On February 2nd the Germans in the enfiladed trenches broke and fled without being attacked.

Deadly British shell fire
Many of them left their rifles and equipments behind—a clear indication of the demoralisation produced by our heavy howitzer shells. It was found out that one German company with a total strength of one hundred and sixty men had lost one hundred and thirty men in six days' work of garrisoning the trenches at Cuinchy. The losses had been entirely due to shells and bombs from our howitzers and mortars. Then on February 1st the remaining thirty men were all killed, wounded, or captured. Two neighbouring companies were reduced to twenty men each. The total German losses on this fragment of the front were four hundred and forty out of four hundred and eighty.

Slight as the incident was, it was highly significant of the general conditions under which the Germans were maintaining the great trench campaign throughout the winter; for by far the larger part of the German casualties were the result of the newly-won superiority in artillery power possessed by the Allies. Some of the German trenches round Lille had been deepened to nine feet, with a view to obtaining protection from our 9·2 in. howitzer and the heavy French rifled mortar. The Germans, according to the somewhat sanguine calculations of the French Staff, were losing men amounting to five army corps a month, in the western theatre of war. There was no need to push them back to the shorter line running from the Dutch frontier through Liège, and thence to the Belgian Ardennes to Metz. Far more damage could be done to the enemy by allowing him to retain his existing lines, which he was unable to hold in ample strength, while he was under-

taking an offensive movement against Russia. He was being lured by the hope of obtaining a decision in the eastern theatre of battle in time to resume the offensive in the west in overwhelming strength. Meanwhile his first-line armies were being worn down in their stationary, defensive lines.

Until the Germans stooped to the degrading savagery of employing asphyxiating gases, in extreme contravention of the customs of civilised warfare, there was no need for General Joffre to alter his plan of campaign. The Germans possessed in the coal-fields of Belgium and Northern

The grand prize of the war

France and the iron mines of Lorraine and other regions, the grand prize of the war. This made them equal, if not superior, to the people of the United States in their capacity for coal, iron, and steel production. Indeed, they could look forward to excelling the Americans and becoming the greatest steel producers in the world, if only they could hold the territory they had occupied. This economic advantage of their position tended to induce them

LIEUT. L. G. HAWKER, D.S.O.
Dropped bombs on German airship shed at
Gontrode from a height of only 200 feet.

CAPTAIN F. P. NOSWORTHY, R.E.
Awarded the Military Cross for conspicuous
heroism at Neuve Chapelle.

PRIVATE EDWARD BARBER, V.C.,
Grenadier Guards, awarded the Victoria Cross
for bravery at Neuve Chapelle.

to hold on to every inch of ground they had occupied. Meanwhile their new formations were being used up in Russia, as soon as they were prepared for the field. None could be spared in the winter for any movement of importance in France and Flanders.

All these things entered into the scheme of strategy of the great Frenchman of genius who directed the armies of the western Allies. He did not want to break through the German lines in the winter. As against the sacrifice of men which the Germans were making, General Joffre sacrificed some of the principal economic interests of France and Belgium. The sufferings of the oppressed civil population of Belgians and Frenchmen behind the German lines scarcely entered into the calculation, for it was doubtful if they would not suffer more than they were doing if the tide of battle ebbed over their fields, villages, towns, and cities. The allied armies would

General Joffre's economic sacrifice have been compelled to bring their artillery to bear upon all the positions occupied by the German rearguard. Hence the anguish and misery of non-combatants in Belgium and Northern France were likely to be increased by a sweeping offensive movement of the allied armies.

The almost stationary method of French warfare appeared to be preferable from the French and Belgian point of view, especially as the British Expeditionary Force had only been augmented by a few additional army corps. Sir John French now had two main armies, one under the command of Sir Horace Smith-Dorrien at Ypres, and another under the command of Sir Douglas Haig near La Bassée. But they only held about the same length of front as the original three army corps and the 7th Division. Great Britain was not yet in a position to make a great military effort. A very considerable number of the men and company officers composing our original Expeditionary Force had been put out of action. Our comparative losses, however, were slight when contrasted with

278

LANCE-CORPL. W. D. FULLER, V.C.
Another Grenadier who won the V.C. at
Neuve Chapelle.

SERGEANT MICHAEL O'LEARY, V.C.,
Irish Guardsman, who killed eight Germans and
captured two at Cuinchy.

those of the French and the Russians. They were still very much slighter when contrasted with those of the Germans and Austrians. Heavily as our heroic little regular army had suffered, the vital resources of our Empire were barely touched by the terrible campaign of six months. We had, in fact, escaped lightly from the dreadful crippling effects of the greatest war ever waged on earth, and yet we had given, by means of our sea-power, no small assistance to France and Russia.

If the German Fleet had been able to blockade the French coasts, when France had lost nearly all her coal and iron mines, the result would have been deplorable. Not only would the French have been threatened by a landing of German troops in their rear, but they would have been unable to draw upon the factories of the United States for munitions of war. In the same way a German squadron might have **Influence of British** cut off Russia from **sea-power** the factories of Japan and America, and the German Fleet would have allowed Germany to develop practically all the resources of her own country and the mining regions of Belgium and France, with no competition from the manufacturers of war material in oversea nations, benevolently neutral to the Allies.

All this was prevented by British sea-power. The French Commander-in-Chief was able to look without anxiety at the temporary loss of his chief mining districts, for the French armament firms obtained from abroad all the coal, iron, and other ores they could not produce at home. By great expense of treasure General Joffre effected a great saving in the blood of his people. The underlying principle of his conduct of the war was, in fact, his magnificent economy of French lives. He never forgot that Germany had a population of 68,000,000, increasing at the rate of 800,000 every year, while France had a population of under 40,000,000, which was diminishing instead of augmenting.

STRONGLY - FORTIFIED BRITISH TRENCH AT NEUVE CHAPELLE.

General Joffre was a statesman as well as a soldier, and he fought with an eye on the future of his race. It was the profound and blank spirit of pessimism, produced in all the educated French classes by the results of the previous war with Germany, that had sapped the vital breeding power of France. The glorious renaissance of the entire French nation, foreshadowed by the resurgence of soul ensuing on the victory of the Marne, could be trusted to produce after the war an expansion of life-energy that would gradually heal the terrible gaps in French manhood. In the meantime General Joffre had to take full toll from the German nation for every French life lost. He wanted three dead Germans for every one dead Frenchman. So he continued to increase his artillery and store of shells, and keep the Germans outstretched between the North Sea and Switzerland. His aim was to kill the enemy—kill and wound him at the rate of a quarter of a million a month— instead of trying to drive him back on to a shorter and stronger line. Not until the new German formations began to appear in April, 1915, in the western field of war did the subtle, far-seeing, and sternly logical Commander-in-Chief of the Allied Armies alter his plan.

On the other hand, he had to maintain the threat of a general offensive movement, in order to continue to relieve the pressure on Russia. To this end he secretly accumulated a vast store of shells around Perthes, on the Champagne sector. At the same time he made the feint of a decisive attack against the weakest part of the German lines at St. Mihiel, between Verdun and Toul. At the beginning of the new year the French troops round Perthes were four miles from a railway in the German lines, which fed the German front and helped to link the German army in Champagne with the German army in the Argonne. The loss of this cross-country railway would have been serious for Germany, and if an attack were made in over-whelming force, with cavalry and motor-artillery ready to make a sweeping movement through the gap, the result would have been decisive. Perthes was, in fact, one of the most inviting places for the grand French offensive which General Joffre had been deceitfully threatening since the middle of December, 1914.

So, in the second week of February, 1915, a French army of a quarter of a million men was collected near Perthes, in front of a section of German trenches not more than twelve miles long. The sec- **French pressure** tion extended from the village of Souain **near Perthes** to Ville-sur-Tourbe in the Argonne. The German line in this region was at first only held by two divisions of Rhinelanders. But the French wore them down early in the year by superior heavy gun fire directed by able and daring aviators. In this region French airmen, from January to March, made three observation flights for every one made by the enemy, and the fire of the French artillerymen, directed by their airmen, was also thrice as powerful. The consequence was that the German commander became alarmed at the pressure exerted upon this part of his line, for the French infantry continually made short rushes against the bombarded German trenches, which were being pushed back at the rate of a few yards a day. This part of the front rested mainly on a chalk soil, through which the rain drained rapidly, leaving the surface—a rolling waste with the rises topped by fir plantations—dry enough for military movements. The Germans brought up 80,000 more men. Some of them came from the La Bassée position, others were fresh troops originally intended for an offensive movement in the north.

BRITISH WOUNDED FROM NEUVE CHAPELLE: A PHOTOGRAPH TAKEN AT A FRENCH RAILWAY STATION.

It was the knowledge that the Germans were bringing up reinforcements in order to attempt to resume the offensive that led General Joffre to concentrate in great force at Perthes.

He wished to impose his will upon the enemy commander and to direct the movement of the German troops. This he did by throwing a quarter of a million men against the hostile lines in Champagne. The German troops then

The Battle of Champagne

massed just where he required them so to do. The battle lasted twenty days, from February 16th to March 7th. The French won scarcely a mile of ground in depth, capturing a ridge overlooking the railway line feeding and connecting the German armies. At the rate at which they progressed it would have taken them a lifetime to push the enemy over the frontier. The achievement of the long battle was not, however, the capture of the ridge overlooking the railway, for the French artillery had already been able to bombard this hostile line of communication by indirect fire from the former French line.

The sole object of the French commander, General de Langle de Cary, was to press against the enemy and force him to concentrate round Perthes. This pressure was continued, until at least 220,000 German troops were massed against the 250,000 French troops who were attacking. Then an enormous number of French howitzers and guns, brought up behind the twelve-mile front, opened fire in an extraordinary way. Over a hundred thousand shells were dropped into the packed German lines, and though the Germans in turn brought up sixty-four field batteries, twenty-two batteries of heavy guns, and an additional regiment of field artillery, the vast volume of French shell fire could not be kept down. The French artilleryman commanded the field—a thing he had not done in such overwhelming power since the days when Napoleon taught men that shell fire was a solution of the problem of trench warfare.

In the small area of ground which the French won they picked up and buried ten thousand dead Germans. There must have been several thousand more corpses in the new German lines running through the village of Tahure. The French aviators, directing the French batteries, maintained the practical command of the air all through the long action, and kept gun and howitzer fixed on the large targets presented in the movement of 220,000 hostile troops. Altogether it was reckoned by the French Staff that from 55,000 to 60,000 German soldiers were put out of action. So terrible were the German losses that the Great German Staff made the frank confession that they had lost more men against the French on the narrow front at Perthes than in the campaign of their fourteen army corps in East Prussia against the Russians. The Germans did not lose a single gun, but at least one-quarter of the finest battalions of their first-line armies in France were killed or seriously wounded. The French losses, on the other hand, were not more than ten thousand. Such was the war of attrition, as General Joffre conducted it when he was fully supplied with the armament needed in

the modern trench warfare. But the terrible wastage of the German garrison of the lines in the Perthes section was only one consequence of General Joffre's scheme of operations. He was anxious to know from what parts of the rest of the front General von Falkenhayn had drawn troops to assist in holding back the menace of a great French advance. In the last week in February it was discovered that at least six batteries of field artillery, six battalions of the Prussian Guard, and two heavy batteries of the Guard had come from Neuve Chapelle and the region north of La Bassée. It therefore followed that Sir Douglas Haig's army round Neuve Chapelle was being weakly held, and that the German demonstrations between La Bassée and Ypres were only meant to mask the enfeeblement of the enemy's forces there. So out of the French victory at Perthes there grew the even more important later British victory at Neuve Chapelle

At this time the condition of our men in the trenches was remarkably good. They had had a hard time of it through the winter in the region south of the Lys, for the Germans held the higher ground about Lille, and entrenched on ridges, hills, and slopes with a good drainage. Our troops, on the other hand, occupied the flat, water-logged plain, almost the only dry spot being at Givenchy, where there was some rising ground, over against the German stronghold of La Bassée. Our lines came through clay soil, holding the water that ran from the high German positions. It was in this shell-pitted, undrainable bog, in a land of mist, rain, and bitter winter winds, that Lord Roberts caught a chill in the second week in November, 1914, which resulted in an attack of pneumonia. He had been visiting the Indian

Elliott & Fry.
LIEUT.-GENERAL SIR JAMES WILLCOCKS, K.C.B., K.C.S.I., K.C.M.G., D.S.O.
Commanding the Indian Army Corps.

Corps round Givenchy, and the brave old master-gunner died within sound of the guns at the town of St. Omer on November 14th. The circumstances of the death of the hero of Kandahar were such as he would have chosen. For it was given to him, in his old age, to pass away on the battlefield. But our soldiers could not help regretting that his wise old kindly face would be seen no more.

It was then that King George conceived the happy idea of paying a visit of honour to our Expeditionary Force. No pinchbeck War Lord was he, trying to keep up in an era of intense military specialisation the pretence of being the chief captain of his people on the battlefield. He left to the men who had given their whole lives to apprenticeship in the art of high command the full honour of their positions.

King George at the Front

He was a trained sailor who could take a light cruiser into action, but claimed no more knowledge of practical warfare than that. He came to his Army on December 1st, 1914, as the civic leader of all his peoples. By his presence on the field of battle he desired to show his incomparable soldiers what their country thought of their heroic achievements from Mons to Le Cateau, from the Marne to the Aisne, and—greatest feat of all—the defence of Ypres. In days of peace he had paid visits of honour abroad to Emperors, Kings, and Presidents.

CONSTRUCTING A BRUSHWOOD GUN-SHELTER.
How our artillerymen disguised their guns from the prying eyes of enemy airmen.

Now he travelled to the Continent to make a visit of honour to the British private soldier and the Indian private soldier. This memorable act of State began on Tuesday, December 1st, with a tour to the Indian troops and the Fourth Army Corps. Two boy gunners, neither twenty years of age, had the Victoria Cross pinned on their tunics by their King. Then the troops lining the roads close to the enemy's trenches gave a fierce, long-sustained shout that must have startled the Germans and set them wondering. The King went walking down the lines, his eyes sparkling with interest, his face radiant with happy pride in the fighting men of his Empire. He inspected their trench kit of goatskins and strawbags and decorated their luckiest heroes.

So far-stretched was the British front that the next morning, Wednesday, King George had to motor seventy miles to visit his Third Army Corps.

Greetings of loyal affection All branches of the service greeted him with loyal affection, and, keen on practical details, he inspected their rest-homes, their baths, and the places in which they made charcoal for use in warming braziers in the trenches.

On Thursday the gallant First and Second Army Corps were visited by his Majesty. They were the veterans of the battlefield, having come into action at Mons on August 22nd, and fought for a month without a single day's rest till they entrenched on the Aisne. From the headquarters of the Second Corps King George went on to the battlefield. On his right were the factory chimneys of Lille; on his left was the ruined Cloth Hall of Ypres, with German howitzer shells bursting in the town as he watched, and sending up their columns of black smoke. A British battery, close at hand, opened fire in turn on the enemy's trenches. The King now stood in the centre of the conflict. All through his visit the sound of the enemy's guns and the thunder of the British batteries had rung in his ears. Hostile aeroplanes, with bombs, had risen on the northern skyline, but their pilots had not approached. Far over the head of our Imperial King circled for days a guard of airmen. The British Army knew how to defend its monarch against every form of attack. It had the lordship of the air as well as an invincible front.

To find the last really historic companion picture to the

TYPICAL BRITISH SAND-BAG BARRICADE.
Constructed by men of the H.A.C. at the front.

King's visit we should have to go back five hundred years, and then turn to the plain of Agincourt, close to the upper course of the same River Lys by which our khaki-clad troops were now entrenched. There Henry of Monmouth, in the autumn of 1415, had reviewed a few thousand English men-at-arms and archers, after their victory over forces four times as numerous.

Our troops were greatly cheered by the visit of honour from their King. And they needed cheering in their soaking trenches and dug-outs, as winter wore on. In December and January, especially, they suffered very badly from a malady of the legs which was called frost-bite. It was really occasioned by a stoppage of **Malady of the** the circulation of the blood in the feet; **trenches** the wet, tight puttees of the troops, the chill dampness of the trenches, and long hours of stationary trench work were among the causes of it. A system of rousing exercises behind the firing-line and a regular and frequent relief from garrison work helped to restore the health of the men and to keep them in good spirits. The

GERMAN PATROL ADVANCING
CAUTIOUSLY IN THE FOREST
OF THE ARGONNE.

GERMAN SCOUTING PARTY IN THE ARGONNE.
While one officer is seen carefully scanning a map, and another searching the landscape through his field-glasses, the horses are kept ready at hand for immediate flight.

upon. But what would they now achieve, in their stale condition, against an enemy famous for his military skill and protected by all the defences that modern technical science could construct ? Such was the question to which the British victory of Neuve Chapelle was to be a decisive answer.

Sir John French, no mean judge of the character of fighting men, had discerned in advance the sterling qualities of his new troops. He was, in fact, relying upon his knowledge, which he shared only with his officers, to produce a surprise effect. It was notorious that the German estimate of the new British troops was very low. The Germans were loud in praise of our young regular troops, saying that each private soldier who fought from Mons to Ypres was equal to a first-class non-commissioned officer. But they reckoned, when our casualties began to exceed the number of troops we had first sent out, that the character of our Army would be found to be weakened. In short, they thought that Britain had struck her hardest blow by land, and that the German conscript soldier would henceforward meet only **A surprise for the enemy** very inferior fighting material before him in the British lines. Neuve Chapelle was again to show the German that he was wrong.

The British commander had a surprise for the enemy, not only in the quality of his new troops, but in the tactics of battle. Like the French commander at Perthes, who had prepared the way for our advance, we were secretly arranging in the first week of March, 1915, for a sudden, disconcerting development of the Napoleonic use of artillery power. Battle tactics were developing with surprising rapidity on the western front, and the Germans, who

Indian troops were the surprise of the winter campaign. It might have been expected that they would have found the cold, misty, wet climate and water-logged ground more trying to their health than was the case with British troops. But things fell out contrariwise ; for there was less sickness in the ranks of the Indian soldiers throughout the long wearing winter than among their comrades from the British Isles.

In addition to the problem of the health of the much-tried troops, the position of affairs in our Expeditionary Force at the opening of the spring campaign in 1915 was not without anxiety. The character of Sir John French's Army had considerably changed. Many of the veteran regular troops were dead, crippled, or recovering from their wounds, and their place was supplied by drafts of reservists, Territorials, and units of the new national forces. Nearly all these men had to endure the rigour of an almost immobile winter campaign, living in earthworks such as the cave-men of the early Stone Age would have scorned as shelters. Had they all come fresh into the fight, their vigour of body and native stubbornness of character could have been depended

GERMAN ARMY CORPS MARCHING INTO GALICIA TO
RELIEVE THE HARD-PRESSED AUSTRIANS.

thought themselves safe in their deep trenches, were holding
to an antiquated idea.

The French, with their alert, inventive minds, and
the British, somewhat slower of intellect, but with a
fine constructive power of imagination, had discussed
things together and made trial experiments against
the German trenches, with the result that they had
arrived, in a month or two, at some startlingly novel
doctrines in regard to the method of attack. Perthes had
been just a preliminary essay; Neuve Chapelle was
designed to reveal fully the new development in modern
warfare.

Sir John French planned the accumulation of a huge
store of shells in front of Neuve Chapelle, and ordered
some three hundred and fifty guns and howitzers to
be hauled to sites commanding only two or three
miles of the German trenches. While this was being
done our Royal Flying Corps held the air all around
our lines, where the secret concentration
Our secret   was being made. The enemy's trenches
concentration were photographed from the sky and
the photographs were measured and
studied by the artillery officers of our First Army. Then
the ordnance was laid in advance, and a few trial shots
fired under aerial observation, to make quite sure that
the target was covered.

At the same time the German system of espionage
working at our base, along our lines of communication,
and even at our front, had to be checked. Trains and
supply columns were marked for destinations at which
they did not arrive, and gigantic masses of shells were
received in unusual ways by the First Army, and
stored handy to the batteries, yet in very inconspicuous
places.

For a week the secret work of preparation went
on, our airmen chasing away every enemy machine which
attempted to reconnoitre over our lines. In other parts
of the front our artillery had to fire more than usual, to
palliate the slight weakening of our front caused by the
concentration of ordnance against Neuve Chapelle. All
this delicate, difficult, intricate preliminary labour was
brought to a promising end without the enemy getting
any warning of the coming event from his airmen or
Intelligence Department.

RUSSIAN PRISONERS OF WAR COMPELLED TO HELP IN
THE TRANSPORT OF SHELLS.

WITH THE GERMAN ARMY IN POLAND.
German soldiers returning in the evening from the trenches carrying
machine-guns on their backs.

283

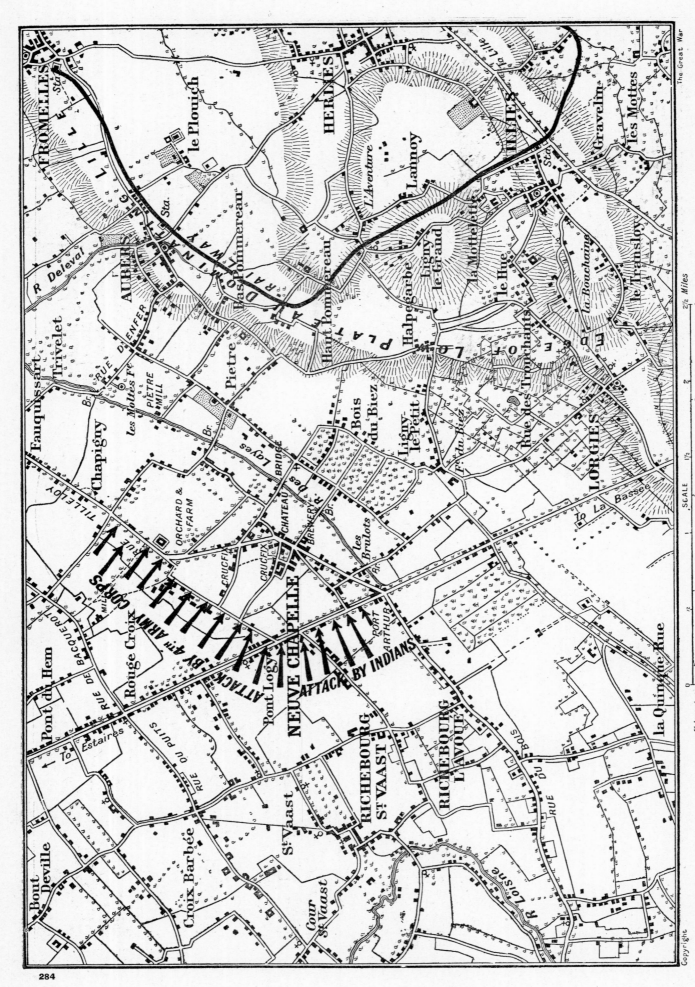

MAP OF NEUVE CHAPELLE AND AUBERS, SHOWING THE LINES OF ATTACK BY THE FOURTH ARMY CORPS AND THE INDIAN ARMY CORPS.

"DUMMY" FRENCH BATTERY | CHAPTER LVIII. | TO DECEIVE ENEMY AIRMEN.

THE STORMING OF NEUVE CHAPELLE AND THE BATTLE FOR THE RIDGE.

Sir John French Prepares a Surprise for the Enemy—How Guns and Shells were Secretly Accumulated in Front of Neuve Chapelle—The New Shock Tactics in Trench Warfare—Our Airmen Attack the Enemy's Rear and Bombard His Railways—Our Artillery Gives the Germans Another Terrible Lesson in Modern Warfare—The Fourth Army and the Indian Corps Storm the Enemy's Lines—The 23rd Brigade Held Up by Barbed Wire—The Lincolns, Berkshires, and Garhwalis Capture the Village—Hitch Caused by the Destruction of Our Field Telephone—The 25th Brigade Works Through Neuve Chapelle and Releases the Middlesex and Scottish Rifles—The Checks at " Port Arthur " and Pietre Mill—Unfortunate Delay in Bringing Up the British Reserves—Neuve Chapelle Won in a Single Hour—All Further Progress Prevented by German Reinforcements—Magnificent Charge by London Territorials and Leicesters—Enthusiasm of the Indian Troops after Witnessing the Power of Our Guns—Mist Interferes with Our Further Artillery Attack Upon the German Position—Enemy Counter-attacks in Great Force, but is Beaten—The Fourth Army Corps Swings Up Against Aubers Ridge—Our Cavalry Prepares to Charge the German Guns and Open a Path to Lille—We are Defeated Just When a Grand Victory Seemed Almost to Have Been Won.

T HE action of the British army in March, 1915, at Neuve Chapelle was designed to have a more magnificent scope than the action General de Langle de Cary's forces had the month previous at Perthes. The British troops were to crown, by a sudden, violent effort, the long, gradual labours of their French comrades. The French soldiers had attracted and were still holding firmly a considerable part of the German garrison of the trenches between La Bassée and Lille. The enemy's lines in front of our First Army were seriously weakened, and the only force capable of reinforcing the menaced trench garrison was a body of Saxons and Bavarians, resting at Tourcoing after a turn in the trenches near Ypres. It was hoped that the immortal 7th Division and the 8th Division, forming the Fourth Army Corps, and the Indian Army Corps, composed of the Meerut Division and Lahore Division, would break through the German front and recapture Lille, while our First Army Corps advanced against La Bassée.

One of the reasons why this was not done was the difficult nature of the ground. Beyond our trenches, set in low-lying, flat, marshy country, was the village of Neuve Chapelle, also on the plain. But east of Neuve Chapelle, and near the hamlets of Aubers, Illies, and Fromelles there was a large, low, horse-shoe ridge, formed by the edge of an upland running towards Lille, Roubaix, and Tourcoing, three of the most important industrial cities of France, lying just below the easternmost slopes. On the upland were the principal batteries defending the captured centres of French industry, and defended themselves by the last earthworks of German infantry at Neuve Chapelle. Our advance in October, 1914, had been arrested at Illies on the ridge, when we were trying to turn the German position at La Bassée. In short, our troops now had to move across boggy ground, through barrier after barrier of wire entanglements, over streams, past hedges, fortified houses, ditches, orchards, and woods, with hostile artillery sending a plunging fire from the horse-shoe ridge ahead.

Then, instead of employing a quarter of a million men on a narrow front, as the French commander could do with his national Army of four and a half million troops, Sir John French could only muster 48,000 bayonets for the most important offensive movement in the western field of war since the Battle of the Marne. He had no more troops to spare in order to make a more comprehensive effort.

[Lafayette.
GENERAL SIR BRUCE M. HAMILTON, K.C.B.
Commanding the Sixth Army.

BRITISH MARKSMEN BEHIND A SAND-BAG BARRICADE.
Often the shallow nature of the ground in Flanders did not allow of effective trench-digging, and our men fought from behind fortifications constructed with sand-bags and carts.

wastage of six months' struggle with fifty to fifty-two enemy army corps, our new army in March, 1915, was not remarkable in number and efficiency. It consisted of six army corps, numbering 144,000 bayonets, and arranged in two armies under Sir Douglas Haig and Sir Horace Smith-Dorrien. The men in the field were excellent—excellent in strength of character and in fighting skill—but there was still not enough of them.

In these circumstances, Sir John French improved upon the example of the commander of the great French army round Perthes, and **Shells in the place of lives** massed still more artillery than usual in support of his storming parties. Against a front of German trenches just over two miles in length we had four hundred guns and howitzers. We were using shells in the place of men's lives, and using them in such enormous quantities as to produce quite as overwhelming an effect as the charge of dense formations of infantry in German fashion. It was really new tactics, this gigantic employment of artillery power. For the British commander

At home, new battalions of otherwise well-drilled soldiers of the new volunteer armies were still waiting for rifles and cartridges in order to begin their musketry training. The artillerymen necessary to support them in battle were either waiting for guns or for shells in order to acquire battle efficiency by actual practice. Neither in camp nor in munition factories had the work yet been carried out necessary to equip a large, national British Army. Moreover, the recruiting was not proceeding at such a rate as would justify the expectation of our putting an army of the modern Continental size into the field.

In spite of the official optimism of some of our politicians, we still seemed likely **Our Army in March, 1915** to remain, as in the days of Napoleon, a great sea-power with a comparatively small military force. Our Army was growing larger, it is true, but it was only growing enormous in comparison with our very small regular force. Compared with Germany's original military resources of seven and a half million men, and even with France's wonderful production of an Army of four and a half million men, after the

AFTER NEUVE CHAPELLE.
Three wounded Germans photographed with a British lieutenant and an interested group of British soldiers after taking part in the fateful Battle of Neuve Chapelle.

intended to use in half an hour almost as many shells as the French General at Perthes had employed in a week.

In addition, Sir John French and his Chief of Staff, Sir William Robertson, with the General of the First Army, Sir Douglas Haig, were planning to use the striking force of some of the British Flying Corps in a novel manner, as already explained in Chapter LIV., when dealing with the development of aerial power in the war. Bomb-throwing aviators in speedy machines were designated to impede the enemy's communications while his front was being attacked In particular, the railway bridge at Menin, over which reinforcements from the Duke of Würtemberg's army might be sent to the help of Prince Rupert of Bavaria's forces, was marked for bombardment. Also

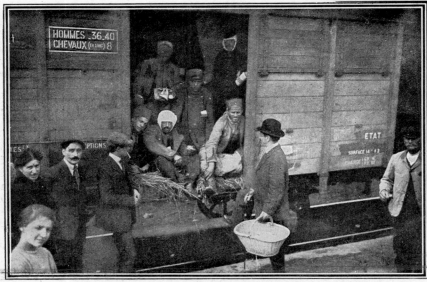

COMRADES IN SUFFERING RETURNING TO THE BASE.
This photograph, taken at a French wayside station, shows the rough-and-ready conveyance of the wounded in horse-waggons to the hospital base.

FRENCH RED CROSS DOGS FOR THE FRONT.
Returning from a review in the Tuileries Gardens, Paris.

BELGIAN DOGS OF WAR.
These animals were used to draw the lighter machine-guns. Our
photograph shows them being fed by Belgian artillerymen.

the Courtrai railway junction, by which German troops could come southward from neighbouring Belgian depots, was selected for attack. In the course of the battle one of our airmen, Captain G. I. Carmichael, flying at a height of only one hundred and twenty feet above Menin bridge, dropped a 100 lb. bomb, which destroyed a pier, and another aviator wrecked Courtrai railway-station. Later, the railway junction at Don was bombarded, and part of a train destroyed there, by Captain G. F. Pretyman, and Douai junction was also badly damaged. Our artillery also took part in this bombardment of the enemy's lines of communication. On March 10th the railway-station at Quesnoy, east of Armentières, was shelled just as German troops were entraining to reinforce the fighting-line. Many casualties were caused by this long-range fire, directed by a British aerial observer.

British airmen's effective work

The idea was to cut the attacked German force at and around Neuve Chapelle from any considerable channel of reinforcements. In a more immediate manner, our massed artillery was partly directed at a critical moment in the action to the same end. Altogether, the planning of the battle was distinguished by a masterly boldness and originality. All the practical lessons of the Great War were digested into a sound, brilliant, classic example of modern offensive tactics.

Only by a surprise attack could a position of such strength as the Germans occupied be carried. And the opening surprise was complete. At a quarter past seven on Wednesday morning, March 10th, 1915, our artillery was lazily shelling the enemy's lines. It seemed just the customary way of disturbing the slumbers of the Bavarians ; but, in matter of fact, our artillerymen were making sure of their ranges. Then, at half-past seven, began the most terribly concentrated bombardment yet known. Pieces of every kind took part in it. The field-guns, unable to pitch their shells into the German trenches, fired low over them to smash paths through the wire entanglements for our charging infantry. The howitzers sent a plunging fire of 15 in., 9·2 in., and 6 in. high-explosive shells into the excavated earthworks in front of the doomed village. In the distance could be seen great masses of flame, smoke,

earth, and brickwork, all ascending together as the great shells burst among the hostile entrenchments and houses. The noise deafened and appalled. The shrieking of the shells in the air, their explosions, the thunder of the guns merged into a single volume of terrific sound. The discharges of the pieces were so rapid that they resembled the fire of a gigantic machine-gun. During the thirty-five minutes of the incessant bombardment our troops could show themselves freely and walk about in safety. But the fumes of the deadly lyddite were blown back towards the neighbouring British trenches, and in one place the upper half of a German officer's body was cast by the explosion into our lines.

Path of advance opened

At five minutes past eight the gunners lengthened their fuses and pitched their shells clean into Neuve Chapelle village. This left open the path of advance to the bombarded hostile trenches, and signal whistles sounded along the British front. Out ran our men, their officers leading. The Indian troops advanced in a flanking movement, the 25th Brigade were lucky. For the German wire entanglements in front of them had been reduced to four-inch lengths, and blown over with their supporting posts into the German trenches. This result had been achieved by very accurate fire from our field artillery, shooting just over our own trench lines, with the guns anchored on specially-prepared platforms. It was the first time in the war that the direct fire of field-cannon had been scientifically used in this novel manner. It saved the lives of thousands of our soldiers, and practically revolutionised the conditions of modern trench warfare. Combined with a plunging, heavy howitzer fire on the entrenchments, it enabled the attack in favourable circumstances to be carried out at less cost than the defence.

It was the second grand lesson in modern tactics that our "contemptible little army" had taught the Germans. First our infantry had defeated the rushing charges in dense formation, according **A lesson in modern** to the Prussian system, and had **tactics** annihilated the enemy at fifty yards by the mad minute of rapid fire. This had led to the Germans adopting the same defensive method, which they extended into the great campaign of trench warfare. But now the British artilleryman, with an inventiveness equal to that of our musketry instructors, had devised another new system for breaking down wire entanglements and blowing up trenches, which cleared the field for a surprise attack by our rapid-firing riflemen.

The success of the action depended mainly upon the extreme accuracy of direct fire by our light field-guns, for where the gunners had not shot away the German wire entanglements our troops were held up by these obstacles. Such was the case with our 23rd Brigade that rushed forward on the left of the 25th Brigade, but was held up by an unbroken tangle of barbed-wire in front of the first German trench. Most of the Germans left alive in the deep trenches were maddened with fright,

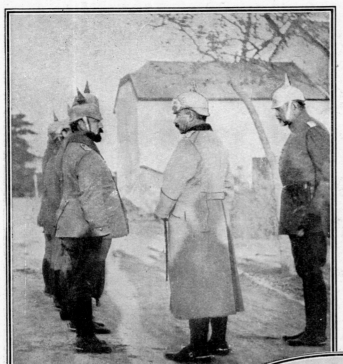

THE KAISER INSPECTING A GROUP OF GERMAN ARMY DOCTORS.

from Richebourg St. Vaast and the Rue de Bois, against the south side of Neuve Chapelle; the British troops swept up in rushes against the main western German position in front of the village; for the weakness of the German lines at Neuve Chapelle was that they formed a salient, jutting into the British front. The salient was attacked on two sides, just as the enemy had continually assailed our salient at Ypres.

The design was to envelop, by attacks directed both west and south of the village, the enemy force that would be driven by the dreadful artillery fire from the entrenchments into the houses. As a matter of fact, when the British and Indian troops met in Neuve Chapelle they captured or killed the Germans in the village, taking in all some two thousand prisoners. This result was largely due to the effective plan of attack arranged by Sir Douglas Haig. Against the German trenches on the north-west of the village there advanced the 23rd Brigade and the 25th Brigade, forming part of Sir Henry Rawlinson's corps. Then against the German entrenchments south of Neuve Chapelle went forward the Garhwal Brigade of Sir James Willcocks's Indian Army Corps. Both the Garhwal Brigade and

KAISER WILHELM IN EAST PRUSSIA.

PRUSSIA'S WAR-LORD DECORATING OFFICERS OF THE GERMAN FLYING CORPS WITH THE IRON CROSS.

THE KING OF BAVARIA IN THE TRENCHES.
King Leopold of Bavaria visited the German trenches in Flanders and made stirring speeches of encouragement to the troops.

GERMAN CROWN PRINCE AND HIS UNCLE.
The Kaiser's eldest son in conversation with Prince Henry of Prussia during the latter's visit to the Crown Prince's Headquarters at the front.

half-dazed by the explosions, and eager to surrender. But where the wire was still unbroken, two undaunted German officers with a machine-gun stood firm and cool, and poured a galling fire into our baulked men. The leading companies of the "Diehards" (Middlesex) and the Scottish Rifles suffered heavily. The utmost the 23rd Brigade could do was to lie down and scrape up cover under a murderous fire, and thus hold the enemy.

Meanwhile the two more fortunate brigades, better served by their artillery, swept along unimpeded, taking more prisoners than they wanted at the moment, and capturing trenches. The Lincolns and Berkshires seem to have led the British Brigade, while the Second 39th Garhwalis were the foremost troops of the Indian Brigade. With hand-grenade work and bayonets they cleared the first hostile line of all Germans who showed fight, assembled the prisoners, and then held the captured positions in preparation for the next step of the advance.

Behind the Lincolns and Berkshires were **Field telephones cut by fire** waiting the Royal Irish Rifles and the Rifle Brigade. It had been arranged that, on capturing the trenches, the leading troops should swerve to right and left, so as to let the Irishmen and the Rifle Brigade through to capture the village. In the same way the Second 39th Garhwalis had to stay in the trenches they took, and let the First 39th Garhwalis rush out and capture the dense woodland of the Bois du Biez, behind Neuve Chapelle. But at this point there was a hitch in the execution of the brilliant plan of Sir Douglas Haig. The trenches had been captured in a swift rush, much quicker than had been expected by our artillery officers. Our guns were still forming an impassable curtain of fire in front of Neuve Chapelle, to prevent any German supports in the village reinforcing the firing-line. But the firing-line had been captured, and our own gun fire prevented our men from making a surprise attack on the village. Such things always happen in war. As a matter of fact, all our field telephones had been cut by the enemy's

fire, and there was no communication between our advanced infantry and the enormous number of guns and howitzers, some of which were placed miles in our rear.

No soldier ever grumbles over a mishap of this sort, for the effect of an enemy's fire in a hotly-contested action usually disarranges some of the delicate machinery of a modern army. This is one of the reasons why soldiers are conservatively distrustful of all newly-invented instruments of warfare. The new weapons may work excellently on the peaceful, undisturbed testing ground; but shell and shrapnel charges, streams of bullets from

FRENCH "75" ON A REVOLVING
PLATFORM.

machine-guns, and chance rifle shots upset all things on a battle-field. A battery suddenly chang-ing position in a moment of extreme urgency, when only the effect of the guns can be thought of, sometimes crushes and breaks all the ground wire on a large section of the fighting-front. Thus the accident to our field telephones was nothing unusual.

In spite, moreover, of this interruption, the village of Neuve Chapelle and the roads leading north and south-west from its eastern end were captured in the morning; for at ten o'clock the Rifle Brigade raced head-long into Neuve Chapelle, where they were met by the little muscular hill-men of Nepaul, the 3rd Gurkhas. The two regiments had known each other and worked together when brigaded in India, and when they met in the captured village,

ON OUTPOST DUTY—"SOMEWHERE ON THE
CONTINENT."

smeared with the dust and blood of victory in an advance conducted from dif-ferent directions, Briton and Indian hailed each other in triumphant friendship.

**A wild and
terrible scene**

Wild and terrible was the scene around them. In the autumn of 1914 Neuve Chapelle had been a quiet, pleasant, pic-turesque French village, with a white, old-fashioned manor house, a mill-stream and a mill, farmhouses set in apple orchards, and a little churchyard, with a great crucifix rising by the side of the church.

But when our guns had done with it, Neuve Chapelle was more desolate than the scene of an earthquake. Only the shell of the church remained. In the churchyard, skeletons had been blown out of their coffins by the great shells, and the bones of the dead forefathers of the hamlet were scattered on the

grey-clad corpses of the bar-barians of Germany. All the houses were unroofed, with their rooms blown out, and great gaps made in the walls. But two things strangely remained erect amid the ruins—the great crucifix in the churchyard and another large cross by the old white manor house. Pitted with bullet-marks, these emblems of the faith of Christendom remained above the wreck and rubble of the hamlet.

But there was little time for our troops to remain spectators of the scene. They could scarcely hear each other speak, for our massed artillery was still maintaining a curtain of shrapnel fire beyond Neuve Chapelle to keep off the German reinforcements. **Annihilating shrapnel fire** The Germans on the slopes of the distant ridge tried to work down through the wood, with the intention of forcing our men back in a hand-to-hand combat. But they could not get through the curtain of death flung out from our guns. As our prisoners afterwards reported, all attempts made by the enemy to strengthen his fighting-line were checked by the annihilating fire of our guns.

Practically, therefore, all the German troops in the village were for the time in a state of siege. Through the thick pall of shell-smoke on all sides some of them emerged from cellars and dug-outs, holding their hands above their heads, all their fighting spirit knocked out of them by our terrifying guns. Others, still gallantly lusting for battle, dodged round the shattered buildings, fired from the blown-in windows, from behind carts, and even from a barricade of tombstones. Then there were unroofed houses from which the brave survivors of machine-gun

MASKED BRITISH GUN THAT WORKED HAVOC IN ENEMY'S RANKS NEAR YPRES.

parties tried to sweep away our leading sections. But the 25th Brigade soon worked round to the left of Neuve Chapelle, and, turning the flank of the Germans entrenched behind the unbroken wire entanglements, released the heroic Middlesex Regiment and the Scottish Rifles. This completed the capture of the whole of the village of Neuve Chapelle, which was accomplished by eleven o'clock in the morning.

After this, however, there was considerable delay in the general British advance. The check to the left of the 23rd Brigade had kept back other forces of our 8th Division, and had compelled part of the 25th Brigade to turn and fight northward, out of its proper line of advance. All the leading infantry was much disorganised by the violent effort of fighting through the enemy's trenches, and then shooting and bayoneting a way through the buildings of the village. Also, the interruption of telephone communications between our outflung front and our distant rear still hindered our guns from accurately co-operating with our attacking infantry. Houses held by German machine-gun parties might have been quickly shattered if our guns could have been brought to bear upon them at once. As it was, our infantry often lost heavily in trying to capture such difficult positions simply by rifle-shot and bayonet. In particular, there were three fortified German posts which were difficult for unaided infantry to attack. One lay at the extreme right of the line, where a German trench defended by barbed-wire remained uninjured, with its garrison, by a group of ruined houses. This was called by our soldiers "Port Arthur." By the other end of the line was a still stronger German position at Pietre Mill. In between Pietre Mill and "Port Arthur" was a bridge over the stream Des Layes. This bridge was also fortified and held by Germans with machine-

"Port Arthur" and Pietre Mill

guns. Besides these hostile strongholds, there were more German machine-guns posted in the houses along the Pietre road. So, altogether, there was much work to be done around the captured village before our two army corps could hope to advance towards the ridge leading to Lille.

The reorganisation of the leading brigades of the Fourth Corps and the re-establishment of telephonic communications between our advanced front at Neuve Chapelle and our rear took some hours. It was half-past three in the afternoon of that glorious Wednesday before Sir Henry Rawlinson's troops were able to renew their attack. And the gallant Indian warriors, under Sir James Willcocks, were in similar difficulties, and were not prepared to advance farther until about the same time.

Fourth Corps reorganisation

During the interval there was carried on the vitally necessary work of forming our new line in the rear of Neuve Chapelle, making deep trenches, with parapets and shrapnel cover against the enemy's batteries on the ridge, with communicating trenches and support earthworks. Meanwhile, Sir Douglas Haig was employing all the leading

BRITISH ARMY SERVICE CONVOY ON THE ROAD. INSET: VIEW OF THE ROAD FROM NOORDSCHOOTE TO PYPEGALE.

forces of the rest of the First British Army in keeping the enemy engaged on his front. His famous First Army Corps, that had fought from Mons to the Marne and stormed the northern heights of the Aisne in September, 1914, and then held Ypres in October against all the forces that the German Emperor could concentrate against it, was now holding the positions at Givenchy and Cuinchy **Held up by barbed** and the brickfields round La Bassée. Sim-**wire** ultaneously with the attack on Neuve Chapelle the First Army Corps advanced from Givenchy on the German lines in front of La Bassée. But here our field-guns, in their preliminary bombardment, had not succeeded in destroying the German wire entanglements. The fact was that only one or two of our brigades of light artillery had at once mastered all the exceeding difficulties of their strange new task. After the battle, the most successful of the light field artillerymen at Neuve Chapelle were sent as instructors in the novel art of wire-entanglement destroying along our front. But at the first essay there were many failures, and round Givenchy

was thrown out of gear, and when at last the village was won, with various German strongholds still resisting fiercely, a new plan of action had to be thought out quickly. This, again, is usually what happens in battle. Deep-laid preparations, such as the Germans often stake everything on, are merely the work of industrious talent for war. They assume a passive enemy who fights in routine fashion. The commander of genius has a faculty for improvising rapidly new means of attack or defence to suit the continually changing situations of actual warfare.

It was in between Neuve Chapelle and Aubers that the most impregnable German machine-gun positions were situated. There was an orchard north of Neuve Chapelle from which the Germans threatened the flank of any advance on the Aubers ridge. Then further eastwards was the Pietre Mill stronghold, strengthened by a defended work and roadside houses with hostile machine-guns, that held up our 22nd Brigade. Farther to the south an entrenched German garrison at the cross-roads, six hundred yards north-west of Pietre, stayed the forward movement of the 24th Brigade. All these checks in the neighbourhood of the ridge impeded any forward movement of the 7th Division.

But about eleven o'clock in the morning, when the interval of reorganisation occurred in Neuve Chapelle, some of the troops of Sir Henry Rawlinson's renowned Division were ordered to advance towards Aubers. This was partly done to stretch out to the full the enemy's available forces, and help to weaken the resistance behind the captured village. By this time the German artillery, though greatly outnumbered by our massed guns, began to act vigorously and shell our front.

Two battalions rushed forward in long waves and disappeared in the battle smoke. Then the rest of the brigades charged. All through the day the men were magnificent. Anywhere their officers led them they went. The air was alive with shells and bullets, making a buzzing noise as in a tropical forest in midsummer. There was an open stretch swept by a terrible gun fire. The troops crossed it in rushes and gained the shelter of some houses. The advanced battalions had captured a trench beyond, and the Germans tried a counter-attack, but were repulsed. The remnant of a leading regiment passed by, sixty men going to the rear. An officer asked them where they were going. " We've stormed every —— trench and every —— village in this —— country," said one of the men. " All our officers are shot, and we thought it about time someone else had a go."

By half-past five in the afternoon part of the Division had, by heroic fighting, worked its way almost opposite to Aubers. There it was ordered to storm some of the outlying houses. Crawling out **The attack on** of their trenches, our troops advanced **Aubers** across the open under a heavy fire from the enemy's artillery. But our guns had still some ammunition to spare, and though they could not silence the opposing batteries, they did great damage to the German entrenchments. However, our advanced infantry could not make much progress, and as darkness fell they dug themselves in on the ground they won. All night they were incessantly bombarded. Then at dawn on March 11th they tried again to carry Aubers, but the enemy's shell fire from the ridge was overwhelming. The attack failed. But, in matter of fact, it was only a strong demonstration; for the situation at Neuve Chapelle, on which a success at

MAP OF THE FIERCELY-CONTESTED AREA IN THE VICINITY OF NEUVE CHAPELLE.
With smaller scale plan of the country between Ypres and La Bassée.

especially the hostile tangles of barbed-wire were insufficiently cut to enable the infantrymen to make progress. All they could do was to pin the German troops in their entrenchments and prevent them from reinforcing the Neuve Chapelle front. In short, our First Army Corps only demonstrated.

Equally unsuccessful, through no fault of theirs, was the 7th Division of the Fourth Corps, operating to the left of Neuve Chapelle, against the Aubers ridge. The Immortal Division, the heroes of Ypres, had bad luck. As Sir Douglas Haig appears to have planned the action, the 7th Division was to wait until the leading brigades of the 8th Division had captured the German trenches and take Neuve Chapelle; then, as the German position at Aubers was shaken by a flanking movement, they were to advance and storm through Aubers and win the ridge running towards Fournes and Lille.

But when the 23rd Brigade was held up by unbroken wire, north-west of Neuve Chapelle, the provisional scheme fell through. The movement of the 8th Division

Speaight.

General Sir Henry Macleod Leslie Rundle, Commanding the Fifth Army.

Remarkable instantaneous photograph of a small isolated Russian force surrendering to Austrians

A scene behind Austrian earthworks during a battle in the Carpathians.

Troop of Uhlans leaving cover in Champagne district to charge the French.

Field=Marshal French makes a wayside inspection of infantry on their way to the trenches.

The capture of Steinbach by the French in the first week of January, 1915.

Aubers depended, had not much improved since the previous day.

It is important neither to underestimate nor to exaggerate our achievement at Neuve Chapelle. Our plan of attack there was brilliantly conceived, and executed generally with remarkable skill and noble gallantry. The slight check in regard to the breaking of telephone communications and the failure to destroy part of the hostile wire entanglements were ordinary inci-**Ground won in a** dents of battle. Such things, and even **single hour** more of them than occurred, were allowed for in advance, for our actual success was so rapidly achieved that its quickness was a surprise to our Staff. We won more ground at Neuve Chapelle by artillery fire and infantry charges in a single hour than a quarter of a million of our French comrades at Perthes had gained in a week. And we only deployed 48,000 men to obtain this result.

But great as our success was, it might have been far greater. In the considered opinion of Sir John French, the fault that prevented the grand extension of our offensive movement rested with Sir Henry Rawlinson, commanding the Fourth Army Corps. He did not use his reserves at the critical moment. He was rather too cautious and prudent, content with sure, small gains rather than foresightful adventurous ones. He should have thrown his reserves forward into the fight on the morning of March 10th. At eleven o'clock on that morning when the village had been won, the disorder in our fighting-line, caused apparently by tactical errors, might at once have been restored if strong reserves had at once taken on the work of pushing the enemy back. For the Germans were then still reeling from the tremendous surprise attack, and their line might have been completely pierced with comparatively little loss if the entire weight of the Fourth Army Corps had been brought to bear quickly at the critical point.

A delay of four and a half hours in restarting the attack prevented us from making progress ere night fell, and interrupted the work; for by the next morning the enemy had recovered from his dismay and surprise, and by making new entrenchments and bringing up strong reinforcements he was able to check our advance. Our victory of Neuve Chapelle was won in three hours on the morning of March 10th, and won with comparatively little loss. It was afterwards that we had 1,751 men and officers taken prisoners, and 10,000 officers and men killed or wounded. Of our total losses of 12,811 men less perhaps than 2,000 were in the actual victory. "The difficulties might have been overcome at an earlier period of the day," says Sir John French in his despatch, "if the general officer commanding the Fourth Corps had been able to bring his reserve brigades more speedily into action."

By noon on Wednesday the German position by the orchard and farm in the north-east of the village was carried by the troops of the Fourth Corps. There our 21st Brigade had at first been able to form up in the open, without a shot being fired at it, owing to the enemy's resistance being paralysed by our terrific gun fire. But when the Worcesters afterwards came to the farmhouse, the Germans had recovered from their dismay. Still, they

could not put up such a fight as they afterwards did at Pietre Mill. The Worcesters chased them round the orchard trees with the bayonet and captured the farmhouse, and found one remarkably fat German trying to squeeze his body up the chimney. On the other side of Neuve Chapelle, however, where the Indian Brigades were operating, "Port Arthur" still held out strongly. The First 39th Garhwalis made an heroic effort to storm it. At the sound of a whistle the men leaped from their trenches and charged across the ground. But they were raked by machine-gun fire; before they reached the barbed-wire entanglements all the officers of the leading companies were killed, with many of the men. Staggering under the terrible fire, the battalion swerved to the right, and after a wild, sharp, hand-to-hand fight they captured part of the trench. But there they were fixed by German troops occupying the other trenches. The battalion had twenty officers and three hundred and fifty men killed and wounded before the fight ended. Cut off from the rest of the army, the gallant little hillmen held on, till the 2nd

MAKING THE BEST OF IT.
An impression of the lot of the British despatch-rider in rain-soaked Flanders.

Leicesters came to them with a rush, and one of their bombing parties crept down the communication trench and pelted the Germans with hand-grenades, forcing them out into the open. About half-past five in the afternoon "Port Arthur" was stormed at the point of the bayonet. We were then in possession of all the enemy's trenches on a front of four hundred yards, having driven in to a depth of three-quarters of a mile from our own lines.

Among the regiments who greatly distinguished themselves in the second part of the attack was the Territorial Battalion of the Royal Fusiliers. The Londoners made a magnificent charge **Territorials'** on the last German stronghold. Yelling, **magnificent charge** they tore across the shelled field, dropping men as they went along, while some of our regular soldiers cheered them as they passed. No German machine-gun could stop them, and in a swift and violent attack with cold steel they stormed the enemy's position and rounded off the conquest of the village.

Meanwhile the delay in bringing up our reserves enabled the Germans to bring up reinforcements, and to organise a stubborn resistance along the Pietre road, and on the edge of Biez Wood by the stream of Des Layes. It is known that at the German headquarters at Lille preparations for a general retirement had commenced, so overwhelming had been the first unexpected onset of the British forces. But every German soldier that could possibly be collected was sent over the ridge to stop the gap. More machine-guns were brought down to the new German firing-line, and the Bavarian and Saxon troops resting at Tourcoing were hurried up towards Aubers and Biez Wood. On the evening of the day of victory the Gurkhas made a gallant attempt to drive through the new German lines. They stormed up the rising ground and penetrated into the wood. But the Germans had a machine-gun stronghold northward, at the bridge over the stream, and from

DESOLATE FLEMISH BATTLE AREA.
Embankment built by the German invaders in Flanders.

this position they got a blast of enfilading fire on the Indian troops, which compelled our men to retire. Sir Douglas Haig then brought up three battalions of the First Army Corps, while his guns were shelling the fortified bridge over the River Des Layes. But by this time the enemy was also reinforced in great strength, and all that the Indian Corps and the Fourth Army Corps could do was to entrench on the ground they had won, and labour with the utmost energy to make good shelters against the enemy's artillery fire.

When day broke on Thursday, March 11th, the fortunes of war were against us, as the weather was very foggy. We were relying on our artillery to break **German artillerymen's** down the houses and other defended **advantage** positions which the Germans were holding all along our front. But our airmen could not see clearly enough to direct the fire of our guns, and our engineers had not been able to get the quantity of material necessary to restore all our telephonic communications.

The German artillerymen on the ridge had the advantage of knowing exactly the range of all the lost entrenchments of their infantry, and having brought up new supplies of munitions in the night they opened a furious shrapnel

fire. As a matter of fact, there were few veritable trenches along the ground we had won, for the soil was so marshy that water was struck at a depth of two feet. So instead of excavating earthworks on both sides in this region, we built up barricades of sand-bags, with ordinary wire entanglements in front of them. As a general rule, the enemy's defences were superior to ours, with loopholes of bullet-proof steel and concrete work, and immense quantities of timber, making altogether comfortable and secure shelters. But round Neuve **Our sand-bag** Chapelle the German works were inferior **barricades** to ours in construction, drainage, and sanitation, and though our men set to work to alter and improve some of them, and reversed the position of the sand-bags, barricades, and wire posts, many of our defences were new constructions thrown up in the night close to the new German lines. These lines were of an extraordinary strength. For instance, on one section of the German front, two hundred and fifty yards in length, there were fifteen machine-guns. Their concentrated fire made any attack by our infantry impossible of success. Only our guns could break a path, and, unfortunately, the weather was adverse to our system of aerial fire-control.

EN ROUTE TO THE TRENCHES.
Across wooden pathways made over the marshy land in Flanders.

On the other hand, our rifle fire was remarkably good. If, as was reported, the Germans had eight machine-guns to a battalion, yet our more capacious magazine rifles helped to restore the balance of fire. After their bombardment on Thursday morning the German troops came down in close order to recapture Neuve Chapelle. Our men held their fire till the enemy was forty paces away, and then knocked the deep, dense German lines to pieces. Not only was the attack beaten back, and hundreds of prisoners taken, but both the Indian and British troops advanced in bayonet charges against their beaten foes. The Highland Light Infantry, however, had a hard struggle to maintain

PEACE AND WAR.
A ploughman tilling the soil in Northern France. Meanwhile the officer in charge of a French armoured motor-car, map in hand, is keeping a keen look-out for the enemy.

"THE WATCHED POT."
Preparing a meal in a British out-door kitchen on the Continent.

their ground. Overwhelmed by masses of Germans, they were driven out of the trenches they had taken, but they swept out again, and in a fierce struggle with bayonets and grenades they recaptured the position. Again they were driven out, yet again they returned in one more magnificent charge and captured the trenches a third time, and held them. The London Brigade, already seen at the top of their fighting on Wednesday, fought with the same tenacity and skill, and proved themselves soldiers of the first order. And grand work was done southward by our regular troops, the Irishmen especially shining by the progress they made.

Grand work by Irishmen As for the troops of the Indian Corps, fighting round Biez Wood, they were wildly happy. Our overpowering bombardment of the enemy's trenches the day before had been a revelation to them. Hitherto they had bravely and stubbornly fought the campaign, thinking that the odds in artillery power were heavy against them. They did not know what havoc our howitzers were working in the enemy's lines, but they had abundant evidence of the deadly work of the high-explosive shell and shrapnel charges blown from the German batteries on the high ground in front of them. So they had come to the conclusion that the German-log were the masters of all the world in artillery, while Indians and Britons excelled in personal courage. They themselves never faltered while they had an officer to lead them; but until Neuve Chapelle they could not help feeling despondent over our apparent inferiority in guns.

What they saw at half-past seven on Tuesday morning took them with amazement. Their trenches were close to the German lines, and they could see these lines suddenly transformed into a wall of leaping fire and thunder-blast as thousands of our high-explosive shells struck home. Then, for the first time in France, the Indian troops drank the full delight of battle in the manner of their fighting forefathers. For months they had patiently endured the enemy's gun fire, accepting it with a sort of fatalism as a thing that their generals would never be able to master. But suddenly their grim and steady desperation was changed into vehement and soaring hopefulness. They had always been ready to die, but now it seemed to them that death on the battlefield when all the odds were equal was a happy thing. It was the wounded Indian troops who smiled most in their pain, for what had depressed them was the fear that the German-log, though inferior in manly fighting, would win by their modern machines of

war. Some of the officers of British regiments had had the same dread. While recognising the personal courage of the German machine-gun officers, who in many cases were quite equal to any Briton in cool and fearless daring, they did not think that the average German soldier was as good a fighting man as the average British soldier. Nevertheless, they thought that Germany might win by reason of the remarkable ability of German Staff work, the remarkable number of the enemy's pieces of heavy artillery and machine-guns.

All through the British Army there was a feeling of personal ascendancy, dashed by a half-admiring dread of the superiority of the German machinery of war. Our new Chief of Staff, Sir William Robertson, was well aware of this doubtful feeling. He had risen from the ranks, and he knew the mind of both the British and the Indian private. He had a chief part **Sir William** in planning our tremendous opening artil- **Robertson's success** lery attack, and he designed it with the double purpose of renewing the spirit of confidence in all our troops and of destroying the enemy's entrenchments at little cost of life to us.

But if the British soldier was cheered by our unexpected display of artillery power, the Indians were excited to enthusiasm. In some places on Thursday and Friday they could not be kept in their trenches. They clambered

299

up on to the parapets in order to use their rifles more freely and get a clear view of the enemy. In some of the captured trenches there was not standing room on the raised step, or banquette, for all the men to shoot at the same time. The troops below could not restrain their impatience. They wanted turn and turn about, and some of them pulled down the men in front and sprang up in their places.

Throughout Thursday, March 11th, the fighting continued almost as fiercely as on the previous day. Our store of shells had, of course, been much reduced, and as our war factories at home were, for want

ELABORATE GERMAN CAVALRY SHELTERS.
These shelters, photographed in the western war area, were thatched with straw and carpeted with hay to protect the horses from cold and wet.

GERMAN OFFICERS' UNDERGROUND DWELLINGS.
To increase the comfort of these quarters doors and windows were torn from houses in devastated districts. Even mats were not forgotten, and telephonic facilities were provided.

of foresight and organisation, inadequate to supply the needs of our fighting men, the Germans, with their superior organisation for the production of munitions, began to recover the advantage. The mist also helped the hostile batteries to escape being again mastered by our guns, and the artillery on both sides kept up a rain of shrapnel on the opposing infantry. Our gunners were principally interested in Biez Wood, in which the German troops gathered for their counter-attacks. When these attacks were beaten off, our guns opened on the wood. They searched it from end to end with rafales—or squalls of fire—to use the technical term by which the brilliant French artillerymen described the deadly method in which they handled their quick-firers. Not a patch of

ground in and behind the wood was untouched by our gun fire, and the enemy's losses must have been very heavy.

The general situation on Thursday night was the same as on Wednesday night. We could make little further progress, and the Germans, on their part, could not drive us back.

But the Crown Prince of Bavaria, commanding the Westphalian Army Corps, the Münster Army Corps, and Bavarian troops in this little section of the front, was determined not to lose Neuve Chapelle without a still fiercer struggle than any that had yet occurred We have seen that it took the German Commander-in-Chief four days to reinforce in overwhelming strength his lines near Mulhouse. It then took him nearly two days to strengthen his line at Perthes. On the present occasion it also took him two days to bring up three army corps against our Fourth and Indian Corps. The Westphalian troops had been shattered by the storming of their lines and the defeat of their counter-attack, and the destruction by our aviators of railway points on the German line added to the difficulties of Rupert of Bavaria. But by Friday morning, March 12th, he had collected **Prince Rupert's counter-attack** sufficient men to attempt the reconquest of Neuve Chapelle.

On the following day a thick mist covered the plain and the ridge, and checked the fire of our artillery. Our airmen had to drop two or three hundred yards above the enemy's position in order to reconnoitre for our guns. The enemy's shells continued to break the telephone wires between our leading brigades, and the artillery officers with them directed the fire of the guns from advanced observation posts. At half-past nine in the morning, for instance, over a hundred feet of our wire was destroyed, and there was a long delay in getting it mended. At forty minutes past ten the Germans made their grand attempt to get back Neuve Chapelle. They came down in masses along the whole front round the village and to the north of it. The troops that tried to debouch from Biez Wood were blown away by our guns, some of our batteries having loaded and laid on this mark, waiting only for a signal from the observation officer to curtain the wood off with shrapnel. Elsewhere the Germans were broken by four bursts of rapid fire from our breastworks, and thrown back with heavy loss. The ease with which the Germans were repulsed was so remarkable that they only reached our trenches at one point north-east of the village. There they were driven out and pursued with the bayonet. As the afternoon wore on the Westphalians especially began to surrender in companies. Many of the men were exhausted. They said they had had no food for days, that all their officers were killed, and whole battalions destroyed.

This condition of things induced Sir Douglas Haig to counter-attack in turn. At half-past two in the afternoon there was another overwhelming outburst by our artillery. Every British gun was brought to bear on Aubers ridge, north of Neuve Chapelle. This was the battle in which we lost most heavily. From Neuve Chapelle our men could be seen through field-glasses advancing just where the shrapnel appeared to be thickest. The 2nd Scots Guards, the 1st Grenadier Guards, the Borderers, the 2nd Gordons, and their 6th Territorial Battalion were among the troops that tried to storm the ridge. For four hours the struggle went on. Near to Neuve Chapelle there was a fierce contest round Pietre Mill, where the 6th Gordons, under Lieutenant-Colonel Maclean, fought their way up to the houses, using grenades and bayonets. The Colonel fell with a bullet in his body by a trench, and a subaltern brought some morphia to ease his agony. "Thank you," said the dying Scottish leader. "And now, my boy, your place is not here. Go about your duty!"

Rifle Brigade's heroic effort The Rifle Brigade made heroic attempts to reach the ridge. They rushed through the zone of shrapnel, and then faced the German machine-guns and rifles, and with terrific losses took a trench. There they stayed with their dead and wounded around them, the latter being unable to raise their heads owing to the devastating fire that swept the ground. More troops tried to advance towards Aubers, and reached the line by the Rifle Brigade, but could not get any farther. Aubers, wrecked by shells from our guns, was taken, but none of our men could reach the ridge just above.

At one time it looked as though Sir Henry Rawlinson, with the Fourth Army Corps and its supports, would achieve one of the grand successes of the war. Our 2nd Cavalry Division, under General Gough, came from Estaires, along with the North Midland Division. At four o'clock on Friday afternoon the 5th Cavalry Brigade, under Sir Philip Chetwode, rode out for immediate action along the Rue Bacquerot, fronting the Aubers ridge. The cavalrymen were to charge through the gap made by the infantry, take the enemy's batteries on the high ground, and open the road for a general advance to Lille. But our infantry attack against the heights failed just when it seemed to be almost success- **Offensive operations** ful. Our troops could not win the ridge, **suspended** and as Sir John French had no reserve army corps to use up in battering a way through the German lines, he directed Sir Douglas Haig on Friday night to suspend offensive operations and hold and consolidate the ground won by the Fourth and Indian Corps. "Most of the objects for which the operations had been undertaken had been obtained, and there were reasons why I considered it inadvisable to continue the attack at that time." Thus the British Commander-in-Chief afterwards wrote in his despatches on the battle.

Our losses in the three days' fighting were very severe, especially among company officers killed or wounded while leading their men onward. A considerable number of our "missing" troops consisted of advanced companies isolated in the trenches they had captured round Aubers and then overwhelmed by the enemy's counter-attacks. The casualties on both sides were about equal.

ON THE YPRES-POELCAPELLE ROAD AFTER THE FIGHTING ON APRIL 25TH-27TH, 1915.
Inset: A striking photograph illustrating the amazing proximity of the conflicting armies. In the foreground is a French communication trench across a village road, with barrels on the parapets for protection against the fire of the enemy. It would have been fatal to cross the road except by means of the trench.

We captured Neuve Chapelle with slight losses, and punished the enemy terribly when he counter-attacked in vain endeavours to recover the village. But he in turn inflicted terrible losses on our troops when we tried to extend our victory by winning the Aubers ridge. But, seeing our gallant attempt on the ridge involved mighty issues for France—the recapture of Lille and the mining district, and the breaking of the German front, leading perhaps to a general retreat—our men did not die in vain. If there was a defect in the plan of attack on the Aubers ridge it was one that could not be avoided. We had too few men.

The nation and the victory The operation was carried out by the left wing of the Fourth Army Corps, numbering possibly little more than ten thousand bayonets. Our Army in the field had not increased sufficiently in number by the middle of March, 1915—after seven and a half months of volunteering, drilling, rifle-making, gun-making, and ammunition manufacture—to enable our commander to strike with any force. Where Hindenburg could launch seven Divisions of Death on a narrow opposing front that he wished to break, our General could not afford to sacrifice twelve thousand men.

Even as it was, our nation seemed to be staggered by the cost of the victory of Neuve Chapelle. A predecessor of General Joffre, in the high command of the French Army—General Bonnal—had refused to look to our country for help against Germany, because of this tendency of our people to want a victory without paying the price for it. He thought a fighting alliance with Great Britain in a great Continental war would lead to a moral disaster to France, as our outcry against the unavoidable heavy losses of each important battle would undermine the temper of the French public. Happily we were made of sterner stuff than General Bonnal supposed, and, though some of our organs of public opinion complained of the casualties in the Neuve Chapelle-Aubers Battle, the people generally took the matter in the way our soldiers did. The partial achievement was of so striking a character that it was well worth the full cost. The fact that the German front had been driven in, despite a formidable system of fortifications developed for five months by the enemy, was a surprise to friend and foe. The thing that seemed to be a practical impossibility was proved to be an achieved fact.

Then, as our victory at Neuve Chapelle was connected with the previous French victory at Perthes, so from our success General Maud'huy's army round Arras built up another triumph for the allied cause. For part of the German reinforcements that held the ridge were drawn from the position of Notre Dame de Lorette, between La Bassée and Lens, and fronting General Maud'huy's troops. As soon as this was known, the French soldiers in turn bombarded and attacked the hill of Notre Dame de Lorette, and gained a footing thereon, leading to the great victory of Carency in May, 1915. All things considered, Neuve Chapelle is one of the high glories of the British and Indian Army. Sir John French's estimate of the achievement is set out in a Special Order of the Day addressed to Sir Douglas Haig and the First Army: "I am anxious to express to you personally my warmest appreciation of the skilful manner in which you have carried out your orders, and my fervent and most heartfelt appreciation of the magnificent gallantry and devoted, tenacious courage displayed by all ranks whom you have ably led to success and victory."

The effect of Neuve Chapelle on the enemy was extraordinary. He was overwhelmed by the blow struck by our artillery—the arm in which he confidently reckoned his superiority was beyond contest. So desperate indeed was the state of mind of the German General Staff that soon after the battle orders were given for a series of experiments on animals with cylinders of asphyxiating gases. Meanwhile the defences of the ridge at Lille were strengthened by concrete **Germany resorts** works and armour-plate covers. Only a **to poison** quarter of a million of the new German troops were allocated for an attempt at offensive action on the western front. The main new formations were sent against Russia in the hope of obtaining a rapid decision on what appeared to be the weaker side of the allied forces. The Franco-British lines were regarded as being too strong for an immediate attack. Thus again the tactical initiative was left in the hands of General Joffre, and, in a vain essay to steal it from him by an inhuman surprise Hindenburg came west to see to the employment of poisonous gases—already used against the Russians by means of bombs—while General Falkenhayn went east to beat down Russia by heavy artillery attack before she could be munitioned through the port of Archangel.

WITH THE H.A.C. IN NORTHERN FRANCE.
Trenches captured from the Germans. Note the zigzag formation.

CHAPTER LIX.

ORGANISING THE DEFENCE OF THE REALM : A RETROSPECT.

German and British Plans Contrasted—Individual Rights Sunk in Interest of the Commonwealth—Money Markets and the Coming Danger—Banks and the Gold Supply—Mr. Lloyd George and Lord Rothschild—The Moratorium—How the Threatened Panic was Stayed—War and Trade—Harmony Between Employers and Employed—Government and the Railways—State Insurance of British Shipping—Regulation of Food Supplies—Defence of the Realm Act—Equipment of the New Armies—A Committee of Production—Drink Factor and the Shell Supply—The King's Example—Problem of the Alien Enemy and How it was Met—German Spies—The Cases of Karl Lody and Karl Ernst—Sinking of the Lusitania—Anti-German Riots—Mr. Asquith's Statement.

AT this stage of our historical record it will be well to make a brief survey of the extraordinary economic conditions resulting from the declaration of war, and to show how the British Government grappled with the stupendous task of organising the nation on a war footing. Germany had prepared as carefully for the financial and industrial struggle that was bound to follow the outbreak of war as she did for her fighting in the field. Britain left most of her preparations until war began.

The German organisers knew what was wanted. Their first need was gold. An intimation was evidently given to certain banking organisations holding large quantities of international securities to turn them into sterling, and for months before war actually came they were engaged in a steady process of selling stocks and bonds abroad, securing the gold and banking it in Germany. Raw material was also accumulated, particularly raw material required for the manufacture of explosives.

Industrial experts classified the factories and workmen. Every man had his task marked out for him. The very supply of chloroform and artificial limbs for the wounded had been arranged for. All that remained when war was declared was for the nation to fall into line and carry out its instructions.

On our side there were no corresponding plans. Our ideal had been individual freedom. Capital was free to do as it pleased; labour was free to work where it wished. Suddenly this

THE DOCKERS' BATTALION.
Lord Derby and Captain Williams, Adjutant of the Dockers' Battalion, after the inspection of the Dockers at Liverpool on April 12th, 1915.

old fundamental idea of the supremacy of personal rights had to go. The State, we realised, must now come first, and the ancient rights of the private person must for the time take second place. The factory must manufacture, not what was most profitable to the owner, but what was most useful for the Empire. The workman must labour, not where he pleased, but where his services were most required. The railways passed, almost without notice, into the hands of the Government. The financier and property owner discovered that the "sacred rights of property" had been amazingly curtailed. The Stock Exchange was closed for a time, and then only allowed to do what business the authorities approved. The newspaper was no longer able to publish what it pleased. Private correspondence became subject to censorship. During some months any citizen charged with acts detrimental to the safety of the State could be tried by courts-martial.

Let it be said at once that this curtailment of individual rights was made with the consent of the nation. Here and there objection may have been raised to some particular demand. But the nation as a whole recognised that in time of war individual rights must be sunk in the interest of the commonwealth. The story of the change covers a very interesting period in the history of the war. Up to the beginning of the first week in August the great majority of people in Great Britain did not believe there would be war. A strong party in the Cabinet was known to be opposed

BRINGING UP A "4·7," A STIRRING REMINISCENCE OF TRAINING MANŒUVRES, THE OUTCOME OF WHICH WAS SEEN
IN MANY A FAR MORE STIRRING INCIDENT AT THE FRONT.

to it; newspapers like the "Daily News," the "Manchester Guardian," and the "Nation" were striving for non-intervention; organisations like the International Arbitration League declared that: "It is the clear duty of the Government to remain strictly neutral." The average man was influenced not so much by these as by his own knowledge that a European war had often before been threatened and never came. He was confident that at the last moment some way out would be found.

The first signs of the urgency of the coming danger were seen in the money markets. The stock exchanges of Europe began to face ruin. Everyone wanted to sell, none to buy.

Alarm in the money markets — Prices fell to what a week before would have seemed impossible figures. In London, firm after firm, including one of those best known on the Stock Exchange, were broken. On Wednesday, July 29th, seven firms were hammered. Foreign houses, particularly German and Austrian, were pouring securities on London, and selling them for whatever they would fetch. The Stock Exchange had to close its doors on Friday, July 31st, to prevent general collapse. On July 22nd the bank rate was three per cent. On July 29th it was raised to four per cent., then to eight per cent., and then, on Saturday, August 1st, to the impossible figure of ten per cent.

At the same time the banks began to guard their gold. The Bank of England took steps to protect itself, and banks generally met demands on them with banknotes in place of sterling. These notes were transferable into gold at the Bank of England on demand, and on Friday and Saturday that week London witnessed the extraordinary spectacle of a queue of people waiting outside the Bank of England to obtain gold for paper. It seemed that a great financial panic was inevitable. We were face to face with the possibility of the entire overthrow of our credit system and of a general run upon our banking institutions.

It was fortunate that the first Monday in August is a Bank Holiday. This pause gave the authorities opportunity to prepare to meet the situation. Mr. Lloyd George, the Chancellor of the Exchequer, who up to this time had been regarded by the City of London as its worst enemy, now won confidence and gratitude by his courageous action. He called the financial kings of London into conference on that memorable first Sunday in August. He and Lord Rothschild had been open foes. They sank their enmity, and with the heads of the great banks laid common plans to meet the crisis. The Bank Holiday was extended for three days more. A moratorium proclamation was issued on Monday, August 3rd, and was subsequently extended to November 4th, with an extension for a month for bills that fell due up to that date. To meet the shortage of gold, one-pound and ten-shilling Treasury notes were put into circulation. Steps were taken to prevent people from withdrawing their deposits from banks through panic and for the purpose of hoarding.

"Nobody should be so foolish and indeed wicked as to add to the difficulties of the financial and commercial situation by selfishly drawing out unnecessary amounts of money in groundless apprehension that it is advisable to hoard it during the crisis. If a man's credit is good there is no advantage to be gained by keeping more money in hand now than at any other time." This quotation is typical of the exhortations that appeared in all the newspapers about this time.

For a few days people in Britain were faced with a very real shortage of money. The Bank Holiday had been extended from the Monday until the Friday morning. No cheques could be cashed. The banks on the previous Saturday had paid out cheques, wherever possible, in £5 notes. **The threatened panic stayed** — Restaurants, shops, and even clubs refused to cash these notes, declaring that they were stocked up with them. The result was that many well-to-do people could not find sufficient money to pay their current minor expenses. This, however, was a very temporary trouble. During the time of the long Bank Holiday people had opportunity to think over the situation. Almost every man decided in his own mind that it would be not only a disloyal but an absurd thing to doubt our national financial stability. He would leave his money in the bank, and

GETTING A "4·7" INTO POSITION. THIS TYPE OF GUN, WHICH PROVED SO SERVICEABLE IN THE SOUTH AFRICAN
WAR, HELPED TO MAKE HISTORY AGAIN IN FLANDERS.

would go on with his normal life as usual. And so when
the banks reopened there was no fresh rush on them. Here
and there a super-nervous individual tried to withdraw
large sums. The banks had now the power to refuse to
pay him, which power they used.

The threatened panic was stayed, but the financial and
industrial situation in Britain during the first week in
August was anything but promising. When the average
merchant or manufacturer returned to his desk after the
holiday he found himself face to face with very perilous
prospects. His investments were not now immediately
available. He could not sell them even at a ruinous
sacrifice, for the Stock Exchange was closed. He could
not borrow on them, for the banks were chary in making
loans. Foreign payments had ceased to arrive, and debts
on the Continent of Europe could not be collected. Business
men who had been able a month before to command scores
of thousands of pounds now found themselves hard pressed
to raise enough money to pay their weekly wages bill.
Debts owing by them could not, it is true, be enforced under
the moratorium proclamation. But the British business
man did not want to damage his own credit by pleading
the moratorium.

Business was immediately curtailed. A large part
of British trade had been with abroad. Most of this
ceased immediately, especially so far as
the Continent of Europe was concerned.
Home buying dropped. The wholesaler
would not lay in further supplies which
he might not be able to sell ; the retailer would not accept
extra stocks. Thus day by day during that first week in
August the manufacturers found their mail composed of
little more than letters cancelling orders. To many of them
it seemed that business had come to an end.

Articles of luxury, objets d'art, pictures, and the like
became suddenly unsaleable. The West End dressmaker
found that her best customers were no longer thinking of
fresh stocks of costly and beautiful attire, but were absorbed
in work for the sick or in preparations for the wounded.
Entertaining ceased, and the army of caterers for the
luxuries of the well-to-do found themselves idle. Holiday-

**Our foreign
trade relations**

makers returned home as soon as war was declared, and
the tens of thousands of lodging-house keepers and hotel-
keepers at the seaside and in the country found their living
gone. Advertising largely ceased. No new business was
promoted, and old business was paralysed.

This condition of things naturally told on employment.
Thousands of young women shorthand typists and general
assistants were thrown out of work by the closing down
of financial offices. Some factories ran
on half time, and some shut altogether.
Here and there patriotic business men,
possessed of unusual resources, did not
permit their people to suffer. "You have stood by us
in good times. We will stand by you in bad," they said ;
and they paid wages in full and kept their staffs unbroken.

**Employer and
employed**

Others who could not do this made often enough great
sacrifices. Nothing was more remarkable at this time
than the coming together of employers and employed.
Factory owners kept open at heavy loss, so that there
might be something doing for their people. Employers in
some cases met their men and discussed the situation
with them. Here and there the workers took the initiative.
"We recognise that there is not enough business coming
in to keep all of us employed," the workers in one large
house wrote to their chief. "We know that some read-
justment must be made. We should be glad if, in place
of discharging part of the staff, you would allow us to
keep together, to share the loss in common, and to have
wages reduced all round rather than some be discharged
and others kept on at full wages."

The crisis brought out in remarkable fashion the
good relations existing, as a whole, between British
employers and their hands. There were, of course, exceptions. But in the vast majority of cases they faced the
crisis together. Still, the industrial outlook during the
month of August was black. It seemed as though Britain
must inevitably face a winter of general unemployment
and of deep distress. How this forecast was completely
falsified will be shown later. Between Sunday, August
2nd, and Tuesday, August 4th, when the Cabinet, after
long consideration, decided to support the neutrality of

305

Belgium by force of arms if necessary, a great change passed over Great Britain. Plans for home defence, which had been carefully worked out by the War Office, came into effect. Railway-stations, bridges, and water and lighting works were suddenly placed under military guard. News came up from a hundred points around the coast of the digging of trenches, the barricading of streets, and the like. At first people refused to take these measures seriously, and laughingly declared that it might be imagined the authorities thought the Germans would invade us. The note of

good-humoured banter soon changed to a more serious tone. A number of Germans suspected of espionage were suddenly arrested, and it is said that a very carefully - planned German scheme was thus crushed. A bill enabling the authorities to move or restrain the movements of undesirable aliens was passed through the Commons on the day war was announced. The navigation of aircraft of every kind, and particularly over the whole of the United Kingdom, was prohibited. Shipping was placed at the command of the authorities, who were given power to commandeer what boats they required for the service of the Government.

Two of the most important measures carried out in the first week for the nationalisation of our resources were the taking over of the railways by the State and the establishment of a Government scheme for the insurance of shipping against war risks.

The State control of railways was announced on Tuesday night, August 4th, **Government and** and it at once **the railways** came into force. Under an Act of Parliament, passed in 1871, the Government possessed power to assume supreme control over the railways of the United Kingdom, in order that the lines, locomotives, rolling-stock, and staff might be used as one complete unit in the service of the State for the movement of troops, stores, and food supplies. The Order-

in-Council, announcing that this power was to be used, stated: "It is expedient that the Government should have control over the railroads of Great Britain. . . . Although the railway facilities for other than Naval and Military purposes may for a time be somewhat restricted, the effect of the use of the powers under this Act will be to co-ordinate the demands on the railways of the civil community with those necessary to meet the special requirements of the Naval and Military Authorities. More normal conditions will in due course be restored, and it is hoped the public will recognise the necessity for the special conditions, and will in the general interest accommodate themselves to the inconvenience involved."

Unsuspected by the country at large, this step had been fully prepared for long before **War Office foresight** war began. For this we have to thank the War Office. A War Railway Council was in existence, under the direction of the Army, and included representatives of the Admiralty and the Board of Trade. The work of this Council was to lay down general schemes of what the railways were required to do in the way of moving troops and supplies. The actual executive administration of the lines was placed in the hands of the Railway Executive Committee, a board composed of the general managers of the railways. Behind it was an organisation, the Engineer and Railway Staff Corps, consisting of the very pick of the railway world, whose members were at once placed in high administrative transportation posts,

HOMES FOR BRITISH WAR WORKERS.
The top photograph is of houses in course of construction in the new munition-workers' town at Well Hall Station, near Woolwich. In the spring of 1915 twelve hundred dwellings were being erected where once were one hundred acres of cultivated ground. Centre: One of the houses nearer completion. At foot: General view of a street in the new town.

not only at home but on the Continent. The primary work of the Staff Corps was to assume the running of the railways in case of invasion.

The Government guaranteed that during the time of official control the receipts of the railways should equal

WOMEN AND GIRLS IN OUR MUNITION FACTORIES.
Photographs taken in a Leeds ammunition factory. Left: Machine-workers making metal cartridge-cases. Right: Cartridge-making.
Centre: Inspecting cartridge-cases.

STAMPING PIECES OF METAL FOR CARTRIDGE-CAPS.

those they had recently been earning. The result of this guarantee was far-reaching. From now on it was no longer the aim of the railways to attract traffic by special means to their lines, but to meet the Government needs. All the usual railway propaganda, advertising campaigns, canvassing for passengers, and the like, were cut off in a day. Trains were held up or lines closed whenever necessary. Excursion facilities gradually lessened until, in the spring of 1915, it was announced that on account of the military requirements cheap fares and excursion rates would be cancelled altogether. The private traveller suffered to some extent, although not so much as might have been expected. But the work for the Army was done with splendid efficiency. The way in which the First Expeditionary Force was carried to the South Coast and embarked secretly, rapidly, and without a hitch, will go down in history among the greatest of railway feats.

A memorable railway feat
Still more important, if anything, than the conveyance of the Expeditionary Force southwards was the constant preparation to keep our lines day and night ready so that at any moment a defence army of, maybe, 200,000 men, drawn from many centres, could be concentrated on one spot to resist an attempt at invasion. When it is borne in mind that the railways were working very short-handed, a large number of their men being at the war, that they had lost some of their chief organisers for administrative work on the Continent, and that they were primarily from August onwards working for the Government, it will be realised that the way in which they still catered for the civilian element stands to their great credit.

The scheme for insuring British shipping against war risks was necessary if our shipping was to continue its work freely. Everyone assumed before war began that Germany would have large numbers of armed cruisers scattered over the seas, and that these would for a time, until we could hunt them down, destroy an appreciable percentage of our ships. The Germans, it turned out, were not so well prepared with their cruisers as we expected. But the fear of them alone was enough to force insurance to an impossible figure if nothing was done. A State Insurance Office was started in London, and the State announced that it was prepared to insure eighty per cent. of the risks on ships and to insure cargoes at moderate fixed rates.

The result of this State guarantee, and of the protection afforded to our shipping by the Fleet, was soon made

The Cabinet formed a Committee on Food Supplies, which met the representatives of the multiple grocery firms and of the Grocers' Federation, and it was decided to set up a maximum retail figure announced by the Government for certain staple foods, such as sugar, butter, cheese, lard, bacon, and margarine. The Government went further than this. The price of sugar had been forced up to, in some instances, as much as 7d. a pound. The State purchased an immense quantity of sugar, sufficient for the national supply for many months, and arranged its distribution through the wholesale trade at a much more reasonable price.

The problem of the anticipated winter distress and unemployment among the working classes engaged widespread attention during August and September.

The Dominion of Canada sent a million bags of flour for the relief of our poor, and other dominions and provinces

Fresh industrial enterprises

followed suit. The Prince of Wales's Fund was established to meet the distress—a fund that within nine months was to exceed five million pounds. The Board of Trade established a new department for the promotion of fresh industrial enterprises. This department, managed with an initiative and zeal such as are not usually looked for among officials, brought all manner of fresh enterprises to the attention of our tradesmen. The chairmakers of Luton were lacking work; a Board of Trade official showed them how to make bentwood furniture so as to capture the Austrian trade. Nottingham mills were given samples of fresh lines wanted abroad. Dundee was put in touch with new Continental buyers. The East End little master was shown how to make fasteners or bag frames, and where to sell them when made.

CANADIANS REPLENISHING THEIR WATER-CART.
A scene on the River Avon, near the camp of the Canadians on Salisbury Plain.

manifest. A number of merchant vessels were taken over by the Government for transport work. The others were insufficient for the work awaiting them. The great German mercantile fleets had been driven from the seas by the British Navy. France had no ships to spare. Japan, with her growing shipping, gained enormously. But the main benefit fell to the British shipowners. There came the greatest boom shipping had ever known. Rates doubled, trebled, and quadrupled in a very short time. Old ships almost derelict, which a few weeks before had been unsaleable, now fetched more than they cost when new. Shipowners who had struggled along with small fleets of tramp boats now found that every boat left to them by the Government was a little gold-mine. Sailors and officers demanded much higher wages, and got them. This represented a very small share of the gains. Many men made fortunes from their ships in the autumn and winter of 1914-15.

The steadily growing activities of the State revealed themselves in another direction. Immediately war grew probable, a number of middle-class people started hastily buying large supplies of foodstuffs against

Regulation of food prices

any emergency. In some cases they laid in fantastic quantities of preserved foods, more than they would consume in a year in the normal course of things. Some shopkeepers tried to meet this rush by refusing to supply anyone except their regular customers, only selling them their usual quantities. Others, including some great wholesale houses, quickly raised prices. This rise fell most heavily on small and struggling retailers in poor districts, who could not afford to keep large stocks. As a result they had to increase prices for their customers, and the poorest classes were made to pay.

A WATER—NOT A GAS MAIN.
Engineers laying down a water-supply system in the North of France.

CHANNEL ISLANDERS IN WAR TIME.
Detachment of the Royal Guernsey Light Infantry (Guernsey Militia), marching off after parade. This island force has a history dating back hundreds of years.

There was much talk of a business war against Germany. While our soldiers were fighting the German armies in the field, our merchants and manufacturers were to establish British trade where German had formerly prevailed. We were to reconquer the South American market, to make an end of German manufactures in Canada, to do the business formerly done by Germany in China, and to have Australian trade once more to ourselves. This talk was very popular for a time. Then it died away, as people came to realise that we had something very much more important to do than to make fresh trade conquests. Our business was to beat Germany in the field of war. That required all our efforts, and the public mind had to be **Temporary talk of** devoted to that. People felt that there **trade conquests** was something a little paltry in so much talk of trade benefits at this crisis. Hence various campaigns, such as the " Business as Usual " campaign, faded out of sight as the serious purpose of the war loomed larger and larger.

When arrangements had to be made for the arming, clothing, and equipping of Lord Kitchener's New Army of a million men, it was found that it was hardly possible for the Yorkshire mills to turn out the khaki, for Sheffield to produce the guns and bayonets required, or for Birmingham to find the small arms. Every firm which catered for the soldier in any way was quickly overwhelmed with orders. Firms that had never done military work before transformed their plant. The Birmingham steel-pen maker now turned to the manufacture of buttons by the million, and cartridge-cases by the ten million. The Hawick manufacturer of fine tartans was commanded to make khaki. At first traders sought for Government work. After a time the Government came to them, with directions that they were to turn out certain amounts in a given time, and with stern intimation that if they did not they might expect to have military representatives take the control of their mills from them.

This threat was rendered possible by a remarkable measure, passed in the early days of the war, the Defence of the Realm Act.

The Defence of the Realm Act was in many ways the most extraordinary legislative measure passed by the British Parliament for many years. It specified a number of acts for which civilians could be tried by court-martial. These acts included communicating with the enemy, spreading false reports or reports likely to cause disaffection, giving assistance to the enemy or endangering the successful prosecution of the war. The person deemed by the military authorities guilty of any of these offences could be arrested and tried as if subject to military law, and as if **Defence of the** he or she had, on active service, **Realm Act** committed an offence under the Army Act. In other words, the military authorities could arrest any persons they pleased and, after court-martial, inflict any sentence on them short of death. In addition, the military authorities were allowed to demand the whole or part of the output of any factory or workshop dealing with military supplies, and to take possession of any factory or workshop they required. They were also allowed to take any land they needed. This, in effect, made the civil administration of the country entirely subservient to the military administration.

The Act created surprise, and while the majority of people were willing to accept it, believing that the powers under it would not be abused, a number of eminent peers, including several famous judges, among them such men as Lord Halsbury, Lord Parmoor, Lord Loreburn, and Lord Bryce, objected. Lord Halsbury declared that he saw no necessity to get rid of the fabric of personal liberty that had been built up for many generations. "I do not think that the liberty of the subject is so trifling a matter that it can be swept away in a moment because some of us are in a panic."

ROYAL GUERNSEY ARTILLERY AT PRACTICE.
An officer directing the fire of his battery from behind a mass of granite boulders.

MM

EAST ANGLIAN COASTGUARD AWHEEL.
A picturesque photographic study of Essex Cycle Scouts riding along one of the coast roads, which they patrolled day and night on the look-out for the approach of enemy raiders by sea or air.

The Act, nevertheless, passed into law, and the military authorities, as expected, used their great powers prudently. But the feeling grew that it was not right that all the ancient limitations on the supreme authority should go, and when the House of Lords met on January 7th, 1915, Lord Parmoor introduced an amending Bill, to restore to citizens their right to be tried by ordinary courts. The Government promised, if this was withdrawn, to bring in a similar measure itself. It did so, and a new law was passed, giving any accused civilian the right to choose whether he should be tried by civil court or court-martial. It was provided, however, that in case of special emergency, such as invasion, this choice would be withdrawn. The change was welcomed in responsible circles. Even great emergency did not justify the Government, it was felt, in maintaining a law under which legitimate criticism could be suppressed. The effect of the law, even after amendment, was, however, to vest in the Government authority such as it never had before the war began.

Unemployment almost abolished

By the beginning of 1915 the industrial position in Britain was very different from what had been anticipated. The war, in place of leading to a shortage of employment, had almost abolished unemployment. The Army and Navy required vast quantities of guns, shells, and equipment. More warships had to be built, and those partly built had to be pushed on night and day to be ready in the shortest possible time. The great shipyards on the Tyne, on the Clyde, and at Belfast were almost overwhelmed. Private orders could scarcely be looked at, and small yards unsuitable for naval work were sending their men to help in the bigger warship yards. At Newcastle firms like Armstrong's were bringing down miners from the coalfields to help

to build their new sheds, and were employing armies of women to fill shells and to aid in other work. Glasgow manufacturers were conducting an active advertising campaign in many other parts of the country to attract workmen, urging them to go and help in Government work. In Birmingham, in the expressive phrase of one manufacturer: "Having secured all the good workmen, and all the poor workmen, they were now bringing in women and boys, one-armed men and one-legged men to help." Northampton had never been so prosperous before in its history. Our great manufacturing centres were producing goods not alone for the British, but for the French, Russian, and Belgian Governments. In many centres they were working seven days a week, with day and night shifts.

Government control of workshops

Even this was not enough. The Government obtained further powers enabling it to acquire and control factories and workshops. It appointed a Committee of Production, with extensive powers, and mapped Great Britain out into a series of districts. The scheme was gradually evolved of allotting a certain amount of war work to each district and expecting it to produce it. The amount was sufficient to keep all available labour busy then.

Still the authorities were not satisfied. Lord Kitchener led the demand for more shells. "The output," said he, "is not only not equal to our necessities, but does not fulfil our expectations. The progress of equipping our new armies and also in supplying the necessary war material for our forces in the field has been seriously hampered by the failure to obtain sufficient labour, and by delays in production of the necessary plant." He declared with the utmost emphasis that unless the whole nation worked, not only in supplying manhood for the fighting field, but also in supplying the necessary arms, ammunition, and equipment, successful operations would be delayed.

Lord Kitchener and Mr. Lloyd George both emphasised the delay caused in factories by slack work and irregular time-keeping, due to excessive drinking among workmen. Having acquired many approved factories, and transformed them for producing war material, the Government now set about getting the utmost out of the men. Two steps were proposed to insure this—an appeal to the patriotism of the workmen themselves, and the restriction of temptations to drink. The appeal to the workmen was carried out by a series of meetings throughout the country, notably by a great meeting at Newcastle-on-Tyne on April 20th, 1915, when Mr. Asquith talked with the Tyneside men, face to face, about their share in helping the nation to carry on the war. He declared that he did not come there to accuse the men of remissness. "The miner, the shipbuilder, the engineer, the iron and textile worker, the railwayman, and the docker—everyone who contributes, whether by brain or by muscle, to maintain and increase the supply of munitions, upon which the efficiency of the fighting forces depends—is, in as true a sense as any of our gallant sailors and soldiers, a patriot and a combatant," said he. "Success in this war is a question of munitions," said Mr. Lloyd George.

The appeal to the workmen was on the whole successful. In some centres they went back to their tasks with

MEN OF THE ROYAL NAVAL DIVISION IN TRAINING AT THE CRYSTAL PALACE, SYDENHAM.

MARCH-PAST OF THE PARIS GARRISON BEFORE GENERAL GALOPIN, WHO SUCCEEDED GENERAL GALLIENI AS GÓVERNOR.

renewed zeal. They agreed to the temporary suspension of many of their Trade Union regulations, and recognised that in war time even Unionism must be modified. " Shall we deliver the goods ? " asked one of the men's leaders at the close of a great gathering. The answering " Yes ! " came like a thunderclap

The campaign against drinking was not so successful. The King led the way by pledging himself and his household to personal abstinence during the war, and Lord Kitchener and numbers of our leading men followed. But when it was proposed by the Government to increase the taxation on spirits, beers, and wines to an almost prohibitive degree, such opposition was set up by many of their own supporters in the Liberal ranks, by the entire Irish Party, and by strong sections of the Opposition and the Labour group, that this proposal had to be withdrawn.

By the early summer of 1915 the civil life of Great Britain had been largely transformed. Parliament had fallen for the time to a comparatively minor place, while the administrative authority of the heads of the Government had increased enormously. Section after section of industrial life, that had formerly been under private control, was now supervised and controlled by the State.

MILL AS OBSERVATION POST.
British artillery officer on the look-out for the enemy—" somewhere in France."

War work took the main place in every industrial centre. There was a scarcity of workmen, due to the large numbers who had joined the new armies, and in some cases their places were taken by women. The civilian was no longer free to go where he pleased, should the military authorities desire to stop him. The task of leaving or entering a country was made one of great difficulty by severe passport regulations. The visitor to a strange place had to fill up a form declaring **Necessary sacrifice** his identity, hotel guests had to be **of private rights** registered in the same way as had long prevailed on the Continent. Great Britain was fighting for her life, and her people knew that, faced with this supreme issue, the rights and privileges of ordinary times must of necessity go.

The sacrifice of personal rights had been gladly made by the nation. It was a temporary sacrifice made to save honour and Empire, the safety of our women and the honour of our homes.

The Government at the outbreak of the war was called upon to decide what should be done with the very large

numbers of Germans in Britain. For years Germans had come and settled here in growing hosts. German financiers were among the leaders in our banking world ; German stockbrokers formed a section of their own on the Stock Exchange ; German importers and exporters dominated branch after branch of commerce in London and in many of our great provincial cities. It was notorious that the young German clerk, speaking three languages and requiring little wage, had ousted the British from thousands of offices. Most of our great hotels were run by Germans or Austrians, while as waiters the only serious competitors of the German were Italians and Swiss. The old English waiter had almost disappeared. Germans had captured the greater part of the baking trade of London, and their food stores were scattered over the City and the West End. Many people **Enemy aliens** with German names and of German **in our midst** descent were naturalised ; very many more were not. We had German clubs and unions galore. Whole sections of Bloomsbury, Highgate, and St. Pancras were overwhelmingly Teutonic.

What was to be done with these people ? The problem was admittedly not easy. Among the German and Austrian subjects were some, like the Czechs, who hated Germanism more than ourselves, and who had fled to this country as a refuge against its tyrannous rule. There were others who had lived here for many years, had married English wives, whose sons were serving in the British Army, and who were passionately English. But these were the exceptions. The vast majority of the Germans here were, as might be expected, devoted to their Fatherland. Tens of thousands of the young men were German Army reservists, eager to return to their regiments to fight us. Among them there existed an elaborate and carefully-organised spy system, fastened on Great Britain like a leech on its victim.

The Government hesitated to employ its authority against these people. Even when it was seen that British subjects caught in Germany at the beginning of the war were to be treated in the harshest possible fashion, our authorities still held their hand. Known spies were arrested and some two hundred suspected spies were kept under watch. A few hours after war broke out the Home Secretary issued a notice allowing Germans to leave this country during the subsequent six days. Thanks to this extraordinary permission, young German reservists, amounting in numbers to a division of the Army, were enabled to return home, rejoin their colours, and fight against us. Some wholly inadequate precautions were taken. German financial undertakings were placed under special supervision, and a series of minor checks on alien enemies were instituted. Espionage was made a military offence, punishable with death. Alien enemies were not allowed to keep carrier pigeons, photographic apparatus, or arms. The houses of Germans and Austrians were raided and searched. Later on a certain number of Germans and Austrians of military age—at first nine thousand, rising afterwards to nineteen thousand —were arrested and confined in detention camps as prisoners of war. A number of Germans and Austrians attempted to change their names in order to pass as British. This was forbidden by a special Order-in-Council.

Germans and Austrians remaining in Britain were ordered to register, and to submit to certain regulations limiting their right to travel over the country. Many of them evaded these regulations in every possible way.

It soon became evident, however, that these measures were utterly insufficient to counteract the activity of German secret agents in this country. There were a certain number of outrages, particularly in Government works, unexplainable except as the deliberate work of active enemies. Some of these—as, for example, the series of fires that took place in Portsmouth Dockyard—were not allowed to be published at the time, owing to the system

BRINGING UP A TANK OF WATER FOR THE TROOPS. AN INDIAN MULE-DRIVER IS SEEN IN THE REAR.

TAKING STOCK OF SUPPLIES IN A TOWN AT THE REAR OF THE FIRING-LINE.

WITH THE MEN OF OUR ARMY SERVICE CORPS AT THE FRONT.

Unloading sacks of provender at a supply base. Never before had the men of our Army Service Corps so many varied calls upon their resourcefulness, and never before the Great War had these "universal providers" of the Army worked more splendidly or efficiently than they did under the skilled direction of the Quartermaster-General.

of secrecy then enforced here. Cases that came before the courts increased the public uneasiness. Thus one boarding-house keeper in Bloomsbury was shown to be the wife of a German general. Spy after spy was brought to trial, and the evidence afforded best proof of the dangers of their system. Two of the most noted cases were those of Karl Lody, a German naval lieutenant who was shot after trial at the Tower of London for espionage, and Karl Ernst, a naturalised British subject, a hairdresser in North London, who was sentenced to seven years' penal servitude for acting as distributor of letters for one of the German spy organisers. Many Germans settled on the East Coast at possible invasion points. Some of them were found in possession of wireless apparatus. It was quite evident months after the war broke out that German agents in this country were succeeding, by some means or another, in communicating valuable information to our enemies. The authorities tried to check such leakages by making it more difficult for people to leave the country and by subjecting travellers to minute search and investigation. But every official step against the Germans themselves in Britain was taken with evident reluctance, and many of the aliens who were first interned were gradually released. Attacks on this leniency met with the reply that everything was done with the approval, if not at the direction of, the military authorities.

Here and there the activity of the authorities was quickened by slight displays of public resentment against German businessmen. But until the spring of 1915 these displays were very rare. People contented themselves for a time with very generally refusing to employ German subjects. Thousands of Germans and Austrians had, in consequence, to come on to the public funds for relief. The Germans in this country did little to conciliate public opinion. Numbers of them adopted an exceedingly belli-cose attitude—rejoicing openly over German victories,

Rejoicing over German victories

boasting what would happen to England when German armies came here, and aggressively flaunting their views in a way that aroused the wonder of neutral visitors at the patience of the British people in submitting to them.

This patience was finally subjected to too great a strain. On May 7th, 1915, came the news of the sinking of the Lusitania. Some Germans in England were foolish enough to show their glee. As details were published in this country of women and children in the monster liner done to death without warning, the popular passion flared up. The butchers of Smithfield ordered German butchers away. The merchants of the Baltic Exchange told Germans there they would no longer endure their company. On the Stock Exchange men of German descent were warned to go. Starting in East London, there came a number of riots against German tradesmen, that spread widely over the country. As is nearly always the case in popular rioting, the demonstrations were taken up by mere pillagers who attacked shops generally, and who were less influenced by the desire to demonstrate against Germans than by the wish to rob and steal.

Effect of anti-German riots

The anti-German riots, deplorable as they were, had one immediate effect. The Government was stirred to action. In a speech in the House of Commons on May 14th, 1915, Mr. Asquith stated that of the alien enemies in this country there were some nineteen thousand interned, and some twenty-four thousand males and sixteen thousand women at large. He proposed that, with certain excep-tions, all adult male enemy aliens should, for their own safety and for that of the community, be segregated and interned or, if over military age, be repatriated. Women and children of suitable age were also to be repatriated, exceptions being made in special circumstances. As for the people of German birth who had become naturalised and who were, therefore, in law British subjects, they were only to be proceeded against in cases of proved necessity.

INSTANTANEOUS CAMERA RECORD OF SHRAPNEL BURSTING OVER THE BELGIAN TRENCHES IN FLANDERS.

Shrapnel bursting over the Turkish troops opposing

CHAPTER LX.

the landing of forces from a British transport.

THE FIGHT FOR THE DARDANELLES.

The Lesson of the German Fortification of the Belgian Coast—German Guns Drive off British Ships—Scheme for Combined Greek, French, and British Landing Force Falls Through—British Cabinet Decides to try first a Naval Bombardment—Political Considerations Underlying this Adventurous Policy—How the Germans Strengthened the Defences of the Dardanelles—Entrance Forts Destroyed by Close-range Fire—Allies' Apparent Success in the First Basin of the Dardanelles—Gallant Work by the Mine-Sweepers—The Queen Elizabeth Intervenes—Important Part Played by Naval Air Squadrons—Mishap to the Amethyst—Opening of the Grand Attack on the Turco-German Forts—Admirable Skill and Patience of German Gunners—Loss of Bouvet, Irresistible, and Ocean—Complete Failure of the Naval Operations—Fleet Waits for the Help of Mediterranean Expeditionary Force—The Great Landing Battles.

WE have seen that in the third week of October, 1914, a squadron of British warships began to operate off the Belgian coast and assist the French and Belgian troops along the Yser. In spite of the valuable aid of our long-range naval guns, the German Army succeeded in bringing up heavy batteries, and, though we had 12 in. guns in our battleships, skilfully directed by observers in flying machines, our ships were at last compelled to withdraw. Our warships carried out their main work of assisting the Belgian Army to hold its positions in the inundated polders north of Fournes, but they were unable to prevent the German artillerymen from fortifying the coast and establishing a dangerous submarine base at Zeebrugge. The work which the Germans did under continual bombardment by our naval guns was of remarkable importance. It was an achievement that settled the question of the power of ships against land batteries in the conditions of modern warfare. By using part of his siege train from Antwerp, including several of the monster Krupp howitzers, the enemy was able to fortify all the coast, and lay a new minefield round Zeebrugge, despite the fact that our squadrons off the Belgian coast were heavily reinforced.

Seeing, therefore, that we had not been able to master a short stretch of coast with our naval guns, and hinder the enemy from fortifying it, it did not seem likely that any naval attack upon a strong line of forts guarding a winding, narrow waterway would be successful. But in

January, 1915, Mr. Winston Churchill, the First Lord of the Admiralty, appears to have decided for himself that the Dardanelles ought to be opened, and that they could be forced by the British Fleet. Lord Fisher, the First Sea Lord, was opposed to the scheme, as he maintained that the aid of a large army was indispensable to the bombarding squadrons. This seemed also to have been the opinion of the experienced chiefs of the French Navy. At the outset it was hoped that some part of the Greek Army would assist in the operations. A small French Expeditionary Force, composed of Senegalese troops and Zouaves, was collected in North Africa, under the command of General d'Amade. There may also have been some arrangement for detaching a small portion of our forces in Egypt to help in attacking the gates of Constantinople and the Black Sea. But all this part of the scheme fell through when the King of Greece refused to follow the advice of his Prime Minister, M. Venizelos. M. Venizelos seems only to have promised the Allies to send one division (20,000 men) to the Dardanelles, but King Constantine would not agree even to this small amount of aid being given. The effect was that practically no military help against the Fifth Turkish Army, entrenched on the Gallipoli Peninsula, could at the time be granted to the combined British and French squadrons which were preparing to attack the Dardanelles forts. In these circumstances it might have been well, from a military point of view, to postpone the attack on the Turkish straits until a decision had been obtained in the western

GENERAL SIR IAN HAMILTON, G.C.B., D.S.O.
Commanding the Expeditionary Forces in the Dardanelles.

Lafayette.

SANATORIUM ON HALKI, ONE OF THE PRINCE'S ISLANDS, FORTIFIED ON ACCOUNT OF THE WAR.

BRITISH ADMIRALTY YACHT IMOGENE OFF THERAPIA.
A photograph taken a few weeks before war was declared on Turkey.

theatre of war against the first-line armies of Germany. The danger of a purely naval expedition up the Dardanelles was well known to the naval officers at the Admiralty. It had been placed on record in 1877 by that great leader Admiral Hornby, who in that year was directed to force a way to Constantinople. He warned the authorities at home that, while it was practicable for a squadron to run past the forts—which were far weaker in those days, and were not supplemented by mines and torpedoes—the fleet would, none the less, be helpless in the Sea of Marmora. Its supply of coal, ammunition, and food would be cut off, because the enemy would be certain to mount guns on the cliffs, which for more than six miles overhang the northern shore of the Dardanelles at the point where the channel closes to little over half a mile. It is never more than two miles in width. "Guns thus placed," he said, "could not fail to stop transports and colliers," and the fleet would be exposed to terrible danger. He therefore urged the necessity of occupying the Gallipoli Peninsula with British troops before entering the Sea of Marmora. When, by a stroke of singular daring aided by good luck, he passed the Dardanelles, the Turks offered no resistance. But he had no illusions as to his position. "There seems to be an idea," he wrote from the Sea of Marmora to the First Lord of the Admiralty, "that this fleet can keep the Dardanelles open. Nothing can be more visionary. Not all the fleets in the world can keep them open for unarmoured ships. Small earthworks on the cliffs would always prevent their passage."

Admiral Hornby's warning

Still earlier, in the days of the old sailing ship, Admiral Duckworth, who with a British squadron ran past the forts and anchored before Constantinople in 1807, pronounced the operation "the most dangerous and difficult ever undertaken." It was also fruitless, as the Turks refused to be terrified, and he had to beat a speedy retreat as the only alternative to finding himself without water and food. The evidence of history was certainly not encouraging.

The advice of naval officers seems to have been overridden by Mr. Winston Churchill, the first Lord of the Admiralty, in consideration of the critical condition of the political problems of the Mediterranean. Both the British

and the French Navy had a large number of powerfully-armed warships, which were too slow to take part in the manœuvres of a general fleet action. There were battleships, such as those of the Canopus class, which were slower than the latest type of German submarines. They could not be used in the North Sea with our swift super-Dreadnoughts. Moreover, our Grand Fleet was so strong in both gun power and speed that even our newest battleship with 15 in. guns—the Queen Elizabeth—could safely be detached from it. There were also battle-cruisers, like the Inflexible, which could safely be spared from Sir John Jellicoe's command.

Altogether, we had a surplus of naval force, over and above our Grand Fleet and Mediterranean Fleet, and no immediate use for it could be found except in the Dardanelles. A considerable portion of this surplus was composed of old and slow types that were destined for the scrap-heap at the end of the war. But their guns in most cases were very powerful, and it seemed well worth while to use them against the land forts of the Dardanelles, even at the risk of serious injury to the ships in an attempt to force a passage. As had been seen in the case of the Canopus in the action off the Falkland Islands, her low speed made her practically valueless in a running engagement. It was clear that any great battle in the North Sea would be a running fight. Any slow British battleships present

Gunpower a deciding factor

THE FAMOUS MOSQUE OF ST. SOPHIA, CONSTANTINOPLE.

PANORAMIC VIEW OF CANDILLE, THE BRITISH COLONY ON THE BOSPHORUS.

THE "TOUR BRULÉE," CONSTANTINOPLE.
There is a legend that when this iron-bound tower falls the Ottoman Power will fall with it.

THE LARGEST MOSQUE IN THE TURKISH CAPITAL.
The Egyptian obelisk (left) is on the site of the old Byzantine Hippodrome, where executions once took place. This and other views on this page were photographed on the eve of the war with Turkey.

THE SULTAN'S PALACE ON THE BOSPHORUS.
Part of the Imperial yacht is seen on the right of the photograph.

DIAGRAMMATIC VIEW OF THE ENTRANCE TO THE DARDANELLES, ILLUSTRATING THE WORK OF THE BRITISH FLEET IN THE EARLY DAYS OF MARCH, 1915.

would tail off during such an engagement, and be left without the protection of destroyers—a prey to enemy submarines.

There were at least three reasons for attempting to force the passage of the Dardanelles, at a foreseen loss of some of our obsolescent warships. In the first place, a stroke at the heart of the Ottoman Empire would be the best defence against Turkish operations against Egypt and on the Persian Gulf. If successful, it would check the Turco-German intrigues in Persia, Afghanistan, and the Indian border.

In the second place, an attack upon the **The foreseen and** waterway between the Mediterranean and **the unforeseen** the Black Sea would appeal to Italian sympathy, steady Bulgaria, and stimulate Rumania. Indeed, the mere fact that Britain and France were assailing in force the heart of Turkey would be sufficient to paralyse all German and Austrian designs in the Balkans. Then, in the third place, the success of the scheme would, by opening a warm water road for the munitioning of Russia, have a profound and practically decisive effect upon the course of the main land campaign; for Russia was sadly deficient in heavy artillery and shells. It was foreseen that her position in regard to war material would become critical by the spring of 1915. The opening of the Dardanelles would enable guns, shells, and rifles to be landed at the Black Sea ports, close to the main lines of battle.

One thing, however, was clearly not foreseen by Mr. Winston Churchill and the members of the Liberal Cabinet who supported his plan. When the attack on the Dardanelles had proceeded as far as the first severe check to the British and French bombarding fleet, no withdrawal from the situation created thereby was possible. Britain, France, and Russia were important Mohammedan Powers. They were fighting the Ottoman Caliphate, which, though a usurpation, had for centuries been recognised by Moslems as the practical directing force of their religious world. So long as the Powers of the Triple Entente conserved their military prestige, the Ottoman Sultan and the Young Turk war party using him as their marionette were unable to influence seriously the Mohammedan subjects of the Christian nations. For the Ottomans themselves were leagued with Christian Germans, Austrians, and Hungarians. There was no sound pretext for a Holy War. On the other hand, if the prestige of Britain and France were temporarily lowered in the Orient by a great Turkish victory in the Dardanelles, the consequences might be gravely felt in India, Egypt, and Northern Africa. Thus, even in the political field, the advantages won in one quarter by a serious display of activity might be fully balanced by disadvantages elsewhere, unless the naval attack on the Dardanelles by the Fleet were backed by the landing of a very large Franco-British army.

There were thus complications upon complications in the affair, and our French allies, with their passion for logic and clarity of thought, would have preferred to do one thing at a time, and settle the main struggle with the Germans before detaching a large army for action far outside the grand theatre of conflict. But our Cabinet, led in the matter by the dashing and enterprising Mr. Churchill, somewhat reluctantly consented to face serious risks in the chief field of operations for the sporting chance of winning a great Mediterranean victory by a swift, single **A serious preliminary** stroke. It is at once our failing and our **failure** strength as a nation that we lack prudence, and almost delight in hazardous enterprises. Instead of always calculating the means to an end, we engage in great risks, and rely on the standing luck of our fighting men, which, in ultimate analysis, means that we trust, in the event of preliminary failure, to win through at last by our large, general reserves of strength.

Certainly the Dardanelles campaign opened with a preliminary failure of a serious nature. As Lord Fisher had foreseen from the naval bombardment of the Belgian coast, the old saying that ships alone were useless against forts still held true under modern conditions of artillery fire. Even in the summer of 1912 the Italians had hesitated to attack with both troops and ships the Straits leading to Constantinople.

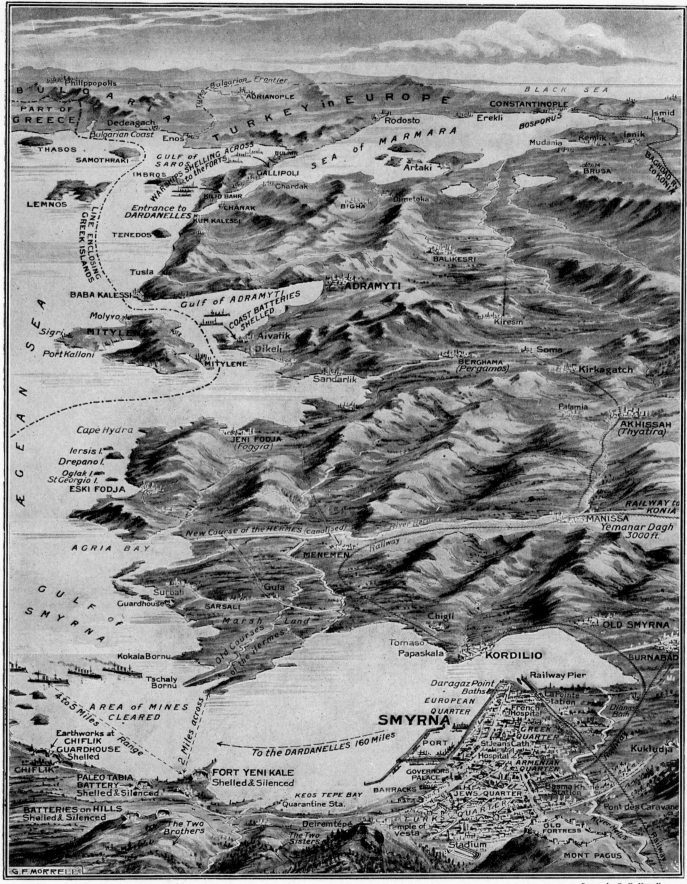

THE TURKISH PORT OF SMYRNA, WHICH WAS BOMBARDED BY A FORCE UNDER
VICE-ADMIRAL SIR RICHARD PEIRSE IN MARCH, 1915.

The Admiralty officially stated that the reduction of the Turkish defences at Smryna were " a necessary incident in the main operation."

At that time the Turkish defences were weak, the forts were out-of-date, and the minefield at Dardanus was covered by batteries which mounted few guns of large calibre. Passing the minefield one reached the Narrows, where the forts of Kilid Bahr and Chanak were armed only with plunging fire batteries. So weak were the defences in 1912 that another minefield was laid in front of the Narrows to supplement the batteries. Nevertheless, the Italians were so daunted by the difficulties of that tortuous and insidious waterway that they would not risk their fleet in attempting to force the passage.

The Turks began to strengthen the defences of the Dardanelles in September, 1914, some months before they opened hostilities against the Allies. They were greatly helped by a cargo of mines brought to Constantinople in the second week in August by a German steamer that accompanied the Goeben and the Breslau in their flight from Mediterranean waters. A considerable number of powerful guns and howitzers, some of 14 in. calibre, were obtained from the Teutonic Empires. Motor-batteries, worked by German gunners, were largely used, and rails were laid on one shore at least for the employment of very heavy but mobile howitzers. In the Gallipoli Peninsula four distinct lines of trenches were dug near Krithia, and carried from this point round all the important heights which dominate the line of advance towards the Narrows. The works at Bulair, in the neck of the Peninsula, which had proved a strong defence against the Bulgarian Army in the Balkan War, were further strengthened. Forty thousand troops were entrenched on the Peninsula to prevent the forts on the European side of the Straits from being attacked in the rear by the Franco-British landing-force. Another Turkish army corps was held ready to reinforce the Gallipoli garrison if need should require. The forts on the Asiatic shore were supported by well-entrenched troops, amounting to at least another army corps. Large reinforcements were available in the interior of Asia Minor and round Smyrna. It looked as though an army of half a million British and French troops would be needed to attack from the land the forts and Turkish armies on both sides of the Dardanelles. At the time it was quite impossible to spare

WITH THE AUSTRALIANS AT THE DARDANELLES.
The men were photographed as they were climbing down the side of a transport into the small boats in which they were rowed ashore.

this immense force from the Franco-Belgian front. So the fleet was ordered to try to carry the waterway by naval gun-power alone.

Chief among the bombarding warships was the Queen Elizabeth, with her eight 15 in. guns, each throwing a shell weighing 1,720 lb. to a distance of fifteen miles or more. She possessed besides twelve 6 in. guns, and a powerful anti-aircraft armament. She used only oil fuel, giving her a designed speed of 25 knots. She was 650 feet long, with a displacement of 27,500 tons. It was reckoned that one of her shrapnel shells threw out something like two thousand bullets. Her high-explosive shell, when it made a direct hit at a distance of ten miles or so, produced the most tremendous destructive effect of any missile used by man. "Black Bess," or "Lizzie," as the pride of the British Navy was called by our admiring seamen, was a potent influence on the political side of the action by the Allies It might be said that she did more harm to the Turks by the popular interest she excited in the Balkan States than by the blows she dealt to the Turkish forts.

When neutrals saw that our Grand Fleet in the North Sea was so strong that a new battleship with eight 15 in. guns could be spared from the Mediterranean, their confidence in the eventual victory of the Allies was restored. Among the other important ships was the early battle-cruiser the Inflexible, with a nominal speed of 25 knots, and eight 12 in. guns, and the two last pre-Dreadnought battleships, the Lord Nelson and the Agamemnon, with a speed of about 18·5 knots, each armed with four 12 in. guns and ten 9·2 in. guns. Then there were several older battleships, armed with four 12 in. guns and twelve 6 in. weapons apiece. Such were the Irresistible, Duncan, Cornwallis, Vengeance, Ocean, Goliath, Albion, and Canopus.

Of the same general type, but still more ancient, were the battleships Majestic and Prince George. The Swiftsure and Triumph were newer ships, purchased from Chili in 1903. They mounted four 10 in. guns and fourteen 7·5 in. guns apiece. A number of cruisers, such as the Euryalus, Amethyst, Dublin, and Sapphire, with destroyer flotillas, mine-trawlers, and a seaplane-carrier, the Ark Royal, made up the British fleet. The French Navy, whose main forces were

A camp of the Australians on the Gallipoli Peninsula.

Transports and battleships in the Dardanelles.

Australians disembarked and ready to move forward in the Dardanelles operations.

The great attack on the Turkish defences of the Dardan

Kum Kale Fort on fire, while one of the British landing-partie

: *Australian troops preparing for the assault by land.*

sheltering under the glacis of the immense Turkish stronghold.

The sinking of H.M.S. Irresistible during an attack on the forts at the Narrows of the Dardanelles, March 18th, 1915.

occupied in the Adriatic, detached a group of old battle-ships. These were the Suffren, with four 12 in. guns and ten 6·4 in. guns; the Bouvet, with two 12 in., two 10·8 in., and eight 5·5 in. guns; the Gaulois, with four 12 in. and ten 5·5 in. guns; and the Charlemagne, equally ancient, with four 12 in. and ten 5·5 in. guns. The top speed of the Suffren was only 16 knots, and that of the three older ships was less. The only representative of the Russian Navy was the Askold, a 1903 cruiser, with twelve 6 in. guns.

The allied fleet was at first commanded by Vice-Admiral Sackville Carden, but he retired indisposed a couple of days before the main action against the forts was undertaken, and was succeeded by Vice-Admiral de Robeck. The French squadron was commanded by Rear-Admiral Guépratte, who carried out his part of the work very gallantly from his flagship the Suffren, while not concealing his opinion that the naval attack was useless without the simultaneous co-operation of a large allied military force.

Naval leaders of importance

Vice-Admiral Peirse, with some of the ships of our East India Squadron, conducted operations against Smyrna and neighbouring points, with a view to distracting the enemy by the feint of a landing on the Asiatic coast. Another naval leader of importance in the allied attack was Captain Johnson, who directed the difficult and dangerous work of the mine-trawlers in the Dardanelles. Then Wing-Commander Samson, with some of the squadrons which had done much good work in France and Flanders, came to direct the aerial work of reconnaissance and fire control by the officers of the Royal Naval Air Service.

The German Emperor had sent one of his best naval men, Admiral Usedom, with a large number of gunnery officers and gunners, to direct the defences of the Dardanelles. A German general, Liman von Sanders, with a multitude of German officers, controlled the Turkish land forces in Gallipoli. According to a German war correspondent, the Ottoman troops were everywhere commanded by German officers in the Dardanelles operations. Deeply embedded between the hills were enormous position-guns, with ammunition chambers dug out of the earth, and filled with waggon-loads of explosives and vast quantities of shells. Close at hand were tents in which the officers had been living for months past. In the Sea of Marmora a great flotilla of boats maintained communications at night between the Gallipoli Peninsula and the Asiatic shore, thus preventing any attempt at reduction by famine in the case of the Allies getting command of the Bulair lines at the neck of the Peninsula.

For some months before the main attack opened there had been desultory firing at the entrance forts to the Dardanelles, just by way of keeping the Turks and Germans there in a state of anxiety. But the main attack was a surprise for the enemy, for they had then ceased to expect that we should attempt so daring a thing as the forcing of the greatly-strengthened defences of the Straits. On February 14th, 1915, the gunnery-lieutenants of some of our battleships set out in a destroyer to have a good look at the forts they were to attack. Four miles off the land they came under fire, but the shooting was very bad, and none of the German shells struck the reconnoitring

ADMIRAL DE ROBECK (LEFT) WITH HIS STAFF INSPECTING MARINES.
The Admiral, whose photograph is inset, succeeded Vice-Admiral Sackville Carden as Commander of the Allied Fleet in the Dardanelles.

little warship. At eight o'clock on Friday, February 19th, 1915, the historic engagement began.

The allied fleet of battleships and battle-cruisers steamed off with bands playing to their positions, and at a quarter to ten the bugles sounded "Action Stations," and everybody disappeared under cover. About ten minutes afterwards the fore turret of the leading British battleship opened fire. Its 12 in. shell fell over the forts. The next fell short, but near. Then, by these bracketing shots, the range was obtained; the third shell got home, and a great cloud of stone and brickwork rose high in the air. For an hour the leading ships worked hard at their guns. Then, about noon, the leading ships drew back, and another squadron of big-gunned vessels took their place. At each crash of the guns great clouds of grey smoke rose from the forts, and flames appeared from a

LANDING ON THE GALLIPOLI PENINSULA.
Troops disembarking by means of a trawler.

Turkish camp on the hillside and from a large barracks in the town by the forts. The Germans and Turks attempted no reply, as the allied fleet kept beyond the range of their guns.

But the long-range bombardment had not put the hostile batteries out of action. An exciting time followed when at three o'clock in the afternoon the Vengeance, Cornwallis, and Triumph, with the Suffren, Gaulois, and Bouvet, closed in to try and finish off the first forts of the Dardanelles. Far out to sea the Inflexible and Agamemnon kept up a long-range covering bombardment with their 12 in. guns, while the ships that closed in used only their secondary armament. By nightfall the forts round Cape Helles had been very badly battered, and had ceased to reply, and on the other side of the Straits only **Operations stayed** one battery remained active. The Ger-**by bad weather** man shells had pitched close to the French and British ships, and some had passed between the masts. But the enemy's shooting was not good; not a single hit was obtained on any unit of the fleet.

For a week afterwards the great battle between ships and forts was interrupted. There was a hurricane of wind, with short, high, hurrying seas, that made aerial reconnaissance and steady naval gunnery impossible. But the weather became quieter from February 25th, and the attacking fleet steamed up again to see if anything were left of the forts. Our naval airmen found that in the interval the enemy had prepared several new gun-positions, but no guns had been mounted in them. Two

or three of the guns, overturned by the first bombardment, seem also to have been set up again. But the entrance forts, with their nineteen guns, ranging from 6 in. to 11 in., and their smaller armament of another eleven guns less than 6 in. calibre, were not able to withstand the terrific fire brought against them. The Germans seem to have left the old entrance forts unstrengthened, except for one new earthwork and a mobile howitzer battery working behind Kum Kale.

By Monday, March 1st, both entrance forts and their magazines were destroyed, and under the shelter of our battleships the mine-sweepers began to clear away a line of mines which had **Mine-sweeping** been observed by our naval airmen. **by night** At eleven o'clock in the morning the Triumph, Ocean, and Albion entered the Straits and bombarded White Cliff Fort and Dardanus Fort, some ten miles up the Dardanelles, towards the Narrows. In the night the mine-sweepers, with remarkable daring and skill, swept within a mile and a half of Kephez Point, with land batteries and field-guns firing at them

ACTIVITY IN THE ÆGEAN SEA.
British landing-party setting out in the ship's boats.

GUN CREW OF THE FRENCH BATTLESHIP CHARLEMAGNE.
This remarkable photograph was taken during the operations in the Dardanelles. The men are seen on the hammock-protected upper deck, and are wearing anti-concussion caps to lessen the effect of the firing of the big guns.

Xeros and bombarded the forts on the Bulair line, blowing up several ammunition depots. On Thursday our battleships were able to advance about four miles into the Straits, which brought them to within two miles of the danger zone. Ten miles ahead of them was Chanak, with Kilid Bahr opposite, where the channel narrowed to a breadth of less than two miles. Here it was that forts, field-batteries, and mobile howitzers were thickly clustered on both sides of the waters leading to Nagara Point. In addition to their numerous guns of position, their field-howitzers, shore torpedoes, and electric mines fixed on the bed of the channel, the Germans and Turks had a formidable weapon of defence in the strong current flowing from the Black Sea to the Mediterranean. In the month of March the rivers of the Black Sea were in flood, and the consequence was that there was a great volume of water flowing with fierce, swift current through the Narrows. A modern torpedo, the Leon, was admirably suited to the circumstances. It consisted of a powerful floating mine which could be set in torpedo fashion to drift in a current, bobbing up and down, and with a good knowledge of the direction of the current it could be employed with deadly effect against any target in narrow waters.

The only protection used against this torpedo was an old-fashioned torpedo-net round each battleship. But by reason of its curious oscillating movement the Leon mine was likely to pass under the net and explode on the ship's hull. Moreover, if a battleship went into action with her torpedo-nets out, her speed was much reduced, and the old slow vessels, constituting the main part of the attacking fleet, wanted to get every knot possible out of their engines. It was by moving in curves in Erenkoi Bay, within the basin of the Dardanelles, that they managed to disconcert the German and Turkish gunners and escape from the shells pitched at them. Thus, for what seemed at the time good reason, no means of protection was used against the Leon torpedoes.

In the meantime the main business of destroying the modern-gunned and newly-strengthened defences of the Narrows was taken in hand. On March 6th the Queen Elizabeth opened fire from the Gulf of Xeros, throwing her huge shells over the Gallipoli Peninsula and across the Narrows on to the forts of the Asiatic coast around Chanak. The 12 in. guns of the Agamemnon and Ocean fired in the same way at a range of 21,000 yards on forts Hamidieh I. and Hamidieh III. by Chanak. These forts had each four 14 in. guns, together with eight 9·4 in., one 8·2 in., and four 5·9 in. But they were utterly helpless against the far-flung indirect fire of "Big Lizzie" and her companions, coming over the hills from the unseen Ægean Sea.

Attack on Narrows' defences

furiously as they worked along. A squadron of allied destroyers answered the hostile guns and succeeded in keeping down their fire. The next day Fort Dardanus, on the Asiatic side, and Fort Suandere, on the Gallipoli side, were bombarded by the Canopus, Swiftsure, and Cornwallis. The German Ottomans then began to fight the fleet with greater power and fury. Every available field-gun and howitzer on Achibaba, or Tree Hill, and on the southern slopes of Pasha Dagh pitched high-explosive shells against the three British battleships. And Fort Suandere worked all its guns with the utmost speed. Each ship was struck, but their armour held good, and the only casualty was one man slightly wounded. At ten minutes to five on the winter evening the forts ceased to fire, being apparently badly damaged, and after continuing the bombardment for another forty minutes the battleships withdrew.

A fog the next day prevented observations as to the effect of the bombardment, but our landing-parties found that forty of the enemy's guns had been destroyed, including six modern field-guns near Cape Helles. On Wednesday, March 3rd, the French squadron steamed into the Gulf of

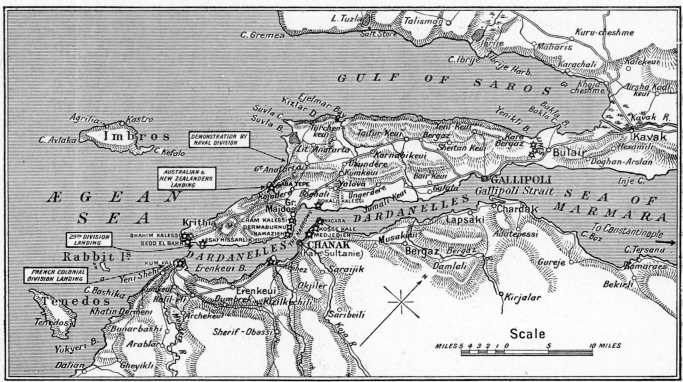

EXPLANATORY MAP OF THE OPENING OPERATIONS IN THE FIGHT FOR THE DARDANELLES.

We were then fighting the Turks and their German masters mainly with seaplanes. It was entirely the modern flying machine, carrying an officer with range-finding instruments and an instrument for wireless telegraphy, that made the bombardment of the Narrows practicable. Our naval airmen, darting about the sky, were alone able to direct the elevation and traverse of the great battleships' guns. The gunnery officers of the Queen Elizabeth could see nothing except the sandstone cliffs of the Gallipoli Peninsula and the scrub-covered heights of the Pasha Dagh beyond. Even if observation balloons had been used, at a distance of thirteen miles from the low-placed and masked forts and earthworks, no exact work of position-finding and spotting would have been possible. In some cases officers in the fire-control stations of battleships circling within the Straits were able to watch certain of the bombarded forts and signal the results of the fire to the Queen Elizabeth and her companions in the Gulf of Xeros. But this was not practicable in the attack on the most difficult defences of the Narrows. The task of directing the guns had to be carried out by airmen, and whenever there was a fog, or even a mist, the work of the fleet was seriously interrupted. The conditions of this extraordinary naval action were the same as those governing the action of land artillery in Flanders and France. Everything depended upon the clear vision of the observing airman. He worked at his best when the clouds were high and the weather calm. When the scene of action was veiled

Forts blanketed by mist

with haze, the guns could only be trained by means of measurements on the map, and as the effect of their fire was then incapable of being known, they were just as likely to be wasting costly ammunition and wearing away uselessly the tubing of the great naval guns, as to be damaging the enemy.

Little progress therefore was made in the bombardment during hazy weather, and there were also continual delays owing to storms. The tail-end of winter was indeed the worst of all seasons for naval operations in and round the Dardanelles. And as it was a mild winter, the flooding of the Black Sea set up an especially strong current in the Straits in February and March, and the general moisture of the air at the opening of spring led to the hostile forts and field-batteries being blanketed by mist for a week or more at a time. The upshot was that, soon after every hostile bombardment, the Germans were able to repair much of the

damage done. Only the old forts at the entrance were quite destroyed, and even at Helles and Kum Kale motor-batteries and new gun-sites were prepared close to the landing places, thus making the destruction of the old entrance forts an affair of small permanent importance.

The most notable achievement of the allied fleet in the first week of March was the effect produced upon the Italian mind. The "Giornale D'Italia," a newspaper closely connected with the Government of Signor Salandra and Baron Sonnino, urged the necessity for an Anglo-Italian agreement with the view to the intervention of Italy

Alarm in Constantinople

on the side of the Triple Entente. Other powerful organs of Italian opinion advocated the same policy, and the Government began to act in a most vigorous way with a view to the denunciation of the treaty with Austria and Germany. In Bulgaria and Rumania there was a similar strong current of public opinion in favour of intervention on the side of the Allies, the Bulgarians especially being excited by the prospect of renewing their struggle with their old enemies the Turks. In Constantinople was a deep and widespread feeling of alarm. Even the wife of General Liman von Sanders and the wives of many German officers fled to Bucharest, and the Germans were hissed by the crowd when they appeared in the streets.

All this, however, was due more to the prestige of the British Navy and to the British reputation for tenacity than to the actual amount of progress made in forcing the Dardanelles. But on March 9th the Queen Elizabeth entered the Straits for the first time and attacked the forts in the Narrows by direct fire. In the afternoon the fog again interrupted the bombardment, but the next day it was resumed with more fury, and with so much success that German military writers began to prepare their public for the forcing of the Narrows and the bombardment of Constantinople. The town of Chanak was wrecked, and only two minefields were said to be still intact. So by the end of the second week in March the Straits had been swept for twelve miles up to Kephez Point, and only a desultory fire from the field-guns assailed the ships using this stretch of water.

A grave mishap to the British cruiser, Amethyst, however, revealed the signal dangers of the whole enterprise. While inside the Dardanelles, apparently covering the mine-sweepers, she was suddenly fired upon by a concealed Turkish battery, and suffered terrible loss in a few minutes. As the result of a dozen hits by the Turkish guns one-fifth of her crew were put out of action. No detailed account of this unhappy affair, in which her men displayed the utmost gallantry, was published by the Admiralty, and this led to the absurdest legends obtaining credence. Thus it was said that she had run through the Narrows and entered the Sea of Marmora. The nation was thus allowed to rest under a complete misconception of the tremendous difficulty of the task before its Navy. For if a single light

Mishap to the Amethyst

ship could pass the Turkish batteries, it seemed to the uninstructed that it would be a simple matter for a fleet of battleships, protected by stout armour, to make the passage. Even German naval writers appeared at the time to suppose that the Amethyst had run through the Narrows, as far as Nagara Point, but this seems to have been only a modern Greek myth.

The Teutonic defenders of the Straits displayed an admirable patience and restraint in handling their big guns, allowing small targets, such as destroyers and light cruisers sent to draw their fire, to steam up without being attacked. Only the German motor-batteries, as a rule, fired on these small vessels. The allied naval commander naturally wanted to discover the positions of all the enemy's guns; and, like a chess-player sacrificing pawns with a design to get a strong line of attack on his opponent's more important pieces, Admiral de Robeck threw out his destroyers and a light cruiser or two and watched for the flashes from the great guns along the waterway. But the Germans were not to be drawn in this fashion. They suffered terribly at times from the long-range fire of the allied battleships, and if Turkish officers had been controlling the forts and earthworks the position of all the guns would quickly have been revealed. The Teutonic discipline, endurance, energy, and ingenuity with which the defence of the Dardanelles was conducted deserved high praise.

The Germans had their full reward when the first great attempt was made to approach the Narrows. This took place on Thursday, March 18th, a day of good weather and clear air, when the entire scene of operations was spread out in a bright picture at the feet of the observers on the island mountain of Tenedos. Above the low-lying hills on the Asiatic shore the view extended down to the wide first basin of the Dardanelles, with the shattered forts of Seddul Bahr by Cape Helles, and the stretch of low land at the village of Krithia, rising up to Tree Hill. Beyond Tree Hill was the valley of Suandere, from which mounted the great rocky clump of the Pasha Dagh. At the foot of the Pasha Dagh were the white walls of the village of Kilid Bahr, and it was here that the chief defences of the Straits were concentrated. They consisted of ten forts, lying opposite to the forts on the Asiatic side at Chanak. Immediately north and south of the main forts were five other batteries at the base of Pasha Dagh. On the Chanak side there were also three additional forts. Then, farther to the north, in the rocky bend of the Narrows by Nagara, there were two forts on the Gallipoli cliffs and three forts on the Asiatic promontory. As already explained, the Germans also had guns on the hillsides, some of them running on rails in and out of

excavated caves, while others were moved by motor-vehicles, or hauled along on a light railway track. Below the Narrows there was a fort at Kephez Point, and another fort opposite it on the Gallipoli cliff. Still more southward there was another fort by the ravine of Suandere. This was thought to have been silenced, as for some days it had made no reply to the fire of our ships, and the forts almost opposite it at Dardanus and White Cliffs seemed to have been put out of action. But, as a matter of fact, Suandere and Kephez forts, guarding the first narrow strait, were not much damaged by the preliminary long-range bombardment. The German gunners there were only reserving their fire for the great struggle.

At a quarter to eleven o'clock on Thursday morning the Triumph and Prince George entered the basin and began to shell these two forts. Then from the entrance to the Dardanelles the Queen Elizabeth, Inflexible, Agamemnon, and Lord Nelson shelled the forts at Kilid Bahr and Chanak. Every gun and howitzer on both sides of the Straits returned the fire, when at about twenty-two

WITH OUR NAVAL MEN IN THE DARDANELLES.
A big gun and its crew with ammunition in readiness. A transport is lying off the landing-stage.

minutes past twelve Admiral Guépratte led his squadron up the Dardanelles and engaged the forts at close range. All the ten battleships engaged were hit, but they silenced every gun at Dardanus and Suandere, and put Fort J at Kilid Bahr and Fort U at Chanak out of action. A German war correspondent at Chanak said that the town looked like being reduced to a rubbish heap. Gigantic walls, that had stood all the storms of four and a half centuries and seemed to have been built for eternity, heaved under the earthquake shock of the great shells and went up in hurtling lumps of earth and stone. Ship after ship steamed into the bay, fired her guns, and

The bombardment of Chanak

then swerved round in an ellipse, followed by other vessels, each in turn coming into the firing-line. Shells flew in all directions towards Dardanus and the howitzer batteries by Suandere and on the forts on both sides of the Narrows.

At Chanak there was a tremendous fire caused by the great shells of the Queen Elizabeth. The camp, barracks, and buildings used by the Germans were a heap of rubbish, and though according to the German statement only one

THE SINKING BOUVET—A FEW MOMENTS BEFORE
SHE DISAPPEARED.

A FEW OF THE SURVIVORS OF THE BOUVET ON BOARD A BRITISH
WARSHIP.

gun was destroyed, most of the others were overthrown
and buried in the earth, or otherwise temporarily disabled.
The same condition of things seemed to obtain round
Kilid Bahr when the action ceased at nightfall. Most
of the batteries were upset or covered with earth or thrown
out of position by great holes made beneath them. Had
it been entirely a contest of gun against gun, the battleships
would have dominated the Narrows sufficiently to allow
landing-parties of the Royal Naval Division to complete
the work of destroying the enemy's main defences. The
forts on the Gallipoli side especially suffered badly from the

**Work of the
Queen Elizabeth**

long-range fire which the Queen Elizabeth
poured into them from her position
under Kum Kale. One of her shells produced a tremendous outburst of flames,
rising like a volcanic eruption above the hills, and followed
by a great canopy of smoke. She also exploded a
powder magazine at Chanak.

Only two of the allied ships were seriously damaged
by the enemy's shells. The battle-cruiser Inflexible was
heavily hit, and her forward control position shattered by
a heavy shell, and the old Gaulois was also badly

damaged by the hostile batteries. All this, however, was less injury to the fleet than had been
reckoned in the most hopeful estimate of the cost
of the grand attack at close quarters. But just
when things were going well the first disaster
occurred. At twenty-five minutes past one all
the forts ceased firing, and six more of our old
battleships steamed inside the Straits to relieve
the Suffren, Gaulois, Charlemagne, and Bouvet,
with the Triumph and Prince George. But as the
Bouvet was returning in the basin, north of Erenkoi
village, she was struck by a mine. There was a
column of vapour followed by a spout of dense
black smoke, and in less than three minutes the old
battleship sank with most of her crew, six hundred
officers and men. There was only
a patch of bubbling water when
the Charlemagne steamed up to
try to rescue the drowning sailors.

**Loss of Bouvet
and Irresistible**

The ammunition of the Bouvet seems to have been
exploded by the mine, and the internal explosion caused
the ship to sink so quickly that only a few of the crew
had time to jump overboard.

It seemed pretty clear that the Germans were sending
Leon torpedoes down with the current, the torpedoes being
adjusted to float out of sight below the surface of the
water and strike the battleships at a considerable depth;
for as soon as the Bouvet sank, our mine-sweepers came out
under the terrible fire of the enemy's artillery and gallantly
swept the channel again through the minefield at the
approach of the Narrows. Nearly every night the Turks
used to row out in small craft from the shore, towing mines
with them, which they released in the middle of the
channel so that they would drift towards the entrance to
the Straits. This practice was well known, and the battleships always made a roundabout course in leaving Tenedos
Roads for the Dardanelles, in order to avoid the currents
along which the ordinary mines drifted.

Mine-sweeping, however, could not protect the fleet
against the Leon torpedoes; for about nine minutes past
four in the afternoon, as the Irresistible was steaming

THE LAST OF THE FRENCH BATTLESHIP BOUVET.
The Bouvet was blown up by a drifting mine in the Dardanelles on March 18th, 1915, and sank so rapidly that only 64 of her crew of 621 were saved.
The above photograph, obtained from another warship close by, gives a vivid impression of the vessel heeling over after striking the mine.

TRANSPORTS AT THE ENTRANCE TO THE DARDANELLES.

along in the firing-line, she also was blown up, and began to list heavily. Happily, she remained afloat for nearly an hour and three-quarters, and, in spite of the massed fire which the German guns poured upon her and upon all vessels that stood by to save her crew, our destroyers managed to save most of the officers and men. But scarcely had this been done when, at five minutes past six, the Ocean was also struck by one of the deadly missiles which M. Leon had invented. Again, with great skill and gallantry, practically the whole of the crew was safely removed under a hot fire. The work of rescue was done in a way that excited the admiration of the French sailors. The loss of life on the British ships was slight, having regard to the large scope and importance of the operations. But the loss of three old and slow battleships was a heavy price to pay for an unsuccessful attack upon all the principal fortresses of the Dardanelles. Our fleet had been badly defeated. Though the Secretary

Hidden instruments of defence of the Admiralty remarked at the time, "The power of the fleet to dominate the fortresses by superiority of fire seems to be established," this appears to have been a surprisingly sanguine interpretation of a series of staggering disasters.

For unfortunately it was not a question only of the comparative strength in gun fire of the ships and the forts. The German defenders of the Dardanelles had torpedoes of a new type, in addition perhaps to ordinary torpedo-tubes firing from the shore, and electrically-controlled mines along the channel. By these hidden instruments of defence they undoubtedly transformed the artillery duel on March 18th into an important victory over the bombarding fleet. The admiral in command of the allied naval forces was unable to resume the attack upon the forts until means had been devised for protecting the ships against floating torpedoes and drifting mines. Then a large allied army had also to be employed. The check was an affair of a more serious nature than the British Government were inclined to admit at the time.

The Ottoman victory in the Dardanelles much heartened the Turks and their German masters. Moreover, it greatly lowered the traditional prestige of Britain throughout the Ottoman dominions, and in the more independent Moslem world of Southern Arabia, Persia, and Afghanistan. Even in the bazaars of Egypt some gossipers began to speculate about a possible renaissance of the lordly power of the ancient Ottomans. In characteristic British fashion we had entered upon one of the grandest adventures of empire at a time when we were hard put to it in another direction. We had converted the Turk, with his traditions of French and British invincibility, dating from the Crimean War, from a half-dispirited opponent into a confident enemy. Such was the result of amateurish interference in the gravest problems of national strategy.

TURKISH SHELL FALLING PERILOUSLY NEAR H.M.S. ALBION IN THE DARDANELLES. INSET: VILLAGE AND FORT OF KUM KALE ON FIRE DURING THE BOMBARDMENT OF MARCH 4TH, 1915.

GREEK VOLUNTEERS WITH THE FRENCH IN THE NEAR EAST.

A BURIAL SERVICE—THE DEAD HONOURED BY THE FLAG.

ALGERIANS SALUTING THE WOUNDED IN THE DARDANELLES.

TURKISH PRISONERS CAPTURED IN THE DARDANELLES.

332

The Turk, after being badly defeated by Bulgarians, Serbians, and Greeks in the recent Balkan War, had come to Gallipoli and Chanak oppressed by the legend of the invincible British and with a romantic sympathy for the gallantry and daring of the French. Without the help of the German he would certainly have crumpled up and broke out in riot in Constantinople when the allied fleet assailed him with 12 in. and 15 in. shells. But the upshot of his victory in the Dardanelles was that the Turk fully recovered his self-confidence and **Turks' self-confidence** became, as his fathers had done at **recovered** Plevna, one of the most formidable fighting men of the world.

Equally important was the result of their victory upon the minds of the German commanders and officers who had conducted the principal work of defending the Dardanelles. They had been almost ready to accept defeat when the bombardment was proceeding vigorously. But when night fell on March 18th they became inspired to more severe efforts by a success with which they were themselves surprised. For example, the German officer in charge of the battery at Chanak had most of his guns damaged when

BREAD FOR THE TROOPS IN THE NEAR EAST.

FRENCH TROOPS ON THE MARCH AT MUDROS.

he ceased fire at half-past six on Thursday evening. But by working all night at high pressure he repaired the battery, and on Friday morning all the guns except one were again ready for battle. By the end of March even Kum Kale Fort, at the entrance to the Straits, was again active, a motor-battery having been placed in operation there by the Germans. Then across the water at Seddul Bahr field-guns were placed in earthworks to command the bay. Every night for five weeks, from March 18th to April 25th, the work of strengthening all the Gallipoli Peninsula and the Asiatic shore went on under the direction of the German officers. Our airmen could see long camel transport trains coming from the interior of Asia Minor towards the coast, and troops were concentrated from north and south to form the large Fifth Army, under the command of General Liman von Sanders.

It was in these difficult circumstances that the British nation benefited by the deeds of its fighting men of old. For though the puppet Sultan at Constantinople was proclaimed Ghazni, or victorious, by the Germans and Germanised Turks—who directed all the attitudes of the old feeble man—the ancient reputation for tenacity of Englishmen, going back to the days of Richard Cœur de Lion, served us well in all the Mediterranean countries

and in the independent Moslem States. It was not doubted that the surprising check to our imposing naval forces would quickly be retrieved. For some time the general opinion held that the allied fleet, which was reinforced by three more battleships—the French Henri IV. and the British Queen and Implacable—would again attempt to force the Dardanelles without waiting for a landing army. But stormy weather set in, and though the Black Sea Fleet of the Russian Navy tried to disconcert the enemy on March 29th by bombarding the outside forts and batteries of the Bosphorus, the attack on the Dardanelles was not resumed.

The fact was that the allied admirals had decided at a council of war that nothing more could be done without the help of a large army. The difficulties of the situation continued to increase. After the intervention policy of the Greek Prime Minister, M. Venizelos, was defeated by King Constantine, everything went wrong. As originally planned, the attack on the Straits was to have been a combined affair, in which twenty thousand Greek troops and eighty thousand French, Australian, New Zealand, British, and Indian soldiers **The Greek offer** would have taken part. It was the **withdrawn** withdrawal of the offer of Greek aid that led to the disastrous use of naval forces alone. For the Allies lost their arranged bases at Salonica and Mitylene, and though with the tacit consent of M. Venizelos the fleet continued to use as a base the Greek island of Lemnos, this very slight measure of assistance was also withdrawn by the new Greek Premier, M. Gounaris.

No spot remained near the scene of operations at which the allied troops could be collected, for the two neighbouring Turkish islands of Imbros and Tenedos were small and

TURKISH TORPEDO ATTACK ON THE BRITISH TRANSPORT MANITOU.

The Manitou was attacked in the Ægean Sea on April 19th, 1915, by a Turkish torpedo boat, which fired three torpedoes, all of which missed. The torpedo boat was chased, run ashore, and destroyed on the coast of Chios. Expecting the destruction of the transport (seen on the right), the troops took to the boats. Our photograph shows boats picking up men in the water, some of them from a partly submerged boat of the transport.

almost waste, with little accommodation. The bases to which the attacking force was reduced after the loss of Lemnos were Alexandria and Cyprus—both more than two days' steaming for transports going to the Dardanelles. Many more steamers had, therefore, to be engaged for the transporting, provisioning, and munitioning of the troops, with the result that the work of preparation occupied five weeks.

All this was a great gain to the Turks and Germans.

Prussian intrigues at Greek Court The Prussian intrigues at the Greek Court, leading to the sudden fall of the great Cretan fighting statesman, M. Venizelos, practically saved for a while the Ottoman Empire, and cost us many battleships and the lives of tens of thousands of men, When the Kaiser arranged for his sister to marry the Danish King of Greece, he accomplished without knowing it at the time one of the most brilliant strokes of diplomacy in history. For, as a well-known German military expert, Colonel Gaedke, stated in the first week in April, the Allies would have had a good chance of success had they launched both ships and troops against the Dardanelles early in March, according to the plan originally arranged with M. Venizelos.

As it was, when the allied army was ready to attempt to carry the Gallipoli Peninsula its task had become an almost impossible one. With five weeks' more work the German engineers had turned the hilly tongue of land into one of the most formidable fortresses in existence. From the lines of Bulair to the pom-pom battery at Cape Helles the Peninsula was about forty miles long. Its greatest breadth, just above the Narrows, was thirteen miles, but in other places southward it varied from one and a half miles to seven miles. The main attacks of the Allies were delivered against the narrow mile and a half tip, and the seven-mile mountain tract extending from the Ægean Sea to the forts round Kilid Bahr. The Turks had chiefly to defend about seventeen miles of coast, behind which were three clumps of high, broken ground, and a series of ridges and valleys. They had trenches on every cliff, arranged in lines one above the other; they had artificial caves containing machine-guns and small quick-firers; they had thousands of dug-outs, each containing a week's food and ammunition for a sniper. They had also some hundreds of miles of wire entanglements, usually concealed in the low thorny bushes that covered the hills, and line after line of entrenchments on every ridge; while the powerful German artillery was hidden in every possible way, especially by dug-out chambers in the hillsides.

Along the rampart of cliffs were only a few beaches, where landings could be made. Here the German sappers

A MAN FROM THE MANITOU ALONE ON A RAFT.

The casualties in connection with the attack on the Manitou were twenty-four drowned and twenty-seven missing. The above photograph was taken from a vessel which took part in the rescue. One of the survivors was rescued from a raft on which he was found floating alone.

PART OF THE WALLS OF SEDDUL BAHR AND OLD CANNON LYING IN THE SEA AFTER THE BOMBARDMENT.

INSIDE VIEW OF THE FORTIFICATIONS OF SEDDUL BAHR SHATTERED BY SHELLS FROM THE ALLIED FLEET.

ONE OF THE HEAVY CANNON USED IN THE DEFENCE OF SEDDUL BAHR.

THE BEGINNING OF THE FIGHT FOR THE DARDANELLES.

Remarkable camera pictures of the Turkish defences at the western entrance to the Dardanelles after the Franco-British bombardment. The lower photograph shows part of the outer walls of the fortifications. In circle: Trenches and cannon behind Seddul Bahr, with panoramic view of the Turkish fortress town.

had constructed wire entanglements beneath the shallowing sea, to hold up the troops as they left the boats and waded to the shore. In all cases these underwater obstacles were commanded by machine-guns hidden in holes in the rock or earth, and invisible to any reconnaissance from the decks or fighting-tops of the battleships. The exact number of Turkish troops with German officers garrisoning this " Gibraltar " of the Dardanelles is not known. About 100,000 men were available at the beginning of the action, but they were enormously reinforced from Adrianople and from Asia Minor, and at last a considerable part of the army opposing the Russians in the Caucasus Mountains was transported to this most vital area of conflict. Through the Bulair lines northward and across the Narrows eastward the Army of Gallipoli, as it weakened under the immense slaughter, was continually **Shells to Turkey** strengthened by three-quarters of the **through Bulgaria** entire military forces of the Ottoman Empire. Moreover, the Germans and Austrians were able, in spite of the strain upon their cartridge and shell factories, to pour a great store of ammunition into Turkey through Bulgaria. Our attacks on the Dardanelles in March and April so used up our supplies of shells that our First Expeditionary Force between Ypres and La Bassée was for a time starved of high-explosive shells in some critical weeks of the spring campaign.

Altogether the cost to Great Britain of the attempts to force the Straits between the Mediterranean and the Black Sea was very heavy ; and no small part of this cost was borne by Sir John French and his men in Flanders. A considerable number of our best troops, who would otherwise have been available in the main theatre of the war, were diverted, together with enormous stores of shells and war material, to the attack upon the Dardanelles. But it must always be remembered that our strong and tenacious action in this apparently secondary field of warfare may have brought about, in May, 1915, the intervention of Italy and the launching of her great Army on the flank of Austria-Hungary. Our naval losses also were more than compensated when the battle squadrons of Italy stripped for action and prepared to engage the Austrian Fleet. On the other hand it might be more strongly contended that Italy was moved at last more by the difficulties of the Allies than by their successes. She joined the Triple Entente after a series of grave reverses,

notably the Russian defeat in Galicia and the British defeat in the Dardanelles.

Certainly, from a military point of view, the operations in the Gallipoli Peninsula were extremely serious. Sir Ian Hamilton, one of our most distinguished generals, who had first been designated to lead our new Fourth Army in France, was now appointed Commander-in-Chief of the Mediterranean Expeditionary Force. Serving under him were General d'Amade, the conqueror of Morocco, commanding a division of Senegalese troops and Zouaves, Major-General **Sir Ian Hamilton's** Birdwood, commanding the Australian **appointment** and New Zealand contingents, and Major-General Hunter-Weston, commanding the British 29th Division. There were sixteen battalions of Australian infantry and some four battalions of New Zealand infantry, with engineers and artillery. A British naval division, an armoured-car division, and a number of naval air squadrons took part in the battles. A hundred and fifty ships were needed to transport the troops from their Egyptian base.

These set out on April 21st, but instead of making direct

SEDDUL BAHR DEFENCES.
Part of the Turkish fortifications at Seddul Bahr after the bombardment by the Allied Fleet.

for the Turkish coasts they put into the roomy Bay of Mudros, on Lemnos Island, waiting for the most favourable weather.

The spectacle in the great bay was wonderfully imposing. The ships varied in size from the Queen Elizabeth to the blue fishing smacks of the islanders. Famous liners, which have carried the British flag in every sea, were collected into a fleet of transports of the largest size ever seen, and the warships covering the entrance to the bay with their guns formed one of the mightiest naval forces.

AFTER THE BOMBARDMENT OF SEDDUL BAHR.
Seddul Bahr is situated on the north side of the entrance to the Dardanelles. Our photograph shows a mill that was struck during the naval shell fire.

CHURCH SERVICE ABOARD H.M.S. QUEEN ELIZABETH IN THE DARDANELLES.
Above are seen the huge muzzles of the warship's 15 in. guns. The photograph was taken by the official photographer to the Dardanelles Expedition.

This great fleet, composed of spare vessels of the British and French Navies, had to guard against an attack by hostile torpedo craft. The thoughts of many Frenchmen and Britons went back to the days when their forefathers set out under Richard of England and St. Louis of France on the early Crusades. Now men from lands undiscovered in the days when the Turks first rose to power were uniting with their kinsmen of the chief crusading nations of Europe in what was probably the last crusade the Christian world would ever make against the Turks.

Even in the age of St. Louis a German Emperor had been ready to conclude peace with the Saracens in order to have his hands free to ravage the fairest cities in Northern Italy. Now the infidel Hohenstaufen was

Hohenzollern and Hohenstaufen succeeded by another Suaban tyrant, the Hohenzollern, who had reduced the Turks to vassalage with a view to a greater attempt to reduce the enlarged modern world into a German dominion. It was notorious that the mad dream of the Hohenzollern was based upon romantic memories of the Hohenstaufen, whose excessive lust of conquest had ruined Germany and had crippled her for six centuries. But, by forcing the Turks to league with him, the new German Emperor had shown less talent for statecraft than his mediæval model; for Turkey had at once become the pivot of a new turning movement in the politics of the Balkans and the Mediterranean countries. By putting an end to the Turkish neutrality the German intriguer had given the Allies a lever by which they might bring Italy, Rumania, and even Bulgaria, over to their side simply by undertaking the last and the greatest of the Crusades.

For three days the huge fleet of transports and warships in Mudros Bay waited for the period of calm, settled weather that was needed to make a landing. Sir Ian Hamilton was faced with a larger and more difficult task than his fellow Scotsman Sir Ralph Abercromby had undertaken in March, 1801, in Aboukir Bay. In one day's violent action on a flat shore, commanded only by sandhills, Abercromby had made a landing in Egypt in the face of a storm of shot and had driven back the enemy. From the fighting-tops of our ships our modern soldiers and sailors could see through their glasses the beach in Asia Minor where Abercromby had practised landing tactics for weeks with all his troops and **Hamilton follows Abercromby's example** seamen before he sailed for Egypt. Sir Ian Hamilton followed Abercromby's example, and while the fleet waited at Mudros Bay every soldier was taken from the transports and trained at embarking and disembarking from warships and troopships to the shore and from the shore to the ships. The bluejackets showed the men, heavily laden with their kits and rifles, how to climb up and down the ships' sides by means of rope ladders, how to row and steer the disembarking boats, and how to use boathooks.

By general consent the Australian, New Zealand, and Tasmanian troops were the finest body of men ever sent forth by any country to the field of battle. The average height in some of the battalions was close on six feet, and every man looked like a trained athlete. Many of the privates held better positions in civil life than their officers.

THE TOWN OF GALLIPOLI AT THE ENTRANCE TO THE SEA OF MARMORA.

these operations were dependent on the state of the capricious spring weather, and a rough sea would leave one part of our army ashore while its main force and its supplies were held off the coast. The beaches were very few in number, the rampart of steep cliff being practically continuous, especially on the side where the Australasians proposed to land. Above the cliffs were hostile gun-positions on the inland hills commanding every line of approach.

This led to an intensely democratic spirit in the Australasian Army, with excellent discipline, however, and a keenness for battle which was quite extraordinary. The attack on the Suez Canal had been a disappointment to the men from the lands of the Southern Cross. They were eager for as tough a job as the regular British Army had undertaken at the Aisne, at Ypres, and at Neuve Chapelle. In the Dardanelles they obtained what they wanted. For in the new Plevna the stubborn courage and magnificent endurance of the Turks and the powerful armament and superb organising skill of the German Staff gave our Second Expeditionary Force, consisting of about a hundred and fifty thousand men, one of the most arduous and terrible combats in all the annals of warfare. To speak

No surprise attack was possible at the end of the Peninsula. There were only six beaches there, and the 29th Division, under Major-General Hunter-Weston, made a straight rush from the boats at each landing-place, and by hard, furious, and unceasing fighting drove the Turks back and obtained a footing. The Australasians, however, were

Imposing spectacle
at Enos

LIGHTHOUSE AND ROCKS, GALLIPOLI.

VILLAGE OF BULAIR FROM THE SOUTH-WEST.

quite plainly, we were faced in the Dardanelles with a task that verged on the impossible. Half a million men at least were needed to carry it through. Even with half a million men it would have been a hard, long, and costly operation. The Turks and Germans had

Accomplishing the seemingly impossible good reason to suppose that they could drive every landing-party back into the sea, as in the first weeks of the battle they announced they had done. Only men of British stock, exalted to a height of heroism surpassing that of their forefathers, could have accomplished what our Second Expeditionary Force achieved. For they accomplished the seemingly impossible.

Sir Ian Hamilton had to land an army in the face of an enemy who had had full warning for two months that a landing in force would be attempted. He had to put on shore food, water, guns, horses, ammunition, and a thousand articles necessary to keep an army in the field, and to make arrangements to remove a large number of sick and wounded. All

luckier. It seems to have been originally planned that they should row to a beach by the promontory of Gaba Tepe, on the Ægean coast, some miles northwest of the point which the British were storming. In order to weaken the opposition which the Australasians would meet, our Naval Division set out in advance of them, and made great preparations to force a landing more northward near Suvla Bay. This was only a continuation of the earlier demonstrations by our fleet. Our sailors had steamed to Enos, close to the Bulgarian frontier, and made a show of clearing the way for the landing of the whole of the Expeditionary Force there. The spectacle at Enos was so imposing that the King of the Bulgarians came to watch the great landing battle. But it was only a British ruse to draw Turkish troops away from the Gallipoli Peninsula and misdirect any immediate reinforcement from the real field of conflict. The demonstration against Suvla

BRIDGE AT KAVAK DESTROYED BY FIRE OF ALLIED BATTLESHIPS IN MARCH, 1915.

Bay later was similarly intended to move the Turkish troops away from Gaba Tepe. It was successful in achieving this end, and it prepared the way for the splendidly audacious feat of the Colonial contingents.

On Friday morning, April 23rd, the stormy weather subsided, and at five o'clock in the afternoon the first transport steamed out of Mudros Bay, followed by other huge liners, all their decks yellow with khaki battalions. The bands of the fleet played them out, and the crews of the warships cheered them on to victory. The last salutation from the fleet was answered by a deafening cheer from the soldiers on the troopships. Then the Australasian division of liners, with its assistant battleships, steamed towards Gaba Tepe, which was made about one o'clock a.m. on Sunday, April 25th. It was a beautiful, calm night, with the sea lit by a brilliant crescent moon ; the soldiers rested in preparation for their tremendous exertion, and were afterwards served with a last hot meal. At twenty minutes past one the boats were lowered, and the troops fell in on deck and embarked in the boats, in complete silence and with great rapidity, without a hitch or accident of any kind.

The steam-pinnaces towed the boats towards the shore, the great battleships also steaming towards the land. By ten minutes past four the three battleships arrived two hundred and fifty yards from the coast, which was just discernible in the starry darkness, the moon having sunk. The boats, which had been towed behind the great warships, now went ahead, in snake-lines of twelve, each boat being crowded with troops so that the gunwale was almost flush with the water. The operation was timed

An historic Sabbath morn so as to allow the boats to reach the beach in darkness before daybreak, so that the Turks would not be able to see the targets before the Australasians reached the land. Every eye was fixed on the grim, sombre sweep of cliff and hill just in front, which was so dark and silent that it seemed as if the enemy had been completely surprised.

But at ten minutes to five, as the leading boats approached the beach, an alarm light on the hill flashed for ten minutes. It was soon followed by a burst of rifle fire from the beach, where the Turks were entrenched. Soon a British cheer rang out and the rifle firing diminished as the dawn broke in a haze at half-past five on this historic Sabbath morn.

As some of the steam-pinnaces returned men learnt what had happened. When the Australians were about two hundred yards from shore the enemy opened fire with rifles and machine-guns. Happily, most of the bullets went high, yet many men were hit in the crowded boats. In grim silence the others rowed with all their might till they reached the five-foot watermark. Then, without waiting for orders, the troops leaped into the sea and waded to the beach, and there, forming up roughly, they charged at the line of flame marking the first Turkish trench. The men of the landing-party had been warned not to fill their magazine rifles until daybreak, as a hot rifle fire from them would have given the enemy's batteries the target they were vainly searching for in the darkness. The Australians, therefore, used only their bayonets.

Australians use their bayonets

In about a minute they had taken the trench on the beach, captured a Maxim gun, and killed or dispersed all the defenders. Facing the small victorious force was a steep cliff, like the cliffs of Folkestone. It was covered

HOISTING THE "AERIAL" AT A NEW WIRELESS STATION ON THE SUEZ CANAL. IN CIRCLE : FIXING WIRELESS APPARATUS FOR FIELD WORK. THE INDIANS WERE PARTICULARLY INTERESTED.

with thick undergrowth, and about halfway up it was another trench, from which the enemy directed a terrible fire on the beach and on the boats. Three boat-loads of men were wiped out before they could land, and the troops of the first landing-party dropped in large numbers from bullets poured on them from three sides. The Australians flung down their packs and climbed up the cliff, lifting themselves up from foothold to foothold by clutching at the shrubs. In less than a quarter of an hour most of the Turks holding the **A complete surprise** cliff trench were killed by the bayonet **attack** or put to flight. The Australians cut through the wire entanglements just before the sky whitened at daybreak and made a complete surprise attack.

When the sun rose, and the outlines of the yellow coast and the green hills beyond became clear, it was seen that a happy mistake had been made. Instead of landing at Gaba Tepe, just north of the rocks, the boats had turned in the darkness towards Sari Bair, a great clump of sand-stone rock rising from nine hundred and fifty to nine hundred and seventy-one feet. At the intended landing-place there was a long slope from which the enemy

seamen pulling each boat. They had to row the troops to the beach under fire, return under fire for more troops, and continually repeat the process during the early part of the day, in which it was impossible to check the enemy's fire. It was here that British midshipmen, many of them boys of sixteen fresh from Dartmouth, where they had only received a few months' training, conducted themselves with an heroic coolness recalling the best traditions of the midshipmen of Nelson's days. To the older men, naturally, the extraordinary gallantry of the lads was very moving.

It is indeed said that some of our sailors were at last unable to resist the temptation to join in the fight. Taking rifles from the wounded troops, they left their boats and fought with the soldiers. One party of seven sailors attacked a band of two hundred and fifty Turks, and the Colonial troops were delighted with their helpers, and induced them to stay on with them. This was the reason why so many small boats were abandoned on the Gallipoli coast. It was not altogether in keeping with good naval discipline, but the blood of the sailors was up, and they could not resist an opportunity for joining in the fight on the slightest pretext. The admiration felt by the seamen for the soldiers was high and intense. The two Services were soldered together by that manly love of comrades which is the supreme source of the fighting spirit of heroic peoples. There were times when our men melted like women and stooped above their dead, kissed them, and then went out in white, Berserker-like fury to fall in their turn upon the foe. Heroism, like panic, is contagious. It was an epidemic of heroism that kept our men going at Gallipoli as it had kept them going at Ypres. Modern education, and particularly the general habit of daily newspaper reading, had made all men of British stock somewhat more susceptible in mind than their forefathers. But this suscepti-bility of intelligence had not weakened the old fundamental qualities of character. The Australasians, especially, were quite a new type of Britons. They were both fire and granite —volcanic lava—and the fight they put up on Sari Bair

VIEW TAKEN BY OFFICIAL PHOTOGRAPHER OF THE INTERIOR OF THE DISMANTLED FORTRESS OF SEDDUL BAHR.

could have poured a terrible fire. But at Sari Bair there was only a forty-foot stretch of sand, where the sand-stone cliff rose almost sheer from the edge of the water at flood-tide. After the Australians had stormed the cliff in the darkness the situation of the Colonial contingent was by far the best throughout the expeditionary force. There was no slope down which hostile infantry could fire, and the bluffs, ridges, and broken ground formed good cover to the troops after they had passed the beach.

In other respects, however, affairs were extremely difficult when the sun rose. For it shone right in the eyes of the gunners on the battleships, and prevented them from supporting our infantry attacks. On the other hand, the Turkish sharpshooters, with the light behind them and the clear breadth of sea in front, could direct a deadly fusillade upon every target. Some boats, having broken away from their tows, drifted down the coast under fire. One came near the shore with only two Australians un-wounded in it. The two men jumped into the water and dashed furiously into the fight. Meanwhile, the task of the seamen running the boats from the beach to the troopships became very perilous. There were from six to eight

was a thing of epic quality.

The speed, violence, and drive of their first attack were unparalleled in British warfare. The ground they worked over was a confused triangle of ridges, ravines, bluffs, dales, and long slopes, stretching across the Peninsula to a point above the Narrows. The surface was either bare, crumbly, yellow sandstone, or a dense undergrowth of shrub about six feet in height. It was so broken that Turkish snipers were able to work a few yards in front of our lines without being spotted. No movement on a large scale could be regu-   **First landing** larly organised, for as soon as the men   **battle won** moved forward in open order they were lost to the view of their officers in the thick scrub. It was the most remarkable of all soldiers' battles, for the winning quality was the initiative and resource of the leading men of each section, clambering over cliffs, working their way up and down ridges, much of the work being done even without directions from the corporals.

By the time the sun had fully risen the Australians had gained the first ridge of Sari Bair, and by a quarter-past nine the first landing battle was won; for the

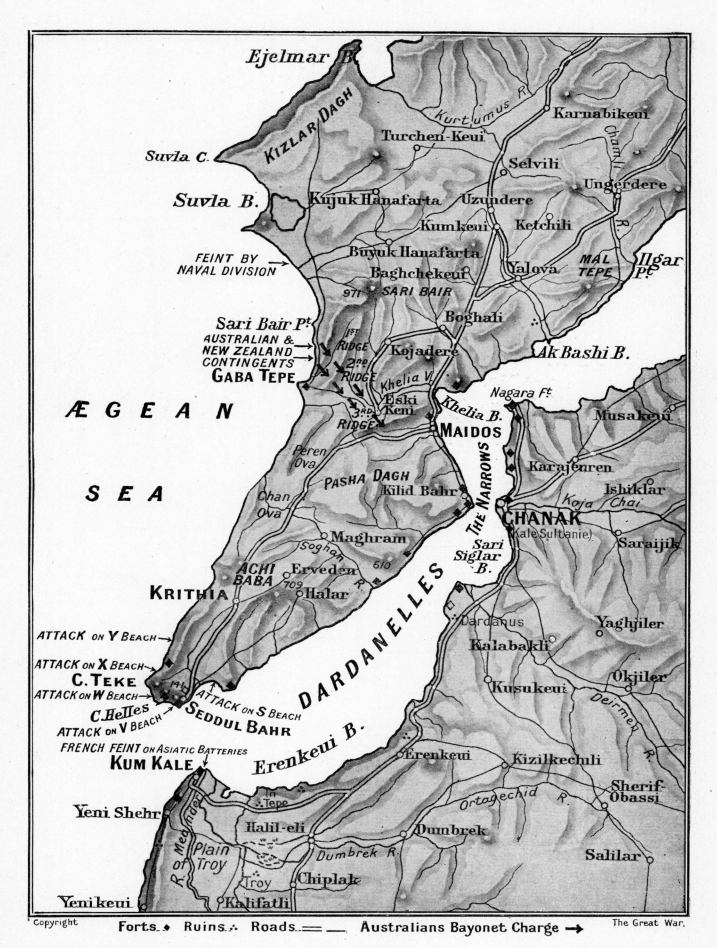

Ejelmar B.

KIZLAR DAGH

Suvla C.

Suvla B.

Karnabikeui

Turchen-Keui

Selvili

Kujuk Hanafarta   *Uzundere*

Kumkeui   *Ketchili*

Buyuk Hanafarta

FEINT BY
NAVAL DIVISION

Baghchekeui

971   SARI BAIR

Yalova

Ungerdere

MAL
TEPE

Ilgar
Pt.

Sari Bair Pt.
AUSTRALIAN &
NEW ZEALAND
CONTINGENTS

GABA TEPE

1ST
RIDGE

2ND
RIDGE

Boghali

Kojadere

Ak Bashi B.

Nagara Ft.

Khelia V.

Eski
Keui

3RD
RIDGE

Khelia B.

MAIDOS

Musakeui

Æ G E A N

S E A

*Peren
Ova*

PASHA DAGH

*Chan
Ova*

Kilid Bahr

THE NARROWS

Karajenren

Ishiklar

Koja Chai

CHANAK
(Kale Sultanie)

Saraijik

Maghram

*Soghan
R.*

610

*Sari
Siglar
B.*

ACHI
BABA

Erveden

709   *Halar*

Dardanus

Yaghjiler

KRITHIA

Kalabakli

Okjiler

ATTACK ON Y BEACH

ATTACK ON X BEACH

C. TEKE

ATTACK ON W BEACH

141

ATTACK ON S BEACH

C. Helles

ATTACK ON V BEACH

SEDDUL BAHR

FRENCH FEINT ON ASIATIC BATTERIES

KUM KALE

Erenkeui B.

D A R D A N E L L E S

Kusukeui

Deirmen R.

Erenkeui

Kizilkechili

Sherif-
Obassi

Yeni Shehr

In.
Tepe

Halil-eli

R. Medinder

Plain
of
Troy

Troy

Dumbrek

Dumbrek R.

Ortagechid R.

Salilar

Chiplak

Yenikeui

Kalifatli

Copyright   Forts◆ Ruins∴ Roads═══ Australians Bayonet Charge ➔   The Great War.

MAP OF THE DARDANELLES AND GALLIPOLI PENINSULA, SPECIALLY DRAWN TO ILLUSTRATE
THE OPERATIONS BY LAND AND WATER WHICH BEGAN IN THE SPRING OF 1915.

FRENCH SOLDIERS IN CAMP AT SEDDUL BAHR SORTING OUT THE KITS OF THEIR DEAD AND WOUNDED COMRADES.

covering force of Australians held such a firm footing on the crest that the intense fire of the enemy died away, and though sniping went on throughout the day the dis-embarkation of the remainder of the force proceeded without interruption save from shrapnel shells. The position of the victorious battalions was, however, very difficult. The proper thing for them to have done was to have entrenched on the conquered ridge and waited for the main force to disembark. But the ground **Surprise for** was so broken and scrubby that it was **German commander** hard to find a good entrenching line. When the troops thought they had cleared a space they were still subjected to a continual and punishing fire from the snipers.

Then as the light became good the German gunners on the heights brought their artillery into action. There were first two guns at Gaba Tepe, which enfiladed the landing beach with shrapnel. But one of our cruisers moved in close to the shore and battered the sandstone rocks with high-explosive shell so that the enemy guns there were silenced. In the meantime the Australians on the crest, smitten on both flanks and worried all along their front, began to move out in search of their foes. The fact was their landing at Sari Bair had been quite a surprise for the German commander. Only a weak force had held the beach, and only a scattered body of snipers occupied the mountain, trying to hold back the Australians until the Turkish divisions, sent towards the wrong places round Suvla Bay in the north and Gaba Tepe in the south, collected in the afternoon at Sari Bair.

The Australians worked northward and eastward in a series of fierce bayonet rushes. Then, encouraged by the slight opposition they met, they went ahead in a burst of charges down the ravines and up the ridges. The

Turks and Germans played every possible trick. They had machine-guns in the scrub, the men working the guns having their hands and faces stained green, with boughs and bushes tied about them. There were dug-outs every-where, each with its sniper, a German or Macedonian marks-man, with several days' food, and ammunition up to two thousand rounds. Some of them would fire till the Australians were five yards off, and then ask for quarter. Naturally they did not get it. Others tried the stretcher game on the raw recruits from oversea. A stretcher-party dressed in a uniform of khaki came to a trench crying " Make way for the stretcher-party!" However, the Australians had been doing a good deal of newspaper reading in Egypt, and something in the accent and the look of the stretcher-bearers made them suspicious. They opened fire, killed a German and a dozen painted Turks, and found in one stretcher a machine-gun and in the others three boxes of ammunition.

When the Australians in turn found an enemy trench they did not take the trouble to capture it by a ruse. One of the first works on the heights was stormed by a man famous for his reach and great strength. He jumped into the trench and lifted the Turks out of it with his bayonet, driving the steel **Fury of** through their bodies, and then flinging **Australian onset** them over his shoulder in a movement that released the blade for the next stroke. He killed five men in this way, but could do no more, because his com-panions had finished the other Ottomans. This bayonet work went on all the morning, the Australians still advancing by the fury and rapidity of their onset. Their leading troops worked down the Khelia Valley, and by one of the most tre-mendous efforts in history they seem to have crossed the last and third ridge and got within a few hundred yards of

BRITISH ENCAMPMENT IN THE VICINITY OF THE DARDANELLES. VESSELS OF THE ALLIED FLEET IN THE OFFING.

ROAD-MAKING UNDER THE PROTECTION OF THE GUNS—ONE OF MR. ASHMEAD-BARTLETT'S DARDANELLES PHOTOGRAPHS.

ANOTHER VIEW OF A BRITISH BEACH ENCAMPMENT NEAR THE WESTERN ENTRANCE OF THE DARDANELLES.

TURKISH DEFENCES ON THE GALLIPOLI PENINSULA SHATTERED BY THE FIRE OF THE ALLIED FLEET.

In the fighting on Sunday the Colonial contingents probably lost more men than did the enemy through the covering force advancing across the Peninsula without waiting for their supports. Whatever the losses of the Australians were, they and the New Zealanders and Indians had their full revenge when they held the ridge and prevented the Turks from driving them into the sea; for the Turks attacked in dense formations all during Sunday night and Monday morning. Our troops met them in the British way—reserved their fire, and then emptied their magazines at point-blank range into the advancing masses. A single Australian platoon, supported by

Maidos, the key to the Narrows. In front of them, across the water, was Nagara Point. Had it been possible to make this attack in force and bring up guns and entrench on the ground won in the extraordinarily impetuous charge, the road to Constantinople would practically have been conquered in a few hours.

But the vehement covering force of Australians had gained more ground than it could hold. There were only two or three thousand troops, without food or guns, and lacking even in Maxims. Most of their work had been done with the bayonet, and in the afternoon the German commander brought his main force against them and almost outflanked them. But at the critical moment the New Zealanders came to the help of the Australians, and after retiring from the third ridge back to their early position on the first ridge, the gallant Colonial troops dug themselves in. Then the Indian troops disembarked, and after the second rush of the Austral-asians, the combined and strengthened force of Australians, New Zealanders, and Indians again advanced to the third ridge, after repulsing some furious counter-attacks by the Turks.

Turks' horrible torture of wounded

As twilight fell the enemy brought up more reinforcements, and his counter-attacks were supported by a heavy bombardment of our position from hostile batteries which our naval guns could not reach. So dangerous did the pressure on our lines become that Major-General Birdwood drew the troops back to the first ridge during the night, and his Staff devoted all their energies to strengthening the position and getting some field-guns ashore to deal with the enemy's artillery. The Australians had suffered heavily in their first retreat from the point near Maidos. Nearly a fourth of their force was put out of action, and by a dreadful misfortune the wounded men of their leading companies fell into the hands of the Turks and were horribly tortured and mutilated before being put to death.

RUINS ON GALLIPOLI PENINSULA AFTER THE BOMBARDMENT.

Marines, was charged by half a battalion of Turks. They waited till the Turks were ten yards away, gave them the mad minute of rapid fire, and then leaped forward in turn and smote the remaining upright figures with hand-grenades. No Ottoman who took part in that charge escaped. All along the front on Sunday night the conflict continued with an intensity like that of Le Cateau and Ypres, for Liman von Sandars had a similar advantage in artillery power, and he used the Turks in shoulder-to-shoulder lines, advancing in human billows against the British front.

When Monday morning dawned the landing battle at Sari Bair was won, in spite of the fact that another Turkish army corps was moving up on the north-east for the grand assault which was to drive our men into the sea. The German artillerymen had brought all their guns into play and had moved up more batteries for the final bombardment. During the whole of Sunday **Landing under** night the hostile gunners had maintained **rain of shrapnel** a rain of shrapnel over the landing beach, with a view to hindering our disembarking operations and disabling our troops when they were impotent to defend themselves. Our battleships had tried to support the troops by a heavy fire from their secondary armament, but as the enemy's gun-positions at this time were not known our ships could not do much to keep down the enemy's fire.

But on Monday morning the position was reversed. The Turks could clearly be seen moving in large numbers along the heights, and the position of their supporting batteries could be spotted by their flames. Moreover, every time they had fired in the darkness of Sunday night naval fire-control officers in the fighting-tops of our battleships had been spotting the flashes and comparing notes and measurements. The Queen Elizabeth and seven other warships steamed up to take part in the grand battle. The seven older ships moved close inshore,

Turkish barbarities avenged each of their chief gunnery lieutenants having a marked map of this section of the enemy's territory. "Lizzie" stood farther out to sea, so as to get a howitzer effect with her guns by pitching the shells as high as possible into the dales, where our airmen reported the enemy were gathering for shelter preparatory to the advance.

Then, as the Turkish infantry moved forward to the attack, they were punished for all that they had done to the Australian wounded. Every kind of shell carried by our warships was thrown at them, from the 15 in. shrapnel of the Queen Elizabeth to the little shell of the 12-pounders. The thunder and concussion made by the

was visible, and a similar cloud of cordite could be seen southward of Cape Tekeh, where another division of British battleships was canopying the hill of Achibaba with another continual burst of shrapnel fumes. Nearer at hand a battleship and a cruiser, close inshore at Gaba Tepe, were covering the low ground with their secondary armament and dropping shells into the Straits on the other side. Then beyond the battleships the great liners, in which the troops had been transported, lay out to sea to avoid the Turkish guns.

On land we still kept the enemy back by rifle and machine-gun fire. For two hours the Turks pressed their attack, while our naval guns inflicted terrible losses on them and our infantry smote them down in heaps before our trenches. But in spite of all the scientific instruments of slaughter employed on both sides, the great landing battle ended in a primitive way. It could be seen that the Turks were becoming demoralised by the overwhelming fire of our naval guns. The German officers found it difficult to bring them up to the attack, and had to pack them closer than ever in order to keep control over them.

Major - General Birdwood at last let **Position at Sari Bair** them advance through our shrapnel zone, **secured** gave a general order for rapid fire, and then, after the magazine rifles and machine-guns had done their work, there was a flash of steel along the trenches. The Colonial troops leaped out with the bayonet and charged the staggered, reeling Turks, who broke and fled.

They were bayoneted in the back as far as the shrapnel zone. But here our troops fell back, and, in answer to a wireless message, the eight warships turned all their guns on the fugitive enemy and pounded them with shrapnel. On Monday afternoon our position at Sari Bair was secure. The trenches were deepened so that our men could not be shaken by shrapnel fire, and though the Turks were still in overwhelming numbers in

THE BROKEN FORTRESS OF SEDDUL BAHR.

entire armament of the great naval squadron were beyond description. The hills on which the Turks were collecting were transformed into smoking volcanoes, the common shell forming craters hung with black smoke, while the 15 in. and the 12 in. shrapnel burst in white canopies over the exploded rocks and uprooted bushes. An enemy warship tried to reply across the Peninsula, but the Triumph nearly struck her with two 10 in. shells, and she retired to a safer position, from which she was able to do no damage. Our ships were soon hidden from the troops they were protecting by vast rolling clouds of cordite. But the day was so clear that all the coast-line

CORNER OF THE FORTRESS OF SEDDUL BAHR AFTER BOMBARDMENT BY THE BIG GUNS OF THE QUEEN ELIZABETH.

LANDING OPERATIONS IN THE DARDANELLES. REMARKABLE CAMERA-RECORD OF THE VARIED ACTIVITIES ON BEACH V, TAKEN BY THE OFFICIAL PHOTOGRAPHER FROM THE S.S. RIVER CLYDE.

comparison with the troops we had put ashore, they were too much demoralised to attempt another attack in force. Only their snipers continued to harass our lines on Monday night. Some of our field-guns were landed, with several Indian mounted batteries, and our entrenchments were firmly established on a wide front, covering the whole of the foreshore on which disembarking operations were still proceeding.

Like General von Kluck at Maubeuge, who announced to his General Staff that he had got the British army in a ring of iron, General von Sanders had been so confident of the success of his plan that he had proclaimed in advance that he had driven our Second Expeditionary Force into

Von Sanders' over-confidence

the sea. This news was published at Constantinople in the same way as Kluck's anticipation of an event which never happened was wirelessed to all the world from Berlin. The German General at Gallipoli had expected to find at Sari Bair a line thinly held by Colonial troops exhausted by their losses and labours of the previous day of landing. His aim was to force this thin line into the sea by a great concentration of infantry and an unceasing bombardment by shrapnel shells. But, as of old, thin lines held by men of British stock were not easy to break. The Australians and New Zealanders had from the first been determined to a man to die rather than give up the ground they had won at such heavy cost on Sunday, for they knew it would have been impossible to re embark the army if the ring of hills commanding the beach had been lost.

Most of the men were volunteers who had only had a few months' training, and had come under fire for the

346

first time in circumstances calculated to try the nerve of veteran troops. The sixteen thousand Australian infantrymen had suffered badly on Sunday, and should have been, therefore, capable of being demoralised by an attack in overwhelming numbers. But the Australians were not made that way. All they wanted to do was to avenge their dead. No man cared what happened to himself, except that he regretted when he was wounded and so prevented from killing more Turks. Not since the French Revolution have new recruits fought with such combined impetuosity, steadfastness, and long-sustained fury as the Australians and New Zealanders displayed when their foes gave them the opportunity of exacting full revenge. For every mutilated, tortured Australian soldier left in the bush in the retreat from the Narrows a hundred Turks died the next day.

Australasians' impetuous valour

On Tuesday morning, April 27th, a fresh Turkish division was brought up to Sari Bair and launched against our trenches after a heavy bombardment by the German batteries. But the result was the same as on Monday. The Turks came on time after time, and were shot down in multitudes, and by three o'clock in the afternoon all the spirit of the twelve thousand fresh hostile infantrymen was broken. The Australasians again advanced with the bayonet and won more ground, enabling them to strengthen their defences. All that the German commander then could do was to maintain a curtain of shrapnel over the beach and the neighbouring waters, in order to impede the disembarking operations. But the hail of bullets made little impression on the work on the pinnaces, boats, lighters, and tugs, and the seamen who manned them; for though the shrapnel bullets churned up the water with the spectacular effect of a hailstorm, the material damage inflicted by the intense and costly bombardment was slight. Certainly it was out of all proportion to the expense, labour, and intrigue which the Turks and Germans had been put to in collecting their store of munitions in Gallipoli. The more shells they used on "Folkestone Leas,"

Shells on "Folkestone Leas" as the stretch of foreshore and cliff was called, the less shells they would have when the final tussle opened. Nothing could budge the Colonial troops, and by all working like frenzied navvies, building roads, making concrete works, dragging guns up the cliff, constructing bomb-proof shelters, and turning their stretch of foreshore into an invisible town, they fortified their position between Sari Bair and Gaba Tepe so that they were able to reduce the garrison and send a considerable force to help the British troops at Seddul Bahr, at the end of the Peninsula.

As in Flanders, France, and Egypt, so in the Dardanelles the Indian troops proved themselves of high and splendid courage, fighting with great skill and tenacity. To their help the Australians were much indebted. But owing to the widely separated scenes in which the warriors of India continually fought—at La Bassée and Neuve Chapelle, along the Suez Canal, and at Sari Bair and the southern end of the Gallipoli Peninsula—the achievements of the Indian peoples in all the work of the war is difficult to appreciate. So it may be worth while, at this important point in their warlike task, to interrupt the main narrative and bring out the value and scope of the aid given by India to the Empire. Then in the following chapter we can continue the story of the Dardanelles operations and describe the series of magnificent feats accomplished by the 29th Division on the beaches of the southern end of Gallipoli Peninsula.

INDIAN TROOPS, JUST LANDED FROM THE DARDANELLES TRANSPORTS, ON THEIR WAY TO THE FIRING-LINE
UPPER PHOTOGRAPH: LOADING AMMUNITION FOR USE AGAINST THE TURKS.

INDIAN MAXIM SECTION

CHAPTER LXI.

IN THE FIELD.

THE GREAT WAVE OF LOYALTY AND IMPERIAL ENTHUSIASM IN INDIA.

Bernhardi's False Prophecy—Germany's Mistake—Lord Hardinge's Splendid Work—Caste, Customs, Prejudices, and Religious Differences Placed Aside—Surendranath Banerjee's Eloquent Testimony—Loyal Attitude of Responsible Moslems—The King-Emperor's Message—India's Military Strength—Importance of the Native States—Contributions of the Ruling Princes—Their Offers of Personal Service—Arrival of the Indian Expeditionary Force at Marseilles—A Royal Greeting—Sir James Willcocks's Stirring Order of the Day—How the Indians Bore Themselves in the Field—Memorable Charge of the Bengal Lancers—German Plans to Confuse and Perplex the Indians—An Example of Prussian Audacity—Lord Roberts's Visit to His Old Comrades-in-Arms—The Indians at Neuve Chapelle—Effect on India's Future of the Services of Her Sons in Europe—A Typical List of Gifts to the Indian Government.

NO more confident prediction was made in Germany in the days before the Great War than that immediately Britain was fighting for her existence India would rise in revolt against her.

The Indian chiefs—Nizam and Nawab, Maharaja and Raja, Shah and Prince, Sawbwa and Rao, princes of ancient lineage and hereditary power—were one and all to seize this chance of striking off the shackles of our rule. Moslem races, fired to fanaticism by the careful preaching of a Holy War from Constantinople, were to fly to arms against Great Britain. The ancient jealousies of the hundred and one peoples who make up our vast Eastern Empire were to be rekindled, and a greater mutiny was to drive the hated British into the sea. Here a Maharaja was to lead his old troops upon us; there the advocates of native rights were to provoke the people to rise. A witches' cauldron of hatred and strife was to be stirred, and Britain was to be robbed of the brightest jewel in her crown.

Bernhardi, the prophet of the new Germany, exultantly forecasted this. "There is another danger," he said, "which concerns England more closely, and directly threatens her vitality. This is due to the Nationalist movement in India and Egypt, to the growing power of Islam, to the agitation for independence

in the great Colonies, as well as to the supremacy of the Low German element in South Africa. In India some 70,000,000 of Mussulmans live under English rule; but now that a pronounced revolutionary and Nationalist tendency shows itself amongst the Hindu population, the danger is imminent that Pan-Islamism will unite with the revolutionary elements of Bengal. The co-operation of these elements might create a very grave danger capable of shaking the foundation of England's high position in the world."

This was what many sober and carefully informed German leaders expected. For years they had studied India microscopically. Numbers of German officials, representatives, and secret agents —from the Crown Prince on a visit of State to the underling whose work it was to promote unrest in the bazaars—had examined and reported on India from east to west. They knew all about the secret societies plotting against Britain. Every speech railing at us was carefully noted. Every bomb-thrower's deed was marked as another nail in the coffin of our Empire.

The Germans made one great mistake. They took notice of the slight movements of unrest which came to the surface as the scum rises to the top of the great waters. But they did not realise that for every one revolutionist there were a thousand satisfied supporters of our rule, and ten thousand who were content to live

VISCOUNT HARDINGE OF PENSHURST, VICEROY OF INDIA SINCE 1910.

[Elliott & Fry.

348

Bourne & Shepherd.]

H.H. The Nizam of Hyderabad.

[Bourne & Shepherd.

H.H. The Gaekwar of Baroda.

Barton, Son & Co.]

H.H. The Maharaja of Mysore.

[C. Vandyk.

H.H. The Maharaja of Gwalior.

Mobile mountain battery from the frontier of Afghanistan in use in France.

Detachment of Indian cavalry on the march near the Franco=Belgian frontier.

Indian infantry carrying Maxims into action under fire in France.

Indian infantry on their way to support the British at the front in Northern France.

351

Bourne & Shepherd.]

H.H. The Maharaja of Kashmir.

[C. Vandyk.

Sir Pertab Singh, Regent of Jodhpur.

C. Vandyk.]

H.H. The Maharaja of Bikaner.

[Bourne & Shepherd.

H.H. The Maharaja of Patiala.

their life peaceably under the British Raj, without troubling their heads with affairs of State. The native rulers, whom they pictured as shackled and fretting under the limitations of British supremacy, knew very well that never before had they or their people enjoyed such sustained abundance, such general prosperity, and such peace. Part of the unrest which the Germans observed so closely was actually due to the fact that in India there was little for the ancient warrior tribes to do. The old dominant and dominating races—the men of Hyderabad, Jaipur,

Wonderful harvests of goodwill and Gwalior—now found their fighting arms growing stiff for want of exercise. Idleness sometimes leads to mischief.

The Germans did not understand that in recent years the British Government had, by a policy of Imperial reform, done everything in its power to meet the natural native demands for increased self-government. Lord Morley had introduced schemes which now were bearing wonderful harvests of goodwill. The King-Emperor and the Queen-Empress, by their visit to India at the close of 1911, and their solemn crowning at Delhi, had made themselves real personalities to their Indian subjects, and their visible power, dignities, and goodwill appealed forcibly to the imagination of an Oriental nation. India was fortunate in having Lord Hardinge as Viceroy at this time, a statesman whose great work for India was even more appreciated by the rulers and people there than understood by people at home.

If our enemies were astonished and disconcerted at the conduct of India immediately after the outbreak of war, it may be admitted that they were not the only people to be surprised. The British did not expect that India would be so blind to her own interests as to play into the hands of Germany. But few among us had the imagination or the courage to anticipate the overwhelming wave of loyalty and Imperial enthusiasm which swept over the race. As the news travelled over the wires that the Empire was at war, the hand of India flew to its sword. Rulers of the great States summoned their armies together and hastened to offer all they had to their Emperor. From the Nizam of Hyderabad down to the chieftains on the Indian frontier ruling over a few villages the response was the same. The great princes offered money—scores of lacs of rupees ; they offered their very jewels ; they presented their soldiers, their horses, and their guns for their Emperor's service. The ruler of the ancient State of Rewa sent one question, "What orders from his Majesty for me and my troops ? " The Punjab Chiefs' Association passed a resolution expressing the determination of the Punjab aristocrats to serve Britain in war as well as in peace. Even the Grand Lama of Tibet proffered his aid. The Bengalee merchants raised big war funds. Most wonderful of all to those who know the East, the women of India broke the conventions that kept them from public life, and, from the Maharanis on their thrones to the humblest wife of Hindu, Moslem, or Parsee, they brought forward their silver and gave their personal gifts for the men at the front. India reached still greater depths of sacrifice. Men broke even the barriers of caste to serve, and as one Indian speaker truly said, " Indians have renounced every-

thing—caste, customs, prejudices, and religious differences —and laid down their lives to fight for their King."

Those Germans who believed that India would aid them had counted especially on two classes—the advocates of greater self-government and the Mohammedans. The former were represented by the Indian National Congress, a gathering in which on some occasions bitter criticisms had been heard of certain aspects of British rule. The Indian National Congress of 1914 opened in December, and for the first time in its history the Governor of the province in which it was held was present. No criticisms of Britain were heard now. Surendranath Banerjee, the famous Nationalist leader, voiced the feelings of his people when he declared : " The best prospects of India are linked up with the permanence of British rule. We desire to proclaim to the Kaiser and to the enemies of England that behind the British Army is the whole Indian people, who as one man will defend the Empire and die for it. The loyalty of India is consecrated by the blood of our fellow-countrymen who have died in Europe. If England demands it, the last pice we have and the last drop of blood

INDIAN SOLDIERS SORTING LETTERS INSIDE AN HOTEL WHICH WAS BEING USED AS A MILITARY POST-OFFICE.

that flows through us will be at the service of the Empire."

" This is not the time to deal with matters upon which we may differ," said the President of the Congress, Bhupendra Nath Basu. " We must present to the world the spectacle of a united Empire. India can put a wall of Indian soldiers in the field against which the German militarism will hurl itself vainly. India is oblivious of the past and impregnated with the future."

The attitude of the Moslems proved **Hindu and Moslem** equally disappointing to our foes. When **loyalty** Germany had succeeded in inducing Turkey to go to war with Great Britain there was a possibility that the Moslem peoples might, under the influence of religious zeal, join in a Jehad against us. The most fantastic stories were spread abroad. The German Emperor had, it was confidently reported, himself become one of the faithful, and was leading the hosts of the faithful against the infidel. Great Britain, it was rumoured, intended

INDIAN MAXIM-GUN SECTION IN FLANDERS.

BENGAL LANCERS—A PHOTOGRAPH TAKEN JUST AFTER THEIR LANDING IN FRANCE.

to make the Caliph—the religious head of the faithful—the mere subordinate of itself, to dictate his appointment, and to control him. Here and there in Central Asia, and in some parts of Africa, the more ignorant Moslem peoples rose to the bait. In India, while there was undoubtedly some danger and much uneasiness from the poorest and most ignorant sections of the Moslem races, the responsible Moslems knew Britain better and threw all the weight of their influence and authority on our side. Many of the ruling chiefs called their peoples together and urged on them that this was no religious war and that the Koran did not require them to fight for Turkey. "Turkey has made herself a tool in Germany's hands," said the great Moslem leader Aga Khan. "She has not only ruined herself, but has forfeited the position of trustee of Islam."

Aga Khan's view of Turkey

The Nizam of Hyderabad, the premier native ruler of India, issued a manifesto declaring that " it is the bounden duty of the Moslems of India to adhere to their old and tried loyalty to the British Government, whose cause I am convinced is right and just. I give expression to the hope," said he, " that as I, following the traditions of my ancestors, hold myself ready to devote my own person and all the resources of my State and all that I possess to the service of Great Britain, so will all the Mohammedans of India, especially my own beloved subjects, hold themselves wholeheartedly ready in the same way."

Even women leaders spoke for us and worked for us. One of the most important of them among Mohammedan rulers is her Highness the Nawab Begum of Bhopal, a progressive modern woman of the East, the only ruler in India of the female sex, who combines a strict Mohammedanism with modern methods. Among the faithful she is famous for having made a pilgrimage to the holy cities of Arabia.

Among westerners she is known, among other things, for the deep interest she takes in education and for her work for the higher education of the sons of the ruling chiefs. Her family is traditionally loyal. Since one great occasion, in 1778, when they stood by Colonel Goddard in days of great danger, the fidelity of the rulers of Bhopal has been proverbial. The Begum rose to the occasion. When the first whispers of disaffection among Mohammedan peoples were heard she called her officers and all her leading men together and addressed them. She told them with the utmost earnestness and conviction that Turkey was wrong, that this was no fight of Islam against Christianity, but a fight in which Great Britain was standing for world-liberty and justice. She did more than talk. She poured out the resources of her State for the Empire, and contributed men, horses, and money for the cause. She sent her heir-apparent, the Nawab Nasrulla Khan, a minor, to the front in command of the Bhopal contingent of troops. She joined forces with the Maharaja of Gwalior in organising and raising funds among the chiefs for the Indian hospital-ship Loyalty, which was to prove so useful in the months ahead.

Begum of Bhopal's example

The Council of the All-India Moslem League, at a meeting at Lucknow, assured the Viceroy " that the participation of Turkey in the present war does not and cannot affect our loyalty in the least degree, and that the Council is confident that no Mussulman in India will swerve even a hair's-breadth from his duty to the Sovereign." Private Moslem gentlemen of influence urged all of their faith to assist the mighty British Empire, pointing out that under the rule of their Emperor they had perfect religious freedom.

The difficulty of giving, in a reasonable space, an adequate idea of the doings of the Indian peoples in the Great War lies in the vast extent of our Eastern Empire and the variety and multitude of its peoples. They are numbered by hundreds of millions. They talk among them twenty-four native languages, apart from minor dialects. They differ among themselves in the most amazing way in religion and in their manner of living. What relation is there, it may be asked, between the fierce fighting tribes of the north and the meek ryot of Bengal? What is the link between Calcutta the Splendid and the barren marches under the shadow of the Himalayas? How, it has often been asked, can all these diverse fabrics be woven into one vast nation? How can a Rajput and Bengalee, Afridi and Hindu, man of Madras and man of Kashmir join in common aspiration and united nationhood?

When war broke out the British Government had to decide whether or not it should use Indian troops against European peoples. The ruling princes of India, the soldiery, the men of the fighting north, and the very Indian students in London demanded the right to serve. They felt that, with the vast issues at stake, unless they showed themselves willing and obtained the right to take actual part in the fighting in the war, India could never hope to rise to the place she desired in the Empire. The British Government had, however, to keep other considerations in mind. Throughout India the people are taught respect for the white man. To many of them he is seen solely as an administrator, a ruler, and a judge. To bring scores of thousands of Indian troops into intimate contact with the working peoples of Europe might, it was felt, lower the white man's prestige. In the Boer War these considerations prevailed, and, greatly to the disappointment of the Indian peoples, and despite their most urgent demands, they were not employed on active service. "This," they were told, "is a white man's war." But early in the Great War the British Government decided that Indian troops were to be employed in Europe, and a message was sent from the King-Emperor to the princes and peoples of India which touched the emotions of the whole of the Far East. The King-Emperor's message, part of which has been quoted already on page 194 of Vol. II., was as follows :—

To the Princes and Peoples of My Indian Empire :
During the past few weeks the peoples of my whole Empire at home and overseas have moved with one mind and purpose to confront and overthrow an unparalleled assault upon the continuity of civilisation and the peace of mankind.
The calamitous conflict is not of my seeking. My voice has been cast throughout on the side of peace. My Ministers earnestly strove to allay the causes of strife and to appease differences with which my Empire was not concerned. Had I stood aside, when, in defiance of pledges to which my Kingdom was a party, the soil of Belgium was violated and her cities laid desolate, when the very life of the French nation was threatened with extinction, I should have sacrificed my honour and given to destruction the liberties of my Empire and mankind. I rejoice that every part of the Empire is with me in this decision.

The King-Emperor's message

Paramount regard for treaty faith and the pledged word of rulers and peoples is the common heritage of Britain and India.
Among the many incidents that have marked the unanimous uprising of the populations of my Empire in defence of its unity and integrity, nothing has moved me more than the passionate devotion to my Throne expressed both by my Indian subjects and by the Feudatory Princes and the Ruling Chiefs of India, and their prodigal offers of their lives and their resources in the cause of the Realm. Their one-voiced demand to be foremost in the conflict has touched my heart and has inspired to the highest issues the love and devotion which, as I well know, have ever linked my Indian subjects and myself. I recall to

mind India's gracious message to the British nation of goodwill and fellowship which greeted my return in February, 1912, after the solemn ceremony of my Coronation Durbar at Delhi, and I find in this hour of trial a full harvest and noble fulfilment of the assurance given by you that the destinies of Great Britain and India were indissolubly linked.

The British Government had considerable forces of different kinds in India upon which it could draw. In the first case there were 75,000 British soldiers, the regular Indian garrison. It would not have been wise to deplete this garrison too much, but it was possible to take away large numbers of trained and hardened soldiers and to replace them by Territorials. Next there came the regular Indian Army, an army strong in numbers, rich in traditions, and trained to a point of high efficiency. The regular Indian Army numbered 160,000 men, including over 3,000 British officers and officials, and it had 40,000 reserves to be drawn upon. It was largely raised from the fighting Mohammedan races, and in the years immediately before the war, starting with the time when Lord Kitchener was Commander-in-Chief, its entire organisation had been remodelled and its artillery and transport brought up to a war standard. It would be difficult in the space of a few paragraphs to give any adequate notion of the traditions that lie behind this Army, traditions which even the hour of madness of the Great Mutiny could not wholly wipe out. The Indian Army is drawn in the first place largely from the military peoples of the Punjab. High in rank among its soldiers are the Sikhs, acclaimed by many as some of the finest fighting men in the world. They are the military adventurers of the Far East. They

India's military resources

SIKHS ON THE MARCH IN FRANCE. THE SMALLER PHOTOGRAPH AFFORDS A GLIMPSE OF THE GURKHAS EN ROUTE FOR THE FRONT.

AN INDIAN SCOUT ON DUTY ON A WAR-WORN HIGHWAY OF FRANCE.

Sweden ! I wonder if everyone calls to mind that the Maharaja of Gwalior has more subjects than the King of Denmark ; or that the Nizam of Hyderabad governs a people twice as numerous as the people of the Netherlands and three times as numerous as the people of Ireland."

The native States are a series of semi-independent kingdoms and principalities, some of vast extent, rivalling England in size, some mere collections of hill-side huts, whose entire area can be surveyed from a neighbouring height. In all they cover about 700,000 square miles. Their princes retain, with some limitations, their ancient state and dignities. External affairs are controlled by the Indian Government. In each State there is a British Resident, a carefully selected high official who exercises a certain limited supervision and guides the ruling prince when necessary, by friendly counsel, in promoting honest administration and good government. It is not his business to interfere in any way with the ordinary affairs of State. But it is his business to be a man to whom the prince and his advisers can go in hours of real need for advice and aid. If a bad ruler arises, who wastes the resources of his State in notorious corruption and extravagance, the British Resident endeavours to restrain him, and if he fails, the ruler may even be deposed. The reigning families are encouraged to bring up

adhered to our side in the days of the Mutiny, and have done much good work for us since, and are men of fine physique, strong principles, born soldiers. The Rajputs, the fighting tribes of the Punjab, have served us well, as have the Dogras, the Pathans, the hillmen of the north, the Afridis, the Baluchi, the Jats, and the Sujars. The Brahmin regiments, charged through and through with pride of race and pride of caste, boast of their soldiery. Then come the little Gurkhas, whose reputation as hill fighters, as stealthy breakers into enemy entrenchments, as scouts, and as men who with their knives alone are more dangerous than most soldiers with magazine rifles, spread throughout the German ranks long before they reached Europe. The Garhwalis, fighting hillmen, small and lithe, are very like the Gurkhas, and yet distinct from them. The Mahrattas, drawn from the Deccan, have given us many regiments. The Mohammedan peoples of the Eastern Punjab and of Hindustan are represented both in infantry and in cavalry. From the Madras

Importance of Indian Native States Presidency come admirable regiments of Mohammedans, Tamils, and Pariahs.

In addition to the regular Indian Army there were other forces for the Crown to draw upon, the volunteers, including Anglo-Indians, numbering some 40,000 and the Imperial Service troops from the native States, numbering over 20,000, and capable of being increased to eight or ten times that total within a reasonable time.

Few people outside of India realise the great place the Indian native States hold there. " I wonder," said the Marquis of Lansdowne on one occasion, " whether everyone realises that the Maharaja of Mysore rules over a population which exceeds in numbers the whole of the population of

their young princes in the hardy, open-air fashion, and with the discipline of European royal families, rather than in the old luxury traditional for princes in the East.

The result of this British influence, wise, prudent and constantly applied, had been to create a revolution in the ways of many of the native States. The palace of the prince no longer continued to be the centre of elaborate celebration, but had become the organising headquarters of capable, strenuous, reforming rulers. Education, sanitation, and modern medicine had been introduced, and more rights for the women had been granted and secured. The prince, formerly rarely seen abroad, save in hours of state when, decked with jewels, he lolled lazily atop of his elephant, moving through his obsequious subjects, went freely among his people in his Norfolk jacket and riding-breeches. Often enough he drove his own motor-car. He was alive and alert. " Our fathers were brought up to be idle," said one of the great rulers of India recently to a European visitor.

The lesson of " Noblesse oblige " " Enjoyment and extravagance were held up before their eyes as the most sacred duties. It is in our English schools that we have been taught the lesson of *noblesse oblige*. Where our forebears were living riotously at the cost of their subjects, Indian princes to-day are working hard to advance the weal of their people."* Britain had given to these Indian princes, the rulers of the native States, security on their thrones, and peace for their people, and had aided them to make the most of the resources of their States. Many years ago the question arose what return in the way of military service they could make to us. The rulers of

* " A German Staff Officer in India." London, 1910.

the different States desired to maintain large armies of their own at their own cost, and in the old days they did so. There were, however, two drawbacks to this. The expense of these armies ate considerably into the State revenues, and, in the hands of doubtful princes they were always a potential danger. On the other hand, it was recognised that they were also a source of potential strength. This was proved in the Indian Mutiny, when troops from the native States helped the British splendidly. In 1885, after the Pendjeh incident, when Britain seemed at the point of war with Russia, it was decided to regularise the military system of the native princes. Regiments were raised in each State, under the control of their own rulers, known as the Imperial Service troops, whose training, equipment, and arms were similar to those of the regular Indian Army. They were supervised by an Inspector-General, and represented a force of 20,000 of as good fighting men as could be wished for. It was understood that they would be at the call of the Imperial Government when required.

From the beginning it was the ambition of the ruling princes to have their soldiers employed in the battles of the Empire. At every sign of war they were among the first to come forward with the offer of their armies, accompanied often enough by the offer of themselves. In many of the border expeditions, in Somaliland, at the relief of Chitral, and in the expedition to China the Imperial Service troops did well. All who knew India were confident that the native princes would again hasten with offers of help, and this expectation was not disappointed.

Let us go down the list of these rulers, whose names and dignities themselves give us a glimpse of the romance and splendour of India, and note what they did at this time. First come the Nizam of Hyderabad, the Gaekwar of Baroda, and the Maharaja of Mysore, the three rulers each entitled to a salute of twenty-one guns, the outward symbol of their rank.

The Nizam of Hyderabad, ruler of the largest and most important State in India, who governs a population of over thirteen million people, and who measures his domains by the scores of thousands of square miles, **Nizam of Hyderabad's princely gift** made gifts worthy of his position and State. He sent a contribution of sixty lacs of rupees (about £400,000) towards the expenses of the war, the largest individual donation received by the Government of India. He desired to make his contribution equal to that of his late father, who subscribed a similar amount to the British Government during the Russian crisis of 1885. The rulers of Hyderabad have been ever loyal, and in accepting the Nizam's gift

the Viceroy wrote that it was only one more proof, if such were needed, of the Nizam's intense patriotism and devotion to the British Raj. In addition to this, the Nizam also expressed a desire to defray the entire cost, while on active service, of the 1st Hyderabad Imperial Service Lancers and of the 20th Deccan Horse, of both of which regiments he was honorary colonel. These State troops were among the first to be accepted for active service with the Expeditionary Force, and did marked service on the Continent.

The Maharaja of Mysore made a magnificent gift of fifty lacs of rupees (£333,000) for expenditure in connection with the Indian Expeditionary Force, a gift which stands out as one of the most munificent of the princely contributions received by the Indian Government. The Maharaja also placed at the disposal of the Government his cavalry—the Mysore Imperial Service Lancers—a splendidly-equipped regiment of picked men and horses, which was soon to earn distinction on the field of battle in France.

A RUDE CHANGE FOR INDIANS: FROM THEIR NATIVE SUNSHINE TO THE FROZEN TRENCHES OF FRANCE.

The Maharaja of Mysore, his Highness Shri Sir Krishnaraja Wadiyar Bahadur—who rules, as has already been said, over a population which exceeds in numbers the whole of the population of Sweden—is a prominent example of many of the great Indian princes, who by their personal example are bringing their people to new stages of efficiency. The success and prosperity of his great State is known everywhere. Its progress owes much to his own fine leading. "It is not government, nor forms of government, that have made the great industrial nations of the world," he declared in a notable speech, "but the spirit of the people and the energy of one and all working to a common end."

THE INDIAN TURBAN IN A FRENCH RURAL SETTING.

The Maharaja of Mysore is essentially a working prince, who not only devotes his time and attention to the affairs of his State, but who has displayed throughout his reign sound sense and real business ability. He is well known as a fine horseman, a keen rider to hounds, a polo and racquet player, and a musician of taste and skill. He is deeply interested in racing, and his colours are familiar at the great race meetings of India. He is also interested in motors, and frequently drives his own cars with nerve and ability.

The Gaekwar of Baroda, his Highness Shri Sir Sayaji Rao III., has long been a familiar figure in England and America, where **Baroda a modernised East** his princely splendour, his great hospitality, and his essentially modern outlook on life have made him the object of much attention. His State is one of the richest and most fertile in India, and maintains an army of 1,500 cavalry, 3,182 infantry, and 93 artillery. He has for years been active in the introduction of reforms among his people. Believing that the mastery of the modern world will be won by the educated, he has enforced compulsory education among his subjects. Baroda under his rule represents a modernised East. In the Boer War his

Highness offered to supply the British Government with horses for mounted troops in South Africa, an offer that was gratefully accepted. Now, in addition to subscribing liberally to the leading war funds, he placed all his State troops and all his resources at the service of the King-Emperor.

There is, perhaps, no more outstanding figure in India to-day than Major-General Sir Pertab Singh, the veteran chief of the fighting Rajputs and Regent-Maharaja of Jodhpur. Sir Pertab Singh demonstrated years ago that the fire of his race burns in his veins with undiminished power. He is a great soldier and has seen much active service—in China, in the frontier campaigns, and elsewhere. Lord Roberts **The veteran Sir Pertab Singh** counted him among his closest personal friends. The Rajput chief was seventy years old when war broke out. He at once demanded that he should be allowed to serve in person with the Expeditionary Force, and before he left for the front in company with his young nephew the Maharaja of Jodhpur, who was only sixteen years old, and with four of his sons, he made a touching farewell speech in the forenoon to the great crowds that assembled to bid him farewell. "Englishmen are shedding their blood like water for the great cause," said he. "Now is the time for the Rajputs to show their gratitude

INDIAN INFANTRY TAKING MAXIM GUN FROM MULES TO CARRY IT INTO ACTION AGAINST THE GERMANS.

to the British Raj and shed their blood for the King-Emperor." As the train left, the crowd sent up a shout of "Victory to the British Emperor!"

Another great military figure in India was the Maharaja of Gwalior, who also saw active service in China and in the Chitral and Tirah campaigns. His Highness was particularly anxious to accompany the Gwalior State troops with the Indian Expeditionary Force, but, to his great regret, this was found impossible owing to reasons of State. Unable to serve in the field personally, he devoted himself to helping the cause in other ways. He provided thousands of horses for remounts, contributed handsomely

[Ernest Brooks.

H.H. THE BEGUM OF BHOPAL.

[Bourne & Shepherd.

H.H. THE MAHARAJA OF BARIA.

[Backhouse.

THE NAWAB OF SACHIN.

[B. Framji.

H.H. THE RAJA OF SITAMAU.

[Bourne & Shepherd.

H.H. THE MAHARAWAL OF DUNGARPUR.

to the Prince of Wales's Fund, sent £5,000 for the sufferers in Belgium, and planned, in co-operation with the Begum of Bhopal, the hospital-ship Loyalty for the Indian wounded. The Maharaja's best-known gift was the splendid motor-ambulance fleet, purchased at a cost of £22,000. When King George inspected this fleet of motor-cars, motor-lorries, and motor-cycles at Buckingham Palace, and accepted them in the name of the Navy and the Army,

Gift of motor-ambulance fleet he telegraphed to the Maharaja : " This is yet another proof of your unswerving loyalty to my throne and person, and of your thoughtful interest in the welfare of the Empire."

The ruler of the State of Kashmir, Major-General his Highness Maharaja Sir Partab Singh Bahadur, subscribed to the Indian Fund for the equipment of the Expeditionary Force, and spoke at a great meeting of twenty thousand persons at Srinagar in support of the fund. He worked enthusiastically at the task of stirring

Service Transport Corps, which he had raised, for service with the Indian Expeditionary Force, an offer gratefully accepted by the Imperial Government. This corps had already seen service in the Chitral and Tirah campaigns, and consisted of 1,200 ponies, 558 folding iron carts, 16 ambulance tongas, and 775 officers and men.

Another of the ruling princes who volunteered for active service at the front was the Maharaja of Bikaner, one of the most popular of the Rajput chiefs. Colonel his Highness Sir Ganga Singh Bahadur of Bikaner had long been known in India for his splendid public and military services. As far back as 1899, when, a young man in his teens, his State was threatened with ruin through the great famine of that year, he organised the resources of his people, and provided for relief in a way remarkable in one little more than a lad. Then came the British Expedition to China in 1900. The Maharaja commanded the Camel Corps from his own State, which did most valuable service both there and later on in Somaliland. In the days of peace which followed he showed ability to adjust himself to the new conditions of New Asia. He inaugurated a representative assembly for his State in order that his people might be developed along the way of constitutional government. When news came of the outbreak of war he placed himself and the entire resources of his State at the service of the Crown.

He wrote to the Viceroy and offered both his Camel Corps and the Sadul Light Infantry for immediate service, and offered to enrol and equip 25,000 of his subjects as a special emergency Imperial Service Contingent. As he reminded Lord Hardinge, his ancestors had done similar service in the Mutiny. The Maharaja's Camel Corps proved of great service in Egypt. On one occasion when patrolling to the east of the Suez Canal it came on a much larger Turkish force, attacked it and beat it off.

It is well known that the fighting Rajput chiefs took part in the war against Germany with special vehemence, because some of them had been subjected to constant insults by German officers during the Allied Expedition to Peking

SOME OF THE OFFICERS OF OUR INDIAN TROOPS IN FRANCE PARTAKING OF A FRUGAL LUNCH IN CAMP.

up his people to support the Government and do everything in their power to bring the war to a speedy and successful conclusion. The troops from his State were soon to distinguish themselves across the water. The Maharaja was sixty-two years old, and his great State, covering just over 79,000 square miles, contains some of the finest and most picturesque scenery in the Empire.

The State of Jaipur ranks among the most prosperous and best governed in India, and for this its people have largely to thank the keenness, the far-sightedness, and the reforming spirit of their present Maharaja. He has spent crores of rupees in modern improvements. He has provided free education throughout Jaipur, and to-day there are 1,135 schools and colleges there. The Jaipur School of Arts is famous throughout the world. His Highness contributed in the most generous manner in men and money for the war. His personal gifts included £19,800 for the Indian Expeditionary Force, £6,600 for the Prince of Wales's Fund, £6,600 for the Imperial Indian Relief Fund, and many minor gifts. He offered the Imperial

in 1900. The Germans had openly treated them as coolies, and flaunted their honours and dignities. The chiefs knew the Germans for what they were. Thus the Maharaja of Bikaner, in talking with an English correspondent about this time, said that even fourteen years before, when he first came **Germany's treatment** into contact with German methods of **of the Indians** warfare, he was pained and astonished to note their ruthlessness. On one occasion, after the capture of Peking, he heard a German officer gloatingly tell a group of British Staff officers that he had raided some villages that day and had killed every Boxer he could find. Asked how he identified the Boxers, he replied that he searched every man to be found, and shot anyone who had on his clothing or about his person anything coloured red, taking that to be sufficient evidence of his identity with the Revolutionist movement. Another Rajput chief, when learning that he could go on service in Flanders, muttered with stern satisfaction," Now I'll show them who's the coolie."

The young Maharaja of Patiala, a prominent member of

[Vandyk.

H.H. THE MAHARAJA OF JODHPUR.

[F. Bremner.

H.H. THE RAJA OF CHUMBA.

[H. Moller.

H.H. THE MAHARAJA OF SIRMOOR.

[London Stereoscopic.

H.H. THE THAKUR SAHIB OF MORVI.

[C. D. Silva.

H.H. THE MAHARAJA BAHADUR
OF CHHATARPUR.

361

INDIAN INFANTRY ADVANCING TO TAKE UP A POSITION AND AVAILING THEMSELVES OF ALL THE COVER THE
GRASSY HILLOCKS AFFORDED.

the Imperial Cadet Corps, joined the Expeditionary Force at the outbreak of war. Besides liberally contributing to war funds in India and in England, his State troops were also accepted for service, and acquitted themselves with credit and distinction. A crack shot, a keen cricketer, and polo player, his athletic skill and sporting instincts now served him in good stead.

The Aga Khan's determined loyalty — The Aga Khan, or to give him his full title, his Highness Aga Sultan Sir Mahomed Shah, Aga Khan, rules over no State, but is one of the greatest religious and social forces in India, the spiritual head of over sixty million of the Khojas community of Mohammedans there. The wonderful history of his sect and the traditions of his family read more like romance than sober fact. Although without a kingdom, the Aga Khan has great revenues, mainly derived from the free-will offerings of his people. He is an all-round sportsman and a strong supporter of the turf. At the outbreak of war he was at Zanzibar, and he at once hurried to England to offer his services to the Imperial Government, and offered, if need be, to serve the King-Emperor as a private in any infantry regiment attached to the Indian Expeditionary Force. He showed in the most unmistakable fashion his determined loyalty, and his attitude in the most critical hours did much to reassure the wavering.

The great Indians serving with the Expeditionary Force included: Honorary Major-General H. H. Sir Pertab Singh, G.C.S.I., G.C.V.O., K.C.B., A.D.C., Maharaja-Regent of Jodhpur; Honorary Lieutenant H. H. the Maharaja of Jodhpur; Honorary Colonel H. H. Sir Ganga Singh Bahadur, G.C.S.I., G.C.I.E., A.D.C., Maharaja of Bikaner; Honorary Major H. H. Sir Madan Singh Bahadur, K.C.S.I., G.C.I.E., Maharaja-Adhiraj of Kishengarh; the Maharaja of Baria; the Nawab of Sachin; the Maharaja of Idar; the Mahajara of Bharatpur; the Raja of Rutlam; the Raja of Akalkot; the Nawab of Rampur; the Mir of Khairpur; Honorary Captain the Honourable Malik Umar Hayat Khan, C.I.E., M.V.O., Tiwana; Honorary Lieutenant Raj-Kumar Hira Singh

ANOTHER IMPRESSION OF OUR INDIAN TROOPS IN ACTION. HERE ALSO THE MEN ARE SEEN MAKING THEIR WAY
WITH THE MAXIMUM OF CAUTION.

[Bourne & Shepherd.

H.H. THE MAHARAJA OF KAPURTHALA.

THE CHIEF OF KALSIA STATE
(S. Rani Shri Singh Sahib Bahadur).

[Johnston & Hoffman.

H.H. THE MAHARAJA OF JAIPUR.

[Vandyk.

H.H. THE MAHARAJA OF KOLHAPUR.

[F. Bremner.

H.H. THE MAHARAJA OF JIND.

[Bourne & Shepherd.

H.H. THE MAHARAJA OF TRAVANCORE.

of Panna ; Honorary Lieutenant Maharaja-Kumar Hitendra Narayan of Cooch Behar ; Lieutenant Malik Mumtaz Mahomed Khan, Native Indian Land Forces ; Resaldar Khwaja Mahomed Khan Bahadur, Queen Victoria's Own Corps of Guides ; Honorary Captain Shah Mirza Beg.

Imperial Service troops were also accepted from the following States, and were later serving at the front : Alwar, Bharatpur, Bikaner, Faridkot, Gwalior, Hyderabad, Indore, Jaipur, Jind, Jodhpur, Kapurthala, Kashmir, Mysore, Patiala, Rampur.

The Indian Expeditionary Force as despatched to Europe in September, 1914, consisted of 70,000 men. This was not all. Other forces were sent to Mesopotamia and elsewhere, and by the spring of 1915 India had put in the field in the several theatres of war, including the British troops sent from India, a force equivalent to nine complete infantry divisions, with artillery, and eight cavalry brigades, besides several smaller bodies of troops, aggregating more than an infantry division, in minor and outlying spheres. She had placed at the disposal of the Empire for service out of India, so Mr. Asquith stated in a notable speech at the Mansion House, London, twenty-eight regiments of cavalry, British Indian, and Imperial, and one hundred and twenty-four regiments of infantry, British, Indian, and Imperial. The Prime Minister declared : " When we look at the actual achievements of the force so spontaneously despatched, so liberally provided for, so magnificently equipped, the battlefields of France and Flanders bear tribute to their bravery." Lord Hardinge, in a speech dealing with the despatch of troops, was able to point with justifiable pride to what had been done, and to declare significantly : " We are not at the end of our military resources."

The voyage of the Expeditionary Force to Europe was carefully planned. It was well known that the Germans intended, if they could, to destroy some of the transports with their raiding cruisers, or to torpedo them en route. The ships, however, were guarded the whole way across by the allied fleets, and the first divisions arrived without loss in Marseilles in the later part of September, to be quickly followed by others. The dark-skinned troops, as they landed and marched through the streets of the rock-bound southern French port, had a remarkable reception. The people of France could not do enough for them They cheered and shouted, broke into their ranks, and heaped gifts on

The voyage to Europe

them. " The troops, who literally leaped ashore," said Mr. Douglas Crawford, writing at the time from Marseilles, " were fighting men to the last ounce, hard and fit, and ready, had the word of command been given and had the thing been practicable, to march straight from the quay to the fighting-line. Not a few of the Sikhs, lithe, black-bearded giants, were deeply concerned to know if I thought the war would be over before they could get to grips with the common enemy, and it was a burden off their minds when I assured them there was absolutely no likelihood of anything of the kind coming to pass. Never has the port of Marseilles, used as it is to cosmopolitan crowds and the multi-coloured habiliments of Africa, witnessed a scene so kaleidoscopic as that presented to-day by the defiling of thousands of soldiers down seemingly numberless gangways and along quays lit up by brilliant sunshine."

The reception at Marseilles

The new-comers when they arrived at Marseilles found messages waiting for them from the King-Emperor. There was one to the British troops expressing the King's implicit confidence in them : " Duty is your watchword, and I know your duty will be nobly done." The message to the Indian troops was in Urdu, and when translated into English read as follows :

I look to all my Indian soldiers to uphold the Izzat of the British Raj against an aggressive and relentless enemy. I know with what readiness my brave and loyal Indian soldiers are prepared to fulfil this sacred trust on the field of battle shoulder to shoulder with their comrades from all parts of the Empire. Rest assured that you will always be in my thoughts and prayers. I bid you to go forward and add fresh lustre to the glorious achievements and noble traditions of courage and chivalry of my Indian Army, whose honour and fame are in your hands.

Lieutenant-General Sir James Willcocks, who commanded the Indian Army Corps, issued a stirring Order of the Day to his troops on October 10th, as they were moving up to the front :—

Soldiers of the Indian Army Corps:
We have all read with pride the gracious message of his Majesty the King-Emperor to his troops from India. On the eve of going into the field to join our British comrades, who have covered themselves with glory in this great war, it is our firm resolve to prove ourselves worthy of the honour which has been conferred on us as representatives of the Army of India. In a few days we shall be fighting as has never been our good fortune to fight before, and against enemies who have a long history. But is their history as long as yours ? You are the descendants of men who have been mighty rulers and great warriors for many centuries. You will never forget this. You will recall the glories of your race.

INDIANS IN ENGLAND : STALWART SONS OF OUR EASTERN EMPIRE GUARDING THE ROUTE AT THE ADMIRALTY ARCH WHEN PARLIAMENT WAS OPENED BY THE KING.

WOUNDED INDIANS RECUPERATING IN CAIRO. FROM THE ROOF OF THE HOSPITAL IN THE CITADEL THEY COULD OBTAIN FINE VIEWS OF THE TOWN AND SURROUNDING COUNTRY.

Hindu and Mohammedan will be fighting side by side with British soldiers and our gallant French allies. You will be helping to make history. You will be the first Indian soldiers of the King-Emperor who have the honour of showing in Europe that the sons of India have lost none of their ancient martial instincts, and are worthy of the confidence reposed in them. In battle you will remember that your religions enjoin on you that to give your life doing your duty is your highest reward. The eyes of your co-religionists and your fellow-countrymen are on you. From the Himalayan Mountains, the banks of the Ganges and Indus, and the plains of Hindustan, they are eagerly waiting for the news of how their brethren conduct themselves when they meet the foe. From mosques and temples their prayers are ascending to the God of all, and you will answer their hopes by the proofs of your valour. You will fight for your King-Emperor and your faith, so that history will record the doings of India's sons, and your children will proudly tell of the deeds of their fathers.

The Expeditionary Force arrived in Europe fully equipped for war. Great care had been taken to study the caste requirements of the troops, to provide the special foods demanded by them, and to meet their particular needs in other ways. The medical arrangements were all complete, with field ambulances, base hospitals, and ample provision for conveying the wounded from the front, including the hospital-ship Loyalty, to which previous reference has been made. A special Indian Soldiers' Fund, under the patronage of Lord Roberts, was opened, and some scores of thousands of pounds were quickly raised to supplement the clothing and comforts already provided by the Government, and to help the men in ways that could hardly be attempted officially.

At the beginning, far-fetched notions were entertained both in Germany and among the Allies as

AN INDIAN BUGLER.

to the fighting capacity of the Indians. They were supposed to possess powers of dash and endurance unequalled by Europeans. The Gurkhas were credited with a marvellous capacity for penetrating the trenches of the enemy without being seen, and the keen knives of these hillmen were said to be more formidable than a rifle in European hands. Similar claims were made for other branches of the Army. Those intimately acquainted with the Indian peoples knew that those who held extravagant ideas of what the Indians could do were bound to be disappointed. That the Indians would do well was taken for granted. But the Indian in Europe was obviously fighting under disadvantages in a climate very different from his own—damp, not dry—among winter conditions that were bound to test his physique to the uttermost, amid methods of war such as he had never experienced before. The Indian's idea of war is to fight in person, to risk your physical strength and skill in arms against the physical strength and skill in arms of your foe, to stand up man to man in a direct, fierce, overwhelming, personal struggle. What he was asked to do now was something very different. It was to engage in a long, dreary trench war; to live day after day, week after week, in sodden, soaking, freezing holes in the ground; to lie still for a week at a time under the heavy fire of the enemy's artillery; to fight a foe whom often enough he never saw. It says much for our Eastern troops that they worthily maintained the honour of their country under these conditions.

The Lahore Division arrived in the concentration area

in the rear of the Second British Army Corps on October 19th and 20th. It was quickly followed by others. When the Meerut Division arrived at the corps' headquarters the Indian Army Corps then took over the line previously held by the Second Corps, enabling some of the British troops to be drawn back into reserve. Two and a half brigades of British infantry and a large part of the artillery of the Second Corps remained to assist the Indian Corps in the defence of this line, until the Ferozepore Brigade, which had been supporting the cavalry farther north, joined the remainder of the Indians, thus enabling two and a half battalions of the British brigades to retire. At the beginning of November the Secunderabad Cavalry Brigade and the Jodhpur Lancers came.

The Indian troops at once found themselves plunged into the heart of the fighting. The Germans were resolutely

INDIAN TROOPS IN ENGLAND.
Before going to the front many Indian units underwent preparatory training in England to fit them for the new and strange conditions of warfare.

endeavouring to push on, determined to clear the road to Calais. No sacrifice was to be too great, no slaughter too heavy to accomplish their aim. They were backed with very heavy artillery. Their troops advanced to the assault time after time, and they displayed, it may be generally admitted, a reckless daring which nothing but the coolness and determination of the numerically weak British troops could have foiled.

The Indians had fought in wars up to now in which artillery had played but little part. Here they found themselves in a war where artillery was the dominating **Trial of Indian** factor. They soon got to know the **nerves** Minenwerfer—the trench mortar of the Germans—which, with a range of some five hundred to six hundred yards, throws a bomb loaded with high explosive weighing up to two hundred pounds. The Indians hated the trenches, with the cold, the wet, and the mud. But they were soon to find that even the deepest trenches were only a partial protection from the

enemies' weapons. They were in a strange land, dependent on their British officers and interpreters for intercourse with the white people around. Everything was strange and bizarre to them, and it would not have been surprising if, amid this novel and terrible maelstrom of death into which they had plunged, their nerves should temporarily have failed.

Nothing of the kind, however, happened. The Indian Cavalry took over some ground previously held by the First French Cavalry Corps and did excellent service. Time after time the Indians stood up against the most constant bombardments and the heaviest advances. Sir John French was able to **Sir John French's** say of them in a general review of the **tribute** situation: "Since their arrival in this country and their occupation of the line allotted to them I have been much impressed by the initiative and resource displayed by the Indian troops. Some of the ruses they have employed to deceive the enemy have been attended with the best results, and have doubtless kept superior forces in front of them at bay. The Corps of the Indian Sappers and Miners have long enjoyed a high reputation for skill and resource. Without going into detail I can confidently assert that throughout their work in this campaign they have fully justified that reputation. The General Officer commanding the Indian Army Corps describes the conduct and bearing of these troops in strange and new surroundings to have been highly satisfactory, and I am enabled from my own observations to fully corroborate his statement."

The story is told of how at one point the Germans had been pressing the British lines heavily for three weeks until our men were almost worn out. They kept up a ceaseless artillery fire, and every now and then they would attempt to charge. The soldiers held the line without flinching, although they were scarcely able to move from sheer fatigue.

INDIAN STRETCHER-BEARERS REMOVING WOUNDED AT A HOSPITAL BASE.
The Indian Red Cross work on the Continent was the subject of general commendation.

At last there came a moment when it seemed that the Germans had a chance of success. The ceaseless artillery fire had been heavier than ever and had cost us dearly. Fresh German infantry came up, and as nightfall approached they started to advance on our wearied lines. One British soldier who was there relates what happened: "Just when they were half-way towards our trenches the Bengal Lancers, who had arrived the day before and were anxious to get into it, were brought up. Splendid fellows they

IN AN INDIAN RED CROSS CAMP
AFTER NEUVE CHAPELLE.
British officers and orderlies taking the roll of
the injured and inspecting preparations for
their care and treatment.

WOUNDED INDIANS ROUND A CAMP-FIRE.
They took the fortune of war with the utmost cheerfulness and found considerable solace in
the cigarette.

looked as they passed us on their fine chargers, and we broke into cheers. They smiled back grimly, with their eyes glancing ahead and their fingers nervously feeling their lance shafts. At the word of command they swept forward, only making a slight detour to get out of our line of fire, and then they swept into the Germans from the left like a whirlwind. The enemy was completely taken aback. The Turcos they knew, but these men with their flashing eyes, dark skins, and white, gleaming teeth, not to mention their terribly keen-edged lances, they could not understand. The Lancers did not give them much

Bengal Lancers' great charge

time to arrive at an understanding. With a shrill yell they rode right through the German infantry, thrusting right and left with their terrible lances, and bringing a man down every time. The Germans broke, and ran for their lives, pursued by the Lancers for about a mile. When they came back from their charge they were cheered wildly all along our line, but they did not think much of what they had done."

The Germans, backed by their admirable system of secret service, laid many plans for confusing and perplexing the Indians. German spies, dressed in Indian uniforms, would go up and give wrong instructions at critical moments. Here is a typical incident told by the "Observer" attached by the Government to the Indian Army Corps :

" The audacity of the enemy cannot be better illustrated than by a well-authenticated statement of what took place last night in a trench held by a Gurkha regiment. A figure silhouetted in the moonlight and wearing a complete Gurkha uniform approached the end of the trench and delivered the message : ' The Gurkhas are to move farther up the trench ; another Gurkha contingent is advancing in support.' Puzzled by this announcement, the officer in charge replied, ' Who are you ? Where do you come from ? ' To which the only answer was : ' You are to move up to make room for other Gurkhas.' The English was good, but something—or many small things—excited

the officer's suspicions. ' Answer, and answer quickly,' he said. ' If you are a Gurkha, by which boat did you cross ? ' The question was, in the circumstances, no easy one to answer, and the German (for such he was) turned at once and fled. But he had not gone five yards before he fell riddled by bullets. If the officer had been deceived, the trench, of course, would have swarmed with Germans almost before the Gurkhas had made room for them."

One of the most remarkable and touching incidents in the early campaign of the Indian troops—an incident which will be remembered generations hence throughout the East—was the farewell visit of Lord Roberts to his old soldiers at the front. Lord Roberts was determined, despite his years and despite the pleadings of his friends, to go to Flanders and do what he could to cheer some of his comrades there. He reached Boulogne on November 11th, and first visited the Indian wounded on the hospital-ship. The stricken Indian soldiers strove as he entered the wards to rise up from their beds and greet

Lord Roberts and the wounded

him. The veteran Commander-in-Chief went from one to the other, with a word of comfort and good cheer for each, unable to conceal his own emotion as he gazed on their battered and stricken forms. From Boulogne he moved on to the headquarters of the Indian Corps, where he was received with great state. He spoke to the Indian regiments in their own tongues, and marched through the ranks of the men drawn up in his honour, his very presence an inspiration to them all. Great Indian commanders who had served under him were there. Men who had fought in the ranks under him time after time in great battles gazed up at the slight figure of the veteran Field-Marshal again.

He had planned to cheer up the wounded in more than one hospital, and to inspect the troops in many lines. But in the course of his tour he was seized with a chill, taken with congestion of the lungs and pleurisy, and was unable to rally. He died at the front after a few hours' illness, amidst the armies for whom he had lived and worked and fought so long. Some people in England

Effect of Lord Roberts' visit

spoke of his end as a tragedy. It must ever be a tragedy for his country to lose so great, disinterested, and simple a leader of men. But for Lord Roberts himself surely there could have been no tragedy in such an end, but rather the worthy culmination of a long life dedicated to the single purpose of loyalty and devotion to monarch and Empire. From end to end of the Indian Army the story of how Roberts Bahadur had come again among them and had died among them, served as a fresh inspiration and a fresh stimulus.

There came days in the fierce October - November struggle around Neuve Chapelle when it seemed that our men must be overwhelmed. Then it was that the Indians stood their ground firmly, doggedly, unflinchingly. Day after day they fought without ceasing, enduring losses rarely equalled up to that time. Their casualties in officers were particularly heavy, and their loss was severely felt. The European officer who leads Indian troops is a picked man, who has lived for years among them, who speaks their own tongue, and who knows them intimately. Some companies, it was said, lost

SIKHS IN CAMP IN FRANCE.
An interval for reading.

every officer in their first engagement. One particular section was reported to have had sixty per cent. of its effectives killed, wounded, or missing. The Anglo-Indian officer could not well be replaced without long delay. The language difficulty alone made it of little use for an officer without special qualifications to attempt to fill his post.

On Wednesday, October 28th, there was a closely contested battle around Neuve Chapelle, in which the Indians played a large part. Two days previously the Germans, advancing in the evening, had attacked this village and captured part of it. A terrific hand-to-hand combat of the most murderous description followed. All day

AN INDIAN BAKERY.
Native cooks baking chupatties (unleavened cakes) at the front.

on Tuesday our men tried again and again to push the enemy back. Then on the Wednesday morning some of the Indian regiments—the 47th Sikhs and the 20th and 21st Companies of the 3rd Sappers and Miners—made a big counter-attack, driving the Germans out of the greater part of the place with the bayonet. As the Germans fled into the fields beyond, the Indians attempted to pursue them. They at once came under the fire of concentrated machine-guns, and could go no farther.

Five days later the Germans attacked a portion of the line to the west of Neuve Chapelle with great determination. They

Colonel Norie's excellent leadership

pierced our line, and for the moment things threatened to be very serious. The situation was saved by the excellent leadership displayed by Colonel Norie, of the 2nd Gurkha Rifles. From October 25th until the end of the first week in November the Indians were practically continuously engaged in the great fight which brought about the holding up of the German winter campaign.

All India was thrilled by the news that in the fighting one Indian soldier, the first of his race, had earned the

"LIGHT REFRESHMENT."
Milking one of the thousands of goats provided for our Indian troops in the field.

Victoria Cross. Khudadad, an infantryman of the 129th Duke of Connaught's Own Baluchis, was in the fighting at Hollebeke, on October 31st. The British officer in charge of his detachment was wounded and helpless, and other guns had been put out of action by a shell. Khudadad, although badly wounded himself, continued working his machine-gun until the other five men of his detachment had been killed. The bestowal of the highest military decoration on this soldier touched the heart of India. Now, indeed, her people felt, India was really sharing danger and honour with Great Britain.

The Indian Cavalry Corps chafed at first at the little use that could be made of them. This fighting gave little or no opportunity for horsemanship. Their commander strongly urged that his men should be allowed to share the work of the trenches. As a result, various units of the Indian Cavalry took their regular turn in trench fighting.

After the great stand of Neuve Chapelle there followed the dreariest time of all, a time infinitely more trying to the Indians than the fiercest battles—the winter trench war. The wet, the cold, and the dreary mud, often up to one's middle, tested the Indian physique to the utmost. "This is not war," they said one to another. As the winter grew more and more severe, it became a question whether it was wise or not to keep them longer at the front during the worst of the weather. Then came fighting at Givenchy, where the Indians suffered very heavy loss. It was thought that the time had now come to give some of the Indian regiments a temporary rest. They were transferred for a time to the South of France, and the Indian line was shortened.

This, however, was only temporary. In the great British advance on Neuve Chapelle on March 10th the Indians once more played a distinguished and prominent part, sharing the honours of the day with the Fourth Army Corps, the attack on the whole German position being entrusted to the Indian Corps on the right and the 4th Army Corps at the centre and left. Following a powerful artillery bombardment of the German position, which wrought terrific destruction, the 23rd and 25th Brigades of the 5th Division stormed the German lines, and simultaneously the Garhwal Brigade of the Meerut Division, which was occupying a position to the south of Neuve Chapelle, rushed forward. Apart from the British attack elsewhere, which it is not necessary to describe here, the Garhwal Brigade, together with the 25th Brigade, carried the German entrenchments and pushed right on into Neuve Chapelle itself. Owing to the delay in bringing up reserves and other causes, our advance was not carried as far as it should have been, but for this the Indians were not to blame. The Indian Corps and the British troops dug themselves in that night. Next morning they attempted a further attack, but it was soon seen that this would be impossible without a renewed heavy artillery bombardment. Weather conditions made this now impossible. The Fourth Corps and the Indians tried again and again, despite the heaviest slaughter, to capture the positions fronting them. The effort was vain. The Germans had recovered from their surprise. Backed by reinforcements, they now had every point well covered

Garhwal Brigade's brilliant advance

with machine-guns, and every attempt to make further progress was repulsed. All that could be done was to hold and consolidate the ground the Fourth Corps and the Indians had gained so brilliantly and at such heavy cost.

A vivid account of the scene after the first advance on the village of Neuve Chapelle was given by Mr. Valentine Williams, the famous war correspondent:

Vivid story of Neuve Chapelle

"It is now half-past eight, the hour when folks in England are comfortably sitting down to their breakfast, when trim maids are bringing tea to the bedsides. Neuve Chapelle is ours, but the German resistance is not broken. Only a few hundred yards from where Riflemen and Gurkhas are fraternising in the first flush of victory, Britons are traversing the last stern stage of a soldier's career in the field—the path of death. . . . . .

"We are with the First 39th Garhwalis, a tough regiment that showed its worth in Burma and in the Tirah campaign. Whistles blow, the men leave their trenches. Instantly they are withered by a fearful blast of fire. The German trench is untouched. So is the barbed-wire, two hundred yards of it. The Garhwalis never waver. All the officers of the leading companies

STRANGE, EXOTIC SCENE ON THE BORDERS OF THE NEW FOREST.
Some of the Indian actors who took part in an entertainment given by the Indian Art and Dramatic Society at Barton-on-Sea, New Milton, on the borders of the New Forest, to the Indian troops at the convalescent hospital there.

are killed, right ahead of their men. The battalion staggers under the blast of fire, loses its direction, swings to the right, and captures, after fierce in-fighting with bayonet and knife, a section of trench there, only to be cut off in the upshot by the Germans in the intact trench. . . .

"Five of the Garhwalis' officers are dead now, killed in the first line after prodigies of bravery. In this fight the battalion is to lose twenty officers and three hundred and fifty men killed and wounded. The Germans have started to shell the Garhwalis' trenches. But the men, though without officers, are steady. These stout little hillmen have seen their officers fall, fearlessly exposing themselves. They remember that, and it keeps them firm."

From now on the Indians shared to the full the summer campaign of the British.

What is to be the effect on India itself of the active share of the Indian troops in the European campaign? It would be idle to deny that from end to end of India there has arisen the expectation that this may be the start of a new era in Indian Government.

THE TRANSPORT RIVER CLYDE AS "THE NEW HORSE OF TROY."
One of the most thrilling stories of the war is that of the transport River Clyde landing British troops on Gallipoli by running ashore, and, under cover of darkness, pouring out her great cargo of men from doors cut in her sides. Photograph taken after the historic landing battle.

THE RIVER CLYDE AFTER THE TERRIBLE LANDING BATTLE AT SEDDUL BAHR.
This photograph shows exactly how the troops contained within "the new Horse of Troy" were got ashore by means of lighters and gangways.

CHAPTER LXII.

THE TERRIBLE LANDING BATTLES ROUND SEDDUL BAHR.

How the Senegalese and Zouaves Stormed Kum Kale—Turkish Entrenchment in Asia Minor Carried—The Five Battle Beaches of the Glorious 29th Division—Lack of High-Explosive Shells for Bombarding Turkish Trenches—How the Implacable by Bold and Skilful Handling Swept the Turks from Cape Tekeh Beach—The Heroic Struggle Round Cape Helles—British Troops Held Up by Wire Entanglements on the Shore—The Death-Trap from which Our Men Fought their Way Out—Success of the Landing-Party in Morto Bay—The Problem of the Impregnable Beach of Seddul Bahr—Extraordinary Ruse of the British Sailors—The New Horse of Troy Advances into the Bay and Rests by a Reef Opposite a Sandbank—The Tragedy of the Sandbank and the First Landing-Party of Fusiliers—Two Thousand British Troops Imprisoned in a Transport Smitten all Day Long by the Fire of the Enemy—Night Falls and the Fusilier Brigade Leaves the New Horse of Troy—Furious Hand-to-Hand Conflict in the Old Castle of Seddul Bahr—How the Dublin Fusiliers with the Munsters and Hants Carried the Hill Above the Beach—Major Doughty-Wylie and Major Grimshaw Lead the Irish Bayonets—Lieut. Bastard's Single-Handed Attack on a Turkish Machine-Gun Fort—The Turkish Army Counter-Attacks in Dense Formation and is Half Destroyed—General British Advance Towards Krithia—Insecure Position of Franco-British Army on Gallipoli Peninsula—Turks Begin the Torpedo Campaign against our Fleet.

O F all the tasks ever set any army, there had been none so desperately difficult as that which faced our troops on Sunday morning, April 25th, 1915, at the southern end of the Galli-poli Peninsula. Even the landing operations by the Australian and New Zealand Army Corps at Sari Bair were easier than those of the 29th Division round Seddul Bahr and Cape Helles. All the beaches there, and especially the wide, open, shallow stretch of Morto Bay, were dominated by mobile German batteries firing from the other side of the Strait behind Kum Kale. It was a vital necessity to master the fire of the enemy on the Asiatic shore, in order to enable the 29th Division to land and establish itself. So, by arrangement with Sir Ian Hamilton, the French Colonial Division, under General d'Amade, steamed in its trans-ports to Kum Kale, protected by three French battleships. The French General selected as his landing-ground the most historic battlefield in the world—the far-famed windy plain of Troy, stretching below the hill on which Troy stood, to the mouth of the Meander, or Simois River. The landing was made west of the river by the mouth of the Meander, where the French

A DISTINGUISHED GROUP AT CAIRO.
Right to left : Lieut.-General Sir John Maxwell (Commander of the Forces in Egypt), Harvey Pasha (Chief of Cairo Police), Prince Alexander of Battenberg, and (in front) the Sultan of Egypt.

transports poured the Marines and Senegalese troops into small boats early on Sunday morning, April 25th, when the landing conflicts were raging on the other side of the Strait. The boats were towed by trawlers and torpedo craft to the mouth of the river at half-past nine in the morning, under a fire of shells and bullets from the ruined citadel of Kum Kale. Some distant German batteries at In Tepe were also rained on the French Marines and coloured troops. Every man in one boat was put out of action by a shell bursting in it.

A French captain was the first to wade ashore, and though wounded he charged the fort, followed by his men from Senegal. The place where the French troops had to win a foothold was only a few yards in extent, forming a ledge, under the grim, overhanging, black mass of the citadel of Kum Kale. In this holed, shattered, and dismantled entrance fortress, bombarded into ruins by the fleet two months previously, the Germans had placed machine-guns and riflemen sheltered beneath the old thick walls. There was also a machine-gun on a neighbouring windmill, while the mobile German batteries operated behind the next village of Yeni Shehr. All the defences were well and cleverly organised, but

INDIAN BAGGAGE WAGGON PROCEEDING TO THE POINT OF EMBARKATION FOR THE DARDANELLES.
In the foreground is a native with some of the goats provided to supply the troops with milk.

the battleships still retained their advantage over this narrow line of hilly land between the river and the Asia Minor coast.

As the French captain and his Senegalese troops scaled the breach in the walls of the fortress the machine-gun on the windmill opened fire. But a shell from a French battleship knocked the gun and all its crew from the top of the mill into atoms, and the French troops pushed on with heroic determination through a storm of shrapnel and machine-gun fire, and bayoneted the Turks out of the old courts and then advanced on the village. In the French division were Zouaves who had come from Nieuport and the Yser. In the judgment of these veterans the hurricane of shell and machine-gun fire that swept them at Kum Kale was the most terrible thing they had encountered in the war. It showed again that the German organisers of the defences of the Dardanelles were **Heroism triumphs over machinery** fully justified in thinking that they could prevent any opponent landing upon Ottoman soil.

But heroism triumphed over all the machinery of slaughter. House by house the covering force of some 3,500 men fought their way onward. In one place some five hundred Turks surrendered, but, seeing how few were their captors, they shot down two of the French officers and ran away. Then, strongly reinforced, they returned and recaptured part of the village together with a French machine-gun. But the French, in violent and unceasing hand-to-hand fighting, with no artillery to help them and no trenches as cover against the continual rain of shrapnel, fought and held nearly a mile of ground. They recaptured the machine-gun and again drove the enemy back. They found it safer to keep in hand-to-hand conflict with their foes, getting so well mixed up that the hostile guns could not play on the fighting front without killing more of their own men than French troops.

The main effort of the enemy was made on Sunday night, when a fresh division was pushed up to support the attack. Four times in succession did the German officers lead the Turks against the houses and bits of broken wall held by the French. But each time a dense, charging multitude, coming up in wave after wave, was broken by infantry fire and machine-gun fire and then routed at the point of the bayonet. On Monday morning the French could see hundreds of corpses on every hundred yards' depth beyond their front. They had shattered brigade after brigade by fire directed by the searchlights. The Turks had at last retired in the darkness and entrenched between the coast and the river in front of Yeni Shehr.

Meanwhile our magnificent Allies had landed in the night a battery of their deadly light field-guns—the "75's." These were trained on the Turkish trench. Then the French battleships and an auxiliary cruiser opened a flanking fire on the trench, while the field battery swept the hostile position with a frontal fire. The affair was all over in a few minutes. Most of the Turks bolted inland, only to be slain in a shrapnel zone formed by the battle-ships' guns. The remaining five hundred men saw that they could not escape and, throwing down their weapons, they came towards the French, waving handkerchiefs and white flags. The resistance at Kum Kale was thus completely broken during the critical period in the landing of British troops two miles across the Straits, where reinforcements had been got ashore at Seddul Bahr, and our troops were holding the first line of hills that saddled the Peninsula. **Kum Kale resistance broken**

Having thus accomplished with splendid heroism its preliminary work at Kum Kale, the French covering force re-embarked with no attempt at attack by the Turkish infantry. Only the distant batteries inflicted some losses by shrapnel fire, but the guns of the French battleships took full revenge; for the Turks were caught by high-explosive shells in the village of Yeni Shehr, and not a house was left standing. Every building in the country round about holding snipers and machine-gun parties, was blown up by the "75's" or the naval guns, and though the Turco-German Staff at Constantinople claimed that the French division had been driven back into the sea, not a single Turkish infantryman or a single German gun occupied the land around Kum Kale when the French returned to their boats on Monday night.

This part of the operations was excellently planned and executed; for if the German batteries had been able to fire from behind Kum Kale the task of our 29th Division would have been quite impossible. Even as it was the landing battles round the southern end of the Peninsula of Gallipoli were long, terrible, and arduous. They rank with the attack on the Aisne plateau, the defence of Ypres, and the conflicts on the crests of the Carpathians. We have seen that the Australians escaped their worst landing difficulties by a surprise embarkation on a part of the coast where even they had not expected to land. But the 29th Division could make no surprise attack. The cliffs at Cape Tekeh, Cape Helles, Seddul Bahr, and De Totts Battery, at the eastern point of Morto Bay, rose from fifty to a hundred feet. Above the cliffs was an open plateau, rising in places not far from the sea's edge to 138 feet, 141 feet, and 256 feet. Two miles inland the hills began sloping up to the dominating ridge of Achibaba, or Tree Hill, 730 feet above sea level. Then, hill over hill, the ground ran to the rocky, broken clump of Pasha Dagh, at the Narrows. The Germans had everywhere the finest possible field for direct gun fire, innumerable ravines and hollows, in which to shelter their howitzers, and mile-long slopes like the glacis of a mighty fortress, down which their entrenched infantry could shoot with their machine-guns helping them, and preparing for their charges.

Long and terrible landing battles

In many places at the end of the Peninsula there was no foreshore, and jagged rocks made a landing impossible. But five beaches were selected for the operations. On the Ægean shore was a gap where a stream, flowing north of the village of Krithia, broke down the high cliff. This was known as Beach Y. South of it, and north of Cape Tekeh, was Beach X. Then just south of the promontory of Tekeh was Beach W. Full south, between Cape Helles and Seddul Bahr, was Beach V. Then in Morto Bay, between Seddul Bahr and De Totts Battery, was our fifth and last landing-place, known as Beach S.

The plan of attack was different from that at Sari Bair. No surprise in the darkness was possible, as the beaches were defended by underwater wire entanglements and by the main forces of the Fifth Turkish Army entrenched on the high ground and flanking all the beaches. The defending troops were supported by light field-guns and 6 in. howitzer batteries in formidable numbers, working with marked ranges, and completely swept the whole field of fire. Our troops were transferred just before dawn to tow-boats, some of which were towed by the battleships and others by steam-trawlers and pinnaces. The trawlers were to cast off the boats on nearing the beach, leaving the soldiers to row ashore with the help of a few seamen. It was hoped that a terrific bombardment of the enemy's positions by every gun in the battleships, including the Queen Elizabeth, would master the enemy's fire.

Underwater wire entanglements

But as the ships, apparently, used shrapnel shell chiefly, against which the German engineers had skilfully made

RESTING UNDER THE SHADOW OF SHATTERED TURKISH DEFENCE WORKS.
Photograph taken after the huge fortifications had been reduced and our men were firmly established where they landed.

deep trenches, the extraordinary volume and fury of our naval bombardment did not in most cases have an effect commensurate with the tremendous effort made. What was needed was high-explosive shell in immense quantities. Only high-explosive shell could smash up the enemy's earthworks. But as is well known, shell of this kind was sadly lacking in our munition stores at home. Sir John French in Flanders could not get all the high-explosive shells he needed, and even at Neuve Chapelle the French artillery had to come to our aid. At the Dardanelles, where the enemy was magnificently entrenched for a long siege warfare, the lack of high-

Lack of high-explosive shell

explosive shell seems to have been the principal factor of failure in the military operations.

These operations had been suddenly designed and ordered. allowing no time for the efficient preparation and organisation of our instruments of attack. Fleet and army had to get to work with all possible speed, and make use of such means as were available. Shrapnel was plentiful, as it had been found of little use in trench warfare; the Navy had a fair supply of common shell, but high-explosive shell was very rare. This was the principal reason why the landing battles cost us so many lives and why, after the landing, the progress of our troops was so very slow. From beginning to end we were fighting against a superbly entrenched enemy without the proper means of destroying his entrenchments.

In ultimate analysis this condition of affairs was due to the fact that our military authorities before the war broke out were unable to get as good a fuse for high-explosive shell as the Germans possessed. Either through a total failure of the scientific intellect of our Empire, or through the neglect by the Government to put the problem of the high-explosive shell into the hands of men of science capable of solving it, **Implacable captain's** our shell remained inferior to both the **bold tactics** French and the German shell. The fuse was so delicate that when this type of projectile was first introduced shells were known to explode if jolted over a rough road.

The only real success in the preliminary bombardment was obtained round Beach X, north of Cape Tekeh. It was due to the bold tactics of the captain of the Implacable. At dawn the covering ship, the Swiftsure, started a fierce and continual fire against the cliffs—using, of course,

AUSTRALIANS AND BLUEJACKETS ON BOARD A WARSHIP IN THE DARDANELLES.
In circle : Turkish torpedo-boat driven ashore on the coast of Chios, after its attack on the British transport Manitou.

WATER DISTRIBUTION TO THE TURKISH PRISONERS AT
SEDDUL BAHR.

shrapnel. But at eight minutes to six the Implacable, also
employing shrapnel for her 12 in. and 6 in. guns, closed for
action. Instead, however, of remaining in deep water, the
captain navigated his ship within five hundred yards of
the shore, till there were only six fathoms of water to float
the old battleship that displaced 15,000 tons. With her
four 12 in. and her twelve 6 in. guns she smote the cliffs
at point-blank range, so that the shrapnel smashed into the
enemy's trenches and machine-gun chambers in the sand-
stone with a battering effect. Not a Turk was able to
show his head above the bluff of shrub-grown rock, and our
troops were towed into the beach and
The enemy again   there they landed without any opposi-
surprised   tion, climbed up the cliff and entrenched.
When they advanced inland they were
badly worried by a Turkish battery at the village of Krithia.
But again the gunnery lieutenants of the Implacable came
to their aid, and when the position of the battery was signalled to the battleship the guns were knocked out of action.
Had the other naval bombardments of the enemy's positions
by the seashore been as rapidly successful as the affair
on Beach X, remarkable progress might have been made.

The landing on Beach Y, northward nearer Krithia, also
went well. The embarkation at this point was a greater
surprise to the enemy than the operations round the end
of the Peninsula. Only three light cruisers, the Dublin,
Amethyst, and Sapphire, helped with their guns—the
Dublin having eight 6 in., and the two older warships
twelve 4 in. pieces each. But the light draught of these
unarmoured cruisers enabled them to get close to the shore,
and with their small guns they bombarded the high cliff so
that a covering force of two battalions and one company
landed with scarcely any resistance from the Turks and
obtained a firm footing on the heights.

Far more difficult was the disembarkation on the next
beach southward, known as Beach W. It consisted of a
bay with a wide stretch of sand running like the mouth of
a funnel into an inland valley, dominated on one side by
the hills extending to Cape Tekeh, and commanded on the
other side by the cliffs ending in Cape Helles. The natural
defensive strength of the position was extraordinary,
for the covering force had to land on a shelterless stretch
of sand, with the enemy holding in front of them a crescent
of broken, rising ground, pouring down a flanking fire on
both sides and a frontal fire from the centre. The

GENERALS IN CONSULTATION.
General d'Amade talking with a British military attaché and General
Gouraud conversing with Colonel Descains at the military headquarters in
the Dardanelles.

German engineers had much improved the natural advantages of the ground. There were wire entanglements
in profusion, and a great system of shrapnel-proof trenches.
In vain did the battleships bombard the Turkish
defences with all their armament for three-quarters of an
hour. The guns were not able to destroy even the lines
of barbed-wire on the foreshore. The boats that made
for the beach were confronted by a hedge of undamaged
wire entanglements, and the crowded troops were exposed
to a murderous cross-fire from pom-poms, machine-guns,
and entrenched riflemen. In the centre
of the bay every brave man who waded   **Murderous defences**
ashore and heroically dashed forward to   **of Beach W**
cut the wire was shot down. Meanwhile,
another beach party, consisting of Engineers and Royal
Naval Division men, made for the shelter of Cape Tekeh
in the second line of tow-boats. Here another landing-
party had got into difficulties, and after rowing through a
heavy fire the men climbed the cliff, holding on to the
extreme edge of it with desperate courage.

Hearing the shouts of these men the party in the second
tows came to their assistance, scrambling up the cliff
rifles in hand. The two parties then advanced and

captured a Turkish trench in a furious bayonet charge, and thus checked the enfilading fire which was still being poured on the foreshore. About the same time the cliffs on the other side of the bay were carried by our men, and both our landing-parties on the horns of the crescent displayed such marksmanship that the Turks were afraid to leave their trenches and charge them. At ten o'clock another regiment was landed. The reinforced covering column then worked up the valley and cleared the enemy from their central position. Only then was it possible to cut the barbed-wire entanglements, remove our wounded from the beach, and begin disembarking ammunition and stores. For we then held the crests commanding the terrible death-trap of Beach W. The men there were in somewhat the same position as the Australians and New Zealanders between Sari Bair and Gaba Tepe. Snipers and distant hostile batteries rained rifle and shrapnel bullets over the disembarking operations; but the holes

AT THE GATES OF THE DARDANELLES.
British torpedo-boat destroyer on patrol duty opposite Seddul Bahr after this place had been reduced by the fire of the Franco-British battleships.

in the cliffs from which the German machine-guns had been firing were in our possession.

All round the southern part of the coast, however, the troops were not able to advance. They were most successful when they merely entrenched on the cliffs they had won and covered the principal work of disembarkation. At Beach Y the men tried to work inland, and thus clear all the southern plateau from the opposing Turks. But our troops were outflanked and punished so heavily that all the force at Beach Y re-embarked on Monday morning. This was the only landing failure the British had in the Peninsula.

The troops at the next landing-place, Beach X, also moved forward on Sunday morning, according to the co-ordinated plan of attack arranged by the General. They were checked, after fighting their way inland for a thousand yards. At this point the landing-force on their right at Beach W had been timed to meet them. But, as we have seen, Beach W had proved to be a death-trap, and the men there had enough to do to win a footing. The consequence was that the right flank of the troops advancing from Beach X was exposed, and the men retired towards the cliff, where a desperate **Desperate Sunday** battle went on all Sunday night. It **night battle** ended, however, in a British victory, and on Monday morning the troops north of Cape Tekeh again advanced.

On the other side of the end of the Peninsula. at Beach S, by Morto Bay and De Totts Battery, the landing was effected with few losses and a fine dash. For though the enemy had a trench along the shore, the British battleship at this point was more successful than the ships that fired at the wire entanglements on the death-trap beach. The Turkish position was well battered by the naval guns, and then carried at the point of the bayonet by a landing-party of seven hundred men.

The enemy howitzers then swept the lost beach

with shrapnel, but our troops were in a fairly safe position in the circumstances, as they were swarming up the cliff and also working round the shoulder of a hill on the left. They reached the old battery on the top by ten o'clock in the morning, and in the afternoon they had made a line of trenches on the plateau, from which they were able to hold the 2,000 Turks in front of them. They formed the right wing of the force that was trying to get astride of the **The worst** Peninsula, occupying the position it **landing-place** was intended that the French troops should work from when the demonstration against Kum Kale was completed. On Tuesday morning the Zouaves, Senegalese, and some Paris regiments took over the trenches by De Totts Battery, leaving our successful little landing-force free to strengthen the British line on the left.

Between De Totts Battery and the death-trap of Beach W was the worst of all the landing-places. This was Beach V, lying under the old castle of Seddul Bahr, and extending towards the high cliff that rose sharply from the foreshore round Cape Helles. The beach was only a few hundred yards wide, and the strong current of the Dardanelles swept round it with great power, making any landing by row-boats a disastrous affair. The lie of the ground was similar to that of Beach W, with a smaller sandy foreshore,

TURKISH SHELL EXPLODING IN THE SEA.
Falling wide of its mark, the missile only sent up a fountain of steaming foam.

fronted by a broken valley and enfiladed from the heights on either hand. On the left, at Seddul Bahr, was the modern entrance fort to the Dardanelles. Its two great guns had been dismantled by our fleet, but the bomb-proof chambers were intact, and the German engineers had constructed a system of trenches and barbed-wire entanglements extending round the valley and connecting with the solid masses of masonry of the old ruined castle. The ruins still afforded excellent cover to sharpshooters and Maxim-gun parties, and the broken walls of the village of Seddul Bahr had also been skilfully worked into the enemy's new system of earthwork defences. Behind the village was a hill one hundred and forty-one

H.M.S. Majestic, which was torpedoed on May 27th, 1915, leaving Mudros Bay.

British troops going ashore at the Dardanelles from the transport Nile.

Carrying stores to the Australian camp on the Gallipoli Peninsula.

Tending wounded Australians who landed on Gallipoli Peninsula under heavy fire.

Men of the Australian Light Horse who fought so gallantly on the Gallipoli Peninsula.

Australians hauling the first gun to be landed by the Allies in the Dardanelles.

Ruins of Seddul Bahr with foreshore where the troops landed in May, 1915.

Major=General Birdwood, C.B., in command of the Australian troops.

feet high, now famous as Doughty-Wylie's Hill. On this commanding position the enemy had constructed a maze of trenches and barbed-wire hedges from which the beach was dominated at point-blank range. As in the case of Beach W, the foreshore and valley were also trenched and set with barbed-wire. Farther inland were the heavy howitzer batteries of this terrible fortress, which even in the ordinary way would have been one of the most formidable positions that any troops had ever been called upon to take. But instead of coming overland against the stronghold and entrenching against the enemy's fire and working forward by saps, our troops had to attack without any cover from the sea, advancing in little boats against an adverse current of the great Strait.

INTERIOR OF THE TURKISH BATTERY AT CAPE HELLES.
Heavy cannon on a turn-table guarding the entrance to the Dardanelles.

THE LIGHTHOUSE AT SEDDUL BAHR.
Part of the old fortifications is shown, with obsolete cannon and stacks of ammunition.

Only the ingenuity of Admiral de Robeck and his Staff made the landing attack practicable. Two miles across the Strait was the town of Troy, which the ancient Greeks had captured after a long siege by means of the ruse of the wooden horse. Very likely memories of Homer inspired our fighting seamen with the idea which they had been reducing to practice during the weeks of preparation.

Admiral de Robeck's ingenuity They took a large collier, the River Clyde, cut great doors in her steel sides, and filled her with 2,000 troops on Saturday night, April 24th. Her bridge was turned into a fort by means of steel plates, and casemates were built in her bows and lower bridge, from which twelve machine-guns were worked by the Maxim section of the Naval Division. A string of lighters, towed by a steam-hopper, moved by the side of the new Horse of Troy, the lighters being intended to form a sort of pontoon bridge from the ship to the shore if need required.

It was proposed that the River Clyde should run herself ashore on Seddul Bahr beach, as high up as possible. But the current swung her out of her course, and she went too far eastward close to a reef of rocks. The water above the reef was too deep for the men to wade through, but the steam-hopper also beached herself alongside, forming a gangway. Under a tornado of fire from the enemy, a lighter was also got into position, and the most difficult of all the landings began. While the River Clyde was grounding, a covering party in eight tows also reached the shore But fifty yards from the water's edge was a barbed-wire obstruction spanning the beach. It was undamaged by our naval guns, and the enemy waited **Tragedy of the sandbank** till our covering party was held up on the wire, and then played on them with three machine-guns. All our men would have perished entirely but for the fact that there was near the sea a sandbank about five feet high. Under the lee of this shelter the survivors dug themselves in. All the while the River Clyde was rattling under the tempest of pom-pom shells, machine-gun fire, and shrapnel. One of the gangways was destroyed as soon as it was let down, and though our Maxims from the bridge and casemates answered the enemy's fire, they could not beat it down.

It was death to venture outside But at the word of command, part of the Fusilier Brigade, under General Napier, dashed out and tried to reach the foreshore. The short-range fire of the Turkish machine-guns swept them off the planks as they ran, mowed them down in the barges, knocked them over in the water, and took a ghastly toll of those who reached the beach and rushed for cover to the sandbank. Of those who fell into the water during the race down the gangway and across the barges, many were drowned. Wounded and weighed down by their packs and full cartridge-belts, many an heroic Fusilier perished in quite shallow water. Yet there was no hanging back. General Napier, who was hit by three bullets early in the conflict, lived just long enough to send his men a message. He said he would like to kiss the whole Fusilier Brigade.

There were the Dublin Fusiliers, who had three companies wiped out; the Lancashires, who went with the first tows and suffered terribly, and the Munsters, some of whose platoons also reached the sandbank. It was wonderful to see how the men conducted that race with death to the shore. The Lancashires got caught in an underwater entanglement, and were there swept by machine-guns. The survivors struggled out of the water into a minefield, and those who extricated themselves from this new peril were again enfiladed by machine-guns. Only fifteen men were left alive in the platoon that reached the beach. But with an undauntedness glorious alike to the annals of their regiments and their country, they held on gamely, and tried to rush a Turkish trench. It was an impossible feat. The Turks poured a shower of bullets at them and then charged with the bayonet. Somebody in H.M.S. Majestic was watching the Lancashires. Two shells from the battleship's guns struck the trench as the Turks were rising to the charge, and the survivors of the fifteen Fusiliers thereby accomplished the apparently impossible. For, rushing on the staggered enemy, they shot or bayoneted those that did not flee, and captured the trench.

Miracles of courage were performed by the men under the sandbank, who went out and brought to shelter their wounded comrades struggling in the **Miracles of courage performed** water. Some of the rescuers also got the wounded men into the boats and away to the ships. Often the rescuers were killed and the wounded men shot a second time. The grandest figure in the scene of horror and heroism was a seaman from the River Clyde. Calmly smoking a pipe, he went about the beach amid a hurricane of bullets, getting the wounded into safety, and working all the time with an amazing unconcernedness. Meanwhile a party of the Fusiliers, who had landed in tow-boats, scaled the cliff to the village of Seddul Bahr and carried on a close-range rifle fight with the Turkish infantry in the streets and ruined buildings. But our men were too few in number and too much exposed in position to force their way into the town. They had at last to give up the unequal combat and scrambled down the cliff to the shelter on the beach.

By the afternoon there were about two hundred men under the sandbank. Digging holes in the sand, they crawled under cover, and there they had to remain until nightfall. It had been seen that any further attempt at a landing would mean the entire destruction of the Fusilier Brigade and the 2nd Battalion of the Hampshires working with them. So the new Horse of Troy—the River Clyde— remained all day by the beach with 2,000 men inside her. Meanwhile the situation had been greatly improved by the success of the landing on Beach W, under Cape Helles. A battalion of infantry there began to climb up the steep slopes of the crest. So quickly did they move that the sailors watching from the battleship could hardly realise that the troops were meeting fierce resistance and losing heavily at every step. But there was no stopping to count the cost. The troops swarmed out on the crest of Cape Helles and entrenched there, and in the afternoon a couple of guns were landed. It was hoped that the men holding Cape Helles would be able to work round towards Seddul Bahr and facilitate the operations of the Fusilier Brigade by clearing the high ground round the sandbank.

The German engineers had foreseen everything. They had reckoned on losing Cape Helles, while holding up our landing-party at Seddul Bahr. Round the plateau eastward of Cape Helles lighthouse was a barrier. It consisted of meshes of wire, the barbs **German science** only an inch apart, supported on iron **and foresight** posts. This barrier was ten yards in width. It ran from Cape Helles to Seddul Bahr Fort. Behind it was a series of trenches, zigzagging in a rough circle, forming a redoubt held by a strong body of German infantrymen, who were able to fire in any direction in order to prevent any force which might force a landing at Cape Helles from giving any help to the landing-party in difficulties at Seddul Bahr. It was precisely this situation which had arisen, all of which goes to show what science and foresight the Germans employed in fortifying the Gallipoli Peninsula.

Yet, supported by the fire of our warships, the troops at Cape Helles worked up to the very edge of the barbed-wire by the end of Sunday afternoon. Then, as nonchalantly as if they were clipping a hedgerow at home, they began to cut a path through the jungle of barbs, while enduring a furious fire from the redoubt. And when some of our infantry tried to dash through in daylight the Turkish fire

ARRIVAL AT CAIRO OF RED CROSS TRAIN WITH WOUNDED FROM THE DARDANELLES.

OOPS WITH THEIR RIFLES IN READINESS AS
PORT STEAMS SHOREWARD AT THE WESTERN
ENTRANCE TO THE DARDANELLES.

GUNNER IN BRITISH BATTLESHIP IN THE DARDANELLES
TAKES A HURRIED MEAL WHILE WAITING ORDERS BY
TELEPHONE.

for an advance on so small a front as had been
ugh the wire barrier. Not till night fell were
ble to work forward and get some command over
holding up the landing on Seddul Bahr beach.
darkness of Sunday night the two thousand
the River Clyde at last managed to get ashore
single further casualty. The operation was con-
ith such silent skill that the enemy did not peril it was too late that anything was happening.
y opened a raging rifle fire on the ship, and maintained it until close upon dawn. But

used the ship was empty, and while it was

decoy serving as a decoy target the troops,
having got ashore with all the ammu-
food, and water they needed, began to push up
e shelter of the cliffs below the castle.
even o'clock at night the Turks became seriously
, and swept the entire beach with a violent fusil-
But our men were lying down under cover and
little loss. Again they went forward in the
ss, and worked their way into part of the ruined
and the shattered fort. Our centre also advanced,
n a firm hold on the shore ; and when day broke
nday, April 26th, an attempt was made to close
the enemy from the castle cliff on one side and the
beach. The attack, however, was held up by
ne-guns from one of the towers of the castle, and
en had again to take cover until the Cornwallis
ed the towers down with her guns. Then, by hard
ng through the ruined village behind the castle, the
h troops worked out in the open country, only to be
held up by the principal work of defence of the
an engineers—the Doughty-Wylie Hill.

This green mound, one hundred and forty-one feet
above sea-level, had been converted into a system of
earthworks and wire entanglements, from which the
German machine-gun officers, pom-pom crews, and
Turkish infantry swept the beach in front, Cape Helles
on their right and Seddul Bahr on their left. The condition
of our wasted and weary troops, who had
been fighting all night and morning and   **A critical**
losing heavily, was very serious. The   **situation**
loss in officers during the landing had
been disastrous, and though all the men they had got
through unwounded were desperately eager to close with the
enemy, there was in many cases nobody left to lead them.

It was in these circumstances that Colonel Doughty-
Wylie came ashore and began to talk to the men. He
was a Staff officer, and he had no business to be where
he was. But the situation was critical, and it was because

GHEZIREH PALACE HOTEL, CAIRO.
Converted into a Red Cross hospital where Australians and New Zealanders, wounded in the Dardanelles, were attended to.

THE WORLD'S LARGEST HOTEL AS A HOSPITAL.
Heliopolis Grand Hotel, Cairo, used as a hospital for Australasian wounded. It contained 800 rooms, with saloons annexed to each.

SIDE VIEW OF GHEZIREH PALACE HOTEL.

them all thrown back by a sweeping fire from the machine-gun. While the men took cover Lieutenant Bastard ran forward to the opening through which the machine-gun was playing, thrust in his revolver, and emptied all its chambers. He must have killed or wounded some of the gunners, for the fire was at once reduced. The young lieutenant escaped at the time by a miracle, but afterwards, while **The glorious 29th** passing a loophole in the fort, he got a **Division** bullet through his cheek.

The speed and dash with which the Irishmen took the fortified hill were, according to the soldiers themselves, the grand feature of the most remarkable landing battle in military history. One of the Worcesters afterwards said that he did not mind being wounded when he saw what the Irish Fusiliers did. But the fact was every regiment of the 29th Division distinguished itself by its dauntless skill and invincible tenacity. In addition to the first battalions of the Dublin, Munster, Lancashire, and Inniskilling Fusiliers, and the second battalion of the Royal Fusiliers, the landing battles at the southern end of the Gallipoli Peninsula were fought by the 1st Essex Regiment, the 2nd Hants, and 1st Scottish Borderers, 2nd South Wales Borderers, 1st Border Regiment, 4th Worcesters, and 5th Territorial Battalion of the Royal Scots. Magnificent work was also done by the Chatham, Deal, Portsmouth, and Plymouth Marine Light Infantry, and the Drake, Hood, Nelson, Howe, and Anson Battalions of the Naval Division.

It was at noon on Monday, April 26th, that the Turks fled from their last defences on the hill, enabling Beach V to be cleared. This prepared the way for a further advance inland, enabling our line to be stretched right across the southern end of the Peninsula. When General Liman von Sanders came down in great force on April 28th to make the grand attack which was to push our troops back into the sea, we in turn had constructed a system of trenches from the Ægean coast to the Dardanelles shore. Against our trenches the packed lines of Turks fell in thousands, for our veteran troops of the 29th Division were the flower of our little regular Army. Among them were officers and men who had fought from Mons to the Marne, and from the Aisne to Ypres. The Turkish infantry of the line shot poorly and could not attack in extended order. The enemy's machine-gun parties were both brave and skilful, and their sharpshooters, mostly Moslem Macedonian refugees, were also courageous and marksmanlike. But the Turkish infantry could not attack in a scientific manner. The men bunched together too much, and heavy though our losses had been in the landing battle, we gave the enemy more than we had received when he made his first attempts to drive back and drown us in the sea.

In a sustained effort on the night of Wednesday, April

he knew the men had lost their officers that he assumed command. Carrying only a small cane, he walked about in the tempest of fire, talked to the men, cheered and rallied them, and formed them up for the charge. At his orders they fixed their bayonets, and, leading them with his cane, he took them up the fortress hill, and fell dead in front of them. The Fusiliers passed over his body, cut through the barbed-wire, **Doughty-Wylie's** bayoneted the Turks, and captured **heroic death** the height. And in honour of the man who led them they called it Colonel Doughty-Wylie's Hill.

The Dublin Fusiliers, with the Munsters on their left and the Hants on their right, made the great charge. Major Grimshaw, of the Dublin Fusiliers, was as heroic as Colonel Doughty-Wylie, and fell like him on the field of battle. A younger hero of the Dublins was Lieutenant Bastard. He led his men against the fort, only to have

WOUNDED TURKISH PRISONERS, WITH NURSES, WALKING IN THE GROUNDS OF THE NEW RED CRESCENT HOSPITAL OPENED AT CAIRO UNDER THE PATRONAGE OF THE SULTAN OF EGYPT.

FIRST BATCH OF GERMAN AND TURKISH PRISONERS FROM THE DARDANELLES ARRIVING AT CAIRO UNDER AUSTRALIAN ESCORT.

28th, the Turks pressed forward in close-order formation on our thinly-held line, intending, after the manner of the Germans, to smash their way through by sheer weight of numbers. But they were everywhere repulsed. Long lines of their dead lying in front of our trenches marked the high-water mark of their onslaughts. They also attacked the French in dense masses on the same night, but they withered under the rapid fire of the Lebels, and were routed by a fierce counter-attack at the point of the bayonet. Again on the following Saturday the Turks concentrated against the French front, while making only a spasmodic effort on our lines. Some of the Senegalese troops on Saturday gave way after their officers had fallen. But the Zouaves went forward in a grand bayonet charge and recaptured the ground.

CARRYING AUSTRALIAN WOUNDED FROM CAMP HOSPITAL TO TRANSPORT.
On the left is a remarkable photograph, also from the Dardanelles, showing how the wounded were raised on board ship by means of cranes.

The Peninsula had to be reduced by slow and laborious siege-work against the most skilful military engineers in the world. It was impossible to dispute the excellence of the leadership of the German officers. Brutal and overbearing they may have been, but they held the Turks together in a superb way, and by their tenacity in attack got all that was best out of the fatalistic temperament of the Ottoman peasantry. Indeed, they got more out of the Turk than Osman had done at Plevna, and gave us in the Gallipoli Peninsula the most difficult feat our Army had ever to accomplish.

Our soldiers and sailors worked as well as they fought. By the beaches piers were built out into deep water so that the largest lighters could come alongside. Roads were cut along the cliffs, and a system of lighting devised to allow the work to go on in darkness as well as in daylight. At night the southern end of the Peninsula, formerly so barren and deserted, had the appearance of being one of the world's greatest seaports. The multitude of

The first stage of the great battle ended in the middle of May with the Turks entrenched across the slopes of Achibaba, and the allied troops holding the ground south of Krithia village. The campaign had become a matter of trench warfare, and the winning of the Peninsula was a question of how many men we could afford to lose in order to capture each trench and each hundred yards of ground. Nothing could be done without large reinforcements and an enormous supply of ammunition. For our Mediterranean Expeditionary Force was only starting on its labours after its series of heroic contests for the landing beaches.

THE SULTAN OF EGYPT AND LIEUT.-GENERAL SIR JOHN MAXWELL TALKING TO A DARDANELLES PATIENT IN THE HOSPITAL AT HELIOPOLIS, CAIRO.

ONE OF THE 15 IN. GUNS OF H.M.S. QUEEN ELIZABETH.
Each of these guns is capable of sending a shell weighing about a ton a distance of twenty-four miles.

lights ashore made the coast look as though several towns had sprung up, and out to sea, like an enormous mass of ocean commerce, were a hundred great transports, and a mighty fleet of warships lay packed outside the still-bolted path to Constantinople.

The position of our fleet remained insecure. In the middle of April one of our new submarines, the E15, entered the Dardanelles at night to make a reconnaissance of the minefield at the end of the first basin. But it was caught by a strong current and carried towards Kephez Point, where it grounded, most of the crew being captured by the Turks. A day or two afterwards a Turkish torpedo-boat, officered by Germans, slipped out of the Dardanelles and made a torpedo attack on the West Hartlepool steamer the Manitou, which was full of British troops. Though three torpedoes were fired at the transport all of them missed, but twenty-four men were drowned, owing to one boat capsizing in the water, and another boat being lost through the breaking of a davit. In addition to the men drowned twenty-seven were reported missing. The hostile torpedo-boat, a small craft of ninety-seven tons, was chased by the Minerva and some British destroyers and destroyed on the coast of Chios. The crew of thirty-four men, including seven Germans from the Goeben, were made prisoners.

This was a poor beginning of the torpedo campaign

PRINCE SAID HALIM PASHA.
The Turkish Grand Vizier.

DSCHEWAT PASHA.
In charge of Dardanelles Defences.

against our immense fleet of battleships and transports. But the German seamen who conducted it were to improve with practice, and to introduce by means of a flotilla of submarines a new and powerful factor antagonistic to the success of our naval and military operations against the Dardanelles. All things considered, the situation round the Gallipoli Peninsula in the middle of May was one of great anxiety.

In regard to the control of the operations of our united Services by brilliant and daring politicians, it is usual to refer to the exploits of the elder Pitt, as related by ordinary historians. According to the works of these men Pitt, though a mere politician, was the most masterly leader of our naval and military forces we ever possessed. But we must point out that our leading military historian, Mr. Fortescue, after studying very closely the operations conducted by Pitt, came to the conclusion that this famous politician, with the advantage of having only two effete and badly governed countries to act against, not infrequently wrought more mischief than good when he interfered. Pitt's example was certainly misleading to the inexpert modern politicians, who, at a time when we were opposed by the mightiest military empire in the world, acted as amateur strategists and dictated plans of campaign with the best intentions but without the knowledge and experience required.

BRITISH WARSHIP ATTACKING THE OUTER FORTS OF THE DARDANELLES.

GERMAN SUBMARINE THAT SUNK THE FALABA.

THE PIRATE CRAFT SEEN FROM DECK OF THE FALABA.

PASSENGERS WAITING TO BE TAKEN OFF THE VESSEL.

TWO OF THE FALABA'S BOATS "TURNED TURTLE."

PASSENGERS CLINGING TO FALABA'S UPTURNED BOAT.

CHAPTER LXIII.

DEVELOPMENT OF THE SUBMARINE WARFARE TO THE SINKING OF THE LUSITANIA.

By Percival A. Hislam, author of "The North Sea Problem," "The Navy of To-Day," etc.

British Submarines in the Mediterranean—Perilous Exploit of the B11—The First Naval V.C. in the War—Hostile Underwater Craft in the Channel—Loss of the Formidable—Captain Loxley's Heroic Message—German Mines on British Trade Routes—Sinking of the Viknor—The Clan McNaughton Mystery—French Naval Watch on the Strait of Otranto—Austria's Initial Essay in Submarine Warfare—The Léon Gambetta Torpedoed—Disregard of the Rights of Neutrals—A Ten Months' Record of Losses—Why the Enemy's Boats Concentrated on Merchantmen—The German "Blockade"—Delight of the German Press—Blood-Lust and the Falaba—The War Against North Sea Fishermen—Captain J. W. Bell of the Thordis Retaliates—Attack on the Transport Wayfarer—Blockade of German Ports Declared by Great Britain—The U28 and U29 Sent to the Bottom—Treatment of Submarine Prisoners—Aircraft Aid in Submarine Attacks—The Most Horrible Crime in Civilised Warfare—German Jubilation over the Torpedoed Lusitania.

ALTHOUGH the watch of British submarines on the German coast, which had begun a few hours after the declaration of war, was maintained with undiminished zeal, the increased precautions taken by the Germans after the sinking of the Hela and the S116 proved sufficient for many months to save the enemy's fleet from further loss. The impossibility of putting to sea without serious risk of meeting superior British forces would alone have sufficed to reduce the surface-keeping ships of the enemy to a state of impotence. The submarines, however, besides adding to the firmness of our grip on the enemy, were able to do some extremely useful work as scouts, penetrating hostile anchorages and returning with information of vital importance to the commander-in-chief.

But although our submarine flotillas in home waters had little opportunity for proving their fighting worth, the turn of events at the eastern end of the Mediterranean enabled them to show the world that the coming of new weapons had not detracted from the old-time skill and daring of the British seaman. In the late autumn a combined British and French fleet, under the command of Vice-Admiral Sackville H. Carden, had carried out a brief bombardment of the Turkish forts at the entrance to the Dardanelles, more to test the

nature of the defences than for any other reason, and the ships then withdrew, leaving only a patrol to blockade the Strait, while plans for the grand assault were matured.

Among the vessels left behind to maintain the blockade were the submarines of the B class, which had been stationed in the Mediterranean for a few years before the outbreak of war, and in the early morning of December 13th, 1914, the B11, commanded by Lieutenant-Commander Holbrook, set out on the perilous task of reconnoitring the interior of the Strait. The B11 belonged to one of our earliest classes of submarines. She was launched in 1906, and had a displacement of only three hundred and sixteen tons, while her best speed when submerged was only eight knots, allowing a margin of no more than three or four knots over the powerful current that runs through the Dardanelles from the Sea of Marmora into the Ægean. With this little craft, manned by a crew of two officers and fourteen men, Lieutenant-Commander Holbrook set out to perform one of the most difficult pieces of submarine navigation ever attempted.

It was three o'clock in the morning when the B11 left her parent ship, and in view of the perilous nature of the enterprise everyone left letters behind to be sent to those dearest to him if the vessel never returned. As the entrance to the Strait was approached the vessel submerged, in order that she might not be seen from

THE U36 CROSSING THE BOWS OF THE DUTCH STEAMER BATAVIER V.

the look-out stations ashore. Once within the Dardanelles progress was difficult. The current was strong and treacherous, but the B11 battled bravely against it, and slowly won her way ahead. The channel was known to have been liberally mined by the Turks, and it was necessary to proceed at a considerable depth below the surface. The greater part of the journey was made at a depth of sixty feet, the vessel rising occasionally so that a swift glimpse of her whereabouts and surroundings might be obtained through the periscope.

Under five rows of mines The B11 had been under way nearly nine hours when, having successfully passed under five rows of mines, she came to the surface within striking distance of a Turkish battleship that had been stationed on the inner side of the field to prevent its being swept or countermined. As soon as Lieutenant-Commander Holbrook sighted the ship he took his boat down to a depth of forty feet while the torpedo was made ready for firing, and then slowly brought his vessel up until she was no more than fifteen feet from the surface and a clear view of the Turkish vessel could be obtained. Almost at the moment of the torpedo's

ARMED GERMAN SUBMARINE TENDER WAITING TO CAPTURE THE DUTCH STEAMER ZAANSTROOM.

discharge the submarine was sighted, and instantly guns began to blaze away at her from the shore and the ships in the vicinity. But the Whitehead had been truly aimed, and as the B11 dived again a tremendous explosion was heard as the weapon reached its mark.

The B11 had performed more than she set out to do; but she had a very narrow escape from disaster herself, for as she dived to escape the enemy's fire she struck the bottom in thirty feet of water. It was an anxious moment for all on board. Other submarines that attempted later to emulate the feat of the B11 were brought to disaster in just this way. But the crew had full confidence in their commander, and he justified it. For some distance the submarine crept along the bottom, scraping the shingle as she went, and then, happily, she found herself in deep water again, and was able to get down to sixty feet. Then Lieutenant-Commander Holbrook made a "porpoise" leap to the surface, and had the satisfaction of seeing the battleship settling fast by the stern; but he also saw that several of the enemy's torpedo-boats and destroyers were scouring the Strait for a sign of his craft, and he promptly went down again, and did not reascend to the surface until he had got well clear of the Strait nine and a half hours later. To keep a vessel of the B class submerged for this length of time was in itself no mean feat.

The torpedoed battleship proved to be the Messudiyeh, which had been launched on the Thames in 1874, and reconstructed and fitted with new armour and guns in 1901. One hundred of those on board were killed, including several German officers; and an extraordinary touch of comedy was added to the incident by the official Turkish announcement that " the old battleship Messudiyeh sank at her anchorage as the result of a leak." It was a leak, in all truth; but it was caused by the explosion of two hundred pounds of British gun-cotton.

" For most conspicuous bravery" displayed in this exploit Lieutenant-Commander Holbrook was awarded the Victoria Cross. This was the first announcement of a naval V.C. in the war; but in April it was stated that Commander H. P. Ritchie had been awarded the coveted decoration for gallantry at Dar-es-Salaam in November, so that the distinction of priority belongs to this officer. Lieutenant Sydney T. Winn, second-in-command of the B11, received the Distinguished Service Order, and the fourteen petty-officers and men who were on board were all granted the Distinguished Service Medal.

The following day the B9 entered the Strait, but she had not proceeded far before her periscope was seen from the shore, and no fewer than eight observation mines were exploded round her. Providentially she escaped injury, and she got away safely after diving to eighty-five feet. A month later the French submarine Saphir endeavoured to get through. Entering the Dardanelles on January 15th, 1915, she got as far as Nagara when, in diving to avoid mines, she struck the bottom and was compelled to come to the surface in a disabled condition. The shore batteries at once opened fire, and in a few moments the vessel was sinking. Many of her crew were killed, but ten were picked up by the Turks; the commander gallantly refused to be saved and went down with his ship. The Saphir was a vessel of three hundred and eighty-six tons, launched in 1908, and carried an armament of six torpedo-tubes.

In home waters the New Year was ushered in with disaster. Hostile submarines had occasionally been seen in the Channel, and towards the end of November two British merchantmen, the Malachite and Primo, had been sunk by these vessels in the neighbourhood of Havre. Our warships, however, had become more accustomed to the tactics of submarines, and although the patrols were maintained in undiminished force, no successful attack was made on them from November 11th, when the old gunboat Niger was sunk off Deal, down to the end of the year. Then the spell of immunity was suddenly broken. Among the ships engaged in the patrol of the Channel was a squadron of obsolescent battleships under the command of Vice-Admiral Sir Lewis Bayly, who cruised more or less regularly between Devonport and the mouth of the Thames. The activity of the enemy's submarines in the North Sea had already shown how unwise it was to employ old and big ships of low speed upon patrol work, and it is obvious that adherence to anything like a settled programme would enable the enemy to lay his plans some time in advance and place himself in a favourable position for delivering an attack.

On the night of December 31st, 1914, the squadron was

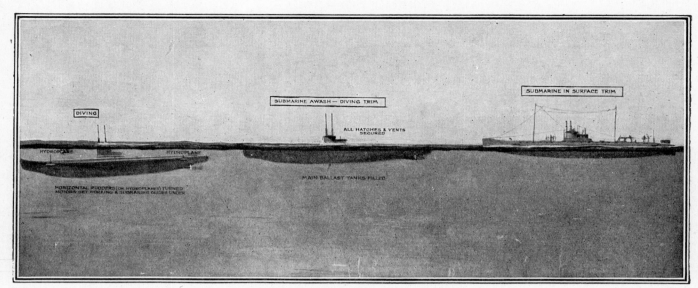

First Stage—From surface trim to diving.

Second Stage—Discharging a torpedo while submerged.

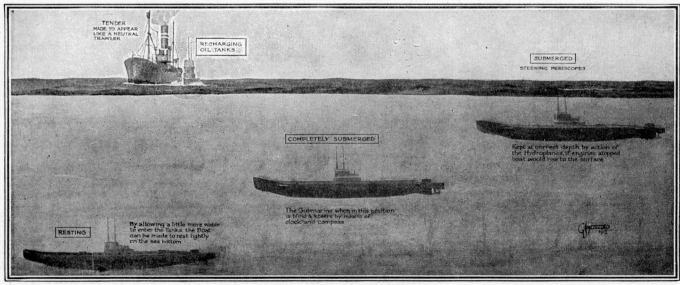

Third Stage—Submerged after sinking its prey.

HOW THE GERMAN SUBMARINE WENT ABOUT ITS DEADLY WORK.

THE CAPTURE OF THE ZAANSTROOM.
On the left the U36; in centre, the Zaanstroom; on right, the armed tender to U36.

GERMAN PILOT APPROACHING THE ZAANSTROOM.

steaming slowly down the Channel through a heavy sea, the end of the line of battleships being brought up by the Formidable, under the command of Captain Arthur Noel Loxley. There were no destroyers in company, although the experiences of our ships when bombarding the Germans on the Belgian coast had conclusively proved that vessels of this type offered the best possible protection against submarine attack; and the great ships went leisurely on their way at a speed of seven or eight knots. Officers and men had welcomed the coming of the New Year, and everything had settled down again to order and watchfulness, when suddenly at about half-past two in the morning a torpedo struck the Formidable on the starboard side just abaft the fore magazines. Had the

Loss of the Formidable

vessel been hit a few feet nearer the bows she would probably have been blown to atoms almost instantly. As it was, she remained afloat long enough to adorn our naval history with one of the most noble episodes of which it can boast.

It was realised from the first that the ship was doomed. Captain Loxley had won his way to the hearts of his men, and was loved as few officers have been since Nelson, and now in a heavy gale and a torrent of rain, facing certain death, he gave the last and greatest proof of his worth. As the ship began slowly to list the men came rushing up from below, many with hardly a shred of clothing on

them. Captain Loxley was on the bridge, his little terrier Bruce by his side, and for three hours he remained there, giving orders and encouraging the men by his wonderful coolness, until the great ship slowly turned over and took him to the bottom. His first words to the men as they assembled on the sloping, sea-swept decks were: "Steady, men! No panic! Keep cool and be British. There's tons of life in the old ship yet." The men needed no reminder of their duty. Boats were hoisted out, many of them to be smashed against the ship's side, while some that got safely away were swamped and sunk by the heavy seas.

The noise of the exploding torpedo was heard in one of the other ships, and immediately she came to stand by and give what assistance she could. But Captain Loxley would not have it. The Formidable had been attacked by a sub-marine, and he knew that if another vessel

Captain Loxley's heroic message

came to his aid she would probably share her fate. Instantly, therefore, he gave the order for the signal to be sent: "Keep off. Submarines about." The sending of that signal made his own end doubly certain, but it probably saved the lives of many hundreds of men in the ship coming to his aid. "That," said the Earl of Crewe in the House of Lords, "was a very gallant act, and worthy of the highest traditions of the British Navy."

Under the orders of Commander C. F. Ballard and Lieutenant H. D. Simonds, some of the boats got safely away. After some time the light cruiser Topaze endeavoured to get near the sinking ship to pick up survivors, but the heavy seas made it impossible. She did manage, however, to throw a line into a cutter containing thirty-five men, who were hauled safely on board. The coxswain in charge of the boat was no less a hero than his captain. He refused to leave it, and called to his crew to go with him back to the Formidable and get another load of men.

BRITISH DESTROYERS ON PATROL DUTY OFF THE COAST OF FRANCE.

THE DESTROYER DESTROYED—CREW OF THE SINKING GERMAN SUBMARINE U8 SIGNALLING OFF DOVER TO BRITISH WARSHIPS FOR ASSISTANCE, MARCH 5TH, 1915.

To do so would have been impossible, but nothing would make the man abandon his intention until an officer dropped into the boat and literally forced him out of it.

Captain Loxley remained at his post to the end. Those who were saved from the disaster stated that as they left the ship the men on board were calmly smoking, awaiting the inevitable end, and singing the song which had swelled through the ship in such different circumstances only a few hours before—" Auld Lang Syne." The captain himself never left the bridge, but remained **Captain Loxley's** there, a type of the British sea spirit to **last words** the last, a cigarette between his lips and his faithful dog by his side. He spoke a few words of praise to Lieutenant Simonds for the manner in which that officer had attended to the boats; and the last words he was heard to utter were : " Good-bye, lads. Every man for himself, and God help you all ! "

The men who had succeeded in getting into the boats still had a fearful battle for life before them, and many died of exposure before they reached the shore or help came to them. One of the most heroic of the many gallant deeds done that wild winter's morning was accomplished by William Pillar, skipper of the Brixham trawler Providence. The little vessel was running for shelter to Brixham before a heavy gale, and had to heave-to owing to the violence of the wind. Suddenly the crew caught sight of an open boat driving through the mountainous seas, hidden some-

times for minutes together in the trough of the waves. Captain Pillar swung the Providence clear. The crew, with almost superhuman efforts, took another reef in the mainsail and set the storm-jib, for until that had been done it would have been disastrous to attempt a rescue. The warship's cutter was seen to be drifting to leeward, and the captain decided to jib (take the wind on the opposite quarter)—a perilous manœuvre in such weather, since the mast was liable to give way.

Four times did the gallant smacks-**Brixham trawler's** men seek to get a rope to the cutter, **gallant skipper** and at last success attended their efforts. The boat was hauled as close alongside as the seas permitted, and one by one the exhausted sailors leaped on board the trawler. Seventy-one men owed their lives to the magnificent seamanship of Captain Pillar and the splendid courage of his crew of three, and the story of the rescue thrilled the country as greatly as the heroism displayed by everyone on board the lost battleship. Captain Pillar and his men were decorated by the King with the medal for gallantry in saving life at sea, and gifts of money were made to them by the Admiralty.

In the sinking of the Formidable there were lost, besides Captain Loxley, thirty-three officers and five hundred and thirteen men. The ship was of 15,000 tons, and had been completed at Portsmouth in 1901 at a cost of £1,022,745. She was armed with four 12 in. and twelve 6 in. guns.

A DEED OF HEROISM IN THE DARDANELLES.
Lieutenant Brooke Webb and some of the men who destroyed the E15 on the night of April 18th, 1915, when the submarine ran aground and was in danger of falling into the hands of the Turks.

FUNNEL
DAMAGED
BOAT DECK

PROMENADE DECK

SHELTER DECK

← Dotted line →
represents
approximate
height of water
& debris thrown
up by the explosion

Approximate size
of vast hole caused
by Torpedo.

Torpedo

← Area affected (Rivets started Etc) →

APPROXIMATE VIEW OF THE CAVERNOUS HOLE THROUGH WHICH THE SEA RUSHED WHEN THE LUSITANIA WAS TORPEDOED BY THE GERMAN SUBMARINE U21 OFF THE IRISH COAST ON MAY 7TH, 1915.

with the steamer Erivan and went to the bottom with all on board—three officers of the Naval Reserve and eleven men. Much more serious was the loss of the armed merchantman Viknor, which before the war was a well-known pleasure steamer called the Viking. Towards the end of October it became known through the sinking of merchantmen that the Germans, probably by means of ships flying neutral flags, had succeeded in laying large numbers of mines on the trade routes that lead to England round the north coast of Ireland. All possible precautions were taken to protect our ships from these weapons, but on January 26th the Admiralty announced that the Viknor, which had been engaged on patrol work in these waters, had not been heard of for some days, and it therefore had to be assumed that she had been lost with every officer and man on board. The cause of her loss was uncertain, but as some bodies and wreckage were washed ashore on the north coast of Ireland it was presumed that during the bad weather the vessel either foundered or—being carried out of her course—struck one of the enemy's mines in the waters where the Germans were known to have laid them. Questions were raised as to whether the mounting of guns on her upper deck might have affected her seaworthiness and increased her liability to founder, but nothing could be proved on that point. Commander E. O. Ballantyne, twenty-one other officers, and about two hundred men were lost with the ship.

A month later, on February 25th, the Admiralty announced the loss of another armed merchantman—the Clan McNaughton—with twenty officers and two hundred and sixty men. The cause of her disappearance was never discovered. She was last heard of on February 3rd, and the discovery of wreckage belonging to her led to the conclusion that she, too, had probably foundered in a gale. Commander Robert Jeffreys was the officer in command. In our last great naval war we lost about three times as many ships by wreck as we did in action with the enemy.

The circumstances attending her loss were the subject of much comment. Lord Charles Beresford, in particular, complained that battleships should not have been sent to cruise at slow speed in waters where hostile submarines were known to be without an escort of fast torpedo craft. This was the first occasion on which a ship was attacked and destroyed by a submarine during the hours of darkness, and the exploit was one which reflected much credit on the efficiency and skill with which the attacking vessel was handled.

During the few weeks following this calamity we sustained some heavy losses among the vessels that had been taken over by the Admiralty from the mercantile marine at the outbreak of war and commissioned for various naval duties. In the early morning of January 16th, 1915, the Char, a small vessel engaged in examining the cargoes of suspected ships sent into the Downs, collided

On March 11th another large auxiliary cruiser was lost, but the victim in this case—the Bayano—was torpedoed by a hostile submarine. The cruiser was patrolling off the south-western coast of Scotland when, at about five o'clock in the morning, a violent explosion occurred near her bows. This was quickly followed by a second— German submarines usually fire two torpedoes in quick succession when attacking a large ship—and such was the effect of the weapons that the Bayano rapidly settled down by the head and went to the bottom in less than four

Loss of the Bayano

minutes, leaving such of the crew as were able to get on deck to save themselves if they could by clinging to the floating wreckage. There was no time to launch the boats, but two of the three rafts were cut adrift, and on these a number of men were saved. No one on board the cruiser saw any sign of a submarine, but one or two of the vessels that hurried up in response to the brief wireless call for help were chased away by an enemy craft. Subsequently, however, the survivors were picked up, but there were only twenty-six out of a total crew of two hundred and forty. The captain, Commander Henry C. Carr, and eleven men of the Newfoundland Naval Reserve were among the lost.

It was not only the British Fleet that was exposed to the attack of hostile submarines. In the Mediterranean the gallant Navy of our French Ally was charged with a duty very similar to that of the Grand Fleet, for while the latter had to prevent German warships from getting on to the Atlantic trade routes, and from interfering with the transports that were constantly crossing and recrossing the Channel, the French forces in the Mediterranean had to exercise a similar control over the Austrian Fleet in the Adriatic. Using Malta as his base, the French commander-in-chief, Admiral Boué de Lapeyrère, maintained a close watch over the Strait of Otranto—a task that became increasingly imperative as the Allies began to concentrate their forces for the opening of the Dardanelles. This guard could not be maintained without exposing the French ships to the risk of torpedo attack, but it hardly needs saying that the risks were cheerfully accepted in the common cause.

At the beginning of the war Austria had seven submarines in service, and seven in various stages of construction. From time to time reports were published of the arrival of new vessels at Pola, sent in sections overland from Germany to be put together in the Austrian dockyard. It was not until the war had been in progress nearly five months, however, that the enemy's underwater craft made any attempt on the French Fleet. On December 21st submarine U12, command by Lieutenant Egon Lerch, reached the southern end of the Adriatic, and there, after lying in wait for some time, she succeeded in stalking the French Dreadnought Jean Bart. She fired two torpedoes, one of which missed its mark by a hundred yards, but the other struck the 23,000-ton battleship in the bows and tore a huge rent in her side. Fortunately, however, the Jean Bart was solidly built in accordance with the latest ideas of naval architecture. Her bulkheads and watertight doors stood out against the strain, and she was able to make her way into port, some hundreds of miles distant, under her own steam and without further

mishap. One of the ship's officers, in writing of the incident to a French newspaper, told a little story which affords an admirable illustrat.on of the spirit of the French Navy. "What I shall remember all my life," he said, "is the sight of my master carpenter. He was on the forward deck when the explosion took place, and for a moment was completely stupefied. Quickly recovering himself, his thought was only of the outlet valves, and he rushed below to **Master carpenter's** open them. He was not so quick as **heroism** the water, though, and when I went below myself I perceived my master carpenter swimming about in the hold in the middle of the wine barrels. The work took him an hour, but he accomplished it."

The Austrian version of the affair was not without its amusing side. The enemy declared that it was the Dreadnought Courbet that was torpedoed, and that she sank after colliding with the Jean Bart. As a matter of fact, the Courbet was nowhere near the scene, while the Jean Bart was repaired and had rejoined the fleet in less than two months.

Three days after this incident the French submarine

RESCUE WORK AFTER THE DISAPPEARANCE OF THE LUSITANIA.
It was announced in June, 1915, that the Kaiser had conferred on Captain-Lieutenant Hersing, commander of the U21, the Order "Pour le Mérite," in recognition of his "gallant act" in torpedoing the Lusitania. The same submarine sank the Pathfinder in September, 1914.

DESTRUCTION OF THE DRESDEN OFF JUAN FERNANDEZ ON MARCH 14TH, 1915.

The Dresden was the last of the regular German cruisers on the high seas, and to the loss of these vessels is attributed in large degree Germany's indiscriminate war on peaceful trading ships, unarmed men, and defenceless women.

Curie, a small but modern vessel of three hundred and ninety tons, carrying seven torpedo-tubes, made a plucky attempt to enter the harbour at Pola with the object of attacking the Austrian ships within. She safely passed the outer defences, and was creeping slowly along towards the inner harbour, when she was suddenly fouled by a heavy steel net rigged across the entrance. In extricating herself from this obstruction the submarine rose to the surface, and the Austrians, having been warned by the movements of the buoys supporting the net, immediately opened a heavy fire, which rapidly smashed in the sides of the submarine and sent her to the bottom. All the crew were picked up, with the exception of the commander, who chose to go down with his ship.

The second Austrian submarine attack on the French Fleet was, unfortunately, much more successful than the first. On the night of April 26th-27th the armoured cruiser Léon Gambetta, flying the flag of Rear-Admiral Sénès, was steaming slowly across the mouth of the Adriatic, en route to Malta. Without any warning of impending attack, a terrific explosion occurred amidships, in the neighbourhood of the engine-room. The dynamos were wrecked, and the whole vessel plunged into darkness, while the wireless apparatus was destroyed, so that it was impossible for the ship to send for help. Those who had not been killed or injured by the explosion rushed on deck, but there was no sign of panic. Orders were given for the guns to be manned in case a glimpse might be caught of the enemy. Down below the engineers worked frantically to get the dynamos going again, but all to no purpose. A few minutes after the first explosion, when

SOMEWHERE AMID THE NORTHERN MISTS.
British naval officer's impression of the quarter-deck of one of the ships of the Grand Fleet at night after a snowfall.

the ship was already heeling dangerously, a second torpedo struck her, and she began to settle down rapidly. One or two boats full of men got away, and one or two were swamped as the 12,000-ton ship disappeared beneath the waves. The men in one of the boats, seeing her gallant commander on the bridge, called to him to jump, so that they might pick him up. With a farewell wave of the hand, he answered :

Last of the Leon Gambetta " No. Think of your own lives. My destiny is here   I die with my ship. Vive la France ! "

All the officers of the doomed ship gathered on the bridge, and not one of them was saved. The noise of the explosions was fortunately heard at the lighthouse on Cape Santa Maria di Leuca, and a flotilla of Italian torpedo craft was immediately sent out to search for survivors. It was a most gallant action on the part of the nation that was shortly to join hands with the Allies in the most chivalrous war since the Crusades, for the boats might

easily have been mistaken for French vessels, and fired upon or torpedoed by the Austrians. They searched the sea for hours, but were only able to pick up one hundred and thirty-seven survivors out of a crew of some seven hundred and twenty. All the bodies that could be recovered were taken ashore and given reverent burial.

The Léon Gambetta was a serviceable armoured cruiser of 12,000 tons, completed in 1905, and armed with four 7·6 in. and sixteen 6·5 in. guns. Her successful assailant was the U5, a submarine of two hundred and sixty-nine tons submerged displacement, carrying two torpedo-tubes, and commanded by Lieutenant Georg Ritter von Trapp. The French fleet of armoured cruisers was so strong in comparison with that of Austria that the sacrifice of the Gambetta was by no means a shattering blow for our Ally ; and, although the loss of nearly six hundred brave men is no light matter even for the greatest of sea Powers, the manner in which they faced death will always remain an inspiration for France, and so, perhaps, prove

THE LOSS OF THE FRENCH CRUISER LÉON GAMBETTA, TORPEDOED IN THE STRAIT OF OTRANTO, APRIL 26-27TH, 1915.
As the vessel went down all her officers were at their posts. Her gallant commander's last words were : " I die with my ship. Vive la France !" Our illustration is from the painting by Paul Lévéré.

of even greater value than the ship and her mortal crew.

To the British mind the idea of carrying on warfare by means of submarines, mines, and similar methods has always been repugnant, but by the custom of nations the use of these weapons has come to be regarded as legitimate and proper, so long as they conform to the laws relating to the general conduct of war. The use of submarines is a legalised form of warfare ; but a submarine has no more right than a battleship or a cruiser to disregard the rights of neutrals, wantonly to attack and destroy the lives of non-combatants, or even to sink a merchant ship without taking the proper steps to ascertain its real enemy character. For the first few month Germany conducted the war at sea in a manner which, in comparison with the behaviour of her armies in Belgium and France, was almost honourable ; but as the pressure of the sea-power of the Allies began to make itself more and more strongly felt, so our enemies fell rapidly away from their earlier standards, until at last their submarine flotillas became little better than a horde of savages, scattering death and destruction among men, women, and children, reckless of the flag under which they sailed, careless of international agreements to which the seal of Germany had been set, and subject in not the remotest degree to the elementary dictates of common humanity.

The genesis of this indiscriminate war waged upon peaceful trading ships, unarmed men, and defenceless women is to be traced to two main sources, and the principal of these was undoubtedly the utter failure of those deeply-laid schemes which Germany had prepared for the embarrassment and destruction **Genesis of indiscriminate war** of our oversea trade. The Dresden, the last of the regular German cruisers on the high seas, was destroyed on March 14th off the island of Juan Fernandez. The Kronprinz Wilhelm, the last of the auxiliary cruisers specially commissioned for the annihilation of our commerce, sought refuge in an American port in April, and in due course was interned for the remainder of the war. From the opening of hostilities down to the inglorious exit of the Kronprinz Wilhelm, a period of nearly nine months, German cruisers succeeded in capturing or destroying a total of only fifty-four British merchantmen out of a total of over twenty thousand. Every regular cruiser engaged in this work was sent to the bottom ; and two of the armed merchantmen had been sunk, others captured, and the remainder interned in neutral ports. The definite and complete collapse of a campaign of which so much was expected drove the enemy to the adoption of other means for achieving the same end.

Another point which weighed heavily with him was the dwindling success of his submarines when used for their legitimate purpose of attacking warships. In the first few weeks of the war these vessels cost us many good ships and hundreds of valuable lives ; but the Fleet rapidly adapted itself to the new conditions. In the first five months of the war enemy submarines destroyed eight of our warships in home waters, their total tonnage being 67,700. In the second five months the record fell to two ships of 6,333 tons, and only one of these— the old destroyer Recruit, of 385 tons — was a regular warship. Therefore, besides having learned by costly experience that his surface-keeping ships were useless for attacking our commerce, the enemy also came to realise that his submarines were becoming less and less valuable for attacking our warships. The result was that the submarines were

ship to France a large number of troops and a great quantity of war material. We shall act against these transports with all the military means at our disposal." Whatever the instructions issued to the enemy's submarines in the Channel, they were interpreted in the most barbarous spirit. In the afternoon of February 1st a deliberate attempt was made to sink the British hospital-ship Asturias. This vessel, carrying a full hospital staff of doctors and nurses, was making for Havre in order to embark wounded British soldiers and bring them across to England. In accordance with the Hague Conventions, to which Germany had subscribed, she was painted white, with a broad band of green running from stem to stern, and huge red crosses painted in prominent positions on her sides. According to the sworn statement of the master of the ship, it was broad daylight when, at about five o'clock in the afternoon, the conning-tower of

Dastardly attack on hospital-ship a German submarine was sighted at a distance of about five hundred yards, and immediately afterwards the track of a torpedo was seen making directly towards the ship. The master immediately altered his course, and rang down to the engine-room for full speed, with the result that the torpedo missed its aim and passed close under the stern; but it was not Germany's fault that her list of crimes at sea was not swollen by the sinking of a ship whose character she was pledged by her own word and by every impulse of humanity to respect. It is true that some weeks later a sort of official apology was issued, but it perverted the facts to such an extent as to amount to no more than an attempt to justify the crime.

The apparent success of the war upon unarmed merchantmen gave rise to wild shrieks of delight in the German Press, where it was freely advocated that all ships entering the " war area " should be sunk on sight, without regard to their nationality or to the safety of whatever passengers they might be carrying. But the German Navy seems to have required little encouragement in this direction, as the incidents already described conclusively prove, though many officers in command of submarines seem to have been unable to descend to the depths of inhumanity and callous murder demanded of them by their Government and their countrymen. The majority, however, had no qualms about it, and those who made the slightest effort to save the lives of men, women, and children

came to be looked upon in this country as the Prussian equivalent of a gentleman.

There was great confidence in Germany in the moral effect of the " submarine blockade." It was firmly believed that, with this menace facing them, British ship-owners would refuse to risk their ships at sea, and that officers and men would decline to place their lives in jeopardy. The enemy made no allowance for the fact that the British merchant seaman comes of fighting stock, and is not frightened merely because he is told he ought to be. The enemy received his first lesson in this direction a week before the official opening of the " blockade." On February 10th the steamer Laertes, bound for Amsterdam, was intercepted in the North Sea by a German submarine, and peremptorily ordered to stop, and the skipper of the submarine must have been more than a little surprised when, instead of doing so, the Laertes clapped on extra speed and proceeded to steer an erratic course in order to avoid the torpedoes that the Germans were expected to fire. The Laertes hoisted the Dutch flag, and the submarine had no means of knowing she was not Dutch. But a torpedo was fired, and the Laertes dodged it; and then the submarine uncovered a gun and opened fire on the ship. Even this did not impress the steamer. She kept on her way at full speed, and soon had the pleasure of seeing the submarine drop astern and give up the chase. It was Germany's first taste of the spirit of the British merchant service, and the Admiralty were so delighted with the example which Captain William H. Propert, of the **Plucky example of the Laertes** Laertes, had set to his brother officers in the mercantile marine, that they awarded him the Distinguished Service Cross, and gave him a commission as a lieutenant in the Royal Naval Reserve.

The inauguration of the blockade was accompanied by no diminution of British shipping or in the volume of traffic dealt with at our ports. Ships were torpedoed and crews were wantonly murdered. On February 19th the Cardiff steamer Cambank was attacked without warning off Anglesey, and three men were killed by the explosion, while a fourth was drowned. On the same day the campaign against neutral shipping was opened by the torpedoing off Folkestone of the Belridge, a Norwegian ship carrying oil from New Orleans to Amsterdam, and having therefore nothing whatever to do with

LIEUT.-COMMANDER HOLBROOK, V.C., AND CREW OF THE B11, PHOTOGRAPHED ON BOARD THE SUBMARINE'S PARENT SHIP, AFTER SINKING THE TURKISH BATTLESHIP MESSUDIYEH IN THE DARDANELLES, DECEMBER 13TH, 1914.

THE MARCH OF THE MILLIONS: RUSSIAN TROOPS ON THE WAY TO CRACOW.

RUSSIAN INFANTRY FORMING UP OUTSIDE A VILLAGE IN READINESS FOR AN ADVANCE.

NEW RUSSIAN TROOPS EN ROUTE TO THE WARSAW BATTLE-LINE.

MACHINE-GUN IN ACTION IN AUSTRIAN TRENCH.

this country or even with a British port. Fortunately, the vessel did not sink, and was towed into the Thames, where pieces of a German torpedo were found on board.

It is not necessary to give a detailed account of the " warfare " conducted by German ships against merchantmen. In a few instances the officers of the enemy ships showed some little consideration for the crews of the vessels they attacked, giving them ample time to take to their boats and even, in some cases, towing the boats towards the shore. When the Delmira was sunk off the French coast on March 25th the submarine U32 came up alongside the boats and asked the officers if they would like a bottle of wine—an offer, needless to say, that was refused. In the great majority of cases, however, the conduct of the Germans was marked by a callous brutality, and a mad blood-recklessness that was in every way worthy of the doings of their countrymen ashore. German submarines killed their first woman victim on March 15th, when the Fingal was torpedoed without warning off the Northumberland coast. **Germans' mad** Of her crew of twenty-seven, six **blood-recklessness** men and the stewardess were murdered.

It was at the end of the same month that the character of the German submarine service was revealed in its naked iniquity. On March 27th the steamship Aguila was intercepted in the Irish Sea by the U28 and ordered to stop. Instead of doing so the vessel put on her best speed in an endeavour to escape; but the submarine proved the faster, and when at last the Aguila was overhauled and came to a standstill the exasperated Germans gave the passengers and crew only four minutes to take to the boats. Almost before it was possible to begin to get the boats out the submarine opened fire on them. Three of the engine-room staff were killed by shells as they were scrambling into the boats and many of the seamen were wounded. A heavy sea was running, and in the confusion caused by the enemy's fire one of the boats was capsized, adding two women victims to the record of German infamy. On the very same day, however, this exhibition of blood-lust was eclipsed. The steamer Falaba, outward bound from Liverpool, and carrying nearly two hundred passengers— men, women, and children—was stopped at the mouth of

WITH THE FORCES OF THE EMPEROR FRANZ JOSEF IN EAST GALICIA.
The troops are seen trying to save a village which has been set on fire by shell. In circle: Austrian troops firing from behind a stone barricade.

OPEN-AIR BANQUET GIVEN TO TROOPS AND REFUGEES BY RUSSIAN OFFICERS TO CELEBRATE A VICTORY OVER THE GERMAN INVADERS.

the St. George's Channel by the U36. In spite of the large number of people on board, the submarine gave them only ten minutes to get into the boats and away. It was, of course, absolutely impossible to do this in anything like the time, and the expiration of the ten minutes found many of the passengers still on board, while others were in boats that still lay alongside the ship, waiting for passengers to jump into them. The submarine was only a short distance away, with numbers of her officers and men on her decks. They watched the frantic efforts of the people on the Falaba to save their lives; they could hear the agonised cries of women and children as they ran about in search of safety; they could see the decks still crowded, and the loaded boats in the water close by; and with all these things happening within less than two hundred yards they slewed the submarine round and drove a torpedo into the ship.

The scene that followed can be imagined. Many were killed by the explosion. Boats were shattered and their occupants thrown into the water, while the liner rapidly took a heavy list that precipitated the others into the sea. The submarine came slowly on, a score of men on her decks. By reaching out their hands they could have pulled a few children—or even, perhaps, a woman or two—on board.

The Falaba horror

They did nothing of the sort. On the contrary, those who were fortunate enough to survive the massacre agree almost unanimously that the officers and men on the submarine laughed and jeered as their vessel forged its way slowly among their drowning victims. One hundred and twenty-one lives—innocent lives—were destroyed. The German Navy had another victory to inscribe on its banners.

Our gallant fishermen in the North Sea were selected as special targets for these murderous attacks. Some were fired upon with guns, which killed or wounded members of their crews. On April 18th a German submarine tor-

pedoed the trawler Vanilla without warning, and when another fishing vessel came along to pick up the crew, the submarine turned her guns upon the would-be rescuers and forced them to let their comrades drown. Instances of the same thing could be multiplied, and it is satisfactory to know that a full and complete record of these atrocities is kept by the Admiralty. Refugee ships, hospital ships, passenger ships, fishing-boats—all came alike to these Germans who disgraced the name of seamen; but there were not many things in their record much worse than the sinking of the Harpalyce. This ship was engaged in bringing relief from the United States for the stricken and impoverished people of Belgium. She flew a large flag to indicate her business. Along her sides, in letters

Belgian relief ship sunk

visible at a distance of eight miles, were painted the words, "Commission for Belgian Relief." Above and beyond all this, she carried a safe conduct issued by the German Minister at The Hague, which was intended, or pretended, to save her from all interference at the hands of German warships. Yet on April 10th this ship was deliberately torpedoed in the North Sea by a German submarine and sent to the bottom, three of her crew being killed. It was another instance of the value attached by a German to his pledged word.

Many were the occasions when a threatened British ship refused to be cowed by these murderous pirates. The feat of Captain Propert, of the Laertes, has been already recorded. It was repeated under even more difficult circumstances by Captain John Green, of the steamer Vosges. On March 27th this ship was attacked by a submarine. The captain at once ordered all the firemen below, and called for volunteers from among his passengers to assist them. The submarine chased and opened fire from straight astern. The first round was blank, but the next hit the ship in the after part. All this time the vessel was going at top speed, and altering her course as necessary

403

IN GALICIA : HELPING A WOUNDED RUSSIAN INTO AN AMBULANCE.

to keep the submarine well astern. The chase continued for an hour and a half, during which time the Vosges was repeatedly hit and the engine-room badly pierced by shrapnel. The chief engineer was killed near the stokehold while he was exhorting the firemen and volunteers to further efforts. Several of the crew were injured, and a lady passenger received a slight wound in the foot. At last the submarine sheered off; but the steamer was in a sinking condition, and it was fortunate that she met a patrol-boat, to which every-one was transferred, for she went down two hours after the chase was ended. All the crew were rewarded, and Captain Green received the Distinguished Service Cross and a commission in the Naval Reserve.

Equally plucky was the behaviour of the steam-tug Homer. On April 8th this little vessel was towing the French sailing-ship General de Sonis up the Channel, when, off the Isle of Wight, a German

Merchantman sinks a submarine

submarine appeared and called upon them to surrender. Captain Gibson, of the Homer, paid no attention, but, awaiting his opportunity, slipped the tow-rope and steered straight for the submarine under a shower of bullets from the enemy's machine-gun. The Homer missed the submarine's stern by no more than a yard and then steered for the Owers Lightship, pursued by the enemy, who fired a torpedo that missed its mark. The tug got safely into port with seven bullet holes in her, and the General de Sonis arrived later under sail.

The first merchantman which actually sank a submarine was the Thordis, a vessel of less than eight hundred tons, commanded by Captain J. W. Bell. The incident occurred on February 28th, when the ship was off Beachy Head. The look-

out suddenly sighted a submarine, and Captain Bell immediately ordered all hands on deck in case of emergency. In a few minutes the track of a torpedo was seen making towards the vessel; but the stopping of her machinery upset the enemy's calculations, and the weapon passed clear. Something then appeared to go wrong with the submarine's engines, for she drifted towards the Thordis, and the latter was steered so as to bring her bows on to the vessel. A heavy wave came and lifted the steamer on its crest, and when she descended there was a tremendous crash as she fell on to the hull of the submarine. Large quantities of oil appeared on the surface, and the submarine was not seen again. An expert investigation by naval officers convinced them, by the condition of the hull of the steamer, that she had actually sent the

Enemy attacks on transports

vessel to the bottom. Many rewards of money had been offered for this effective sort of work, and the officers and men shared a total of £1,160, while Captain Bell was made a lieutenant in the Naval Reserve, and was awarded the Distinguished Service Cross.

In view of the fact that the German declarations relating to attacks on merchant shipping had laid special stress on the assumption that we were about to ship large numbers of men and quantities of material to France, their failure to attack our transports with any success was most remarkable. Many thousands of journeys had been made across the Channel by ships loaded with men, munitions, and stores, presenting a perfectly legitimate target for German attack. In the first ten months of the war only one vessel was even hit. This was the liner Wayfarer, torpedoed one hundred miles off the Scilly Isles on April 11th. She was towed into Queenstown, where a hole forty feet long and several feet wide was found in her side. No detailed statement of the in-

WOUNDED AUSTRIAN HELPED BY FRIEND AND FOE.

cident was issued, but on May 28th the following Army Order was published :

"The Secretary of State for War desires to place on record his warm appreciation of the gallant conduct and devotion to duty displayed by Major R. A. Richardson,

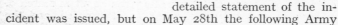

RUSSIAN RED CROSS WORKERS LENDING SUCCOUR TO WOUNDED PRUSSIAN PRISONERS.

The sinking of the German submarine U8 off Dover, March 5th, 1915.

Germany's "grand coup" in crime: The sinking of the Lusitania and the

...rder of over 1,200 non=combatants off the Old Head of Kinsale, May 7th, 1915.

With the Russian Army—Communion Service before battle.

and the officers, non-commissioned officers, and men of the 1st Warwickshire Yeomanry on the occasion of a torpedo attack on the transport Wayfarer on April 11th, 1915. Through the prompt action of Major Richardson, and the marked efficiency of the officers and men under his command, only five lives were lost out of a total of one hundred and eighty-nine men, and all the horses, seven hundred and sixty-three in number, were brought safely to shore. The Secretary of State for War is proud of the behaviour of the troops, and regards it as a good example of the

Premier and "submarine blockade" advantages of subordination and strict discipline. He cannot close this order without expressing his admiration of the coolness and courage of Captain David Cownie and the officers and crew of the Wayfarer."

Although the details are meagre, the incident must be placed on record as the first instance of a submarine—or any other—attack on a British transport, vessels of which class must have travelled many hundreds of thousands of miles in the first ten months of the war.

It was not until March 1st that the British Government announced any special retaliatory measures against the "submarine blockade." Hitherto, although the enemy's shipping had been wiped off the seas, commerce was still carried on with German ports by neutrals, provided that they were not carrying contraband. On March 1st, in the House of Commons, Mr. Asquith reviewed the policy and behaviour of German submarines, and added :

"Germany is adopting these methods against peaceful shipping and non-combatant crews with the avowed object of preventing commodities of all kinds, including food for the civil population, from reaching or leaving the British Isles or Northern France. Her opponents are therefore driven to frame retaliatory measures in order, in their turn, to prevent commodities of any kind from reaching or leaving the German Empire. These measures will, however, be enforced by the British and French Governments without risk to neutral ships or to neutral or non-combatant lives, and with strict observance of the dictates of humanity. The British and French Governments will therefore hold themselves free to detain and take into port ships carrying goods of presumed enemy destination, ownership, or origin."

In short, the British Government at last declared a blockade of German ports—a measure which, in the opinion of many, should have been taken much earlier in the war.

In the meantime the British Navy had not been idle in dealing with the menace of the submarine. A very large number of vessels—torpedo craft, cruisers, and specially commissioned auxiliaries—were kept in all the waters known to be infested by these craft; but the submarine, unfortunately, is in the position of being able to make fairly certain that the ground is clear before coming to the surface. If, when the periscope was raised a few feet above the water, a hostile warship were discovered, the submarine could, without the least difficulty, descend again to await a more favourable opportunity. A large, slow-moving warship might be attacked, as several were in the early days of the war ; but when a submarine sights a fast vessel, such as a destroyer, her safest plan is to get

out of sight as quickly as possible. It must be remembered, too, that the submarine was a new weapon, calling for new means of defence or counter-attack, and it was necessary that the Admiralty should take every care not to give the slightest hint to the enemy as to the means that had been devised for dealing with these craft. In most cases, therefore, the authorities contented themselves with announcing the bare fact of the destruction of a hostile submarine, without giving any details, and there were other cases in which even that information was not given, but held back until its publication could not be of the slightest use to the enemy. It is therefore advisable to give only those details which the Admiralty saw fit to make public at the time.

The first enemy submarine to be accounted for by our Fleet after the institution of the "submarine blockade" was the U8, which was sighted off Dover on March 5th by a flotilla of British destroyers. Captain C. D. Johnson, commanding the flotilla, immediately made such dispositions that when the submarine came to the surface again one or more destroyers were bound to be in the vicinity. Success attended his efforts. When the U8 rose again she was promptly attacked by the destroyers

AUSTRIAN GENERAL STAFF'S INSTRUCTIONS BEING SIGNALLED TO THE VARIOUS COMMANDERS DURING THE FIERCE FIGHTING IN POLAND.

Ghurka and Maori, and damaged so that she quickly sank. The whole of her crew were taken prisoners, and in connection with them the Admiralty issued the following announcement : " The Board do not feel justified in extending honourable treatment to the twenty-nine officers and men rescued from the submarine U8. This vessel has been operating in the Strait of Dover and the English Channel during the last few weeks, and there is strong probability that she has been guilty of attacking and sinking unarmed merchantmen, and firing torpedoes at ships carrying non-combatants, neutrals, and women. There is, of course, great difficulty in bringing **Admiralty and the** home particular crimes to any individual **crew of U8** German submarine, and it may be that the evidence necessary to establish a conviction will not be obtained until after the conclusion of peace. In the meantime, persons against whom such charges are pending must be the subject of special restriction, cannot be accorded the distinctions of their rank or be allowed to mingle with other prisoners of war." This was a perfectly correct attitude to take up. Indeed, the ends of justice would have been no more than served if those submarine murderers

THE TSAR GREETING HIS OFFICERS IN THE FIELD.

TSAR'S BROTHER AT THE FRONT.
The above picture was obtained on the Upper San River south of Przemysl. The figure in the foreground is the Grand Duke Michael Alexandrovitch the Tsar's only brother. He has had a very distinguished career in the Russian Army.

had been treated as pirates were in the old days, and strung up on gibbets in prominent places *pour encourager les autres*. Unfortunately, however, Germany was in a position to retaliate, and it was promptly announced that if any distinction were drawn against the crews of submarines reprisals would be exacted upon an equal number of British prisoners in the hands of Germany. This was, in fact, done. Twenty-nine British Army officers, prisoners in Germany, including near relatives of Sir Edward Grey and Sir Edward Goschen, were placed in solitary confinement in isolated fortresses, and allowed only the usual

rations of a private soldier. The British Government shrank from carrying the policy of reprisals to sterner lengths ; and the irony of the situation lay in the fact that the submarine prisoners were, in fact, treated in exactly the same way as the others, but were kept in different quarters. Even this small degree of discrimination was abandoned after a few weeks, much to the general satisfaction.

Another enemy submarine, the U12, was destroyed on March 10th off the Firth of Forth. The first intimation of her whereabouts was given by two trawlers, and a hunt was immediately organised. The submarine discharged two torpedoes at the destroyer Attack, and as she came to the surface to see the result, was discovered by the destroyer Ariel (Lieut.-Commander J. V. Creagh), which proceeded to charge full speed at the vessel. The submarine dived, but she was too slow in sinking. The Ariel, keeping dead on her course, sped over the spot where the **Destruction of U12 and U29** submarine had disappeared, and as she did so she struck the periscope and bent it completely over in such a way that it prevented the hood of the conning-tower from being raised. The loss of the periscope blinded the submarine. She came to the surface again, and the Ariel and other destroyers immediately opened fire on her, maintaining it until the crew came out of the hatches with their hands raised in token of surrender. Eighteen of the crew of twenty-eight were drowned.

The next success was recorded by the Admiralty on March 26th in the following brief statement : " The Admiralty have good reason to believe that the German submarine U29 has been sunk with all hands." This achievement, the method of which was not announced, was one of the greatest so far attained, for the lost boat was commanded by Commander Otto Weddigen, who, when in command of the U9, had sunk the Aboukir, Hogue, Cressy, and Hawke. The loss of this capable officer caused much regret in Germany, where it was even proposed that his memory should be immortalised by always using the word "Weddigen" instead of torpedo The French Ministry of Marine issued statements on February 24th, March 5th, and March 31st, claiming the destruction of German submarines, but in no case was the number given of the vessel alleged to have been sunk. Further, many other merchant ships besides the Thordis undoubtedly struck submerged bodies of one sort or another, but in such cases, where no prisoners were taken and no relics recovered, it was naturally a matter of very great difficulty to be certain of the destruction of the vessel.

Aircraft, both seaplanes and dirigibles, took part in these attacks on merchant shipping, but with no success. Many bombs were wasted in attempts to destroy British vessels, but an American steamer, the Cushing, was struck on the taffrail, while the Norwegian ship Diana was assailed by an aeroplane from which hundreds of **Aircraft attacks** eight-inch steel darts were dropped on to **on shipping** the decks. Many of the crew would undoubtedly have been killed or injured had they not taken refuge below when the aircraft came in sight. Submarines joined with a will in these attacks on neutrals. The Dutch steamer Medea was sunk in the Channel by the U28 on March 25th, after she had been stopped and her papers examined, so that the Germans could have been in no doubt as to what they were doing. At about the same time the Italian steamer Luigi Paradi was sunk, to be followed early in April by the Swedish vessel Folke. The most glaring example of this wild policy of indiscriminate destruction occurred on April 14th. The Dutch steamer Katwyk, carrying a cargo of grain from Baltimore for Rotterdam consigned to the Dutch Government, came to anchor in the evening a few miles from the Noordhinder Lightship. The necessary lights were placed in position, and the Dutch flags fore and aft were illuminated by special electric lights. The name of the ship and of her port—Rotterdam—were painted in huge letters along the side. Without the slightest warning this vessel, carrying the property of the Dutch Government, was torpedoed by a submarine and sent to the bottom, the crew fortunately being able to save themselves. The German Admiralty at first insisted that it must have been a British vessel that fired the torpedo, but later they admitted it to have been one of their own craft. Norwegian, Danish, and Greek vessels were treated in the same way, and the Germans did not even hesitate to insult the American flag. The aerial attack on the Cushing has been recorded. On May 1st the United States steamer Gulflight, carrying a cargo of oil, was torpedoed off the Scilly Isles. She did not sink, but the captain died of heart failure, while

two men were thrown overboard and drowned. Other neutral Powers appeared to be indifferent to the damage inflicted upon their citizens by this peculiar method of making war, but the case of the Gulflight gave rise to serious diplomatic tension between the American and German Governments.

There has now to be recorded the most horrible and outrageous crime in the history of civilised warfare.

Driven to desperation by her impotence to affect our position seriously, Germany planned a grand coup. She advertised her intentions extensively in America. On May 1st, 1915, the giant Cunard liner Lusitania was due to leave New York for England, and the same morning the following announcement, issued from the "Imperial German Embassy, Washington," appeared in a number of American newspapers :

Travellers intending to embark for an Atlantic voyage are reminded that a state of war exists between Germany and her Allies and Great Britain and her Allies ; that the zone of war includes the waters adjacent to the British Isles ; that, in accordance with the formal notice given by the Imperial German Government, vessels flying the flag of Great Britain or any of her Allies are liable to destruction in those waters ; and that travellers sailing in the war zone in ships of Great Britain or her Allies do so at their own risk.

To emphasise the warning, most of the prominent Americans who had booked a **Evidence of** passage by the Lusitania received a **premeditated crime** telegram on the morning of the vessel's departure in these terms : " Have it on definite authority Lusitania is to be torpedoed. You had better cancel passage

IN THE ADVANCED GERMAN TRENCHES BEHIND MLAWA. THE SMALLER PICTURE SHOWS GERMAN SNIPERS ON THE ROOF OF A FARMHOUSE IN POLAND.

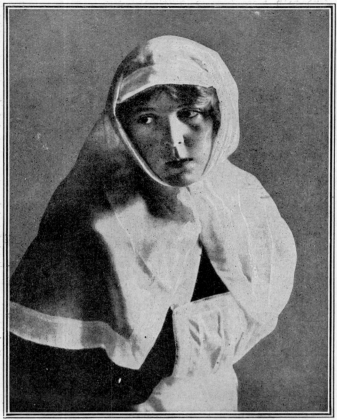

BRITISH AMBASSADOR'S DAUGHTER AS NURSE.
Miss Meriel Buchanan, only child of the British Ambassador at Petrograd.
She took a deep interest in the work of the British Hospital in the
Russian capital.

immediately"; and the message was signed either "John Smith" or "George Jones." Hardly anyone paid serious attention to these things.

And so the Lusitania set out on what was to prove her last voyage. Her commander, Captain W. T. Turner, when interviewed in America before the sailing, expressed his belief that the warnings were merely "bluff," and that in any case the speed of his ship would enable him to avoid a possible assailant. As the unhappy event proved, however, when the critical moment came the Lusitania was not using that high turn of speed in which her commander had placed such confidence.

The normal course of the Lusitania lay across the Atlantic to the south-western point of Ireland, whence she would steam along the south of that island, and so up the Irish Sea to Liverpool. During the week of her last crossing there was a remarkable outburst of submarine activity in these waters, and particularly in those between Dingle Bay on the west and Queenstown. The collier Fulgent was sunk off the north of Valencia Island on April 30th ; on May 5th the sailing ship Earl of Lathom was sunk off the Fastnet, while another British vessel narrowly avoided a torpedo thereabouts on the same day.

The Lusitania's voyage of doom Other submarines were reported as having been sighted in the mouth of the Shannon, and in Dunmanus Bay, so that all the evidence pointed to a large concentration of these craft having been made off the south-west coast of Ireland for some particular purpose.

The Lusitania crossed the Atlantic at a speed of twenty-one knots—considerably below the rate she was capable of. As she got into the British seas the vessel reduced speed to about eighteen knots, so that she might arrive off the Mersey at such a time as to be able to proceed straight in without waiting for the tide. It has been remarked that in view of the known presence of submarines in the waters through which the ship would pass, it would have been better to direct her to take a more circuitous route at her full pace rather than to reduce her speed. At a speed of eighteen knots she steamed along the south of Ireland on a lovely spring day, only a few miles off the coast, not even taking the trouble to steer a zigzag course. Such assurance did the Admiralty feel in her capacity to elude the hostile submarines that no attempt was made to provide an escort for her.

It was well past mid-day, and many of the passengers were down below at lunch. Everything seemed to promise well for a happy ending to the voyage. The look-outs had been doubled, and Captain Turner was pacing the bridge anxious, no doubt, but confident.

Suddenly from the other end of the **Tragedy of misplaced** bridge there came the cry, " There's a **confidence** torpedo!" Captain Turner rushed across, but it was too late to do anything to save the ship. Almost as soon as he had seen the track caused by the ejection of compressed air from the weapon, the torpedo struck the Lusitania on the starboard side between the third and fourth funnels.

Instantly the great ship began to heel, but never at any time was there the slightest disorder among the passengers or crew. The vessel was so huge that many on board did not for a moment imagine that the dull boom they heard was the explosion of a torpedo against her hull, and those who did know what had happened were confident that a vessel of such a size would not succumb. Every available boat was ordered to be launched at once. Lifebelts were served out, and as the ship listed more and more, confidence gave way to despair. The boats on the port side could not be lowered—they simply dropped against the side of the ship ; and many of those on the starboard side had to be attended to by the passengers themselves. The tragedy was over, so far as the ship was concerned, in eighteen minutes. She was struck by the torpedo just before 2.15 p.m. on May 7th, 1915. She gave a final lurch and disappeared just after 2.30.

There was no ship in the vicinity at the time.

FRENCH VOLUNTEER WITH THE RUSSIAN FORCES.
M. Gabriel Elchain, a volunteer in a Siberian regiment, receiving a gift from a member of a deputation from the municipality of Petrograd.

AUSTRIAN OFFICERS WATCHING EFFECT OF ARTILLERY FIRE IN THE CARPATHIANS.

THE ARCHDUKE CHARLES FRANCIS JOSEPH, HEIR TO THE AUSTRIAN THRONE, PHOTOGRAPHED IN A RAILWAY CARRIAGE WHILE ON A TOUR OF INSPECTION.

THE AUSTRIAN ARCHDUKE FRANCIS SALVATOR IN CONVERSATION WITH A GERMAN OFFICER.

But fortunately there were watchers ashore who in the far distance had seen the disaster, and with all possible despatch a swarm of vessels was sent out from Queenstown. But this was locking the stable door after the horse had been stolen, and the rescuers arrived only to save those who had been fortunate enough to get into the boats, or to find some other sure means of keeping afloat.

There had been 2,016 people on board the Lusitania, and over 1,200 had been murdered in cold blood, including score upon score of women and children, and people of all nationalities. The whole world rose in execration of Germany at this unparalleled crime. That it had been premeditated there was ample proof; and because a warning had been issued that wholesale murder was intended there was no palliation of the heinous offence. Out of two hundred and eighteen American citizens on board only seventy-nine were saved.

World's horror at Lusitania crime The depraved German mind found it possible to justify and rejoice over this act of barbarity. They asserted that the Lusitania was armed and carried ammunition. Collector Malone, of the Customs service of the port of New York, asserted positively that there were no guns, either mounted or unmounted, on board. There was not an ounce of explosive on board.

Great as Germany's crimes had been before, nothing could have set the feeling of the world against her so strongly as this fiendish and useless massacre. American opinion especially was strongly roused because of the number and prominence of the United States citizens who were lost. Germany had, in short, deliberately challenged another enemy to enter the field against her. From the military point of view that was the only result of the sinking of the Lusitania. One of the victims was a member of large firm of manufacturers in Connecticut which had previously refused on moral grounds to manufacture munitions for the Allies. The murder of a partner changed their attitude, and the firm promptly laid down the plant required for turning out shells.

There was a wide impression that, in view of all the circumstances, the Admiralty should have taken some special measures for the protection of the Lusitania. The official reply to that suggestion was that **British Admiralty's** even two destroyers could not be **lame excuse** spared from their other duties, and as the decision of the Admiralty must be paramount in war, that reason had to be accepted. But it carried no conviction to those who remembered that the cost of the Navy had always been regarded as, in part, an insurance premium for the protection of the mercantile marine. This was, in fact, one of the gravest mistakes of the war.

413

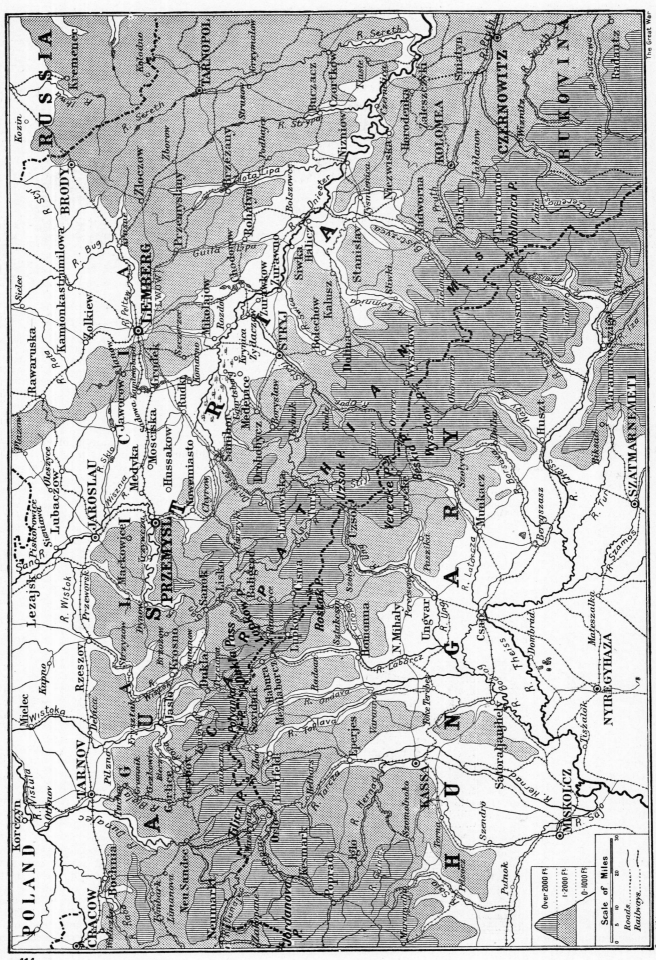

MAP OF THE REGION OF PRZEMYSL AND THE BATTLES OF THE MOUNTAINS AND RIVERS OF GALICIA.

Copyright

The Great War

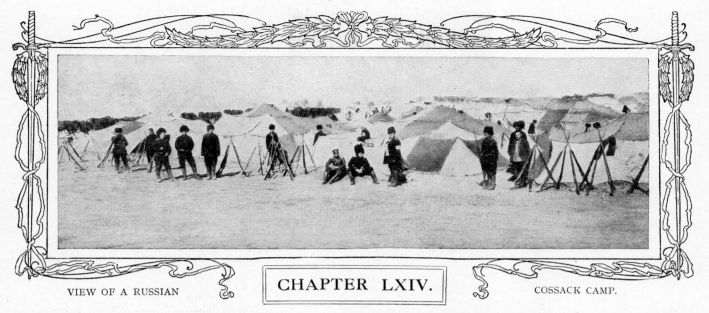

CHAPTER LXIV.

PRZEMYSL & THE BATTLES OF THE MOUNTAINS & RIVERS.

Russians Rely on the Spring Floods to Defend their Northern Front—Surprise Attack on Seaport of Memel—Failure of Both German and Austrian Flank Attacks—Russians Strike at Hungary Over the Carpathian Passes—Russians' Disadvantages in Munitions and Equipment—Fierce Mountain Conflicts in Hungary and Galicia—Terrible Sufferings of Austrian and Hungarian Troops in Winter Battles on the Snow-covered Heights—Przemysl Blocks the Railway Communications of Southern Russian Army—Lacking Siege-Guns, the Russians Resolve to Starve Out Garrison—Extraordinary Condition of Affairs at Przemysl—Kusmanek has More Troops than He Can Feed—Tries to Save Food by Sending His Soldiers Out to Die in Sorties—Austrian and German Relieving Armies Fight their Way Towards the Beleaguered Fortress—Furious Battles Upon the Crests and Slopes of the Mountains—Complete Failure of the Austro-German Relieving Armies—Surrender of Przemysl.

T the beginning of March, 1915, the victory which the Russians had gained at Prasnysch had a definite effect on all the operations along the whole East Prussian frontier. The German commanders, Eichhorn and Bülow, strove in vain to retrieve their defeat by making another concentration at Willenberg and striking again at Warsaw through the frontier town of Chorzele. With its central thrust and flanking movement, the battle extended in the first week in March from Suwalki to Plock. The Russian general, owing to the magnificent tenacity of his advanced troops, had been able to throw forward from Kovno a force at least equal to the combined armies of Eichhorn and Bülow. For a week the Russians held the enemy all along the line, and then slowly drove forward in fierce and incessant conflicts, in which both sides employed in a daring fashion, amid the thawing river-marshes, squadrons of armoured motor-cars with quick-firers and machine-guns. The Russians especially used the modern war-chariots round Prasnysch in the old way, sending them in front of the infantry in a charge against the German trenches. The cars and their crews were sacrificed to break the German line, where they fought to the death with a view to producing such disorder in the hostile front as would allow the Russian infantry to follow in their wake and smash through.

Having suffered from the success of this new form of attack on their entrenchments, the Germans attempted on

March 9th to use their armoured motor-cars in the same manner. Every available squadron of them was collected in the neighbourhood of the fortress of Osoviec. There the position was very intricate. The armoured cars formed the advanced force of a column which was engaged in trying to outflank the Russian column that in turn was attempting to outflank the German line in front of Osoviec. But our Allies were prepared for the onrush of the hostile war-chariots. They countered the charge by a furious sweeping fire from the screened batteries of their field-guns, and in spite of the swerving, zigzagging manœuvres of the car-drivers, the Russian gunners got home on the leading cars, and smashed them up before they could operate against the infantry.

The Russian commander, however, did not pursue on the East Prussian frontier the advantages he had won, for he had no desire to get the Russian Army again entangled in the Masurian Lakes district. All he fought for was to gain time so as to allow the forces of Nature to co-operate in the defensive tactics which the Grand Duke Nicholas had imposed upon the Warsaw-Petrograd line of communication. For though the weather in the second week of March continued to be surprisingly cold, remaining at freezing-point in the shade, the great thaw was likely to occur as soon as the wind changed. The released water, owing to the unusual delay in the arrival of the warm spring wind, would flood the Niemen, Bobr, Narew, and the other frontier rivers and streams. Consequently,

GENERAL ARTAMONOV, THE RUSSIAN COMMANDANT AND MILITARY GOVERNOR OF PRZEMYSL, AT LUNCH WITH HIS STAFF.

RUINS AT PRZEMYSL WHEN SURRENDERED BY THE
AUSTRIANS.

some hundreds of miles of swamp would protect the Russian frontier in a most effectual manner. There would only be a few causeways to defend, and forts and earthworks with batteries already commanded these lines of invasion. Hindenburg's attempt to work around and behind Warsaw before the thaw took place had been defeated, and so far as the Russians were concerned this was an end to the matter. Instead of engaging in any further adventure in East Prussia, they **Russian attack** wanted to use their new Kovno army **on Memel** to reinforce their lines on the Bzura, Pilica, and Nida Rivers.

But before doing this a single brigade of the Kovno army undertook one surprising adventure. On March 17th it worked round the northern stretches of the Niemen River and surprised another small German force near Tauroggen. Having captured two guns and motor-lorries full of ammunition, the Russians employed this welcome addition to their slight artillery power in an attack upon the German seaport of Memel. Making a long night-march by one of these feats of physical endurance that distinguish the Russian peasant, the attacking force surprised the city and tried to carry it in a bayonet charge. But the German Landsturm troops were assisted in the house-to-house fighting by most of the German population. From the German point of view it was a fine patriotic thing for German non-combatants to fight for their homes. Francs-tireurs were only criminals when they were Belgians, Frenchmen, Russians, Serbians, and Italians. The Germans massacred the population of a village if a single person there used any means of defence, and they burned down towns if a shot were fired, even by a militiaman. But these extraordinary rules of warfare only applied to the lesser breeds who lack the light of "kultur." There was a higher law for German villagers and townsmen, as was seen at Memel.

The Russians, however, were not to be denied. They used the captured German guns and German ammunition against the barricades, which were being defended by two regiments of Landsturm and a large number of civilian inhabitants. The shells broke down the resistance of the Germans, and the remnant of the garrison and population fled to the sandy peninsula that protects the harbour, and there German warships steamed up and covered them with their guns. The position which the German authorities took up in regard to this flagrant example of

franc-tireur practice on the part of their own people was a revelation of the qualities of the modern German mind. For they proclaimed that if Memel were burnt down, according to the Teutonic law in such cases, they would burn down towns and villages in Poland by way of reprisal. The Russians, however, acted in the ordinary civilised manner. Having defeated the civilian force opposed to them, they did not dream of taking vengeance upon the more peaceful part of the population. They held Memel until the Germans weakened their frontier force by bringing up a fresh army against them; then, having accomplished their object of distracting the enemy and insulting the pride

CUPOLA OF TOWER, FORT NO. 11, PRZEMYSL, DESTROYED
BY THE AUSTRIANS BEFORE SURRENDER.

of the Prussian aristocracy by the occupation of an important Prussian seaport, they withdrew fighting over the frontier into Courland. So deeply were the Prussians vexed by this unimportant little raid that they gathered a strong force and tried to conquer Courland. And for this they were able to spare men in both the eastern and western **The battle in the** theatres of war, where great battles **Carpathians** were raging.

On the eastern front, after the victory of Prasnysch, Hungary became the danger-area in the Teutonic Empires. From the point of view of the German Commander-in-Chief, the indecisive operations north of Warsaw remained useful only as long as they detained there a large Russian force. After Prasnysch Hindenburg had to submit to the will of the Grand Duke Nicholas and agree to the Carpathians being the critical field of battle. The German attempt on the left flank had failed by the Niemen and Narew; the Austrian attempt on the right flank in the Bukovina had also been checked. All along the central river front—along the Bzura, Pilica, Nida, Vistula, and Dunajec—the Austro-German forces were for the time completely exhausted by their enormous losses, and on both sides of this section of the fighting-line a condition of stationary trench warfare obtained.

This left the Russian commander free to choose his own point of attack and concentrate all available troops there. There was, however, one very important factor that interfered with his free choice of the scene of his offensive movement. He had fewer guns and howitzers of the heavy class than the enemy possessed. What was worse, his store of large, high-explosive shells was almost exhausted, and even his field-artillery had to be exceedingly economical in the use of ammunition. In these circumstances he could not take the proper line of attack and drive in on Cracow and the industrial

OUTWORKS OF A FORT AT PRZEMYSL, HIT BY AN AUSTRIAN 42 CM. MORTAR.

RUSSIAN 18·5 CM. GUN IN FORT NO. 10, PRZEMYSL, AFTER BOMBARDMENT BY AUSTRIAN ARTILLERY.

region of Silesia. The mighty agricultural population of the Russian Empire, stretching almost across two continents, was baffled by the culminating achievements of all the slow and involved forces of urban civilisation. For the second time in history " the little **Strength of the** street-bred people " of the city were **"street-bred people"** more powerful than the men who led open-air lives in field and forest.

For thousands of years the saddle had been master of the plough. Loose congregations of semi-nomad tribes of horse-rearers and cattle-breeders had been the practical lords of the world. Never had the more settled and more peaceful farming races been able to resist the charging squadrons of wild horsemen from the steppes. Every era in the early agricultural stage of civilisation was broken by the irruption of the barbaric horsemen. They overturned every ancient empire. Then came the rise of the little inventive city States, which managed, by the elaboration of new instruments of slaughter and novel tactics, to check the larger forces of the sturdier barbarians. But with the invention of gunpowder the advantages which the cities enjoyed were spread more equally among the peasantry of Europe. The free cities fell under the power of kings,

largely because the king was able to arm the serf and yeoman with weapons equal to those employed by city dwellers.

This condition of things obtained down to our day. The sturdy and more enduring countryman could outmarch, and therefore outmanœuvre, the more intelligent, but less strongly-built townsman. The Germans depended almost entirely upon their peasantry for their first-line troops, and one of the chief reasons why their Government checked free trade in **German fear of** agricultural produce was to enable the **the moujik** peasantry to flourish at the expense of the urban industrial population. France was still regarded with respect because, owing to the fertility of her soil, she was principally a nation of small-holding peasants, likely to prove good marchers and steady fighters on the field of battle. But the Germans feared most of all the Russian moujik, because of his famous powers of physical endurance. Great Britain was supposed to have lost the chief source of her ancient valour by reason of her system of free trade, which had oppressed, impoverished, and depopulated the countryside for the sake of obtaining cheap food for the less vigorous stocks in all the industrial centres.

This was the German idea of the matter, and owing to Germany's success in the Danish, Austrian, and French wars it was generally agreed that the correctness of this idea was established by German military successes. All that the British people hoped was that their public health system had mitigated some of the principal disasters of their general movement towards urbanisation. We trusted that with the French people we should be able to hold out until the vast agricultural population of Russia began to press with irresistible force against Germany. But to everybody's surprise it was discovered, when the war had lasted for four months or less, that the working man of the urban class, when perfectly organised and disciplined, held the fate of the world in his hands. So tremendous had been the development of modern applied science that the factory dominated the battlefield. It was one of the greatest revolutions in class values in history. The cities were supreme over farm and cattle range. For the cities produced, in continually increasing volumes of production, the terrible machinery of slaughter, without which the civilised intelligent peasant infantryman was as helpless as the Zulu armed only with spear and assegai.

This extraordinary change in the conditions of modern warfare told most heavily against the soldiery of Russia, for the activities of the Russians were almost entirely agricultural. General Sukhomlinoff, the Russian Chief of Staff, displayed great energy in mobilising all available factories in the Empire. But, unfortunately, the only industrial region of much importance in Russia was that extending from Lodz to the frontier of Silesia, and it was in the possession of the enemy. Most of the Russian seaports were closed by ice, and though some ammunition was obtained through Port Arthur it was not sufficient for the needs of the Russian armies. The result was that our heroic allies had to rely on the bayonet and the shrapnel-proof trench. Millions of Russian peasants were ready to take the field, but were held back by a lack of rifles and artillery.

Russia's lack of munitions

In these circumstances the Grand Duke Nicholas, on recovering the initiative, selected as his region of attack the high-wooded sandstone heights of the Eastern Carpathians. Here, in a mean altitude rising from 3,250 feet near the sources of the tributaries of the Dunajec to 5,000 feet south of the sources of the San, one of the greatest

Tyrolean regiments, but the Russians, moving on snow-shoes in superior numbers, ambushed and slaughtered the brave and splendid Tyroleans. Austria had no more troops of the same class to supply their place, and in both the Carpathian field of war and the later area of mountain conflict in the Alps the early disasters to the Tyrolean troops had bitter and serious consequences.

We have seen in a previous chapter the tactics employed by the Russian commander General Brussiloff in the first phase of the Battle of the Carpathians. His subordinate general officer, General Dimitrieff, was entrenched along the Dunajec and Biala Rivers, where he resisted for months all Austro-German attacks from the direction of Cracow and the Neumarkt Pass. With his left wing near Gorlice, Dimitrieff helped also to fight back all attempts made to relieve Przemysl from the south-west. The main forces of the Russian southern army held the Dukla Pass, some fifty miles south-west of Przemysl, and were fighting their way towards the next important break in the mountain ridge—the Lupkow Pass. Some forty miles south-west of Lupkow is another important mountain road and mountain railway—the Uzsok Pass—which was being held by the enemy, and attacked by the Russians. Then another twenty miles farther south-west was the Tuchla Pass, controlling the road from the town of Munkacz, on the Hungarian plain, to the town of Stry, on the Carpathian foothills below Lemberg, in Western Galicia.

The main lines of the situation remained unchanged for months. The Russians tried to work down from the Dukla Pass; the Austro-Germans tried to work up from the Tuchla Pass. Between these two passes stretched 180 miles of mountain ridge, with a breadth of about fifteen to twenty miles, the altitude running from 2,000 feet on the lower northern scarps, to 5,000 feet on the central summit. Some of the heights were over 6,000 feet, and at times men on either side would try to get a machine-gun near the summit of one of these treeless, breezy mountain-tops. There was another field of conflict farther south,

TRANSMITTING ORDERS BY TELEPHONE FROM THE RUSSIAN HEADQUARTERS STAFF TO THE FIRING-LINE.

battles in the annals of the human race was fought. It began in midwinter when the mountains were covered with snow, and the wind in the high passes was so chill that the water in the bottles carried by the troops froze as they walked. Immense stretches of pine forest covered the slopes, walls, and peaks of yellow rock. The consequence was that there was seldom a clear field of fire for the enemy's superior artillery. The vast mountain forests, breast-deep in snow and cloaked often with low-hanging clouds, gave back to the Russian infantryman his natural advantage over his opponent.

For one thing the terrible climate suited him. He was accustomed to bear a greater rigour of Arctic cold than any other European. The Austrians of the plains were killed or crippled in hundreds of thousands by the severity of the winter mountain weather. The Bavarians showed more powers of endurance, yet they also suffered from frost-bitten feet, while the Russian troops lost no men whatever from this cause. The only men in the Teutonic Empire who could fight in the snow on the Carpathian heights with anything like the resisting powers of the Russians were the Tyrolean sharpshooters. Good men they were, and greatly enduring, but there were too few of them. Austria weakened her southern mountain defences against Italy by denuding the Tyrol of the

where the Austrians advanced through the passes leading towards Stanislav and Kolomea. Then more southward still, with the altitude of the Carpathians rising higher as they trended to the Rumanian frontier, were the forested heights of the Bukovina.

The position of the Russians was excellent at Dukla. The mountains in this region were low and bare, and the passes were broad, well-made roads, rising by easy gradients from the plain. The high ground was also lacking in breadth. All this made the maintenance of Russian communications an easy matter. The enemy, on the other hand, had worked southward over higher mountains and across a far broader stretch of broken highland country, where the forests were more extensive, **Rival positions at Dukla** the population scantier, and the roads fewer and steeper. The maintenance of Austro-German communications was therefore difficult. At the extreme end of the hostile front in the Bukovina the breadth of mountainous land was enormous—some three hundred miles.

At the other end of the Carpathian battle-line, round Dukla, the Russians had only nine or ten miles of falling mountain slopes in front of them before they reached the Hungarian river-valley. There were ten of these river-valleys running south from the Carpathian heights, and the

HURKO FORT, PRZEMYSL, AFTER THE AUSTRIANS HAD SURRENDERED TO THE RUSSIANS.

RUINED DEFENCES OF PRZEMYSL, AS FOUND BY OUR RUSSIAN ALLIES, AND LEFT BY THEM FOR THE AUSTRO-GERMANS.

passes extending from the river valleys formed the means of operations from Dukla to Kolomea. But all the ten river valleys converged quickly in the Hungarian plain, where the mountain streams flowed into the Theiss River. The Russians had only to work round the Ondava valley, from which the Dukla Pass ran; then, on a front of twenty miles or so, they would get astride the branching lines of communication, which were feeding the Austro-German front of one hundred and fifty miles in Galicia and the Carpathian rampart. In other words, by advancing southward from the Dukla Pass the Russians could turn completely the enemy's front and attack him in the rear, after cutting off all his supplies.

How Brussiloff saved Calais

This was the reason why General Brussiloff held on only to the Dukla region, and slowly pushed forward there against a desperately stubborn resistance. On all the rest of the front he was content to hold back the Austrians and Germans. He occupied at Dukla the decisive position, and by continually pressing forward he compelled the hostile commanders to mass against him for the defence of the Austrian communications. So hard pressed were the Austrians that three Bavarian army corps, under the command of General von Linsingen, were sent to the Carpathians to assist them. The Bavarians held the Lupkow, Uzsok, and Tuchla Passes. But they were not strong enough for their task. More German aid had to be sent, until the German forces under von Linsingen amounted to half a million men. Great was the tax upon the military strength of Germany. The Germans had to stand entirely on the defensive in France and Flanders, and also in Poland, when half a million of their best troops were urgently required in the Carpathians for the defence of Hungary. But unless this large measure of help had been given, the Hungarians would have been compelled to make terms with the Triple Entente, with the result that the Austrians would also have followed the same course. Bavaria in particular was drained of men of military age for the sake of Hungary. The German aid was not willingly given; it was the consequence of some very outspoken statements of the Hungarian position made by Count Tisza.

As we shall afterwards see, the pressure which General Brussiloff exerted against Hungary from his commanding position on the Dukla Pass saved Calais from falling into the hands of the Germans in May, 1915. General Brussiloff in the spring of that year was able to do what neither General Joffre nor Lord Kitchener in combination could effect. He was able to force General von Falkenhayn to employ, on a given stretch of front in Galicia, all the new and tremendous machinery of war which Germany had been building up for nine months.

The Russians had won the Dukla Pass at Christmas, 1914, but for eight weeks afterwards they could do little more than hold on to their new position and strengthen it. All along the eastern front our heroic allies were still outnumbered by the German, Austrian, and Hungarian forces controlled by Field-Marshal von Hindenburg. It was not until the end of March, 1915, that the Kitchener of Russia, General Sukhomlinoff, was able to place at the

disposal of the Grand Duke Nicholas the new army which at last gave the Russian Commander-in-Chief a full equality in infantry force with that of the enemy. It was the arrival of a considerable supply of rifles, cartridges, and light quick-firing guns in March and April, 1915, that enabled the Russians at last to put into the field forces nearly equal in number to those of their foes.

Until this was done General Brussiloff remained on the defensive without losing the initiative. The Austrians and Germans had continually to attack him on the front he chose, by reason of the two advantages he possessed. He held at Dukla the gate into Hungary, and he also encircled at Przemysl a fortress of the importance of Metz, with a garrison of 150,000 German and Austrian troops. Therefore, the tasks he set the enemy were to drive him from the Dukla Pass and to relieve Przemysl.

The Bavarian army tried to carry out both these extremely important undertakings by advancing from the Lupkow and Uzsok Passes to the upper reaches of the San River. For months unending furious battles went on along the San and its tributary streams, by the towns of Baligrod and Lutoviska. The aim of the enemy was to reach the Sanok-Sambor railway, which was only about ten miles north of Baligrod. Then, less than forty miles north of the railway, was Przemysl. At almost any time, two days' hard marching would have brought Linsingen's army to the beleaguered fortress city of Galicia. So his nights and days were spent in massing his troops for attack after attack on the lines held by the Russian southern army on the outlying heights and foothills of the Lupkow-Uzsok section of the Carpathian battle-front.

At the same time the Austrian Arab commander, Böhm Ermolli, with equal incessancy, tried to drive through towards Lemberg from the Tuchla and Jabloniska Passes. The operations of the Austrian Arab general, however were only of secondary importance. Except when he managed to threaten one of Brussiloff's lines of railway communication by an advance against Stanislav, Böhm Ermolli succeeded only in amusing himself, without endangering the Russian conquest of Eastern Galicia.

His Austrian and Hungarian troops had the most difficult country to work in, and they weakened fearfully in the bitter winter weather. Tens of thousands of them were killed by their own army contractors. Their winter uniforms, supposed to be made from thick wool material costing thirteen shillings a yard, were really fashioned out of thin, light, summer dress material for women, worth at the most half-a-crown a yard. The Government had given the full price, and the army contractors,

Killed by army contractors

after paying bribes to the officers entrusted with the duty of examining the quality of the uniforms, made a fortune. They did not enjoy their enormous profits for many months, being, in fact, shot or sentenced to penal servitude, together with the officers whom they had bribed. But this tardy act of justice did not save the troops from death by exposure. In less than two weeks' fighting and marching through the snow and brambled undergrowth of the mountain forests the clothes of the men were worn to rags.

PLAN OF THE DEFENCES OF PRZEMYSL.

TWENTIETH-CENTURY "CAVALRY" SCOUTS—A MOTOR RECONNOITRING PARTY.

They had to sleep in the open air with the temperature far below freezing-point, and in the first week of March, when warm spring weather was expected, there was another deadly cold snap, in which the temperature fell again below freezing-point even in the plains. On the northern slopes of the mountains, 3,000 to 6,000 feet above sea-level, where the battle continually raged, the last ounce of endurance was worn out of the Austrian soldiers. More than 100,000 of the troops were put out of action by frost-bite. Then another 120,000 men in the Carpathian battles were stricken with pneumonia or consumption. Of the cases of frost-bite, 50,000 recovered, but of the pneumonia and consumption casualties only 20,400 were, after hospital treatment, made fit enough to resume fighting. In order to fill the gaps in the fighting-line the Dual Monarchy, in the spring of 1915, had practically to resort to a general levy of the people. All men up to the age of fifty were called out for military service, except in the case of persons engaged in armament work and vital food industries.

Never had the tottering structure of the Austrian monarchy been so terribly tested. At the beginning of the war the available resources of Austria-Hungary were excellent. A thorough and honest system of organisation and administration would have enabled the Hapsburg Empire to crush rapidly and easily the attacks of the peasantry of Russia. The Austrian Army was large; the Austrian system of railways excellent, permitting the rapid movement of troops; and the Skoda armament works at Pilsen and Trieste surpassed those of Krupp in the production of very heavy and yet mobile howitzers. But the Austrian nobility was a vain,

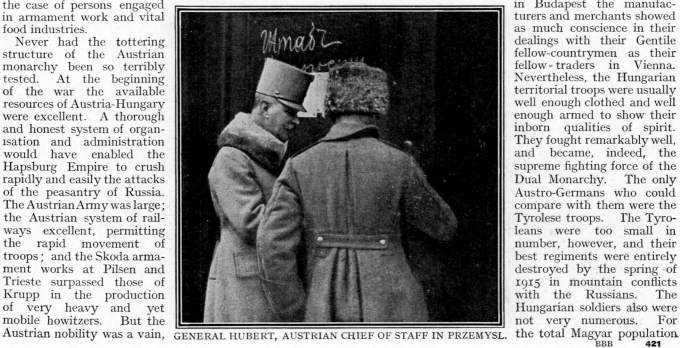

GENERAL HUBERT, AUSTRIAN CHIEF OF STAFF IN PRZEMYSL.

empty, self-complacent, and miserably inefficient class, with no constructive intelligence and no gift for leadership. The merchant class, largely composed of able but avaricious aliens, was eager to make money out of the necessities and misfortunes of the nation. The number of scandals concerning army contracts was enormous, not only in regard to the supply of ladies' summer dress material to the army fighting in winter in the Carpathians, but in regard to army stores of almost every kind. The aristocratic Austrian officer had ever been remarkable for being in need of money, and as inspector of army stores he let what patriotism he possessed rest in a cheerful faith in the heroism of the working classes, while he worked with the contractors in as profitable a manner as possible.

The Hungarian magnates, many of them men of great wealth and strength of character, proved themselves on the whole an efficient fighting aristocracy. There were army scandals in Budapest as well as in Vienna. For in Budapest the manufacturers and merchants showed as much conscience in their dealings with their Gentile fellow-countrymen as their fellow-traders in Vienna. Nevertheless, the Hungarian territorial troops were usually well enough clothed and well enough armed to show their inborn qualities of spirit. They fought remarkably well, and became, indeed, the supreme fighting force of the Dual Monarchy. The only Austro-Germans who could compare with them were the Tyrolese troops. The Tyroleans were too small in number, however, and their best regiments were entirely destroyed by the spring of 1915 in mountain conflicts with the Russians. The Hungarian soldiers also were not very numerous. For the total Magyar population

SENTENCED TO DEATH—RUTHENIAN SPIES UNDER AUSTRIAN GUARD IN GALICIA AWAITING THEIR TURN FOR EXECUTION.

of both sexes and all ages was at the beginning of the war only about ten million. So it was upon the Teutonic, Bohemian, Russian, Polish, Rumanian, Italian, Croatian, Serbian, and Mohammedan mixture of races—the most extraordinary in the world—that the main task of defending the Hapsburg Empire fell. As there was no common bond of veritable patriotism in this medley of peoples, the officers and army contractors often combined to diminish their means of warlike strength by every possible kind of malpractice. There were several large mutinies, ending in the shooting of thousands of the soldiers, and the general disruption and corruption were so great that it needed only a Russian descent into the Hungarian plain for the Empire of the Hapsburgs to fall into inter-militant fragments.

There was a time when it seemed that the fortress of Przemysl would decide the fate of the mosaic Empire it was built to defend. The Austrian stronghold on the San River had been remodelled and strengthened by a famous Swiss engineer after the affair of Agadir in 1911, when the Teutonic Empires decided to open hostilities in three years, and bent all their energies in the interval to the work of preparing for the tremendous struggle. When the new fortifications of Przemysl were completed in 1913 the experts of the German Great Staff examined the fortress very carefully, and congratulated the Austrian Staff upon the strength of the new works. In the considered judgment of the German authorities, Przemysl had been transformed into a strong place superior to Thorn, and at least equal to Metz. That was as much **Przemysl, the Austrian Metz** as to say that it was the finest modern fortress in Central Europe. It consisted of nine main works, arranged in a circle around the town.

In these main works were guns of enormous size, mounted in armoured towers, operated by electricity, and automatically disappearing after the gun had discharged its shot. Each of these works was placed on one of the foothills of the Carpathians, at an altitude of 1,000 to 1,350 feet above sea-level. The distance between the main works ran from 2,000 yards to 10,000 yards, there being marshes and other natural obstacles in the wider spaces to help in the defence. In the gaps between the main works there were nine smaller forts, with armour-plate cupolas, quick-firing guns, armoured machine-guns, and motor-batteries. Further, in the course of the siege, a considerable number of temporary works were erected all along the twenty-five-mile ring. There was also a girdle of closed trenches, wire entanglements, and land mines, the last-named being worked from the forts by means of electric current. The railway running from the Russian frontier to Lemberg and Cracow was bent round so as to pass through Przemysl.

PLAYING A RUSSIAN REGIMENT TO THE TRENCHES.

RUSSIAN CAVALRY CROSSING A RIVER SOMEWHERE ALONG THE EASTERN BATTLE-FRONT.

So as long as the fortress garden-city of the Carpathians held out, an invading army fed from Kieff would lack the use of the main railway when operating in Eastern Galicia. This is what occurred when the armies of Generals Brussiloff and Dimitrieff advanced in September, 1914, from Lemberg towards Cracow. Their railway communications were cut by Przemysl, and all through the autumn, winter, and early spring General Dimitrieff in particular had to rely entirely upon the small branch railway bending up and down by Ravaruska. The Russian forces at the Dukla Pass were also hindered by the control over the Galician railway system exercised by the enemy at Przemysl. The Russians could not maintain their offensive movement over the Dukla Pass against Hungary by a long, strong, persistent culminating effort until the trunk railway was in their hands. In other words, the Russians could not feed and munition an overwhelmingly numerous army in the Battle of the Carpathians until they had captured Przemysl.

The railway factor in Galicia

But, as we have seen, the Russian War Minister, General Sukhomlinoff, could not arm his new armies for the winter campaign. So the fall of Przemysl was not an urgent necessity in the Russian plan. There had been an occasion when its swift capture would have been a great benefit to the Russian forces. This was in September, 1914, when General Dimitrieff, advancing with amazing speed from Lemberg, hoped to take Cracow by surprise and capture it. Przemysl stood in his way. He massed his artillery against two of the forts, shattered them in a fierce, swift hurricane of shell, and then launched an army corps at the gap. But the main works of defence held good, and the leading Russian brigades were felled in thousands with such rapidity that the attempt to rush Przemysl by a quick, violent, storming attack came abruptly to an end. Then in the middle of October, 1914, Field-Marshal von Hindenburg's advance against Warsaw and Ivangorod compelled the Russian Commander-in-Chief to alter his entire front; for the Germans and Austrians were superior in number to the Russians and were able to choose their points of attack and to force the Russians to concentrate in answer to their movements. The troops investing Przemysl had to be drawn off to strengthen the fighting front.

But when Hindenburg was thrown violently back, and his right wing, composed of Austrian and Hungarian troops under General Dankl, was severely handled and almost broken on the Upper Vistula and the Lower San, the situation in Przemysl became curious. General Kusmanek, the commander of the fortress, did not at first know whether the strength of his position had been augmented or decreased. His proper garrison numbered

THE POISONERS' WAR—A LESSON IN THE USE OF A RESPIRATOR.

about eighty thousand troops. But after the smashing blow delivered by General Dimitrieff against the Austro-German force, seventy thousand more fugitives—German, Austrian, and Hungarian soldiers—retired into the fortress to avoid capture. The result was that Kusmanek had on November 12th, 1914, when the second siege began, double the number of troops that had originally been assigned to the defence of the stronghold. In itself this was a matter of congratulation, for the ring of forts measured twenty-five miles round. The proper garrison for a system of trenches of this extent, reckoning on the Continental estimate of two men to a yard, was eighty-eight thousand men. That left no reserve of the original

fugitive troops in strong and vehement sorties before they brought his stock of provisions down to danger point. His superfluous troops were so numerous that it was likely they could battle their way through the investing force near the road to the Lupkow Pass, at a time when the main Russian southern army near Lupkow was straining every nerve to meet the **Kusmanek's hopeful** attacks of the relieving army from **calculations** Hungary. If only the troops making the sortie could break through the line of investment they would take Brussiloff's men in the rear at the moment when the relieving forces were pressing on the Russian front. The result of this would be something more important than the relief of Przemysl. The Russian forces round the Dukla Pass would be cut off, together with a considerable portion of Dimitrieff's army fronting Cracow, in Western Galicia. All the land between Cracow and Przemysl would be cleared of Russians, and there would be an admirable opportunity, after the Russian front was broken, of turning and encircling the entire Russian forces in Galicia. In short, what was contemplated, as the result of an overwhelming sortie from Przemysl, was the complete destruction of the southern Russian army under General Brussiloff.

Brussiloff had no siege-artillery, and even his available force of field-guns was not large. No idea

KITCHEN IN WAR PRISONERS' CAMP AT KÖNIGSBRUCK, NEAR DRESDEN.

garrison to fill the gaps caused by casualties and sickness, and to provide for the sorties in great strength which would be required when the Russian front was pressed by the grand relieving army of Austrians and Germans. Thus, from a purely military point of view, General Kusmanek could look with pleasure on the enormous increase of his forces.

Unhappily for him, the economic situation was not so favourable. The store of food in Przemysl had been measured only by the requirements of the original garrison. Since the fall of Lemberg streams of civilian and military fugitives had passed into the city, with somewhat the effect of a locust swarm. By the middle of November, 1914, the year's food supplies had so diminished that even

FRENCH AND RUSSIAN PRISONERS PEELING POTATOES IN A DETENTION CAMP.
These two pictures are from German sources, and purposely exaggerate the provisioning of the camps.

the original garrison would not have **Przemysl's diminished** been able to live on the stores for more **food supplies** than eight months. The enormous addition of seventy thousand more soldiers reduced the period for which the fortress could hold out, without further supplies, to five months.

Yet, on the whole, General Kusmanek does not seem to have been discontented with the position of affairs. He reckoned on being able to use the larger part of the

of a bombardment duel with the great pieces of ordnance at Przemysl could be entertained. The Russian commander could profit only by the enormous number of troops in the fortress and revert to the old-fashioned method of reduction by famine. Only five divisions of Russian troops of the third class, old reservists more than forty years of age, were detached for the siege operations. They were placed under the command of General Selivanov, a veteran of seventy years, who had served in all the Russian wars since the Turkish war of 1877. His forces at first were much inferior to the Przemysl garrison, there being

WAR TIME IN AUSTRIA'S SERBIAN PROVINCES—A GERMAN ARTIST'S IMPRESSION OF A STONE QUARRY WHERE MEN OF THE HERZEGOVINIAN LANDSTURM WERE AT WORK.

about 100,000 Russians to 170,000 Germans, Austrians, and Hungarians. General Selivanov's field-guns were largely the outworn artillery of the southern army, the tubes having lost their exact rifling by constant use since the beginning of the previous August. When new field-artillery arrived for the army in Galicia General Brussiloff, instead of sending the old guns back to Kieff to be re-rifled, gave them to General Selivanov.

The old general kept his batteries well out of range of the great new guns of Przemysl, and entrenched on a wide circle of hills at a long distance **Russian and Austrian** from the girdle of forts. His sole object **chivalry** was to stop anybody from getting in or out of the beleaguered fortress-city. He made no attack, but simply waited until General Kusmanek attempted a sortie. Then, as the enemy troops advanced beyond the shelter of their great guns of position, they were shot down close to the wire entanglements in front of the Russian trenches.

No serious attempt was made to break the ring of investment until December 10th. General Kusmanek was then informed by wireless that a relieving army was advancing from the Carpathians and steadily gaining ground towards Limanova. Thereupon the garrison of Przemysl began to make sorties in great force. Although they helped the relieving army to gain a little more ground, they did not succeed themselves in breaking through Selivanov's circle of defences, for the besieging commander was reinforced at some expense to the Russian fighting-line on the Carpathian front, and all that Kusmanek achieved was to reduce considerably the amount of mouths he had to feed. The siege then went on in a quiet, leisurely manner for a month. The situation at Christmas was quite friendly and peaceful. By means of their airmen the Russians distributed thousands of Christmas-cards over the invested fortress. "We wish a happy and a peaceful Christmas to the heroic defenders of Przemysl. Let peace reign on earth, and happiness in the hearts of men." Thus ran one of the cards of greeting. On January 12th, the Russian Christmas, the garrison returned this act of Christian chivalry. Not a shot was fired, and the Austrian outposts came forward to the Russian advanced guard and gave

them Christmas-trees. But in the middle of January Kusmanek began to grow seriously alarmed at the rapid diminution of his food supply. More of the garrison was sacrificed in vain attempts at a successful sortie, while the Russian sappers began to drive their trenches closer to the ring of forts. The decisive struggle took place in the middle of February, when the southern Russian army was swinging round from its position on the Dukla Pass and winning ground towards Lupkow. Instead of the relieving army in the Carpathians helping the garrison of Przemysl, the garrison troops had to fling themselves out in fierce night attacks, less with a view to breaking through than with the design to compel Selivanov to ask for more reinforcements.

The old Russian general had a difficult task. As his lines ran in a much larger circle than the ring of forts he was investing, he needed many more troops than the men he was wearing down. As the power of making attacks really rested with the beleaguered Austrians, they could mass at night and break forth for an advance in any direction they chose. The Russian commander could not concentrate in advance against them, but had to leave the defence of the assailed section of trenches in the hands of the ordinary number of men there. The only consequence of the repeated attempts to break through the investing line, conducted by the valiant Hungarian General Tamassy, was that General Selivanov was compelled to use the proper number of men in garrisoning his trenches —two to a yard—which, on a circular **Fall of outer** front of fifty miles required an army of **fortifications** 176,000 troops. These were infantry-men, and the total Russian besieging forces may at last have amounted to 200,000 men.

Even this was not very much more than the number of foes against whom they were operating. And these foes had an overwhelming superiority in heavy artillery. But with undaunted courage the Russians sapped forward, building their trenches by special devices, perfected since the outbreak of hostilities, which gave some protection to the troops against even the heaviest projectiles. The outer forts and field fortifications soon fell into the hands of the Russians, who mined and counter-mined, completing each

425

piece of their mole-like work by a night attack with bayonets and hand-grenades.

But though they were able to push their trenches so near as to bring in view the churches and roofs of Przemysl, they remained incapable of capturing one of the main forts. The Austrians asserted that from November 12th, 1914, to March 1st, 1915, merely three shells fell in the city. Having only short-range artillery, all that the Russian commander could do with it was to cover every path and road by which the enemy could make sorties. He relied almost entirely on shrapnel, which he employed against the hostile troops as they came into the open. Every night the Russian searchlights on the distant hills swept all the country in a regular, constant manner, seeking for signs of a sortie, and telegraphing to the gunners the range and direction of any advancing body of hostile troops.

In the second week of March the situation of the defenders became desperate. For some time they had been subsisting on short rations, but these had given out suddenly ; for it was found that a large store of tinned meat had been either supplied in an old, rotten condition by some fraudulent army contractor, or else had gone wrong

SPOILS OF WAR—RIFLES AND MUNITIONS CAPTURED BY AUSTRIANS IN THE CARPATHIAN CAMPAIGN.

through being kept too long by the military authorities. The preserved meat was quite putrescent ; it was impossible to use it in any way, and there was nothing left for the garrison to eat.

General Kusmanek informed the Austro-German armies along the Carpathians of the situation by wireless messages, with the result that everything possible was done to relieve the falling fortress. The battles upon the crest and slopes of the mountains raged with terrific fury. Large German reinforcements arrived for General von Linsingen, and every man that Austria-Hungary could at once put into the field was railed up through the Latorcza valley to strengthen General Böhm Ermolli. In a magnificent spirit of heroism the Germans, Austrians, and Hungarians fought their way through the snow, ascending and descending the frozen rampart of rock, and deploying around the upper vast reaches of the San River. Holding again the Lupkow Pass, the Austrians swept out towards Baligrod, and at the same time advanced from the Uzsok Pass northward. By a tremendous effort and an enormous sacrifice of men the Teutons and Hungarians almost touched the railway thirty miles south of Przemysl. Unfortunately for them, General

Attacks of relieving armies

Brussiloff, knowing the position of affairs in Przemysl, had foreseen all the attacks of the relieving armies. Indeed, one of the chief reasons why only three shells fell in the beleaguered city during the siege of five months was that the Austrian movements had been long foreseen. The shells had been saved with a design to employ them in shattering the supreme attack by the relieving armies.

To General Brussiloff the condition of Przemysl was a matter of only secondary importance. His main object was to defeat all the forces that Germany, Austria, and Hungary could bring against him across the Carpathian Mountains. The Hungarian plain, sown with winter wheat, sufficient to nourish the Central Empires for months, was the grand objective of the southern Russian army. Przemysl was only valuable as a means of luring the hostile relieving armies into a difficult position during the winter months, when the Russian War Minister could not arm the million or more new Russian troops waiting for equipment.

General Brussiloff was offered a powerful park of heavy siege-guns in January, 1915, but he said he could do without it, if it could be used with effect elsewhere. The park was, in fact, employed along the opposite flank of the great Russian battle-front, and the Siege of Przemysl went on with extraordinary quietness except for the sorties of the famishing garrison. When, however, in March, 1915, the offensive movement of the German and Austrian relieving armies culminated in an attack upon Brussiloff's Carpathian front, there was no need to prolong any further the agony of the beleaguered fortress town. By then the siege had served its main purpose, and had dragged the forces of Austria-Hungary beyond the limit of their strength. To complete his grand design Brussiloff needed at once the 200,000 men detained around Przemysl. So General Selivanov was at last ordered to close in upon the doomed city and carry it, if need be, by storm.

On Sunday, March 14th, the veteran general opened the attack, for which all the means had been available since the previous January. The operations were started in the north by the village of Malkovice, along the railway line from Jaroslav. Heavy howitzers were brought up by the railway, and the bombardment of the strong main fort dominating the highway to the north was begun. At the same time the smaller works on this northern section were assailed, and the hostile batteries were so well mastered that on Tuesday, March 16th, the Russian infantry carried the heights and entrenched themselves within rifle-shot of the forts. The Austrians tried to recover some of the ground by using an armoured train along the railway. The train came along at night with a large body of troops in the hinder carriages, but the Russian searchlight men spotted it and directed the guns on it, and the armoured train was swiftly and completely wrecked by shell fire.

The Russians advanced in open formation, by crawling in short rushes, and drove the defenders from the miles of trenches along the high-road and railway. The ground was covered with snow, making it easy for searchlights on both sides to light up advancing or retreating troops, who then came under a tempest of shrapnel. Happily, there was a birch wood, with a stretch of thick, short undergrowth, along the line the Russians were taking, and it served them as cover from observation till they were close on the railway.

Brussiloff's grand objective

AUSTRIAN HOWITZER BATTERY IN ACTION.

we should fall into the power of the enemy like a helpless crowd. Hero-soldiers, we must break through, and we shall!"

This impassioned and moving appeal appears to have been made to all the infantry and cavalry forces of the garrison. But such was the feeling of utter dispiritment, due perhaps partly to want of sufficient food, that only 20,000 men answered it. These were mainly Hungarians, comprising the 23rd Honved Division, part of the 23rd Landwehr Brigade, and the 4th Regiment of Hussars. Led by the brave Hungarian General Tamassy, this fighting remnant of the garrison marched out beyond the forts

All through the night the screech of shells and hum of bullets were terrible, and in the blue light of the bursting bombs and in the lanes of flame from the searchlights, with a fort exploding on the skyline, the scene was a sort of ghastly modern Doomsday. The soldiers' faces in the blue radiance had a strange and eerie appearance.

The great forts tried to retrieve the defeat on the northern section by a continual bombardment of the closing-in lines of Russian trenches. Twenty thousand rounds of big-gun ammunition were fired daily on March 15th and March 16th. But the Russians were too deeply entrenched to be shattered by even this terrific fire. They continued to advance from the south as well as from the north, **Kusmanek's eloquent** occupying the village of Krasiczyn south-**proclamation** westward. It was against the southern Russian trenches that most of the great shells were flung on March 17th, preparatory to the final sortie of the garrison. General Kusmanek served out the last rations, and issued a proclamation to the troops:

"Soldiers, half a year has passed while we children of almost all the nationalities of our beloved country have incessantly stood shoulder to shoulder against the enemy. Thanks to God's help and your bravery, I have succeeded, despite the enemy's attacks, despite cold and privations, in defending the fortress against the enemy. You have already done much to win the acknowledgments of the Commander-in-Chief, the gratitude of the country, and even the respect of the enemy.

"Yonder in our beloved country, thousands and thousands of hearts are beating for us. Millions are waiting with held breath for news of us.

"Heroes, I am about to make my last demand of you. The honour of our Army and country requires it. I am going to lead you out, a steel wedge, to break through the iron ring of the foe, and then, with unflagging efforts, move farther and farther till we rejoin our Army, which, at the price of stubborn battles, has already approached quite near to us. We are on the eve of a big fight, for the enemy will not willingly allow the booty to slip through his fingers. But, remember, gallant defenders of Przemysl, each one of you must be possessed by the single idea, 'Forward, ever forward!' All that stands in our way must be crushed.

"Soldiers, we have distributed our last stores; and the honour of our country, and of every one of us, forbids that after such a hard-fought, glorious, and victorious struggle

AUSTRIAN ARTILLERY IN THE CARPATHIANS.

at five o'clock on Friday morning, March 19th. They advanced in an easterly direction in a determined manner, but were unable after nine hours' fighting to reach the Russian trenches. Eight thousand of them were killed, and nearly four thousand were taken prisoners.

At the same time as the Przemysl garrison made its last vain essay to break through, a furious battle was opened all round Przemysl by the relieving armies. The attack raged especially west and east of Gorlice. The Austro-Hungarians used 12 in. howitzer fire, under cover of which twenty battalions flung themselves against the Russian trenches, but they were held up on the wire entanglements, and there shot down by machine-guns and magazine rifles. Another attack was **Quarter not asked** delivered by a Honved brigade against the **nor given** height held by our allies near Ciezkovice.

Only a Russian battalion held the position at first, and their line was taken, but they counter-attacked, with two battalions hurrying to their aid, and beat the enemy back by noon. An hour afterwards the entire 39th Honved Division swept out in a great charge. Despite their heavy losses, the Hungarians got through the wire entanglements and took the height. But the Russians were reinforced, and drove them back. Three times the position was lost and won, but at four o'clock in the afternoon the remnant of Russians made a fourth counter-attack. Such was the frenzy of battle on both sides that neither asked nor gave quarter ; and after slaughtering all their foes the Russians recovered their trenches. The swaying battle-line extended from Gorlice in Western Galicia, across the Carpathians, to Svidnik in Hungary, then back over the Carpathians near the Lupkow Pass, to Baligrod and Lutoviska ; thence over the Dniester and along the Stry River. In no place did the relieving armies break through. All their vigorous and costly attacks were intended solely to withdraw attention from Przemysl, and to provide favourable conditions for the final sortie of the garrison.

But, as we have seen, the larger part of the troops in Przemysl were much too enfeebled to attempt to break out. After the Hungarian division was repulsed, no course was left to General Kusmanek but to prepare for the act of surrender.

Meanwhile the Russians pressed the attack relentlessly on Friday night and Saturday against the east and north front. But across the sound of the guns there suddenly came a series of still more thunderous explosions. Shocks

RUSSIAN ARMOURED MOTOR-CAR IN USE ON THE GALICIAN FRONT.

like earthquakes were felt. The Austrians were blowing up the great forts, motor-batteries, magazines, bridges, and everything likely to be useful to the victors. One of the smaller forts with quick-firing guns was captured by the Russians in time to save it from entire destruction. But all the main works of defence were so thoroughly dynamited that Przemysl lost all its importance as a place of strength. The famous 12 in. Skoda howitzers were exploded into fragments. Then every soldier was ordered to destroy his rifle. It was a pitiful sight to see them do it. Many kissed the rifle first, and wept while hammering it to bits.

This had to be done, as there was no time to gather the rifles and destroy them in one pile. **The main forts dynamited** Then, as the Russian shells began to fall on the aeroplane sheds, four Austrian airmen made their last voyage from the fortress in the two last machines left intact. The scene below them was indescribably terrible. From the exploding ammunition stores smoke and flame shot up in clouds, the military buildings and warehouses were on fire, and the flying machines were in danger of being overturned by the force of the explosions. Then on Monday morning, March 22nd, 1915, General Kusmanek,

who had opened negotiations for surrender on Saturday, gave up the fortress.

It was not the first time that Przemysl had been taken by a Russian force. It had been first captured by the Russian Duke Oleg in the year 907. It was afterwards lost, but again besieged and retaken in 1031 by the Grand Duke Jaroslav. Under the successors of this prince of the House of Moscow the whole of Galicia became an important Russian Duchy, peopled almost entirely by Russians. But when Russia weakened under the attacks of the Mongols, their neighbours, the Poles, became the leaders of the Slav world, and the Polish King Casimir, after a long **Fruit of a hundred victories** struggle, got possession of Przemysl, and subdued all the Russians in Galicia. Then at the time of the division of Poland, the Russians were compelled to allow their old Duchy of Galicia to fall into the hands of a still more alien race than the Poles—the Austrians.

The recovery of the "Gibraltar" of Galicia was thus a matter of great rejoicing among the Russians. It marked the beginning of the last stage of the slow, painful development of the great Slav race. At the time when the Mongols were overwhelming China, destroying Mohammedan culture, sweeping down towards India, and finally menacing the entire destruction of European civilisation, Russia had been the breakwater of the white races. The breakwater had been submerged by the Mongolian flood, but before going under it had sufficiently broken the force of the barbaric hordes to enable Poland, Silesia, and Hungary to drive out the invaders. Then, after remaining vassals for two centuries to the Mongolian power, the Russians, under the leadership of their princes of the House of Moscow, conquered their conquerors, and by winning all the Mongolian land of Siberia, established a great empire without thinking to do so ; for all they first set out to achieve was to break the Mongolian power so as to render impossible another great invasion from the east. Meanwhile the old Russian Duchy of Galicia, in which the native Russians, under first Polish and then Austrian and Hungarian tyranny, had sunk into the condition of half-savage peasants living in extreme poverty in mud huts, excited the attention of the free Russian races. For, in spite of centuries of persecution, most of the Russians of Galicia still held to the Russian form of religion. Their religion, their language, and their folk-lore were indeed the only elements of national culture remaining to the lost and oppressed Galicians, who by the irony of historic memories of their former wealth were still known as "Red-Gold" Russians.

All this goes to explain the general enthusiasm excited in the people of all the Russias by the news of the recapture of Przemysl. To them it was something more important than a victory. It was the long-desired fruit of a hundred victories, beginning with the uprising against the Mongols, and concluding with the recent defeat of the first-line armies of Austria and Hungary. Before the Poles captured Galicia from their weakened fellow-Slavs, the town of the Carpathian foothills had been known by its original Russian name of Peremysl—the Polish form of Przemysl was a later growth. To the Russians it was a mournful memory of ancient national disasters. So, as in the case of Lemberg, one of their first acts was to restore to the Russian city its old Russian name.

From a military point of view the fall of Przemysl, which gave the Russians control over the trunk railway of Galicia, and thus strengthened their hold on the recovered duchy, was an event of high importance ; for the Austrians then lost about one quarter of the territory of the Dual Monarchy, with a population of eight million. As Galicia had contributed to the Austro-Hungarian Army about one-fifth of its recruits, the effect of the loss was increased. Moreover, Galicia was a province of enormous natural wealth. It was the only centre of oil production in the Teutonic Empire ; its coal reserves were calculated at twenty-five thousand million tons, and its great salt-

THE LONELY SHRINE—GERMAN ARTILLERYMEN GREET THEIR AUSTRIAN ALLIES BESIDE A WAYSIDE SYMBOL OF THE PRINCE OF PEACE.

WITH THE AUSTRIANS IN THE SNOW-COVERED CARPATHIANS—GUNNER ABOUT TO FIRE ONE OF THE HEAVY HOWITZERS WHICH PROVED SO EFFECTIVE IN SIEGE OPERATIONS.

mines, almost within reach of Dimitrieff's army, were the salt-treasury of Europe.

The last matter did not seem of much importance on March 22nd, 1915. The question whether the Germans and Austrians would lack an abundance of salt did not seem to have much bearing upon the course of the war. But common salt is properly known as sodium chloride. It can easily be resolved into its elements of sodium and chlorine. Chlorine can be obtained in vast quantities from the Galician salt-mines in the form of a greenish-yellow gas, which eats the lungs out of the men that breathe it, leaving their dead, agonised bodies purple from lack of oxygen. This was why the fall of Przemysl was a matter of extreme concern to the German and Austrian General Staffs.

The fall of the fortress released General Selivanov's army, together with a large part of the army of General Dimitrieff, which had assisted in the final operations. General Dimitrieff was holding the Dunajec at Tarnov, and the great salt-mines were only about forty miles distant from his front. By the fall of Przemysl his railway communications through Lemberg to Kieff were much strengthened. His army could now be fed with a stream of munitions that would be calculated to carry him quickly towards the salt-mines at Wieliczka. Indeed, he had reached these mines in his first fierce swoop towards Cracow during the previous autumn. As we now know, the secret new plan of campaign with poison gases, drawn up by the German Staff and approved by the Austrian Staff, was based upon the resources of the Galician salt-mines. The Russians, trusting to the signature of the German plenipotentiary appended to the Hague Convention forbidding the use of asphyxiating gases in civilised warfare, did not guess at the time how menacing was their position from the German point of view. Had only the diabolical German scheme been suspected, it could have been at once countered by using the quarter of a million troops set free by the fall of Przemysl to reinforce the Dunajec line for an immediate advance to the next river, the Raba, where from the surrounding heights the salt-mines could have been bombarded and captured. As we shall see, it was partly the fear that the Russians should get information of what was going on and attempt to capture the salt resources of the Teutons, that determined the future course of the campaign in both the eastern and western theatres of war. The guilty are always suspicious, and though the Allies do not seem clearly to have foreknown what the Germans intended doing, the Germans were apprehensive of being attacked before they had fully prepared their new, ghastly, scientifically-savage instrument of torture and destruction.

Salt-mines and poison gas

Although the Russian Secret Service is often regarded as superior to the similar Intelligence system of the Germans, no foreknowledge was obtained of the vital importance of the Galician salt-mines. So far as could be seen, their capture would only interfere with the enemy's cookery and means of preserving meat, and the Russian Commander-in-Chief thought that a descent on the Hungarian plain, though a far slower and more difficult operation than the short advance on the salt-mines, promised results of more importance; for the condition of affairs in Przemysl when the Russians entered the fallen city was significant of a spirit of general disintegration in the Austro-Hungarian Army. The captured garrison consisted of 131,000 men and nearly 4,000 officers. Very few of the officers cared anything about the hardships endured by their men, or made any attempt to relieve their condition. Up to the last they had their three meals a day, with fresh meat, wines, and every luxury, while their own orderlies begged for a slice of bread. The private soldiers were seen to fall in the street from lack of nourishment. Yet the officers, until the day before the surrender, retained a large store of oats to feed their 2,000 private thoroughbred riding-horses. The horses were at last killed to prevent them from falling into the hands of the Russians; and when the conquerors entered the town, they found the Austrian and Hungarian soldiers, half-crazed for want of food, gouging into the bodies of the slaughtered thoroughbreds, their faces and hands smeared red with blood as they devoured the raw and dripping flesh. Some of the Cossacks, who are by no means men of a sentimental or delicate disposition, wept like women when they beheld the shocking spectacle of starving men gorging themselves on raw meat with the fury of starving wolves.

Fallen fortress's ghastly contrasts

It was because the Austrian officers in Przemysl conducted themselves in this manner that most of their men had refused to march out and fight in answer to the appeal of General Kusmanek. Kusmanek, a Bohemian by race, was distinguished from the Austrian officers. A carrier pigeon was cooked for his last meal, but instead of eating it, he gave it to a wounded soldier. His great defect was, in fact, his general kindness of heart. He should have sent half of his garrison, at least, in December, to fight their way out, or to be killed or captured. He should have despatched all the fugitive troops that had taken shelter in the fortress, and turned the guns on them if they tried to return. Przemysl might then have held out for a year, as the probability would have been against the Russians capturing it. But as General Kusmanek was in constant communication with the Archdukes and Court favourites forming the high command of the Austrian forces, it is likely that this course was ordered by his superior officers.

WAR DOGS OF THE RUSSIAN ISMAILLOVSKY REGIMENT.

CHAPTER LXV.

PRZEMYSL AND THE ADVANCE OF THE GREAT GERMAN PHALANX.

Capture of Lupkow Pass and Menace to Hungary—Disgrace and Dismissal of Hindenburg and Rise of Mackensen—Falkenhayn Creates the Grand Phalanx to Capture Calais—Position of Hungary Compels him to Swing the Phalanx against the Southern Russian Army—Tremendous Hurricane Fire against the Short Russian Front in Western Galicia—Radko Dimitrieff Stands Up against the Withering Blast—Holding the Austrian Archduke on the Dunajec, he Withdraws the Remnant of his Men from the Biala River—Mackensen's Phalanx Tries to Advance Through the Gap and Get to the Rear of the Southern Russian Army— Magnificent and Decisive Stand Made by Dimitrieff against Terrible Odds—General Ivanoff Sweeps into the Battlefield with Strong Reinforcements—Mackensen Defeated by Superior Strategy on the Wisloka—General Brussiloff's Victories in Bukovina and South of Lemberg—Battles of Jaroslav and Sieniawa—The Army of the Austrian Archduke Defeated in Poland and Northern Galicia—Russians Win a Week's Breathing Space owing to the Slow Movement of the Grand Phalanx—Why the German Commander Could only Move his Enormous Fighting Force at the Rate of Three Miles a Day—Russian Front in Peril at the Salient of Przemysl—Having Removed all their Stores, the Russian Troops Retire from the Town.

AFTER the fall of Przemysl it was known, both from the reports of prisoners and from information received from Russian Intelligence officers, that the general condition of Austrian troops along the Carpathian battle-line was deplorable. For the Austrian officers were more careful in looking after their own interests than in tending to the well-being of the soldiers under their command. We have given in the previous chapter some of the extraordinary figures concerning the sickness prevailing in the Austrian Army. It was fairly evident to General Brussiloff that the military forces of the Dual Monarchy were approaching a condition of extreme weakness. Only by the help of half a million German troops did they still hold the rampart of the Carpathians. The Russian design was, therefore, to press the enemy most strongly at his weakest point, and while holding the main German eastern armies from the Niemen to the Lower Vistula, to advance over the Carpathians into Hungary.

The advance began the day after the fall of Przemysl. Half of the 200,000 troops released by the success of the

GENERAL ARTAMONOV.
The Russian Governor of Przemysl photographed in his quarters during the Russian occupation. Note the portrait of the Emperor of Austria untouched. Had the situation been reversed, it is certain a portrait of the Tsar would have been defaced by the Austro-Germans.

siege operations were sent southward towards the Dukla and Lupkow Passes. There they strengthened the front of the Russian southern army, and the reinforced troops began steadily to push both the Austrians and the Germans over the crests of the mountains. In the neighbourhood of the Dukla the three road passes of Polyanka, the Dukla, and the Jaliska were won by the Russians, and they descended the Hungarian slopes towards Bartfeld, Svidnik, and the valley of the Laborcz River. Then in the higher and more densely-wooded heights between the Lupkow and the Uzsok Passes our Allies conquered, in the first week of April, 1915, the towering forested ridge of the Polonina Mountains and approached Rostok Pass. From this point they progressed by fierce and incessant forest fighting through the high snows to the Smolink Hills, situated beyond the main Carpathian ridge, on the Hungarian decline. The only reverse the Russians met with was around the railway-station of Mesolaborcz, in Hungary, where one of their divisions was trapped in a valley and badly cut up.

But this was only a small, temporary check in a great and steadily-successful advance by something like three-

IN A RUSSIAN TRENCH—AWAITING THE ORDER FOR A BAYONET CHARGE.

quarters of a million men of the southern army. Every day the Russians took from 2,000 to 7,000 prisoners, with a few mountain guns and a dozen machine-guns. This was the regular result of the steady process of attrition by which all the hostile forces were being worn down and forced back in disorder into the Hungarian plain. In the second week in April the enemy's powers of resistance suddenly weakened in a general manner, and the Russians were able to advance twenty miles in twenty-four hours between the Dukla and Uzsok Passes. About this time a heavy snowstorm raged on the great heights, and the more robust Russian peasants advanced through it on a ninety-mile front, over pathless steeps, with six feet of drifted snow in places. By sheer superiority of physique they pushed back, in the frozen tempest, the less enduring Teutons and Magyars, and fought their way to the upper waters of the Uzsok River. The German regiments sent to relieve the Austrian army had to renew their front

Fighting on Carpathian Heights

line four times. Then they, too, fell back towards the lower slopes on the Hungarian side. where the snow was melting in the warmer climate.

In one month's fighting on the Carpathian heights the Russians captured 40,000 men and 4,000 officers, twenty guns, and an immense number of machine-guns. The Austrians had four distinct armies deployed along the mountain range from Bartfeld to the Rumanian frontier. Assisting them were ten German army corps. Then another Austrian army, operating from Cracow, faced General Dimitrieff along the Dunajec River. Every available man from the Dual Monarchy was thus massed against the southern Russian army which General Brussiloff was pushing over the Carpathians into the Hungarian wheat-plain. So fierce and relentless was the pressure exercised from Galicia against Hungary that the German General Staff had to stand on the defensive in France, Flanders, and Poland in order to collect the army corps needed to save Hungary. At the beginning of the third week in April it was reckoned that the opposing forces on the Carpathians numbered 3,000,000 men.

The main points in the conflict were the Homonna Railway, ascending the Lupkow Pass, and the Munkacs Railway, crossing near the Tuchla Pass. On the Homonna line the Russians by mid-April were twenty miles into Hungary. On the Munkacs line the Germans were still trying to advance towards Stry. But they were in danger of having their lines of communication cut by a sharp Russian advance into the valley of the Theiss. On April 18th the weather changed at last and brought the Russians for a time to a standstill. For the warm spring rain washed the snow from the Carpathian peaks, with the result that the mountain torrents were turned into turbulent floods and the lower valleys into lakes,

Capture of Lupkow Pass

while in many places land which had been hard and frozen was transformed into impassable swamps. Being mainly on the southern slope of the mountains, with a web of railways close behind them, the Austrians and Germans tried to profit by the spring floods, and brought up heavy artillery—8 in., 11 in., and 12 in. howitzers—into the Carpathian region. Then, in the last week of April, they delivered a great massed attack against the heights held by the Russians upon the Homonna and Munkacs lines. But the Russians beat them down by machine-gun and rifle fire and hand-grenades.

The Lupkow Pass was captured and an advance was made from the Hungarian side against the Uzsok Pass. This threatened to cut off the German force defending the pass, and when this was done there would be a gap of seventy miles in the Carpathian defences—quite a large enough door for Brussiloff to flood the Hungarian plain with a large force of troops. Such was the position in the last week in April, 1915. On Field-Marshal von Hindenburg, who was responsible for the disastrous situation, fell the disgrace of the disaster. He had completely failed. In his bull-like rushes against Ivangorod and Warsaw, Grodno and Prasnysch, he had wasted army corps after army corps. Possessing, in a railway system designed by the elder Moltke, the finest instrument of invasion in the world, he had done little more than turn it into a huge platform for military acrobatics that wasted men by the hundred thousand without producing a single definite important gain.

A council of war was held on the eastern front, at which the Emperor William decided to dismiss Hindenburg from his high command. The decision was not made public, by reason of the extraordinary popular faith in the victor of Tannenberg. But for all that the act of dismissal was carried out. Hindenburg retired for a time at least from the Army, and devoted himself once more to the pleasures of the punch-bowl and a country life. His appearance at Ypres was merely a pretence. He was not in command there, but was sent, for the sake of his false

Last moments of H.M.S. Majestic, torpedoed off Gallipoli May 27th, 1915.

A trench in Flanders—where British soldiers fought and died.

German shrapnel bursting behind a hastily=built French barricade.

French engineers constructing a reserve trench behind the firing=lines.

Kaiser (left) and General von Emmich at German headquarters in France.

reputation as a conqueror, to hearten the troops of the Duke of Würtemberg and the Crown Prince of Bavaria.

The former Minister for War, General von Falkenhayn, who had succeeded the younger Moltke as Chief of Staff, took over the enormous task of directing operations on both the eastern and the western fronts. General von Mackensen, who had become the favourite general of the Kaiser by reason of the skill and fury in attack he had shown in the battles round Lodz, was appointed to lead the main German forces in Galicia. General von Linsingen, commanding the German troops on the **Mackensen succeeds** Munkacs-Stry line, was further reinforced **Hindenburg** and given larger powers of command. The Austrian Archduke Friedrich, nominally in chief command over the Austro-Hungarian forces, was placed under the control of Mackensen ; the Archduke Ferdinand, commanding the army along the Dunajec, was also subordinated to Mackensen, and all the other Austrian and Hungarian commands were also strictly subjected to German leadership.

What especially angered General von Falkenhayn was the lack of strategical insight displayed by Field-Marshal von Hindenburg and Hindenburg's Chief of Staff, General von Ludendorff. After their failure along the Bzura and Pilica front, and along the East Prussian borders, they had responded too blindly to the offensive movement made by the Russians in the Carpathian region. All they had done, when General Brussiloff pressed over the Dukla Pass and menaced the Lupkow Pass, was to concentrate against the advancing Russian lines. In the opinion of General von Falkenhayn, the Russian pressure should have been countered by a sudden and sharp flank attack from Cracow against the Dunajec and Biala river lines. To this purpose the formidable German reinforcements should have been used, instead of being wasted in indecisive mountain conflicts on the Russian positions in the Carpathians.

The correctness of this view was generally admitted at the Austro-German council of war, and the Kaiser entrusted Falkenhayn with the task of remedying Hindenburg's and Ludendorff's mistakes. Ever since Falkenhayn's failure on the western front to break through at Ypres and capture Calais, he had been preparing to make good this plan of his in the spring of 1915. All through the winter and early spring the German artillerymen in France and Flanders had been ordered to observe a strict economy in the use of high-explosive shells. This was the explanation of the momentary allied ascendancy in artillery power, remarked by both the French and British commanders at the close of 1914. Germany was quite as formidable in heavy armament as she had been, and it was calculated that in the manufacture of munitions she was still seventy-five per cent. more efficient than Britain and France combined. In all German and Austrian armament factories the work had been kept going day and night by three eight-hour shifts in the early months of the war. But after the defeat at Ypres the supply of munitions was increased, by engrossing every power-lathe formerly used for ordinary work, and setting the armament mechanics and labourers on a general twelve-hour shift,, the men working in weekly turns of twelve hours' day work and twelve hours' night work.

The fierce winter battle on the Bzura, Pilica, and Nieder

Rivers, and the operations of the German army of half a million men north of Warsaw along the Bobr, Narew, and Niemen Rivers, necessitated the use of a vast number of high-explosive shells. In all their battles against the Russians the Germans used their superior artillery power in a wasteful manner. This waste was partly balanced by the economy observed upon the western front, and with the extreme speeding up of all the gun-making work and munition factories, General Falkenhayn had his new war machine ready for operations by the middle of April, 1915. Krupp and Skoda and other gunmakers had provided him with two thousand new heavy pieces of ordnance, and three millions of large, heavy, high-explosive shells. There were also 2,000 new or fairly unworn pieces of field-artillery, and for these also there were thousands of truckloads of high-explosive shell ready. At the same time the manufacture of machine-guns had gone on at high speed, enabling the ordinary fire-power of the infantry to be enormously increased.

It was Falkenhayn's original intention to use this new war-machine to break the Franco-British front, either at the western end near Calais, where he made his first

FIELD-TELEPHONE STATION NEAR THE AUSTRIAN HEADQUARTERS IN GALICIA.

attempt, or at the eastern end near Metz, where the nephew of the elder Moltke had proposed to attack before he was superseded as Chief of Staff by Falkenhayn. But with Hindenburg's complete failure in both strategy and tactics, in the eastern theatre of war, Falkenhayn's scheme for a decisive spring campaign in the west had to be postponed. So successful was the southern Russian army under General Brussiloff that by the middle of April it was in a position to advance into the Hungarian plain and cut the communications of all the German and Austrian troops on the **Falkenhayn's Western** Carpathian front. By his extraordinary **scheme postponed** success, combined with the general lack of munitions of war in Russia, General Brussiloff drew on his men the crushing blow intended originally for the French and British troops.

The position of the southern Russian army was very curious. It was advancing in great force all along the Carpathians on a front of more than one hundred and fifty miles ; but on its right flank, looking towards Cracow, there was a lateral position of about seventy miles, held only by a small entrenched army of 160,000 men, under the Bulgarian commander, General Dimitrieff. By selecting for attack two places on this short lateral front, the

IN PRZEMYSL AFTER THE FALL.

existence of all the Russian armies in Galicia and Hungary could be menaced. The Austro - German means of communication round Cracow were excellent. There were two lines of railways running from Cracow to Dimitrieff's positions at Tarnov, near the Dunajec River, and at Gorlice, on the Ropa stream. Then, midway between Cracow and Tarnov, the two railways were connected by a cross-country line, enabling troops to be manœuvred in trains from south to north or north to south. In the south, on the Lower Dunajec, was the railway junction of Neu Sandez, from which another railway ran into Northern

Hurricane fire against Dimitrieff

Hungary. There were thus three rail-ways, by means of which the thousands of heavy howitzers and the millions of high-explosive shells could be transported for action against the narrow lateral Russian front in Western Galicia.

Towards the end of April General Dimitrieff observed the concentration of enemy forces against his line. He was far from suspecting that the greatest military machine known in history was being brought against his com-paratively small forces. He asked for reinforcements, and General Ivanoff, on the Nida front north of him, and General Brussiloff, on the Carpathian front south of him, sent what men and guns they could spare.

But when the blow fell on the night of April 30th, 1915, the force of it was beyond anything that man had experienced.

In estimates published before the war, the entire artillery power of Ger-many was placed at 4,000 guns and howitzers. This was a larger number of pieces of ordnance than either France or Russia was credited with possessing. Our Army, for instance, only had seven hundred guns. About seven hundred

guns was the number used by General Dimitrieff to defend his lines along the Dunajec and the Biala Rivers until the fall of Przemysl enabled him to increase his artillery. When reinforced, he had about 250,000 troops between the Lower Vistula and the Carpathian heights, but a good many of them lacked their artillery corps, as there was still a serious shortage of munitions. Massed against them were more than a million Germans, Austrians, and Hungarians, with their artillery corps of about 2,000 guns, behind which was Falkenhayn's enormous new siege train of 2,000 heavy pieces, including some howitzers of 17 in. calibre.

The front was far too short for the deployment of the enemy forces. Both the guns and the troops were arranged in a step for-mation, or echelon system. Yet the echelons were so close together that there was a practically solid line of front from the point where the Dunajec flowed into the Vistula to the point where the Biala valley merged into the Carpathian heights. The Austrian army of the Archduke Ferdinand ad-vanced on the night of April 30th against the Dunajec front. Mackensen, with part of his troops and 1,000 pieces of siege-artillery in addition to his ordinary artillery corps, attacked south of Tarnov, between that town and Gorlice.

Falkenhayn's enor-mous siege-train

The Archduke was unfortunate, as Austrian Archdukes sometimes are on the field of battle. Some of his forces advanced in the darkness down the Vistula at the junction point between General Ivanoff's army in Poland and General Dimitrieff's army in Western Galicia. He was given German troops for this important operation, and they managed to entrench by the river, forming themselves into a spear-head driven between the two Russian armies.

DEPARTURE OF THE AUSTRIAN GARRISON FROM PRZEMYSL.

AUSTRIAN OFFICERS LEAVING PRZEMYSL.

On paper their position appeared to constitute a formidable menace to their opponents, but the Russian infantry attacked them on the night of May 2nd and annihilated them with the bayonet. Elsewhere along the high banks of the Lower Dunajec the Austrian army was unable to advance. The gunners used hundreds of thousands of shells against the Russian positions, but they did not succeed in putting the Russian light field-artillery out of action. The result was that every attempt made by the Archduke to throw pontoon bridges over the stream by day or night was defeated by our Allies' shrapnel fire.

Only at one point, between the outflow into the Vistula and Tarnov, did the Austrians succeed in **2,000 men for a** crossing the river. At **bridge-head** the town of Oftinov there had been a ferry in peace time, but the river flowed between two very high artificial banks, and the Russian artillery was so well hidden that even the hurricane fire from the enemy's howitzers could not find it, though hundreds of Austrian and German airmen were searching for the Russian guns and directing the fire of their own pieces. But the German engineers had been working for some weeks round the ferry. They had driven several large tunnels through the bank on their side, leaving only a wall of earth on the river frontage. In the tunnels ran pontoons, fitted with wheels, and filled with men. In the night the wall of earth was blown up, and twenty pontoons were wheeled out and floated across the river under cover of a terrific bombardment. It was an exceedingly ingenious plan of attack, yet the troops, who floated across the river in the darkness, did not succeed as well as they expected. For, though the Russians were surprised, they sank nine

RUSSIAN PROVISION COLUMN ENTERING PRZEMYSL.

FIXING A RUSSIAN NOTICE OUTSIDE A PUBLIC BUILDING IN PRZEMYSL.

of the pontoons and killed or wounded most of the men in the remaining eleven bridge-boats. At a loss of two thousand men a bridge-head was won on the opposite side of the Dunajec on the morning of May 1st. But the Archduke's army could get no farther than the bridge-head. All the Lower Dunajec was firmly held by the Russians for a full week, from April 30th to May 6th. It was only at 10 a.m. on May 6th that Tarnov was reoccupied by the Austrians, and until four o'clock in the afternoon of the same day the Russians held some **Archduke** of the commanding heights on the east **Ferdinand's failure** bank of the Lower Dunajec. Considering the overwhelming power of artillery and men possessed by the Archduke Ferdinand, and the extraordinary skill of his engineers, the surprise attack on the Russian positions on the Lower Dunajec was a ridiculous failure. With everything in his favour, he took six to seven days to win two or three hundred yards of water and land. In the meantime General Ivanoff, commanding the Russian army in Central Poland, was able to march hundreds of thousands of men across the Vistula to the help of General Dimitrieff's small army. Even the Caucasian corps, formerly on the Bzura front near Warsaw, was able to march into Western Galicia before the Archduke Ferdinand brought his army across the Dunajec. The Austrian command and the Austrian troops were absolutely incompetent. Their incompetency, joined with the heroic intrepidity and fighting skill of Dimitrieff and his men, saved the Russian Empire from a vast and decisive disaster. Along the Biala, above Tarnov, the enemy started with an advantage in the lie of the land, for in many places the banks were higher on the western side of the river than on the eastern side. It was along the Biala, with his centre at Ciezkovice, that General von

RUSSIAN DETACHMENT PASSING THROUGH A STREET IN PRZEMYSL.

Mackensen attacked. His front extended only about twenty-five miles, from Tuchov to Gorlice. He had at least half a million men, including all the remnants of the Prussian Guard and the best Bavarian and Saxon troops from the French and Flemish front. His crack troops numbered 150,000, and the rest of his men were mainly drawn from the First German Reserve. He had 1,500 heavy guns, including most of the available 17 in. howitzers. Opposed to him were two army corps of General Dimitrieff's army, reduced by the wastage of war to 60,000 men. There was thus somewhat less than one Russian to every yard of front, and as there were three lines of Russian trenches the trench garrisons amounted to about one man to four yards. Mackensen began the attack with what the Germans called a hurricane fire. For four hours every gun and howitzer was worked as fast as human hands could work it, and 700,000 high-explosive shells were pitched into the Russian trenches—more than

SLOVAK OUTPOSTS IN SOME OLD RUINS IN THE
CARPATHIANS.

ten shells to each Russian soldier. The quantity of projectiles used by Mackensen on this narrow front in four hours was double the amount usually regarded as necessary for a six months' siege of a great and well-provisioned fortress.

Falkenhayn had been inspired by the British artillery achievement at Neuve Chapelle. The plan, execution of which he had entrusted to Mackensen, merely consisted in a grandiose, but quite unoriginal, imitation of the new tactics of rapid, heavy artillery fire invented by Sir John French, Sir William Robertson, and General Foch. There was no escape from the 17 in. Skoda shells, or Pilseners, as the Russians named them. Each shell weighed 2,800 pounds ; in its flight it rose nearly five miles in the air, and it penetrated twenty feet into soft ground before it exploded. Every living thing within one hundred and fifty yards of the explosion was killed, and many persons farther off

were also slain. The main damage was not done by the metal fragments, but by the enormous pressure of the exploding gas. The gas got into the body cavities, and in its further process of expansion tore the flesh apart. Men who happened to be close by entirely disappeared ; not the slightest remains of their clothes or of their flesh could be found. Their rifles melted like metal struck by lightning. Scores of men at a distance who escaped metal fragments, stones, and showers of earth, were killed, lacerated, or blinded by the pressure of **Awful effect of** gas. The gas also broke in the partitions **Skoda shells** and bomb-proof roofs of shelters, and as the force of the explosion travelled everywhere along the air, no winding of the trenches was a defence against the terrible pressure.

At Ciezkovice on May 1st the Russians managed for a time to hold their ground even under the hurricane of shells. They remained silent and motionless until the German infantry advanced to occupy the wrecked trenches ; then they opened fire at six hundred paces and repulsed them. But more southward, at Gorlice, there was no battle. The famous naphtha town was battered into a heap of ruins, only one wall with a tower standing in the midst of unimaginable devastation. The immense oil-tanks were set on fire at the first attack, and for days the flames shot up into the clouds, making the place look in the distance like a gigantic torch. The Russians who survived the first inferno of shell fire beat back the advancing infantry and retired in the night north-eastward to Biecz.

Then, on the fourteen-mile front from Tuchov-Biecz, Mackensen, by means of long-range fire from his heavy artillery and a bombardment at shorter range by his field guns, delivered another attack on May 2nd. But between Tuchov and Biecz there are three streams and the Branka Mountain, with a peak 1,600 feet high. The peak dominates a considerable stretch of the lower course of the Biala. General Dimitrieff made full use of this advantage in the lie of the land, and though he had only light field-artillery firing shrapnel he held the enemy up for another three days. It was not until May 5th that the Grand Phalanx, as Mackensen's enormously-gunned army was called, succeeded in blowing a path through the Russians' three lines of defences east of the Biala. In other words, General Dimitrieff, by a magnificent six days' resistance on his southern front and flank, gave the southern Russian army, operating in Hungary from the Zboro, Dukla, and Lupkow Passes, full time to withdraw in good order away from the mountains and back to the San. Only the 48th Russian Division, under General Korniloff, was cut off by the enemy while retiring from the Dukla Pass on May 6th. Korniloff's troops were surrounded on all sides, but their commander skilfully massed them in the direction of the **Dimitrieff's** San Valley, and by a violent attacking **magnificent stand** movement through the densely-wooded foothills the division shot and bayoneted its way out of the German ring of flame and steel and rejoined its parent corps on Friday, May 7th.

With this brilliant exception, there was no disaster to the Russian movement of withdrawal, for though a gap was forced between the two army corps holding the Biala line, and the right flank of one corps was crushed by the hurricane shell fire, the brigades which lost most heavily retired undemoralised. Some regiments had only three hundred men left, but still remained full of fight, and practically all the hostile infantry attacks, led on this front by the Prussian Guard, were defeated ; for the two corps held out so stubbornly that the famous Caucasian corps arrived in time, after an all-night march, and went forthwith into battle and closed the gap. Every time the Germans advanced beyond the cover of their guns the Russian infantry moved out and counter-attacked. The Russian losses were heavy, and many of the regiments were reduced to half or a quarter of their number. But the men had

REMARKABLE FLANK VIEW OF THREE ADVANCED RUSSIAN
TRENCHES ON THE EASTERN FRONT.

WHERE THE GROUND BRISTLED WITH BAYONETS.
A noticeable feature of the top photograph is the shallow pit dug between the foremost trenches for the officer. In the lower view a Russian officer
is seen scanning the enemy's position through binoculars while the men, with bayonets fixed, are waiting for the word to charge. In oval: A
Russian howitzer battery.

AUSTRIAN FIELD-GUN BATTERY
IN THE CARPATHIANS.

ARCHDUKE CHARLES FRANCIS JOSEPH INSPECTING TROOPS IN POLAND.

the scheme of General von Falkenhayn. Falkenhayn had not massed a million men, with four thousand guns, against the short Dunajec and Biala line merely with a view to pushing back the four Russian army corps there and recapturing Przemysl; for the front on which he worked was so narrow that he could not employ his men along it. Only five German army corps went into action on the Biala front against the two Russian army corps holding the position, and along the Dunajec the Archduke Ferdinand used only about three Austrians to one Russian. The main Austro-German force was waiting in the rear of the fighting-line until the time came for it to perform its special duties. What was intended was to blow a hole about thirty to forty miles wide in the Russian front. Then through this hole all Mackensen's troops, with only their light field-artillery, were to dash against Lemberg and get in the rear of General Brussiloff's forces.

Falkenhayn's grandiose project

Mackensen's task, in short, was to envelop entirely the southern Russian army, against which Linsingen and Böhm Ermolli were still pressing on the south.

In addition to this grand operation, another great encircling movement was intended against the central Russian army, under General Ivanoff, entrenched along the Pilica and Nida Rivers, and linking with Dimitrieff's forces near the junction of the Vistula and the Dunajec. For while one half of the Grand Phalanx swung through the gap to the rear of Brussiloff's army in the south, the other half of the Phalanx, according to Falkenhayn's plan, was to move through the gap and turn northward across the Vistula and get in the rear of Ivanoff's army, cutting its communications with Ivangorod. It will be seen that the scheme was of a grandiose nature, and the power employed in its attempted execution was of incomparable magnitude. Had it prospered, Russian armies amounting to two million men would have been destroyed. The Russians, besides, would have lost the greater part of their artillery, leaving the Empire permanently crippled. The army in front of Warsaw would have been left in the air and compelled hastily to retreat, dragging with it all the Russian forces guarding the Warsaw-Petrograd Railway.

scarcely any bullet-wounds—it was entirely shell fire that had pounded them out of the trenches. For this reason the Russians remained in wonderfully good spirits. All they desired was to catch the German infantry away from the big guns and show that, man for man, they could outfight the enemy.

"Wait until it gets dark, little brothers!" the Russian privates would say, looking towards the Germans, and intending the message for them. And when darkness fell on the battlefield and the squadrons of hostile aeroplanes were unable to direct the fire of the big guns, the Russian soldier got to work in the woods on the flank of the enemy's foremost columns. Then the enemy began to keep up an intense bombardment all night. Under cover of this fire, his troops went forward, but as soon as the guns had exhausted their temporary stock of shells the Russians turned back at dawn and recaptured their trenches by a furious charge, retreating when the German gunners got a fresh supply of ammunition and resumed the hurricane fire. The Third Army lost about fifty guns, most of them being destroyed by heavy shells. A few of the batteries were deliberately sacrificed in covering the retreat of the infantry, and according to the accounts of a Hungarian novelist, who was an eye-witness of the scene, the Russian gunners of the rearguard fought on, amid an overpowering tempest of fire, until they had used all their shells.

Third Russian Army's tenacity

The result of the extraordinary tenacity of the Third Russian Army was magnificent. It completely defeated

The Germans and Austrians would then have been able to conduct the summer campaign into the heart of Russia, if need be; or, as they hoped to do, they could have then held the enfeebled Russians back with part of their forces while they swung the victorious Grand Phalanx across Central Europe and launched it against its original target in France or Flanders.

As soon as the magnitude of the force employed by Mackensen was revealed, every intelligent man could see how enormous was the scope of Falkenhayn's plan. For this reason the entire civilised world looked with feverish anxiety to the conflict in Western Galicia. But for a time the situation was saved by the marvellous endurance of the diminishing troops of the Third Russian Army and the heroic skill of their commander, General Dimitrieff. It may be doubted if there can be found in military history any man to compare with Radko Dimitrieff. Neither the retreat of Sir John Moore to Corunna nor that of Sir John French to the Marne was as difficult as the operation conducted by the great Bulgarian. Indeed, **A great Bulgarian soldier** the greatest of all retreats in modern times—the retreat of the Russians under Barclay du Tolly and Kutusoff before the Grand Army of Napoleon—was not so magnificent an achievement as that which Radko Dimitrieff accomplished.

At the beginning of May he gave ground at Gorlice in the south, but hung on the upper course of the Dunajec with desperate tenacity. By this means he kept in connection with General Ivanoff's army and obtained reinforcements from it; and when the town of Tarnov fell, the two linked Russian armies withdrew down the Vistula towards the next great tributary, the Wistoka. At the

same time, by a more sudden retirement from Gorlice towards Jaslo, Dimitrieff removed from the zone of high-explosive shell fire on his southern flank, while keeping in close touch with General Brussiloff's forces round the Dukla Pass. Then when the three Russian armies— Ivanoff's, Dimitrieff's, and Brussiloff's—were closely linked together, the direction of all the combined operations was taken over by the oldest of the three commanders—the veteran General Ivanoff. Behind him was the Grand Duke Nicholas and the Russian Staff, who decided the national lines of strategy; but the great retreat was chiefly fought by Ivanoff, with Dimitrieff and Brussiloff assisting him. By May 7th the position of the Russians was secure; for though they were compelled to continue to give ground, the cohesion of their forces, instead of being weakened by the blow from the German battering-ram, was strengthened. **Mackensen outmanœuvred** Before the blow fell, General Dimitrieff, trusting to his formidable system of trenches to maintain his defensive action, had lent a division of his two southern army corps for operations on the Carpathians. Mackensen knew of this position of affairs from his spies, and launched the Grand Phalanx against the weakened place in Dimitrieff's front. And when, after a week's furious and incessant fighting, Dimitrieff's front remained unbroken, the position in regard to infantry power was improved. Reinforcements were poured into Galicia, and a considerable new army was collected in the Lublin province. Munitions were railed eastward from Kieff to Lemberg, and brought westward from Ivangorod and sent down to Jaroslav. Brussiloff shortened his line, enabling him to lend men, and Ivanoff withdrew from the Nida, in Poland, and

CHEERS FOR THEIR BRITISH ALLIES.
With their rifles at the salute the men of the famous Fongorijski Regiment are giving " Three cheers for King George ! "

STRIKING CAMERA-PICTURE OF A FULL-DRESS PARADE OF RUSSIAN TROOPS—SOMEWHERE ON THE EASTERN BATTLE-FRONT.

abandoned Kielce, with its copper-mines, and established a new line running from the Pilica and over the Lysa Gora heights through Opatov to Sandomierz, close to the junction of the Vistula and the San Rivers. This considerable shortening of his line enabled him also to throw large bodies of men and guns into the Galician battles.

What, however, the Russian commander could not do was to extemporise an artillery power equal to that of the enemy. A thousand heavy guns of position are not made in a day or a month, and three million high-explosive shells from 6 in. to 17 in. in diameter cannot be manufactured on the spur of the moment. The port of Archangel was closed to ordinary traffic in May to enable the British and French Governments to pour into Russia every gun and shell, rifle and cartridge that could be spared. The operations of our First Expeditionary Force **Outside help for Russia** were interrupted, and our large reinforcements were to some extent delayed by the necessity to loyally help our great Ally when, in the midst of great difficulties, she was fighting with heroic efficacy the common battle of civilisation; for Russia was withstanding the blow that might have been aimed at France, Britain, and Belgium, and the Western Allies naturally did all they could to pour warlike stores and weapons in a continual stream through Archangel. At the same time the Siberian Railway was working at high pressure, connecting the Galician battlefield with the armament factories of Japan and America. With all this outside help Russia could not, in a few weeks, get anything like the artillery power of her enemies; but she did equip a fresh army and get some hundreds of howitzers of a lighter model, which were the most useful of all in battles of manœuvres on the open field.

The Grand Phalanx which Falkenhayn had built up had one very serious defect. It was the hugest battering-ram mortal man had ever constructed. The difficulty was that it would only act in battering-ram fashion. Placed in position, with a solid definite obstacle to work against, it could quickly smash that obstacle into fragments. But when the obstacle withdrew at a speed of twenty miles a day, the battering-ram could not at once pursue it and immediately get to work again. Mackensen's extraordinary number of heavy artillery, and his store of millions of high-explosive shells, some weighing more than a ton each, could only be moved along a railway by means of hundreds of trains. The Russians thoroughly destroyed all railway lines as they retreated, and badly damaged every metalled roadway. The consequence was that the battering-ram could only move forward at the speed which the Germans and Austrians were able to rebuild the railway. The speed varied from three miles to five miles a day at the most. Something like four miles a day was therefore the average rate of progress of Mackensen's army and its enormous siege train.

The German Commander-in-Chief had sacrificed mobility to power. Basing his plan entirely on the conditions of the trench warfare system obtaining throughout the western front, and extending over the larger section of the eastern front, **Defect of the grand phalanx** he had constructed a war-machine that could break through any trench system and shatter any fortress, but which could not pursue an enemy. As a matter of fact, both the Germans and the Austrians were too eager to pursue. On each occasion when the Russian lines withdrew from the zone of heavy shell fire the attacking infantry advanced in an attempt to transform the retreat into a rout. The Russians waited for them with light field-guns, machine-guns, and infantry concealed in woods and ditches from the eyes of reconnoitring hostile airmen. It was then that our Allies got in time after time a damaging counter-blow.

This was also the explanation of the extraordinary and continual conflict of statement in the Russian and Austro-German official reports on the Galician struggle.

RUSSIAN OFFICERS AS PRISONERS OF WAR.
A captured Cossack general walks at the head of this sad procession in the town of Augustowo.

The Austrians and Germans made premature claims to victories on all the chief points of attack along the Wisloka, Wislok, and San Rivers. Mackensen, for instance, claimed to have captured Rymano on Wednesday, May 5th, and to have forced the passage of the Wislok. But two days afterwards he again claimed to have captured Rymano. The town of Debica, on the Lower Wisloka, was also apparently won twice by the army of the Archduke Ferdinand. In both cases the explanation was that the Russians withdrew from a hurricane of shell fire, only to return and slaughter the German and Austrian infantry when it advanced too confidently to occupy the position. At Debica railway-station the Russians used armoured motor-cars with terrible effect against a hostile division that tried to move quicker than the battering-ram behind it.

There was, however, one occasion when Mackensen's army almost succeeded in retrieving its failure to break

through on the Russian front on the Biala River. On Sunday, May 9th, Mackensen's army was further reinforced from Cracow. It crossed the Wislok at Krosno, and the troops deployed in dense lines along the high range of hills running from Stryschov on the Wislok to Brozov on the tributary stream of the Stobnica. It was only a sixteen-mile front, ending about thirty miles west of Przemysl. Covered only by their light field-artillery, the German troops, with the battered Prussian Guards still at their head, manœuvred in a brilliant and impetuous manner under the most brilliant of German commanders, and making a frontal attack against the Russian centre, broke it by pressure of massed numbers. It was a well-fought, well-managed victory in the old, orthodox Prussian manner. Mackensen sacrificed his men in tens of thousands at the decisive point until they had advanced so close that neither the Russian bayonet nor the Russian shrapnel could master its final charge of the surviving locked and roaring ranks of Germans

This time no orderly retreat was possible. Mackensen had repeated his **Ivanoff's swift** achievement at the Piontek marshes, **counter-manœuvre** north of Lodz. He had clean broken through the Russian front. No orderly retirement was possible for our Allies. But as General Russky at Lodz had changed Mackensen's triumph into a disaster, so now General Ivanoff, with heavier odds against him, turned a defeat into a glorious feat of arms. He gave way in his centre, making no attempt

PRUSSIAN CAVALRY ON THE MARCH.
This very striking photograph was taken in the evening twilight near Prasnysch.

to retrieve the position there, but sent all his reserve troops in a long, swift march southward towards Krosno. By means of their magnificent marching powers the Russians rounded the enemy's flank, and in a series of furious charges worked round still farther and menaced his rear. First a German division gave way, then an army corps, enabling the Russians in front also to advance southward to take part in the surprise turning movement. By Sunday evening Mackensen was losing on his right flank double what he was winning on his advanced centre. In fact, his whole line was in process of crumbling up, the Russians having got a hook round it. He had to draw back his victorious troops and send them to his rear, and check the Russian flanking movement. The Russian commander was not able to press his advantage, through lack of a decisive number of men on the Przemysl front. But he completely stopped Mackensen's advance and was able to retreat to the San River in a tranquil manner.

One of the reasons why the Russian counter-stroke was not fully driven home at Krosno was that a large part of the new reinforcements was operating in the Bukovina. Here, on the same Sunday evening as Mackensen in Galicia received his first severe check, a battle was raging on a forty-mile front from Obertyn to

RUSSIAN ORDERLIES ATTACHED TO THE CAUCASIAN NATIVE DIVISION.

Czernovitz. A large Austrian army, under the Archduke Eugene, was trying to work up to the Dniester, and then, in co-operation with the German army moving towards Stry, envelop Lemberg from the east, and cut the Russian communications with Kieff. In conjunction with the severe pressure that the armies of the Archduke Ferdinand and Mackensen were exercising on the east, and the army of Linsingen and the army of Böhm Ermolli were exercising from the south, the enemy's flanking movement in the Bukovina was a very serious matter. But General Brussiloff had good railway communications with Russia at Tarnopol, north of the Dniester. That is to say, he could get reinforcements and munitions quickly, and his local commander-in-chief, General Ivanoff, agreed that the Bukovina front was the best suited for a counter-blow.

Russian victory at Czernovitz

So on May 9th the Russians offered battle round Czernovitz, and advanced in impetuous attack for two days, throwing the enemy back with heavy losses. Some 5,000 prisoners were taken and six guns, and the advanced enemy forces holding the bridge-head on the Dniester at the railway town of Zalestchiki were routed. At the same time a strong attack was made upon the hostile forces working up from the Carpathian Mountains. More

than 5,000 bodies were found in front of the Russians on the mountain slopes of the Javornik range. In five days 20,000 prisoners were taken between the Dniester and the Pruth Rivers, and the Russians captured the town of Nadvorna, and cut the railway between Bukovina and Austria. This for the time being put an end to the Austrian attempt at a flanking movement from the Bukovina. A new commander, General Pflanzer, replaced the Archduke Eugene, the latter going to the Italian front.

German advance on Lemberg.

The Austrians still lacked driving power. All the chief work in the struggle for Galicia was done by German troops under Mackensen or Linsingen. Linsingen's fighting army was the chief force in the south. It worked with Pflanzer's Austrian army in the Bukovina on its left, and on its right was Böhm Ermolli's Austrian army, working through the Uzsok Pass towards Sambor, and General von Marwitz's Austro-German army, advancing through the Dukla and Lupkow Passes, and linking with Mackensen's Grand Phalanx. Of all these four southern armies Linsingen's was the chief striking force. It was composed largely of Bavarian troops, and operated along the Munkacs-Stry railway, with a direct aim against Lemberg. More than half a million men were employed by Linsingen, with a large amount of light field-artillery, including many 6 in. howitzers. Some 12 in. pieces of ordnance were also brought up over the mountain range as the railway was rebuilt. But the difficulties of communication were so great that the heavy artillery power of this second great German army remained very much inferior to that of Mackensen's force.

The result was that Linsingen, having to meet Brussiloff on fairly equal terms, was continually defeated in his advance against Lemberg. Indeed, Linsingen was only able to advance when Brussiloff resolved to shorten his line with a view to assisting the Third Russian Army.

As General Ivanoff viewed the situation, the entire success of Falkenhayn's scheme depended on the progress made by Linsingen. Mackensen and his mighty Phalanx, crawling forward at a speed of four miles a day, had failed to break the Russian front and encircle the southern Russian army. The movement of the Phalanx was therefore no longer a menace, but merely a new development of the war of attrition. The vast and cumbrous moving siege train could be left to exhaust itself in continual frontal attacks, with the Russians giving way very slowly as they wore down the enemy. If necessary, this kind of Russian retreat could be carried on for months, at the rate of four miles a day, without Mackensen getting farther into Russian territory than the Austrian Archduke Friedrich had done in August, 1914, before he was completely overthrown and routed.

But the position of Linsingen's army was different. It was making a flank attack against the Russians at the same time as the Phalanx was making a frontal attack. If the flank attack succeeded, the consequence would be an overwhelming disaster to all the Russian forces in Galicia. So both General Ivanoff and the Grand Duke Nicholas devoted special attention to the struggle between Linsingen and Brussiloff. Brussiloff completely retired from the Carpathian front in the middle of May, and took his stand in the valley of the Dniester from Drohobycz

PIRATE SUBMARINE U12, RAMMED BY THE BRITISH DESTROYER ARIEL AND FIRED ON BY H.M.S. ATTACK, MARCH 10TH, 1915.
Out of the submarine's crew of twenty-eight the number saved was ten.

diverted from the vain hunt for our battleships and cruisers and concentrated upon the merchantmen using our ports.

It has been seen already that the submarines first began their attacks upon our merchantmen in October, when the Glitra was sunk in the North Sea, after ample opportunity had been given to her crew to save themselves. But in December Admiral von Tirpitz gave a very plain hint at a new development that was in contemplation. Early in November the British Admiralty, ascertaining that the German Government had been strewing mines on the high seas by employing apparently innocent trading ships flying neutral colours, declared the whole of the North Sea a "military area," warning merchant ships of all nations that they must only use certain routes, from which they would deviate at their peril, either from mines or from patrolling British warships. The object was to increase the strictness of the examination service, so that no German minelayer in disguise might be able to get out.

The dependence which Germany had placed upon the abuse of neutral flags was shown by the execration with which this announcement was received. For some reason or another, however, neutral Powers declined to see that the measure would ruin them, obstinately as the German tried to convince them of the fact. The climax of these arguments was reached when Von Tirpitz addressed the United States through an interviewer in the following terms : " America did not raise her voice in protest, and has done nothing, or very little, against the closing by Great Britain of the North Sea against neutral shipping. What would America say if Germany should declare a submarine war against all enemy trading vessels ? " Incidentally, Great Britain had not " closed the North Sea."

German " blockade " declared   A few weeks later a definite declaration of policy was made. " Just as Britain has designated the area between Scotland and Norway as an area of war," ran the official German memorandum, " so Germany now declares all the waters surrounding Great Britain and Ireland, including the entire English Channel, as an area of war. For this purpose, beginning from February 18th, 1915, it will endeavour to destroy every enemy merchant ship that is found in this area of war, without its always being possible to avert the peril that this threatens to persons and cargoes. Neutrals are therefore warned against further entrusting crews and passengers and wares to such ships. Their attention is also called to the fact that it is advisable for their ships to avoid entering this area, for even though the German naval forces have instructions to avoid violence to neutral ships in so far as they are recognisable, in view of the misuse of neutral flags ordered by the British Government and the contingencies of naval warfare, their becoming victims of an attack directed against enemy ships cannot always be averted."

Thus did Germany declare indiscriminate war upon merchant ships of whatever nationality that might be found by their submarines in the waters surrounding the British Isles. The reference to the " misuse of neutral flags " by this country was based upon the fact that on one occasion when approaching Liverpool and passing through waters where hostile submarines were known to be lurking, the Cunard liner Lusitania had flown the American flag ; but this, as the Admiralty pointed out, had always been regarded as a legitimate *ruse de guerre* so long as the ship flying the neutral flag committed no act of war until she had hoisted her own colours.

" Misuse of neutral flags "

The organised " submarine blockade " was not due to start until February 18th, but it really began at the end of January, although, of course, numerous merchantmen had been sunk before then. On the 31st of that month half a dozen British merchantmen were attacked, in most cases without the least warning being given to the crews so that they might have an opportunity of saving their lives, even if not their personal belongings. Some were torpedoed in the neighbourhood of Liverpool and some in the Channel, and among the latter was the steamship Tokomaru, which was bringing from New Zealand 97,000 carcases of mutton, the proceeds of a fund raised in that Dominion for the relief of Belgian people who had been driven from their homes by the Germans and deprived of their means of livelihood. No warning was given in this case, but the vessel took an hour and a half to sink, and the crew were saved by French torpedo-boats.

The submarine in the Irish Sea, the U21, behaved with comparative decency towards its victims, giving the crews time to leave before sending the ships to the bottom. But the vessels in the Channel were either commanded by men of a different stamp or they were acting under a different set of orders. The latter seems the more probable explanation, in view of an official statement issued by the German Admiralty at this time, which ran : " England is about to